THE FIRST AND SECOND LETTERS TO TIMOTHY

VOLUME 35A

THE ANCHOR BIBLE is a fresh approach to the world's greatest classic. Its object is to make the Bible accessible to the modern reader; its method is to arrive at the meaning of biblical literature through exact translation and extended exposition, and to reconstruct the ancient setting of the biblical story, as well as the circumstances of its transcription and the characteristics of its transcribers.

THE ANCHOR BIBLE is a project of international and interfaith scope: Protestant, Catholic, and Jewish scholars from many countries contribute individual volumes. The project is not sponsored by any ecclesiastical organization and is not intended to reflect any particular theological doctrine. Prepared under our joint supervision, THE ANCHOR BIBLE is an effort to make available all the significant historical and linguistic knowledge which bears on the interpretation of the biblical record.

THE ANCHOR BIBLE is aimed at the general reader with no special formal training in biblical studies; yet it is written with the most exacting standards of scholarship, reflecting the highest technical accomplishment.

This project marks the beginning of a new era of cooperation among scholars in biblical research, thus forming a common body of knowledge to be shared by all.

William Foxwell Albright
David Noel Freedman
GENERAL EDITORS

THE ANCHOR BIBLE

THE FIRST AND SECOND LETTERS TO TIMOTHY

◆

A New Translation
with Introduction and Commentary

LUKE TIMOTHY JOHNSON

THE ANCHOR BIBLE
Doubleday
New York   London   Toronto   Sydney   Auckland

THE ANCHOR BIBLE
PUBLISHED BY DOUBLEDAY
a division of Random House, Inc.
1540 Broadway, New York, New York 10036

THE ANCHOR BIBLE DOUBLEDAY, and the portrayal of an anchor
with the letters A and B are trademarks of Doubleday,
a division of Random House, Inc.

LIBRARY OF CONGRESS CATALOGING-IN-PUBLICATION DATA

Bible, N.T. Timothy. English. Johnson. 2001.
The first and second letters to Timothy : a new translation with
introduction and commentary / Luke Timothy Johnson–1st ed.
        p. cm.   (The Anchor Bible ; v. 35A)
Includes bibliographical references and index.
1. Bible. N.T. Timothy—Commentaries.   I. Johnson, Luke Timothy.
II. Title. III. Bible
English. Anchor Bible. 1964: v. 35A.
BS192.2.A1 1964 .G3 vol. 35a
[BS2743]
227′.83077—dc21   00-029023

ISBN 0-385-48422-4

Copyright © 2001 by Doubleday, a division of Random House, Inc.

All Rights Reserved
Printed in the United States of America
March 2001

First Edition

10   9   8   7   6   5   4   3   2   1

TO MY YALE TEACHERS

Nils Dahl
Rowan Greer
Abraham J. Malherbe
Wayne A. Meeks

CONTENTS

◆

BIBLIOGRAPHY

FIRST TIMOTHY: AN INTRODUCTION

FIRST TIMOTHY: TRANSLATION, NOTES, AND COMMENTS

SECOND TIMOTHY: AN INTRODUCTION

SECOND TIMOTHY: TRANSLATION, NOTES, AND COMMENTS

INDEXES

PREFACE

◆

The letters of Paul to his delegate Timothy do not make for easy reading in today's world. There is much in them that is difficult to figure out. There is much in them that present-day readers find distasteful and even offensive. But there is much in them also that is powerful and even prophetic.

A commentary on these letters inevitably must deal with the issue of their authenticity, and I do so at considerable length. I interpret 1 and 2 Timothy from the perspective of Pauline authorship, which means, at the very least, that they were composed under his authority during his lifetime. I didn't always think they should be read this way. As a student I was happy to accept the majority position that claimed the letters were pseudonymous. I had no particular historical or theological bone to pick with what seemed both a massive and reasonable consensus. It was only when I began teaching New Testament Introduction at Yale Divinity School in 1976 that I started to question that position. The reason was that in trying to explain the bases for the conventional wisdom, I could not make the arguments convincing even to myself. So I began the process of reexamination, the result of which you have before you.

In an age when the question, "Why another commentary" ought to be the first asked of a book like this, it is perhaps appropriate to identify the features of this particular commentary that make it, if not unique, at least distinctive.

1. The commentary gives more than ordinary attention to the history of interpretation before the 19th century, including patristic and medieval commentaries;
2. it seeks to reconstruct in some detail the movement toward a scholarly consensus in the 19th century, taking into account the sociological and theological dimensions of the debate;
3. it identifies and analyzes at the theoretical level the various criteria used for determining authenticity;
4. it brings to bear the best recent scholarship on the ministry and correspondence of Paul, particularly from the side of Greco-Roman rhetoric and moral philosophy;
5. it analyzes the letters on their own terms consistently as distinct literary compositions;
6. it argues that the critical factor in making the content and language of

these compositions distinctive within the Pauline corpus is their classification as types of letters;

7. it adduces a substantial amount of primary source material, especially from Hellenistic moral discourse.

Although the commentary is informed by the wide range of contemporary scholarship, you will not find here extensive side-discussions of particular points. There are other commentaries that do this, and specialized reference works abound. This commentary seeks to interpret the meaning of the text.

Many students have worked through these letters with me, both at Yale Divinity School and at Candler School of Theology. I thank them for their courage and their intelligence. I am grateful to the faculties of the Immanuel School of Religion in Johnson City, Tennessee, and of Christian Theological Seminary in Indianapolis, Indiana, for allowing me to lecture on these writings. Thanks for the intellectual companionship offered by the Society of Biblical Literature's Seminar on the Theology of the Disputed Pauline Letters, especially Vic Furnish, Beth Johnson, Jerry Sumney, and Steve Kraftchick. Two students (Steven Thompson and Patrick Gray) worked through my translation and offered helpful suggestions. Other students gave help in bibliographic research, including Julia Fogg, Michael Williams, and above all, David Charnon, who brought together a world of learning for me to read a year before I could get to it. Thanks also to the superb staff at the Pitts Theological Library of Emory University, especially Patrick Graham, Ida Boers, and Douglas Cragg. I am deeply grateful for the editorial care and skill of David Noel Freedman, whose vision difficulties during the time he had this manuscript did not keep him from seeing many things in need of correction.

Thanks also to Chase Peeples, who worked through the references, checking for accuracy.

I dedicate this book to my teachers in New Testament at Yale. The more the years pass, the more I know I owe them. Although my debt to all of them is great, in the case of this book, most is owed to Abraham Johannes Malherbe, who started me working on the Greco-Roman moralists in 1971, and who is responsible for many of the best insights in this volume.

And as always, from a full and grateful heart, my thanks to Joy.

Luke Timothy Johnson
May 25, 1999

ABBREVIATIONS

◆

Abbreviations of all ancient writings are those found in *The SBL Handbook of Style for Ancient Near Eastern Biblical, and Early Christian Studies,* ed. by P. H. Alexander and D. L. Petersen (Peabody, Mass.: Hendrickson Publishers, 1999).

AnBib	Analecta Biblica
ANRW	W. Haase and H. Temporini, *Aufstieg und Niedergang der Römischen Welt*
BAGD	W. Bauer, W. F. Arndt, F. W. Gingrich, F. Danker, *Greek-English Lexicon of the New Testament*
Bib	*Biblica*
BJRL	*Bulletin of the John Rylands Library*
BWANT	Beiträge zur Wissenschaft vom Alten und Neuen Testaments
BZ	*Biblische Zeitschrift*
CBQ	*Catholic Biblical Quarterly*
CRINT	Compendium Rerum Iudicarum ad Novum Testamentum
EBib	Études Bibliques
ExpT	*Expository Times*
FzB	*Forschung zur Bibel*
FRLANT	Forschungen zur Religion und Literatur des Alten und Neuen Testaments
HKNT	Handkommentar zum Neuen Testament
HNT	Handbuch zum Neuen Testament
HTKNT	Herders theologischer Kommentar zum Neuen Testament
HTR	*Harvard Theological Review*
ICC	International Critical Commentary
Int	*Interpretation*
JAAR	*Journal of the American Academy of Religion*
JAC	Jahrbuch für Antike und Christentum
JB	Jerusalem Bible
JBL	*Journal of Biblical Literature*
JHC	*Journal of Higher Criticism*
JRH	*Journal of Religious History*
JRS	*Journal of Religious Studies*
JSJ	*Journal for the Study of Judaism*

JSNT	*Journal for the Study of the New Testament*
JSNTS	Journal for the Study of the New Testament Supplement
JTS	*Journal of Theological Studies*
KD	*Kerygma and Dogma*
KJV	King James Version
LXX	Septuagint
MS(S)	Manuscript(s)
MT	Masoretic Text
NAB	New American Bible
NEB	New English Bible
Neot	*Neotestamentica*
Nestle	Aland E. Nestle and E. Aland, *Novum Testamentum Graece*, 27th ed.
NIV	New International Version
NovT	*Novum Testamentum*
NovTSup	Novum Testamentum, Supplements
NRSV	New Revised Standard Version
NT	New Testament
NTS	*New Testament Studies*
OT	Old Testament
PG	J. Migne, ed., *Patrologia Graeca*
PL	J. Migne, ed., *Patrologia Latina*
QD	Quaestiones Disputatae
RB	*Revue biblique*
ResQ	*Restoration Quarterly*
RHE	*Revue d'histoire ecclésiastique*
RHPR	*Revue d'histoire et de philosophie religieuses*
RSPT	*Revue des sciences philosophiques et théologiques*
RSR	*Recherches de science religieuse*
RSV	Revised Standard Version
SB	Sources Bibliques
SBLDS	Society of Biblical Literature Dissertation Series
SBLMS	Society of Biblical Literature Monograph Series
SNTSMS	Studiorum Novi Testamenti Societas, Monograph Series
ST	*Studia Theologica*
THKNT	Theologischer Handkommentar zum Neuen Testament
TQ	*Theologische Quartalschrift*
TS	*Theological Studies*
TSK	*Theologische Studien und Kritiken*
TZ	*Theologische Zeitschrift*
WUNT	Wissenschaftliche Untersuchungen zum Neuen Testament
ZNW	*Zeitschrift für die neutestamentliche Wissenschaft*
ZWT	*Zeitschrift für wissenschaftliche Theologie*

THE FIRST AND SECOND LETTERS TO TIMOTHY: A TRANSLATION

◆

FIRST TIMOTHY

◆

1 [1]From Paul, an apostle of Christ Jesus by the command of God our savior and of Christ Jesus our hope, [2]to Timothy, my genuine child in faith: grace, mercy, and peace from God Father and from Christ Jesus our Lord.

[3]As I exhorted you when I left for Macedonia: stay in Ephesus so that you can command certain people not to teach different doctrine [4]or devote themselves to myths and endless genealogies. These encourage speculations rather than faithful attention to God's way of ordering things. [5]But the aim of the commandment is love that comes from a pure heart and a good conscience, and a sincere faith. [6]Missing out on these, some people have turned aside to foolish chatter. [7]They want to be teachers of law without understanding either the things about which they are speaking or the things concerning which they insist. [8]But we know that the law is good if anyone use it appropriately. [9]We understand this: law is not laid down for a righteous person, but for the lawless and the reckless, the godless and the sinners, the unholy and the profane: people who kill fathers, who kill mothers, [10]who are murderers; people who are fornicators, sexual perverts, slave dealers; people who are liars, perjurers, and who do whatever else is opposed to the healthy teaching [11]that accords with the glorious good news from the blessed God, with which I have been entrusted.

[12]I give thanks to the one who has empowered me, Christ Jesus our Lord, for he has considered me faithful by putting me into service. [13]I was earlier a blasphemer. I was a persecutor. I was an insolent person. But I was shown mercy because in ignorance I acted with faithlessness. [14]And the gift of our Lord with the faith and love that are in Christ Jesus was extravagant. [15]This saying is reliable and worthy of all acceptance, that Christ Jesus came into the world to save sinners. I am the first among them! [16]But I was shown mercy for this reason, that Christ Jesus might demonstrate all possible forbearance in me first, as an example for those who would come to believe in him unto eternal life. [17]To the king of the ages, to the immortal, invisible, only God, be honor and glory for ever and ever. Amen.

[18]My child Timothy, I entrust this commandment to you according to the earlier prophecies made concerning you, so that you might continue fighting the noble battle by means of them, [19]having faith and a good conscience, which some people have spurned and have suffered shipwreck concerning the faith! [20]Among such are Hymenaios and Alexander. I have handed them over to Satan, so that they may be taught not to blaspheme.

2 [1]I am requesting first of all, therefore, that entreaties, prayers, petitions, and thanksgivings be made in behalf of all people, [2]for kings and all those who are

in positions of authority, so that we might lead a peaceful and quiet life in complete piety and dignity. [3]This is a noble thing to do, and pleasing in the sight of our savior God, [4]who wants all people to be saved and to come to the recognition of truth. [5]For God is one. One also is the mediator between God and humans, the human being Christ Jesus. [6]He gave himself as a ransom in behalf of all. The testimony was given at the right time. [7]I have been appointed its herald and apostle—I speak the truth and do not lie—a teacher of Gentiles in faith and truth.

[8]Therefore I want the men in every place to pray with their hands lifted up with piety, removed from anger and argument. [9]Likewise also women should adorn themselves in appropriate dress with modesty and discretion, not in braids or gold or pearls or costly apparel, [10]but in a way fitting to women dedicated to the service of God, through good works. [11]Let a woman learn quietly in complete subordination. [12]I do not entrust teaching to a woman, nor authority over a man. She is to stay quiet. [13]For Adam was made first, then Eve. [14]Also, Adam was not deceived, but the woman, once she was deceived, fell into transgression. [15]Yet she will be saved through childbearing, if they remain in faith and love and holiness with moral discretion.

3   [1a]This is a reliable opinion.

[1b]If anyone seeks to be a supervisor, it is a noble role that he desires. [2]The supervisor must therefore be blameless, the husband of one wife, sober, prudent, respectable, hospitable, an apt teacher. [3]He must not be addicted to wine, nor be violent, but should be gentle, neither given to battle nor a lover of money. [4]He should be ruling well over his own household, with his children in subordination with complete reverence. [5]For if someone does not know how to rule his own household, how can he take charge of God's assembly? [6]He should not be a recent convert in order that he not get a false sense of his own importance and fall into the judgment reserved for the devil. [7]And he should also have the commendation of outsiders, so that he does not fall into disgrace and the trap of the devil.

[8]Helpers likewise should be dignified. They should not be duplicitous, overfond of wine, or willing to do anything for a profit. [9]They should hold unto the mystery of faith with a pure conscience. [10]They also should first be tested, and then, being blameless, they can carry out their service. [11]Women helpers likewise should be dignified, should not be gossipers, should be sober, and should be faithful in every respect. [12]Let the helpers be men who have one wife, who manage their children and their own household affairs well. [13]Those who have served well have thereby gained a good position for themselves and much confidence in the faith that is in Christ Jesus. [14]I am writing these things to you even though I hope to come to you shortly. [15]But if I am delayed, you should know how it is necessary to behave in the household of God, which is the church of the living God, as a pillar and support for the truth. [16]The mystery of godliness is—we confess—a great one: He was manifested in flesh, he was made righteous by spirit, he appeared to messengers, he was preached among nations, he was believed in by the world, he was taken up in glory.

4 ¹Now the spirit expressly declares that in later times some people will distance themselves from the faith. They will devote themselves to deceiving spirits and the teachings of demons. ²In hypocrisy they speak falsely, since their own consciences have been cauterized. ³They forbid marriage, forbid eating foods. These are things that God created to be shared with thanksgiving by those who are faithful and have come to a recognition of the truth, ⁴because every creature of God is good. Nothing is to be rejected if it is received with thanksgiving. ⁵For it is made holy by God's word and by prayer. ⁶If you propose these things to the brethren, you will be a good helper of Christ Jesus, nourished by the words of faith and by the noble teaching in which you have followed. ⁷But stay away from profane and old-women myths. Instead, train yourself for godliness. ⁸Training the body is useful in a limited way. Godliness, however, is useful in every way. It bears a promise of life both now and in the future. ⁹The word is faithful and worthy of complete acceptance. ¹⁰For this is why we labor and struggle, because we have come to hope in a living God who is the savior of all human beings, above all those who are faithful. ¹¹Command these things. Teach them. ¹²Let no one despise your youth. Become, rather, a model to those who are faithful, in speech and in behavior, by love, by faith, by purity. ¹³Until I arrive, pay attention to the reading, to exhortation, and to teaching. ¹⁴Do not be careless with the special gift for service within you. It was given to you through prophecy with a laying on of hands by the board of elders. ¹⁵Pay attention to these things. Live by them, so that your moral progress is manifest to all. ¹⁶Be attentive to yourself and to the teaching, and remain steady in both. For if you do this, you will save both yourself and those who are listening to you.

5 ¹Do not castigate an older man. Instead, exhort him as if he were your father. Act toward younger men as toward brothers, ²toward older women as toward mothers, toward younger women as toward sisters, that is, in all purity. ³Provide financial support for widows who are truly widows. ⁴But if any widow has children or grandchildren, let them learn first of all to show godliness in their own household and to give back some repayment to those who gave them birth. For this is an acceptable thing before God. ⁵Now the real widow is one who, having been left alone, has put her hope in God and continues to make petitions and prayers night and day. ⁶In contrast, the woman who lives self-indulgently has already died even though she is alive. ⁷And you should command these things so that they can stay without reproach. ⁸But if people do not provide for their own relatives, especially if they are members of their household, they have denied the faith and are worse than unbelievers. ⁹A widow should be enrolled. She should not be less than sixty years old, married only once. ¹⁰She should have a reputation for good deeds, such as rearing her children, showing hospitality to strangers, washing the feet of the saints, helping those in trouble; in short, she has been dedicated to every sort of good deed. ¹¹But avoid younger widows. For they want to marry when they have grown wanton against Christ. ¹²They earn condemnation because they have put aside their first commitment. ¹³Moreover, they immediately learn to be idlers, going from house to house.

They are not only idlers but also gossips and busybodies, saying things that they should not. [14]I therefore want younger women to marry, to bear children, to run their households, giving no opportunity for reviling to the one who opposes us. [15]For some women have already turned aside after Satan. [16]If any faithful woman has relatives who are widows, she should provide for them. The church should not be burdened, in order that it might support those who are real widows. [17]Elders who govern well should be considered worthy of double compensation, especially those who labor in speech and in teaching. [18]For the Scripture says, "Do not muzzle an ox that is threshing," and, "The worker deserves his pay." [19]Do not consider an accusation against an elder unless two or three witnesses support it. [20]Those who are sinning, rebuke in the presence of all, so that the rest might be afraid. [21]I am charging you before God and before Jesus Christ and before the elect angels, that you observe these matters without favoritism. Do nothing on the basis of partiality. [22]Do not lay hands on anyone hastily. Do not associate yourself with other people's sins. Keep yourself pure. [23]Do not keep drinking only water. Use a little wine for the sake of digestion and for your frequent weakness. [24]The sins of some people are obvious, parading before them into judgment. The sins of some others trail behind. [25]In the same way, good deeds are also obvious, and deeds that are not cannot remain hidden.

6   [1]Let those who are slaves under a yoke regard their own masters as worthy of all respect, so that the name of God and the teaching not be blasphemed. [2a]And those who have believers as masters should not despise them because they are brothers. Rather they should serve them better because those who are receiving their benefaction are believers and beloved.

[2b]Teach and urge these things. [3]If anyone teaches otherwise and does not attend to the healthy words of our Lord Jesus Christ and the teaching that accords with godliness, [4]that person is deluded, understanding nothing. Instead he is sick from debates and controversies, from which come envy and strife and reviling speech, evil suspicions, [5]the constant wranglings of people with corrupted minds. And defrauded from the truth, they think that godliness is a means of financial gain. [6]Now godliness is a great source of gain, when it is accompanied by self-sufficiency. [7]For we brought nothing into the world, because neither can we take anything out of it. [8]But if we have food to eat and a covering, with these we shall be content. [9]Now those who want to be rich are falling into temptation and a trap, and into many senseless and harmful cravings that plunge people into ruin and destruction. [10]For the love of money is a root for every kind of wickedness. By pursuing it some people have been led astray from the faith and have tortured themselves with many agonies.

[11]But you, O Man of God, flee these things! Instead, pursue righteousness, godliness, faith, love, endurance, and a generous temper. [12]Engage the noble athletic contest for the faith. Take hold of the eternal life. You were called to it. And you pronounced the noble profession before many witnesses. [13]I command you before the God who gives life to all things, and before Jesus Christ who testified to the noble profession before Pontius Pilate, [14]keep the commandment spotless and blameless until the appearance of our Lord Jesus Christ,

[15]which God will reveal at the proper season. He is the blessed and only ruler, the King of kings, and the Lord of lords. [16]He alone possesses immortality. He dwells in unapproachable light. No human being has ever seen Him. No one can ever see Him. To Him be eternal honor and power. Amen. [17]Tell the rich in this world not to be arrogant and not to put their hope upon the uncertainty of wealth, but rather upon God who supplies us with all things richly for our enjoyment. [18]Tell them to do good work, to be wealthy in noble deeds, to be generous in giving, to be sharers of possessions, [19]thereby storing up for themselves a noble foundation for the future, so that they can lay hold of real life. [20]O Timothy! Protect the tradition! Avoid the profane chattering and contradictions of so-called knowledge. [21]Some have professed it. They have missed the mark concerning faith. Grace be with you.

SECOND TIMOTHY

◆

1 ¹From Paul, an apostle of Christ Jesus because God wills it, and based on the promise of life found in Christ Jesus, ²to Timothy my beloved child. May you have grace, mercy, and peace from God who is Father and from Christ Jesus our Lord.

³I thank the God whom I serve, as did my forebears, with a pure conscience. I hold you constantly in my memory as I pray night and day. ⁴I long to see you, as I remember your tears, that I might be filled with joy, ⁵holding in memory your sincere faith, the same kind that dwelt in your grandmother Lois and in your mother Eunice before you. I trust it is in you as well.

⁶For this reason, I remind you to revivify that special gift for service that God gave you through the laying on of my hands. ⁷God did not give us a spirit of cowardice. He gave us a spirit of power, of love, and of self-control. ⁸Do not be ashamed, therefore, of the witness of our Lord or of me, a prisoner for him. But as God gives you power, take your share of suffering for the good news. ⁹God saved us and called us by a holy calling. He did this, not on the basis of our own accomplishments, but on the basis of his own purpose and gift. The gift was given to us before the ages in Christ Jesus. ¹⁰But it has been revealed now through the appearance of our savior, Christ Jesus. He has abolished death. He has manifested life and incorruptibility, and this through the good news ¹¹whose proclaimer, apostle, and teacher I have been appointed. ¹²For this reason I suffer even these things. But I am not ashamed, for I know the one I have trusted. I am positive he is able to preserve that which has been entrusted to me until that day. ¹³Keep holding to the example of healthy teaching that you heard from me. In the faith and love that are in Christ Jesus, ¹⁴protect the precious deposit through the Holy Spirit that dwells in us.

¹⁵You know this fact: that all those in Asia, among them Phygelos and Hermogenes, have abandoned me. ¹⁶May the Lord grant mercy to Onesiphorus's household! Many times he refreshed me. He was not ashamed of my chains! ¹⁷Rather, once in Rome, he sought me eagerly and he found me. ¹⁸May the Lord grant him to find mercy in that day. And you know well how many services he rendered in Ephesus.

2 ¹Be strengthened therefore, my child, by the gift that is in Christ Jesus. ²The things that you heard me say in the presence of many witnesses you must entrust to men who are faithful and will be competent enough to teach others as well. ³Take your share of suffering as a good soldier of Christ Jesus. ⁴No one serving military duty allows himself to become entangled in everyday matters—so that he might please his recruiter. ⁵And also, if any one competes in an athletic contest

he won't be crowned unless he competes by the rules. [6]The hardworking farmer ought to share first in the fruits of the harvest. [7]Grasp what I am telling you. For the Lord will give you quickness of understanding in all these matters.

[8]Keep on remembering Jesus Christ. According to the good news I preach, he is raised from the dead, he is from the seed of David. [9]For this good news I am suffering even to the point of being enchained as a criminal. But the word of God is not enchained. [10]This is why I endure all things for the sake of the chosen ones, that they also might attain salvation with eternal glory, which is found in Christ Jesus. [11]The word is faithful! For if we have died together, then we shall also live together. [12]If we endure, we shall reign together. If we deny him, he will deny us. [13]If we are unfaithful, he still remains faithful, for he is not able to deny himself.

[14]Remember these things as you admonish before God. Do not engage in polemics that are of no profit but lead to the destruction of those hearing them. [15]Be eager to present yourself as a proven workman to God, one with no reason for shame, as you accurately delineate the word of truth. [16]But keep avoiding profane chatter. Those people are going to make ever greater progress in impiety [17]and their teaching will spread like gangrene. Hymenaios and Philetos are among those [18]who have missed the mark concerning the truth by saying that the resurrection has already happened. They are upsetting some peoples' faith. [19]Nevertheless, God's firm foundation still stands, bearing this seal: "The Lord has known his own," and, "Everyone who names the Lord's name should depart from wickedness." [20]In a great household there are not only gold and silver utensils, but also wooden ones and clay. Some are for noble use, some for ignoble. [21]If then one cleanses oneself from these, one will be a vessel ready for noble use, consecrated, useful to the master, prepared for every good work.

[22]Flee cravings for novelty. Instead pursue righteousness, faithfulness, love, and peace, with all those who call on the Lord's name with a pure heart. [23]Avoid foolish and uneducated disputes. You know that they generate conflicts. [24]The Lord's servant, in contrast, must not engage in conflicts, but must be gentle toward all, an apt teacher and long-suffering. [25]He must teach with mildness those who oppose him. Perhaps God will give them a change of heart so that they recognize truth. [26]And perhaps they will regain their senses, once they have been snatched alive by God from the devil's snare, so that they can do God's will.

3 [1]But know this: difficult times are approaching in the last days. [2]People will be selfish, greedy, boastful, arrogant, blasphemers. They will not be obedient to their parents. They will be ungrateful, unholy, [3]unaffectionate, intractable. They will be slanderers, out of control, wild. They will not care about doing good. [4]They will be traitors, rash and crazed. They will love pleasure more than they love God. [5]They will have the appearance of piety while denying its power. Avoid these people especially. [6]Now from among them are the ones who are sneaking into households and capturing silly women who are beset by sins and driven by various passions, [7]women who are always learning but never capable of reaching a recognition of truth. [8]In the very way that Jannes and Jambres opposed Moses, so also these men oppose the truth. They are corrupted in mind,

untested concerning the faith. [9]But they will not progress much further, for just as it happened with those men, their stupidity will become obvious to everyone.

[10]But you have followed closely my teaching, my way of life, my purpose, my faith, my patience, my love, my endurance, [11]my persecutions, and my sufferings, such as befell me in Antioch, in Iconium, and in Lystra. I endured such persecutions, and the Lord delivered me from them all. [12]And indeed all those who choose to live piously in Christ Jesus will be persecuted. [13]Evil men and charlatans will get even worse. They are deceivers and are themselves deceived. [14]But you, remain in those things that you learned and about which you have become convinced. You are aware of the ones from whom you learned them. [15]And you have known the sacred writings since you were a child. They are capable of making you wise concerning salvation through the faith that is in Christ Jesus. [16]Every scripture is God-inspired and useful for teaching, reproving, correcting, toward an education in righteousness, [17]in order that the man of God might be fit, prepared for every good work.

4 [1]I admonish you before God and before Christ Jesus, who is coming to judge the living and the dead, and in view of his appearance and his kingdom: [2]Preach the word! Apply yourself to it in good times and in bad. Refute and rebuke! Give comfort with every sort of long-suffering and teaching. [3]For there will be a time when, because they have itchy ears, they will not put up with healthy teaching, but will multipy teachers fashioned to their own passions. [4]They will stop listening to the truth. They will turn aside to myths. [5]But you, stay sober in all matters. Endure the hard things. Do the work of proclaiming good news. Fulfill your ministry. [6]For I am already being offered up as a sacrifice, and the time for my death is near. [7]I have fought the noble fight, finished the race, held tight to the faith. [8]There is waiting for me now the crown given to the righteous, which the Lord, the righteous judge, will award me on that day, not only me but all those who have loved his coming.

[9]Make an effort to come to me quickly, [10]for Demas, having fallen in love with this world, has left me and gone to Thessalonica. Crescas has gone to Galatia, Titus to Dalmatia. [11]Only Luke is with me. When you have picked up Mark, bring him along with you, for he is useful to me in service. [12]And I sent Tychichos to Ephesus. [13]When you come, bring along the cloak I left behind at Carpus's place in Troas. Bring also the books and especially the parchments. [14]The coppersmith Alexander has acted badly toward me in many ways. The Lord will repay him according to his deeds. [15]You keep away from him also. He has greatly opposed our words.

[16]No one was beside me at my first defense presentation. Instead they all abandoned me. May it not be counted against them! [17]The Lord, on the other hand, stood by me and gave me strength, so that through me the proclamation might be fulfilled and that all nations might hear. And I was delivered from the mouth of the lion. [18]The Lord will deliver me from every evil deed, and he will save me for his heavenly kingdom. To Him be glory for ever and ever. Amen. [19]Greet Prisca and Aquila and the household of Onesiphorus. [20]Erastus has remained in Corinth. But I left Trophimus ill in Miletus. [21]Try to get here before winter. Eubulus and Pudens and Linus and Claudia, and all the brethren, greet you. [22]The Lord be with your spirit. Grace be with you.

GENERAL
INTRODUCTION

◆

INTRODUCTION TO THE
PASTORAL EPISTLES

◆

Commentaries on biblical books have always started with introductions that propose guidelines for reading the compositions as a whole—directions that commentaries, because of their atomistic approach, are otherwise notoriously poor at providing. For the letters of Paul the Apostle, the so-called Marcionite Prologues of the late second century are the prototype: they sketch the circumstances of the respective letters' composition and the Apostle's purpose for writing.[1] Context and meaning: drawing deductions about the audience and the occasion from the contents of the letter itself, such prologues make suggestions concerning the message. The conversations have become far more complex over the intervening centuries, but the goal remains fundamentally the same. For all biblical books, the task of introduction has been made more complex by the growth of knowledge about antiquity and, with such knowledge, the questioning of the self-presentation of the biblical composition. Some of the debates concerning biblical books began among patristic writers; more arose with the development of critical historiography in the eighteenth century, at the time of the European Enlightenment.[2]

The case of the three letters addressed to Paul's delegates (1 Timothy, 2 Timothy, and Titus), known at least since the eighteenth century as the Pastoral Letters,[3] is particularly complex. They present themselves as three sepa-

---

1. See the insightful comments in N. A. Dahl, "The Origin of the Earliest Prologues to Paul's Epistles," *Semeia* 12 (1978): 233–277.

2. On the history of this scholarship, see particularly W. G. Kümmel, *The New Testament: The History of Its Problems*, trans. S. M. Gilmour (Nashville, Tenn.: Abingdon Press, 1972); S. Neill, *The Interpretation of the New Testament, 1861–1961* (London: Oxford University Press, 1964); W. Baird, *History of New Testament Research*, vol. 1, *From Deism to Tübingen* (Minneapolis: Fortress Press, 1992); and L. Salvatorelli, "From Locke to Reizenstein: The Historical Investigation of the Origins of Christianity," *HTR* 22 (1929): 263–367.

3. Like much about these letters, the origin of this common name is unclear. Was the term first used in a technical sense by Paul Anton in his lectures at Halle (1726–1727), which were edited by J. A. Maier as *Exegetische Abhandlung der Pastoral-Briefe Pauli an Timotheum und Titum* (1753–1755)? Such is the opinion of Theodor Zahn, as reported in P. N. Harrison, *The Problem of the Pastoral Epistles* (Oxford: Oxford University Press, 1921), 13. C. Spicq, *Les Èpîtres pastorales* E Bib; (Paris: Gabalda, 1969) xxi, would like to give the honor to D. N. Berdot, *Exercitatio Theologica Exegetica in Epistolam S. Pauli ad Titum* (Halle, 1703). But as I will indicate in this introduction, Thomas Aquinas in the thirteenth century already referred to 1 Timothy as *quasi pastoralis regula* and to 2 Timothy as *ad curam pastoralem* (as Harrison also acknowledges). Abraham Scultetus also referred to them as *pastoralis* in the mid-seventeenth century.

rate letters written by Paul to two of his closest co-workers. Yet for the past two hundred years, an ever-increasing number of critical scholars has challenged each part of that self-presentation: they are not three separate letters, but a single literary composition; they are not written by Paul, but by a follower after his death; they are not written for first-generation Christians, but for a later time. If meaning is connected to context, then it is obvious that the meaning of this literature will be under dispute as long as its context is not firmly established.

Prospects for scholarly unanimity are slender. The clear majority of scholars today considers the Pastorals as a whole to be pseudonymous. Yet a small but stubborn minority holds—in various ways and with varying degrees of enthusiasm—to the more traditional position that the letters are authentic. There is little communication between the positions. Few converts are won from one side to the other. Symptomatic of the current situation is the fact that Jerome Quinn's commentary on Titus in the Anchor Bible is written from the perspective of pseudonymous composition,[4] while this volume on 1 and 2 Timothy approaches the letters as authentically Pauline.[5]

Virtually everything about these compositions is a matter of dispute, not only the circumstances of their production, but also the character and implications of their message. The Pastorals have managed to offend scholars committed to reformation theology as well as feminists dedicated to liberation theology. Discussions of historical and linguistic issues almost inevitably become entangled with theological and ideological commitments. The issue of Pauline authorship shades imperceptibly toward the question of canonical status and theological authority, and dominates all discussion of this literature.

In order to provide readers with as adequate a basis as possible to make their own judgments, this General Introduction moves deliberately through several stages, seeking both to expose the different dimensions of the writings and to show how they give rise to different conclusions. I begin with the question of the Greek text on which the translation in this book is based. For most introductions, the next consideration would be the respective compositions' style, genre, and setting. But since each of these is at issue, I first provide a sketch of the history of interpretation of these letters. Then I deal with the entire ques-

---

4. J. D. Quinn, *The Letter to Titus*, Anchor Bible 35 (New York: Doubleday, 1990). Jerome Quinn's work on 1 and 2 Timothy has been edited and expanded after Quinn's death by W. C. Wacker, and appeared too late to be used in this book: J. D. Quinn, W. C. Wacker, *The First and Second Letters to Timothy*: A New Translation with Notes and Commentary (The Eerdmans Critical Commentary; Grand Rapids: Eerdmans, 2000).

5. This commentary builds on earlier exercises, including L. T. Johnson, *Introduction to the Letters of Paul III: Colossians, Ephesians, Pastorals*, Invitation to the New Testament (Garden City, N.Y.: Doubleday, 1980); *First Timothy, Second Timothy, Titus*, John Knox Preaching Guides (Atlanta: John Knox Press, 1987); and *Letters to Paul's Delegates: A Commentary on 1 Timothy, 2 Timothy, and Titus*, New Testament in Context (Valley Forge, Pa.: Trinity Press International, 1996).

tion of authenticity in a systematic fashion, introducing the various dimensions of 1 and 2 Timothy in the process. Since the three Pastorals are almost always discussed together—a practice I consider unfortunate and distorting—the Letter to Titus is inevitably included at various places. The letters to Timothy remain, however, my main concern.[6] After the General Introduction, I provide separate INTRODUCTIONS to 1 and 2 Timothy at the beginning of the commentary on each of these letters.

---

6. Quinn provides the standard approach to the PE (as he designates them), from the perspective of pseudonymity and as a group, in *Letter to Titus*, 1–22.

I. THE TEXT OF
1 AND 2 TIMOTHY

◆

At least three reasons make a consideration of the Greek text underlying any translation significant. The first is the most straightforward: establishing the Greek text is itself a constructive act of interpretation and deeply affects translation decisions. The second has to do with the history of the reception of the composition: an early appearance of a composition in papyrus can speak positively for an early dating. The absence of a particular composition in a manuscript, however, is a more ambiguous fact; as with all such cases, arguments from silence are dangerous. The third reason is that textual variants, however unhelpful they may be for the task of establishing the most probable original text, are valuable evidence for the history of interpretation.

A. ESTABLISHING THE TEXT

The translation in the this commentary is based on 27th edition of Nestle–Aland,[7] a critical edition that is eclectic; the text is constituted by a process of selection among witnesses, based on the relative strength of external witness as well as the basic rules of textual criticism, which include a preference for shorter and harder readings.[8] There is no extant papyrus evidence for the letters to Timothy, although for Tit 1:11–15 and 2:3–8 we have $\mathfrak{P}^{32}$ (ca. 200), and for Tit 3:1–5, 8–11, 14–15 there is $\mathfrak{P}^{61}$ (ca. 700).[9] The text of 1 and 2 Timothy is found intact in

---

7. E. Nestle and K. Aland, *Novum Testamentum Graece*, ed. B. Aland, K. Aland, et al. (Stuttgart: Deutsche Bibelgesellschaft, 1993). The text of this edition is the same as that of the 26th edition (1979), but the textual apparatus has been changed (see Nestle–Aland, 45*).

8. For the term "eclectic," see B. M. Metzger, *The Text of the New Testament*, 2nd ed. (New York: Oxford University Press, 1968), 175–179, and E. J. Epp, "The Eclectic Method in New Testament Textual Criticism: Solution or Symptom?" in *Studies in the Theory and Method of New Testament Criticism*, ed. E. J. Epp and G. D. Fee (Grand Rapids, Mich.: Eerdmans, 1993), 141–173. On these writings in particular, see J. K. Elliott, *The Greek Text of the Epistles to Timothy and Titus*, Studies and Documents 31 (Salt Lake City: University of Utah Press, 1968), 1–14.

9. According to Elliott, there has been reported papyrus evidence for 1 Tim 1:4–7, 15–16 (*Greek Text*, 13): K. Treue, "Neuetestamentliche Fragmente der Berliner Papyrussammlung," *Archiv für Papyrusforschung* 18 (1966). But I have not been able to confirm this, and it is not represented in Nestle–Aland. As for the possibility that a fragment of 1 Timothy is attested in a Greek MS from Qumran, see H. Puech, "Des fragments grecs de la grotte 7 et la Nouvelle Testament? 7Q4 et 7Q5 et le Papyrus Magdalen Greg 17-P64," *RB* 102 (1995): 570–584, whose answer is "impossible."

the great fourth-century uncial Codex Sinaiticus (‭א‬) and in the fifth-century uncial Codex Alexandrinus. In the fifth-century Codex Ephraemi Rescriptus, we find 1 Tim 1:1–3:9; 5:20–6:20; 2 Tim 1:1–2. The entire text of both letters is in the fifth-century Codex Bezae Cantabrigiensis (D). Other important witnesses include G (012, ninth century), H (015, sixth century), I (016, fifth century), K (017, ninth century), L (019, ninth century), ψ (044, ninth–tenth centuries), 048 (fifth century), and 049 (ninth century). In the NOTES portion of the commentary, I discuss variant readings with reference to these witnesses, as well as to such versions as the Old Latin, the Vulgate, the Syriac (especially the Peshitta and Harclean), and the Coptic (especially Bohairic and Sahidic), and citations from patristic authors.[10] For the most part, I follow the decisions of Nestle–Aland. At times, my translation provides a solution to some "hard readings" that are close to those represented in some of the variants.[11]

B. THE SIGNIFICANCE OF PAPYRUS EVIDENCE

It is always welcome when the happy accident of a papyrus find helps establish the early dating of a New Testament composition.[12] Caution is appropriate when assessing the absence of such evidence. The fact that the earliest substantial manuscript containing the Pauline letters (𝔓[46], ca. 200) lacks the Pastoral Letters is sometimes cited as an argument against their authenticity. Although it would have been fortunate to have such positive evidence, its absence is mitigated by the following observations:

1. The equally early 𝔓[32] (ca. 200) contains Tit 1:11–15 and 2:3–8. This does not, naturally, stand as evidence for 1 and 2 Timothy, but it does for the existence of "the Pastorals" as such.
2. 𝔓[46] has its own peculiarities: in addition to the three Pastorals, it also lacks 2 Thessalonians and Philemon, while containing instead the Letter to the

---

10. When early papyrus evidence is lacking, the patristic citations from versions are particularly important, not only as indicating the state of the text, but also as evidence for the reception of the composition.

11. Consideration of textual issues throughout the commentary is in conversation with B. M. Metzger, *A Textual Commentary on the Greek New Testament,* rev. ed. (New York: United Bible Societies, 1975), 639–656, and Elliott, *Greek Text.* Readers interested in comparing translations can consult the one provided for all three of the Pastorals in Quinn, *Letter to Titus,* as well as in R. G. Bratcher, *A Translator's Guide to Paul's Letters to Timothy and to Titus,* UBS Handbook Series (London: United Bible Societies, 1983), and D. C. Arichea and H. A. Hatton, *A Handbook of Paul's Letters to Timothy and Titus,* UBS Handbook Series (New York: United Bible Societies, 1995).

12. The most dramatic case is the discovery of papyri containing fragments of the Fourth Gospel (𝔓[52], 𝔓[66], 𝔓[75]) that point to a late-first-century or early-second-century date for composition, thus disproving the very late second-century dating proposed by the Tübingen School. See R. E. Brown, *The Gospel According to John (I–XII),* Anchor Bible 29 (Garden City, N. Y.: Doubleday, 1966), lxxx–lxxxiii.

Hebrews. $\mathfrak{P}^{46}$, in fact, may represent a special sort of collection of Paul's letters to "seven churches," thereby excluding letters to individuals.[13]

3. Other certainly authentic Pauline letters have as slender a representation in early papyri. Although 2 Corinthians is found in $\mathfrak{P}^{46}$, for example, it does not appear in any other papyrus, and large portions of it are also missing from Sinaiticus and Ephraemi. In contrast, the highly disputed Letter to the Ephesians is found not only in $\mathfrak{P}^{46}$, but also in the third-century $\mathfrak{P}^{49}$ and $\mathfrak{P}^{92}$.

4. Patristic citation of 1 and 2 Timothy substantially precedes the earliest MS evidence, certainly by as much as decades, possibly by as much as a century or more. This is especially the case with writers like Tertullian and Cyprian, who are using the Old Latin. For Tertullian to be citing from 1 and 2 Timothy from the Old Latin in the last decade of the second century suggests the existence of that translation—and an acceptance of the letters as Pauline—closer to the middle of the second century.

Arguments from silence are always hazardous, and nowhere more so than in the case of MS evidence. The absence of 1 and 2 Timothy from NT papyri has no significance either for the dating of the letters or for their authenticity.

C. TEXT AND HISTORY OF INTERPRETATION

Just as the ideal of the classic historical-critical method was to discover the pristine form of Christianity within the pages of the New Testament,[14] so classic text-criticism of the New Testament sought the earliest possible form of the text: the ideal critical text would be as close an approximation as possible to a hypothetical "autograph" of the composition. Another perspective on text-criticism is also possible. It recognizes that the critical Greek text is in fact a constructed reality and that no one before post-Enlightenment scholars (and the readers of their translations) had ever read the New Testament in that constructed form. Before the production of critical texts, made possible by the invention of printing, Christians heard the New Testament read liturgically in all the many versions now represented by separate manuscripts. The study of these variants thus

---

13. J. D. Quinn, "P46—The Pauline Canon?" *CBQ* 36 (1974): 379–385; N. A. Dahl, "The Particularity of the Pauline Epistles as a Problem in the Ancient Church," *Neotestamentica et Patristica*, NovTSup 7 (Leiden: Brill, 1962), 261–271.

14. According to F. C. Baur, "the essential nature of Christianity is a purely historical question, whose solution lies only in that Past in which Christianity had its origins; it is a problem which can only be solved by that critical attitude of thought which the consciousness of the present age assumed toward the past" (*Paul, the Apostle of Jesus Christ*, 2nd ed., ed. E. Zeller, trans. A. Menzies [London: Williams and Norgate, 1875], 1:2). Compare P. Wernle, *The Beginnings of Christianity*, trans. G. A. Bienemann (London: Williams and Norgate, 1903), 1:ix–x, and A. C. McGiffert, *A History of Christianity in the Apostolic Age* (New York: Scribner, 1897), 672.

becomes one way of doing the history of biblical interpretation. Those who heard Sinaiticus read liturgically understood Paul to be an apostle according to the promise (*epangelia*) of God, not the command (*epitagē*) of God in 1 Tim 1:1. Hearers of Bezae believed that the goal of the commandment in 1 Tim 1:4 was edification (*oikodomē*) rather than ordering (*oikonomia*). Likewise, the hearers of Bezae thought that Paul was telling Timothy to be an infant (*nēpion*) rather than gentle (*ēpion*) in 2 Tim 2:24, just as the hearers of Sinaiticus were convinced that Crescas had departed for Gaul (*gallia*) rather than Galatia (*galatia*) in 2 Tim 4:10. The analysis of such textual variants is a rich field of study that has yet to be fully exploited.[15]

---

15. For one approach to the topic, see B. D. Ehrman, *The Orthodox Corruption of Scripture: The Effect of Christological Controversies on the Text of the New Testament* (New York: Oxford University Press, 1993).

II. HISTORY OF INTERPRETATION
OF 1 AND 2 TIMOTHY

◆

A. EARLIEST INTERPRETATION

The earliest plausible evidence for the use of 1 and 2 Timothy occurs in Polycarp of Smyrna's *Letter to the Philippians*, written sometime between 110 and 135.[16] In *Phil.* 4:1, there is a double allusion (virtually a citation) of 1 Tim 6:10 and 6:7, appearing shortly after a statement suggesting that Polycarp intends to draw his instructions from Paul's letters and proceeds to shape his language from those letters (3:2–3). A less obvious echo of 1 Tim 1:1 appears in *Phil.* 8:1, and of 1 Tim 2:2 in *Phil.* 12:3. There are also fairly strong allusions to 2 Tim 2:12 in *Phil.* 5:2; 2 Tim 2:11 and 4:10 in *Phil.* 9:2; and 2 Tim 2:25 in *Phil.* 11:3. The use of 1 and 2 Timothy by Polycarp is particularly important, for it sets a baseline for theories of pseudonymous composition. If Polycarp knew and used these letters and considered them to be by Paul, then their composition has to substantially precede his own. The Pastorals could not, therefore, have been written in the middle of the second century, as some have proposed.[17] Because of the critical importance of Polycarp's evidence, it is not surprising that it has been challenged. In the COMMENT on 1 Tim 6:2b–10, I will take up that challenge in some detail.

There is no surprise to the Pastorals being seldom used by the Apologists of the second century, since the Apologists generally use the NT compositions sparingly. In Justin Martyr (ca. 100–165), we find no awareness of the Pastorals or, for that matter, of any other Pauline letters. According to Jerome, the Apologist Tatian (ca. 120–173) rejected 1 Timothy despite his acceptance of Titus, probably because of its position on asceticism.[18] In two of the Apologists, however, there is an almost certain reference to 1 Timothy. In Theophilus of Antioch, *To Autolycus* 14 (late second century), and Athenagoras of Athens, *Legation* 32 (second century), we find the claim that Christians pray for kings and rulers, using

---

16. In my view, the possible allusions in both Ignatius of Antioch and 1 Clement are too disputable to argue for the probable use of the Pastorals. For the evidence, see Spicq, *Épîtres pastorales*, 162–163, and D. A. Hagner, *The Use of the Old and New Testaments in Clement of Rome*, NovTSup 34 (Leiden: Brill, 1973), 236–237.

17. F. C. Baur dated the Pastorals to around 150 in *Die sogennanten Pastoralbriefe des Apostels Paulus auf neue kritisch untersuchte* (Stuttgart: Cotta'sche, 1835), 8–39. The latest date I have seen suggested is between 100 and 180 in E. D. Freed, *The New Testament: A Critical Introduction* (Belmont, Calif.: Wadsworth, 1986), 398.

18. Jerome, Prologue to the *Commentarium in Titum* (PL 26:555).

language very close to that of 1 Tim 2:2 and, more significantly, offering the same rationale: that Christians might live quiet and peaceful lives. The combination tilts the probability toward some knowledge of the Pauline dictum, if not awareness of 1 Timothy as such.

Toward the end of the second century, we find 1 and 2 Timothy being used vigorously in each part of the Christian world. In Gaul, Irenaeus (ca. 120/140–200/203) found these letters a resource for his battle *Against Heresies*, beginning the preface to book 1 with the citation of 1 Tim 1:4, introduced by "as the Apostle says."[19] In Alexandria, Clement (ca. 150–211/215) uses Tit 2:11–13 and 3:3–5 programmatically in *Exhortation* 1. In the *Paidagogue*, he quotes 1 Tim 5:23 (2:2), 6:10 (2:3), 2:9 (3:11, although he misattributes it to Peter!), and 6:2 (3:12). His use of 1 and 2 Timothy in the *Stromateis* is especially frequent. Of special interest is his testimony that the contents of 1 and 2 Timothy caused them to be rejected by some heretics. After citing 1 Tim 6:20, he says, "convicted by this utterance, the heretics reject the epistles to Timothy" (*Stromateis* 2.11).[20] The same account is given about Marcion by Tertullian (ca. 155/160–220) in North Africa. In his polemical treatise *Against Marcion*, Tertullian makes no use of the Pastoral Letters, in sharp contrast to his usual extensive citation of them.[21] The reason has to do with argumentative strategy. Tertullian cannot use these letters to rebut Marcion's reading of Paul because Marcion does not accept them: "He rejected the two epistles to Timothy and the one to Titus, which all treat of ecclesiastical discipline" (*Against Marcion* 5.21).[22] As with the statement in Clement of Alexandria, the phrasing makes clear that these letters were in existence before the time of Marcion and that he

---

19. See also the citation of 1 Tim 1:4 (*Fragment* 36), 1:9 (*Against Heresies* 4.16.3), 2:5 (5.17.1), 3:15 (3.1.1), 4:2 (2.21.2). The passage from 1 Timothy that begs to be cited is 6:20, which condemns *gnōsis* falsely so-called, a text perfect for the rebuttal of gnostic systems (*Against Heresies* 1.23.4; 2.pref.1; 2.14.7). Irenaeus also has two allusions to 2 Tim 3:6 (1.13.7) and 3:7 (5.20.2), as well as an explicit citation of 2 Tim 4:10–11 (3.14.1).

20. See also the citation of 1 Tim 5:21 (*Stromateis* 1.1), 6:3–5 (1.9), 1:18–19 (2.6), 4:1, 3 (3.6, 12), 5:14–15 (3.12), 3:2–4 (3.18), 1:9 (4.3; 7.2), 4:12 (4.16), 6:16 (6.3, 9), 4:10 (6.17), and 2 Tim 1:7–8 (4.7), 2:14 (1.10), 2:23 (1.11; 5.1), 3:2 (1.17), 2:25 (3.12).

21. See, for example, the citation of 1 Tim 2:2 (*Apology* 31), 1 Tim 1:19 and 6:10 (*On Idolatry* 11), 1 Tim 5:23 and 2 Tim 4:13 (*On the Crown* 8), 1 Tim 2:9 and 2 Tim 4:8 (*On the Crown* 14, 15), 1 Tim 1:4 and 3:2 (*On the Soul* 2, 16), 1 Tim 5:22 (*On Baptism* 18), 1 Tim 2:1, 8, and 4:13 (*On Prayer* 3, 13, 15), 1 Tim 6:10 (*On Patience* 7). In *Prescription Against Heresies*, there is the expected citation of 1 Tim 6:20 (25), but see also 1 Tim 1:18 (25), 1:4 and 4:1 (7), 6:3–4 (16), as well as 2 Tim 2:19 (3) and 2:17 (7). Of special interest is the combined use against Marcion and Valentinus of 1 Tim 4:3, 2 Tim 2:3, and 1 Tim 1:4, in *Prescription Against Heresies* 33. In *Against Hermogenes* 1, Tertullian refers to his opponent's antecedent in 2 Tim 1:15. In *Against Praxeas*, he makes particular use of 1 Timothy—see 2:5 (26), 6:16 (15, 16), 1:17 (15), and 6:20 (15)—just as in *Scorpiace* 13, he clusters references to 2 Tim 1:7, 8; 2:11; and 4:6. In *Resurrection of the Flesh*, Tertullian refers to 1 Tim 6:14, 15, 20 (23), 2:5 (51), as well as 2 Tim 1:17 (23) and 1:15 (24).

22. See also the citation of 2 Tim 3:16 (*On the Apparel of Women* 1:3) and 1 Tim 5:9 (*The Veiling of Virgins* 9), 5:9, 13 (*To His Wife* 1:7–8), 3:17, 5:14, and 4:1–3 (*On Monogamy* 12, 13, 15), 4:10, 1:19–20, 2:7, 5:22, and 1:13–15 (*On Modesty* 2, 13, 14, 18), 4:3 and 5:23 (*On Fasting* 1, 9).

chose to reject them.[23] The declarations of Tertullian and Clement are significant because, if true, they demand dating the Pastorals considerably before the year 135.[24]

In the first half of the third century, we can take Hippolytus of Rome (170–236), Cyprian of Carthage (200–258), and Origen of Alexandria (184–254) as representative. Hippolytus makes relatively light use of 1 and 2 Timothy.[25] Cyprian makes vigorous use of both writings in his *Letters*,[26] treatise *On the Unity of the Church*,[27] shorter moral writings,[28] and *Testimonies*.[29] Out of Origen's vast work, we can note only his use of 1 and 2 Timothy in the extant portions of *Commentary on John*,[30] *Commentary on Matthew*,[31] *On First Principles*,[32] and *Against Celsus*.[33] From the latter part of the third century, we see the use of 1 and 2 Timothy in Pseudo-Clement, *First Epistle on Virginity*,[34] in the writings of Novatian of Rome (210–280),[35] and in the epistles of the teachers of the Alexandrian church.[36] We can mention as well the citation of 1 Tim 2:4 by

---

23. In contrast, H. Y. Gamble states a commonly held view: "One traditional component of the Pauline collection was not regularly present in its early editions, namely, the pseudonymous letters to Timothy and Titus. The first explicit witness to their presence in the collection is Irenaeus late in the second century. Prior to that time, their status is unclear. They formed no part of Marcion's edition, *doubtless because Marcion did not know them and not, as Tertullian alleged* (Adv. Marc. 5.21), *because he rejected them* [emphasis added]" (*The New Testament Canon: Its Making and Meaning* [Philadelphia: Fortress Press, 1985] 42). The statement goes considerably beyond what the historian can justifiably say and ignores the evidence from both Clement and Jerome concerning second-century heretics and their nonuse of the Pastorals.

24. For the specific problems connected to the second-century prologues to the Pauline letters and their connection to Marcion, see D. de Bruyne, "Prologues bibliques d'origines marcionite," *Revue bénédictine* 14 (1907):1–16; M. J. LaGrange, "Les Prologues prétendus marcionites," *RB* 35 (1926): 161–173; and Dahl, "Origin of the Earliest Prologues."

25. 1 Tim 4:3 (*Refutation of All Heresies* 7:18), 5:20 (*Commentary on Proverbs*), 37:22 and 2 Tim 2:1–2 (*Christ and Antichrist* 1).

26. 1 Tim 6:3–5 (*Letter* 39:6), 2 Tim 2:20 (50:3, 51:25), 2 Tim 4:12 (64:3), 2 Tim 2:4 (65:1), 1 Tim 1:13 (72:13), 2 Tim 2:17 (72:15), 1 Tim 6:3–5 (73:3).

27. 1 Tim 2:9–10 (*On the Unity of the Church* 8), 6:9 (12), 6:7 (19).

28. 1 Tim 6:7–10 (*Works and Alms* 10) and 2 Tim 2:4–5, 11–12 (*Exhortation to Martyrdom* 5, 8).

29. 1 Tim 2:9–10 (*Testimonies* 36), 2:11–14 (46), 4:3–4 (67), 5:3–12 (75), 5:19 (76), 5:20 (77), and 2 Tim 2:4–5 (11), 2:23–24 (53), 4:3–4 (67), 4:6–8 (16).

30. 2 Tim 3:11, 16 (*Commentary on John* 1.5), 3:4 (10.13), and 1 Tim 3:15 (10.16).

31. 1 Tim 4:13 (*Commentary on Matthew* 2.15), 1:7 (12.41), 6:5 (11.9), 6:10 (11.10), 4:5 (11.14), 3:1 (11.16; 14.22), 3:10 (12.14), 3:12 (14.22), 5:9 (14.22), 6:20 (12.12), and 2 Tim 3:12 (2.18).

32. 2 Tim 1:3 (*On First Principles* 2.4), 1:16–18 (3.1), 2:20–21 (2.9; 3.1), 4:1–3 (2.7).

33. 1 Tim 1:15 (*Against Celsus* 1.63), 2:1–2 (8.73), 3:15 (5.33), 3:16 (3.31), 4:4–5 (8.32), 4:10 (4.28), 6:17–18 (8.21), 6:20 (3.11), and 2 Tim 1:3 (5.61), 1:10 (3.61), 2:11 (2.69), 2:15 (5.1), 2:20 (4.70), 3:8 (4.51), 4:1–3 (5.61), 4:7 (7.52).

34. 1 Tim 5:3 (*First Epistle on Virginity* 11), 6:20 (6), and 2 Tim 2:7 (3), 3:5 (3).

35. 1 Tim 1:17 (*On the Trinity* 3), 2:5 (21), 4:1 (29), 6:16 (30), 6:8 (*On Jewish Meats* 6).

36. Peter of Alexandria (260–311), *Canonical Epistle* 14, for 1 Tim 6:11–12; Alexander of Alexandria (273–326), *Epistles on the Arian Controversy*, for 1 Tim 6:3–4 (1.13) and 2 Tim 2:17 (2.5), 3:4 (1.13).

Methodius of Olympia (260–312) in *Banquet* 2.7, and by Archelaus in *Acts of Disputation with Manes*, written in 277.[37]

This partial survey of uses up to the fourth century shows that 1 and 2 Timothy were used early and widely throughout the church. They are universally cited as Pauline. Those who reject them (possibly Tatian and the Valentinians,[38] certainly Marcion) did so, apparently, on the basis of their contents rather than their authorship.

The ways in which the letters were used are also of interest. As noted several times, both letters lent themselves in obvious ways to the condemnation of heretics. But they were also used as evidence for Paul's life, especially his conversion and imprisonment. Theologically, it is 1 Timothy's portrayal of Jesus as the one mediator between God and humans (2:5) and declaration of God as living in unapproachable light (6:16) that draws the most attention. To a remarkable degree, the use of the letters focuses where the letters themselves focus: on the moral life, especially the dangers of the love of money and the need to share possessions (1 Tim 6:7–10, 17–19). It is also worth noting that texts that we might have supposed to have been used frequently are not; in his treatises on the apparel of women and the veiling of virgins, for example, Tertullian makes no use of 1 Tim 2:8–9. In the literature I have surveyed, the only use of 1 Tim 2:11–15 is in Cyprian of Carthage's *Testimonies* 46: under the heading "That Women Should Be Silent in Church," he cites, with no comment, the passage from 1 Timothy together with 1 Cor 14:34–35. Most of all, the letters to Timothy and Titus are read together with, and contextualized by, the other letters of Paul. And since the dominant way such early readers appropriated Paul was as a moral teacher, this only made the letters to Timothy seem more obviously his own.[39]

The *Apostolic Constitutions*, a church order of the fourth century, probably of Syrian provenance, can usefully provide a summary to this survey of the early use of 1 and 2 Timothy in the church, especially since, as will be discussed later, the Pastorals are sometimes thought to be a stage of development toward church orders. The composition basically provides directions for every imaginable aspect of ecclesial life. In the discussion of the place of women in the church (1.3.7–10), it should be observed, the *Apostolic Constitutions* does not employ 1 Timothy at all. 1 Tim 3:2–6 is cited in support of the character desired in bishops (2.1.2). 2 Tim 2:5 appears by way of allusion in an exhortation to "strive lawfully" (2.3.14), and 2 Tim 2:3–4 is used as guidance to the recognition of wicked people to be avoided (3.6.43). In a discussion of the age of widows in 3.1.1, the composition cites 1 Tim 5:9–11 as authoritative. When the silence of women

---

37. 1 Tim 4:1–4 is applied directly to Manes himself in *Acts of Disputation* 35. See also 1 Tim 1:20 (13), 1:9 (31), and 2 Tim 3:8–9 (45).

38. Tertullian says that the Valentinians used the same Scriptures that he did (*Prescription Against Heresies* 38).

39. D. K. Rensberger, "As the Apostle Teaches: The Development of the Use of Paul's Letters in Second Century Christianity" (Ph.D. diss., Yale University, 1981).

in the church is enjoined (3.1.6), it is not 1 Tim 2:11–15 that is quoted but 1 Cor 14:34. That the clergy should be married is supported by 1 Tim 3:2 and 3:12 (6.3.17). That the ordained should be able rightly to divide the word of God is authorized by 2 Tim 2:15 (7.2.31). That Jannes and Jambres opposed Moses is found in 2 Tim 3:8 (8.1.1). That prayer should be offered for kings and rulers is given warrant by 1 Tim 2:2 (8.2.13), and, finally, that God dwells in light inaccessible is taught by 1 Tim 6:16 (8.2.15).

The impression given by the early patristic use of 1 and 2 Timothy is confirmed by the evidence offered by statements concerning the canonical process. I speak cautiously here, for much recent scholarship has devoted itself to dismantling the premise that there was a canon of the New Testament before the late fourth century.[40] An unfortunate aspect of such research is the tendency to equate the organic process of canonization—which involved the exchange, collection, and selection of writings in many churches—with the much more formal stage of ratification, by which bishops and councils sought to solidify and generalize the results of the earlier process. The two stages need to be distinguished in order to avoid the (thoroughly ahistorical) conclusion that there were no collections of normative texts before the fourth century or that the very idea of canon was a fourth-century invention. Just the contrary is true: although the process reached an unprecedented level of stabilization in the late fourth century, it was under way since Paul's letters were first exchanged between communities. Indeed, it is difficult to know what to call the display of evidence given earlier for the use of these three letters across such a spread of literature if not the signs of an emerging canon of Scripture.

That Origen considered the three letters to be part of Scripture is clear from his reference to Paul and the "fourteen trumpets [he was clearly including Hebrews] of his epistles" in *Homilies on Joshua* 7:1,[41] as well as from the various uses of the letters I have recounted. Tertullian also speaks of confirming opinions out of the Old Testament and out of the New Testament (*Against Praxeas* 15), and although he does not produce a complete list of writings to be included in the New Testament, his objection to Marcion's exclusion of the Pastorals clearly indicates that they were included in his own New Testament (*Against Marcion* 5.21). Considerable dispute now surrounds the Muratorian Canon: Should it be read as a Roman canonical list of around 170 or as a Syrian canonical list from the late fourth century? Despite the arguments brought against an early and Roman dating, I continue to find the reference to the Shepherd of

---

40. See, for example, the revisionist scholarship concerning the so-called Muratorian Canon in A. C. Sundberg, "Canon Muratori: A Fourth Century List," *HTR* 66 (1973): 1–41; G. M. Hahneman, *The Muratorian Fragment and the Development of the Canon* (Oxford: Clarendon Press, 1992); and L. M. McDonald, *The Formation of the Christian Biblical Canon*, rev. ed. (Peabody, Mass.: Hendrickson, 1995).

41. E. R. Kalin throws doubt on Rufinus's translation of this passage in "Re-Examining New Testament Canon History: I. The Canon of Origen," *Currents in Theology and Mission* 17 (1990): 274–282. They are, in my view, insufficient to discredit the testimony of Origen on this point.

Hermas in lines 70–76 convincing evidence for the traditional dating.[42] In any case, the place of the three Pastorals within the list is secure. After listing the letters that Paul wrote to "the seven churches," the document states, "[Paul also wrote] out of affection and love to Philemon, one to Titus, and two to Timothy; and these are held sacred in the esteem of the church catholic for the regulation of ecclesiastical discipline" (lines 59–63).[43] Although the authorship of the four letters to individuals is recognized as Pauline, so is their distinctive character: Philemon is regarded as an affectionate letter, while the Pastorals have to do with ecclesiastical discipline.

Eusebius of Caesarea (260–340) is a key figure in the history of canonization. He traces the implicit canons of the writers antecedent to him and summarizes the state of the question at the time of Constantine. In *Ecclesiastical History* 3.3.1, he lists the "fourteen letters of Paul" (again including Hebrews in this number) among the undisputed compositions in the canon (see also 3.25.3). No special note is taken of the letters to Timothy and Titus because their Pauline authorship is not in question. In his famous *Paschal Letter* of 364, Athanasius (ca. 293–373) lists "fourteen letters of the apostle Paul," enumerating "two letters to Timothy, one to Titus" (*Letter* 39 [*PG* 26:1177]). Cyril of Jerusalem (315–386) also lists "the fourteen epistles of Paul" among the compositions that "belong to the New Testament" and are to be "read in the church" (*Catechetical Lectures* 4:36 [*PG* 33:499]). In the West, the three letters are included among Paul's in the canonical lists of Rufinus (*Commentary on the Creed* 36 [*PL* 21:374]), Augustine (*On Christian Doctrine* 2.13 [*PL* 34:41]), and the Council of Carthage (Canon 39) in 397.[44]

Before turning to the commentaries devoted to 1 and 2 Timothy in the patristic period, we should note the subtle way in which these letters, through the sponsorship of Augustine and John Chrysostom, helped shape the medieval world. In *On Christian Doctrine*, 1.26, Augustine takes 1 Tim 1:5, "the goal of the commandment is love [*agape*]," as the foundation for his central hermeneutical principle for interpreting all Scripture, as well as for the Christian moral life. Difficulties and contradictions in Scripture are to be resolved on the basis of charity. Where many meanings are possible in a text, it is the reading that builds up charity that should be regarded as the best (1.35–36). Such interpretation can be accomplished, however, only by one who reads and who lives "from a pure heart" (again from 1 Tim 1:5 [1.40]). That Augustine has not simply lifted one verse from a letter out of convenience is shown by his development of the ideal of the Christian teacher, based on the portrayal of Paul as

---

42. Even Hahneman, who argues against this time and place, agrees that such is the "plain reading" of the text, and his argument against it is not fully convincing (*Muratorian Fragment*, 33–72). See also P. Henne, "La Datation du *Canon* de Muratori," *RB* 100 (1993): 54–75.

43. The translation is that of B. M. Metzger, *The Canon of the New Testament: Its Origin, Development, and Significance* (Oxford: Clarendon Press, 1987), 305–307.

44. For the text, see A. Souter, *The Text and Canon of the New Testament*, 2nd ed., rev. C. S. C. Williams, Studies in Theology 25 (London: Duckworth, 1954), 204.

"teacher of the nations" (1 Tim 2:7 [4.7]). In *On Christian Doctrine* 4.16, Augustine weaves together 1 Tim 4:11; 5:1; 2 Tim 1:13; 2:15; 4:2; Tit 1:9; 2:12; 2:15–3:1; and 2 Tim 3:14 in an exposition of the qualities that the Christian teacher is to possess. From the second to the fifth century, then, the perception of Paul the teacher in the Pastoral Letters not only helps shape the understanding of Paul as teacher throughout the rest of his correspondence, but also deeply affects the understanding of the style and the goal of Christian pedagogy within the church.

No less significant is the employment of 1 and 2 Timothy in John Chrysostom's *On the Priesthood* (PG 48:623–692). Paul's instructions and exhortations to Timothy are taken by Chrysostom as directly applicable to the *presbyteros* of his own age. Thus the priest must have extraordinary generosity of spirit (2:4 [2 Tim 2:25]), must be of good reputation (2:4 [1 Tim 3:7]), and must desire the work of leadership rather than the honor (3:11 [1 Tim 3:1]). Because of these demands, the office should be entered only with caution (4:1 [1 Tim 5:22]). In *On the Priesthood* 4:8, Chrysostom pulls together a number of citations from Paul "in his epistle to his disciple," quoting in sequence from 1 Tim 4:13; 2 Tim 2:24; 3:4; 3:16; Tit 1:9; and 1 Tim 5:17. Paul in these passages has been "sketching the portrait of the good priest" (6:5). Chrysostom helps secure the function of these letters as a guide for a clerical medieval Christianity. It is no surprise, then, that he also uses 1 Tim 2:12 as the explicit warrant for refusing to consider the claims of some women to be allowed access to priesthood (3:9).

B. PATRISTIC COMMENTARIES

In the East, the earliest genuine commentary on 1 and 2 Timothy is in Syriac by Ephraim Syrus (306–373).[45] His comments weave in and out of the Pauline text. On 1 Tim 1:4, Ephraim is clear that the opponents are Jewish. They indulge in genealogical speculation about descent from Abraham. He sees the contrast between their sponsorship of law and the goal of Paul's commandment: *propter ipsam charitatem ordinata sunt mandata omnia: et ubi charitas est, nihil opus est legis* (all laws were ordained for the sake of love itself, and where there is love there is no need for a law, 244). Concerning the silence of women in the assembly, he adds that they should obey the priests (248)! And somewhat oddly, he renders 3:1 as desire for the presbyterate rather than the bishopric (249). He considers 2 Timothy to have been written before Paul's death so that Paul might be an exemplar to Timothy (256). He considers the error of Hymenaeus and Philetos to be that they taught the immortality of the soul rather than bodily resurrection (261). He makes vigorous use of the Acts of the Apostles to explain the biographical references in the letter (264–265). He considers Alexander the Coppersmith to be an associate of Simon Magus (267).

---

45. Some comments by Origen on Titus 3:10–11 are preserved in Pamphylius (240–309), *Apology* 1, which was translated in the fourth century by Rufinus (PG 17:553–557). Armenian monks translated Ephraim Syrus, *Commentarii in Epistolas D. Pauli* (Venice: St. Lazarus, 1893), 243–268.

Theodore of Mopsuestia (350–428) earns his reputation as an excellent exegete in his commentaries on 1 and 2 Timothy.[46] 1 Timothy is written to Paul's
delegate in Ephesus for the sake of "ecclesiastical order" in the churches throughout Asia, and it remains useful, Theodore says, to contemporary bishops (67–68).
2 Timothy is written at a considerable time after the first letter, and is sent from
Rome during the time of a second imprisonment. Timothy's location is not
known precisely; he is certainly not in Ephesus (191–193 [2 Tim 4:12]).
Theodore is a careful reader of the text, seeking to follow Paul's logic and explaining terms that may seem obscure. He provides a nuanced reading of 1 Tim
2:11–15. Paul's instruction in this passage was generated by the practice of
prophecy, to keep it from disturbing the church (93–94); Paul is not concerned
with domestic discourse, and women are free to teach husbands who are not of
the faith (94). In his explanation of Paul's reading of Genesis, Theodore says
that Paul wanted to avoid "an inference that a state of deception and sin is the
normal condition of womankind" (95). Women are equals with men in the assembly regarding piety, but "it is necessary for them to hold a secondary position in the common life" (96). In short, Theodore seeks to mitigate rather than
exacerbate the force of Paul's instructions. Similarly, he sees 1 Tim 3:11 as referring to women deacons (128). Theodore's sensitivity to the literary texture of
2 Timothy is shown in his recognition that Paul's mention of Onesiphorus
(1:16–17) has an exemplary function (202). He does not engage in much theological reflection, but when he does, it is to good effect (88–89).

John Chrysostom (347–407) devotes eighteen homilies to 1 Timothy and ten
to 2 Timothy.[47] As is the case with those of other ancient commentators, his introductory comments are fairly rudimentary and based largely on the evidence
offered by the letters. In response to the question why Paul wrote to Timothy
and Titus and not to other close associates, however, his answer is simplicity itself: associates like Silvanus and Barnabas stayed at Paul's side, whereas Titus
and Timothy had already been put in charge of conspicuous churches (*PG*
62:503). Chrysostom's commentary can properly be called moralistic. He connects Paul's statement about the *telos* (goal) of the commandment being *agape*
(love, 1 Tim 1:5), for example, with the lack of love shown generally by heretics
throughout the history of the church (2.1 [*PG* 62:510]). He reads 1 Tim 1:12
as an example of Paul's humility (*tapeinophrosynē*, 3–4 [*PG* 62:515–526]). He
turns sections of the letters into extended exhortations of the hearers (see 6.2–3
[*PG* 62:531–535]; 7.3 [*PG* 62:558]). At the same time, Chrysostom provides a
rich set of Pauline parallels and cross-references, reading the letters within the
context of the Pauline correspondence as a whole.

On certain points, the commentary of Theodoret of Cyr (393–466) shows def-

---

46. Theodore of Mopsuestia, *In Epistolas B. Pauli Commentarii: The Latin Edition with Greek
Fragments*, vol 2, *1 Thessalonians–Philemon*, ed. H. B. Swete (Cambridge: Cambridge University
Press, 1882).

47. John Chrysostam, *Homilia in Epistolam Primam ad Timotheum* (PG 62:501–599); *Homilia
in Epistolam Secundum ad Timotheum* (PG 62:599–662).

inite lines of continuity with that of Chrysostom:[48] on 1 Tim 2:15, for example, he agrees that "if they remain" refers to the children rather than the women, but that women have a responsibility to train their children in the faith (*PG* 82:804). He reads 1 Tim 3:11 as referring to women deacons in the church (*PG* 82:809). He brings a greater historical awareness to the task of interpretation. The genealogies and myths in 1 Tim 1:4 are connected to the practice of Jewish interpretation of the Law "called by them the second [*deuterōsis*]," an accurate report on the "second Torah" of the oral tradition (*PG* 82:789).

He deduces (with Theodore of Mopsuestia) that women are being silenced in church because of their practice of prophecy (*PG* 82:802). In 2 Tim 2:18, he understands the teaching of Hymenaios and Philetos to be that resurrection is accomplished through the continuation of biological life in one's offspring (*PG* 82:843)—perhaps a reading influenced by the *Acts of Paul and Thecla* 14. But his interpretation does not lack theological engagement: on 2 Tim 3:16, Theodoret says, "using a distinction, he [Paul] separates Scripture from human wisdom. Scripture is divinely inspired, meaning it is spiritual. For grace was spoken by the divine Spirit through the prophets and apostles. If therefore, as according to the divine apostle, the Holy Spirit is God, then Scripture is inspired by the Spirit of God" (*PG* 82:849).

The commentary of John of Damascus (675–749) is extremely brief, especially for portions of 2 Timothy, which leave sections of the biblical text either without comment or with only a few telegraphic remarks.[49] In places, one can see the way in which commentaries begin to pass on observations derived from predecessors. On 1 Tim 1:20, for example, Damascene carries over the same remark found earlier in Chrysostom and Theodoret, that the phrase *hina paideuthōsin* (in order that they be taught) does not mean that humans are to instruct them, but God (*PG* 95:1003). Likewise, he follows the developing tradition concerning 1 Tim 2:15, that women's role is the education of their children; he makes the point even more strongly by insisting that the women's salvation really depends on their success in saving others—an insistence guaranteed to create overanxious mothers and overinstructed children! He says, "This is no small matter, lifting up children to God, from whom they were given" (*PG* 95:1005). Damascene sees 1 Tim 4:1–3 as a straightforward prediction of the Marcionites and Manicheans (*PG* 95:1009), identifies the lion in 2 Tim 4:17 as Nero (*PG* 95:1023), and names the Linus of 2 Tim 4:21 as the successor of Peter in the bishopric of Rome (*PG* 95:1026). The commentary is not masterful, but neither is it without interest.

In the West, the earliest extant commentary on 1 and 2 Timothy is based on the Old Latin (pre-Vulgate) text. The name Ambrosiaster is given to the anonymous late-fourth-century author who comments on all thirteen of Paul's letters.[50]

---

48. Theodoret of Cyr, *Interpretatio Epistolae I ad Timotheum* (PG 82:787–830); *Interpretatio Epistolae II ad Timotheum* (PG 82:831–858).

49. John of Damascus, *In Epistolam Primam ad Timotheum* (PG 95:997–1016); *In Epistolam Secundam ad Timotheum* (PG 95:1016–1026).

50. In *PL* 17:487–526, it appears under the name Ambrose (it was Erasmus who first coined the designation Ambrosiaster).

His remarks are brief and tend to contemporize the letters with little sense of the historical distance between Paul's time and his own. The commentary shows no influence from the Eastern tradition. The Jews miss the real meaning of the Law because they miss faith in Christ, without whom the Law makes no sense, and the Law is used lawfully when it is read Christologically (1 Tim 1:6–8). Similarly, on 1 Tim 1:15–16, Ambrosiaster reflects Christologically on the logion that Jesus came into the world to save sinners: "Coming down from heaven to earth he accepted the flesh of sin, he mingled with the earthly in order to make it heavenly." On 1 Tim 2:1–4, Ambrosiaster constrains God's will to save all humans by insisting on the need for humans to respond to God's invitation. In contrast, he strengthens Paul's injunction against women speaking in church (1 Tim 2:11–15): they should be subject to the ones from whom they derive! And the salvation of women is now dependent on their children correctly believing in Christ (2:15). Similarly, he rejects the idea that 3:11 speaks of women deacons, blaming the Cataphrygians (followers of Montanus) for such an interpretation. Paul's discussion of the widows in 5:3–16 is read entirely in terms of contemporary ecclesiastical arrangements. In 2 Tim 1:3–5, the sense of distance from Judaism is profound: God was the God of the Jews, but is now the God of Christians!

The next Latin commentary on 1 and 2 Timothy[51] is that of Pelagius (late fourth–early fifth century), who comments on all thirteen Pauline epistles (*PL* 30:917–940).[52] Once again, the merging of the Pauline and contemporary ecclesiastical worlds is observable. In the *Argumentum* to 1 Timothy, Pelagius identifies Timothy simply as "this bishop" (474). Defining "faith" in 4:12, Pelagius notes telegraphically: *in fide. Catholica, vel perfecta* (in faith. Catholic, or perfect, 492). There is a direct link between 2 Tim 2:25 and the Novatian Heresy (517). The word-battles of 1 Tim 6:4 are directly attributed to the Manicheans (499). Pelagius seems to have some awareness of earlier Greek commentaries. On 1 Tim 1:4, he uses the term *deuterōsis* without seeming to recognize its meaning as the "second," or "oral," Torah (475). On the authority of women over men (1 Tim 2:12), he resembles Oecumenius (see below): *publice non permittit: nam filium vel fratrem debet docere privatim* (she cannot do it publicly, for she must teach a son or brother privately, 482). And he sometimes gives several interpretations for a single verse, showing an awareness of earlier readings (2 Tim 2:18 [514–515]; 3:20 [515]; 3:10 [519]; 3:13 [520]). Finally, Pelagius places the letters within the larger context of Scripture, drawing widely from other texts to make points (e.g., 483, 486, 488, 509, 513).

Not properly a commentary but rather a discussion of three difficult passages in 1 and 2 Timothy appears in the *Instructionum Libri Duo ad Salonium* (*PL* 50:808) by Eucherius, a fifth-century bishop of Lyons. His book takes the form

51. There is a commentary on Titus alone by Jerome, *Commentarium in Titum* (*PL* 26:555–600), written around 387 or 388.

52. A. Souter, "Pelagius's Expositions of the Thirteen Epistles of St. Paul," in *Texts and Studies: Contributions to Biblical and Patristic Literature*, ed. J. A. Robinson (Cambridge: Cambridge University Press, 1922), IX 2:474–524.

of questions and answers about Scripture. The first question, on 1 Tim 2:1, asks the differences among the four terms used for prayer—still an exegetical issue—but the answer is in terms of Latin usage and is not terribly illuminating for the Greek. The second question (another good one) concerns the matter of sins preceding one to judgment in 1 Tim 5:19; the answer, unfortunately, refers the passage to the final judgment before God, not—as in the letter itself—an ecclesial setting. The question on 2 Tim 4:14 inquires into the theological appropriateness of Paul's statement there and in Acts 23:3 threatening punishment; the answer is that the verb is future ("God will pay back") rather than subjunctive ("may God pay back").

C. MEDIEVAL COMMENTARIES

In the East, Oecumenius of Tricca (tenth century) provides a full and, in many respects, satisfying commentary on both letters.[53] His interpretation is characterized first by its close attention to the details of language. In 1 Timothy—which he thinks was written from Laodicea (PG 119:134)—he works with the odd syntax of 1:18 (PG 119:146) and recognizes the difficulty of the phrase *hotan katastrēniasōsin* (when they grow wanton) in 5:11 (PG 119:178). Oecumenius seeks to resolve contradictions in the text: he asks how Paul can call himself the first of sinners (1:15) if in Phil 3:6 Paul also said he was without reproach with respect to the Law (PG 119:146). In Paul's more explicitly theological sections, Oecumenius is concerned to make the statements work within the framework of a developed trinitarian theology (PG 119:152). And the typical patristic piety shines through: What does Paul mean for the men to pray with pure hands (1 Tim 2:8)? He means that they should be free from avarice, rapaciousness, and murder, purified by almsgiving (PG 119:153). Oecumenius also has an unusually positive perspective on women in the church. Like his predecessors, he views women's salvation through *teknogonia* as a matter not simply of bearing, but also of educating children in the faith (*kata theon anagagein*, "bringing them up according to God"). But he asks whether this means that widows and virgins without children cannot be saved, and answers *apage* (literally, "get away!"): they also are saved by their virtuous lives; the raising of children is rather an opportunity presented to parents (PG 119:157). The women in 1 Tim 3:11 are deaconesses (PG 119:161). In the discussion of the good works expected of the widows in 1 Tim 5:10, Oecumenius remarks that these are the sort of things that women without children can do (PG 119:172). In 2 Timothy, he remarks on the "encomium" Paul gives to the women who educated Timothy (PG 119:201). In 2 Tim 3:6, he is at pains to point out that Paul does not imply that all women are seducible this way, because "there are women who are virile by nature, just

53. Oecumenius of Tricca, *Pauli Apostoli ad Timotheum Prior Epistola* (PG 119:133–196); *Pauli Apostoli ad Timotheum Epistola Secunda* (PG 119:195–240).

as there are men who are feminine by nature," meaning by this a compliment: women can be strong and resist false teaching, while some men can easily be swayed (*PG* 119:224). Oecumenius notes that Paul lists Priscilla before Aquila in 4:19, because "she was more faithful and more diligent than him" (*PG* 119:240). Finally, he comments on the name Claudia among the greetings: "You see how even women went through fire and were fervent and were crucified to the world. For the gender [*genos*] is not less than that of a man, if she wishes it" (*PG* 119:240).

The eleventh-century Bulgarian archbishop Theophylact follows Oecumenius closely in his commentaries on the two letters to Timothy, as he does in his commentaries on other NT writings.[54] Thus large portions of his exposition are drawn substantially from that of Oecumenius (e.g., *PG* 125:18, 21, 27, 35, 39). Of particular interest are the point-by-point explanations of the virtues and vices listed by Paul in various places (*PG* 125:44, 60, 81, 117). There are some distinguishing touches: Theophylact considers the myths and genealogies to be Greek rather than Jewish (*PG* 125:13), and he entirely lacks the anti-Jewish tendency of Oecumenius. He adds significant lexical comment (*PG* 125:15). In the contemporizing of 1 Tim 4:1–3, he adds the Encratites to the Marcionites and Manicheans (*PG* 125:52). Concerning the prohibition of women teaching, Theophylact argues that Paul's concern was public rather than private: "She is not prohibited from [teaching] in private, in the way that Priscilla instructed Apollos, and the faithful woman catechizes her husband" (*PG* 125:37). Likewise, the women in 1 Tim 3:11 are deacons (*PG* 125:47). Like Oecumenius, Theophylact takes the denial of the resurrection in 2 Tim 2:18 as equivalent to the denial of the final judgment, with its rewards and retributions (*PG* 125:109). He notes concerning 2 Tim 3:6 that Paul does not condemn women as a whole or by nature (*PG* 125:120), and repeats Oecumenius's praise of women occasioned by the name Claudia—although not that concerning Priscilla (*PG* 125:140).

In the West, the *Commentaria in Epistolas S. Pauli* (*PL* 68:659–684), attributed to Primasius, a sixth-century bishop of Hadrumetum in North Africa, is more properly assigned to the school of Cassiodorus (485–580). It is basically a reworking of Pelagius's commentary with few distinctive features. In contrast, the full commentary of Aimon d'Auxerre (d. 855) is a rich and in many ways original creation, the true beginning of the medieval commentary tradition on 1 and 2 Timothy.[55] It elaborates legendary information concerning both Timothy (his mother was a widow, he had a Greek education and was ordained a presbyter before becoming a bishop [*PL* 117:789]) and Paul (his father was from Gischala and lived among nobles in Tarsus [*PL* 117:810]). Aimon has, however,

---

54. Theophylact of Bulgaria, *Epistolae Primae Divi Pauli ad Timotheum Expositio* (*PG* 125:9–87); *Epistolae Secundae Divi Pauli ad Timotheum Expositio* (*PG* 125:87–140). Compare the commentaries of Oecumenius and Theophylact on James.

55. Aimon d'Auxerre, *Expositio in Divi Pauli Epistolas* (*PL* 117:783–810). There is also a commentary on Titus by Alcuin (d. 804), *Tractatus super Sancti Pauli ad Titum Epistolam* (*PL* 100:1009–1026).

access to Greek texts, so he must discuss the difference between the *fidelis sermo* (faithful word) of his Latin in 1 Tim 1:17 and the *anthrōpinos logos* (human word) in the Greek (*PL* 117:785). He also has some knowledge of Jewish lore — probably through Jerome — as shown by his discussion of myths and genealogies in 1 Tim 1:3–4 (*PL* 117:783–784) and by his awareness of apocryphal writings that contain the names Jannes and Jambres (*PL* 117:807). All the instruction concerning church order in 1 Timothy is interpreted in light of medieval practice. Paul directs all bishops and priests (1 Tim 2:1) to celebrate solemn masses (*PL* 117:788)! Paul does not need to address the issue of priests because all bishops are already priests (*PL* 117:792)! Although some want to see women deacons in 1 Tim 3:11, Augustine's authority is invoked to deny the possibility (*PL* 117:792).

Aimon's is, nevertheless, an intelligent and thoughtful commentary: he struggles with the meaning of 1 Tim 2:15 and offers several possible interpretations (*PL* 117:791). On 1 Tim 6:10, he tries to show how both avarice and pride can be called the root of evils by Scripture (*PL* 117:796). But the true sign of medieval imagination coming into play is found in his commentary on 2 Tim 2:3–7: Paul's comment on Timothy's need to have intelligence to grasp his analogies serves as permission for a spiritual reading of the text in addition to the literal (*PL* 117:802). Similarly, the Law is read lawfully only when it is understood completely in terms of moral and spiritual realities pointing to Christ (*PL* 117:785).

Rabanus Maurus (784–856) was not an original theologian, but handed on tradition in a learned fashion. His commentaries on 1 and 2 Timothy have just that character.[56] His discussions are so full that the text almost disappears. He spends over five columns in *PL* on 1 Tim 2:1. There are two reasons for such prolixity: all his cross-references to Scripture are cited in full, and his commentary has abundant borrowings from Jerome, Augustine, Gregory, and Cassiodorus. Much briefer, but with the same anthological tendency, is the curious work by Florus (790–860), a deacon of Lyons, whose compendium circulated widely under the name of the Venerable Bede. His "commentaries" on the letters of Paul consist entirely of extracts from the writings of Augustine.[57] In fact, he does not even provide the full citations from Augustine, but merely the first and final lines of the intended reference, together with the identification of the book from which it was drawn. If not terribly illuminating on the text of the letters, Florus's work shows how the weight of authority bore down on medieval interpreters and how complexly (if narrowly) intertextual their world became.

---

56. Rabanus Maurus, *Expositio in Epistolam I ad Timotheum* (*PL* 112:580–636); *Expositio in Epistolam II ad Timotheum* (*PL* 112:636–654).

57. Florus of Lyons, *Expositio in Epistolam I ad Timotheum* (*PL* 119:397–406); *In Epistolam II ad Timotheum* (*PL* 119:406–410). See the similar construction of "commentaries" on James drawn from the writings of Gregory the Great by Paterius and Alulfus in L. T. Johnson, *The Letter of James*, Anchor Bible 37A (New York: Doubleday, 1995), 138–139.

The "commentaries" of Lanfranc (1010–1089), archbishop of Canterbury, have the same character,[58] with only the bare text of the letter followed by glosses derived from the writings of Ambrosiaster and Augustine, with Lanfranc filling the gaps with glosses of his own. Similar is the work of Anselm of Laon (d. 1117), whose bare comments on the text are considered to be the basis of the *Glossa Ordinaria*.[59] Most of the comments are drawn from the works of Augustine. This tendency reaches its apex in the commentaries of Peter Lombard (1100–1160), whose gloss on the Pauline epistles, like his *Sentences*, itself became a "text" for the comments of scholastic theologians.[60] Lombard's own comments rework previous ones, and his debt to Augustine and Ambrose (Ambrosiaster), is explicit. The major additional feature of Lombard's gloss is the supporting evidence he adduces from other places in Scripture. The effect is to reduce even further the sense of a "Pauline voice" speaking in these letters. It is all Scripture.

Other medieval commentaries have a greater degree of individuality. That of Sedulius Scotus (ninth century) shows some influence of Pelagius and is similar in its terse, almost staccato style.[61] Sedulius is selective in his treatments, often providing a short phrase of explanation (1 Tim 1:18–20), but at times developing a fuller interpretation (e.g., 1 Tim 2:1–3; 3:1–2; 2 Tim 2:1–4). By far his longest discussion is devoted to 1 Tim 2:11–15, where he tries to explicate Paul's reading of Genesis. He agrees ultimately with the earlier tradition that women can exercise authority over men privately, but he makes their salvation a matter of being baptized, a new and distinctive reading (*PL* 103:253). The commentaries of Anton de Verceil (d. 950) are much fuller, but still fall within the tradition deriving from Pelagius.[62] He tends to dwell on the "theological" passages of the Pastorals, with full discussions of the proper way to understand the Law (*PL* 134:664–665), the significance of the incarnation (*PL* 134:665–666, 668–669), and the church as the "great house" (*PL* 134:693). The tone taken toward women is more negative, not so much in the comment on 1 Tim 2:11–15 as in the discussions of 1 Tim 3:11; 5:3–16; 2 Tim 3:1–6 (*PL* 134:670, 672, 678–680, 695).

The commentary on 1 and 2 Timothy by St. Bruno (1032–1101), the founder of the Carthusian order, is marked, above all, by its careful reasoning.[63] Its con-

---

58. Lanfranc, *Commentarii in Omnes Pauli Epistolas* (*PL* 150:345–372). The section devoted to 1 Timothy is *PL* 150: 345–361; that to 2 Timothy *PL* 150:362–372.

59. Anselm of Laon, *Epistola I ad Timotheum* (*PL* 114:632); *Epistola II ad Timotheum* (*PL* 114:633–638). The complexity of the tradition is indicated by the placement of these commentaries in *PL* under the authorship of Walafrid Strabo (808–849).

60. Peter Lombard, *In Epistolam I ad Timotheum* (*PL* 192:325–362); *In Epistolam II ad Timotheum* (*PL* 192:363–384).

61. Sedulius Scotus, *In Epistolam I ad Timotheum* (*PL* 103:229–233); *In Epistolam II ad Timotheum* (*PL* 103:233–242).

62. Anton de Verceil, *Epistola I ad Timotheum* (*PL* 134:663–686); *Epistola II ad Timotheum* (*PL* 134:686–700).

63. Bruno, *Epistola I ad Timotheum* (*PL* 153:425–458); *Epistola II ad Timotheum* (*PL* 153:459–474).

tents are fairly standard, but his way of first presenting the entire section of text, and then proceeding in a conversational manner through the text once more, picking up its phrases and explicating them in a straightforward manner, is attractive. In effect, Bruno enters into the implied conversation between Paul and Timothy: from time to time, he has Timothy ask why Paul has said something to him, and then provides the answer. If a conventional reading of the letters, it is also an unusually engaging one.

The commentary of Hugh of St. Victor (d. 1142) adopts quite a different approach:[64] the posing of scholastic-type questions on portions of the text that are cited in the form of propositions. Thus on 1 Tim 1:1, he proceeds in this fashion:

> Question 2: "And Jesus Christ our hope": again it is asked why hope is specially referred to the son, saying, and Jesus Christ our hope, when we believe and hope in the entire trinity. Solution: we refer our hope therefore toward Christ, because he himself rose from the dead and ascended into heaven; because through his resurrection we hope to attain the glory of a future resurrection. (PL 175:594)

The entire framework is that of a systematic theology, with little or no effort spent in discovering Paul's original sense.

One of the theologically richest commentaries of the medieval period comes from Hervé de Bourg-Dieu (d. 1149).[65] The influence of Augustine can be seen in the careful development of the idea of love as the goal of the Law; but unusually, these observations on 1 Tim 1:5 are joined to an interpretation of the "lawful" way to read the Law in 1 Tim 1:7–11 (PL 181:1405–1408). Likewise, in his reading of 1 Tim 1:12–17, he has a fine statement on the incarnation, giving close attention to Paul's argument as seen through the lens of a scriptural imagination (PL 181:1410–1411). He is an independent reader: against the majority of medieval Western commentators, he thinks that 1 Tim 3:11 refers to deaconesses (PL 181:1424). He offers the views of both Jerome and Augustine on 1 Tim 5:24–25 (PL 181:1439). He shows literary sensitivity, recognizing that Paul presents Onesiphorus to Timothy (2 Tim 1:15–16) ut et Timotheus imitatur (so that Timothy might imitate him, PL 181:1454). Given this range of sensibilities, it is the more painful to see present also the growing sexism of the medieval commentaries. Perhaps part of the reason is that these commentaries are written by monks whose contact with women was limited and whose imaginations were therefore unimpeded by actual experience. In 1 Tim 2:11–15, for example, he grants that women can have authority over other women, but goes out of his way to emphasize the inferiority of women to men. Indeed, he wants

---

64. Hugh of St. Victor, In Epistolam I ad Timotheum (PL 175:593–602); In Epistolam II ad Timotheum (PL 175:601–606).

65. Hervé de Bourg-Dieu, In Epistolam I ad Timotheum (PL 181:1403–1450); In Epistolam II ad Timotheum (PL 181:1450–1478).

the children through whom the childbearing woman will be saved to be virgins (*PL* 181:1419). He does not even see Paul's praise of Timothy's maternal forebears in 2 Tim 1:5, and instead of understanding real women seduced by heretics in 2 Tim 3:6, he takes the language as referring to both males and females, but only those who are "feminine" and therefore weaker and more easily seduced (*PL* 181:1467).

The commentaries of Thomas Aquinas (1224–1274) show his usual virtues as a biblical interpreter.[66] He recognizes the "pastoral" focus in each letter as well as their individual distinctiveness. 1 Timothy is written *quasi pastoralis regula* (as something of a rule for a pastor, 184), whereas 2 Timothy is written with an eye toward *curam pastoralem ac pastorale officium* (pastoral care and pastoral office), which is a matter of *curam gregis* (care for the flock, 230). He makes this distinction: "In the first he instructed him [Timothy] concerning ecclesiastical order. In this second one, however, he deals with a complete pastoral solicitude, that even may undergo martyrdom for the sake of the care for the flock" (230). Thomas's reading is rich in biblical cross-references (see the Prologues to each letter [184, 230] and the treatment of Onesiphorus in 2 Tim 1:16 [236]). He shows exegetical independence, as when he rejects the patristic explanation of the genealogies in 1 Tim 1:4 and identifies them with the Talmud (185). Likewise, in his exceptionally rich discussion of 1 Tim 1:9–11, he rejects the distinctions made by the *Glossa Ordinaria* and enters into a vigorous discussion of Pauline theology on Law and faith that would be worthy of Luther (186–188).

The most disconcerting feature of Aquinas's commentary is its scholastic approach. At times, the multiple distinctions and sub-distinctions make for illumination (e.g., 1 Tim 2:9–10 [195–196]); sometimes they appear artificial. As a student of Aristotle, he is quick to pick up on the elements of moral teaching in these letters, finding Paul to be a good teacher of virtue (e.g., 1 Tim 1:5 [185]). The same Aristotelian influence is less beneficial in his reading of the passages on women. In his discussion of 1 Tim 2:11–15, Thomas thinks it obvious that it has been given to men by God to be teachers, because, as Aristotle notes, male is to reason as female is to sensuality (197)! When he asks about women like Deborah, he answers that they spoke through the spirit of prophecy, which does not distinguish between men and women; plus, they advised privately rather than spoke publicly (197). Again using Aristotle, "a rule by women is a corruption of the family as tyranny is of kingship" (197; see also his discussion of 2 Tim 3:6 [248].[67]

---

66. Thomas Aquinas, *In Omnes S. Pauli Apostoli Epistolas Commentaria* (Turin: Marietti, 1924), 2:183–258. Thomas wrote his Pauline commentaries late in life.

67. I have been unable to locate two important commentaries from the later medieval period: Nicholas of Lyre (d. 1329), *Postillae perpetuae in omnes S. Pauli Epistolas*, characterized by Spicq as "courtes explications du texte, assez souvent exactes, mais sans profondeur ni originalité" (short explications of the text, often enough exact, but without depth or originality, *Épîtres pastorales*, vii), and Dionysius the Carthusian (d. 1471), *In Omnes B. Pauli Epistolas*, which, Spicq says, "contient des notations heureuses, mais souvent éloignées du sense littéral" (contains pleasing notations, but often detached from the literal meaning, *Épîtres pastorales*, vii). Spicq's appreciation corresponds to that I gained of each commentator's work on James (Johnson, *Letter of James*, 139).

D. COMMENTARIES IN THE SIXTEENTH TO EIGHTEENTH CENTURIES

It is striking that when the spirit of the Renaissance began to affect the study of the New Testament, the approach to the Pastorals did not reveal much change for a long time. Lorenzo Valla (1406–1457) detected the historical forgery of the *Donatio Constantini*, but his treatment of the Pastorals in *Collatio Novi Testamenti* (1444) shows nothing of that skeptical spirit. Valla engages only in a critical comparison of the Vulgate and the Greek New Testament without challenging Pauline authorship.[68] Erasmus of Rotterdam (1469–1536) maintains conversation with patristic and medieval authors (Chrysostom, Ambrosiaster, Aquinas), although critically.[69] Indeed, he remains concerned with the theological problem posed by Paul's use of *apodosei* in 2 Tim 4:14 (484). The spirit of criticism emerges mainly in his use of the Greek and particularly in his attention to textual variants (e.g., 1 Tim 2:7 [468]; 3:1 [469]; 2 Tim 4:1–2 [483]. The resemblance of Erasmus's annotations to medieval commentaries is most apparent in his willingness to use the text of Paul for exercising his own concerns, such as his attacks against sophistical theologians and papal authority, using 1 Tim 1:3–4 (464–465) and 1 Tim 6:1–4 (476) as pretext, as well as his deep interest in the marriage of bishops (1 Tim 3:2 [469]).

Much the same sensibility is found in Thomas de Vio (1469–1534), known as Cajetan, in his notes on 1 and 2 Timothy.[70] As with Erasmus, the Renaissance perspective is found primarily in his discussion of textual variants (172) and his appeal to the Greek rather than the Vulgate in certain passages (1 Tim 1:3 [168]). Otherwise, his comments resemble those of his predecessors: the Law is good if it is read Christologically (168); women are to be silent in church, but are able to instruct sons and daughters privately (170); and in 2 Tim 3:6 Paul does not mean that only women can be seduced by false teaching—his word choice of *gynaikaria* indicates a category of person who is weak and susceptible (181). Unlike Erasmus, however, Cajetan enters into no conversation with previous commentators and, in that sense, represents a more decisive break with tradition. Although both Erasmus and Cajetan challenged the genuineness of the Letter of James because of its lack of apostolic gravity, neither shows the slightest inclination to doubt that Paul is the author of 1 and 2 Timothy.[71]

Cajetan identifies the "myths and genealogies" of 1 Tim 1:4 as "talmudic fictions" (168). A more positive engagement with Jewish lore is found in other Renaissance commentators, who begin to cite Hebrew as well as Greek precedents

---

68. Lorenzo Valla's *annotationes* can be found, with those of many of the other authors discussed in this section, in *Critici sacri, sive, Annotata doctissimorum virorum in Vetus ac Novum Testamentum: quibus accedunt tractus varii theologico-philologici*, vol. 7 (Amsterdam: Henricus & Vidua Theodori Broom, 1698).

69. Desiderius Erasmus, *Annotations in Novum Testamentum* (Basel, 1519).

70. T. de Vio (Cajetan), *Epistolae Pauli et aliorum Apostolorum ad Graecum Veritatem castigatae* (Paris: Apud Iod. Badium, 1532).

71. Johnson, *Letter of James*, 140–141.

and parallels in their linguistic observations on 1 and 2 Timothy. The most impressive example is the great humanistic scholar Hugo Grotius (1583–1645), whose *Annotationes* contain an astonishing range of Greco-Roman, Hebrew, and patristic references.[72] Such linguistic contextualization is a step in the direction of a deeper exegetical engagement with the text on its own terms rather than as a mirror of contemporary ecclesiastical arrangements. Mention should also be made of Abraham Scultetus, who in his *Observationes* (written between 1614 and 1690) speaks of Paul's instructions as having to do with being a "good pastor" and of the recipients of these letters as *pastores*.[73]

The interpreters from within the Protestant Reformation shared the same broad tendencies. Martin Luther (1483–1546) began a series of "Lectures on First Timothy" on January 13, 1535.[74] He says that the letter "is not didactic, and it does not establish basic teaching. Rather, it establishes the church and sets it in order. And yet, in the midst of this process Paul does not neglect to add very important doctrinal subjects" (217).[75] His remarks are typically full and lively, with comments on textual issues and Greek syntax (3:16 [303]; 2:6 [267]), as well as attacks on enthusiasts on one side and papists on the other (221, 231, 268, 285–286, 319, 322). Luther clearly appreciates the letter. Paul's teaching on the Law in 1:8, for example, "is a fine passage about the understanding, or knowledge of the law. Paul explains it more fully in Rom 7" (229). On 3:15, he exclaims, "These are all bright and beautiful words!" (302). As might be expected, Luther is fully approving of Paul's domestication of women in 2:11–15: they can have authority where there are no men around, but must defer to men in public—let them argue with their husbands at home (277). Luther must work hard to justify Paul's reading of the Genesis account, and even harder to explain how 2:15 does not clash with the doctrine of salvation by faith (278–279). On 5:11, he offers gratuitously, "to feed a young widow is to nourish a serpent in your bosom!" (342). So far from seeing "women deacons" in 3:11, he changes the Latin of his text from *mulieres* (women) to *uxores* (wives), adding that "the natural function of women, to have something flighty about them, they have by nature" (298).

---

72. Hugo Grotius, *Annotationes in Vetus et Novum Testamentum* (1642). Others making use of Hebrew parallels as well as Greek are Capellus and Drusius, both of whose comments are found in *Critici sacri* (Amsterdam, 1698), as are those of Sebastian Castallio (1515–1563), Isaac Casaubon (1559–1614), John Cameron (1579–1625), and many other sixteenth- and seventeenth-century commentators. None of these scholars, whose knowledge of Greek literature was often impressive, raised any questions about the Pauline character of the Greek in 1 and 2 Timothy.

73. *Critici sacri*, 412, 418.

74. M. Luther, "Lectures on First Timothy," trans. R. J. Dinda, in *Luther's Works*, ed. H. C. Oswald (St. Louis: Concordia, 1973), 28:217–384. See also Luther, "Lectures on Titus," trans. J. Pelikan, in *Luther's Works*, ed. J. Pelikan and W. A. Hanson (St. Louis: Concordia, 1968), 29:4–90.

75. Compare Luther's characterization of the letter as providing "a model to all bishops of what they are to teach and how they are to rule Christendom in the various states of life" and his description of 2 Timothy as "a farewell letter, in which Paul exhorts Timothy to go on propagating the gospel, even as he has begun" in "Prefaces to the New Testament," in *Luther's Works*, ed. H. T. Lehmann, vol. 35, *Word and Sacrament*, ed. E. T. Bachmann (St. Louis: Concordia, 1960), 388–389.

Luther also preached a sermon before certain German princes in Würlitz on November 24, 1532: "Sermon on the Sum of the Christian Life, 1 Tim. 1:5–7."[76] What is remarkable in the sermon is not only its length and power, or even its continuity with the Augustinian tradition, but its wholehearted construal of 1 Timothy as "this text we have taken from St. Paul" (265). Referring to 1 Tim 1:5, Luther declares, "Now these are deep and genuinely Pauline words, and besides they are very rich, so we must explain them somewhat in order that we may understand it a little and become accustomed to his language" (267). It is as the language of Paul that Luther understands the letter, finding in 1 Tim 1:3–11 the same message that he found in Galatians and Romans: "Therefore let us hold on to this text, for it is excellently expressed and a pure, perfect teaching of how we are to be righteous . . . above all it teaches us that we must look to Christ and bring him into it, who 'is the end of the law' [Rom 10:4] and of everything else and our whole righteousness before God" (287). Luther's close associate Philipp Melanchthon (1497–1560) also wrote a commentary on these letters from the perspective of Pauline authorship and, therefore, as teaching Paul's views on righteousness as consistently as in his other letters.[77]

John Calvin (1509–1564) was a superb exegete, who included the letters to Timothy and Titus among his commentaries on the letters of Paul.[78] His insight into literary form and function is exceptional. He argues, for example, that 1 Timothy was written for others more than it was for Timothy himself (228–229), whereas 2 Timothy is clearly a personal letter directed to his delegate alone (296). Calvin's command of ancient rhetoric is everywhere evident. He quotes Quintilian on 1 Tim 3:1 (252), sees 1 Tim 5:10 as an example of *synecdoche* (275), and considers the expression in 2 Tim 2:9 as *hypallage* (303). He realizes that 2 Tim 2:13 functions as an example (306). He quotes Galen on the meaning of gangrene in 2 Tim 2:17 (315), and everywhere clarifies the meanings of Greek terms (e.g., 1 Tim 2:1 [242]; 3:2 [254]). He is in conversation with ancient commentators like Chrysostom (1 Tim 3:3 [255]; 5:2 [271]) and contemporary commentators like Erasmus (1 Tim 5:24 [283]). Calvin is limited by his own cultural and religious biases: everyone agrees, he declares on 1 Tim 2:11, that rule by women is a bad thing (250), and he hammers repeatedly on the "papists" (251, 306, 336). But he also has sensitivity to historical realities: the discussion in 1 Tim 5:3–16 is about a practice in the ancient church; and he rightly understands—against Chrysostom—that the issue in both 5:3 and 5:17 (about *timē*, "honor") is a matter not of respect, but of financial support (271,

76. M. Luther, "Sermon on the Sum of Christian Life: 1 Tim. 1:5–7," in *Luther's Works*, ed. H. T. Lehmann, vol. 51, *Sermons I*, ed. and trans. J. W. Doberstein (Philadelphia: Muhlenberg Press, 1959), 259–287.

77. P. Melanchthon, *Enarratio epistolae I ad Timotheum et duorum capitum secundae, scripta, et dictata in praelectione publica, annos 1550 et 1551* (Wittenburg, 1561). I have not been able to consult this commentary.

78. J. Calvini, *In Omnes Pauli Apostoli Epistolas atque etiam in Epistolam ad Hebraeos Comentarii*, ed. A. Romanos (Halis Saxonum: Sumptibus Librariae Gebauriae, 1831).

278–279). Calvin is especially rich in his use of scriptural cross-references, and it is in this respect that his understanding of the Pastorals as Pauline shines through most clearly. He links the excommunication of Alexander and Hymenaios in 1 Tim 1:20 to that in 1 Cor 5:5 (241). He has no difficulty in understanding the Pauline character of the statement that "the law is good if it is used lawfully" in 1 Tim 1:9 (235). And his rich discussion of the theologoumenon "God is one" in 1 Tim 2:5 invokes both Rom 3:29 and 10:17. Once more, we see a scholar thoroughly at home both in Paul's letters and in ancient rhetoric, raising no objections to the Pauline character of these letters.

This basically conservative appreciation of the Pastorals continues into the eighteenth century. From the Protestant side, notable commentators include Johannes Albertus Bengel (d. 1752), whose first edition of *Gnomon Novi Testamenti* was published in 1734.[79] Bengel makes acute comments on the grammar and syntax of the letters (e.g., 1 Tim 1:3 [815]; 3:2 [827]). He seeks to explicate the meaning of the Greek text, making spare but effective use of ancient parallels from classical literature (1 Tim 3:2 [823]; 5:9 [830]; 2 Tim 4:2 [846]) and of biblical cross-references (1 Tim 3:16 [826]). Among his most intriguing contributions is the attempt to make the final phrase of 1 Tim 3:15, "pillar and foundation of truth," part of a single expression with "this mystery of faith which is confessedly great" in 3:16 (825–826). On 1 Tim 2:15, Bengel points out that ultimate salvation for women cannot be meant, since—in his remarkably compressed fashion—*multae quae pariunt tamen pereunt, quae non pariunt, tamen salvantur* (many women who give birth nevertheless perish, while many women who don't give birth nevertheless are saved, 822). However terse his comments, they are suffused with a real piety. On Paul's statement that all Scripture is divinely inspired (2 Tim 3:16), Bengel notes, "not only when it was being written by God breathing through the writers, but also while it is being read, by God breathing through the Scripture, and with Scripture breathing Him" (846).

The same quiet piety, without the same apparatus of learning, is found in John Wesley's (1703–1791) *Explanatory Notes on the New Testament*, which relied heavily on Bengel's *Gnomon*.[80] Much less overtly pious and much more learned, is John Jacob Wettstein's *Novum Testamentum Graece*, which provides the full Greek text with variants (and evidence supporting them), as well as remarkably full cross-references to biblical, patristic, Jewish, and, especially, Greco-Roman literature.[81] The material is undifferentiated but remains a useful source (see, e.g., the Greco-Roman authors cited on the clothing of women in 1 Tim 2:9–10). Like those of Bengel, his interpretive comments are few and spare. On

---

79. J. A. Bengel, *Gnomon Novi Testamente*, 4th ed., enl. A. E. Bengel and J. Steudel (Tübingen: Fues, 1855).

80. J. Wesley, *Explanatory Notes on the New Testament* (1754; reprint, London: Epworth, 1950), 554–561.

81. J. J. Wettstein, *Novum Testamentum Graece* (Amsterdam: Ex Officiana Dommeriana, 1752), 2:315–368.

1 Tim 2:15, for example, Wettstein notes that since women are so capable of being deceived, they should stay at home and not wander (327).[82]

On the Roman Catholic side, a similar combination of conservative piety and great learning characterizes the commentary of Cornelius à Lapide, whose astonishing commentary on all of Scripture never wavers in clarity and comprehensiveness.[83] Consistent with the entire work, his attention to 1 and 2 Timothy represents a compendium of scholarship prior to 1614. On 1 Tim 1:4, for example, he cites the opinion of some patristic commentators that Paul referred to pagan genealogies and myths, but then adduces specific citations (in full) from Suetonius and Didymus the Grammarian in support. He then turns to the other patristic opinion that these were Jewish genealogies, and draws into that discussion passages from Ignatius of Antioch, Augustine, Josephus, and Eusebius. The possibility that these are Gnostic myths generates views from several of Tertullian's antiheretical writings (8–9). Although Cornelius à Lapide comments on the Vulgate, he is widely learned in languages and pays close attention to the variations in the Greek text; he does not refer directly to manuscript evidence, but he notes how different predecessors used different Greek texts in 1:4, some reading *oikodomē*, some *oikodomia*, and some *oikonomia* (9). His conversation partners are not only from the distant past; Thomas Aquinas is a constant resource, as are more recent scholars such as Erasmus and Vatablus (34–37). As one might expect, his discussion of 1 Tim 2:11–15 draws opinions from the entire tradition (43–47). In this case, unfortunately, the effect is to reinforce the sexism in Paul's own words, since the opinions highlighted repeat and justify Paul's own reasoning. A feel for the Jesuit scholar's own sensibilities is gained from his exclamation at the thought of women leading an assembly: *Monstrum horrendum!* (44).

A similar sustained conversation with the tradition is found in Guglielmus Estius.[84] He recognizes that 1 and 2 Timothy are not like the letters written to Christian communities; they are addressed to bishops and teachers of Christians (632). His commentary is based on the Latin Vulgate, but he pays close attention to the Greek (635) and occasionally enters into a discussion of textual difficulties (638). He regularly makes use of the works of Thomas Aquinas (636, 642) and has an extensive knowledge of patristic and medieval predecessors. On 1 Tim 2:13, for example, he cites Cyprian, Augustine, Peter Lombard, Tertullian, Gregory the Great, Bernard, and Leo the Great (644–646). On 1 Tim

---

82. Other German commentaries of the eighteenth century listed in A. G. E. Leo, *Pauli Epistola Prima ad Timotheum Graece cum Commentario perpetuo* (Leipzig: Kayseri, 1837), are J. L. de Mosheim, *Erklärung der beiden Briefe des Apostels Pauli an den Timotheum* (Hamburg, 1755); Zacharias, *Paraphrastische Erklärung der Brief an Timotheus, Titus, und Philemon* (1775); A. C. Fleischmann, *Interpretatio epistolarum Pauli ad Timotheum et Titum* (Tübingen, 1791); and J. H. Heinrichs, *Pauli Epistolae ad Timotheum, Titum et Philemon Graece* (Göttingen: Apud Dietericum, 1788). I have not been able to consult these firsthand.

83. C. à Lapide, *Commentaria in Omnes Sancti Pauli Epistolas*, ed. A. Padovani (1614; reprint, Turin: Marietti, 1928). References are to page numbers in vol. 3, which contains the Pastorals.

84. G. Estius, *In omnes D. Pauli Epistolas, item in Catholicas commentarii*, 2nd ed. (Mogustiae: Sumptibus Francisci Kirchhenii, 1858–1859), 632–819.

2:11–15, he follows the mitigating tendency of the larger portion of the tradition: women are able to instruct males (such as their children) privately. He considers that teaching is truly an ecclesiastical office reserved to men, but "it is obvious that the teaching office does not pertain to all those who were led by the Holy Spirit [having in mind here the biblical women leaders], for who would deny that such women were governed by the leading of the Holy Spirit?" (666).

The Benedictine scholar Augustine Calmet uses the Latin Vulgate in his commentary, with regular reference to the Greek.[85] Calmet is also in conversation with the entire tradition and adds to it. In his discussion of 2 Tim 3:6, for instance, he brings forward examples of women who were seduced by charlatans, such as the Helen who was the consort of Simon Magus, and the women companions of the Marcosians (385). His note on 2 Tim 3:7 is an extended discussion of the figures Jannes and Jambres, taking into account evidence from Pliny the Elder, Apuleius, the Targum Pseudo-Jonathan, the Babylonian Talmud, Ebenezer and Hiscuri (Jewish scholars), Origen, Ambrosiaster, Artapanus, Palladius, Macarius the Egyptian, and others (385)! On 1 Tim 3:11–12, Calmet insists that Paul is concerned with only public behavior and that women are capable of exercising authority over men privately, such as their children and unbelieving husbands. He brings forward the evidence of female co-workers of Paul in Philippians and 1 Corinthians (362).

The pioneering *Introduction to the New Testament* (1750) by Johann David Michaelis (1717–1791) represents a genuine transition to the controversies of the nineteenth century.[86] On one side, Michaelis is consistently conservative on matters of authorship, considering both 1 and 2 Timothy to have been composed by Paul. In fact, Michaelis rejects the theory that Paul wrote 1 Timothy during a second imprisonment in Rome because it would contradict one of Paul's own statements (in Acts!) and therefore "is not very easy to be reconciled with the notion of St. Paul's infallibility or his divine inspiration" (76). He therefore dates 1 Timothy next in sequence to 1 Corinthians, at the height of Paul's Aegean ministry (76–78).

On the other side, Michaelis is unswervingly committed to history as the way to approach the study of Paul. Thus "it is absolutely necessary to be acquainted with the state of the Ephesian church, in order to understand the Epistles of Paul to Timothy, and to the Ephesians" (79). His depiction of the opposition as consisting of Essenes (79–88) now seems quaint, but it expresses the conviction that will dominate the next two centuries and makes a break with the entire preceding tradition, which read Paul primarily within the context of Scripture.

One intriguing note on his treatment of 1 Timothy, which anticipates a thesis argued in this commentary: Paul wrote the letter not only for Timothy's sake, but to authorize him as a leader among those who might not want to accept his authority: "St. Paul wrote this Epistle, which he might lay before them as a document, in which the Apostle invested him with full powers" (78). Michaelis con-

---

85. A. Calmet, *Commentarius literalis in omnes Libros Veteris et Novi Testamenti*, 2nd ed. (Venice: Colet, 1775), 8:354–391.

86. J. D. Michaelis, *Introduction to the New Testament*, 4th ed., trans. and enl. H. Marsh, vol. 4 (London: Rivington, 1823).

siders 2 Timothy to be Paul's last letter, written during a second imprisonment in Rome; much of his treatment is devoted to demonstrating this point, working to fit the letter within the framework of the canonical literature (165–177). Since 2 Timothy was written to a private individual, Michaelis takes it as revealing Paul's genuine character; it is therefore important in his argument that Paul was not an imposter but a sincere representative of God (179–182). Michaelis was truly a transition figure, for although his conservative position on authorship aligns him with his predecessors, his strictly historical method anticipates the radical critics of the nineteenth century.

E. THE DECISIVE AND DIVISIVE NINETEENTH CENTURY

The beginning of the nineteenth century marks a decisive turn in the history of the interpretation of 1 and 2 Timothy. Over the previous centuries, the letters had been construed as Pauline and, even more important, as Scripture. To be sure, historical questions were put to the letters. But the point of such questioning was the better understanding of their language and of the situations they addressed. In the cases when 1 or 2 Timothy appeared to say something at odds with another letter of Paul's, the tension between them was resolved in a variety of ways, but never by appeal to different authors writing at different periods of time. In the nineteenth century, however, history comes to play another role, that of determining the genuineness of literary attribution. The question of the letters' authenticity—whether they were written by Paul during his lifetime—dominates all discussion of 1 and 2 Timothy over the next two hundred years.

The challenge to the Pauline character of the Pastoral Letters begins with a public letter written by the influential German theologian Friedrich Schleiermacher (1768–1834) to J. C. Gass in 1807.[87] The letter is written in German rather than in Latin, Schleiermacher declares, because the theologian wants the matter to have a public airing (237–239). He assumes twelve of Paul's letters to be authentic, including 2 Timothy and Titus. His concern is to question only 1 Timothy (24). Schleiermacher touches on the fact that the use of the letter by Polycarp is suspect (18) and that it is missing from Marcion's canon (16). The bulk of his argument, however, concerns the diction of 1 Timothy: its author uses vocabulary that is found neither in Paul's other letters nor in the rest of the New Testament (28). Beginning with the verb *heretodidaskalein* in 1 Tim 1:3, Schleiermacher devotes a substantial part of his short book to these *hapax legomena* (words that occur only once), although he also gives some attention to other stylistic elements (90–91). Schleiermacher gains considerable leverage from the contrast be-

---

87. F. Schleiermacher, *Über den sogennanten Ersten Brief des Paulus an den Timotheus: Ein kritisches Senschreiben an J. C. Gass* (Berlin: Realschulbuchhandlung, 1807). Three years earlier, J. E. C. Schmidt (1772–1831) had shown the difficulties of fitting 1 Timothy into the ministry of Paul, in *Historisch-kritische Einleitung in's Neue Testament* (Giessen: Tasche und Muller, 1804), but this was not yet a full-scale challenge to authenticity of the sort that Schleiermacher launched.

tween 1 Timothy and 2 Timothy and Titus. Thus in his discussion of *presbyterion* in 1 Tim 4:14, he emphasizes its difference from 2 Tim 1:6, and he asserts that the same author could not have written both letters (58–59; see also 78). Likewise, he insists that in the elements shared by 1 Timothy and Titus, it is Titus that "holds together more naturally" (145). The bulk of Schleiermacher's analysis, therefore, is linguistic. His premise, which goes unstated, is that there is a consistent Pauline "style" against which a sample can be measured and subsequently shown to be deviant. This will remain a constant criterion through all subsequent discussions, even though its logic is seldom explicitly spelled out.[88]

Schleiermacher also raises a range of other issues that enter into the debate. He observes that 1 Timothy does not fit into Paul's movements as recounted in the Acts of the Apostles (116). The form of the letter is different from that of the other Pauline letters (128–138). The "genealogies and myths" in 1 Tim 1:3 seem to point to Gnostic opponents (86). Most of all, he introduces the issue of thematic or ideological consistency. The term *sōtēr* (savior), for example, reflects a different view of Jesus from that held by Paul (79–80). 1 Tim 2:11–15 contradicts both 1 Cor 14:33–34 *and* 1 Cor 11:3–16 (186), he says, just as 1 Tim 1:20 contradicts 1 Cor 5:5 (105). The outlook in 1:14 is different from that found in Rom 6 or Gal 1 (147, 155). The phrase *pistos ho logos* is not Pauline (168), nor is the concept of a *mesitēs* (177).

Finally, Schleiermacher takes up the issue of church organization, which he says reflects a later time than that of Paul (58–59, 78, 125) and "is not in the least Pauline" (160). Once more, the premise is that there is utter consistency within the remaining twelve Pauline letters such as to provide a steady measure against which to test 1 Timothy. In short, Schleiermacher's opening salvo sets the terms of the debate and manages to touch on all the points that would later be used in arguments against authenticity. What impresses the reader who has moved through all the prior history of interpretation is the sheer self-confidence to declare, with very little substantial argumentation—Schleiermacher's book, after all, is quite short—against the entire preceding tradition.

Schleiermacher concludes that 1 Timothy bears "unmistakable signs of a later date" (230). It contains, in fact, a misunderstood Paulinism (235) and must come from "a date later than the first century" (236). Since it appears under the name of Paul, however, it can only be considered a forgery (233) and therefore raises the question of whether it should be included in the canon (234). Despite the different conclusion on authorship, we observe here a definite line of continuity with Michaelis: authenticity determines the value of the writing. If it is not Pauline yet pretends to be, its presence in the canon renders the moral value of Scripture suspect.

Johann Gottfried Eichhorn (1752–1827) wrote important introductions to both the Old and New Testaments. In his NT introduction, he extends Schleier-

---

88. As Spicq notes, attention to stylistic differences was not lacking in antiquity, since Origen challenged the Pauline authorship of Hebrews on that basis (Eusebius, *Ecclesiastical History* 6.25.11–13), and Jerome declared that Peter could not have been the author of both letters attributed to him because *"stilo inter se et charactere discrepant, structuraque verborum"* (they differ in style and character and in the arrangement of words, (*Letter* 120.11.3) (*Épîtres pastorales*, xii).

macher's attack on authenticity to all three Pastoral Letters.[89] In contrast to his predecessor, he argues first that all three letters must be considered, on the basis of style, to be "without doubt" by the same author (315–317). He then contends that, taken as a group, they stand in contrast to Paul's other letters and could "only with difficulty" be by Paul (317–328). Eichhorn goes on to take up each letter in turn, showing that its circumstances do not fit within Paul's career as we know it (329–380). He concludes that Paul could not have been the author of these letters (380–381). That they were absent from Marcion's canon indicates either that they were already written and Marcion rejected them or that they had not yet been composed; Eichhorn considers the second option to be the more likely (384–385). The letters were therefore written by a "student" (*schuler*) of Paul a considerable time after his death (410).

Eichhorn was quickly followed by Wilhelm M. L. De Wette (1780–1849) in the first edition of *Einleitung ins Neuen Testament* (1826)[90] and in his commentary on the letters.[91] De Wette agrees that "consistent criticism must certainly group all three together in the investigation" (*Historico-Critical Introduction*, 298) and touches on the already standard objections to their genuineness: their lack of literary cohesiveness, their opposition to a heresy that looks much like Gnosticism, and their emphasis on "sound teaching" received from the apostle (*Historico-Critical Introduction*, 298–302). But De Wette adds that the style of writing "betrays an imitator, who writes not from the living fulness of the Apostle's mind, and scarcely knows how to exhaust a single topic" (*Historico-Critical Introduction*, 301). Here we see emerging the theme that to be "different" from Paul is also to be "inferior" to Paul.

De Wette considers that the Pastoral Letters were known and used by Polycarp and therefore cannot be dated too late; 2 Timothy and Titus were written first, and 1 Timothy drew from them both (*Historico-Critical Introduction*, 302). In his commentary, De Wette declares that the inauthenticity of the letters is obvious to anyone with eyes to see (*Kuerze Erklärung*, vi). His introduction to each letter seeks to show the implausibility of their composition in Paul's lifetime (*Kuerze Erklärung*, 1–4, 23–26, 61–64). More intriguing is his understanding of the task of bibical criticism as that of distinguishing between those books that have been handed on in the church through tradition and those that contain the authentic basis for Protestant theology (*Kuerze Erklärung*, vii). De

---

89. J. G. Eichhorn, *Einleitung in das Neue Testament*, vol. 3, pt. 1 (Leipzig: Weidmanischen Buchhandlung, 1812). Eichhorn indicates that he had already been lecturing to this effect even before Schleiermacher's book appeared.

90. A splendid review of the scholarship on authenticity up to the time of the fifth German edition (1847) is in W. M. L. De Wette, *An Historico-Critical Introduction to the Canonical Books of the New Testament*, 5th ed., trans. F. Frothingham (Boston: Crosby, Nichols, 1858), 298–304. It is worth noting that various mediating hypotheses had already been proposed in the first years of the debate, such as an appeal to an amanuensis to account for the difference in style and redacted letters based on authentic notes (De Wette, *Historico-Critical Introduction*, 299).

91. W. M. L. De Wette, *Kurze Erklärung der Brief an Titus, Timotheus und die Hebräer*, Kurzgefasstes exegetisches Handbuch zum Neuen Testament 20 (Leipzig: Weidmann'sche Buchhandlung, 1844).

Wette makes explicit a theological agenda that is operative throughout the debate over authenticity: the quest for a usable Paul.

Ferdinand Christian Baur (1792–1860), the founder of the so-called Tübingen School, which had such a shaping effect on all subsequent study of Christian origins,[92] took up the issue of the Pastorals as an early salvo in his battle to redraw the lines of Christian development in antiquity.[93] Rather than begin with the question of stylistic consistency, Baur approaches from the side of historical setting. In his study of Gnosticism, he came to the conclusion that the heretics opposed by the Pastorals (they are naturally taken as a group) could not have been those of Paul's time, but must have been Gnostics similar to Marcion. Indeed, 1 Tim 6:20, which warns against "so-called *gnōsis*" and *antitheses*, should be read as a direct reference to Marcion, one of whose writings is entitled *Antitheses* (8–39). It follows that the Pastorals must come from the mid-second century.

Other signs of a later date include 1 Timothy's instructions on women, which reflect second-century usage (40–53); the doubtful character of the citation in Polycarp; and the absence from Marcion's canon (136–142). Baur argues that the letters were produced from Rome and reflect that church's hierarchical interests (85–96). The value of the letters is to give a better picture of the development of Christianity (143–144), but not as a guide to authentic Christian existence. Once more, we see the same concern as in De Wette: it is the historian's task to detect among the NT writings those that represent what is "eternal" in Christianity (145–146).

Once Baur dealt with something, he regarded it as done. Thus in his monograph *Paulus, der Apostel Jesu Christi* (1845),[94] he finds it barely necessary to touch on the grounds for the rejection of the Pastorals: their absence from Marcion (1:277), their church order (2:112–113), and the difficulty in placing them in Paul's career (2:114). By this time, Baur had decided that only four of Paul's letters were certainly authentic (Romans, 1 and 2 Corinthians, Galatians), while Ephesians, Philippians, Colossians, Philemon, and 1 and 2 Thessalonians were doubtful. Baur's student Albert Schwegler, writing at the same time, confidently places the Pastorals with Polycarp in the mid-second century as part of an anti-Marcionite movement, and finds them of interest primarily as showing the development of church structure.[95] The strength of Baur's position is found, above all, in what he termed "positive criticism." Not content with challenging traditional authorship, he sought to find a plausible time and motivation for the writings thus displaced from the Apostolic Age. So attractive is the resulting picture that despite the severe criticism of each of its individual points, it continues to exercise a powerful influence: Baur and Schwegler saw the Pastorals as compositions that consolidated an "early catholicism" through the establishment of church order and the repression of diversity.

---

92. For a study of the various members of the movement, see H. Harris, *The Tübingen School* (Oxford: Clarendon Press, 1975).

93. Baur, *Die sogennanten Pastoralbriefe*. The year 1835 was the true birthdate of the school, since it saw the publication also of D. F. Strauss, *Das Leben Jesu kritisch bearbeitet*, 2 vols. (Tübinger: C. F. Osiander, 1835–36), and F. H. Kern, *Der Character und Ursprung des Briefes Jacobi* (Tübingen, Fues, 1835).

94. F. C. Baur, *Paulus, der Apostel Jesu Christi* (Leipzig: Fues, 1866–1867).

95. A. Schwegler, *Das nachapostolische Zeitalter in seiner Hauptmomentum seiner Entwicklung* (Tübingen: Fues, 1846), 3:156–157.

Strong resistance to the rejection of the Pastorals was voiced immediately. Schleiermacher received an immediate response to his arguments.[96] As the titles of these first works indicate, the defense was directed mainly to the first point of attack: 1 Timothy and the question of Pauline diction.[97] When the scope of the attack widened, the defenses became correspondingly more complex, producing discussions of considerable sophistication. Against the premise that the Pastorals are virtually identical, for example, A. L. C. Heydenreich points out that diction is determined by subject matter: Romans and Galatians are not regarded as inauthentic because they share distinctive themes and language not found in the other Pauline letters.[98] Conrad Stephan Matthies insists on the validity of the Polycarp citation, which Schleiermacher so casually dismissed, and begins to construct alternative explanations for the opponents that better fit within the time of Paul, eliminating the need for a post-Marcion dating.[99]

Within two years of the appearance of Baur's book, Michael Baumgarten wrote a substantial monograph (264 pages) by way of rebuttal.[100] He carefully identifies Baur's principles (1–46) and counters them (46–121) before dealing with the false teachers in a fresh way (121–205) and then arguing for the Pauline character of 1 Timothy. The commentary of Martin Joseph Mack (at the Catholic theological faculty of Tübingen) assumes authenticity, but makes only passing reference to the critical challenge.[101] In contrast, Henry Alford offers a substantial response to Schleiermacher, Eichhorn, De Wette, and Baur.[102]

Intellectually most impressive is the response by August Wiesinger.[103] He enters into a vigorous engagement, particularly with the position of Baur concerning the opponents, and makes a number of telling points: for example, the portrait of the opponents in each letter is scarcely uniform; the subject shared by the letters, furthermore, is that of inappropriate and foolish speech; and the Jewish elements in the depictions cannot be expunged (153–168). On the question of church order, he observes tellingly that the arrangements in the Pastorals are extremely simple and not dissonant with the evidence on local authority in

---

96. The first response appeared within a year by H. Planck, *Bemerkungen über den ersten paulinischen Brief an den Timotheus* (Göttingen, 1808). It was followed quickly by J. A. L. Wegscheider, *Der erste Briefe des Apostels Paulus an den Timotheus neu übersetzt und erklärt, mit Beziehung auf die neuesten Untersuchungen über die Authentie dasselben* (Göttingen: Apud Röwerum, 1810), and M. J. H. Beckhaus, *Specimen observationum de vocabulis hapax legomenois et varioribus dicendi formulis in I. epistolam ad Timotheum obviis* (Lingae, 1810).

97. For the continuing defense of 1 Timothy, see Leo, *Pauli Epistola Prima ad Timotheum Graece cum Commentario perpetuo.*

98. A. L. C. Heydenreich, *Die Pastoralbriefe Pauli erlautert* (Habamar: Verlag der neuen Gelehrten-Buchhandlung, 1826), 15.

99. C. S. Matthies, *Erklärung der Pastoralbriefe, mit besonderer Beziehung auf Authentie und Ort und Zeit der Abfassung Derselben* (Greifswald: Mauritius, 1840), 5, 36–48.

100. M. Baumgarten, *Die Ächtheit der Pastoralbriefe* (Berlin: Dehmigke, 1837).

101. M. J. Mack, *Commentar über die Pastoralbriefe des Apostels Paulus* (Tübingen: Osiander, 1836), 199.

102. H. Alford, *The Greek Testament*, 4th ed. (London: Rivington, 1865), 3:70–110.

103. A. Wiesinger, *Biblical Commentary on St. Paul's Epistles*, trans. J. Fulton (Edinburgh: Clark, 1851), 147–256.

other Pauline letters—in sharp contrast to the more hierarchically developed evidence from the second century (168–183). He notes that once the Tübingen mid-second-century dating is abandoned (as in more moderate critics like De Wette), there remains no plausible situation in which to place the letters (189). His discussion throughout is noteworthy for his careful attention to the individual character of the three letters, as when he considers objections to the Pastorals' diction and style: he shows how previous analyses were flawed by not taking seriously enough both the variation in the undisputed letters and the indisputably Pauline elements in the Pastorals (217–241). The main weakness in his position is his dependence, ultimately, on a second imprisonment as a place in which to locate the correspondence (221–222).

Although arguments for and against the authenticity of the Pastorals continued to be made through the mid- and late nineteenth century, the outcome of the debate was almost predictable, for reasons that had little to do with the intrinsic merit of the arguments and much to do with the theological interest suffusing the whole enterprise. It quickly became apparent to more moderate scholars (such as De Wette) that the radical tendencies of the Tübingen School shifted nine of Paul's thirteen letters (not to mention much of the rest of the NT) to the second century. Not only was this done without real historical controls beyond the theoretical dialectic employed by Baur and Schwegler, but it left very little to talk about as nascent Christianity. An even greater threat was posed by scholars who tried to show that the entire Pauline corpus was a forgery.[104] A compromise position was eventually developed: the four letters accepted by Baur, plus Philippians, Philemon, and 1 Thessalonians were accepted as genuine by virtually all scholars; Colossians, Ephesians, and 2 Thessalonians were placed in a disputed category. And the Pastorals were definitively excluded from the Pauline corpus. Heinrich Julius Holzmann's great authority helped secure this compromise position, which has continued to set the framework for discussion to the present day.[105]

---

104. Most notably B. Bauer (1809–1882), *Kritik der paulinischen Briefe* (1850–1852; reprint, Aalen: Scientia, 1972). Salvatorelli says that "Bauer's critical views had no influence" in his own time ("From Locke to Reitzenstein," 297), but that he prepared the way for the later radical Dutch scholars whose sweeping denial of historicity, in Salvatorelli's terms, "represents an important, even an indispensable episode in the elaboration of the history of primitive Christianity" (349). According to Baird, "the endeavors of the Tübingen school encouraged a reactionary conservatism. The fundamental fault, according to many critics, was the dependence on the philosophy of Hegel. For them, a scholar like Bruno Bauer (1809–82) was the horrible example of what happened to theologians who associated with the likes of Strauss and Baur" (*History of New Testament Research*, 1:277–278).

105. H. J. Holzmann, *Lehrbuch der historisch-kritisch Einleitung in das Neue Testament*, 3rd ed., expanded (Freiburg: Mohr [Paul Siebeck], 1892), 272–292. Also influential was Holzmann's own commentary on the letters: *Die Pastoralbriefe kritisch und exegetisch behandelt* (Leipzig: Engelmann, 1880). Holzmann cannot be accused of lack of thoroughness. He devotes fully 282 pages of the commentary to the issue of authenticity, providing a list of authors on the subject before 1880 (7–15). In his discussion of speech and place in ministry, he is much more subtle in his treatment (15–126), and builds his case mainly on the issues of opponents, consistency in teaching, and church order. It is significant that Holzmann also is conscious of the specifically Protestant theological agenda involved in this sort of historical criticism (280–282).

The perspective afforded by distance enables us to see the elements of subjectivity and bias that went into shaping a majority position that was supposedly grounded in the strictest scientific method. Bruno Bauer was a genuine threat precisely because he revealed how the criteria by which some letters were excluded could, if exercised rigorously, end up by excluding them all. Once the Acts of the Apostles is dismissed as unhistorical and tendentious (as Tübingen proposed), there can no longer be a meaningful criterion of "fit within Paul's career." The premise of consistency in diction and theme likewise turns out to be illusory once it is turned on Paul's other letters. It is child's play to find and exploit "contradictions" even within the four letters that Baur thought genuine. The entire process depended on the *assumption* of consistency, but before Bauer argued for the inauthenticity of the entire Pauline corpus, it had not seriously been tested; once tested, it was shown to be false. The compromise position, then, represented a retreat from a genuinely rigorous application of hard criteria applied to all Paul's letters, in favor of a much softer appeal to sensibility, what seemed "more Pauline" to most scholars. And once "most scholars" read from within a single construal, arguments are no longer really needed. Nevertheless, appeal continued to be made to the earlier arguments against the Pastorals, as though most of them could not also be turned against any letters thus isolated, including Romans and Galatians. An observer is tempted to suggest that the expulsion of the Pastorals was the sacrifice required by intellectual self-respect if scholars were to claim critical integrity and still keep the Paul they most wanted—and needed.[106]

The compromise (majority) position was such for only some scholars. Serious defense of the authenticity of all Paul's letters continued to be made by way of special studies through the nineteenth and early twentieth centuries,[107] and

---

106. Genuine arguments continued to be made, but without substantially altering those already established in the first decades of the debate. New Testament studies are nothing if not repetitive! See, for example, A. Hilgenfeld, "Die Hirtenbrief des Paulus," ZWT 40 (1897): 1–86; F. H. Hesse, *Die Entstehung der neutestamentlichen Hirtensbriefe* (Halle: Kämmerer, 1889), who suggests a Pauline basis that was later redacted; and H. H. Maner, *Über die Pastoralbriefe*, FRLANT 3 (Göttingen: Vandenhöck & Ruprecht, 1913), which provides comparisons with *Didascalia Apostolorum* (83–89) and argues that the Pastorals were written in response to the *Acta Pauli* (70–74).

107. See, for example, the massive study by H. Koehling, *Der Erste Briefe Pauli an Timotheus* (Berlin: Rother, 1882, 1887); E. Kühl, *Die Gemeindeordnung in den Pastoralbriefen* (Berlin: Hertz, 1885); J. B. Lightfoot, "The Date of the Pastoral Epistles," in *Biblical Essays* (London: Macmillan, 1893), 399–418; F. J. A. Hort, "The Pastoral Epistles," in *Judaistic Christianity* (London: Macmillan, 1904), 130–146; J. D. James, *The Genuineness and Authorship of the Pastoral Epistles* (London, 1909); F. Maier, *Die Hauptprobleme der Pastoralbriefe Pauli*, Biblische Zeitfragen 3 (Münster: Aschendorff, 1910); F. Torm, "Über die Sprache in den Pastoralbriefen," ZNW 18 (1917–1918): 225–243; and C. Bruston, "De l'authenticité des épîtres pastorales," *Revue de théologie et des questions religieuses* 19 (1910): 346–350; "Les Dernières Épîtres de Saint Paul," *Revue de théologie et des questions religieuses* 22 (1913): 243–264; "De la date de la première épître de Paul à Timothee," *Études théologiques et religieuses* 5 (1930): 272–276.

even into the present period.[108] Commentaries written from the perspective of Pauline authorship of the Pastorals also have appeared regularly over the past 150 years. Those written in the late nineteenth century include (in addition to the ones already mentioned) Weiss,[109] Beck,[110] Ellicott,[111] Fairbairn,[112] Stellhorn,[113] Bernard,[114] and Plummer.[115] Twentieth-century commentaries written from the perspective of Pauline authorship include Belser,[116] Ramsey,[117] White,[118] Knabenbauer,[119] Brown,[120] Hilliard,[121] Parry,[122] Meinertz,[123] Wohlenberg,[124] Lock,[125] Loewe,[126] Molitor,[127] Gardner,[128] Schlatter,[129] Spicq,[130] Am-

---

108. In addition to the arguments found in the commentaries that follow, see W. Michaelis, *Zur Echtheitsfrage der Pastoralbriefe*, Neutestamentliche Forschungen 8; Paulusstudien 6 (Gütersloh: Bertelsmann, 1930); E. E. Ellis, "The Problem of the Authorship of First and Second Timothy," *Review and Expositor* 56 (1959): 343–354, and "Traditions in the Pastoral Epistles," in *Early Jewish and Christian Exegesis* ed. C. A. Evans and W. F. Stinespring (Atlanta: Scholars Press, 1987), 237–253; C. F. D. Moule, "The Problem of the Pastoral Epistles: A Reappraisal," *BJRL* 47 (1964–1965):430–452; and B. M. Metzger, "A Reconsideration of Certain Arguments Against the Pauline Authorship of the Pastoral Epistles," *Exp T* 70 (1958): 91–94.

109. B. Weiss, *Die Briefe Pauli an Timotheus und Titus*, 5th ed., Kritische-exegetische Kommentar (Göttingen: Vandenhöck & Ruprecht, 1902). Weiss lists some twenty-one commentaries written against the Baur position before 1900 (65).

110. J. T. Beck, *Erklärung der Zwei Briefe Pauli an Timotheus* ed. J. Lindenmeyer (Gütersloh: Bertelsmann, 1879).

111. C. J. Ellicott, *The Pastoral Epistles of St. Paul*, 5th ed. (London: Longmans, Greene, 1883).

112. P. Fairbairn, *The Pastoral Epistles* (Edinburgh: Clark, 1874).

113. F. W. Stellhorn, *Die Pastoralbriefe Pauli* (Gütersloh: Bertelsmann, 1899).

114. J. H. Bernard, *The Pastoral Epistles*, Cambridge Greek Testament for Schools and Colleges (Cambridge: Cambridge University Press, 1899).

115. A. Plummer, *The Pastoral Epistles* (New York: Hodder and Stoughton, 1888).

116. J. E. Belser, *Die Briefe des Apostels Paulus an Timotheus und Titus* (Freiburg: Herdersche Verlagshandlung, 1907).

117. W. Ramsey, "A Historical Commentary on the Epistles to Timothy," *Expositor*, ser. 7:7 (1909): 481–494; 8 (1909): 1–21, 167–185, 264–282, 339–357, 399–416, 557–568; 9 (1910): 172–187, 319–333, 433–440, ser. 8:1 (1911): 262–273, 356–375.

118. N. J. D. White, *The First and Second Epistles to Timothy and the Epistle to Titus*, Expositor's Greek Testament 4 (New York: Dodd, Mead, 1910).

119. J. Knabenbauer, *Commentarius in S. Pauli Apostoli Epistolas* (Paris: Lethelleux, 1913).

120. E. F. Brown, *The Pastoral Epistles* (London: Methuen, 1917).

121. A. E. Hilliard, *The Pastoral Epistles of St. Paul* (London: Rivington, 1919).

122. R. St. John Parry, *The Pastoral Epistles* (Cambridge: Cambridge University Press, 1920).

123. M. Meinertz, *Die Pastoralbriefe des Heiligen Paulus*, 2nd ed. (Bonn: Hanstein, 1923).

124. D. G. Wohlenberg, *Die Pastoralbriefe*, 3rd ed., Kommentar zum Neuen Testament 13 (Lepizig: Diechertsche, 1923).

125. W. Lock, *A Critical and Exegetical Commentary on the Pastoral Epistles*, ICC (New York: Scribner, 1924).

126. H. Löwe, *Die Pastoralbriefe des Apostels Paulus* (Cologne: Römke, 1929).

127. H. Molitor, *Die Pastoralbriefe des Hl. Paulus*, Herders Bibelkommentar: Die Heilige Schrift für das Leben erklärt 15 (Freiburg: Herder, 1937).

128. E. A. Gardner, *The Later Pauline Epistles* (New York: Macmillan, 1936).

129. A. Schlatter, *Die Kirche der Griechen im Urteil des Paulus*, 2nd ed. (Stuttgart: Calwer, 1958).

130. Spicq, *Épîtres pastorales*.

broggi,[131] Boudou,[132] Guthrie,[133] Knappe,[134] Kelly,[135] Jeremias,[136] Holtz,[137] Ward,[138] Towner,[139] Ramos,[140] Oden,[141] and Lea and Griffin.[142] By comparison, in fact, commentaries written from the perspective of pseudonymity were, until recently, probably outnumbered.[143] What is striking, indeed, is the way in which contemporary commentaries tend to assert a unanimity of opinion that is not entirely supported.[144]

In this case, counting commentaries is, however, a misleading way of measuring intellectual influence. It was not through commentaries that the major-

---

131. P. de Ambroggi, *Le epistole pastorali di S. Paulo a Timoteo e a Tito* (Rome: Marietti, n.d.).

132. A. Boudou, *Saint Paul: Les Épîtres pastorales,* ed. J. Huby, Verbum Salutis 15 (Paris: Beauchesne, 1950).

133. D. Guthrie, *The Pastoral Epistles,* Tyndale New Testament Comnmentaries (Grand Rapids, Mich.: Eerdmans, 1957).

134. W. Knappe, *Die Brief an Timotheus und Titus* (Kassel: Oncken, 1959).

135. J. N. D. Kelly, *A Commentary on the Pastoral Epistles,* Black's New Testament Commentaries (London: Black, 1963).

136. J. Jeremias, *Die Briefe an Timotheus und Titus,* Das Neue Testament Deutsch 9 (Göttingen: Vandenhöck & Ruprecht, 1981).

137. G. Holtz, *Die Pastoralbriefe,* THKNT 13 (Berlin: Evangelische Verlaganstalt, 1992).

138. R. A. Ward, *Commentary on 1 & 2 Timothy & Titus* (Waco, Tex.: Word Books, 1974), 9–15.

139. P. H. Towner, *1–2 Timothy & Titus,* InterVarsity Press New Commentary 14 (Downer's Grove, Ill.: InterVarsity Press, 1994).

140. M. A. Ramos, *I Timoteo, II Timoteo, y Tito,* Commentario Bíblico Hispanoamericano (Miami: Editorial Caribe, 1992), 56–58.

141. T. C. Oden, *First and Second Timothy and Titus,* Interpretation, a Bible Commentary for Teaching and Preaching (Louisville, Ky.: John Knox Press, 1989), 10–16.

142. T. D. Lea and H. P. Griffin, Jr., *1, 2 Timothy, Titus,* New Broadman Commentary (Nashville, Tenn.: Broadman Press, 1992), 19–40.

143. In addition to those already mentioned, see H. von Soden, *Die Briefe an die Kolosser, Epheser, Philemon, Die Pastoralbriefe,* HKNT 3 (Freiburg: JCB Mohr [Paul Siebeck] 1893); F. Koehler, *Die Pastoralbriefe,* Die Schriften des Neuen Testaments 2 (Göttingen: Vandenhöck & Ruprecht, 1908); P. Leo, *Das anvertraute Gut: Eine Einfuehrung in den ersten Timotheusbriefe,* Die urchristliche Botschaft 15 (Berlin: Furche, 1935); E. F. Scott, *The Pastoral Epistles,* Moffatt New Testament Commentary 13 (London: Hodder and Stoughton, 1936); R. Falconer, *The Pastoral Epistles* (Oxford: Clarendon Press, 1937); J. McCleod, *The Pastoral Epistles,* Speaker's Bible (Grand Rapids, Mich.: Baker Book house, 1963); B. S. Easton, *The Pastoral Epistles* (New York: Scribner, 1947); C. K. Barrett, *The Pastoral Epistles in the New English Bible,* New Clarendon Bible (Oxford: Clarendon Press, 1963); A. T. Hanson, *The Pastoral Letters* (Cambridge: Cambridge University Press, 1966); P. Dornier, *Les Épîtres pastorales,* SB (Paris: Gabalda, 1969); and N. Brox, *Die Pastoralbriefe,* 4th ed., Regensberger Neues Testament 7 (Regensberg: Pustet, 1969).

144. See, for example, L. Oberlinner, *Die Pastoralbriefe,* vol. 1, *Kommentar zum ersten Timotheusbrief,* HTKNT 11 (Freiburg: Herder, 1994), and *Die Pastoralbriefe,* vol. 2, *Kommentar zum zweiten Timotheusbrief,* HTKNT 11 (Freiburg: Herder, 1995); J. Roloff, *Der Erste Brief an Timotheus,* Evangelisch-katholischer Kommentar zum Neuen Testament 15 (Zurich: Benziger, 1988); A. J. Hultgren, *I–II Timothy, Titus,* Augsburg Commentary on the New Testament (Minneapolis: Augsburg, 1984); A. T. Hanson, *The Pastoral Epistles,* New Century Bible (Grand Rapids, Mich.: Eerdmans, 1982); J. L. Houlden, *The Pastoral Epistles,* Trinity Press International New Testament Commentaries (Philadelphia: Trinity Press International, 1976); J. M. Bassler, *1 Timothy, 2 Timothy, Titus,* Abingdon New Testament Commentaries (Nashville, Tenn.: Abingdon Press, 1996); and V. Hasler, *Die Briefe an Timotheus und Titus,* (Züricher Bibelkommentare Neue Testament 12 (Zurich: Theologischer Verlag, 1978).

ity position established itself, but through other instruments. Note, for example, how all histories of early Christianity from the late nineteenth century on presume (but do not argue for) the inauthenticity of the Pastorals, and place them in the development of Christianity only a little before (or, according to Loisy and Pfleiderer, at the same time as) Baur's mid-second-century date.[145] Even more influential are introductions to the New Testament. In the nineteenth century, we find some critical introductions standing for Pauline authorship.[146] But the power of opinion is forcibly felt,[147] and in the twentieth century, very few critical introductions to the New Testament speak in favor of the authenticity of the Pastorals.[148] Increasingly as the century progressed, critical introductions

---

145. See, for example, A. Neander, *History of the Planting and Training of the Christian Church by the Apostles*, trans. J. E. Ryland (London: Bell, 1889), 1:338–339; C. von Weizsäcker, *The Apostolic Age of the Christian Church*, 2nd ed., trans. J. Millar (New York: Putnam, 1899), 393–395; A. C. McGiffert, *History of Christianity in the Apostolic Age*, rev. ed. (New York: Scribner, 1928), 399–413; J. H. Ropes, *The Apostolic Age in the Light of Modern Criticism* (New York: Scribner, 1908), 272; O. Pfleiderer, *Das Urchristentum seine Schriften und Lehren in geschichtlichen Zusammenhang*, 2nd ed. (Berlin: Reimer, 1902), 262–281; J. Weiss, *The History of Primitive Christianity*, completed by R. Knopf, ed. F. C. Grant, trans. by four friends. (New York: Wilson-Erickson, 1937), 1:391–392, 2:565; E. Meyer, *Ursprung und Anfänge des Christentums* (Stuttgart: Cotta'sche, 1924), 3:587–588; A. Loisy, *The Birth of the Christian Religion*, trans. L. P. Jacks (New York: University Books, 1962), 332; E. von Dobschütz, *Christian Life in the Primitive Church*, trans. G. Brenner (New York: Putnam, 1904), 253–263; F. V. Filson, *New Testament History* (Philadelphia: Westminster Press, 1964), 286–288; and H. Köster, *Einführung in das Neue Testament* (Berlin: de Gruyter, 1980), 744. Even as conservative a scholar as F. F. Bruce hesitates to declare on the historical value of the Pastorals for Paul's last days, in *New Testament History* (London: Oliphants, 1969), 346.

146. See, for example, J. L. Hug, *Introduction to the New Testament*, 3rd ed., trans. D. Fosdick (Andover, Mass.: Gould and Newman, 1836), 556–578; J. Condor, *The Literary History of the New Testament* (London: Seeleys, 1850), 380–395; G. Salmon, *A Historical Introduction to the Study of the Books of the New Testament*, 3rd ed. (London: Murray, 1888), 413–432; and the great work by T. Zahn, *Introduction to the New Testament*, 3rd ed., trans. J. M. Trout et al. (Edinburgh: Clark, 1909), 2:1–133.

147. Striking evidence is given by the two editions of New Testament introduction by Samuel Davidson. In *An Introduction to the Study of the New Testament* (London: Bagster, 1840), he devotes an extensive argument to the authenticity of the Pastorals (2:1–153). But things have changed by the time of the second edition, *An Introduction to the Study of the New Testament* (London: Longmans, Green, 1882), in which Davidson spends only pp. 2:1–73 on the Pastorals. He cites the work of De Wette, Ewald, Mangold, Meyer, Hilgenfeld, and Holtzmann, and then says, "The stream of criticism is too strong against the advocates of tradition to be successfully resisted. When moderate theologians like Usterli, Luecke, Neander and Bleck give up the authenticity of the first epistle to Timothy, the other letters cannot be saved from the same fate without logical inconsistency" (72–73). It would be difficult to find a more candid admission that the weight of opinion rather than argument was carrying the day.

148. F. Barth, *Einleitung in das Neue Testament*, 2nd ed. (Gütersloh: Bertelsmann, 1911), 88–109; P. Feine, with J. Behm, *Einleitung in das Neue Testament*, 8th ed. (Leipzig: von Quelle & Meyer, 1936), 198–210; W. Michaelis, *Einleitung in das Neue Testament* (Bern: BEG, 1946), 262–284; A. Wikenhauser, *New Testament Introduction*, trans. J. Cunningham (New York: Herder and Herder, 1963), 437–452; B. Mariani, *Introductio in libros sacros Novi Testamenti* (Rome: Herder, 1962), 367–402; E. F. Harrison, *Introduction to the New Testament* (Grand Rapids, Mich.: Eerdmans, 1964), 326–343; D. Guthrie, *New Testament Introduction*, 2nd ed. (Downer's Grove, Ill: InterVarsity Press, 1975), 584–624; M. C. Tenney, *New Testament Survey*, rev. W. M. Dunnett (Grand Rapids, Mich.: Eerdmans, 1985), 333–343; L. T. Johnson, *Writings of the New Testament: An Interpretation*, 2nd ed. (Minneapolis: Fortress Press, 1999).

placed the Pastorals among the latest writings in the canon as pseudonymous productions of a Pauline school. The more emphatic the assertion, oddly, the less extensive the argumentation brought to bear on the question. The inauthenticity of the Pastorals increasingly becomes a matter of dogma.[149] The most recent critical introduction spends four pages rehearsing the standard arguments on the letters and declares, "The author of the Pastorals was an unknown member of the Pauline school who wrote and circulated the letters in the course of a new edition of the previous corpus of the Pauline letters."[150] Most contemporary monographs on the Pastorals simply assume inauthenticity. Their scholarship, in turn, serves to reinforce that premise.[151]

For scholars on both sides of the question, everything was changed by the debate in the nineteenth century. Those who adopted the majority position based all their discussion of Paul on at most seven of the thirteen letters ascribed to him in the canon. Even those who wanted to retain all thirteen letters found it necessary to deal with six of the seven in a defensive and apologetic fashion. On every side, the historical question dominates the reading of the letters. The observations of Albert Schweitzer are worth quoting in full; speaking of the situation after Holtzmann, he says:

Not even the most conservative of critics had the boldness to place all the letters which have come down under the name of Paul on a footing of equality. Even those who regarded the Epistles to the Ephesians and Colossians as genuine did not fuse the ideas of these Epistles with the system extracted from the four main Epistles, but presented them separately; and any who were not converted to the rejection of the Pastorals at all events took the precaution to

---

149. In addition to those already noted, see A. Hilgenfeld, *Historisch-kritische Einleitung in das Neue Testament* (Leipzig: Fues, 1875), 744–765, dating the Pastorals to around 150 (764); A. Jülicher, *An Introduction to the New Testament*, 2nd ed., trans. J. R. Ward (New York: Putnam, 1904), 174–200; B. W. Bacon, *An Introduction to the New Testament* (New York: Macmillan, 1907), 127–140; A. S. Peake, *A Critical Introduction to the New Testament* (New York: Scribner, 1910), 60–71; J. Moffatt, *An Introduction to the Literature of the New Testament* (New York: Scribner, 1911), 395–420; E. F. Scott, *The Literature of the New Testament* (New York: Columbia University Press, 1932), 191–197; M. Goguel, *Introduction au Nouveau Testament* (Paris: Leroux, 1926), 4, pt. 2:504–561; A. H. McNeile, *An Introduction to the Study of the New Testament* (Oxford: Clarendon Press, 1927), 175–188; K. Lake and S. Lake, *An Introduction to the New Testament* (New York: Harper, 1937), 154–157; E. J. Goodspeed, *An Introduction to the New Testament* (Chicago: University of Chicago Press, 1937), 327–344; M. S. Enslin, *Christian Beginnings* (New York: Harper, 1938), 299–307; A. E. Barnett, *The New Testament: Its Making and Meaning* (New York: Abingdon Press, 1946), 275–292; A. J. F. Klijn, *An Introduction to the New Testament*, trans. M. van den Vathorst-Smit (Leiden: Brill, 1967), 124–134; B. Childs, *The New Testament as Canon: An Introduction* (Philadelphia: Fortress Press, 1984) 386; W. Marxsen, *Introduction to the New Testament* 3rd ed., trans. G. Buswell (Philadelphia: Fortress Press, 1968); and R. E. Brown, *An Introduction to the New Testament*, Anchor Bible Library (New York: Doubleday, 1997), 638–680.

150. U. Schnelle, *The History and Theology of the New Testament Writings*, trans. M. E. Boring (Minneapolis: Fortress Press, 1998), 276–280, 332.

151. This is the scholarship that will be engaged throughout the rest of the General Introduction and the commentary proper. For a review, see W. Schenk, "Die Briefe an Timotheus I und II und an Titus (Die Pastoralbriefe) in der neuerer Forschung," in ANRW II, 25, 4 (Berlin: de Gruyter, 1987), 4:3404–3438.

give a separate chapter to the Pauline theology of these writings [citing here the example of Berhard Weiss, *Neutestamentliche Theologie* (1868)]. If only the personal references might be saved, these Epistles were as completely excluded from the presentation of the Pauline system as if they had been pronounced wholly spurious.[152]

The consequence of the massive challenge to the authenticity of the Pastorals was that no one could any longer truly read them as Pauline. Having the majority position enunciated authoritatively in standard scholarship, having it assumed by all studies of the life and thought of Paul,[153] and having it taught as self-evident in college and seminary classrooms for the past ninety years[154] means that many generations of readers have been shaped by this view, which has come to seem to be a fact of nature rather than a scholarly hypothesis.[155] Those who

---

152. A. Schweitzer, *Paul and His Interpreters: A Critical History*, trans. W. Montgomery 1912 (1911; reprint, New York: Schocken Books, 1964), 27.

153. It is noteworthy that major theologians of Paul in the twentieth century affirm only the seven undisputed letters and, in practice, restrict their "Pauline theology" to the four Pauline letters that Baur considered to be authentic: 1 and 2 Corinthians, Romans, and Galatians. See, for example, the quite diverse works by A. Schweitzer, *The Mysticism of Paul the Apostle*, trans. W. Montgomery (Baltimore: Johns Hopkins University Press, 1931); R. Bultmann, *Theology of the New Testament*, trans. K. Grobel (New York: Scribner, 1951, 1955); C. J. Beker, *Paul the Apostle: The Triumph of God in Life and Thought* (Philadelphia: Fortress Press, 1980); E. P. Sanders, *Paul and Palestinian Judaism* (Philadelphia: Fortress Press, 1977); and J. D. G. Dunn, *The Theology of Paul the Apostle* (Grand Rapids, Mich.: Eerdmans, 1998).

154. In the United States, no medium has more influence on shaping attitudes toward Scripture among collegians and seminarians (some of whom go on to become NT scholars) than the popular introductions that make available the standard scholarly positions. In all the following popular texts, the pseudonymity of the Pastorals is reported as a matter of fact rather than as a hypothesis: E. Lohse, *The Formation of the New Testament*, trans. M. E. Boring (Nashville, Tenn.: Abingdon Press, 1972), 97–105; R. P. Martin, *New Testament Foundations: A Guide for Christian Students* (Grand Rapids, Mich.: Eerdmans, 1978), 298–307; J. L. Price, *Interpreting the New Testament* (New York: Holt, Rinehart and Winston, 1961), 472–484; M. Pregeant, *Engaging the New Testament: An Interdisciplinary Introduction* (Minneapolis: Fortress Press, 1995), 432–439; N. Perrin and D. Duling, *The New Testament, an Introduction: Proclamation and Parenesis, Myth and History*, 2nd ed. (New York: Harcourt Brace Jovanovich, 1982), 384–388; R. A. Spivey and D. M. Smith, Jr., *Anatomy of the New Testament: A Guide to Its Structure and Meaning* (New York: Macmillan, 1969), 367–374; R. W. Crapps, E. V. McKnight, and D. A. Smith, *Introduction to the New Testament* (New York: Ronald Press, 1969), 511–514; Freed, *New Testament*, 398; D. J. Selby, *Introduction to the New Testament* (New York: Macmillan, 1971), 410–418; H. C. Kee, *Understanding the New Testament* 4th ed. (Englewood Cliffs, N.J.: Prentice-Hall, 1983), 311–314; B. Mack, *Who Wrote the New Testament? The Making of the Christian Myth* (San Francisco: HarperSanFrancisco, 1995), 206–207; B. D. Ehrman, *The New Testament: A Historical Introduction* (New York: Oxford University Press, 1997), 332–335. In only two popular introductions are the issues presented in a sufficiently neutral fashion as to allow that more than one solution is reasonable: B. M. Metzger, *The New Testament: Its Background, Growth, and Content* (New York: Abingdon Press, 1965), 218–241, and R. M. Grant, *A Historical Introduction to the New Testament* (New York: Harper & Row, 1963), 208–215. Note that these are the oldest in the group.

155. This statement by J. T. Sanders is not exceptional: "That Colossians, Ephesians, II Thessalonians, 1 and 2 Timothy, Titus, and 1 Peter are pseudonymous and imitate Paul's style and thought is not to be debated here but rather accepted as an assured result of critical historical scholarship" (*Ethics in the New Testament* [Philadelphia: Fortress Press, 1975], 67).

hold the opposite view are considered odd or not truly critical in their thinking. And even those who would wish to keep the conversation open, or who find the arguments against authenticity to be unpersuasive either individually or cumulatively, cannot leap over the critical divide created in the nineteenth century and genuinely read 1 Timothy in the same spirit as they read 1 Corinthians.[156]

The present situation within the American scholarly guild is perhaps best symbolized by the survey of New Testament scholarship sponsored by the Society of Biblical Literature as part of its centennial celebration. In *The New Testament and Its Modern Interpreters*, the article "Pauline Studies" by Victor P. Furnish has only one line devoted to the Pastorals, noting that most scholars still affirm their inauthenticity.[157] More remarkably, there is no further mention of these canonical compositions anywhere else in the volume, even though the survey includes extensive essays on the NT Apocrypha and the Apostolic Fathers. In effect, the Pastorals have been removed not only from the Pauline corpus, but from anything more than purely formal canonicity.

---

156. The mild optimism expressed by E. E. Ellis, "The Authorship of the Pastorals: A Résumé and Assessment of Recent Trends," in *Paul and His Recent Interpreters* (Grand Rapids, Mich.: Eerdmans, 1961), 49–57, concerning the turn of scholarly opinion in favor of authenticity has not been vindicated.

157. V. P. Furnish, "Pauline Studies," in *The New Testament and Its Modern Interpreters*, ed. E. J. Epp and G. W. MacRae (Atlanta: Scholars Press, 1989), 326.

III. Assessing the Authorship of the Pastoral Letters

◆

The term "debate" is surely too strong for the present situation, which is closer to a fixed academic consensus. Little real discussion of the issue of authenticity still occurs. But I remind the reader that this consensus resulted as much from social dynamics as from the independent assessment of the evidence by each individual scholar. For many contemporary scholars, indeed, the inauthenticity of the Pastorals is one of those scholarly dogmas first learned in college and in no need of further examination.[158] To be sure, the existence of a majority opinion is far from a guarantee of the truth of that position. As obvious as the dominant paradigm now seems, it should be remembered that highly intelligent and by no means uncritical scholars read the Pastorals from within an exact opposite construal for six times the period in which the current paradigm has reigned. It is by no means unreasonable, therefore, to engage the issue once more. This is particularly the case since so much of recent scholarship tends to erode the force of the arguments that were used to establish the conventional wisdom in the first place.

A. TENDENCIES IN THE DEBATE

I begin this discussion by identifying certain extra-evidential factors affecting the issue of the authenticity of the Pastorals that are often, precisely because they remain unarticulated and even unconscious, more influential than any amount of exegesis or evidence.

1. The Power of Construal

Construal is the most subtle, yet the most powerful, factor of all. In simplest terms, I mean the way our pre-understanding affects our perceptions. In my review of the interpretation of 1 and 2 Timothy before the time of Schleiermacher, I re-

---

158. Since introductory courses effectively exclude the Pastorals from serious consideration and specific courses on these letters are seldom taught, even in schools of theology, few aspiring scholars even have the opportunity to assess the arguments or the conclusion critically.

marked more than once on the way in which readers simply "saw" things differently then because of their assumption that Paul was the author of all his letters.
A case in point is Luther and Calvin reading 1 Tim 1:8–11. They had no difficulty understanding the passage as one that is in fundamental agreement with
Paul's statements on the Law in Galatians and Romans. Yet for contemporary critics, the same passage is regularly listed as one that most obviously demonstrates
the "un-Pauline" character of the Pastorals. Since the evidence has not changed,
the shift in perception must be due to the overall construal of the situation.

Just as Luther and Calvin were heirs to a long tradition of reading from the perspective of Pauline authorship, so contemporary critics are heirs to a constantly reinforced tradition of reading from the perspective of inauthenticity. Enormous effort is required to shift from one construal to the other. It is remarkable, in fact,
how few scholars seem to have started in one place and ended in the other. Here
is a situation to which the sociology of knowledge is appropriately applied. The
more one construal is handed on to generations that have not examined its premises
and arguments as a settled "fact," the more natural and self-evident it becomes.[159]
The textual evidence itself becomes less relevant. The social fact of consensus is
the primary and convincing argument in favor of one position or another.

2. The Search for a Usable Apostle

For most scholars in the history of biblical scholarship, Paul has preeminently
been "the Apostle."[160] For Protestant critics in particular, as we have seen, the
determination of the letters that were genuinely written by Paul was, in effect,
part of a theological project to ground the Reformation understanding of Christianity in Paul's (authentic) letters.[161] The same tendency continues today. There
is an understandable tendency to find a Paul who corresponds to the scholar's
sense of what is important or essential to Christianity and to reject as unau-
thentic what does not meet that measure. Just as critics of the nineteenth century sought a Paul who is free of moralizing and the institutional, so twentieth-
century critics desire a Paul who is egalitarian rather than hierarchical. This
tendency, it should be observed, works both sides of the ideological street. It is
not entirely by accident that the Pastorals are also thought to be authentic by
scholars who value tradition and ecclesiastical structure and the divine inspira-

---

159. P. Berger and T. Luckmann, *The Social Construction of Reality* (Garden City, N.Y.: Dou-
bleday, Anchor Books, 1967); P. Berger, *The Sacred Canopy: Elements of a Sociology of Religion*
(Garden City, N.Y.: Doubleday, Anchor Books, 1969). It is somewhat amusing to find the theory of
Berger and Luckmann applied to the actual development of the Pastorals, when its real pertinence
is the shaping of the scholarly consensus. I refer to D. Horrell, "Converging Ideologies: Berger and
Luckmann and the Pastoral Epistles," *JSNT* 50 (1993): 85–103.

160. See, for example, the essays in W. A. Meeks, *The Writings of St. Paul* (New York: Norton, 1973).

161. For the role of Protestant theological presuppositions generally in the historical study of
Christian origins, see J. Z. Smith, *Drudgery Divine: On the Comparison of Early Christianities and
the Religions of Late Antiquity* (Chicago: University of Chicago Press, 1990), 1–35, 114–115, and
L. T. Johnson, *Religious Experience in Early Christianity: A Missing Dimension in New Testament
Studies* (Minneapolis: Fortress Press, 1998), 1–33.

tion of Scripture.[162] Scholarship is certainly not entirely determined by such commitments, but neither is it unaffected by them.[163]

3. Authenticity and Worth

The tendency to equate authenticity and worth is related to the quest for a usable Paul. I have pointed out how, for both Michaelis and Schleiermacher, the religious validity of the Pastorals was connected to their actually having been written by Paul. They regarded pseudonymity as straightforward forgery. The canon should not include compositions flying, as it were, under false colors. Later scholars became more sophisticated about pseudonymity, recognizing that it was both prevalent in antiquity and often a transparent fiction that did not seek to deceive. But even today, the value assigned to the Pastorals tends to be connected to composition by Paul rather than canonical status (or even divine inspiration).

In its sharper form, the decision against authenticity means that the Pastorals are automatically secondary (perhaps even tertiary) witnesses to Christian life, since they do not come from the first Christian generation. They are not technically outside the canon, but they may as well be for all the attention they receive, especially when elements in the Pastorals (such as their statements on women) are repugnant to present-day readers. In a milder form, those who reject authenticity often spend so much energy demonstrating the ways in which these letters are *not* by Paul that they can find little positive to say about them as a continuation of the Pauline tradition. Seldom does one find a scholar showing how an element in the Pastorals represents a logical and perhaps even healthy development of something already in the undisputed letters.[164]

---

162. It is almost possible to deduce from a publisher's imprint what direction a book will take on the issue. It was rare indeed that a book published by Putnam or Scribner ever represented a conservative stance, and equally unusual that a book appearing from Eerdmans or Zondervan espouses a liberal position.

163. For a particularly transparent example, see J. C. Beker, *Heirs of Paul: Paul's Legacy in the New Testament and the Church Today* (Minneapolis: Fortress Press, 1991), 36–47, 83–86, 105–108.

164. It is a heartening development to see a change in this respect. Although I bemoan the continuing tendency to treat the Pastorals as a group, there is a growing willingness to consider the letters on their own terms rather than as a contrast to "the authentic Paul." In Christology, for example, see the difference between H. Windisch, "Zur Christologie der Pastoralbriefe," ZNW 34 (1935): 213–238, or W. Foerster, "EUSEBEIA in der Pastoralbriefen," NTS 5 (1958–1959): 213–218, and such recent studies as K. Läger, *Die Christologie der Pastoralbriefe*, Hamburger Theologische Studien 12 (Münster: LIT, 1996); H. Stettler, *Die Christologie der Pastoralbriefe*, WUNT, 2nd ser., 105 (Tübingen: Mohr [Paul Siebeck], 1998); A. Y. Lau, *Manifest in the Flesh: The Epiphany Christology of the Pastoral Epistles*, WUNT, 2nd ser., 86 (Tübingen: Mohr [Paul Siebeck], 1996); and L. Oberlinner, "Die *Epiphaneia* des Heilswillens Gottes in Christus Jesus: Zur Grundstrucktur der Christologie der Pastoralbriefe," ZNW 71 (1980): 192–213. On other subjects, see, for example, U. Wagener, *Die Ordnung des "Hauses Gottes:" Der Ort von Frauen in der Ekklesiologie und Ethik der Pastoralbriefe*, WUNT, 2nd ser., 65 (Tübingen: Mohr [Paul Siebeck], 1994); P. H. Towner, *The Goal of Our Instruction: The Structure of Theology and Ethics in the Pastoral Epistles*, JSNTS 34 (Sheffield: JSOT Press, 1989); R. M. Kidd, *Wealth and Beneficence in the Pastoral Epistles* SBLDS 122 (Atlanta: Scholars Press, 1990); and R. Schwarz, *Bürgerliches Christentum im Neuen Testament? Eine Studien zu Ethik, Amt und Recht in den Pastoralbriefen*, Österreichisches katholisches Studien 4 (Kolsternburg: OBS, 1983).

This tendency also is present on both sides of the debate. Just as some scholars seem to fight the authenticity of the Pastorals because acceptance of them as Pauline would mean also having to grapple with their contents in a more engaged fashion, so it appears that some scholars defend authenticity as a way of championing the same contents. Theologically, questions of religious value and of authorship ought to be kept separate, but they seldom are. The case of the Pastorals shows just how powerful a *theological* instrument the "historical-critical method" has been.

4. The Quality of the Criteria

The decision concerning the authenticity or inauthenticity of the Pastoral Letters ought to be based on the cumulative effect of specific lines of argument rather than on the weight of opinion. It is startling to find, when reading the history of scholarship, how carelessly formulated and executed many of the arguments are. Schleiermacher and his first respondents set the terms of the debate. They worked with premises and criteria that they failed to make explicit or theoretically defend. In light of recent scholarship, the various criteria that were developed willy-nilly—placement in Paul's career, style, church order, consistency in theme—increasingly appear to be simplistic and possibly even misleading. Close examination shows that, at the very least, they are less than stable and reliable norms for measuring anything. Nowhere is there a greater need for serious scholarly engagement than on this point. In this section, I address only methodological issues. I leave until later the substantive discussion.

a. The Meaning of Authorship

The most fundamental category, that of authorship, remains largely unexamined. The model of Pauline authorship therefore remains anachronistic. Recent scholarship shows how the image of Paul as an "author" working through a theological system, or even as a solitary letter writer, is inaccurate. The study of Paul's letters has revealed the complexity of their composition. He often dictated his letters (Rom 16:22; 1 Cor 16:21; Col 4:18; 2 Thess 3:17; possibly Gal 6:11). We do not know what method of dictation Paul used or what freedom of expression he allowed his amanuenses, but the mere fact of dictation points to a more complex process of composition than that of a writer putting pen to papyrus.[165] In writing his letters, Paul also associated others with him in a form of co-sponsorship, writing together with Timothy (2 Cor 1:1; Phil 1:1; Col 1:1; Phm 1), Silas and Timothy (1 Thess 1:1; 2 Thess 1:1), Sosthenes (1 Cor 1:1), and "all the brethren with him" (Gal 1:2). Only Romans, Ephesians, and the three Pastorals are ascribed to Paul alone. Once more, we do not know how to

---

165. O. Roller, *Das Formuler der paulinischen Briefe: Ein Beiträge zur lehre vom antike Briefe*, BWANT 5–6 (Stuttgart: Kohlhammer, 1933); R. Longenecker, "Ancient Amanuenses and the Pauline Epistles," in *New Dimensions in New Testament Study*, ed. R. Longenecker and M. Tenney (Grand Rapids, Mich.: Zondervan, 1974), 281–297.

assess the fact: Was co-sponsorship simply formal, a way of honoring Paul's associates? Or did co-sponsors also contribute to the thought and style of a letter?

These explicit indications of a complex process of composition join two other observations drawn from the analysis of the contents of letters. First, all of Paul's letters make use of traditions drawn from the life of Christian communities. By a kind of literary ripple effect, the use of traditions affects the style and vocabulary of the contexts in which they are placed. In some letters (e.g., Romans, 1 and 2 Corinthians, Galatians), Paul makes extensive use of Torah. In other letters (e.g., Ephesians, 1 and 2 Timothy), he quotes Torah but not extensively. In still others (1 and 2 Thessalonians, Titus, Philippians, Colossians, Philemon), he uses Torah scarcely at all. Paul also makes use of confessional formulas (Rom 10:9; 1 Cor 12:3; 1 Tim 3:16), kerygmatic statements (1 Cor 15:3–8; Rom 4:24–25; 1 Thess 1:9–10; 2 Tim 1:8–11; Tit 3:4–7), hymns (Phil 2:6–11; Col 1:15–20; 1 Tim 3:16; 2 Tim 2:11–13), liturgical traditions (Rom 6:1–11; 8:17; Gal 3:28; 1 Cor 11:23–25; 16:22), and even the words of Jesus (1 Cor 7:10; 9:14; 11:24–25; 1 Tim 5:18). The use of these community traditions inevitably affects the language of the respective compositions. It also suggests a more complex social context for the production of Paul's letters. And it reminds us that "tradition" was part of Paul's enterprise from the start and not something invented after his death.

Second, Paul's letters contain what might be called the literary residue of scholastic processes. By this I mean the clear evidence for the use of the *diatribe* in several of his letters (Romans, Galatians, 1 Corinthians) and the sophisticated use of *midrash* in others (1 Cor 10:1–4; 2 Cor 3–5; Gal 3–4; Eph 2; Rom 9–11; 2 Tim 2:19–21). Both diatribe and midrash were basically modes of teaching within Hellenistic and Jewish schools, the first as a dialogical style of oral argumentation, and the second as a way to study texts. Both modes assume a social context—that of a teacher and students.[166] These sections of Paul's letters may result from arguments that were worked out by him with his coworkers before being included in his letters.

The upshot of these observations—which draw inferences from widespread scholarship on Paul's social world[167]—is that it is reasonable to think of Paul's

---

166. On the diatribe, see S. K. Stowers, *The Diatribe and Paul's Letter to the Romans*, SBLDS 57 (Chico, Calif.: Scholars Press, 1981), 1–78. On midrash, see B. W. Holtz, "Midrash," in *Back to the Sources: Reading the Classic Jewish Texts*, ed. B. W. Holtz (New York: Summit Books, 1984), 177–211; J. L. Kugel and R. A. Greer, "Interpreters of Scripture," in *Early Biblical Interpretation*, Library of Early Christianity 3 (Philadelphia: Westminster Press, 1986), 52–72; and S. Safrai, "Education and the Study of Torah," in *The Jewish People in the First Century: Historical Geography, Political History, Social, Cultural, and Religious Life and Institutions*, ed. S. Safrai and M. Stern, CRINT (Philadelphia: Fortress Press, 1987), 2:945–970.

167. On Paul's social context, see E. A. Judge, "The Early Christians as a Scholastic Community," *JRH* 1 (1960–1961): 4–15, 125–137; A. J. Malherbe, *Social Aspects of Early Christianity*, 2nd ed., enlarged (Philadelphia: Fortress Press, 1983); W. A. Meeks, *The First Urban Christians: The Social World of the Apostle Paul* (New Haven, Conn.: Yale University Press, 1983); R. Hock, *The Social Context of Paul's Ministry: Tentmaking and Apostleship* (Philadelphia: Fortress Press, 1980); E. E. Ellis, "Paul and His Co-Workers," *NTS* 17 (1970–1971): 437–452; and T. Schmeller, "Kollege Paulus: Die Jesusüberlieferung und die Selbstverständnis des Völkerapostels," *ZNW* 88 (1997): 260–283.

"school" as present and operative in the production of his letters even during his lifetime. Paul can be said to have "authored" his letters (even the undisputed ones) in the sense that he authorized them and sent them under his name. But it is most likely that other minds and hearts as well as his own contributed to their composition. The social context of the Pauline correspondence, in a word, is as complex as the social context of his entire ministry.[168]

b. The Meaning of Style

Various elements of the Greek language of the Pastorals have been adduced as evidence that the Paul of the undisputed letters could not have also written the Pastorals; among them are diction (especially the proportional number of *hapax legomena*), sentence structure, the use of particles, and the citation of Scripture. The application of this criterion would be appropriate if (and only if) two assumptions were correct. The first is that Paul's undisputed letters are a unique mode of personal expression (the spontaneous outpouring of an individual consciousness). The second is that the undisputed letters are entirely uniform on these stylistic points.

In fact, however, neither is true. The undisputed letters themselves reveal a range of rhetorical and stylistic patterns. Failure to acknowledge the significant stylistic differences among 1 Thessalonians, 1 and 2 Corinthians, Galatians, Romans, Philippians, and Philemon is serious enough to call into question *any* conclusions drawn from such "comparisons." More serious still, the romantic notion that "the style is the person" is thoroughly anachronistic. In the Hellenistic world, the rhetorical ideal was expressed by *prosōpopoiia*, which means "writing in character," whether in speeches, drama, or narrative. The same ideal applied to the writing of letters in antiquity.[169] Style was a matter of being rhetorically appropriate to circumstances and followed definite conventions.[170] Rhetorical handbooks like those of Pseudo-Demetrius and Pseudo-Libanius provided samples of diverse forms of letters appropriate to different situations and social relations.[171] In Paul's time, style was less a matter of personal expressiveness and more a matter of social presence and rhetorical craft. Writers of such differing gifts and locations as Luke the Evangelist and Lucian the Satirist display a dazzling variety of "styles" that are controlled by a single writer in the service of "writing in character."[172]

---

168. For this argument, see Johnson, *Writings of the New Testament*, 253–259.

169. See, for example, S. K. Stowers, "Romans 7:7–25 as a Speech in Character (*prosopōpoiia*)," in *Paul in His Hellenistic Setting*, ed. T. Engberg-Peterson (Minneapolis: Fortress Press, 1995), 180–202.

170. L. T. Johnson, "Taciturnity and True Religion (James 1:26–27)," in *Greeks, Romans, and Christians*, ed. D. Balch et. al. (Minneapolis: Fortress Press, 1990), 329–334.

171. A. J. Malherbe, "Ancient Epistolary Theory," *Ohio Journal of Religious Studies* 5 (1977): 3–77; S. K. Stowers, "Social Typification and the Classification of Ancient Letters," in *The Social World of Formative Christianity and Judaism*, ed. J. Neusner and H. C. Kee (Philadelphia: Fortress Press, 1988), 78–89.

172. For the rhetorical versatility of Luke, see E. Plümacher, *Lukas als hellenistischer Schriftsteller* (Göttingen: Vandenhöck & Ruprecht, 1972).

c. The Framework of Paul's Ministry

One of the classic ways to test the authenticity of the Pastorals is to determine whether they fit into Paul's ministry as it is recounted in the Acts of the Apostles and Paul's other letters. On the face of it, this is a perfectly sensible criterion, the only one that is truly "hard" in a scientific sense—that is, with some degree of objectivity. If we had a day-by-day or even a week-by-week account of Paul's movements, and if we knew that he was in one place when a letter claimed he was in another place, then the spuriousness of a pretended letter could be demonstrated. But the premise is also the problem: it demands a sufficiently full and accurate account of Paul's movements to place all his letters. That premise is, unfortunately, incapable of being met.

Although Acts is generous in its attention to Paul, devoting most of chapters 13–28 to his mission, it is a notoriously selective source, providing considerable detail for certain movements and scenes (above all, Acts 16–21), but also capable of covering lengthy periods of time in a single line: eighteen months in Corinth (Acts 18:11), over two years in Ephesus (19:10), two years in Caesarea (24:27), and two years in Rome (28:30). Eight of the twelve years between 50 and 62 are dealt with by Acts in four lines. Add the sketchy information that Acts provides for the years before Paul worked in Macedonia and the silence of Acts concerning Paul's last days and death.

Although Acts tests out rather well in what it tells us, measured by our other knowledge of Paul's world,[173] even those who claim a high degree of accuracy for its account do not claim that it is an adequate source for Paul's mission.[174] Even if Acts is fully employed, together with all the undisputed letters, in the effort to reconstruct Paul's ministry, three facts remain dismayingly obvious:

1. There are things that one source tells us about Paul that the other source does not contain; thus Acts never speaks of Paul's mission reaching Illyricum, but Romans does. Likewise, Paul speaks of undergoing multiple imprisonments at a point when Acts has recounted only one. Acts reports an imprisonment of Paul in Philippi that he himself never mentions, and a riot in Ephesus to which he at most alludes.
2. There are conflicts between Acts and the letters that cannot be bridged without further information. What really happened between Paul and the Jerusalem leadership concerning circumcision and table fellowship probably lies somewhere between the two accounts in Acts 15 and Gal 2. Likewise, the timing and nature of Paul's collection for Jerusalem is differently portrayed in each source.

---

173. See, for example, H. J. Cadbury, *The Book of Acts in History* (New York: Harper, 1955), and C. J. Hemer, *The Book of Acts in the Setting of Hellenistic History*, WUNT 49 (Tübingen: Mohr [Paul Siebeck], 1989).

174. M. Hengel, *Acts and the History of Earliest Christianity*, trans. J. Bowden (Philadelphia: Fortress Press, 1980).

3. The most critical omission from Acts is any mention of Paul writing letters at all. Fitting *any* of Paul's letters into the framework of Acts is therefore a process of educated guesswork. At the very best, we can date only five of the thirteen letters attributed to Paul with any degree of probability: 1 and 2 Thessalonians, 1 and 2 Corinthians, and Romans. This assumes the authenticity of 2 Thessalonians and the chronological framework provided by Acts for the Aegean ministry of Paul. Galatians, Philemon, and Philippians (among the undisputed letters), and Colossians, Ephesians, 1 Timothy, 2 Timothy, and Titus (among the disputed letters) cannot be placed with any degree of certainty within the Pauline chronology provided by the letters and Acts.[175]

In fact, however, the same scholars who challenge the authenticity of Paul's letters also question the historical accuracy of Acts (most notoriously, Baur and the Tübingen School, especially Schwegler). Some insist that an account of Paul's career must be based exclusively on the letters[176] or, at best, mainly on the letters with some help from Acts.[177] But, in truth, no real account of Paul's ministry can be given from the letters alone, particularly when the number of letters used for the reconstruction is reduced to seven! When the fashion of fragmenting the Pauline letters into separate sources is followed, the entire process becomes ever more complex, subjective, and circular.[178]

In short, a criterion that appears to be stable and objective, and that has consistently been employed to exclude the Pastorals, turns out itself to be a fragile human construct that even at its best fails to account for the largest part of the Pauline correspondence.

d. Consistency in Theme

The criterion of consistency in theme is reasonable in theory only if two conditions can be met. First, we need a collection of Paul's statements on any particular subject that is systematic and complete—statements that are themselves not conditioned by being responses to highly specific situations that are no longer fully recoverable. Second, we need a treatment of the same subject in another letter not only different from, but also contradictory to, that systematic and complete treatment. Only under such conditions can the criterion of consistency be applied with any precision. Even then, its use would necessarily be cautious: no law of nature forbids an author from changing his or her mind on a specific topic. But at least the criterion could raise significant doubts.

---

175. L. T. Johnson, *The Acts of the Apostles*, Sacra Pagina 5 (Collegeville, Minn.: Liturgical Press, 1992), 3–18.

176. See J. Knox, *Chapters in a Life of Paul* (Nashville, Tenn.: Abingdon Press, 1950).

177. J. Murphy-O'Connor, *Paul: A Critical Life* (London: Oxford University Press, 1996), 1–31.

178. See, for example, H. D. Betz, "2 Cor. 6:14–7:1: An Anti-Pauline Fragment," *JBL* 92 (1973): 88–108; B. D. Rahtjian, "The Three Letters of Paul to the Philippians," *NTS* 6 (1959–1960): 167–173; and A. de Oliveira, *Die Diakonie der Gerechtigkeit und der Versöhnung in der Apologie des 2. Korintherbriefes*, Neutestamentliche Abhandlung 21 (Münster: Aschendorff, 1990), esp. 6–18.

Once more, the facts of the case render the premise inoperable. Any claim of a consistent Pauline teaching on any point must ignore two salient considerations, and have consistently done so! The first is that Paul's thoughts on any particular topic are always conditional and geared to an epistolary situation. He nowhere engages in a complete and systematic treatment of a specific matter. The only possible exception is the thesis concerning God's righteousness in Rom 1:16–17, which is worked out in the course of that letter. Even with Romans, the variety of interpretations given to the letter makes one hesitate to declare overconfidently on Paul's position. The second consideration is that on many major points to which Paul does give sustained attention, there is considerable variety, even tension, among the discussions (e.g., the treatment of Abraham in Rom 4 and Gal 3, or the understanding of eschatology in 1 Thessalonians and 1 Corinthians). The proposition that Paul's undisputed letters have so consistent a teaching on any single theme that the teaching on the same theme in another letter can be declared un-Pauline on the basis of comparison is one that must be demonstrated, rather than assumed.

5. The Consequences of Grouping

The reader will remember that the first objection to the authenticity of the Pastorals (by Schleiermacher in 1807) was addressed to only 1 Timothy, and the argument was carried by contrasting 1 Timothy with 2 Timothy and Titus. Since the time of Eichhorn (1812), however, the Pastorals have consistently been treated as a group, a special set of distinct writings. The consequences of this grouping have too seldom been noted.[179]

The first consequence is that characterizations are drawn from the evidence provided by all three letters as a whole and then (inappropriately) applied to each of them individually, even though a particular letter may lack a trait entirely. Thus the position that "the Pastorals" evince a more elaborate church order than that in the undisputed letters is false when applied to either Titus or 2 Timothy. 2 Timothy has nothing on the subject, and Titus has at most a few (not altogether clear) lines. Similarly, the search for the "opponents in the Pastorals" is one that has always worked with a composite from all three letters, even though each letter has a distinct portrait of the opposition, and the composite fits none of the letters exactly. These generalizations blur the distinctions among the three letters and help strengthen the perception of them as a single literary production.

These composite characterizations are then compared and contrasted with an equally abstract characterization of the "authentic Paul." Once more, the failure is to recognize the intractable diversity of even the undisputed letters. Comparison is not carried out among individual letters, but between groups of letters by way of abstraction. A direct result is that the sense of distance from the undisputed Pauline letters is heightened. It is seldom recognized that the same

---

179. The point I make theoretically has been applied with great effectiveness to the question of style in Torm, "Über die Sprache in den Pastoralbriefen."

effect could be achieved if one were to isolate the Thessalonian letters, read them with reference only to each other, and compare them with the "other Pauline letters" by means of composite characterizations. How easy it is to demonstrate that the collection called "the Thessalonians" has "little genuinely Pauline" about it. Quite another perception results from comparing 1 Thessalonians with 1 Corinthians. Likewise, if Titus is compared point-by-point with Galatians, 1 Timothy is compared point-by-point with 1 Corinthians, and 2 Timothy is compared point-by-point with Philippians, the letters look less alien.

Contrary to the dictum first enunciated by Eichhorn and repeated endlessly since, it simply is *not* necessary to decide for the authenticity or inauthenticity of all three Pastorals together. It is possible to consider the letters separately as distinct literary productions. The majority position on the Pastorals, however, makes any such reexamination difficult, for increasingly it relies on the premise that the three letters are not real correspondence, but a single fictitious literary production.[180] If 2 Timothy could be shown to be authentic, however, with 1 Timothy and Titus pseudonymous compositions based on it, much recent scholarship would require reexamination.

These, then, are five tendencies in the discussion about authenticity that dramatically affect the integrity of the debate on the Pastoral Letters. They are of such fundamental importance that it is surprising, perhaps even shocking, that they have not been thematized and more frequently been made the subject of direct discussion. At the very least, readers of this commentary should be aware of the great and puzzling gap between the massive social fact of the present scholarly consensus and the quality of the methods and arguments purportedly used to support it. The cumulative effect of critical scholarship on every other aspect of Pauline studies over the past thirty years ought, at the very least, allow for a different way of approaching the entire question of the authenticity of the Pastorals.

B. CONSIDERING THE EVIDENCE

Even when prejudicial tendencies have been identified and the weakness of argumentative strategies analyzed, the Pastorals still present substantive issues that require serious consideration.

Everyone recognizes that they are Pauline in at least a broad sense. They are, after all, written in Paul's name, they seek to advance his cause, they present Paul as a positive example, and they contain universally acknowledged elements of Pauline teaching and language. Even those who reject their authenticity recognize them to be part of a Pauline tradition. At the same time, all careful read-

---

180. See, for example, P. Trummer, "Corpus Paulinum—Corpus Pastorale: Zur Ortung der Paulustradition in den Pastoralbriefen," in *Paulus in den neutestamentlichen Spaetschriften*, ed. K. Kertelge, QD 89 (Freiburg: Herder, 1981), 122–145.

ers also recognize that each of these three letters contains just enough divergence from what readers intuitively understand to be "authentically Pauline" as to demand an accounting. It is the way this combination of similarity and difference, of the familiar and the strange, is diversely reckoned that leads to the wide difference of opinion among scholars.

The distinguishing features of 1 and 2 Timothy will be carefully delineated in the commentary proper. In order to understand the current state of scholarship on "the Pastorals" as such, however, it is necessary to continue to consider the three letters as a group, if only to demonstrate, by taking up each point in turn, how that very grouping is problematic and how the data can support more than one position.

1. The Letters and Paul's Ministry

Can the Pastorals be fitted within the framework of Paul's ministry such as it is presented by Acts and the undisputed letters? I have noted the theoretical legitimacy of this way of testing for authenticity. A complete account of Paul's captivity showing that no one named Onesiphorus ever visited him would seriously impugn 2 Tim 1:16. But there would still remain several possible explanations. One would be a fictionalizing later composition. Another would be that Paul was forgetful or mistaken or lying. The larger difficulty is that our knowledge of Paul's movements is anything but full.

We can begin by reviewing the data. 1 Timothy and Titus presuppose that Paul is actively engaged in ministry rather than imprisoned. Little specific information is given by either letter. 1 Timothy has Paul leaving his delegate in Ephesus while he travels to Macedonia (1 Tim 1:3). We are not told whether he wrote the letter before he left, while on the road, or at his destination. Timothy is, in any case, to deal with matters until Paul's return, which should happen shortly (1 Tim 3:14). In principle, such a letter could have been written at almost any time during Paul's extensive Aegean ministry. Our other sources indicate that Paul spent over two years in Ephesus (Acts 19:10) and made at least two trips from there to Macedonia (Acts 20:1–3; 2 Cor 1:16; 2:12–13; 7:5–6).

Titus is much more difficult. Paul writes to his delegate whom he had "left" on Crete (Tit 1:5). Paul's own whereabouts are not named. He plans, however, to spend the winter in Nicopolis (3:12), which could be one of several cities with that name. That Paul's mission should have included the establishment of a church on Crete is not in itself surprising. But we have no evidence at all concerning Paul's work on the island. The only personal presence of Paul on Crete, according to Acts 27:7–15, was a brief stopover as a prisoner when on his way to Rome, and Acts does not name Titus as a companion on that voyage.

2 Timothy is a captivity letter, most probably sent from Rome (2 Tim 1:16–17). By itself, the letter can easily be fitted into the account of Acts 28:30–31, which pictures Paul spending two years in Rome as a prisoner, under a form of house arrest, but able freely to engage in preaching (Acts 28:30–31). But does the reference to his "first defense" in 2 Tim 4:16 indicate that Paul is now in a sec-

ond imprisonment, or does it mean merely that Paul is in a second stage in his trial? In contrast to 1 Timothy and Titus, 2 Timothy contains detailed information about some fifteen of Paul's other helpers in the mission (4:9–21). Their movements, as recorded in the letter, do not for the most part contradict what we know of them from other sources, although the discrepancy about the location of Trophimus has caused considerable dispute: Acts 21:29 places Trophimus with Paul in Jerusalem at the time of his arrest in the Temple there, whereas 2 Tim 4:20 says that Paul left Trophimus ill in Miletus (compare Acts 20:17–37). This would, on the face of it, appear to be one of those impossible-to-resolve contradictions, and it has vexed commentators to the point that some have even suggested an emendation of the place-name! Other information, however, unexpectedly confirms details found in other letters, such as the short remark, "Erastus remained in Corinth" (2 Tim 4:20), which agrees with Rom 16:23 in associating Erastus with that city.

The autobiographical data supplied by the three compositions are evaluated in several ways. Historical placement is more difficult when a hypothesis must include all three letters, for the tendency then is to assume that a shared authorship must also mean an identical time and place for writing. Those who conclude—on this and other grounds—that the Pastorals must be pseudonymous deal with the material in two basic ways. The first is to regard it as entirely fictional, a dimension of pseudepigraphic literature such as is found in the *Testaments of the Twelve Patriarchs* and the *Socratic Letters*.[181] The presence of such autobiographical information as we find in 2 Timothy and Titus has even been proposed as a demonstration of pseudepigraphy,[182] even though several of Paul's undisputed letters contain at least equal amounts of personal information (Galatians, 2 Corinthians, Philemon, Philippians) without thereby being considered inauthentic, whereas the highly disputed Ephesians has no such information.

Others think that although the Pastorals themselves are pseudonymous, the information about Paul may have some historical basis, whether preserved as fragments from lost genuine notes now woven into new compositions,[183] or as

---

181. N. Brox, "Zu den persönlichen Notizen den Pastoralbriefe," *BZ* 13 (1969): 76–94.

182. L. R. Donelson, *Pseudepigraphy and Ethical Argument in the Pastoral Epistles*, Hermeneutische Untersuchungen zur Theologie 22 (Tübingen: Mohr [Paul Siebeck], 1986), 23–66.

183. A version of this was suggested already by Credner, *Einleitung in Neue Testament* (1836) and extensively argued in F. H. Hesse, *Die Entstehung der neutestamentlichen Hirtenbriefe* (Halle: Kämmerer, 1889). The version that has received the most attention and exercised the most influence—especially in England and the United States—is Harrison, *Problem of the Pastoral Epistles*. See also P. N. Harrison, "Important Hypotheses Reconsidered III: The Authorship of the Pastorals Reconsidered," *ExpT* 67 (1955):77–81, and F. Spitta, "Über die persönlichen Notizen im Zweiter Briefe an Timotheus," *TSK* 51 (1878): 582–607. Among the commentaries and introductions that have accepted the fragment hypothesis are Scott, *Pastoral Epistles*; Gardner, *Later Pauline Epistles*; Barrett, *Pastoral Epistles in the New English Bible*; Bacon, *Introduction to the New Testament*; Holtzmann, *Pastoralbriefe*; Hanson, *Pastoral Epistles*; and Dornier, *Épîtres pastorales*, (1942). A new version of the theory has recently appeared in J. D. Miller, *The Pastoral Letters as Composite Documents*, SNTSMS 93 (Cambridge: Cambridge University Press, 1997).

material that was developed folklorically through a process of oral transmission similar to that of the second-century apocryphal writing the *Acts of Paul and Thecla*, whose characters have much in common with those in 2 Timothy.[184]

Scholars who consider—certainly on grounds other than these—that the Pastorals are authentically Pauline have three available options. The first is to squeeze the compositions into the framework provided by Acts and the undisputed letters, an option that requires a considerable amount of ingenuity.[185] The second, the most frequently chosen, is to invoke the ancient tradition (*1 Clement* 5:7) that Paul was released from a first Roman captivity and preached in Spain before being again imprisoned and martyred. The opening provided by a period of time between a first and a second imprisonment enables one to account for the movements reported especially by 2 Timothy and Titus.[186] Partially because it is such an attractive option, the theory of a second imprisonment has also been the special target of those who oppose authenticity; they point out, for example, that even if such a hiatus were historically likely, a mission by Paul in the West scarcely accounts for the movements in the East reported by the letters themselves.[187]

The third option is seldom chosen, but seems most reasonable to me. It begins with the recognition that neither Acts nor Paul's other letters give us an ad-

---

184. D. R. MacDonald, *The Legend and the Apostle: The Battle for Paul in Story and Canon* (Philadelphia: Westminster Press, 1983). For the position that the *AP* were written against the Pastorals, see also J. Rohde, "Pastoralbriefe und *Acta Pauli*," in *Studia Evangelica* ed. F. L. Cross (Berlin: Akademie, 1968), 303–310.

185. See, for example, J. A. T. Robinson, *Redating the New Testament* (Philadelphia: Westminster Press, 1970), 67–85. The thesis of G. S. Duncan, *St. Paul's Ephesian Ministry: A Reconstruction with Special Reference to the Ephesian Origin of the Imprisonment Epistles* (London: Hodder and Stoughton, 1929), seemed to some to open up possibilities for placing the Pastorals, but the thesis has also had its detractors, including P. N. Harrison, "The Pastoral Epistles and Duncan's Ephesian Theory," *NTS* 2 (1955–1956): 250–261; J. Schmid, *Zeit und Ort der paulinischen Gefangenschaftsbriefe* (Freiburg: Herder, 1931), 148–159; and C. Mauer, "Eine Textvariante Klärt die Entstehung der Pastoralbriefe auf," *TZ* 3 (1947): 321–332.

186. See, for example, G. W. Knight, III, *Commentary on the Pastoral Epistles*, New International Greek Commentary (Grand Rapids, Mich.: Eerdmans, 1992), 15–20. Others holding the theory of a second Roman imprisonment are Fairbairn, *Pastoral Epistles*; Plummer, *Pastoral Epistles*; Ellicott, *Pastoral Epistles of St. Paul*; Bernard, *Pastoral Epistles*; White, *First and Second Epistles*; Knabenbauer, *Commentarius*; Brown, *Pastoral Epistles*; Hilliard, *Pastoral Epistles of St. Paul*; Parry, *Pastoral Epistles*; Molitor, *Pastoralbriefe des Hl.Paulus*; Boudou, *Saint Paul*; and Kelly, *Commentary on the Pastoral Epistles*.

187. See, for example, E. Reuss, "La Seconde Captivité de Saint Paul," *Revue de théologie et de philosophie chrétiennes* 1 (1851): 150–171. To such objections, the redoubtable Salmon replied in typically trenchant style: "What is said in answer to this is, that Paul's release from his Roman imprisonment is unhistorical—that it is a mere hypothesis invented to get rid of a difficulty. But this answer exhibits a complete misconception of the logical position; for it is really those who refuse to entertain the idea of Paul's second release who make an unwarrantable hypothesis. Paul's release from his Roman imprisonment, we are told, is unhistorical; so is his non-release. In other words, Luke's history of the life of Paul breaks off without telling us whether he was released or not. Under these circumstances a scientific inquirer ought to hold his mind unbiassed towards either supposition" (*Historical Introduction*, 421).

equate account of his ministry. It also acknowledges that the information in the three Pastorals does not easily fit within the framework offered by Acts and the other letters. But it also leaves open the possibility that the Pastorals may provide important additional information about Paul's career and captivity that are not found in the other sources. In this respect, the Pastorals are put on the same plane as the other letters. 2 Corinthians tells us of imprisonments and beatings experienced by Paul that are otherwise unreported by Acts or his other letters (2 Cor 11:23–24). Galatians informs us that Paul founded churches throughout Phrygia and did so under the burden of a physical affliction, which we would not have learned elsewhere (Gal 1:2; 4:13–14). Romans tells us, as Acts never does, that Paul had a mission in Illyricum (Rom 15:19). All his letters together inform us magnificently of the fact that Acts ignores completely: that Paul wrote letters to his churches! In the same fashion, it is possible that Titus reports on missionary activities in Crete that we learn of nowhere else. And just as 2 Tim 4:10 confirms the information in Rom 16:23 that Erastus was in Corinth, so the note in 2 Tim 4:10 about Titus going to Dalmatia verifies the report in Rom 15:19 about a Pauline mission in Illyricum.[188]

In short, if the Pastorals are difficult to fit into the Pauline mission because of the biographical information they contain, they present problems on this count of no greater magnitude than those presented by Galatians, Philemon, and Philippians. Turned another way, they also provide the basis for expanding our understanding of Paul's movements in exactly the same way the other letters do.

2. Style

Even if the theoretical legitimacy of the criterion of style is granted, it is particularly difficult to apply to the Pastorals with any precision. The early challenge by Schleiermacher was largely impressionistic,[189] and the extended lists of *hapax legomena* posted by other early critics had little methodological point, since they were not compared systematically with other Pauline usage.[190] More recent critics have sought to place the statistical analysis of vocabulary on a more sci-

---

188. To pick up from Salmon, again: "If new evidence presents itself, no good reason either for accepting or rejecting it can be furnished by a preconceived opinion as to the issue of Paul's imprisonment. Now the Pastoral Epistles are a new source of evidence. They come to us with the best possible external attestation; and our opponents will not dispute that if we accept them as Pauline, they lead us to the conclusion that Paul lived to make other journeys than those recorded by St. Luke. We accept this conclusion, not because of any preconceived hypothesis, but because on other grounds we hold the epistles to be genuine. But it is those who say, 'We cannot believe these epistles to be Paul's, because they indicate a release from prison which we know did not take place,' who really make an unwarrantable assumption" (*Historical Introduction*, 421).

189. Schweitzer is perceptive: "Strictly speaking it was not Schleiermacher the critic but Schleiermacher the aesthete who had come to have doubts about 2 [sic] Timothy" *Paul and His Interpreters*, 8). He means, of course, 1 Timothy.

190. De Wette, *Historico-Critical Introduction*, 299–300; Holtzmann, *Pastoralbriefe*, 15–60. The various *hapax legomena* will be identified and discussed separately in the commentary.

entific basis,[191] but even when carried out with some degree of rigor[192] it fails to give adequate attention to the smallness of the sample and the wide variations in the undisputed Pauline corpus.[193]

The study of vocabulary is also distorted by the decision to consider the three letters as a group rather than individually.[194] The vocabulary in 2 Timothy, taken as a whole, is closer to that of the undisputed letters (taken as a whole), whereas the vocabulary of 1 Timothy and Titus diverges more dramatically. When taken as a group, it has frequently been noticed, the Pastorals share a great deal of vocabulary with Luke–Acts. Some have drawn the conclusion that Luke is the author of the Pastorals,[195] perhaps even making these letters the third volume (in effect) of Luke–Acts.[196] But it would be more accurate to say that both Luke and the Pastorals reveal a broader sample of Koine Greek than is attested in the undisputed letters.

It is a critical failure of studies of diction that they do not take seriously the way in which distinctive subject matter shapes vocabulary clusters throughout the Pauline corpus as a whole. This can be demonstrated by playing another sort of vocabulary game than counting *hapax legomena*. Anyone in possession of a concordance can observe the wide variation within the Pauline letters even with respect to some terms that are regarded as "quintessentially Pauline." Note for example that *nomos* (law) occurs seventy-two times in Romans, thirty-one times in Galatians, and eight times in 1 Corinthians, but only three times in Philippians. It occurs also two times in 2 Timothy and one time in Ephesians, but is absent entirely from Colossians, 2 Corinthians, 2 Timothy, 1 Thessalonians, 2 Thessalonians, and Philemon. Similarly, *sarx* (flesh) appears twenty-three

---

191. In *Problem of the Pastoral Epistles*, Harrison tries to establish more precision by developing statistical tables comparing the Pastorals on the one side with the undisputed letters (18–36) and on the other side with second-century literature (67–86). He also touches on other stylistic elements (38–44). Harrison's work is given a higher sheen in K. Graystone and G. Herdan, "The Authorship of the Pastorals in the Light of Statistical Linguistics," *NTS* 6 (1959–1960): 1–15, and D. L. Mealand, "Positional Stylometry Reassessed: Testing a Seven Epistle Theory of Pauline Authorship," *NTS* 35 (1989): 266–286, and "The Extent of the Pauline Corpus: A Multivariate Approach," *JSNT* 59 (1995): 61–92.

192. D. Cook, "The Pastoral Fragments Reconsidered," *JTS* 35 (1984): 120–131; "2 Timothy 4 6–8 and the Epistle to the Philippians," *JTS* 33 (1982): 168–171.

193. T. A. Robinson, "Graystone and Herdan's 'C' Quantity Formula and the Authorship of the Pastorals," *NTS* 30 (1984): 282–288; Metzger, "Reconsideration of Certain Arguments."

194. Parry does a particularly good job of showing how vocabulary in Paul is geared to subject matter in *Pastoral Epistles*, cxi–cxxvi. Torm is brilliant with respect to the implications of *grouping* letters in "Über die Sprache in der Pastoralbriefen." W. Michaelis, severely criticizes Harrison for failing to take Torm's important observations into account in "Pastoralbriefe und Wortstatistik," *ZNW* 28 (1929): 69–76.

195. A. Strobel, "Schreiben des Lukas? Zum sprachlishen Problem der Pastoralbriefe," *NTS* 15 (1968–1969): 191–210; S. G. Wilson, *Luke and the Pastoral Epistles* (London: SPCK, 1979). See the cautionary response by N. Brox, "Lukas als Verfasser der Pastoralbriefe?" *JAC* 13 (1970): 62–77.

196. J. D. Quinn, "The Last Volume of Luke: The Relation of Luke–Acts to the Pastoral Epistles," in *Perspectives on Luke–Acts*, ed. C. H. Talbert (Danville, Va.: Association of Baptist Professors of Religion, 1978), 62–75.

times in Romans, sixteen times in Galatians, nine times each in 1 Corinthians, 2 Corinthians, Ephesians, and Colossians, but, apart from its one use in 1 Timothy and Philemon, is absent from 2 Timothy, Titus, 1 Thessalonians, and 2 Thessalonians.

One might think that the "message of the cross [*stauros*]" would be everywhere in Paul, but, in fact, the noun *stauros* appears three times in Galatians, two times each in 1 Corinthians, Philemon, and Colossians, one time in Ephesians, and not at all in Romans (!), 2 Corinthians (!), 1 Thessalonians, 2 Thessalonians, 1 Timothy, 2 Timothy, Titus, and Philemon. The verb *stauroo* appears four times in 1 Corinthians, three times in Galatians, one time in 2 Corinthians, and not at all in Romans, Philemon, Colossians, Ephesians, 1 Thessalonians, 2 Thessalonians, 1 Timothy, 2 Timothy, Titus, and Philemon. Language about "freedom" (*eleutheria/eleutheros*) appears seven times in Romans, ten times in Galatians, and seven times in 1 Corinthians, but only one time each in 2 Corinthians, Ephesians, and Colossians, and never in Philippians, 1 Thessalonians, 2 Thessalonians, 1 Timothy, 2 Timothy, Titus, and Philemon. By way of contrast, we see that *soteria* (salvation) appears five times in 2 Corinthians, four times in Romans, three times in Philippians, two times each in 1 Thessalonians and 2 Timothy, but not at all in 1 Corinthians, Galatians, 1 Timothy, Colossians, Titus, and Philemon.

If any cluster of vocabulary would seem to characterize Paul, it would be that involving righteousness, but even here, the evidence is mixed: "righteous" (*dikaios*) appears seven times in Romans, two times each in Philippians and 2 Thessalonians, and one time each in Galatians, Ephesians, 1 Timothy, 2 Timothy, and Titus, but is missing from 1 Corinthians, 2 Corinthians, 1 Thessalonians, and Philemon. "Righteousness" (*dikaiosynē*) occurs twelve times in Romans, seven times in 2 Corinthians, five times in Galatians, three times each in Ephesians, Philippians, and 2 Timothy, but one time only in Titus, 1 Timothy, and 1 Corinthians, while appearing not at all in Colossians, Philemon, 1 Thessalonians, and 2 Thessalonians. The verb "to make righteous" (*dikaioō*), in turn, appears fifteen times in Romans, eight times in Galatians, two times in 1 Corinthians, and one time each in 1 Timothy and Titus, while being absent from 2 Corinthians, Philippians, Philemon, Colossians, and Ephesians. The nouns *dikaiōma* and *dikaiōsis* appear only in Romans, five and two times respectively; in contrast, the adverb "righteously" (*dikaiōs*) appears one time only in 1 Corinthians, 1 Thessalonians, and Titus.

We can take "sanctification" language as a final point of diction that would intuitively be thought of as Pauline. But once more, the actual evidence is startling. The adjective *hagios* is widely if unevenly distributed: twenty-one times in Romans, fifteen times in Ephesians, twelve times in 1 Corinthians, seven times in 2 Corinthians, six times each in Colossians and 1 Thessalonians, three times in Philippians, two times each in Philemon and 2 Timothy, and one time each in 1 Timothy and Titus. But the verb *hagiazō* is found in only five letters (three times in 1 Corinthians, and one time each in Romans, Ephesians, 1 Thessalonians, and 1 Timothy); the noun *hagiasmos* is in only four letters (three times in 1 Thessalonians, two times in Romans, and one time each in 1 Corinthians and 2 Thessalonians); the noun *hagiosynē* appears in only three letters (one time each in Romans, 2 Corinthians, and 1 Thessalonians); and the noun *hagiotēs* occurs once in one letter (2 Corinthians). What is most surprising is that the only Pauline letter that utterly lacks "holiness" language in any form is Galatians!

What does all this prove? Nothing. And that is the point. It is clear that even when we take vocabulary that everyone would agree is "characteristically" Pauline, it appears in erratic fashion. Taken as a whole, the three Pastorals share as much of this vocabulary as any other portion of the corpus except Romans. What is most obvious is that the subject matter of a letter has as much to do with vocabulary used as any other factor, and if the topic is left out of consideration, tests of vocabulary are meaningless. Far too little attention has been paid to the fact that vocabulary that is considered "un-Pauline" in the Pastorals tends to be found precisely in those places that take up subjects not discussed in the undisputed letters.

Most of all, vocabulary studies do not take into acount the ancient rhetorical ideal of *prosōpopoiia*, or "writing in character," which calls into the question the entire way of construing authorship as a kind of personal expressiveness and invites consideration of Paul as a rhetorician whose diction is shaped by the situation he faces and the strategies of persuasion he develops.

Stylistic analysis involves more than diction. It entails the analysis of phrases, clauses, and sentences, as well as the arrangement of arguments. The syntax of the Pastorals, taken as a group, is generally smoother and flatter than the more vividly dialogical sections of Romans and Galatians. Sentences tend to be longer and more regular, although they are also marked by frequent anarthous nouns and participles, asyndeton, and dangling clauses. The use of particles is less varied and rich than in some other letters. Such observations are accurate; what they amount to is less obvious. One pertinent question is how much the dialogical style of Galatians, Romans, and 1 Corinthians is due to Paul's use in those letters of the diatribal mode. If the Pastorals are compared with 1 Thessalonians or Philippians, the differences do not seem so severe. It has likewise been pointed out, with considerable justice, that the Pastorals have overall a more distinctly "Greek" sensibility than the "biblical" style of Paul. But it should again be noted that the biblical style is scarcely to be equated with Paul's "natural" mode. In fact, the distinctively biblical idiom is concentrated in some of his letters (especially Galatians and Romans) and is virtually absent from others (such as Philippians and Philemon).

A further complication is that the Pastorals do not manifest a single consistent "hand" in the way that Colossians and Ephesians do. Instead, they appear to alternate sections that are intensely "Pauline" in tone with other sections that are "un-Pauline" (more properly stated, sections we "recognize" as Pauline or un-Pauline). It is this stylistic inconsistency that led to various fragment theories: the "Pauline" sections are accounted for by being lifted from lost notes written by Paul; the "un-Pauline" sections are the work of the later pseudepigrapher. Apart from the difficulties attendant on identifying the "authentic" fragments, the hypothesis invites us to contemplate a forger sufficiently attuned to stylistic niceties to be able to seek the use of the proposed fragments as a way of conveying to others the "Pauline" character of his pseudepigraphy, yet so stylistically inept as to be unable to replicate that style in the portions he writes himself.

Analysis of the style of the three Pastoral letters yields the conclusion that they do have common features not found in other letters. The degree of difference is a matter of judgment. The significance of the difference is a matter of debate. The temptation to decide against authenticity on the basis of style should, however, be chastened by two important considerations. The first is that the same observation can be made about other groups in the Pauline corpus: Galatians and Romans share distinctive features, as do the Corinthian and the Thessalonian letters. When they are isolated and compared with the other letters, they also look "different." The second consideration is the sober reminder that the Pastorals were never challenged on the basis of style in the ancient church, even though criticism of Hebrews on this very point was not lacking. Is it reasonable to propose that the sense of Greek style might have been even better among those who continued to be schooled within the same *paideia* as Paul than among those who learned their Greek in a nineteenth-century German *Gymnasium* or a twentieth-century American preparatory school and seminary?

3. The Identity of Opponents

An early reason for disputing the authenticity of the Pastorals was the identity of the opponents or the nature of the "heresy" they espoused. The basic line of argument is that the evidence suggests forms of deviance not likely to have been existing in the time of Paul, reflecting instead a later period. Thus Baur argued that the mention of "myths and genealogies" (1 Tim 1:3) must be understood as referring to the developed Gnostic Systems of the mid-second century, and that the mention of "falsely called *gnōsis*" and "Antitheses" in 1 Tim 6:20 was directed against the mid-second-century heretic Marcion.[197] Most subsequent scholars have doubted whether the verses could have so specific a referent, but Baur's position continues to be represented in recent scholarship.[198] There have been any number of other efforts to reconstruct the heresy addressed by the letters.[199]

---

197. Baur, *Die sogennanten Pastoralbriefe*, 8–39.

198. W. Bauer, *Orthodoxy and Heresy in Earliest Christianity*, ed. R. A. Kraft and G. Krodel (Philadelphia: Fortress Press, 1971), 222–228; Marxsen, *Introduction to the New Testament*, 199–215; Goodspeed, *Introduction to the New Testament*, 327–344.

199. W. Mangold, *Die Irrlehrer der Pastoralbriefe* (Marburg: Elwertsche Universitäts-Buchhandlung, 1856); W. Lütgert, *Die Irrlehrer der Pastoralbriefe* (Gütersloh: Bertlesmann, 1909); Lock, *Critical and Exegetical Commentary*, xvi–xviii; Spicq, *Épîtres pastorales*, 52–72; Brox, *Pastoralbriefe*, 31–42; F. J. Schierse, *Die Pastoralbriefe* (Düsseldorf: Patmos, 1968), 31; E. Schlarb, *Die Gesunde Lehre: Häresie und Wahrheit im Spiegel der Pastoralbriefe*, Marburger Theologische Studien 28 (Marburg: Elwert, 1990), 14–141; M. Goulder, "The Pastor's Wolves: Jewish Christian Visionaries Behind the Pastoral Epistles," *NovT* 38 (1996): 242–256.

Reconstructions have been frustrated by the fact that the combination of elements presented by all three letters (in composite) does not match precisely the profile of any known heresy: teaching that the resurrection is already past (2 Tim 2:17–18), forbidding marriage and certain foods (1 Tim 4:3), advocating physical asceticism (1 Tim 4:8), being concerned with the observance of the Law (1 Tim 1:7; Tit 3:9), and practicing circumcision and purity regulations (Tit 1:10, 15). For some scholars convinced of pseudonymity on other grounds, this very mixture suggests that the basic message of the Pastorals was simply to counter deviance from orthodoxy in any and every form.[200]

Using the letters to reconstruct a portrait of opponents in the second century has encountered two other difficulties. The first is that each of the elements found in the Pastoral Letters can separately be found in Paul's other letters (e.g., 1 Cor 7:1; 8:1–3; 15:17–19; Gal 4:8–10; Col 2:20–22). The second is the realization that a great deal of the characterization of the opponents is derived from the rhetorical conventions of antiquity governing polemic between opposing teachers.[201] Seeing how much of the language used by each of these letters about the opposition is stereotypical, we should be cautious in using the text as a direct means of access to their positions.[202] The combination of these two factors basically serves to remove the identification of the opponents as a factor in the positive historical placement of the Pastorals.

The manner in which the Pastorals respond to opponents is also sometimes said to be uncharacteristic of the authentic Paul:[203] They rely on polemic, whereas the genuine Paul enters into a serious theological rebuttal of his opponents. The observation is only partly true, since 1 Timothy does engage in substantive theological refutation at least four times (1:8–11; 4:3–5, 7–8; 6:5–10), and the Paul of the undisputed letters shows himself thoroughly capable of using invective against rival teachers (2 Cor 11:13–15; Gal 5:12; 6:13; Rom 16:17–18; Phil 3:2, 18–19).[204] What is distinctive about the polemic in these letters is its pervasiveness and—especially in 1 and 2 Timothy—the literary function it plays (a topic to be taken up in the commentary at several places).[205]

---

200. Barnett, *New Testament*, 286.

201. Some aspects were seen by M. Dibelius, *Die Brief des Apostels Paulus an Timotheus und Titus*, HNT 13 (Tübingen: Mohr [Paul Siebeck], 1913), 149, and developed further by M. Dibelius and H. Conzelmann, *The Pastoral Epistles*, ed. H. Köster, trans. P. Buttolph and A. Yarbro, Hermeneia (Philadelphia: Fortress Press, 1972), 2. See also Spicq, *Épîtres pastorales*, 185–190, and F. H. Colson, "'Myths and Genealogies'—A Note on the Polemic of the Pastoral Epistles," *JTS* 18 (1917–1918): 265–271.

202. See, especially, R. J. Karris, "The Background and Significance of the Polemic of the Pastoral Epistles," *JBL* 92 (1973): 549–564, and "The Function and *Sitz-im-Leben* of the Parenetic Elements in the Pastoral Epistles" (Ph.D. diss., Harvard University, 1971), 3–39.

203. Kümmel, *Introduction to the New Testament*, 380.

204. A. du Toit, "Vilification as a Pragmatic Device in Early Christian Epistolography," *Bib* 75 (1994): 403–412.

205. L. T. Johnson, "II Timothy and the Polemic Against False Teachers: A Reexamination," *JRS* 6–7 (1978–1979): 1–26.

4. The Organization of the Church

A major and persistent reason for doubting the authenticity of the Pastorals has been the structure of the church they are thought to reveal.[206] This is not merely a case of emphasis, as when Colossians alters the image of the church as the body of Christ in 1 Cor 12:12–27 by making Christ the head of the body that is the church (Col 1:18–19). Here, it is argued, we find a historical development from the *ekklēsia* as God's assembly filled with spiritual gifts to an organizational chart for the "Household of God" (1 Tim 3:15), which has a hierarchy of bishops, elders, and deacons, as well as orders of women deacons and widows. For some scholars, such attention to structure virtually defines the Pastorals and locates them in the development of Christianity from sect to church.[207] No clearer evidence could be adduced, it is asserted, that these letters both reflect and help create a church in which the routinization of charism is well on its way to accomplishment.[208] Christianity in the Pastorals has come to grips with the delay of the parousia and is adjusting to continued existence in the world by creating an institutional structure.[209]

Such purported attention to church structure is also sometimes read today as a defensive reaction to powerful egalitarian impulses within Christianity, especially among women,[210] which helps account for the markedly sexist attitudes found in 1 Tim 2:11–15 and 5:3–16.[211] The church order in the Pastorals should be compared with that found in the *Letters* (ca. 115) of Ignatius of Antioch, in which a monarchical episcopate and hierarchical order are instruments in the

---

206. The line is a direct one from Schleiermacher, *Über der sogennanten Ersten Brief des Paulus an den Timotheus*, 58–59, 78, 125, 160, to H. von Campenhausen, *Ecclesiastical Authority and Spiritual Power in the Church of the First Three Centuries*, trans. J. Baker (Stanford, Calif.: Stanford University Press, 1969), 107–120.

207. M. Y. MacDonald, *The Pauline Churches: A Socio-Historical Study of Institutionalization in the Pauline and Deutero-Pauline Writings* SNTSMS (Cambridge: Cambridge University Press, 1988), 159–238.

208. In R. Sohm, *Kirchenrecht*, vol. 1, *Die geschichtliche Grundlagen*, Systematisches Handbuch der deutschen Rechtswissenschaft 8, pt. 1 (Leipzig: Duncker & Humbolt, 1892), note how the opposition is set between *Urchristentum*, which is entirely "charismatic" (22–28), and *Katholicismus*, which is "institutional" (157–227).

209. See, for example, C. von Weizsäcker, "Die Kirchenverfassung des apostolischer Zeitalter," *Jahrbuch für deutsche Theologie* 18 (1873): 631–674; Leo, *Das anvertraute Gut*, 7–13; O. Kuss, "Bemerkungen zu dem Fragenkreis: Jesus und die Kirche im Neuen Testament," *TQ* 135 (1955): 150–183; and W. Oates, "The Conception of Ministry in the Pastoral Epistles," *Review and Expositor* 56 (1959): 388–410.

210. See, for example, D. R. MacDonald, "Virgins, Widows, and Paul in Second-Century Asia Minor," in *1979: Society of Biblical Literature Seminar Papers*, ed. P. Achtemeier (Missoula, Mont.: Scholars Press, 1979), 1:165–184; S. L. Davies, *The Revolt of the Widows: The Social World of the Apocryphal Acts* (Carbondale: Southern Illinois University Press, 1980); and MacDonald, *Pauline Churches*, 181–193.

211. J. Bassler, "The Widow's Tale: A Fresh Look at 1 Timothy 5:3–16," *JBL* 103 (1982): 23–41.

unification of churches throughout Asia Minor against a complex of heretical doctrines.[212]

Although some version of this position is widely held, it is actually one of the weakest arguments against authenticity. The COMMENT on 1 Tim 3:1–7 discusses the evidence in detail, but it is appropriate here to make a series of points in summary fashion:

1. It is inaccurate to speak of the "church order of the Pastorals" as such. There is none in 2 Timothy, and the little there is in Titus does not match precisely what is in 1 Timothy.

2. Elements of organization are touched on in 1 Timothy. They are not defined or described. It is instructive that we are not able to create a full picture from the little that is said.

3. The organization, such as we can reconstruct it, does not resemble the hierarchical arrangement of clergy described in Ignatius's *Letters*. It comes closer to the synagogal structure of diaspora Judaism, an organizational arrangement that, in turn, closely resembled that in Greco-Roman *collegia*. Such arrangements were available in Paul's milieu. No long period of internal development was required for them to emerge.

4. There is a complete absence of legitimation of any organizational element in these letters. Leaders are not designated as priests, and none of their functions are cultic in character. Instead, they are given the sort of secular designations used in clubs, and their functions are practical and quotidian.

5. The letters do not prescribe any organization, but presume one. No job descriptions are given. Rather, there is a concern for the mental and moral qualities of those who are to fill already established positions. This point cuts to the heart of the argument that the Pastorals assert organization as a response to crisis. Nothing in the letters supports the idea that structure is in the process of creation. The casual references (which prevent us from a fully satisfying reconstruction) suggest that the readers were well aware of the arrangements of which the author speaks.

6. Common sense and sociology alike agree that intentional groups move progressively from simpler to more elaborate and eventually more legitimated structures. But it by no means follows that such development requires decades—much less a century—to happen. Indeed, sociological analyses of communes have shown that without strong boundaries, mechanisms for decision making, and social control, survival beyond a few years is unlikely.[213] The assumption that a great amount of time elapsed in early Christianity before the shaping of local structures is counterintuitive. We frequently find charismatic communities to be highly structured. As we have seen, more than a lit-

---

212. Baur, *Paulus*, 2:112–113; Schwegler, *Nachapostolische Zeitalter*, 3:156–157.

213. See, for example, R. Kantor, *Community and Commitment* (Cambridge: Cambridge University Press, 1973), and W. Kephart, *Extraordinary Groups: The Sociology of Unconventional Life-Styles* (New York: St. Martin's Press, 1976).

tle theological tendentiousness is involved in demanding of earliest Christianity a purely charismatic life, with structure appearing as only an element of decline.[214]

7. Attention to the undisputed letters shows that Paul refers by title to the same officers who appear in 1 Timothy (*episkopoi* and *diakonoi*, Phil 1:1; a woman *diakonos*, Rom 16:1). And he is far more concerned with the presence and recognition of authority figures within local communities than is usually acknowledged (Rom 12:8; 1 Cor 6:2–6; 12:28; 16:15–17; Gal 6:6; Col 4:17; 1 Thess 5:12; Phil 4:3).[215] The idea that Paul's communities existed, even during his lifetime, as free-floating cells of charismatic cooperation governed by only the Apostle and his delegates is unsupported by the evidence and is something of a sociological fantasy.

8. The elements of church structure found in 1 Timothy and Titus are far closer to the elements suggested by the undisputed letters of Paul than to the ecclesiastical arrangements outlined by Ignatius of Antioch. For that matter, the structure resembles that in Paul more than it does that found in the writings from the Qumran community, which was contemporary with Paul and whose hierarchical structure was, like Ignatius's, thoroughly legitimated theologically.[216]

9. The way order and organization are addressed in 1 Timothy and Titus can best be understood not as result of the passage of time or as a reaction to new circumstances, but as a function of the nature of the respective compositions and the role of the addressees, who were Paul's delegates to local communities.

When all these points are taken into account, the issue of church order in the Pastorals turns out to be nondeterminative for their authenticity. It does not prove that 1 Timothy and Titus were written by Paul. But it certainly does not demonstrate that they had to have been written after Paul's lifetime. If anything, the evidence suggests an earlier rather than a later time of composition. Nothing in these compositions is anachronistic for church organization in Paul's time, and the elements of structure in them comports best with what we know of first-century synagogues and Pauline *ekklēsiai*.

---

214. Note the statement by Campenhausen at the very beginning of *Ecclesiastical Authority and Spiritual Power*: "In the course of these three centuries the ideal to which Christianity had originally been committed was impaired in various ways: not only do we find rigidities of attitude, curtailment of aspiration, distortion of insight, but also in every department—an indisputable trivialization" (3). And at the very end of his study, he posits as the opposing options "Paul" or "the Pastorals" (301)! For the theological issue of church order in Protestant theology in particular, see H. W. Bartsch, *Die Anfänge urchristlicher Rechtsbildung: Studien zu den Pastoralbriefen*, Theologische Forschung 34 (Hamburg: Evangelische Verlag, 1965), 14–19. For the Pastorals as simply identified with the process of "early Catholicism," see R. Bultmann, *Theology of the New Testament*, trans. K. Grobel (New York: Scribner, 1955), 2:95–118.

215. The evidence is well reported by Weizsäcker in "Kirchenverfassung des apostolischer Zeitalters," although he reaches conclusions different from mine concerning it.

216. B. Reicke, "The Constitution of the Early Church in the Light of Jewish Documents," in *The Scrolls and the New Testament*, ed. K. Stendahl (New York: Harper & Row, 1957), 143–156.

5. Consistency in Teaching

Even though the criterion of consistency, whether applied to style or to content, has serious logical difficulties, it must be acknowledged that at the level of persuasion it is one of the most effective of the arguments against authenticity.[217] Even when full credit is given to Paul's great range of opinion and expression, fair-minded readers must grant that in the Pastorals there are elements that push the margins of what would seem possible for Paul himself to have written, in sufficiently complex combinations as to pose a genuine problem.

The letters clearly contain a number of themes that are distinctively and genuinely Pauline, such as the mission to the Gentiles, the apostolic example, the necessity of suffering in order to share God's glory, the conviction that salvation comes about by the grace of God through Jesus Christ and not through human works, the "gospel" as the measure of life, and the understanding of Jesus as the one "who gave himself."

There are also, however, typically Pauline expressions that are used in ways that seem slightly different from their employment elsewhere. Here we find the Law being spoken of as something that can be "used lawfully" (1 Tim 1:8), and "faith" seems less an obediential response to God's activity and more a matter of belief or community conviction (Tit 1:1; 1 Tim 5:8) or a virtue (2 Tim 2:22). Righteousness (*dikaiosynē*) appears not as a characteristic of God's activity, or even as a state of right relations between God and humans, but as a virtue in the Greek sense of "justice" (1 Tim 6:11; 2 Tim 2:22). Tradition seems to be a deposit of truth that is to be protected (1 Tim 6:20; 2 Tim 1:12–14) rather than a process of transmission within a community (1 Cor 11:2, 23; 15:3). The Christology of the Pastorals puts unusual emphasis on Jesus as savior (*sōtēr*, 2 Tim 1:10; Tit 1:4; 3:6) and on his "appearance" (*epiphaneia*, 1 Tim 6:14; 2 Tim 1:10). Although virtually every one of these terms can also be found in the undisputed letters, the difference here is their combination and concentration.

Critics make the same point, as we have seen, about the understanding of the church and the moral teaching of the Pastorals, which has emphases that appear to some as both different and novel. We do not find, for example, anything approaching Paul's admonition to the Corinthians to live in the world "as though not" (1 Cor 7:29–31) or the Apostle's preference for the radical lifestyle of virginity over marriage (1 Cor 7:32–35). Instead, there is a strong preference for the filling of domestic roles; indeed, the attitudes and aptitudes of life in the household are transferable to the life of the church (e.g., 1 Tim 2:11–15; 3:1–12; 5:3–16; 6:1–2; Tit 2:1–3:1). The distinctive Pauline concept of "conscience" (*syneidēsis*) is here, but is modified not in terms of "weak" and "strong" (as in

---

217. This is a standard element in all discussions. See, for example, Kümmel, *Introduction to the New Testament*, 382–384, and G. Lohfink, "Paulinische Theologie in der Rezeption der Pastoralbriefe," in *Paulus in den neutestamentlichen Spaetschriften*, ed. K. Kertelge, QD 89 (Freiburg: Herder, 1981), 70–121.

1 Cor 8 and Rom 14), but in terms of "good" (1 Tim 1:5, 19) in contrast to "soiled" (Tit 1:15) and "cauterized" (1 Tim 4:2). Especially characteristic of the Pastorals is the contrast between "healthy teaching" (1 Tim 1:10; 6:3; 2 Tim 1:13; 4:3; Tit 1:9; 2:1) and "sick" (2 Tim 2:17; 1 Tim 4:2), expressed, respectively, by a life filled with virtue (1 Tim 1:10; 3:2–4, 11; 4:12; 2 Tim 2:22, 24; 3:10; Tit 1:7–9; 2:7) or vice (1 Tim 1:8–10; 2 Tim 3:2–5; Tit 3:3). Once more, it is possible to find each of these elements in the undisputed letters, but not in the same degree and with the same concentration.

Enumerating such thematic points is easier than evaluating them. At some point, it is necessary to move toward a positive construal that can make sense of both the stylistic and the thematic differences that are found in the Pastorals. Some who favor authenticity and place the letters late in Paul's career during a second imprisonment appeal to the psychological effects of age and imprisonment.[218] This explanation is only as strong as the second-imprisonment hypothesis itself, and there is lacking solid evidence that age or captivity would have had such consequences on style or thought. It must also be remembered that the picture of Paul as aged in 2 Timothy may itself be a literary construct.[219]

Another accounting may be available to those who consider these letters to be authentic. It is based on the appreciation that Paul's "voice" in each of his letters is very much shaped by his subject matter, his audience, the traditions he employs, and the rhetorical conventions demanded by the circumstances. The same factors may be helpful in explaining the distinctive combination of theological and moral emphases in the three letters to his delegates. Does the fact that both Titus and Timothy have at least partly Hellenistic backgrounds and play the role of teachers in Pauline churches help locate the kind of language and the choice of themes found in the letters written to them? How might Paul speak and write when among his more Hellenistically educated associates? Before pursuing this line of inquiry, we must consider in more detail the usual way of accounting for the distinctive elements in the Pastorals, by invoking an author who wrote in a period considerably after Paul's death.

C. THE CONVENTIONAL SOLUTION

The majority of Pauline scholars today work from within the paradigm shaped by the previous two centuries of debate. They posit an "authentic" Paul who wrote seven letters (Romans, Galatians, 1 and 2 Corinthians, 1 Thessalonians, Philippians, and Philemon), which are sufficiently similar to be convincingly by the same author. They next posit a pseudonymous literary production in Paul's name over a period of forty to ninety years after his death. Many scholars consider Colossians, Ephesians, and 2 Thessalonians pseudonymous, al-

---

218. This is classically argued in Spicq, *Épîtres pastorales*, lxxxix–xciv.
219. A. J. Malherbe, "Paulus Senex," *ResQ* 36 (1994):197–207.

though defenders of the authenticity of each can be found. In contrast, the vast majority of scholars think that the Pastorals are pseudonymous and place them toward the end of the process of pseudepigraphic production. All agree, at least implicitly, that there is a sharp difference between the letters written by Paul and those written in his name, with the difference being evaluated as a decline. The pseudonymous letters are a form of tribute to Paul the Apostle that seek to adapt his thought to changing circumstances, but fall short of his genius.

The letters to Timothy and Titus are, therefore, not real letters in the sense that they were sent to actual individuals with the names Timothy and Titus, or even that they were composed separately and sent to anyone. Rather, the three "letters" actually form a *single literary production* in which each "composition" plays a distinct role.[220] The "Pastoral Letters" are, in this understanding, not real correspondence, but the fictional rendering of a correspondence. Thus they are not to be read with reference to Paul's letters (written some generations earlier), but only with reference to one another and, possibly, to other literature considered contemporaneous to their production.

The key to the literary puzzle of the Pastorals is 2 Timothy, which provides the portrait of an aged apostle wishing to hand over tradition to his "delegates" and, through them, to others (2 Tim 2:2). Here is the cipher for the proposed situation: the "faithful teachers" to whom the delegate Timothy passed along the Pauline tradition are the sponsors of this fictional correspondence.[221] They are the ones handing on the proper understanding of Paul to their contemporaries and to future ages. The personal information provided by all three letters is, therefore, entirely fictional, based on the imitation of Paul's genuine letters for the purpose of persuading later readers of Pauline authorship.

The real point of the literary production is found in the polemic, which warns against any divergence from the correct understanding of Paul's message, and in the instructions concerning community life, which form the beginnings of church orders, the manuals of discipline that regulate the behavior of communities. 1 Timothy and Titus therefore find their closest parallel in Polycarp of Smyrna's *Letter to the Philippians*, which, in turn, is related to the *Didache*, the *Didascalia Apostolorum*, the *Apostolic Tradition* of Hippolytus, and the *Apostolic Constitutions*.

Scholars offer several possible situations that might have generated the production of the Pastorals. One proposal regards them as a natural response to what might be called a generational crisis within Pauline Christianity. Communities bereft of their founder needed help adjusting to new circumstances, so disciples of the founder produced these pseudonymous letters to assist the

---

220. Dibelius and Conzelmann, *Pastoral Epistles*, 5; Y. Redalié, *Paul après Paul: Le Temps, le salut, la morale selon les épîtres à Timothee et à Tite* (Geneva: Labor et Fides, 1994), 36–45; P. Trummer, *Die Paulustradition der Pastoralbriefe*, Beiträge zur biblischen Exegese und Theologie 8 (Frankfort: Lang, 1978).

221. M. Wolter, *Pastoralbriefe als Paulustradition*, FRLANT 146 (Göttingen: Vandenhöck & Ruprecht, 1988), 15–17, 243–270; Redalié, *Paul après Paul*, 123–126.

community in its adjustment.[222] An alternative proposal sees the Pastorals in terms of a conservative reaction within Pauline Christianity. In this view, Paul is being championed by groups that the author perceives as dangerous, and the Pastorals are written in order to advance a more conservative form of the Pauline tradition. One version considers Paul to be the hero of ascetic Christians who celebrate the active and itinerant missionary activity of women, the way Thecla is associated with Paul in the *Acts of Paul and Thecla*.[223] The Pastorals are to be seen as working to suppress such tendencies in favor of a patriarchal, household-based church.[224] Alternatively, Paul is being co-opted by heretical movements like Marcion's whose extreme asceticism and dualism appeal to many who are weary of the complexity of life in the body and hope to simplify their existence through fasting and virginity. The author of the Pastorals seeks to claim Paul instead for the more positive view of the world, society, and marriage that we find in these letters.[225] It has even been seriously proposed that Polycarp of Smyrna, the staunch foe of Marcion, was the author of the Pastorals.[226]

Whoever the author of the Pastorals was, he sought to adapt the Pauline message for a new generation, emphasizing structure and order, while resisting ascetic and egalitarian tendencies. In the process, he helped shape a Christianity that adapted to diminished eschatological expectations, growth in organization, and increased accommodation to Greco-Roman culture. The "Paulinism" of the Pastorals is consequently refracted through the prism of second- or third-generation concerns.[227] Paul has receded to the status of a legendary hero who serves mainly to legitimate this new form of Christianity. His voice is reduced to an echo; his startling insights have become the "deposit of faith" for future generations. Paul's eschatological urgency has been reduced to a matter of "good citizenship."[228]

The obvious appeal of this construal is attested to by the number of its adherents. The construal provides a sense of development and continuity within

---

222. See, for example, MacDonald, *Pauline Churches*; R. E. Brown, *The Churches the Apostles Left Behind* (New York: Paulist Press, 1984); Redalié, *Paul après Paul*; Wolter, *Pastoralbriefe als Paulustradition*; and J. S. McDermott, "The Quest for Community Stabilization: A Social Science Interpretation of the Pastoral Epistles" (Ph.D. diss., Drew University, 1991).

223. In *Über die Pastoralbriefe* (1913), 71, H. H. Mayer proposed that the Pastorals were written against the *Acts of Paul and Thecla*; the opposite position is adopted in Rohde, "Pastoralbriefe und Acta Pauli." For the position stated here, see MacDonald, *Legend and the Apostle*, and "Virgins, Widows, and Paul," as well as Davies, *Revolt of the Widows*.

224. Bassler, "Widow's Tale"; E. Schuessler-Fiorenza, *In Memory of Her: A Feminist Theological Reconstruction of Christian Origins* (New York: Crossroad, 1983), 288–291.

225. This position represents a more moderate version of the one staked out by Baur and Schwegler, Baur, *Die Sogennanten Pastoralbriefe*, 8–39; *nachapostolische Zeitalter*, 3:156–157. See, for example, C. K. Barrett, "Pauline Controversies in the Post-Pauline Period," NTS 20 (1973–1974): 229–245, and M. C. de Boer, "Images of Paul in the Post-Apostolic Period," CBQ 42 (1980): 359–380.

226. H. von Campenhausen, *Polykarp von Smyrna und die Pastoralbriefe*, Sitzungsberichte der Heidelberger Akademie der Wissenschaften (Heidelberg: Winter, 1951), esp. 51.

227. This has been extensively argued in Redalié, *Paul après Paul*, esp. 403–454.

228. Dibelius and Conzelmann, *Pastoral Epistles*, 8.

the Pauline tradition. It helps account for the emergence of the "catholic church" in the mid-second century. The Pastorals, together with Acts and Ephesians, become part of the movement of "early catholicism," which resisted Gnosticism while domesticating the radical Paul, enabling his more challenging letters to remain the heart of the New Testament.[229] The position has everything in its favor except an accurate assessment of Paul's correspondence itself.

D. PROBLEMS WITH THE CONVENTIONAL SOLUTION

Having pointed out the difficulties attached to the discussion of authenticity generally and as directed to the Pastorals specifically, I now turn to the majority construal as such. Its weaknesses are both real and significant. That they remain so seldom articulated or examined is surprising. If there are problems fitting these letters within the frame of Paul's career, style, and thought, there are no fewer problems with the conventional hypothesis. The main argument in its favor, in truth, is the simple social fact of so many scholars having espoused it over so many generations. But if this is the case—if the main support for this reading of Paul is tradition—then the hypothesis is essentially no more critical than the construal that obtained over the eighteen centuries before Schleiermacher.

1. Selective Use of Evidence

The conventional hypothesis is based on a selective use of the data in the Pauline corpus. Those elements suggesting discontinuity between the undisputed letters and the Pastorals in style or theme are identified and exploited. Those that suggest continuity are suppressed or minimized. Examples of such continuity in theme include Paul's consistent desire for good order, his use of associates as delegates to local churches, the functions of those delegates, Paul's use of himself as an example for imitation by his readers, his mixed views on women's roles in the assembly, his affirmation of marriage and of the goodness of the created order, his insistence on strong community boundaries, his concern for the good reputation of the community, his hostility toward opponents and rivals, his emphasis on the transformative power of grace, and his expectation that local leaders should have real functions and receive respect. The list could be extended. In the commentary, I will point out many stylistic elements that are equally striking in their continuity with the undisputed letters.

My point is simply that such elements go unreported in most discussions of the Pastorals. But they need to be taken into account when making a decision about authenticity or when constructing a scenario that explains the correspon-

---

229. E. Käsemann, "Paul and Early Catholicism," in *New Testament Questions of Today* (Philadelphia: Fortress Press, 1969), 236–251.

dence. A hypothesis that ignores these elements cannot be considered as having been demonstrated, much less as being self-evident. Three quick examples must suffice. One of the most obvious points of continuity is the command that women keep silent in the assembly (1 Cor 14:33–34; 1 Tim 2:11–14). A parsimonious explanation is that they were issued by the same author. Yet scholars go to great lengths to avoid that conclusion, going so far as to regard the 1 Corinthians passage as an interpolation deriving from the author of the Pastorals. A second example is Paul's action in excommunicating a member of the community who created problems (1 Cor 5:1–5; 1 Tim 1:19–20). The few times this shared reflex is noticed, the differences in detail rather than the deep continuity in sensibility is emphasized. A third example is the way Paul uses the same text from Scripture plus a saying from Jesus in order to support the payment of ministers (1 Cor 9:9, 14; 1 Tim 5:17–18). This is so little noted that the previous edition of Nestle–Aland provides no marginal references from the passage in 1 Timothy to that in 1 Corinthians.

2. Comparison Between Composite Constructs

The comparison between the Pastorals and the other Pauline letters is distorted in several respects. One is the way these three letters are compared with an already reduced sample: if Colossians, Ephesians, and 2 Thessalonians were to be included in the sample for comparison, the results would often shift perceptibly. More critical is the way the comparison is carried out between composites contructed from the three Pastorals and—this is equally important—*also* a composite drawn from the seven universally accepted letters of Paul. On one side, the real and frequently important differences among the undisputed letters is eliminated when the "real" Paul is characterized in terms drawn from only some of them. On the other side, the equally significant differences among the Pastorals is ignored when these comparisons are made.

I have already touched, for example, on one of the most significant differences among them (beyond that of literary form!): the amount of information concerning church structure in each composition. Jerome Murphy-O'Connor has observed some thirty differences between 2 Timothy and the other two Pastoral Letters,[230] and Michael Prior has made a strong argument for reading 2 Timothy on its own terms as authentic.[231] Yet a recent major monograph on the Pastorals relegates such challenges to a footnote, without any engagement with the issues they raise.[232] The majority position, in fact, demands such unitary packaging in order to sustain its theory. To reconsider one of the letters in isolation would be to open up the whole issue once more. But perhaps it is time to do so.

---

230. J. Murphy-O'Connor, "2 Timothy Contrasted with 1 Timothy and Titus," *RB* 98 (1991): 403–410.

231. M. Prior, *Paul the Letter Writer and the Second Letter to Timothy*, JSNTS 23 (Sheffield: JSOT Press, 1989).

232. Redalié, *Paul après Paul*, 18.

3. Assumptions About Pseudonymity

Early critics of the Pastorals put the matter in stark terms: if not authentic, they were forgeries, and serious thought ought to be given their canonical and inspired status. Over the years, that harsh choice has been softened by a better appreciation of pseudonymous literature in antiquity, which was widely used as a way of communicating messages to contemporary audiences in the name of and under the authority of a revered figure of the past.[233] The composition of the Pastorals is frequently so regarded: they are not "forgeries" in the accepted sense, but examples of transparent fiction that meant and did no harm since the conventions were understood by all.[234]

The literature of antiquity gives ample evidence that the production of pseudonymous works was widespread within Jewish and Greco-Roman cultures.[235] For the most part, such literature truly was transparent to readers because the figures in whose name a writing appeared had lived centuries earlier. An Apocalypse attributed to Adam or Enoch could easily be grasped by any but the most credulous reader as a form of literary tribute rather than as an attempt to deceive. The same is true of the Socratic letters, written some four centuries after the death of their eponymous authors.[236]

The assumption that such pseudonymity was regarded as entirely benign by

---

233. Among many other studies, see F. Torm, *Die Psychologie der Pseudonymität im Hinblick auf die Literatur des Urchristentums* (Gütersloh: Bertelsmann, 1932); A. Meyer, "Religiöse Pseudepigraphie als ethisch-religiöse Problem," *ZNW* 35 (1936): 262–279; G. Bardy, "Faux et fraudes littéraires dans l'antiquité chrétienne," *RHE* 32 (1936): 5–23; E. J. Goodspeed, "Pseudonymity and Pseudepigraphy in Early Christian Literature," in *New Chapters in New Testament Study* (New York: Macmillan, 1937), 169–188; L. H. Brockington, "The Problem of Pseudonymity," *JTS* 4 (1953): 15–22; J. C. Fenton, "Pseudonymity in the New Testament," *Theology* 58 (1955): 51–56; D. Guthrie, "The Development of the Idea of Canonical Pseudepigrapha in New Testament Criticism," in *Vox Evangelica: Biblical and Historical Essays* ed. R. P. Martin (London: London Bible College, 1962), 43–49; W. Schneemelcher, "The Origin of the Pseudapostolic Literature," introduction to E. Hennecke, *New Testament Apocrypha*, ed. W. Schneemelcher, trans. R. McL. Wilson (Philadelphia: Westminster Press, 1964), 2:31–34; and D. G. Meade, *Pseudonymity and Canon*, WUNT 39 (Tübingen: Mohr [Paul Siebeck], 1986).

234. Brox, "Zu den persönlichen Notizen der Pastoralbrief"; Donelson, *Pseudepigraphy and Ethical Argument*, 23–66; E. E. Ellis, "Pseudonymity and Canonicity of New Testament Documents," in *Worship, Theology, and Ministry in the Early Church*, ed. J. Wilkins and T. Paige, JSNTS 87 (Sheffield: Sheffield Academic Press, 1992), 212–224.

235. The book of Daniel is a clear biblical example. See also the works attributed to Abraham, Adam, Baruch, Daniel, Enoch, Ezekiel, Ezra, Jacob, Joseph, Moses, Solomon, Zephaniah, and the twelve patriarchs, in *The Old Testament Pseudepigrapha*, ed. J. H. Charlesworth (Garden City, N.Y.: Doubleday, 1983). The same volumes also contain cross-cultural examples, such as the Sibylline Oracles, Pseudo-Hecataeus, the Orphica, and Pseudo-Phocylides. As for the range of pseudepigraphy in the Christian movement, see E. Hennecke, *New Testament Apocrypha*, ed. W. Schneemelcher, trans. R. McL. Wilson (Philadelphia: Westminster Press, 1964), and J. M. Robinson, ed., *The Nag Hammadi Library in English* (San Francisco: Harper & Row, 1977).

236. For an introduction to the Socratic and other Cynic letters, see A. J. Malherbe, *The Cynic Epistles: A Study Edition*, Society of Biblical Literature Sources for Biblical Study 12 (Missoula, Mont.: Scholars Press, 1977), 1–34.

Christians of the first and early second centuries, however, remains only an assumption,[237] in need of serious examination, for the few facts we possess would seem to argue in the opposite direction.[238] Particularly this is the case concerning Paul. He worked and wrote his letters at most ninety years earlier, his letters were specific and circumstantial, and his career was controverted. It cannot simply be assumed that efforts to advance particular interpretations of his thought by means of compositions written in his name would be met with naive acceptance.

I do not challenge the observation that pseudepigraphy was practiced within early Christianity. I am convinced, for example, that 2 Peter must be regarded as pseudonymous, for it is extraordinarily difficult to think of the author of 1 Peter as the author of that letter as well.[239] My question is simply whether it would succeed in the case of a writer like Paul, who, unlike Peter, had a number of his letters already in circulation under his name within thirty years of his death. 2 Thess 2:2, whether it is authentic or not, certainly suggests that producing letters during an assembly purporting to come from Paul would not necessarily be welcomed without question.

The short time between Paul's death (ca. 64–68) and the first certain use of the Pastorals by Polycarp (ca. 120) creates a situation unlike that of the other pseudepigrapha that are adduced as analogies. Here is the basic dilemma: the later the Pastoral Letters are dated (ca. 100–150), the harder it is to sustain the hypothesis of innocent pseudepigraphy, and the easier it is to speak of deliberate forgery. The later the letters are dated, however, the more the premise of ready reception of them by the church would seem to be contradicted by other evidence. We note, for example, that *all* other literary productions associated with the name of Paul—such as 3 *Corinthians*, the *Letter to the Laodiceans*, and the *Letters of Paul and Seneca*—were as universally rejected from the developing NT canon[240] as the Pastorals were universally accepted (with the certain exception of Marcion and the possible exception of Tatian and Valentinus). We do not know exactly when to date 2 Peter, but everyone agrees that it must be one of the latest NT compositions, possibly written in the second century. 2 Pet 3:16 clearly suggests not only that Paul wrote from an earlier generation, but

---

237. K. Aland, "The Problem of Anonymity and Pseudonymity in Christian Literature of the First Two Centuries," *JTS*, n.s., 12 (1961): 39–49.

238. B. M. Metzger, "Literary Forgeries and Canonical Pseudepigrapha," *JBL* 91 (1972): 3–24.

239. Johnson, *Writings of the New Testament*, 442–444.

240. Schneemelcher quotes Knopf-Krueger on the *Letter to the Laodiceans*, a "worthless patching together of Pauline passages and phrases, mainly from the Epistle to the Philippians," in his introduction to Hennecke, *New Testament Apocrypha*, 2:129. The letter was explicitly rejected by the Muratorian Canon. It is uncertain whether the letter was Marcionite in origin. Certainly no comparison can be made between it and the Pastorals at the level of literary, much less theological, merit. The *Letters of Paul and Seneca* appears to have originated in the third century, according to A. Kurfess, *New Testament Apocrypha*, 133–135. The so-called 3 *Corinthians* is actually part of a fictional correspondence between Paul and the church in Corinth embedded in the *Acta Pauli*, dated by Schneemelcher to between 185 and 195 in *New Testament Apocrypha*, 2:375–378.

that his letters exist in some form of collection ("all his letters") and are already the subject of interpretation (and "misinterpretation"). Such is the atmosphere in which three new letters by Paul would need to make their way.

The other earliest Christian literature shows a similar sense of distance between the Apostolic Age and its own. *1 Clement,* usually dated to around 95, is acutely conscious of that gap. Clement makes an explicit allusion to 1 Corinthians (47:1–7), identifying it as a letter by Paul.[241] Ignatius of Antioch (ca. 115) also echoes at least one of Paul's letters in his own (see the allusions to 1 Corinthians in *Eph.* 18:1; *Magnesians* 10:2; *Trallians* 5:1, 9:2; *Rom.* 9:2; *Phild.* 4:3) and makes a sharp distinction between the kind of authority that Paul had as an apostle and his own authority as a bishop, between the Apostolic Age and his own (*Eph.* 12:2; *Rom.* 4:3). Both Clement and Ignatius regard Paul as an example of heroic faith unto death.

Most impressively, Polycarp of Smyrna's *Letter to the Philippians*—written shortly after the death of Ignatius to accompany the collection of Ignatius's letters that Polycarp was sending to the church in Philippi—uses 1 Tim 6:7 and 6:10 in a passage that, as he clearly indicates, he regards as a florilegium of passages drawn from Paul's letters (*Phil.* 4:1). The position that Polycarp and the Pastorals are simply drawing from the same wisdom tradition[242] fails to account for the specific wording and Polycarp's explicit framing. The most reasonable conclusion is that Polycarp was using 1 Timothy, a position held by De Wette.[243]

Finally, a late dating must deal with Tertullian's explicit statement that Marcion "rejected" (*recusavit*) the letters to Timothy and Titus (*Against Marcion* 5:21), signifying at the very least that they were already written and able to be accepted or rejected on the grounds of their contents. In light of these considerations, the question must be asked how likely it would be for these letters both to have been produced between 100 and 150 and to have been so widely distributed and accepted as Pauline. In my view, the burden of proof lies with those who hold the majority position. By no means do these considerations concerning the early acceptance of the Pastorals demonstrate that the Pastorals were written by Paul. It does argue that they were written at a time considerably earlier than the one proposed by the conventional solution, and were thought by readers in the first decades of the second century to have been written by him.

4. Circumstances of Composition

As Baur understood, historical study cannot stop at negative criticism (in this case, the challenge to traditional attribution), but must move to positive criticism, placing the compositions in question in their proper historical setting. Baur

---

241. *1 Clement* also makes use of the Letter to the Hebrews (9:2–4; 17:1; 36:2) and quite probably of James, according to Johnson, *Letter of James,* 72–75.

242. Dibelius and Conzelmann, *Pastoral Epistles,* 2, 84–86.

243. De Wette, *Historico-Critical Introduction,* 303.

thought he had accomplished that by locating the Pastorals in the mid-second century as a response to Marcion. That hypothesis convinced few, however, and since the time of Baur one of the major challenges to the majority view has been the inability to provide a truly convincing setting for the production of these three letters.

Vague allusions to "Pauline tradition" or the generational crisis of "Pauline communities" are inadequate because they have no real specificity. Once more, the problem becomes more acute when the letters are dated later rather than earlier. It makes some sense to speak of a "Pauline church" in the decades between 65 and 95, and to understand how such a community might need to make an adjustment to life without its founder. Or does it? In what sense were any of Paul's communities really his, in the sense that a community would be dependent on him for its day-by-day existence and thrown into a crisis by his death? The longest sojourns with communities we know about lasted about two years each. But granting the point that there were such "Pauline" churches, if they were to have a "generational crisis," it would surely be, on analogy with other intentional groups, immediately after the death of the founder, certainly not eighty or ninety years later.

By the time we get to Clement and Ignatius and Polycarp (95–120), we do find genuine "Pauline Christians" (they quote his letters and honor him as an apostle) who give absolutely no signs of facing a generational crisis. Or if they face one, they find resources within the Pauline letters themselves (as well as other writings) to deal with it.

Proposed motivations for writing—the rehabilitation of Paul, the domestication of his radical edges, the meeting of a generational crisis—eventually need to touch ground. Someone wrote the compositions and deliberately distributed them as Pauline. Unless we think that writings of this complexity simply appear, we must begin to think in terms of specific human authors and readers.

The appeal of Hans von Campenhausen's thesis that Polycarp himself wrote the Pastorals is precisely that it provides a known historical figure in a known place and time with a known allegiance to Paul as well as a reason for writing.[244] In a courtroom, a lawyer would argue means, motive, and opportunity! If he were the author, of course, then we would not be dealing with an innocent pseudepigraphy, but a deliberate forgery whose entire intent would be to deceive readers. We then must ask whether this fits with what else we know of Polycarp's character. We must also ask whether such a ploy would have worked at a time when Paul was already a figure of controversy and when Polycarp's opponent Marcion was already challenging parts of Paul's letters. Then we must ask why, if Polycarp was able to invoke Paul anyway as support for his instructions—which in so many ways resemble those in the Pastorals—and was able to quote from the undisputed letters as authority, he should have needed also to forge these letters. Ultimately, though, the Polycarp hypothesis fails on the ba-

---

244. Campenhausen, *Polykarp von Smyrna und die Pastoralbriefe*, 150.

sis of the strong likelihood that Polycarp was indeed using 1 and 2 Timothy in his *Letter to the Philippians*.

The invocation of a "school" is frequent in New Testament studies to account for a process of composition that is complex and unable to be connected to a specific historical person.[245] A school is an attractive alternative to the unhappy options of charismatic fog and deliberate forgery.[246] It has also been observed that in Greco-Roman schools the imitation of literary exemplars was a standard form of rhetorical training,[247] and that such schools were settings where a corpus of pseudonymous letters (such as the Socratic Letters) could be composed with a specific paraenetic intention. Could such a school setting also account for the production of the Pastorals?[248] A closer look reveals the limitations of the suggestion:

1. What positive evidence do we have for the existence of such a Pauline school after the Apostle's death *apart from the very compositions that are in question?*[249] We have far more evidence that Paul's disciples were at work in his correspondence before he died than that they produced letters in his name after his death.

2. The imitation of literary models as a means of rhetorical training took place at a fairly elementary level. It is a long leap from school exercises to compositions as complex as and serving the proposed purposes of the Pastoral Letters. This is the place where actual comparison with the Socratic Letters is illuminating, for they fall far short of the Pastorals both in length and in rhetorical sophistication.

3. If authentic letters of Paul were being used as exemplars for imitation, why did such students not compose letters written to churches (as is hypothesized for Colossians and Ephesians) rather than letters written to delegates, for which there are no precedents in the undisputed corpus?

4. If students were imitating authentic Pauline letters, why were they not more successful in sustaining the "authentic" Pauline style? This is the same question that applies to fragment theories, except more sharply.

5. If we have a corpus produced by several students in a school, the problem of similarity and diversity in style becomes even more acute, as does the supposition that a group effort could accomplish such a subtle manipulation of the "Pauline tradition" as is envisaged for the Pastoral Letters.

---

245. See the very useful discussion and analysis in R. A. Culpepper, *The Johannine School: An Evaluation of the Johannine-School Hypothesis Based on an Investigation of the Nature of Ancient Schools*, SBLDS 26 (Missoula, Mont.: Scholars Press, 1975).

246. Schnelle, *History and Theology of the New Testament Writings*, 332.

247. Malherbe, "Ancient Epistolary Theory," 12–15.

248. B. Fiore, *The Function of Personal Example in the Socratic and Pastoral Epistles*, AnBib 105 (Rome: Biblical Institute Press, 1986), 107–126, 229.

249. L. T. Johnson, review of *The Pauline Churches*, by M. Y. MacDonald, *JAAR* 58 (1990): 716–719.

A final, very concrete, suggestion for the production of the Pastoral Letters
has been put forward by Quinn, who proposes that they represent the "third volume of Luke–Acts."[250] It is an attractive proposal in many respects, not least because it is so specific. It also helps account for the often noted resemblance between the Pastorals and Luke–Acts in diction and outlook, as in the image of
the Apostle "handing over" the tradition to successors (Acts 20:32). It provides
a mise-en-scène for the two "travel letters," since Titus can have been left on
Crete and Timothy could have been left in charge in Ephesus, and it offers a
perfect setting for a final farewell letter written from a Roman prison. The attacks on false teachers would correspond to the generalized warning against
"wolves" ravaging the flock (Acts 20:29). One cannot object to the theory on the
grounds that these letters were never connected by manuscript or by reception
with Acts, for the same can be said of the Gospel of Luke!

The hypothesis creates, however, as many problems as it solves:

1. Luke would have prepared poorly for this "third volume" by his failure to
   have Paul write letters during the course of his earlier narrative. This would
   be a notable failure, particularly for an author whose specialty is narrative
   anticipation and fulfillment.
2. Luke would have created two farewell discourses, one in Acts 20:17–35
   and the other in 2 Timothy. The more perfect in form is Acts 20:17–35.
   Why have Paul write another?
3. The farewell discourse in Acts 20:17–35 says that the wolves would come
   into the flock after Paul's death. In the Pastorals, they are present and active. Luke would have created a major narrative inconsistency.
4. Luke would, in effect, have created the narrative difficulties that generations of scholars have tried to solve. Why not mention in Acts that Timothy had been left in Ephesus as Paul's representative? Why not indicate
   that Titus had been left on Crete and, for that matter, that churches had
   been founded there by Paul? Why create the inconsistency of Trophimus
   being left at Miletus (2 Timothy) but also present with Paul in Jerusalem
   (Acts)?
5. The many other personal names in the letters become even more difficult
   when placed within Luke's narrative framework. Why would Luke have
   allowed the difficulties of identification attendant on Alexander in 1 Timothy and 2 Timothy, given the appearance of an Alexander in Acts 19:33?
   Why introduce so many new characters (such as Onesiphorus) if the point
   was to establish narrative continuity?
6. There remains unanswered by this thesis the question of the Pauline character of the language in the three Pastoral Letters. The resemblance to

---

250. In "Last Volume of Luke," Quinn views Titus as heading up the group of Luke-composed
letters, which helps account for the length of its greeting and the note that Paul had "left" Titus in
Crete.

Luke is easy to see. But the resemblance to the other letters is certainly stronger. The only reasonable answer from the perspective of the theory is that Luke was using Paul's other letters.[251] But this creates a greater difficulty. Why, if Luke had read Paul's other letters so carefully, does his earlier narrative not reflect the information in Paul's letters more accurately?

These objections are sufficiently severe as to make Quinn's hypothesis, however attractive, unlikely. It does remind us of another way of accounting for the Lukan element in the style of the Pastorals. This is the old theory that Luke was Paul's amanuensis, which takes the cryptic comment "Luke alone is with me" (2 Tim 4:11) as an important clue to the composition of the letters.[252]

5. Variety Among the Letters

The conventional hypothesis does not take into account the irreducible differences among the Pastoral Letters.[253] If these compositions are *both* pseudonymous *and* a single literary production, then we are dealing not with a clumsy imitator, but with an artist of considerable imagination. Each letter is addressed to a situation that close analysis shows to be at once internally consistent and completely inconsistent with the situation addressed by the other two letters.

A pseudonymous author would require the ability to capture precisely the psychology of a prisoner who feels abandoned and alone in 2 Timothy—communicating with subtle touches the difference in mood from the self-presentation of the Apostle in Philippians. Then, in 1 Timothy, he would be able to create the verisimilitude of an established and wealthy church in Ephesus and distinguish it from the needs, in Titus, of a new and unpromising foundation on Crete. The author would be able to construct a portrait of the opponents in each case that fits precisely within that frame, and devise a response to the opponents in each letter that is subtly but suitably distinct.

Our author, in short, is not a hack who writes the same thing over and over in three segments, but an author of considerable literary skill, beyond any we find evidenced in the extant writings of Ignatius, Clement, Polycarp, or any other author of the early to mid-second century. His skill is immediately evident by comparison with the "Pauline letters" that were universally rejected as spurious.[254] It is an artistry sufficient to convince critical readers from Origen through Erasmus to Grotius that the same author who wrote Romans also wrote the Pastorals.

---

251. G. Lohfink, "Die Vermittlung des Paulinismus zu den Pastoralbriefen," *BZ* 32 (1988): 165–188, asserts that the author of the Pastorals certainly knew Romans; probably knew 1 Corinthians, Galatians, and Philippians; and gained the rest of his knowledge of Paul through oral reports.

252. See the carefully argued position of Moule, "Problem of the Pastoral Epistles."

253. A point made well by Spicq, *Épîtres pastorales*, xxiii–xxxi.

254. And, for that matter, by comparison with the Cynic Epistles, most of which are short notes with little literary complexity.

I have proposed five distinct difficulties with the conventional hypothesis concerning the placement of the Pastoral Letters. These difficulties should be added to those examined earlier having to do with the criteria employed to determine inauthenticity in the first place. Perhaps convincing answers can be made to each of these objections. What makes the present state of scholarship on the Pastorals so disheartening is that the difficulties (which are of a fundamental character) are seldom even acknowledged, and even less frequently engaged. As a result, the conventional wisdom concerning authenticity moves farther and farther from any grounding in evidence and argument, farther and farther from the best and most recent scholarship on Paul himself, and perpetuates itself mainly by force of inertia based on an unexamined majority vote by an increasingly uninformed electorate.

IV. ANOTHER APPROACH TO PAUL'S LETTERS TO HIS DELEGATES

◆

I assert emphatically the impossibility of *demonstrating* the authenticity of the Pastoral Letters. It is possible to state, however, that the grounds for declaring them inauthentic are so flawed as to seriously diminish the validity of the scholarly "majority opinion." It is also possible to propose a way of reading these letters that is compatible with placement within Paul's ministry and with Pauline "authorship" in the broad sense that I have previously suggested as appropriate to his complex correspondence. In the following paragraphs, I sketch four important aspects of that approach.

Only the careful analysis of specific passages within the letters themselves will reveal which reading makes the best sense of the compositions. Is 1 Tim 2:11–15 better read within Paul's analogous experiences with the Corinthian church, or *must* it be considered as part of a suppressive strategy by a later sexist author? Is 1 Tim 5:3–16 better understood as Paul's struggle with a church's organized charity efforts—and therefore analogous to the struggles experienced by diaspora synagogues on the same score—or *must* it be regarded as the repression of a proto-feminist movement of the second century? For that matter, should the phrase "likewise also the women" in 1 Tim 3:11 be read as referring to women *diakonoi*, and therefore analogous to Paul's patron Phoebe, or *must* it be read as "wives," since the author of the Pastorals had to be consistent in his exclusion of women from ministry? The real demonstration is in the details.

But the details are also always read within an overall construal. These framing comments, then, set the stage for the commentary proper by stating some fundamentals that the majority position too often overlooks.

A. THE SHAPE OF PAUL'S MINISTRY

Paul's mission was both more extensive and more complex than might be gathered from a casual reading of Acts, which portrays Paul as one in a series of prophetic figures.[255] I have already made the point concerning the extent of his mission, which reaches places that Acts does not report. The complexity of his

---

255. Johnson, *Acts of the Apostles*, 12–18.

mission is evident when we consider that not all these churches were founded or administered by him directly. He writes to the Colossians, for example, as one of his churches, even though it was founded by his associate Epaphras (Col 1:6–8; 4:12).[256] When we pay attention to the number of people Paul regards as co-workers and associates (Rom 16:1–23; 1 Cor 16:10–20; Col 4:10–17), and the way in which he was involved with the coordination of their movements (1 Thess 3:1–6; 2 Cor 2:13; 8:22–23; 12:18), we begin to appreciate what a complex network of relationships—involving over forty persons working in the field—made up the Pauline mission.[257]

In light of these complex endeavors, it is certainly correct to say that Paul was a pastor more than he was a theologian. Perhaps it is more precise to designate him, anachronistically, as a practical theologian. But he was certainly no "pastor-in-place," either. He founded churches, stayed with them for a time, and then left them in the hands of others (1 Cor 16:15–18), as he sought to preach Christ where no one else had gone before him (Rom 15:20). His "daily care for the churches" (2 Cor 11:28) is legitimately listed among Paul's sufferings, for oversight of communities spread across such a geographic expanse and including such diverse and refractory people must have been extraordinarily stressful.

Paul's primary concern was to establish and nurture communities. His interest is not for the individual as such, but only as part of a transformed community. His focus is on "salvation" (sōtēria) as a this-worldly, social reality, just as "sanctification" (hagiasmos) is a quality of community life.[258] It can be argued, indeed, that "edification" (oikodomē) is a constant concern for Paul.[259] The essential thing is "building a house"—that is, creating and maintaining a community of character that manifests in its holiness the presence of the God who calls it into existence (1 Thess 4:3). To shape the moral character of his communities, Paul played the role of the ancient *moral teacher*. One of the most important advances in our understanding of Paul over the past several decades has been in appreciating how pervasively Paul used the techniques and rhetorical *topoi* of Hellenistic moral philosophers.[260]

The point is simply this: when second-century readers appropriated Paul's letters not for their daring theology but for their moral teaching, they were not thereby distorting the "real" Paul, but were in touch with his central concerns. And when the Pastoral Letters portray Paul as "teacher of Gentiles," emphasize life in the community as life in a household, and employ the style and substance

---

256. See the fascinating reconstruction of Paul's mission to the Lycus valley during an Ephesian imprisonment in Murphy-O'Connor, *Paul*, 173–184.

257. Johnson, *Writings of the New Testament*, 248–249.

258. L. T. Johnson, "The Social Dimensions of *Sōtēria* in Luke–Acts and Paul," in *The Society of Biblical Literature 1993 Seminar Papers*, ed. E. H. Lovering (Atlanta: Scholars Press, 1993), 520–536.

259. L. T. Johnson, "Edification as a Formal Criterion for Discernment in the Church," *Sewanee Review* 39 (1996): 362–372.

260. See, especially, A. J. Malherbe, "Hellenistic Moralists and the New Testament," *ANRW* II, 26, 1 (1992): 267–333, and *Paul and the Popular Philosophers* (Minneapolis: Fortress Press, 1989).

of Hellenistic moral teaching (both Greco-Roman and Jewish),[261] they are entirely consistent with the ministry of Paul as found in the undisputed letters.

B. THE CHARACTER OF PAUL'S CORRESPONDENCE

Paul's preferred way of shaping his churches as communities of moral character was through his personal presence; his letters are filled with notices of visits desired, delayed, and deferred (Rom 1:13; 15:23, 32; 1 Cor 4:18; 16:3, 5; 2 Cor 1:15; 2:1; 13:1; Phil 1:8; 1 Thess 3:1–5). When such visits were not possible, Paul sent a trusted delegate, such as Timothy or Titus, to represent him in the community (Rom 16:1–3; 1 Thess 3:2; 1 Cor 4:17; 2 Cor 8:23; Eph 6:21; Col 4:7–8; Phil 2:19). When such a delegation was not possible or prudent or sufficiently prepared, Paul used his third instrument of persuasion: the letter. His letters, then, are to be understood within the ancient conventions of letter writing as a form of personal presence and authority.[262] They were official correspondence from an Apostle chosen by God to churches called into being by God. None of his letters is purely personal correspondence between friends; all of them are shaped by the religious ethos shared by Paul and his readers.[263]

Paul's correspondence is also thoroughly *occasional*, not only in the sense that he wrote when required to write, but in the more precise sense that writing was always generated by a specific *occasion* or situation that required this rhetorical instrument, this modality of his presence. Sometimes the occasion was presented by a situation in the local church that demanded a response; classic examples are 1 Corinthians, 1 and 2 Thessalonians, and Galatians. Other times, the occasion was provided by a project of Paul's, as with 2 Corinthians and Romans. The impossibility of systematizing Paul's "thought"—even granting that there was anything systematic about it in the first place—is connected to this contingent character of his correspondence.[264] That Paul was not entirely successful in his rhetorical efforts is shown by the need to write a second time (or more) in regard to some situations (2 Corinthians; 2 Thessalonians).

There is no generic "Pauline letter," but only a collection of unique missives. Equally, there is no such thing as a "Pauline theology" that stands outside these discrete compositions, but only the specific rhetoric of a pastor and teacher who responds in writing to situations presented by his churches. It may be appropriate to speak of the "theological voice" of Romans, for it can be located within

---

261. F. Weidmann, "The Good Teacher: Social Identity and Community Purpose in the Pastoral Epistles," *JHC* 2 (1995): 100–114.

262. Malherbe, "Ancient Epistolary Theory," 15; S. K. Stowers, *Letter Writing in Greco-Roman Antiquity*, Library of Early Christianity (Philadelphia: Westminster Press, 1986), 58, 69, 144.

263. R. W. Funk, "The Apostolic Parousia: Form and Significance," in *Christian History and Interpretation: Essays Presented to John Knox*, ed. W. B. Farmer, C. F. D. Moule, and R. R. Niebuhr (Cambridge: Cambridge University Press, 1967), 249–269.

264. This has been stated well by Beker, *Paul the Apostle*.

that composition's rhetoric. Attempting larger statements about Paul's theology is always risking a form of abstraction that distorts the flexible and lively thought found in his sentences.

The point of these remarks for the Pastorals is obvious. No more than we can collapse Romans and Galatians and pretend that they are "saying the same thing"—despite their real thematic similarities—can we be allowed to collapse 1 Timothy, 2 Timothy, and Titus, declaring them to be "saying the same thing."

C. THE ROLE OF PAUL'S DELEGATES

From the perspective of the majority construal on the Pastorals, the identity of Paul's addressees is entirely incidental. Timothy and Titus serve as literary types for second- or third-generation disciples of Paul who are to hand on the tradition to others (2 Tim 2:2). A better appreciation of the role played by the delegates in Paul's ministry,[265] together with a closer look at the way they are portrayed in these letters, ought to encourage a reconsideration.

Timothy played a central role among Paul's associates and fellow workers. He was co-sponsor of six of Paul's letters (Philemon, Philippians, 1 Thessalonians, 2 Thessalonians, 2 Corinthians, Colossians). At various times, he served as Paul's representative to the Macedonian churches (Acts 18:5; 19:22) of Thessalonica (1 Thess 3:2) and Philippi (Phil 2:19), as well as to the church in Corinth (1 Cor 4:17; 16:10–11; Rom 16:21). 1 Tim 1:3 portrays him as playing the same role in the Ephesian church.

According to Acts 16:1, Paul met Timothy in Lystra. His mother was a "faithful Jewish woman" or perhaps "a Jewish woman who was a believer." His father, however, as Luke takes pains to mention twice, was a Gentile (Acts 16:1, 2). This would make it likely that he had a Greek style of education as well. From Paul's references to Timothy in his undisputed correspondence, his special role and his place in Paul's affections are obvious. When Paul tells the Corinthians to "imitate me" (1 Cor 4:16), he adds: "Therefore I sent to you Timothy, my beloved and faithful child in the Lord, to remind you of my ways in Christ, as I teach them everywhere in every church" (1 Cor 4:17). Several aspects of this short statement deserve attention. First, we notice Paul's self-characterization as a teacher. Second, we see that he is concerned with consistency in practice throughout his churches. Third, we observe the combination of memory and of imitation: Timothy is to "remind" Paul's community of what Paul himself teaches, so that they can "imitate" the apostle.

Timothy may not have possessed much personal presence or confidence, for Paul also tells the Corinthians: "When Timothy comes, see that you put him at ease among you, for he is doing the work of the Lord as I am. Let no one despise him" (1 Cor 16:10–11).

---

265. M. M. Mitchell, "New Testament Envoys in the Context of Greco-Roman Diplomatic and Epistolary Conventions: The Example of Timothy and Titus," *JBL* 111 (1992): 641–662.

Writing to the Thessalonian church, Paul speaks this way about his delegate: "And we have sent Timothy, our brother and God's servant in the Gospel of Christ, to establish you in the faith and to exhort you, that no one be moved by these afflictions" (1 Thess 3:2). In these last two citations, we see that Paul regards his delegate as fully sharing in his own ministry. Finally, in Philippians Paul writes encomiastically about his delegate:

> I hope in the Lord Jesus to send Timothy to you soon, so that I may be cheered by news of you. I have no one like him, who will be genuinely anxious for your welfare. They all look after their own interests, not those of Jesus Christ. But Timothy's worth you know, how as a son with a father, he has served with me in the Gospel. I hope therefore to send him just as soon as I see how it will go with me. (Phil 2:19–23)

Any attentive reader must be struck by the remarkable correlation between these random notes concerning Timothy in the authentic letters of Paul and the portrayal of him in the two letters addressed to Timothy. In them, he appears as young, timid, and easily despised (1 Tim 4:12; 2 Tim 1:7). He is Paul's "son" who is "beloved" (2 Tim 1:2) or "genuine" (1 Tim 1:2). He is a "servant of God" (*diakonos*, 1 Thess 3:2; *doulos*, 2 Tim 2:24; Phil 1:1). He is to "exhort" others (1 Tim 6:2; 2 Tim 4:2) and to "remind" churches of Paul's teaching (2 Tim 2:14), as well as serve as an example they can imitate (1 Tim 4:12), just as he has an example to imitate in Paul (2 Tim 1:13).

Two reasonable explanations can be offered for this coincidence of details. The first is that a pseudepigrapher scoured Paul's letters to obtain such epithets and reproduced them with stunning efficiency and accuracy.[266] But this explanation must grant that the full range of Paul's letters would have to be available to the pseudepigrapher, for the details do not appear in any single place. The second explanation is simpler and is the one adopted by readers of these letters until the nineteenth century: the letters to Timothy contain Paul's characteristic and habitual perceptions of his delegate and faithfully report them. The most important point—too often overlooked in discussions of these letters—is that the character and functions of the delegate as presented in 1 and 2 Timothy fit perfectly within Paul's own ministry.

We learn far less from the undisputed letters about Titus. He also was of Greek background (Gal 2:3), and Paul makes a considerable point of Titus not undergoing circumcision when accompanying Paul to Jerusalem (Gal 2:1). The connection is only tenuous, but he may in fact be the Titus (or Titius) Justus whom Acts calls a God-fearer and whose house Paul uses after leaving the synagogue in Corinth (Acts 18:7). In any case, Titus is especially linked to Paul's Corinthian ministry (2 Cor 2:13; 7:6, 13–14). He seems to have played a particular role in Paul's collection efforts (2 Cor 8:6, 16, 23; 12:18). He is not the

---

266. H. Maehlum, *Die Vollmacht des Timotheus nach den Pastoralbriefen* (Basel: Reinhardt, 1969).

representative of a local church, but is Paul's "associate/partner" (*koinōnos*) and "fellow worker" (*synergos*) toward the Corinthians (2 Cor 8:23). Paul does not use the same terms of affection for him that he does for Timothy.

There are no other letters in the Pauline corpus addressed to delegates. Paul's letter to Philemon is of another type, being, in effect, a letter of commendation for the slave Onesimus. If we did not have the Pastorals, we could only speculate about what sort of letters Paul might write to delegates with such backgrounds and with such responsibilities. We might, I think, expect personal encouragement concerning the hard work of dealing with lively but willful communities, reminders of the ideals they should follow, slander against rivals, and ad hoc directions about practical affairs. For fellow workers like Timothy and Titus, who were in all likelihood the beneficiaries of Greek education, we might well expect a shaping of the good news that emphasized its godliness/piety (*eusebeia*), a Christology that featured the appearance of a savior, and a moral teaching that stressed the pursuit of virtue and the avoidance of vice. These are, in fact, precisely what we find in the letters to Timothy and Titus. Such a shaping would, in part, be an adaptation by Paul, that most protean of figures, to his readers.[267] But we must not assume that the private Paul did not share some of these characteristics. As so often in antiquity, there were letters available for precisely the concerns Paul wanted to share with his delegates.

D. THE LITERARY FORM OF THE LETTERS

This final consideration is particularly important, for the decision a reader makes concerning the genre of a writing very much affects reading. The significance of genre can be overdone, but it is still a fundamental concern for all informed reading.[268] It matters, in reading Paul's other letters, that we read them first of all as real letters rather than as narratives, fictional correspondence, or philosophical treatises posing as letters.[269] More than that, we have learned in recent years what a difference it can make when we appreciate the conventions attached to different types of letters in the Greco-Roman world.[270]

In the case of the Pastoral Letters, the decision concerning literary form is even more critical, for it can profoundly affect the plausibility of placing the composition within Paul's lifetime. As I have already noted, it is a fundamental

---

267. For the characterization of Paul as protean, see Meeks, "The Christian Proteus," in *Writings of St. Paul*, 435–444.

268. See the discussions in A. Fowler, *Kinds of Literature: An Introduction to the Theory of Genres and Modes* (Cambridge, Mass.: Harvard University Press, 1982), esp. 37–53, 256–276, and T. Kent, *Interpretation and Genre* (Lewisburg, Pa.: Bucknell University Press, 1986), 59–80.

269. The basic point on this matter made by A. Deissmann, *Light from the Ancient East*, 4th ed., trans. L. M. R. Strachan (1922; reprint, Grand Rapids, Mich.: Baker Book House, 1978), 1–61, remains valid, although his applications of it deserve revision. See also Malherbe, *Social Aspects of Early Christianity*, 31–36.

270. Stowers, "Social Typifications and the Classification of Ancient Letters."

part of the conventional wisdom that the Pastorals are *not* "real" letters, but parts of a single literary production. Scholars do recognize some distinctions between 2 Timothy, on one side, and 1 Timothy and Titus, on the other. 2 Timothy is most often considered a *farewell discourse* in the form of a letter. But by its very nature, a farewell discourse is a posthumous production: someone else records the words of the dying sage. Therefore, if 2 Timothy is a farewell discourse, then it cannot be by Paul. Likewise, 1 Timothy and Titus are often considered a stage in the development of *church orders*, again lightly wearing the form of letters because that is the "Pauline way." This literary judgment also tilts the question in the direction of pseudonymity, since we know of such church orders only later in the development of Christianity.

But what if there are well-established letter forms that were available to Paul in his lifetime and that these letters resemble even more? The possibility then emerges that these might be real letters, written by Paul in the manner of other types of letters in his diverse correspondence. In fact, such letter types were available and do fit the form of the Pastorals. 2 Timothy is our most perfect example from antiquity of the *personal paraenetic* letter. 1 Timothy and Titus, in turn, fit the form of royal correspondence called the *mandata principis* (literally, "commandments of a ruler") letter. It is intriguing that although both kinds of letters have been known for some years, they have neither entered into general discussions of NT epistolography[271] nor had any real effect on the issue of the authenticity of the Pastorals.[272] But the finding that there are forms of letters common in Paul's day that were readily available to him, that fit the social circumstances of his relationship with his delegates perfectly, and that render intelligible virtually every detail in 1 and 2 Timothy ought to be of the greatest significance in evaluating the authenticity of these letters. This is truly positive criticism, for if all the standard arguments *against* authenticity are shown to be flawed—and they certainly are—then placement within Paul's ministry becomes the most elegant hypothesis.

---

271. The letters are not represented, for example, in Stowers, *Letter Writing in Greco-Roman Antiquity*.

272. It is intriguing that although three major monographs of recent years—Wolter, *Pastoralbriefe als Paulus tradition*; Fiore, *Function of Personal Example*; and Redalié, *Paul après Paul*—have acknowledged these literary forms, they have continued to view the Pastorals from within the dominant paradigm.

V. THE APPROACH OF THIS COMMENTARY

◆

Since the time of Schleiermacher, the issue of authenticity and historical placement has dominated every discussion of the Pastoral Letters. The reader of this General Introduction will have noticed that until the nineteenth century, it was possible to touch on interpretations of 1 and 2 Timothy without reference to Titus. This is because although the resemblance among the letters was known, they were regarded as real letters written to real people, and therefore to be interpreted, as the rest of Paul's letters, with reference to the situation described in the letters and to the rest of the Pauline corpus. Beginning with Schleiermacher and Eichhorn, however, I have followed the convention of speaking of "the Pastorals," because that is the way the argument was formulated in those fateful years and has been debated ever since.

It is obvious from the entire direction of my argument that I find the reasons for rejecting the letters as inadequate and that I think, at the very least, that a serious attempt should be made to read them within an alternative framework, to test whether the results are more or less plausible than the current theories. In this commentary, I attempt such a reading in the hope that it might provide at least a slight opening to a renewed discussion of these important writings. The commentary will read these letters as much as possible in terms of their self-presentation, an approach that involves at least these three aspects:

1. They are real rather than fictional letters. They were written by Paul to his delegate Timothy and are to be understood within the framework of Paul's ministry, the relationship between Paul and his delegate, and the socio-historical realities of the first century.
2. Each letter addresses a particular situation, has its own literary form, and uses its own mode of argumentation. Each letter must therefore be considered individually and in particular rather than in general and as part of a larger group.
3. The Pauline corpus is assumed to be the appropriate comparative context for each letter. When this premise seems weak, as it does in some cases, the relative strengths and weaknesses of the alternative approach will also be considered.

As with Paul's other letters, each part of 1 and 2 Timothy deserves both loyal and critical engagement. They deserve loyalty as part of the canon of Scripture that has nourished many generations in the faith. They require critical inquiry as well.[273] Some passages in 1 and 2 Timothy appear in the light of contemporary convictions to compromise the good news in favor of cultural conventions. Other passages challenge contemporary cultural conventions through the clear statement of the good news. In this respect, certainly, 1 and 2 Timothy are like all of Paul's other letters. The task of interpretation must begin with establishing the text, elucidating the Greek language, and identifying the cultural and historical contexts that make the compositions intelligible. A commentary ought not, however, end with that descriptive task, even though it is constrained by format and convention to provide help most directly in those matters. Occasionally in the commentary, I have tried to recapture the sense, once natural to all readers of 1 and 2 Timothy, not only that they speak for Paul the Apostle, but that through them Paul the Apostle speaks to us for God.

---

273. F. Young provides a good example of such engagement in the chapter entitled "The Pastorals as Scripture," in *The Theology of the Pastoral Letters* (Cambridge: Cambridge University Press, 1994), 145–161. See also Young, "The Pastoral Epistles and the Ethics of Reading," *JSNT* 45 (1992): 105–120.

BIBLIOGRAPHY

◆

BIBLIOGRAPHY

◆

TEXTS AND TOOLS

Arichea, D. C., and H. A. Hatton. *A Handbook of Paul's Letters to Timothy and Titus.* UBS Handbook Series. New York: United Bible Societies, 1995.

Bauer, W. *A Greek–English Lexicon of the New Testament and Other Early Christian Literature.* 2nd ed. Revised and augmented by F. W. Gingrich and F. W. Danker. Chicago: University of Chicago Press, 1979.

Blass, F., and A. Debrunner. *A Greek Grammar of the New Testament and Other Early Christian Literature.* Translated and revised by R. W. Funk, with supplementary notes by A. Debrunner. Chicago: University of Chicago Press, 1961.

Bratcher, R. G. *A Translator's Guide to Paul's Letters to Timothy and Titus.* UBS Handbook Series. New York: United Bible Societies, 1983.

Burton, E. D. *Syntax of the Moods and Tenses in New Testament Greek.* 3rd ed. Edinburgh: Clark, 1898.

Charlesworth, J. H., ed. *The Old Testament Pseudepigrapha.* Garden City, N.Y.: Doubleday, 1983.

Elliott, J. K. *The Apocryphal New Testament.* Oxford: Clarendon Press, 1993.

————. *The Greek Text of the Epistles to Timothy and Titus.* Studies and Documents 31. Salt Lake City: University of Utah Press, 1968.

Grenfell, B. P., A. S. Hunt, J. G. Smyly. *The Tebtunis Papyri.* University of California Publications in Graeco-Roman Archaeology 1. London: Oxford University Press, 1902.

Hatch, E., and H. A. Redpath. *A Concordance to the Septuagint and Other Greek Versions of the Old Testament.* 2nd ed. Grand Rapids: Baker Books, 1998.

Hennecke, E. *New Testament Apocrypha.* Edited by W. Schneemelcher. Translated by R. McL. Wilson. 2 vols. Philadelphia: Westminster Press, 1963.

Hunt, A. S., and J. G. Smyly. *The Tebtunis Papyri.* Vol. 3, pt. 1. London: Oxford University Press, 1933.

Kittel, G., and G. Friedrich, eds. *Theological Dictionary of the New Testament.* Edited and translated by G. Bromley. 9 vols. Grand Rapids, Mich.: Eerdmans, 1964–1974.

Layton, B. *The Gnostic Scriptures.* Garden City, N.Y.: Doubleday, 1987.

Liddell, H. G., and R. Scott. *A Greek–English Lexicon.* 9th ed. Edited by H. S. Jones and R. McKenzie. Oxford: Clarendon Press, 1925–1940.

Loeb Classical Library. Cambridge, Mass.: Harvard University Press, 1912– .

Martinez, F. G. *The Dead Sea Scrolls Translated: The Qumran Texts in English.* 2nd ed. Translated by W. G. E. Watson. Leiden: Brill, 1996.

Metzger, B. M. *The Text of the New Testament.* 2nd ed. New York: Oxford University Press, 1968.

Moule, C. F. D. *An Idiom-Book of New Testament Greek.* 2nd ed. Cambridge: Cambridge University Press, 1959.

Nestle, E., and K. Aland. *Novum Testamentum Graece.* 27th ed. Edited by B. Eland, K. Eland, M. Black, C. M. Martini, B. M. Metzger, A. Wikgren. Stuttgart: Deutsche Bibelgesellschaft, 1993.

Rahlfs, A., ed. *Septuaginta: Id est vetus testamentum juxta LXX interpretes.* 8th ed. Stuttgart: Würtembergische Bibelanstalt, 1905.

Robinson, J. M., ed. *The Nag Hammadi Library in English.* San Francisco: Harper & Row, 1977.

Zerwick, M., and M. Grosvener. *A Grammatical Analysis of the Greek New Testament.* 2 vols. Rome: Pontifical Biblical Institute, 1996.

COMMENTARIES

Patristic

Ambrose (Ambrosiaster) *Commentaria in Epistolam I B. Pauli ad Timotheum.* PL 17:487–512.

———. *Commentaria in Epistolam II B. Pauli ad Timotheum.* PL 17:511–526.

Chrysostom, John (347–407). *Homilia in Epistolam Primam ad Timotheum.* PG 62:501–599.

———. *Homilia in Epistolam Secundum ad Timotheum.* PG 62:599–662.

Ephraim, Syrus (306–373). *Commentarii in Epistolas D. Pauli.* Venice: St. Lazarus, 1893.

Jerome (347–419/420). *Commentarium in Titum.* PL 26:555–600.

John of Damascus (675–749). *In Epistolam Primam ad Timotheum.* PG 95:997–1016.

———. *In Epistolam Secundam ad Timotheum.* PG 95:1016–1026.

Pelagius. In Primam Epistolam ad Timotheum. PL 30:917–932.

———. In Secundam Epistolam ad Timotheum. PL 30:931–940.

Theodore of Mopsuestia (350–428). *In Epistolas B. Pauli Commentarii: The Latin Edition with Greek Fragments.* Vol. 2, 1 Thessalonians–Philemon. Edited by H. B. Swete. Cambridge: Cambridge University Press, 1882.

Theodoret of Cyr (393–466). *Interpretatio Epistolae I ad Timotheum.* PG 82:787–830.

———. *Interpretatio Epistolae II ad Timotheum.* PG 82:831–858.

Medieval

Aimon d'Auxerre (d. 855). *Expositio in Divini Pauli Epistolas.* PL 117:783–810.

Alcuin (d. 804). *Tractatus super Sancti Pauli ad Titum Epistolam.* PL 100:1009–1026.

Anselm of Laon (d. 1117). *Epistola I ad Timotheum.* PL 114:632.

———. *Epistola II ad Timotheum.* PL 114:633–638.

Aquinas, Thomas (1224–1274). *In Omnes S. Pauli Apostoli Epistolas Commentaria.* Vol. 2. Turin: Marietti, 1924.

Bruno (1032–1101). *Epistola I ad Timotheum.* PL 153:425–458.

———. *Epistola II ad Timotheum.* PL 153:459–474.

de Bourg-Dieu, Hervé (d. 1149). *In Epistolam I ad Timotheum.* PL 181:1403–1450.

———. *In Epistolam II ad Timotheum.* PL 181:1450–1478.

de Verceil, Anton (d. 950). *Epistola I ad Timotheum.* PL 134:663–686.

———. *Epistola II ad Timotheum.* PL 134:686–700.

Dionysius the Carthusian (d. 1471). *In Omnes B. Pauli Epistolas.* Montreuil, 1901.

Florus of Lyons (790–860). *Expositio in Epistolam I ad Timotheum.* PL 119:397–406.

———. *Expositio in Epistolam II ad Timotheum.* PL 119:406–410.

Hugh of St. Victor (d. 1142). *In Epistolam I ad Timotheum.* PL 175:593–602.

———. *In Epistolam II ad Timotheum.* PL 175:601–606.

Lanfranc, Archbishop of Canterbury (1010–1089). *Commentarii in Omnes Pauli Epistolas.* PL 150:345–372.

Lombard, Peter (1100–1160). *In Epistolam I ad Timotheum.* PL 192:325–362.

———. *In Epistolam II ad Timotheum.* PL 192:363–384.

Maurus, Rabanus (784–856). *Expositio in Epistolam I ad Timotheum.* PL 112:580–636.

———. *Expositio in Epistolam II ad Timotheum.* PL 112:636–654.

Nicholas of Lyre (d. 1329). *Postillae perpetuae in Omnes S. Pauli Epistolas.* Douai, 1617.

Oecumenius of Tricca (tenth century). *Pauli Apostoli ad Timotheum Prior Epistola.* PG 119:133–196.

———. *Pauli Apostoli ad Timotheum Epistola Secunda.* PG 119:195–240.

Scotus, Sedulius (ninth century). *In Epistolam I ad Timotheum.* PL 103:229–233.

———. *In Epistolam II ad Timotheum.* PL 103:233–242.

Theophylact of Bulgaria (eleventh century). *Epistolae Primae Divi Pauli ad Timotheum Expositio.* PG 125:9–87.

———. *Epistolae Secundae Divi Pauli ad Timotheum Expositio.* PG 125:87–140.

Sixteenth to Eighteenth Centuries

Bengel, J. A. *Gnomon Novi Testamenti* 4th ed., enl. A. E. Bengel and J. Stendel. Tübingen: Fues, 1855.

Berdot, D. N. *Exercitatio Theologica Exegetica in Epistolam S. Pauli ad Titum.* Halle, 1703.

Cajetan, T. de Vio. *Epistolae Pauli et aliorum Apostolorum ad Graecam veritatem castigat[a]e* . . . Paris: Apud Iod. Badium Ascensium & Ioan. Paruum, & Ioannem Roigny, 1532.

Calmet, A. *Commentarius literalis in omnes Libros Veteris et Novi Testamenti.* 2nd ed. Vol. 8. Venice: Colet, 1775.

Calvini, J. *In omnes Pauli apostoli Epistolas atque etiam in Epistolam ad Hebraeos commentarii.* Edited by A. Romanos. 2 vols. Halis Saxonum: Sumptibus Librariae Gebaueriae, 1831.

Critici sacri, sive, Annotata doctissimorum virorum in Vetus ac Novum Testamentum: quibus accedunt tractatus varii theologico-philologici. Vol. 7. Amsterdam: Henricus & Vidua Theodori Boom, 1698.

Estius, G. *In omnes D. Pauli Epistolas, item in Catholicas commentarii.* 2nd ed. 3 vols. Mogustiae: Sumptibus Francisci Kirchhemii, 1858–1859.

Fleischmann, A. C. *Interpretatio epistolarum Pauli ad Timotheum et Titum.* Tübingen, 1791.

Heinrichs, J. H. *Pauli Epistolae ad Timotheum, Titum et Philemon Graece.* Göttingen: Apud Dietericum, 1788.

Lapide, C. à *Commentaria in Omnes Sancti Pauli epistolas.* Edited by A. Padovani. 3 vols. 1614. Reprint. Turin: Marietti, 1928.

Luther, M. "Lectures on First Timothy." Translated by R. J. Dinda. In *Luther's Works*, edited by H. C. Oswald, 28:217–384. St. Louis: Concordia, 1973.

———. "Lectures on Titus." Translated by J. Pelikan. In *Luther's Works*, edited by J. Pelikan and W. A. Hanson, 29:4–90. St. Louis: Concordia, 1968.

———. "Prefaces to the New Testament." In *Luther's Works*, edited by H. T. Lehmann. Vol. 35, *Word and Sacrament*, edited by E. T. Bachmann, 388–389. St. Louis: Concordia, 1960.

———. "Sermon on the Sum of the Christian Life: 1 Tim. 1:5–7." In *Luther's Works*, edited by H. T. Lehmann. Vol. 51, *Sermons I*, edited and translated by J. W. Doberstein, 259–287. Philadelphia: Muhlenberg Press, 1959.

Melanchthon, P. *Enarratio epistolae I ad Timotheum et duorum capitum secundae, scripta, et dictata in praelectione publica, annos 1550 et 1551.* Wittenburg, 1561.

Mosheim, J. L. de. *Erklärung der beiden Briefe des Apostels Pauli an den Timotheum.* Hamburg, 1755.

Wesley, J. *Explanatory Notes on the New Testament.* 1754. Reprint. London: Epworth, 1950.

Wettstein, J. J. *Novum Testamentum Graece.* 2 vols. Amsterdam: Ex Officicana Dommeriana, 1752.

Nineteenth and Twentieth Centuries

Alford, H. *The Greek Testament.* 4th ed. 4 vols. London: Rivington, 1865.

de Ambroggi, P. *Le epistole pastorali di S. Paulo a Timoteo e a Tito.* Rome: Marietti, n.d.

Barrett, C. K. *The Pastoral Epistles in the New English Bible.* New Clarendon Bible (New Testament). Oxford: Clarendon Press, 1963.

Bassler, J. M. *1 Timothy, 2 Timothy, Titus.* Abingdon New Testament Commentaries. Nashville, Tenn.: Abingdon Press, 1996.

Beck, J. T. *Erklärung der Zwei Briefe Pauli an Timotheus.* Edited by J. Lindenmeyer. Gütersloh: Bertelsmann, 1879.

Belser, J. E. *Die Briefe des Apostels Paulus an Timotheus und Titus.* Freiburg: Herdersche Verlagshandlung, 1907.

Bernard, J. H. *The Pastoral Epistles.* Cambridge Greek Testament for Schools and Colleges. Cambridge: Cambridge University Press, 1899.

Boudou, A. *Saint Paul: Les Épîtres pastorales*. Edited by J. Huby. Verbum Salutis 15. Paris: Beauchesne, 1950.

Brown, E. F. *The Pastoral Epistles*. London: Methuen, 1917.

Brown, R. E. *The Gospel According to John (I–XII)*. Anchor Bible 29. Garden City, N.Y.: Doubleday, 1966.

Brox, N. *Die Pastoralbriefe*. 4th ed. Regensburger Neues Testament 7. Regensburg: Pustet, 1969.

De Wette, W. M. L. *Kurze Erklärung der Brief an Titus, Timotheus und die Hebräer*. Kurzgefasstes exegetisches Handbuch zum Neuen Testament 20. Leipzig: Weidmannn'sche Buchhandlung, 1844.

Dewey, J. "1 Timothy." In *The Women's Bible Commentary*, edited by C. A. Newsom and S. H. Ringe, 353–358. Louisville, Ky.: Westminster/John Knox Press, 1992.

Dibelius, M. *Die Briefe des Apostels Paulus an Timotheus und Titus*. HNT 13. Tübingen: J. C. B. Mohr (Paul Siebeck), 1913.

Dibelius, M., and H. Conzelmann. *The Pastoral Epistles*. Edited by H. Köster. Translated by P. Buttolph and A. Yarbro. Hermeneia. Philadelphia: Fortress Press, 1972.

Dornier, P. *Les Épîtres pastorales*. SB. Paris: Gabalda, 1969.

Easton, B. S. *The Pastoral Epistles*. New York: Scribner, 1947.

Ellicott, C. J. *The Pastoral Epistles of St. Paul*. 5th ed. London: Longmans, Greene, 1883.

Fairbairn, P. *The Pastoral Epistles*. Edinburgh: Clark, 1874.

Falconer, R. *The Pastoral Epistles*. Oxford: Clarendon Press, 1937.

Gardner, E. A. *The Later Pauline Epistles*. New York: Macmillan, 1936.

Guthrie, D. *The Pastoral Epistles*. Tyndale New Testament Commentaries. Grand Rapids, Mich.: Eerdmans, 1957.

Hanson, A. T. *The Pastoral Epistles*. New Century Bible. Grand Rapids, Mich.: Eerdmans, 1982.

———. *The Pastoral Letters*. Cambridge: Cambridge University Press, 1966.

Hasler, V. *Die Briefe an Timotheus und Titus*. Züricher Bibelkommentare Neue Testament 12. Zurich: Theologischer Verlag, 1978.

Heydenreich, A. L. C. *Die Pastoralbriefe Pauli erlautert*. Habamar: Verlag der neuen Gelehrten-Buchhandlung, 1826.

Hilliard, A. E. *The Pastoral Epistles of St. Paul*. London: Rivington, 1919.

Holtz, G. *Die Pastoralbriefe*. THKNT 12. Berlin: Evangelische Verlaganstalt, 1992.

———. *Die Pastoralbriefe kritisch und exegetisch behandelt*. Leipzig: Engelmann, 1880.

Houlden, J. L. *The Pastoral Epistles*. Trinity Press International New Testament Commentaries. Philadelphia: Trinity Press International, 1976.

Hultgren, A. J. *I–II Timothy, Titus*. Augsburg Commentary on the New Testament. Minneapolis: Augsburg, 1984.

Jeremias, J. *Die Briefe an Timotheus und Titus*. Das Neue Testament Deutsch 9. Göttingen: Vandenhöck & Ruprecht, 1981.

Johnson, L. T. *First Timothy, Second Timothy, Titus*. John Knox Preaching Guides. Atlanta: John Knox Press, 1987.

————. *The Gospel of Luke*. Sacra Pagina 3. Collegeville, Minn.: Liturgical Press, 1991.

————. *Introduction to the Letters of Paul III: Colossians, Ephesians, Pastorals.* Invitation to the New Testament. Garden City, N.Y.: Doubleday, 1980.

————. *The Letter of James*. Anchor Bible 37A. New York: Doubleday, 1995.

————. *Letters to Paul's Delegates: A Commentary on 1 Timothy, 2 Timothy, and Titus*. New Testament in Context. Valley Forge, Pa.: Trinity Press International, 1996.

————. *Reading Romans: A Literary and Theological Commentary*. New York: Crossroad, 1996.

Kelly, J. N. D. *A Commentary on the Pastoral Epistles*. Black's New Testament Commentaries. London: Black, 1963.

Knabenbauer, J. *Commentarius in S. Pauli Apostoli Epistolas*. Paris: Lethelleux, 1913.

Knappe, W. *Die Briefe an Timotheus und Titus*. Kassel: Oncken, 1959.

Knight, G. W. *Commentary on the Pastoral Epistles*. New International Greek Commentary. Grand Rapids, Mich.: Eerdmans, 1992.

Koehler, F. *Die Pastoralbriefe*. Die Schriften des Neuen Testaments 2. Göttingen: Vandenhöck & Ruprecht, 1908.

Lea, T. D., and H. P. Griffin, Jr. *1, 2 Timothy, Titus*. New Broadman Commentary. Nashville, Tenn.: Broadman Press, 1992.

Leo, A. G. E. *Pauli Epistola Prima ad Timotheum Graece cum Commentario perpetuo*. Leipzig: Kayseri, 1837.

Leo, P. *Das anvertraute Gut: Eine Einführung in den ersten Timotheusbriefe*. Die urchristliche Botschaft 15. Berlin: Furche, 1935.

Lock, W. A. *A Critical and Exegetical Commentary on the Pastoral Epistles*. ICC. New York: Scribner, 1924.

Löwe, H. *Die Pastoralbriefe des Apostels Paulus*. Cologne: Römke, 1929.

Mack, M. J. *Commentar über die Pastoralbriefe des Apostels Paulus*. Tübingen: Osiander, 1836.

Maloney, L. M. "The Pastoral Epistles." In *Searching the Scriptures*. Vol. 2, A *Feminist Commentary*, edited by E. Schuessler-Fiorenza, 361–380. New York: Crossroad, 1994.

Matthies, C. S. *Erklärung der Pastoralbriefe, mit besonderer Beziehung auf Authentie und Ort und Zeit der Abfassung Derselben*. Greifswald: Mauritius, 1840.

Mayer, H. H. *Über die Pastoralbriefe (I II Tim Tit)*. Göttingen: Vandenhöeck & Ruprecht, 1913.

McCleod, J. *The Pastoral Epistles*. Speaker's Bible. Grand Rapids, Mich.: Baker Book House, 1963.

Meinertz, M. *Die Pastoralbriefe des Heiligen Paulus*. 2nd ed. Bonn: Hanstein, 1923.

Metzger, B. M. *A Textual Commentary on the Greek New Testament*. Rev. ed. New York: United Bible Societies, 1975.

Molitor, H. *Die Pastoralbriefe des Hl. Paulus*. Herders Bibelkommentar: Die Heilige Schrift für das Leben erklärt 15. Freiburg: Herder, 1937.

Oberlinner, L. *Die Pastoralbriefe.* Vol. 1, *Kommentar zum ersten Timotheusbrief.* HTKNT 11. Freiburg: Herder, 1994.

———. *Die Pastoralbriefe.* Vol. 2, *Kommentar zum zweiten Timotheusbrief.* HTKNT 11. Freiburg: Herder, 1995.

Oden, T. C. *First and Second Timothy and Titus.* Interpretation, a Bible Commentary for Teaching and Preaching. Louisville, Ky.: John Knox Press, 1989.

Parry, R. St. John. *The Pastoral Epistles.* Cambridge: Cambridge University Press, 1920.

Plummer, A. *The Pastoral Epistles.* New York: Hodder and Stoughton, 1888.

Quinn, J. D. *The Letter to Titus.* Anchor Bible 35. New York: Doubleday, 1990.

Quinn, J. D., W. C. Wacker, *The First and Second Letters to Timothy.* A New Translation with Notes and Commentary. The Eerdmans Critical Commentary; Grand Rapids: Eerdmans, 2000.

Ramos, M. A. *Timoteo, II Timoteo, y Tito.* Commentario Bíblico Hispanoamericano. Miami: Editorial Caribe, 1992.

Ramsey, W. "A Historical Commentary on the Epistles to Timothy." *Expositor,* ser. 7: 7 (1909): 481–494; 8 (1909): 1–21, 167–185, 264–282, 339–357, 399–416, 557–568; 9 (1910): 172–187, 319–333, 433–440; ser. 8: 1 (1911): 262–273, 356–375.

Roloff, J. *Der Erste Briefe an Timotheus.* Evangelisch-katholischer Kommentar zum Neuen Testament 15. Zurich: Benziger, 1988.

Schierse, F. J. *Die Pastoralbriefe.* Düsseldorf: Patmos, 1968.

Schlatter, A. *Die Kirche der Griechen im Urteil des Paulus.* 2nd ed. Stuttgart: Calwer, 1958.

Scott, E. F. *The Pastoral Epistles.* Moffatt New Testament Commentary 13. London: Hodder and Stoughton, 1936.

Spicq, C. *Les Épîtres pastorales.* EBib. Paris: Gabalda, 1969.

Stellhorn, F. W. *Die Pastoralbriefe Pauli.* Gütersloh: Bertelsmann, 1899.

Towner, P. H. *1–2 Timothy & Titus.* InterVarsity Press New Testament Commentary 14. Downer's Grove, Ill.: InterVarsity Press, 1994.

von Soden, H. *Die Briefe an die Kolosser, Epheser, Philemon, Die Pastoralbriefe.* HKNT 3. Freiburg: J. C. B. Mohr (Paul Siebeck), 1893.

Ward, R. A. *Commentary on 1 & 2 Timothy & Titus.* Waco, Tex.: Word Books, 1974.

Wegscheider, J. A. L. *Der erste Briefe des Apostels Paulus an den Timotheus neu übersetzt und erklärt, mit Beziehung auf die neuesten Untersuchungen über die Authentie dasselben.* Göttingen: Apud Röwerum, 1810.

Weiss, B. *Die Briefe Pauli an Timotheus und Titus.* 5th ed. Kritische-exegetische Kommentar Göttingen: Vandenhöck & Ruprecht, 1902.

White, N. J. D. *The First and Second Epistles to Timothy and the Epistle to Titus.* Expositor's Greek Testament 4. New York: Dodd, Mead, 1910.

Wiesinger, A. *Biblical Commentary on St. Paul's Epistles.* Translated by J. Fulton. Edinburgh: Clark, 1851.

Wohlenberg, D. G. *Die Pastoralbriefe.* 3rd ed. Kommentar zum Neuen Testament 13. Leipzig: Diechertsche, 1923.

STUDIES

Aageson, J. W. "2 Timothy and Its Theology: In Search of a Theological Pattern." In *The Society of Biblical Literature 1997 Seminar Papers*, 692–714. Atlanta: Scholars Press.

Adler, N. "Die Handauflegung im Neue Testament bereits ein Bussritus?" In *Neutestamentliche Aufsätze*, 1–6. Regensburg: Pustet, 1963.

Aland, K. "The Problem of Anonymity and Pseudonymity in Christian Literature of the First Two Centuries." *JTS*, n.s., 12 (1961): 39–49.

Allen, J. A. "The 'In Christ' Formula in the Pastoral Epistles." *NTS* 10 (1963): 115–121.

Allison, R. W. "Let Women Be Silent in the Churches (1 Cor. 14:33b–36): What Did Paul Really Say, and What Did It Mean?" *JSNT* 31 (1987): 27–60.

Appelbaum, S. "The Organization of the Jewish Communities in the Diaspora." In *The Jewish People in the First Century: Historical Geography, Political History, Social, Cultural and Religious Life and Institutions*, edited by S. Safrai and M. Stern, 1:464–503. CRINT 1. Philadelphia: Fortress Press, 1974.

Bacon, B. W. *An Introduction to the New Testament*. New York: Macmillan, 1907.

Baird, W. *History of New Testament Research*. Vol. 1, *From Deism to Tübingen*. Minneapolis: Fortress Press, 1992.

Balch, D. L. *Let Wives Be Submissive: The Domestic Code in 1 Peter*. SBLMS 26. Chico, Calif.: Scholars Press, 1981.

Baldersperger, G. "Il a rendue témoignage devant Ponce Pilate." *RHPR* 2 (1922): 1–25.

Baldwin, H. S. "*authenteō* in Ancient Greek Literature." In *Women in the Church*, edited by A. J. Koestenberger, T. R. Schreiner, and H. S. Baldwin, 269–306. Grand Rapids, Mich.: Baker Book House, 1995.

Balsdon, J. P. V. D. *Roman Women: Their History and Habits*. New York: Barnes and Noble, 1962.

Bardy, G. "Faux et fraudes littéraires dans l'antiquité chrétienne." *RHE* 32 (1936): 5–23.

Barnett, A. E. *The New Testament: Its Making and Meaning*. New York: Abingdon Press, 1946.

Barr, J. *The Semantics of Biblical Language*. London: Oxford University Press, 1961.

Barrett, C. K. "Pauline Controversies in the Post-Pauline Period." *NTS* 20 (1973–1974): 229–245.

———. "Things Sacrificed to Idols." *NTS* 11 (1964–1965): 138–153.

Bartchey, S. S. *MALLON CHRĒSAI: First Century Slavery and the Interpretation of 1 Corinthians 7:21*. SBLDS 11. Missoula, Mont.: Scholars Press, 1973.

Barth, F. *Einleitung in das Neue Testament*. 2nd ed. Gütersloh: Bertelsmann, 1911.

Barton, J. M. T. "Bonum Certamen Certavi . . . Fidem Servavi." *Bib* 40 (1959): 878–884.

Bartsch, H. W. *Die Anfänge urchristlicher Rechtsbildung: Studien zu den Pastoralbriefen*. Theologische Forschung 34. Hamburg: Evangelische Verlag, 1965.

Bassler, J. "The Widow's Tale: A Fresh Look at 1 Timothy 5:3–16." *JBL* 103 (1984): 23–41.

Bauer, B. *Kritik der paulinischen Briefe*. 3 vols. in 1. 1850–1852. Reprint. Aalen: Scientia, 1972.

Bauer, W. *Orthodoxy and Heresy in Earliest Christianity*. Edited by R. A. Kraft and G. Krodel. Philadelphia: Fortress Press, 1971.

Baumgarten, M. *Die Ächtheit der Pastoralbriefe*. Berlin: Dehmigke, 1837.

Baur, F. C. *Paul, the Apostle of Jesus Christ*. 2nd ed. Edited by E. Zeller. Translated by A. Menzies. 2 vols. London: Williams and Norgate, 1875.

———. *Paulus, der Apostel Jesu Christi*. 2 vols. Leipzig: Fues, 1866, 1867.

———. *Die sogennanten Pastoralbriefe des Apostels Paulus auf neue kritisch untersucht*. Stuttgart: Cotta'sche 1835.

Beckhaus, M. J. H. *Specimen observationum de vocabulis hapax legomenois et varioribus dicendi formulis in I. epistolam ad Timotheum obviis*. Lingae, 1810.

Beker, J. C. *Heirs of Paul: Paul's Legacy in the New Testament and the Church Today*. Minneapolis: Fortress Press, 1991.

———. *Paul the Apostle: The Triumph of God in Life and Thought*. Philadelphia: Fortress Press, 1980.

Berge, P. " 'Our Great God and Savior': A Study of *Sōtēr* as a Christological Title in Titus 2:11–14." Ph.D. diss., Union Theological Seminary, 1974.

Berger, P. *The Sacred Canopy: Elements of a Sociology of Religion*. Garden City, N.Y.: Doubleday, Anchor Books, 1969.

Berger, P., and T. Luckmann. *The Social Construction of Reality*. Garden City, N.Y.: Doubleday, Anchor Books, 1967.

Betz, H. D. "2 Cor. 6:14–7:1: An Anti-Pauline Fragment." *JBL* 19 (1973): 88–108.

Bjerkland, C. J. *Parakalō: Form, Funktion, und Sinn der Parakalō-sätze in den paulinischen Briefen*. Biblioteca Theologica Norvegica 1. Oslo: Universitetsverlag, 1967.

Blackburn, B. C. "The Identity of 'The Women' in 1 Tim. 3:11." In *Essays on Women in Early Christianitiy*, edited by C. D. Osburn, 1:303–319. Joplin, Mo.: College Press, 1995.

Bouyer, L. *Eucharist: Theology and Spirituality of the Eucharistic Prayer*. Translated by C. U. Quinn. Notre Dame, Ind.: Notre Dame University Press, 1968.

Bover, J. M. "*Fidelis Sermo*." *Bib* 19 (1938): 74–79.

Brockington, L. H. "The Problem of Pseudonymity." *JTS* 4 (1953): 15–22.

Brockmuehl, M. N. A. "Das Verb *phaneroō* im Neuen Testament." *BZ* 32 (1988): 87–99.

Brooten, B. J. "Inscriptional Evidence for Women as Leaders of the Ancient Synagogue." Ph.D. diss., Harvard University, 1982.

Brown, L. A. "Asceticism and Ideology: The Language of Power in the Pastoral Epistles." In *Discursive Formations, Ascetic Piety, and the Interpretation of Early Christian Literature*, edited by V. L. Wimbush, pt. 1: 77–94. Atlanta: Scholars Press, 1992.

Brown, R. E. *The Churches the Apostles Left Behind.* New York: Paulist Press, 1984.

———. "*Episkopē* and *Episkopos*: The New Testament Evidence." *TS* 41 (1980): 322–338.

———. *An Introduction to the New Testament.* Anchor Bible Library. New York: Doubleday, 1997.

Brox, N. "Lukas als Verfasser der Pastoralbriefe?" *JAC* 13 (1970): 62–77.

———. "Zu den persönlichen Notizen den Pastoralbriefe." *BZ* 13 (1969): 76–94.

Bruce, F. F. *New Testament History.* London: Oliphants, 1966.

Bruston, C. "De la date de la première épître de Paul á Timothee." *Études théologiques et religieuses* 5 (1930): 272–276.

———. "De l'authenticité des épîtres pastorales." *Revue de théologie et des questions religieuses* 19 (1910): 346–350.

———. "Les dernières épîtres de Saint Paul." *Revue de théologie et des questions religieuses* 22 (1913): 243–264.

Bultmann, R. *Theology of the New Testament.* Translated by K. Grobel. 2 vols. New York: Scribner, 1951, 1955.

Burtchaell, J. T. *From Synagogue to Church: Public Services and Offices in the Earliest Christian Communities.* Cambridge: Cambridge University Press, 1992.

Bush, P. G. "A Note on the Structure of 1 Timothy." *NTS* 36 (1990): 152–156.

Cadbury, H. J. *The Book of Acts in History.* New York: Harper, 1955.

———. "Erastus of Corinth." *JBL* 50 (1931): 42–58.

Cameron, A., and A. Kuhrt. *Images of Women in Antiquity.* Rev. ed. London: Routledge, 1993.

Campbell, J. Y. "*Koinōnia* and Its Cognates in the New Testament." *JBL* 51 (1932): 352–380.

Campbell, R. A. *The Elders: Seniority Within Earliest Christianity.* Edinburgh: Clark, 1994.

———. "Identifying the Faithful Sayings in the Pastoral Epistles." *JSNT* 54 (1994): 73–86.

———. "*kai malista oikeiōn*: A New Look at 1 Tim. 5:8." *NTS* 41 (1995): 157–160.

Charue, A. "L'Appel aux ordres dans les épîtres pastorales." *Collationes Namurcenses* 33 (1939): 323–334.

———. "Les Directives pastorales de Saint Paul â Timothee et à Tite." *Collationes Namurcenses* 34 (1940): 1–12.

Chesnutt, R. D. "Jewish Women in the Greco-Roman Era." In *Essays on Women in Early Christianity*, edited by C. D. Osburn, 1:93–130. Joplin, Mo.: College Press, 1995.

Childs, B. *The New Testament as Canon: An Introduction.* Philadelphia: Fortress Press, 1984.

Colson, F. H. " 'Myths and Genealogies'—A Note on the Polemic of the Pastoral Epistles." *JTS* 18 (1917–1918): 265–271.

Condor, J. *The Literary History of the New Testament.* London: Seeleys, 1850.

Conzelmann, H. *A Commentary on First Corinthians.* Translated by J. W. Leitch. Hermeneia. Philadelphia: Fortress Press, 1975.

Cook, D. "The Pastoral Fragments Reconsidered." *JTS* 35 (1984): 120–131.

———. "2 Timothy 4:6–8 and the Epistle to the Philippians." *JTS* 33 (1982): 168–171.

Countryman, L. W. *The Rich Christian in the Church of the Early Empire: Contradictions and Accommodations.* Texts and Studies in Religion 7. New York: Mellen, 1980.

Crapps, R. W., E. V. McKnight, and D. A. Smith. *Introduction to the New Testament.* New York: Ronald Press, 1969.

Croy, N. C. *Endurance in Suffering: Hebrews 12:1–13 in Its Rhetorical, Religious, and Philosophical Context.* SNTSMS 98. Cambridge: Cambridge University Press, 1998.

Culpepper, R. A. *The Johannine School: An Evaluation of the Johannine-School Hypothesis Based on an Investigation of the Nature of Ancient Schools.* SBLDS 26. Missoula, Mont.: Scholars Press, 1975.

Dahl, N. A. "Form-Critical Observations on Early Christian Preaching." In *Jesus in the Memory of the Early Church,* 30–36. Minneapolis: Augsburg, 1976.

———. "The Origin of the Earliest Prologues to Paul's Epistles." *Semeia* 12 (1978): 233–277.

———. "The Particularity of the Pauline Epistles as a Problem in the Ancient Church." In *Neotestamentica et Patristica.* NovTSup 7, 261–271. Leiden: Brill, 1962.

D'Ales, A. "La Signification des termes *monandros* et *univera*: Coup d'oeil sur la famille romaine aux premièrs siècles de notre ère." *RSR* 20 (1930): 48–60.

Danker, F. *Benefactor: Epigraphic Study of a Greco-Roman and New Testament Semantic Field.* St. Louis: Clayton, 1982.

Davidson, S. *An Introduction to the Study of the New Testament.* 4 vols. London: Bagster, 1840.

———. *An Introduction to the Study of the New Testament.* 2 vols. London: Longmans, Green, 1882.

Davies, S. L. *The Revolt of the Widows: The Social World of the Apocryphal Acts.* Carbondale: Southern Illinois: University Press, 1980.

de Boer, M. C. "Images of Paul in the Post-Apostolic Period." *CBQ* 42 (1980): 359–380.

de Bruyne, D. "Prologues bibliques d'origines marcionite." *Revue bénédictine* 14 (1907): 1–16.

Deissmann, A. *Light from the Ancient East.* 4th ed. Translated by L. M. R. Strachan. 1922. Reprint. Grand Rapids: Baker Book House, 1978.

de Lacey, D. R. "Jesus as Mediator." *JSNT* 29 (1987): 101–121.

de Oliveira, A. *Die Diakonie der Gerechtigkeit und der Versöhnung in der Apologie des 2. Korintherbriefes.* Neutestamentliche Abhandlung 21. Münster: Aschendorff, 1990.

De Silva, D. *Despising Shame: Honor Discourse and Community Maintenance in the Epistle to the Hebrews.* SBLDS 152. Atlanta: Scholars Press, 1995.

———. *The Hope of Glory: Honor, Discourse, and New Testament Interpretation.* Collegeville, Minn.: Liturgical Press, 1999.

De Wette, W. M. L. *An Historico-Critical Introduction to the Canonical Books of the New Testament.* 5th ed. Translated by F. Frothingham. Boston: Crosby, Nichols, 1858.

Dibelius, M. "*epignōsis alētheias.*" In *Neutestamentliche Studien Georg Heinrici,* 176–189. Leipzig: Hinrichs'sche Buchhandlung, 1914.

Dill, S. *Roman Society from Nero to Marcus Aurelius.* 2nd ed. 1905. Reprint. New York: World, 1956.

Donelson, L. R. *Pseudepigraphy and Ethical Argument in the Pastoral Epistles.* Hermeneutische Untersuchungen zur Theologie 22. Tübingen: J. C. B. Mohr (Paul Siebeck), 1986.

———. "Studying Paul: 2 Timothy as Remembrance." In *The Society of Biblical Literature 1997 Seminar Papers,* 715–731. Atlanta: Scholars Press.

Doriani, D. "History of Interpretation of 1 Tim. 2." In *Women in the Church,* edited by A. J. Koestenberger, T. R. Schreiner, and H. S. Baldwin, 213–267. Grand Rapids, Mich.: Baker Book House, 1995.

Dschulnigg, P. "Warnung am Richtung und Ermahnung der Reichen. 1 Tim. 6:6–10, 17–19 im Rahmen des Schussteils 6:3–21." *BZ* 37 (1993): 60–77.

Duncan, G. S. *St. Paul's Ephesian Ministry: A Reconstruction with Special Reference to the Ephesian Origin of the Imprisonment Epistles.* London: Hodder and Stoughton, 1929.

Duncan, J. G. "Pistos ho Logos." *ExpT* 35 (1923–1924): 124.

Dunn, J. D. G. *The Theology of Paul the Apostle.* Grand Rapids, Mich.: Eerdmans, 1998.

Dupont, J. *Syn Christō: L'Union avec le Christ suivant Saint Paul.* Paris: Desclée et Brouwer, 1952.

du Toit, A. "Vilification as a Pragmatic Device in Early Christian Epistolography." *Bib* 75 (1994): 403–412.

Ehrman, B. D. *The New Testament: A Historical Introduction.* New York: Oxford University Press, 1997.

———. *The Orthodox Corruption of Scripture: The Effect of Christological Controversies on the Text of the New Testament.* New York: Oxford University Press, 1993.

Eichhorn, J. G. *Einleitung in das Neue Testament.* Vol. 3. Leipzig: Weidmanischen Buchhandlung, 1812.

Ellis, E. E. "The Authorship of the Pastorals: A Résumé and Assessment of Recent Trends." In *Paul and His Recent Interpreters,* 49–57. Grand Rapids, Mich.: Eerdmans, 1961.

———. "Paul and His Co-Workers." *NTS* 19 (1970–1971): 437–452.

———. "The Problem of the Authorship of First and Second Timothy." *Review and Expositor* 56 (1959): 343–354.

————. "Pseudonimity and Canonicity of New Testament Documents." In *Worship, Theology and Ministry in the Early Church*, edited by J. Wilkins and T. Paige, 212–224. JSNTS 87. Sheffield: Sheffield Academic Press, 1992.

————. "Traditions in the Pastoral Epistles." In *Early Jewish and Christian Exegesis*, edited by C. A. Evans and W. F. Stinespring, 237–253. Atlanta: Scholars Press, 1987.

Enslin, M. S. *Christian Beginnings*. New York: Harper, 1938.

Epp, E. J. "The Eclectic Method in New Testament Textual Criticism: Solution or Symptom?" In *Studies in the Theory and Method of New Testament Criticism*, edited by E. J. Epp and G. D. Fee, 141–173. Grand Rapids, Mich.: Eerdmans, 1993.

Erbe, K. "Zeit und Ziel der Grüsse Rom. 16:3–15 und der Mitteilungen 2 Tim. 4:9–21." *ZNW* 10 (1901): 185–218.

Fee, G. D. *The First Epistle to the Corinthians*. Grand Rapids, Mich.: Eerdmans, 1987.

————. "Toward a Theology of 2 Timothy—From a Pauline Perspective." In *The Society of Biblical Literature 1997 Seminar Papers*, 732–749. Atlanta: Scholars Press.

Feine, P., with J. Behm. *Einleitung in das Neue Testament*. 8th ed. Leipzig: von Quelle & Meyer, 1936.

Fenton, J. C. "Pseudonymity in the New Testament." *Theology* 58 (1955): 51–56.

Filson, F. V. *New Testament History*. Philadelphia: Westminster Press, 1964.

Finley, M. I. *Ancient Slavery and Modern Ideology*. New York: Penguin, 1980.

Fiore, B. *The Function of Personal Example in the Socratic and Pastoral Epistles*. AnBib 105. Rome: Biblical Institute Press, 1986.

Fitzgerald, J. T. "Virtue/Vice Lists." In *The Anchor Bible Dictionary*, edited by D. N. Freedman, 6:858–859. New York: Doubleday, 1992.

Foerster, W. "*EUSÉBEIA* in der Pastoralbriefen." *NTS* 5 (1958–1959): 213–218.

Ford, J. M. "A Note on Protomontanism in the Pastoral Epistles." *NTS* 17 (1970–1971): 338–346.

Fowler, A. *Kinds of Literature: An Introduction to the Theory of Genres and Modes*. Cambridge, Mass.: Harvard University Press, 1982.

Francis, F. O. "Humility and Angelic Worship in Col. 2:18." *ST* 16 (1963): 109–134.

Frankel, L. "Charity and Charitable Institutions." In *The Jewish Encyclopedia*, edited by I. Singer, 3:667–670. New York: Funk & Wagnall, 1903.

Freed, E. D. *The New Testament: A Critical Introduction*. Belmont, Calif.: Wadsworth, 1986.

Friesen, S. J. *Twice Neōkoros: Ephesus, Asia, and the Flavian Imperial Family*. Leiden: Brill, 1993.

Fuller, J. W. "Of Elders and Triads in 1 Timothy 5:19–25." *NTS* 29 (1983): 258–263.

Funk, R. W. "The Apostolic Parousia: Form and Significance." In *Christian History and Interpretation: Essays Presented to John Knox*, edited by W. B. Farmer, C. F. D. Moule, and R. R. Niebuhr, 249–269. Cambridge: Cambridge University Press, 1967.

Furnish, V. P. "Pauline Studies." In *The New Testament and Its Modern Interpreters*, edited by E. J. Epp and G. W. MacRae, 321–350. Atlanta: Scholars Press, 1989.

Galtier, P. "La Réconciliation des pécheurs dans la première épître à Timothee." In *Mélange Jules Lebreton I. RSR* 39 (1951–1952): 317–320.

Gamble, H. Y. *The New Testament Canon: Its Making and Meaning*. Philadelphia: Fortress Press, 1985.

Gardner, J. F. *Women in Roman Law and Society*. Bloomington: Indiana University Press, 1986.

Garnsey, P., and R. Saller. *The Roman Empire: Economy, Society, and Culture*. Berkeley: University of California Press, 1987.

Gero, S. "Parerga to the Book of Jannes and Jambres." *Journal for the Study of Pseudepigrapha* 9 (1991): 67–85.

Goguel, M. *Introduction au Nouveau Testament*. Vol. 4. Paris: Leroux, 1926.

Goodspeed, E. J. *An Introduction to the New Testament*. Chicago: University of Chicago Press, 1937.

———. "Pseudonymity and Pseudepigraphy in Early Christian Literature." In *New Chapters in New Testament Study*, 169–188. New York: Macmillan, 1937.

Goodwin, M. J. "The Pauline Background of the Living God as Interpretive Context for 1 Tim. 4:10." *JSNT* 61 (1996): 65–85.

Goulder, M. "The Pastors Wolves: Jewish Christian Visionaries Behind the Pastoral Epistles." *NovT* 38 (1996): 242–256.

Grabbe, L. L. "The Jannes/Jambres Tradition in Targum Pseudo-Jonathan and Its Date." *JBL* 98 (1979): 393–401.

Graebbe, P. J. "*Dynamis* (in the Sense of Power) in the Main Pauline Letters." *BZ* 36 (1992): 226–235.

Grant, R. M. *A Historical Introduction to the New Testament*. New York: Harper & Row, 1963.

Graystone, K., and G. Herdan. "The Authorship of the Pastorals in the Light of Statistical Linguistics." *NTS* 6 (1959–1960): 1–15.

Greer, T. C. "Admonitions to Women in 1 Tim. 2:8–15." In *Essays on Women in Early Christianity*, edited by C. D. Osburn, 1:281–302. Joplin, Mo.: College Press, 1995.

Gritz, S. H. *Paul, Women Teachers, and the Mother Goddess at Ephesus: A Study of 1 Tim. 2:9–15 in Light of the Religious and Cultural Milieu of the First Century*. New York: University Press of America, 1991.

Gundry, R. H. "The Form, Meaning, and Background of the Hymn Quoted in 1 Tim. 3:16." In *Apostolic History and the Gospel*, edited by W. Gasque and R. P. Martin, 203–222. Grand Rapids, Mich.: Eerdmans, 1970.

Guthrie, D. "The Development of the Idea of Canonical Pseudepigrapha in

New Testament Criticism." In *Vox Evangelica: Biblical and Historical Essays*, edited by R. P. Martin, 43–49. London: London Bible College, 1962.

―――. *New Testament Introduction*. 2nd ed. Downer's Grove, Ill.: InterVarsity Press, 1975.

Hagner, D. A. *The Use of the Old and New Testaments in Clement of Rome*. NovTSup 34. Leiden: Brill, 1973.

Hahneman, G. M. *The Muratorian Fragment and the Development of the Canon*. Oxford: Clarendon Press, 1992.

Hamel, G. *Poverty and Charity in Roman Palestine, First Three Centuries C.E.* Near Eastern Center Series 23. Berkeley: University of California Press, 1990.

Hands, A. R. *Charities and Social Aid in Greece and Rome*. Ithaca, N.Y.: Cornell University Press, 1968.

Hanson, A. T. *Studies in the Pastoral Epistles*. London: SPCK, 1968.

Harris, H. *The Tübingen School*. Oxford: Clarendon Press, 1975.

Harrison, E. F. *Introduction to the New Testament*. Grand Rapids, Mich.: Eerdmans, 1964.

Harrison, P. N. "Important Hypotheses Reconsidered III: The Authorship of the Pastorals Reconsidered." *ExpT* 67 (1955): 77–81.

―――. "The Pastoral Epistles and Duncan's Ephesian Theory." *NTS* 2 (1955–1956): 250–261.

―――. *The Problem of the Pastoral Epistles*. Oxford: Oxford University Press, 1921.

Harvey, A. E. "Elders." *JTS* 25 (1974): 318–322.

Hemer, C. J. *The Book of Acts in the Setting of Hellenistic History*. WUNT 49. Tübingen: Mohr (Paul Siebeck), 1989.

Hengel, M. *Acts and the History of Earliest Christianity*. Translated by J. Bowden. Philadelphia: Fortress Press, 1980.

Hengel, M. *Crucifixion in the Ancient World and the Message of the Cross*. Translated by J. Bowden. London: SCM Press, 1977.

Henne, P. "La Datation du *Canon* de Muratori." *RB* 100 (1993): 54–75.

Hesse, F. H. *Die Entstehung der neutestamentlichen Hirtensbriefe* Halle: Kämmerer, 1889.

Hilgenfeld, A. "Die Hirtenbriefe des Paulus." *ZWT* 40 (1897): 1–86.

―――. *Historisch-kritische Einleitung in das Neue Testament*. Leipzig: Fues, 1875.

Hock, R. *The Social Context of Paul's Ministry: Tentmaking and Apostleship*. Philadelphia: Fortress Press, 1980.

Holladay, C. R. "1 Corinthians 13: Paul as Apostolic Paradigm." In *Greeks, Romans, and Christians*, edited by D. L. Balch, E. Ferguson, W. A. Meeks, 80–98. Minneapolis: Fortress Press, 1990.

Holmberg, B. *Paul and Power: The Structure of Authority in the Primitive Church as Reflected in the Pauline Epistles*. Lund: CWK Gleerup, 1978.

Holtz, B. W. "Midrash." In *Back to the Sources: Reading the Classic Jewish Texts*, edited by B. W. Holtz, 177–211. New York: Summit Books, 1984.

Holtzmann, H. J. *Lehrbuch der historisch-kritisch Einleitung in das Neue Testament.* 3rd ed. Freiburg: J. C. B. Mohr (Paul Siebeck), 1882.

Holzmeister, U. "Si Quis Episcopum Desiderat, Bonum Opus Desiderat." *Bib* 12 (1931): 41–69.

Horrell, D. "Converging Ideologies: Berger and Luckmann and the Pastoral Epistles." *JSNT* 50 (1993): 85–103.

Hort, F. J. A. "The Pastoral Epistles." In *Judaistic Christianity*, 130–146. London: Macmillan, 1904.

Howard, G. E. "Christ the End of the Law: The Meaning of Romans 10:4ff." *JBL* 88 (1969): 331–337.

Hug, J. L. *Introduction to the New Testament.* 3rd ed. Translated by D. Fosdick. Andover, Mass.: Gould and Newman, 1836.

James, J. D. *The Genuineness and Authorship of the Pastoral Epistles.* London, 1909.

Jeremias, J. "*presbyterion* ausserchristlich bezeugt." ZNW 48 (1957): 127.

Johnson, L. T. *The Acts of the Apostles.* Sacra Pagina 5. Collegeville, Minn.: Liturgical Press, 1992.

———. "Edification as a Formal Criterion for Discernment in the Church." *Sewanee Review* 39 (1996): 362–372.

———. "James 3:13–4:10 and the *Topos* PERI PHTHONOU." *NovT* 25 (1983): 327–347.

———. *The Literary Function of Possession in Luke–Acts.* SBLDS 49. Missoula, Mont.: Scholars Press, 1977.

———. "The New Testament's Anti-Jewish Slander and the Conventions of Ancient Polemic." *JBL* 109 (1989): 419–441.

———. *Religious Experience in Early Christianity: A Missing Dimension in New Testament Studies.* Minneapolis: Fortress Press, 1998.

———. "Religious Rights and Christian Texts." In *Religious Human Rights in Global Perspective*, edited by J. Witte, Jr., and J. D. van der Vyver, 1:65–95. The Hague: Nijhoff, 1996.

———. Review of *The Pauline Churches*, by M. Y. MacDonald. *JAAR* 58 (1990): 716–719.

———. "Romans 3:21–26 and the Faith of Jesus." *CBQ* 44 (1982): 77–90.

———. *Scripture and Discernment: Decision Making in the Church.* Nashville, Tenn.: Abingdon Press, 1996.

———. *Sharing Possessions: Mandate and Symbol of Faith.* Overtures to Biblical Theology. Philadelphia: Fortress Press, 1981.

———. "The Social Dimensions of *Sōtēria* in Luke–Acts and Paul." In *The Society of Biblical Literature 1993 Seminar Papers*, edited by E. H. Lovering, 520–536. Atlanta: Scholars Press, 1993.

———. "Taciturnity and True Religion (James 1:26–27)." In *Greeks, Romans, and Christians*, edited by D. Balch, E. Ferguson, W. A. Meeks, 329–339. Minneapolis: Fortress Press, 1990.

———. "II Timothy and the Polemic Against False Teachers: A Reexamination." *JRS* 6–7 (1978–1979): 1–26.

————. *Writings of the New Testament: An Interpretation*. 2nd ed. Minneapolis: Fortress Press, 1999.

Judge, E. A. "The Early Christians as a Scholastic Community." *JRH* 1 (1960–1961): 4–15, 125–137.

Jülicher, A. *An Introduction to the New Testament*. 2nd ed. Translated by J. R. Ward. New York: Putnam, 1904.

————. "Paul and Early Catholicism." In *New Testament Questions of Today*, 236–251. Philadelphia: Fortress Press, 1969.

————. "Sätze heiligen Rechts im Neuen Testament." *NTS* 1 (1954–1955): 248–260.

Kalin, E. R. "Re-Examining New Testament Canon History I: The Canon of Origen." *Currents in Theology and Mission* 17 (1990): 274–282.

Kantor, R. *Community and Commitment*. Cambridge: Cambridge University Press, 1973.

Karris, R. J. "The Background and Significance of the Polemic of the Pastoral Epistles." *JBL* 92 (1973): 549–564.

————. "The Function and *Sitz-im-Leben* of the Parenetic Elements in the Pastoral Epistles." Ph.D. diss., Harvard University, 1971.

Käsemann, E. "Das Formular einer neutestamentlichen Ordinationsparänese." In *Neutestamentliche Studien für Rudolf Bultmann*, 261–268. Berlin: Töpelmann, 1954.

Kautsky, K. *Foundations of Christianity*. Translated by H. F. Mins. New York: Russell, 1953.

Kee, H. C. *Understanding the New Testament*. 4th ed. Englewood Cliffs, N.J.: Prentice-Hall, 1983.

Kent, T. *Interpretation and Genre*. Lewisburg, Pa.: Bucknell University Press, 1986.

Kephart, W. *Extraordinary Groups: The Sociology of Unconventional Life-Styles*. New York: St. Martin's Press, 1976.

Kidd, R. M. *Wealth and Beneficence in the Pastoral Epistles: A "Bourgeois" Form of Early Christianity?* SBLDS 122. Atlanta: Scholars Press, 1990.

Kittel, G. "*Genealogia* des Pastoralbriefe." *ZNW* 20 (1921): 49–69.

Klijn, A. J. F. *An Introduction to the New Testament*. 3rd ed. Translated by G. Buswell. Leiden: Brill, 1967.

Kloppenborg, J. "Edwin Hatch, Churches and *Collegia*." In *Origins and Method: Towards a New Understanding of Judaism and Christianity: Essays in Honour of John C. Hurd*, edited by B. H. McLean, 212–238. JSNTS 86. Sheffield: Sheffield Academic Press, 1993.

Klopper, D. A. "Zur Christologie der Pastoralbriefe (1 Tim. 3, 16)." *ZWT* 45 (1902): 339–361.

Knight, G. W., III. "ΑΥΤΗΕΝΤΕΟ in Reference to Women in 1 Tim. 2:12." *NTS* 30 (1984): 143–157.

————. *The Faithful Sayings in the Pastoral Letters*. Grand Rapids, Mich.: Baker Book House, 1979.

Knox, J. *Chapters in a Life of Paul*. Nashville, Tenn.: Abingdon Press, 1950.

Koch, K. "Das Lamm, das Ägypten vernichtet: Ein Fragment aus Jannes und Jambres und sein geschichtlichen Hintergrund." ZNW 57 (1966): 79–93.

Koehling, H. *Der Erste Briefe Pauli an Timotheus*. 2 vols. Berlin: Rother, 1882, 1887.

Koenig, J. *New Testament Hospitality: Partnership with Strangers as Promise and Missions*. Minneapolis: Augsburg, 1985.

———. "Ephesos in Early Christian Literature." In *Ephesos: Metropolis of Asia*, edited by H. Köster, 119–140. Harvard Theological Studies 41. Valley Forge, Pa.: Trinity International Press, 1995.

Kolenkow, A. B. "The Genre Testament and Forecasts of the Future in the Hellenistic Jewish Milieu." *JSJ* 6 (1975): 57–71.

Köster, H. *Einführung in das Neue Testament*. Berlin: de Gruyter, 1980.

Kümmel, W. G. *Introduction to the New Testament*. 17th rev. ed. Translated by H. C. Kee. Nashville, Tenn.: Abingdon Press, 1975.

———. *The New Testament: The History of Its Problems*. Translated by S. M. Gilmour. Nashville, Tenn.: Abingdon Press, 1972.

Kugel, J. L., and R. A. Greer. "Interpreters of Scripture." In *Early Biblical Interpretation*, 52–72. Library of Early Christianity 3. Philadelphia: Westminster Press, 1986.

Kühl, E. *Die Gemeindeordnung in den Pastoralbriefen*. Berlin: Hertz, 1885.

Kurz, W. *Farewell Addresses in the New Testament*. Collegeville, Minn.: Liturgical Press, 1990.

———. "Kenotic Imitation of Paul and Christ in Phil. 2 and 3." In *Discipleship in the New Testament*, edited by F. Segovia, 103–126. Philadelphia: Fortress Press, 1985.

———. "Luke 22:14–38 and Greco-Roman and Biblical Farwell Addresses." *JBL* 104 (1985): 251–268.

Kuss, O. "Bemerkungen zu dem Fragenkreis: Jesus und die Kirche im Neuen Testament." *TQ* 135 (1955): 150–183.

Kysar, R. *John: The Maverick Gospel*. 2nd ed. Louisville, Ky.: Westminster/John Knox Press, 1996.

Läger, K. *Die Christologie der Pastoralbriefe*. Hamburger Theologische Studien 12. Münster: LIT, 1996.

LaGrange, M. J. "Les Prologues prétendus marcionites." *RB* 35 (1926): 161–173.

Lake, K., and S. Lake. *An Introduction to the New Testament*. New York: Harper, 1937.

Lakoff, G., and M. Johnson. *Metaphors We Live By*. Chicago: University of Chicago Press, 1980.

Lau, A. Y. *Manifest in the Flesh: The Epiphany Christology of the Pastoral Epistles*. WUNT, 2nd ser., 86. Tübingen: J. C. B. Mohr (Paul Siebeck), 1996.

Lee, E. K. "Words Denoting 'Pattern' in the New Testament." *NTS* 8 (1962–1963): 167–173.

Lefkowitz, M. R., and M. B. Fant. *Women's Life in Greece and Rome*. 2nd ed. Baltimore: Johns Hopkins University Press, 1992.

Lightfoot, J. B. "The Date of the Pastoral Epistles." In *Biblical Essays*, 399–418. London: Macmillan, 1893.

Lohfink, G. "Paulinische Theologie in der Rezeption der Pastoralbriefe." In *Paulus in den neutestamentlichen Spätschriften*, edited by K. Kertelge, 70–121. QD 89. Freiburg: Herder, 1981.

———. "Die Vermittlung des Paulinismus zu den Pastoralbriefen." *BZ* 32 (1988): 165–188.

Lohse, E. *The Formation of the New Testament*. Translated by M. E. Boring. Nashville, Tenn.: Abingdon Press, 1972.

Loisy, A. *The Birth of the Christian Religion*. Translated by L. P. Jacks. New York: University Books, 1962.

Longenecker, R. "Ancient Amanuenses and the Pauline Epistles." In *New Dimensions in New Testament Study*, edited by R. Longenecker and M. Tenney, 281–297. Grand Rapids, Mich.: Zondervan, 1974.

Lütgert, W. *Die Irrlehrer der Pastoralbriefe*. Gütersloh: Bertelsmann, 1909.

MacDonald, D. R. *The Legend and the Apostle: The Battle for Paul in Story and Canon*. Philadelphia: Westminster Press, 1983.

———. "Virgins, Widows, and Paul in Second-Century Asia Minor." In *1979: Society of Biblical Literature Seminar Papers*, edited by P. Achtemeier, 1:165–184. Missoula, Mont.: Scholars Press, 1979.

MacDonald, M. Y. *The Pauline Churches: A Socio-Historical Study of Institutionalization in the Pauline and Deutero-Pauline Writings*. SNTSMS 60. Cambridge: Cambridge University Press, 1988.

Mack, B. *Who Wrote the New Testament? The Making of the Christian Myth*. San Francisco: HarperSanFrancisco, 1995.

MacMullen, R. *Roman Social Relations, 50 B.C. to A.D. 284*. New Haven, Conn.: Yale University Press, 1974.

Maehlum, H. *Die Vollmacht des Timotheus nach den Pastoralbriefen*. Basel: Reinhardt, 1969.

Maier, F. *Die Hauptprobleme der Pastoralbriefe Pauli*. Biblische Zeitfragen 3. Münster: Aschendorff, 1910.

Malherbe, A. J. "Ancient Epistolary Theory." *Ohio Journal of Religious Studies* 5 (1977): 3–77.

———. "Antisthenes and Odysseus, and Paul at War." In *Paul and the Popular Philosophers*, 91–119. Minneapolis: Fortress Press, 1989.

———. "The Beasts at Ephesus." In *Paul and the Popular Philosophers*, 79–90. Minneapolis: Fortress Press, 1989.

———. *The Cynic Epistles: A Study Edition*. Society of Biblical Literature Sources for Biblical Study 12. Missoula, Mont.: Scholars Press, 1977.

———. "Gentle as a Nurse: The Cynic Background of 1 Thess. 2." In *Paul and the Popular Philosophers*, 35–48. Minneapolis: Fortress Press, 1989.

———. "Hellenistic Moralists and the New Testament." ANRW II, 26, 1:267–333. Berlin: W. de Gruyter, 1992.

———. " 'In Season and Out of Season': 2 Timothy 4:2." In *Paul and the Popular Philosophers*, 137–145. Minneapolis: Fortress Press, 1989.

———. "Medical Imagery in the Pastorals." In *Paul and the Popular Philosophers*, 121–136. Minneapolis: Fortress Press, 1989.

————. *Moral Exhortation: A Greco-Roman Handbook*. Library of Early Christianity. Philadelphia: Westminster Press, 1986.

————. "Paulus Senex." *ResQ* 36 (1994): 197–207.

————. "Self Definition Among the Cynics." In *Paul and the Popular Philosophers*, 11–24. Minneapolis: Fortress Press, 1989.

————. *Social Aspects of Early Christianity*. 2nd ed., enlarged. Philadelphia: Fortress Press, 1983.

Malina, J. B. *The New Testament World: Insights from Cultural Anthropology*. Louisville, Ky.: John Knox Press, 1981.

Malina, J. B., and J. H. Neyrey. "Honor and Shame in Luke–Acts: Pivotal Values of the Mediterranean World." In *The Social World of Luke–Acts: Models for Interpretation*, edited by J. H. Neyrey, 25–65. Peabody, Mass.: Hendrickson, 1991.

Maner, H. H. *Über die Pastoralbriefe*. FRLANT 3. Göttingen: Vandenhöck & Ruprecht, 1913.

Mangold, W. *Die Irrlehrer der Pastoralbriefe*. Marburg: Elwertsche Universitäts-Buchhandlung, 1856.

Mariani, B. *Introductio in libros sacros Novi Testamenti*. Rome: Herder, 1962.

Marshall, I. H. "Salvation, Grace, and Works in the Later Writings in the Pauline Corpus." *NTS* 42 (1996): 339–358.

Martin, D. *Slavery as Salvation: the Metaphor of Slavery in Pauline Christianity*. New Haven: Yale University Press, 1990.

Martin, R. P. *New Testament Foundations: A Guide for Christian Students*. Grand Rapids, Mich.: Eerdmans, 1978.

Martin, S. C. *Pauli Testamentum: 2 Timothy and the Last Words of Moses*. Rome: Editrice Universita Gregoriana, 1997.

Marxsen, W. *Introduction to the New Testament*. 3rd ed. Translated by G. Buswell. Philadelphia: Fortress Press, 1968.

Mauer, C. "Eine textvariente Klärt die Entestehung der Pastoralbriefe auf." *TZ* 3 (1947): 321–332.

McDermott, J. S. "The Quest for Community Stabilization: A Social Science Interpretation of the Pastoral Epistles." Ph.D. diss., Drew University, 1991.

McDonald, L. M. *The Formation of the Christian Biblical Canon*. Rev. ed. Peabody, Mass.: Hendrickson, 1995.

McEleny, N. J. "The Vice-Lists of the Pastoral Epistles." *CBQ* 36 (1974): 203–219.

McGiffert, A. C. *A History of Christianity in the Apostolic Age*. New York: Scribner, 1897. 2nd Edition, 1928.

McLean, B. H. "The Agrippinilla Inscription: Religious Associations and Early Christian Formation." In *Origins and Method: Towards a New Understanding of Judaism and Christianity: Essays in Honour of John C. Hurd*, edited by B. H. McLean, 239–270. JSNTS 86. Sheffield: Sheffield Academic Press, 1993.

McNeile, H. *An Introduction to the Study of the New Testament.* Oxford: Claren-don Press, 1927.

Meade, D. G. *Pseudonymity and Canon.* WUNT 39. Tübingen: J. C. B. Mohr (Paul Siebeck), 1986.

Mealand, D. L. "Positional Stylometry Reassessed: Testing a Seven Epistle The-ory of Pauline Authorship." *NTS* 35 (1989): 266–286.

———. "The Extent of the Pauline Corpus: A Multivariate Approach." *JSNT* 59 (1995): 61–92.

Meeks, W. A. *The First Urban Christians: The Social World of the Apostle Paul.* New Haven, Conn.: Yale University Press, 1983.

———.*The Writings of St. Paul.* New York: Norton, 1973.

Meggitt, J. J. *Paul, Poverty, and Survival.* Edinburgh: Clark, 1998.

Meier, J. P. "*presbyteros* in the Pastoral Epistles." *CBQ* 35 (1973): 325–345.

Methuen, C. "The 'Virgin Widow': A Problematic Social Role for the Early Church?" *HTR* 90 (1997): 285–298.

Metzger, B. M. *The Canon of the New Testament: Its Origin, Development, and Significance.* Oxford: Clarendon Press, 1987.

———. "Literary Forgeries and Canonical Pseudepigrapha." *JBL* 91 (1972): 3–24.

———. *The New Testament: Its Background, Growth, and Content.* New York: Abington Press, 1965.

———. "A Reconsideration of Certain Arguments Against the Pauline Author-ship of the Pastoral Epistles." *ExpT* 70 (1958): 91–94.

Metzger, H. "Zur Stellung der liturgischen Beamten Ägyptens in frührömischen Zeit." *Museum Helveticum* 2 (1945): 54–62.

Meyer, A. "Religiöse Pseudepigraphie als ethisch-religiöse Problem." *ZNW* 35 (1936): 262–279.

Meyer, E. *Ursprung und Anfänge des Christentums.* 3 vols. Stuttgart: Cotta'sche, 1924.

Michaelis, J. D. *Introduction to the New Testament.* 4th ed. Translated and en-larged by H. Marsh. Vol. 4. London: Rivington, 1823.

Michaelis, W. *Einleitung in das Neue Testament.* Bern: BEG, 1946.

———. "Pastoralbriefe und Wortstatistik." *ZNW* 18 (1918–1919): 69–76.

———. *Zur Echtheitsfrage der Pastoralbriefe.* Neutestamenmtliche Forschun-gen 8. Paulusstudien 6. Gütersloh: Bertelsmann, 1930.

Miller, J. F. *The Pastoral Letters as Composite Documents.* SNTSMS 93. Cam-bridge: Cambridge University Press, 1997.

Mitchell, A. C. "1 Cor. 6:1–11: Group Boundaries and the Courts of Corinth." Ph.D. diss., Yale University, 1986.

Mitchell, M. M. "New Testament Envoys in the Context of Greco-Roman Diplo-matic and Epistolary Conventions: The Example of Timothy and Titus." *JBL* 111 (1992): 641–662.

Moffatt, J. *An Introduction to the Literature of the New Testament.* New York: Scribner, 1911.

Moore, G. F. *Judaism in the First Three Centuries of the Christian Era*. 3 vols. 1927–1930. Reprint. New York: Schocken Books, 1971.

Mott, S. C. "The Power of Giving and Receiving: Reciprocity in Hellenistic Benevolence." In *Current Issues in Biblical and Patristic Interpretation*, edited by G. Hawthorne, 60–72. Grand Rapids, Mich.: Eerdmans, 1975.

Moule, C. F. D. "The Problem of the Pastoral Epistles: A Reappraisal." *BJRL* 47 (1964–1965): 430–452.

Moule, H. C. G. *Studies in II Timothy*. Kregel Popular Commentary. Reprint. Grand Rapids, Mich.: Kregel, 1977.

Müller-Bardorff, J. "Zum Exegese von 1 Timotheus 5:3–16." In *Gott und die Götter: Festgabe für Erich Fascher*, 113–133. Berlin: Evangelische Verlag, 1958.

Munck, J. "Discours d'adieu dans le Nouveau Testament et dans la littérature biblique." In *Aux sources des traditions chrétiennes*, 155–170. Paris: Neuchatel, 1950.

Murphy-O'Connor, J. "Interpolations in 1 Corinthians." *CBQ* 48 (1986): 81–96.

———. *Paul: A Critical Life*. London: Oxford University Press, 1996.

———. "2 Timothy Contrasted with 1 Timothy and Titus." *RB* 98 (1991): 403–410.

Neander, A. *History of the Planting and Training of the Christian Church by the Apostles*. Translated by J. E. Ryland. 2 vols. London: Bell, 1889, 1891.

Neill, S. *The Interpretation of the New Testament, 1861–1961*. London: Oxford University Press, 1964.

Nock, A. D. *Conversion: The Old and the New in Religion from Alexander the Great to Augustine of Hippo*. Oxford: Clarendon Press, 1933.

North, J. L. " 'Human Speech' in Paul and the Pastorals: The Investigation of the Meaning of *anthrōpinos ho logos* (1 Tim. 3:1)." *NovT* 37 (1995): 56–67.

———. "Paul's Protest that He Does Not Lie in the Light of His Cilician Origin." *JTS* 47 (1996): 439–463.

Nussbaum, M. C. *The Therapy of Desire: Theory and Practice in Hellenistic Ethics*. Princeton, N.J.: Princeton University Press, 1994.

Oates, W. "The Conception of Ministry in the Pastoral Epistles." *Review and Expositor* 56 (1959): 388–410.

Oberlinner, L. "Die *Epiphaneia* des Heilswillens Gottes in Christus Jesus: Zur Grundstrucktur der Christologie der Pastoralbriefe." *ZNW* 71 (1980): 192–213.

O'Brien, P. T. *Introductory Thanksgiving in the Letters of Paul*. Leiden: Brill, 1977.

Osburn, C. D. "The Interpretation of 1 Cor. 14:34–35." In *Essays on Women in Early Christianity*, edited by C. D. Osburn, 1:219–242. Joplin, Mo.: College Press, 1995.

Padgett, A. "Wealthy Women at Ephesus: 1 Timothy 2:8–15 in Context." *Int* 41 (1987): 19–31.

Page, S. "Marital Expectations of Church Leaders in the Pastoral Epistles." *JSNT* 50 (1993): 105–120.

Peake, A. S. *A Critical Introduction to the New Testament*. New York: Scribner, 1910.

Pearson, B. A. "Philanthropy in the Greco-Roman World and in Early Christianity." In *The Emergence of the Christian Religion*, 186–213. Harrisburg, Pa.: Trinity Press International, 1997.

Perrin, N., and D. Duling. *The New Testament, an Introduction: Proclamation and Parenesis, Myth and History*. 2nd ed. New York: Harcourt Brace Jovanovich, 1982.

Pfister, F. "Zur Wendung *apokeitai moi ho tēs dikaiosynēs stephanos*." ZNW 15 (1914): 84–86.

Pfleiderer, O. *Das Urchristentum seine Schriften und Lehren in geschichtlichen Zusammenhang*. 2nd ed. Berlin: Reimer, 1902.

Planck, H. *Bemerkungen über den ersten paulinischen Brief an den Timotheus*. Göttingen, 1808.

Plevnik, J. *Paul and the Parousia: An Exegetical and Theological Investigation*. Peabody, Mass.: Hendrickson, 1997.

Plümacher, E. *Lukas als hellenisticher Schiftsteller*. Göttingen: Vandenhöck & Ruprecht, 1972.

Porter, S. E. "What Does It Mean to Be 'Saved by Childbirth' (1 Timothy 2:15)?" *JSNT* 49 (1993): 87–102.

Prast, F. *Presbyter und Evangelium in nachapostolisher Zeit: Die Abschiedsrede Paulus in Milet (Apg 20, 17–38) im Rahmen der lukanishen Konzeption der Evangeliumsverkuendigung*. FzB 29. Stuttgart: Katholisches Bibelwerk, 1979.

Pregeant, M. *Engaging the New Testament: An Interdisciplinary Introduction*. Minneapolis: Fortress Press, 1995.

Price, J. L. *Interpreting the New Testament*. New York: Holt, Rinehart and Winston, 1961.

Price, S. R. F. *Rituals and Power: The Roman Imperial Cult in Asia Minor*. Cambridge: Cambridge University Press, 1984.

Prior, M. *Paul the Letter Writer and the Second Letter to Timothy*. JSNTS 23. Sheffield: JSOT Press, 1989.

Puech, H. "Des fragments grecs de la grotte 7 et la Nouvelle Testament? 7Q4 et 7Q5 et le Papyrus Magdalen Greg 17–P64." *RB* 102 (1995): 570–584.

Quinn, J. D. "The Last Volume of Luke: The Relation of Luke–Acts to the Pastoral Epistles." In *Perspectives on Luke–Acts*, edited by C. H. Talbert, 62–75. Danville, Va.: Association of Baptist Professors of Religion, 1978.

———. "𝔓46—The Pauline Canon? *CBQ* 36 (1974): 379–385.

Rahner, K. *Inspiration in the Bible*. QD. New York: Herder and Herder, 1961.

Rahtjian, B. D. "The Three Letters of Paul to the Philippians." *NTS* 6 (1959–1960): 163–173.

Redalié, Y. *Paul après Paul: Le temps, le salut, la morale selon les épîtres à Timothee et à Tite*. Geneva: Labor et Fides, 1994.

Reed, J. T. "Cohesive Ties in 1 Timothy: In Defense of the Epistle's Unity." *Neot* 26 (1992): 131–156.

Reicke, B. "The Constitution of the Early Church in the Light of Jewish Documents." In *The Scrolls and the New Testament*, edited by K. Stendahl, 143–156. New York: Harper & Row, 1957.

Rensberger, D. K. "As the Apostle Teaches: The Development of the Use of Paul's Letters in Second Century Christianity." Ph.D. diss., Yale University, 1981.

Reumann, J. "Church Office in Paul, Especially in Philippians." In *Origins and Method: Towards a New Understanding of Judaism and Christianity: Essays in Honour of John C. Hurd*, edited by B. H. McLean, 82–91. JSNTS 86. Sheffield: Sheffield Academic Press, 1993.

Reuss, E. "La Seconde Captivité de Saint Paul." *Revue de théologie et de philosophie chrétiennes* 1 (1851): 150–171.

Reuther, R. R. "The Feminist Critique in Religious Studies." *Soundings* 64 (1981): 388–402.

Robbins, V. K. *The Tapestry of Early Christian Discourse: Rhetoric, Society, and Ideology*. London: Routledge, 1996.

Robinson, J. A. T. *Redating the New Testament*. Philadelphia: Westminster Press, 1970.

Robinson, T. A. "Graystone and Herdan's 'C' Quantity Formula and the Authorship of the Pastorals." *NTS* 30 (1984): 282–288.

Rohde, J. "Pastoralbriefe und *Acta Pauli*." In *Studia Evangelica*, edited by F. L. Cross, 5:303–310. Berlin: Akademie, 1968.

Roller, O. *Das Formuler der paulinschen Briefe: Ein Beiträg zur Lehre vom antike Briefe*. BWANT 5–6. Stuttgart: Kohlhammer, 1933.

Romaniuk, K. "Was Phoebe in Rom. 16:1 a Deaconess?" *ZNW* 81 (1990): 130–134.

Ropes, J. H. *The Apostolic Age in the Light of Modern Criticism*. New York: Scribner, 1908.

Safrai, S. "Education and the Study of Torah." In *The Jewish People in the First Century: Historical Geography, Political History, Social, Cultural and Religious Life and Institutions*, edited by S. Safrai and M. Stern, 2:945–970. CRINT 2. Philadelphia: Fortress Press, 1987.

———. "The Synagogue." In *The Jewish People in the First Century: Historical Geography, Political History, Social, Cultural and Religious Life and Institutions*, edited by S. Safrai and M. Stern, 2:908–944. CRINT 2. Philadelphia: Fortress Press, 1987.

Saller, R. *Personal Patronage Under the Early Empire*. Cambridge: Cambridge University Press, 1982.

Salmon, G. *A Historical Introduction to the Study of the Books of the New Testament*. 3rd ed. London: Murray, 1888.

Salvatorelli, L. "From Locke to Reizenstein: The Historical Investigation of the Origins of Christianity." *HTR* 22 (1929): 263–367.

Sanders, E. P. *Paul and Palestinian Judaism*. Philadelphia: Fortress Press, 1977.

Sanders, J. T. *Ethics in the New Testament*. Philadelphia: Fortress Press, 1975.

Schenk, W. "Die Briefe an Timotheus I und II und an Titus (Die Pastoralbriefe) in der neuerer Forschung." ANRW, II, 25, 4:3404–3438. Berlin: de Gruyter, 1987.

Schlarb, E. *Die Gesunde Lehre: Häresie und wahrheit im Spiegel der Pastoralbriefe*. Marburger Theologische Studien 28. Marburg: Elwert, 1990.

Schleiermacher, F. *Über den sogennanten Ersten Brief des Paulus an den Timotheus: Ein kritisches Sendschreiben an J. C. Gass*. Berlin: Realschulbuchhandlung, 1807.

Schmeller, T. "Kollege Paulus: Die Jesusüberlieferung und die Selbstverständnis des Völkerapostels." ZNW 88 (1997): 260–283.

Schmid, J. *Zeit und Ort der paulinischen Gefangenschaftsbriefe*. Freiburg: Herder, 1931.

Schmidt, J. E. C. *Historisch-Kritische Einleitung in's Neue Testament*. Giessen: Tasche und Muller, 1804.

Schneemelcher, W. "The Origin of the Pseudapostolic Literature." Introduction to *New Testament Apocrypha*, by E. Hennecke. Edited by W. Schneemelcher. Translated by R. McL. Wilson. 2 vols. Philadelphia: Westminster Press, 1963.

Schneiders, S. *The Revelatory Text*. San Francisco: HarperCollins, 1991.

Schnelle, U. *The History and Theology of the New Testament Writings*. Translated by M. E. Boring. Minneapolis: Fortress Press, 1998.

Scholem, G. *Major Trends in Jewish Mysticism*. New York: Schocken Books, 1941.

Schreiner, T. R. "An Interpretation of 1 Timothy 2:9–15: A Dialogue with Scholarship." In *Women in the Church*, edited by A. J. Koestenberger, T. R. Schreiner, and H. S. Baldwin, 105–154. Grand Rapids, Mich.: Baker Book House, 1995.

Schubert, P. *The Form and Function of the Pauline Thanksgiving*. Berlin: Töpelmann, 1939.

Schuessler-Fiorenza, E. *Bread Not Stone: The Challenge of Feminist Biblical Interpretation*. Boston: Beacon Press, 1984.

———. *In Memory of Her: A Feminist Theological Reconstruction of Christian Origins*. New York: Crossroad, 1983.

Schulze, W. A. " 'Ein Bischof sei eines Weiber Mann,' zur Exegese von 1 Tim. 3, 2 und Tit. 1, 6." KD 41 (1958): 287–300.

Schwarz, R. *Bürgerliches Christentem im Neuen Testament? Ein Studie zu Ethick, Amt und Recht in den Pastoralbriefen*. Österreichisches katholisches Studien 4. Kolsternburg: OBS, 1983.

Schwegler, A. *Das nachapostolische Zeitalter in den Hauptmomentum seiner Entwicklung*. Tübingen: Fues, 1846.

Schweitzer, A. *The Mysticism of Paul the Apostle*. Translated by W. Montgomery. Baltimore: Johns Hopkins University Press, 1931.

———. *Paul and His Interpreters: A Critical History*. Translated by W. Montgomery. 1912. Reprint. New York: Schocken Books, 1964.

Scott, E. F. *The Literature of the New Testament*. New York: Columbia University Press, 1932.

Scroggs, R. "Paul and the Eschatological Woman." *JAAR* 40 (1972): 283–303.

Selby, D. J. *Introduction to the New Testament.* New York: Macmillan, 1971.

Skeat, T. C. " 'Especially the Parchments': A Note on 2 Timothy 4:13." *JTS* 30 (1979): 173–177.

Smith, J. Z. *Drudgery Divine: On the Comparison of Early Christianities and the Religions of Late Antiquity.* Chicago: University of Chicago Press, 1990.

Sohm, R. *Kirchenrecht.* Vol. 1, *Die geschichtlichen Grundlagen.* Systematisches Handbuch der deutschen Rechtswissenschaft 8, pt. 1. Leipzig: Duncker & Humbolt, 1892.

Souter, A. "Pelagius's Expositions of the Thirteen Epistles of St. Paul." In *Texts and Studies: Contributions to Biblical and Patristic Literature,* edited by J. A. Robinson, vol. 9, Cambridge: Cambridge University Press, 1922.

———. *The Text and Canon of the New Testament.* 2nd ed. Revised by C. S. C. Williams. Studies in Theology 25. London: Duckworth, 1954.

Spicq, C. *Agape in the New Testament.* Translated by M. A. McNamara and M. H. Richter. 3 vols. St. Louis: Herder, 1963, 1965, 1966.

———. "La Philanthropie hellénistique, vertu divine et royale." *ST* 12 (1958): 169–191.

———. "Saint Paul et la loi des dépôts." *RB* 40 (1931): 481–502.

———. " 'Si Quis Epicopum Desiderat' (I Tim. 3, 1)." *RSPT* 29 (1940): 316–325.

Spitta, F. "Über die persönlichen Notizen im Zweiter Briefe an Timotheus." *TSK* 51 (1878): 582–607.

Spivey, R. A., and D. M. Smith, Jr. *Anatomy of the New Testament: A Guide to Its Structure and Meaning.* New York: Macmillan, 1969.

Stanton, E. C. *Women's Bible.* 2 vols. New York: European, 1895, 1898.

Stegner, W. "Der Christushymnus in 1 Tim. 3, 16." *Trierer theologischer Zeitschrift* 70 (1969): 33–49.

———. *Der Christushymnus in 1 Tim. 3, 16: Ein strukturanalytusche Untersuchung.* Regensburger Studien zur Theologie 6. Bern: Lang, 1977.

Steifel, J. H. "Women Deacons in 1 Timothy: A Linguistic and Literary Look at 'Women likewise . . .' (1 Tim. 3:11)." *NTS* 41 (1995): 442–457.

Sterling, G. E. "Women in the Hellenistic and Roman Worlds (323 B.C.E.– 138 C.E.)." In *Essays on Women in Early Christianity,* edited by C. D. Osburn, 1:41–92. Joplin, Mo.: College Press, 1995.

Stettler, H. *Die Christologie der Pastoralbriefe.* WUNT, 2nd ser., 105. Tübingen: J. C. B. Mohr (Paul Siebeck), 1998.

Stevenson, G. "Power and Place: The Symbolism of the Temple in the Book of Revelation." Ph.D. diss., Emory University, 1999.

Stowers, S. K. *The Diatribe and Paul's Letter to the Romans.* SBLDS 57. Chico, Calif.: Scholars Press, 1981.

———. *Letter Writing in Greco-Roman Antiquity.* Library of Early Christianity. Philadelphia: Westminster Press, 1986.

———. "Romans 7:7–25 as a Speech in Character (*prosōpopoiia*)." In *Paul in*

His Hellenistic Setting, edited by T. Engberg-Peterson, 180–202. Minneapolis: Fortress Press, 1995.

———. "Social Typification and the Classification of Ancient Letters." In *The Social World of Formative Christianity and Judaism*, edited by J. Neusner and H. C. Kee, 78–89. Philadelphia: Fortress Press, 1988.

Strange, J. F. "A Critical and Exegetical Study of 1 Timothy 3:16: An Essay in *Traditionsgeschichte*." Ph.D. diss., Drew University, 1970.

Strobel, A. "Schreiben des Lukas? Zum sprachlichen Problem der Pastoralbriefe." *NTS* 15 (1968–1969): 191–210.

Sundberg, A. C. "Canon Muratori: A Fourth Century List." *HTR* 66 (1973): 1–41.

Tenney, M. C. *New Testament Survey*. Revised by W. M. Dunnett. Grand Rapids, Mich.: Eerdmans, 1985.

Theissen, G. *The Social Setting of Pauline Christianity: Essays on Corinth*. Translated by J. Schuetz. Philadelphia: Fortress Press, 1982.

Thiselton, A. C. "Realized Eschatology in Corinth." *NTS* 24 (1977–1978): 520–526.

Thurston, B. B. *The Widows: A Women's Ministry in the Early Church*. Minneapolis: Fortress Press, 1989.

Torm, F. *Die Psychologie der Pseudonymität im Hinblick auf die Literatur des Urchristentums*. Gütersloh: Bertelsmann, 1932.

———. "Über die Sprache in der Pastoralbriefen." *ZNW* 18 (1917–1918): 225–243.

Towner, P. H. "Gnosis and Realized Eschatology in Ephesus (of the Pastoral Epistles) and the Corinthian Enthusiasm." *JSNT* 31 (1987): 95–124.

———. *The Goal of Our Instruction: The Structure of Theology and Ethics in the Pastoral Epistles*. JSNTS 34. Sheffield: JSOT Press, 1989.

———. "The Present Age in the Eschatology of the Pastoral Epistles." *NTS* 32 (1986): 427–428.

Treue, K. "Neuetestamentliche Fragmente der Berliner Papyrussammlung." *Archiv für Papyrusforschung* 18 (1966).

Trible, P. *Texts of Terror: Literary-Feminist Readings of Biblical Narratives*. Philadelphia: Fortress Press, 1984.

Trummer, P. "Corpus Paulinum—Corpus Pastorale: Zur Ortung der Paulustradition in den Pastoralbriefen." In *Paulus in den neutestamentlichen Spätschriften*, edited by K. Kertelge, 122–145. QD 89. Freiburg: Herder, 1981.

———. "Mantel und Schriften." *BZ* 18 (1974): 193–207.

———. *Die Paulustradition der Pastoralbriefe*. Beiträge zur biblischen Exegese und Theologie 8. Frankfort: Lang, 1978.

Turmel, J. "Histoire de l'interprétation de I Tim. II, 4." *Revue d'histoire et de littérature religieuses* 5 (1900): 385–415.

Van Vliet, H. *No Single Testimony: A Study on the Adaptation of the Law of Deut . 19:15 Par. into the New Testament*. Utrecht: Kreminck en Zoon, 1958.

Verner, D. C. *The Household of God: The Social World of the Pastoral Epistles.* SBLDS 71. Chico, Calif.: Scholars Press, 1983.

Viviano, B. T. "The Genre of Matt. 1–2: Light from I Tim. 1:4." *RB* 97 (1990): 31–53.

von Campenhausen, H. *Ecclesiastical Authority and Spiritual Power in the Church of the First Three Centuries.* Translated by J. Baker. Stanford: Stanford University Press, 1969.

———. *Polykarp von Smyrna und die Pastoralbriefe.* Sitzungsberichte der Heidelberger Akademie der Wissenschaften. Heidelberg: Winter, 1951.

von Dobschütz, E. *Christian Life in the Primitive Church.* Translated by G. Brenner. New York: Putnam, 1904.

von Weizsäcker, C. *The Apostolic Age of the Christian Church.* 2nd ed. Translated by J. Millar. New York: Putnam, 1899.

———. "Die Kirchenverfassung des apostolischer Zeitalter." *Jahrbuch für deutsche Theologie* 18 (1873): 631–674.

Wagener, U. *Die Ordnung des "Hauses Gottes": Der Ort von Frauen in der Ekklesiologie und Ethik der Pastoralbriefe.* WUNT, 2nd ser., 65. Tübingen: J. C. B. Mohr (Paul Siebeck), 1994.

Warfield, B. *Biblical Foundations.* Grand Rapids, Mich.: Eerdmans, 1958.

Weidmann, F. "The Good Teacher: Social Identity and Community Purpose in the Pastoral Epistles." *JHC* 2 (1995): 100–114.

Weiss, J. *The History of Primitive Christianity.* 2 vol. Completed by R. Knopf. Edited by F. C. Grant. Translated by Four Friends New York: Wilson-Erikson, 1937.

Welles, C. B. *Royal Correspondence in the Hellenistic Period: A Study in Greek Epigraphy.* New Haven, Conn.: Yale University Press, 1934.

Wendland, P. "Betrogene Beträger." *Rheinisches Museum für Philologie.* 49 (1894): 309–310.

Wernle, P. *The Beginnings of Christianity.* Translated by G. A. Bienemann. 2 vols. London: Williams and Norgate, 1903.

White, L. M. "Urban Development and Social Change in Imperial Ephesos." In *Ephesos: Metropolis of Asia,* edited by H. Köster, 27–79. Harvard Theological Studies 41. Valley Forge, Pa.: Trinity International Press, 1995.

Wikenhauser, A. *New Testament Introduction.* Translated by J. Cunningham. New York: Herder and Herder, 1963.

Wilshire, L. E. "The TLG Computer and Further Reference to AUTHENTEŌ in 1 Timothy 2:12." *NTS* 34 (1988): 120–134.

Wilson, S. G. *Luke and the Pastoral Epistles.* London: SPCK, 1979.

Windisch, H. "Sinn und Geltung des apostolischen Mulier Taceat in Ecclesia." *Christliche Welt* 9 (1930): 411–425.

———. "Zur Christologie der Pastoralbriefe." *ZNW* 34 (1935): 213–238.

Wire, A. *The Corinthian Women Prophets.* Minneapolis: Fortress Press, 1990.

Wolter, M. *Der Pastoralbriefe als Paulustradition.* FRLANT 146. Göttingen: Vandenhöck & Ruprecht, 1988.

Yarbrough, R. W. "The Hermeneutics of 1 Tim. 2: 9–15." In *Women in the*

Church, edited by A. J. Koestenberger, T. R. Schreiner, and H. S. Baldwin, 155–196. Grand Rapids, Mich.: Baker Book House, 1995.

Young, F. "The Pastoral Epistles and the Ethics of Reading." *JSNT* 45 (1992): 105–120.

———. *The Theology of the Pastoral Letters*. Cambridge: Cambridge University Press, 1994.

Zahn, T. *Introduction to the New Testament*. 3rd ed. Translated by J. M. Trout et al. 3 vols. Edinburgh: Clark, 1909.

FIRST TIMOTHY:
AN INTRODUCTION

◆

INTRODUCTION

◆

As a first step toward modifying the conventional wisdom concerning the letters to Paul's delegates, it is crucial to consider each composition carefully on its own terms as a separate letter. There are certainly similarities among 1 Timothy, 2 Timothy, and Titus, but there are as many dissimilarities. Each letter also has very real points of contact with other letters in the Pauline corpus that are obscured when they are read as a separate literary production.

In a neutral system of classification, 1 Timothy would be grouped with Paul's travel or mission letters. Paul is not in prison, but actively carrying out his work. There is no sense that he is at any particular turning point in his mission. Rather, the impression given by the letter is that Paul writes as though in mid-stride. The amount of information actually provided about Paul or his delegate is sparse. Paul has left for Macedonia, and Timothy is to represent him in the Ephesian church (1:3) until Paul's return, which is expected to be soon (3:14). Ostensibly, Paul writes in order to provide instructions to Timothy in his absence (4:13), "so that you may know how it is necessary to behave in the household of God, which is the church of the living God—a pillar and support for the truth" (3:15).

PLACEMENT IN PAUL'S MINISTRY

The first question facing the reader of 1 Timothy is the plausibility of the situation as presented by the letter. This involves assessing the respective roles that the letter assigns to Paul and Timothy, as well as the possible occasion for this particular sequence within Paul's ministry. I discuss the role of Paul's delegates as a whole in the General Introduction. I need only repeat here that the picture of Paul's delegate spending time in a local church as Paul's representative while Paul travels is essentially consonant with the evidence provided in the undisputed letters. In Acts, Timothy travels with Paul, but also carries out missions for him in other places. He stays for a time in Macedonia with Silas while Paul begins his work in Corinth (Acts 18:5). He and Erastos are sent to Macedonia while Paul remains in Ephesus (Acts 19:22). Although Timothy is so frequently by Paul's side that he is listed as co-sponsor of six letters (2 Cor 1:1; Phil 1:1; Col 1:1; 1 Thess 1:1; 2 Thess 1:1; Phm 1), and is with Paul in Corinth as he writes Romans (Rom 16:21), he is also sent on missions of shorter or longer duration. His role in such cases is to represent Paul.

Three examples are noteworthy. Paul sends Timothy to Thessalonica to "strengthen and exhort" the members of the church so that they will not be confused by the afflictions they are experiencing; Timothy performs his task and reports back to Paul (1 Thess 3:2, 6). In 1 Corinthians (a letter not co-sponsored by Timothy), Paul tells the community that although he plans—if God is willing—to visit them quickly, he has sent Timothy precisely to remind them of Paul's ways as he teaches them everywhere in every church (1 Cor 4:17). At the end of the letter, he seeks to pave Timothy's way, asking the church not to scorn him (1 Cor 16:10–11). Finally, Paul tells the Philippians (in Macedonia) that he hopes to send Timothy to them quickly, to deliver news about Paul and to bring back news about them. This is despite Paul's hope to come to them quickly himself (Phil 2:19–24). In short, the scenario suggested by 1 Timothy corresponds perfectly with the role given to Paul's delegates in our other sources.

The other side of the question is whether the specific situation suggested by 1 Timothy can be fitted within Paul's career as we reconstruct it from the available sources. To engage this issue, we must remember the basic difficulty presented by those sources: that they are neither complete nor disinterested in their account of Paul's movements. Although they tell us something about Ephesus, Macedonia, and the movements of Paul and Timothy with respect to those two locations, we cannot be confident that we have a full report.

We can approach the problem by reviewing the evidence, starting at the beginning, which is Paul's mission to Macedonia. Macedonia is the landmass bounded on the west by Illyria, on the east by Thrace, and on the south by Thessaly (Greece). Formerly a kingdom that under Alexander the Great became the basis of the Hellenistic Empire, Macedonia became a Roman province under Augustus in 27 B.C.E. In C.E. 15, it was linked with Moesia and Achaia into a single province, but under Claudius in C.E. 44 it became once more a separate province.

According to Acts 16–18, Timothy accompanies Paul in his mission to the chief churches in eastern Macedonia, namely, the Roman colony of Philippi and the capital city of Thessalonica. When Paul arrives in Corinth, he sends Timothy back to Thessalonica to strengthen the church there (1 Thess 3:2). Paul spends at least eighteen months in Corinth, joined by Timothy and Silas (Acts 18:4). After that period, Paul makes his first contact with Ephesus, the capital city of the province of Asia (Acts 18:19). After a side trip to Jerusalem, Paul returns to Ephesus and stays there for at least two years, probably longer (Acts 19:10). Acts does not tell us of any more trips made by Paul during that two-year period before the great riot in the city (Acts 19:23–41), which places Paul in peril and makes him move again. But in 19:22, Acts has Paul make plans for a trip to Jerusalem and then to Rome, and he sends Erastos and Timothy to Macedonia, while he stays on a while longer in Ephesus.

According to Acts 20:1, Paul then leaves Ephesus for Macedonia and travels through that territory (20:2) before returning to Greece (20:2) for three months. It is precisely in this interval of Paul's traveling in Macedonia—with Timothy's whereabouts unreported—that it is possible to fit Timothy's serving as Paul's representative in the Ephesian church, if Timothy in the meantime had returned there to take up such a post. After his three months in Greece, Paul departs again for Macedonia (Acts 20:3), specifically Philippi. From there he crosses over to Troas (20:5), where he begins his final journey to Jerusalem. Note that

Acts places Timothy again as one of Paul's companions in Greece (Corinth?) as he departs for Macedonia (20:4). The window of opportunity for 1 Timothy is consequently not large, if we restrict ourselves to the account in Acts.

Paul's Letters to the Corinthians confirm that Paul traveled frequently among Asia, Macedonia, and Achaia, but it is difficult to make their evidence fit precisely with that in Acts. It is generally assumed by scholars that 1 and 2 Corinthians are written by Paul from Ephesus, although that cannot definitively be proved (2 Corinthians, for example, which is co-sponsored by Timothy, might have been written from Macedonia). In 1 Cor 16:1–4, Paul states his plan to travel to Jerusalem with a collection, and says in 16:5 that he plans to pass through Corinth on his way to Macedonia. In 2 Cor 1:15–16, Paul repeats that this had been his plan. But, in fact, Paul had gone instead to Macedonia by way of Troas (2 Cor 2:12–13), arriving there to meet with Titus, who brought good news of his reconciliation with the Corinthian community (2 Cor 7:5–7). In 2 Cor 8:1–5 and 11:9, we learn simply that the Macedonian churches had supported Paul financially, which is confirmed by Phil 4:10–20.

In summary, it is difficult, although not impossible, to fit 1 Timothy within the information we have about Paul's movements from Acts and the letters. But it is also possible to recognize that both sources are limited in what they tell us and to suggest that 1 Timothy itself might be taken as a positive source of information about Paul's career. In any case, the mis-en-scène for 1 Timothy is plausible, if not probative. It matches perfectly the assignments given to delegates, and it reflects as well the busy traffic among Macedonia, Corinth, and Ephesus that is revealed in our other sources. There is nothing historically disqualifying or anachronistic in its self-presentation.

LITERARY GENRE

Coming to grips with 1 Timothy as a literary composition has always been difficult, for—in company with Titus—it appears to be so different from anything else in the Pauline collection. Before discussing its possible genre, we can observe some features of the composition.

Its many instructions or commandments give 1 Timothy its distinctive character. The verb *parangellō* (command/instruct) occurs more frequently here than in any other Pauline letter (1 Tim 1:3; 4:11; 5:7; 6:13, 17; compare 2 Thess 3:4, 6, 10, 12; 1 Thess 4:11; 1 Cor 7:10; 11:17), and the noun *parangelia* (commandment/instruction) appears twice (1 Tim 1:5, 18; otherwise in Paul, only in 1 Thess 4:2), together with *entolē* (commandment) in 1 Tim 6:14. The actual instructions deal with a range of subjects: prayer in the assembly and the respective liturgical roles of men and women (1 Tim 2:1–15); the qualifications of supervisors (*episkopoi*, 3:1–7), helpers (*diakonoi*, 3:8–10, 12–13), and women helpers (3:11); the care of widows (5:3–16); the resolution of charges against elders (*presbyteroi*, 5:19–22); and the attitudes of slaves (6:1–2) and the wealthy (6:17–19).

Three things about these directives strike the reader:

1. Although they employ the language of the household (*oikos*), their concern is with the *ekklēsia*, the public life of the community. This stands in contrast to 2 Timothy, which has no public *entolai*, and Titus, whose *entolai* are, with the exception of 1:5–9 (dealing with the supervisor/elder), aimed at the household (Tit 2:1–3:2).
2. They are consistently ad hoc and nonsystematic. Only in 5:3–16 is there anything resembling a full or elaborated development of a topic, and it leaves many things unsaid that we would like to know.
3. The instructions alternate with sections devoted to Paul's delegate Timothy: his attitudes, his practices, and the ways he is to rebut the errors of his opponents.

If it were possible simply to lift out the discrete sections containing the instructions about the community's life, leaving only the verses dealing with Timothy and his opponents, we would find a letter that looked like an abbreviated version of 2 Timothy. In those sections, we find the elements of personal paraenesis and protreptic that are discussed more extensively in the introduction to 2 Timothy: the presentation of Paul as a model for believers (1 Tim 1:16) and the exhortation that Timothy also present himself as a model to the Ephesian community (4:12) together with the use of maxims concerning Timothy's behavior set in antithesis to the stereotypical polemic used to describe the opponents (6:1–5, 11–16).

At first glance, then, 1 Timothy appears to lack any literary coherence.[274] It certainly does not resemble any other Pauline letter except Titus, whose brevity camouflages the problem. Such literary disjointedness was one of the reasons, as we have seen, that Schleiermacher rejected the authenticity of 1 Timothy and began the entire process of questioning the Pauline letters on the basis of stylistic or thematic consistency.[275] In addition, 1 Timothy did not seem to fit any known classification of ancient letter. Scholars therefore concluded that 1 Timothy was a transitional literary form, a stage toward the development of Christian church orders.[276] Such documents began to emerge in the early second century with the *Didache* (full title, *Teaching of the Twelve Apostles*), grew in size and complexity through the *Didascalia Apostolorum* (third century), and culminated in the massive *Apostolic Constitutions* (fourth century). Despite differences in size, date, and provenance, it is clear that they served first of all to regulate community life—especially in matters of worship—and to do so in the

---

274. A more positive view of 1 Timothy's structure is expressed in P. G. Bush, "A Note on the Structure of 1 Timothy," *NTS* 36 (1990): 152–156, and J. T. Reed, "Cohesive Ties in 1 Timothy: In Defense of the Epistle's Unity," *Neot* 26 (1992): 131–156.

275. Schleiermacher considered that Titus, in comparison with 1 Timothy, "held together more naturally" (*Über den sogennanten Ersten Brief des Paulus an den Timotheus*, 45).

276. See, for example, Dibelius and Conzelmann, *Pastoral Epistles*, 5–7.

name of the apostles, thus intimating that however innovative the practices enjoined, they had the authority of the Apostolic Age behind them.

It was not difficult for scholars to regard I Timothy (and Titus), therefore, as examples of a literary form that developed distinctively within the Christian tradition, continuing the apostolic letter form (for purposes of authority) but adapting Pauline teaching for a later generation. The striking similarity on a number of points between 1 Timothy and Polycarp's *Letter to the Philippians*—written shortly after the death of Ignatius of Antioch as a cover letter for the collection of Ignatius's letters—is taken as evidence that Polycarp and the author of 1 Timothy, if not the same person, were on the same track. This, despite the fact that Polycarp draws a sharp distinction between his own age and that of the Apostles (*Phil.* 3; 11), and despite the fact that Polycarp in all likelihood actually alludes to 1 Timothy (*Phil.* 4).

1 Timothy resists classification as an early church order on three other counts. First, it presents itself as written by Paul himself, rather than the anonymous authority of "the apostles." Second, its attention to Paul's delegate and the theological rebuttal of diverse teachings is sufficiently detailed and specific to make dismissal of this element as an accoutrement of pseudepigraphy improbable. Third, its actual *parangeliai* are so related to specific situations and (with the partial exception of 5:3–16) so brief that it is hard to imagine them functioning as an official regulatory document. Nevertheless, the contrast with the other extant Pauline letters, and the slight similarity to known church orders, was sufficient to persuade scholars that 1 Timothy was a distinctively inner-Christian development. It is obvious that if this designation is correct, it also both assumes and reinforces the position that 1 Timothy is pseudonymous.

More recent research has enabled another possibility to be entertained. There is a body of letter writing that can be termed broadly "royal correspondence," and that is extant partially through inscriptions[277] and partially through papyri fragments.[278] The collections include a variety of communications between royal officials and cities, as well as between royal officials and their subordinates. The latter category is of special significance, for it provides an analogy to the social relationship in 1 Timothy: a superior writes to a representative or delegate with instructions concerning the delegate's mission.

Examples of letters from Seleucid kings to the governors of various territories in their care can be dated to the third century B.C.E.[279] Of particular importance is the fact that these letters are now found on inscriptions, which means that such correspondence not only was published by being read aloud, but was memorialized by inscription on stone erected in a public place.[280] The subject matter

---

277. C. B. Welles, *Royal Correspondence in the Hellenistic Period: A Study in Greek Epigraphy* (New Haven, Conn.: Yale University Press, 1934).

278. B. P. Grenfell, A. S. Hunt, J. G. Smyly, *The Tebtunis Papyri*, University of California Publications in Graeco-Roman Archaeology 1 (London: Oxford University Press, 1902).

279. Welles, *Royal Correspondence*, no. 9, 54–60; nos. 18–20, 89–104.

280. Welles, *Royal Correspondence*, 60–71.

of the Seleucid letters touches on affairs from the protection of temples to the disposition of property and the appointment of priests.[281]

Some scholars have recognized the literary resemblance between such letters and 1 Timothy and Titus,[282] categorizing them as a whole as *mandata principis* (commandments of a ruler) letters, in recognition of the dominant place held by commandments (*entolai, parangeliai*) in them. Some such letters were carried as memorandums by a newly appointed delegate to a district or province, summarizing the mandates to be carried out in the course of his administration. Although addressed to an individual, the delegate in question, the letters had at least a quasi-public character, for the *entolai* were to be heard by others as well as the delegate. In some instances, such mandates were accompanied by personal instructions and exhortations to the delegate having to do less with specific actions and more with general attitude and behavior.

Papyrus evidence from Egypt confirms the same practice among Ptolemaic rulers of the Hellenistic period.[283] An almost perfect example is provided by the Tebtunis Papyrus 703. In it we find a senior Egyptian official instructing a subordinate—probably a financial manager—in some of his responsibilities.[284] Much of the letter is taken up with the specific public works that the delegate is to oversee: the maintenance of waterworks (lines 29–40), the weaving industry (lines 87–117), and runaway soldiers and sailors (lines 215–222). The letter makes clear that these detailed instructions are meant as a "reminder" or memorandum (line 235): "I thought it well to write down for you in this memorandum what I told you in sending you to the nome" (line 260). But in addition to such *mandata/entolai* is a passage that focuses on the character of the delegate and his manner of conducting himself in his new position (lines 260–280). He is to behave in a manner without reproach, fleeing any form of vice. And he can find an example of such "behavior and striving" (*anastrophē kai agonia*) in the superior who sends the letter (*kath' hēmas*, lines 270–271).[285]

The Roman Empire followed the same practice. In a letter written to his friend Atticus while on his way to assume the proconsulship of Cilicia in 51 B.C.E., Cicero reports on his efforts to fulfill the Senate's decree of 60 B.C.E. not to exploit the provinces, efforts encouraged also by his friend Atticus. From the letter, we learn how an actual delegate responded to the demand of exemplary behavior: "every day I think of how to fulfill your [Atticus's] often-repeated exhortations (which fell on willing ears) to get through this abnormal duty with the strictest decency and propriety, and so I impress on my companions, and so in fact I do" (Cicero, *Letters to Atticus* 5.9.1). In a later letter, Cicero says, "My strictness with regard to your precepts is so remarkable that I am afraid I shall have to raise a

---

281. Welles, *Royal Correspondence*, no. 9, 54; no. 10, 61; no. 18, 90–91; no. 30, 137; no. 36, 157–158.

282. Fiore, *Function of Personal Example*; Wolter, *Pastoralbriefe als Paulustradition*.

283. See the full discussion in A. S. Hunt and J. G. Smyly, *The Tebtunis Papyri* (London: Oxford University Press, 1933), 66–73.

284. Hunt and Smyly, *Tebtunis Papyri*, 73–102.

285. See also Tebtunis Papyrus 27 in Grenfell, Hunt, *Tebtunis Papyri*, 105–114.

loan" (*Letters to Atticus* 5.15.2). Atticus did not hold the position of the consul or the senate, and Cicero was not a subordinate but his friend. Stiu, these excerpts reveal something of the situation reflected in the official letters I am discussing and exhibit the same kind of concern for avoiding avarice that is found in the verbal citation by Ulpian (d. 223) of one such *mandata* letter.[286]

According to Dio Cassius, such letters were routinely sent to Roman proconsuls and prefects as early as the first century B.C.E.: "The emperor gives instructions [*entolas*] to the procurators, the proconsuls, and the propraetors, in order that they may be under definite orders [*epi rhētois*] when they go out to their provinces" (*Roman History* 53.15.4). Philo's *Against Flaccus* gives an example of the sort of mandate (*entolē*) that Augustus sent to Magiûs Maximus, his prefect in Egypt, as does the excerpt *ex entolōn* of Mettius Rufus in the reign of Trajan.[287]

A delegate carrying such a letter from his superior and having it read aloud in the assembly of the city to which he was commissioned—even for such a short period as envisaged by 1 Timothy—would accomplish two things. First, the provisions for the community would be perceived as the will of the superior and not simply the whim of the delegate. As a result, the instructions would be legitimated. Second, those parts of the letter exhorting the delegate to good behavior provided the community with a norm by which to measure the delegate's behavior as the leader's representative. The populace would thereby have a basis for appeal to the leader if the delegate fell significantly below the standards established by the letter.

1 Timothy (and Titus) find their appropriate literary antecedent in such *mandata principis* letters, which are addressed to a social situation analogous to that presented by Paul's letters: Paul has sent Timothy and Titus to specific locations as his representatives with specific *parangeliai* (commandments/instructions) to administer. Examples like the Tebtunis Papyrus 703 also help account for the odd mixture of personal and public elements in 1 Timothy and Titus, since the combination is found in such letters. Finally, reading 1 Timothy and Titus as *mandata principis* letters makes more intelligible their decidedly detached tone. They are less personal and intense than 2 Timothy precisely because they are not genuinely private letters; they are intended from the beginning to be read in public, both to support Paul's delegate in his work and to hold the delegate to a standard of personal behavior that is exemplary.

By no means does the categorization of 1 Timothy as a *mandata principis* letter demonstrate its authenticity. A pseudepigrapher, after all, could have made use of this genre as easily as any other. But the existence of such a well-attested

---

286. Ulpian, *Duties of a Proconsul*, Book 8, in *The Digest of Justinian* 47, 11, 6; Latin Text edited by Theoder Mommsen with the aid of Paul Krueger; English Translation edited by A. Watson (Philadelphia: University of Pennsylvania Press, 1985) 4:784.

287. H. Metzger, "Zur Stellung der liturgischen Beamten Ägyptens in frührömischen Zeit," *Museum Helveticum* 2 (1945): 54–62; Wolter, *Pastoralbriefe als Paulustradition*, 164–165; Fiore, *Function of Personal Example*, 61–63.

letter form in widespread use by officials centuries before Paul's time—with some samples, we remember, inscribed on steles and visible to all—means at the very least that the literary shape of 1 Timothy does not necessitate its being pseudonymous. Indeed, it ought to shift the discussion concerning authenticity significantly. The otherwise strange combination of elements can now be seen not as the clumsy effort of someone trying to imitate other letters, but as belonging to the well-established conventions of an epistolary form that Paul uses with the same flexibility and freedom that he did other conventional letter forms in the amazing range of letters found in the Pauline collection. And it opens the way to a serious consideration of the situation faced by Paul's delegate, not as a fictional setting, but perhaps as the real-life occasion for the letter.

THE SITUATION IN THE EPHESIAN CHURCH

Ephesus was "the first and greatest metropolis of Asia," as many of its inscriptions proclaimed. It was made the capital of the province of Asia under Augustus in 29 B.C.E. (Dio Cassius, *Roman History* 51.20.6). Both its size and its prosperity as a market are attested by archaeological and literary evidence (e.g., Strabo, *Geography* 14.1.24; Philostratus, *Life of Apollonius of Tyana* 8.7.8). Its population during the early empire was probably between 100,000 and 150,000, making it rank only below Rome and Alexandria in size as an urban center.[288] Inscriptions also confirm the city's wealth and demographic diversity,[289] which, as in the case of Corinth across the Aegean, owed much to its position as the major port of the region. The city's pride was its role as the *neōkoros* (temple keeper) of the goddess Artemis (Strabo, *Geography* 14.1.22–23; Xenophon, *The Ephesians* 1.2.2–7), a cult that had spread even into Greece (Pausanias, *Description of Greece* 2.2.6; 4.31.8) and whose jealously guarded prerogatives are vividly sketched in the account of the Ephesian riot caused by the Ephesian silversmiths in Acts 19:23–41.

Christianity at Ephesus was probably a pluriform phenomenon from the beginning. It was certainly not a Pauline foundation in the same sense that Thessalonica, Philippi, and Corinth were. In Acts, Luke gives an unusual amount of attention to Paul's first contacts with the city (19:1–20). As important as Ephesus turns out to be in the history of Christianity, Luke may give it so much attention precisely because it was not a church founded by an apostle. His stories about Priscilla and Aquila and Apollos and the Twelve Disciples of John the Baptist (Acts 18:24–19:7) may deflect attention from the fact that Paul himself did not found the church there, but only stopped there the first time on his way to Jerusalem (18:19–21). In Paul's absence, there were already "brethren" in Ephesus able to

---

288. L. M. White, "Urban Development and Social Change in Imperial Ephesos," in *Ephesos: Metropolis of Asia*, ed. H. Köster, Harvard Theological Studies 41 (Valley Forge, Pa.: Trinity International Press, 1995), 27–79.

289. White, "Urban Development and Social Change," 60–79.

communicate with the Corinthians and commission Apollos (18:27).[290] Notice that, writing from Ephesus to the Corinthians, Paul refers to "the churches of Asia" as well as to "Aquila and Prisca together with the church that meets in their house" (1 Cor 16:19). There are also traditions linking Johannine Christianity to Ephesus, and the book of Revelation—written by a John from Patmos, probably toward the end of the first century—addresses the church in Ephesus (Rev 2:1–7).[291]

Christianity in Ephesus may also have been troubled from the beginning. Acts gives us the account of the riot in 19:23–41, carefully removing Paul from direct involvement (19:30), yet, revealingly, having Paul avoid Ephesus when he later sails from Troas to Miletus (20:15). Luke explains this in terms of Paul's desire to be in Jerusalem by Pentecost (20:16), but his intention "not to spend time in Asia" may have been motivated as much by danger as by haste.[292] Writing from Ephesus to the Corinthians, Paul says that he has an opportunity for work there, but "there are many adversaries" (*antikeimenoi polloi*, 1 Cor 16:9). Earlier, he spoke of "fighting with the beasts at Ephesus" (*thēriomachein*, 1 Cor 15:32). This could be taken literally, but could also be combined with 16:9 to reflect dealing with human adversaries.[293] In 2 Cor 1:8–9, Paul mentions a *thlipsis* (affliction) he endured in Asia that overwhelmed him and brought him to the very point of death, a "deadly peril" from which God rescued him. Does this refer to an imprisonment, as some scholars think,[294] or to some other tribulation? In any case, it is clear that Paul's experience in Ephesus was not entirely positive, despite the evidence given by Acts of his powerful ministry there (Acts 19:10–20). Indeed, the polemic in Rev 2:6 against the Nicolaitans has been taken by some scholars as reflecting an animus against relatively more liberal Pauline Christians.[295] Finally, there is the evidence provided by 1 Timothy itself concerning rival interpretations of the good news.

According to 1 Timothy, Paul's delegate is to deal with matters in the church at Ephesus (1:3) in accordance with his commandment (*parangelia*, 1:5). A precise reconstruction of how matters stood in Ephesus at the time of writing— even if it is a fictional rendering—is difficult. The reader gains the distinct impression that this church—in sharp contrast to the situation addressed by Titus—is already well established. It has had the basic organizational structures in place long enough to make plausible the warning against a "new convert" (*neophytos*) becoming a supervisor (3:6). How long would a community have to exist before such structures were in place? 1 Thess 5:12 speaks of authority fig-

---

290. Johnson, *Acts of the Apostles*, 342–344.

291. For a review of all the evidence, see H. Köster, "Ephesos in Early Christian Literature," in *Ephesos: Metropolis of Asia*, ed. H. Köster, Harvard Theological Studies 41 (Valley Forge, Pa.: Trinity International Press, 1995), 119–140.

292. Johnson, *Acts of the Apostles*, 356.

293. A. J. Malherbe, "The Beasts at Ephesus," in *Paul and the Popular Philosophers* (Minneapolis: Fortress Press, 1989), 79–90.

294. Duncan, *St. Paul's Ephesian Ministry*.

295. C. K. Barrett, "Things Sacrificed to Idols," *NTS* 11 (1964–1965): 138–153.

ures in the Thessalonian community after only a few months of its founding. According to Acts, as we have noted, there were Christians in Ephesus even before Paul's involvement (Acts 18:24–28), and his own sojourn there lasted for at least two years before the riot (19:10). This is more than sufficient time for a community not only to develop an organization, but even to experience some difficulties within it. There is the need for good people to fill the positions of supervisor and helper (1 Tim 3:1–13), and charges are being brought against certain elders (5:19). Apparently, all is not well in the Ephesian *presbyterion* (4:14).

It is instructive to observe how many parallels there are between the situation sketched by 1 Timothy and that presented by 1 Corinthians—a letter to the church across the Aegean that is universally recognized as authentic and as one of our most important sources for recovering the social history of Pauline Christianity.[296] In each case, Paul uses his delegate Timothy as his representative to remind the church of his teaching and his "ways" (1 Cor 4:17; 16:10–11/1 Tim 1:3; 4:11–14). In each case, Paul reinforces boundaries by "handing over to Satan" those who are upsetting the community (1 Cor 5:1–5/1 Tim 1:20). Each community contains a certain number of wealthy people who can disrupt worship by their display of social status (1 Cor 11:17–22/1 Tim 2:9–10), and whose ownership of slaves can occasion questions about the relationship of Christian identity to social class (1 Cor 1:11; 7:21–23/1 Tim 6:1–2). In each church, heads of households are recommended as leaders (1 Cor 16:15–18/1 Tim 3:4, 12). In each letter, the metaphor "house of God" is applied by Paul to the church (*theou oikodomē*, 1 Cor 3:9; *oikos theou*, 1 Tim 3:15).

The two letters also present remarkably similar sets of behavioral issues. Some in each community consider themselves possessed of a superior wisdom or knowledge (*gnōsis*, 1 Cor 1:17; 3:18–19; 8:1/1 Tim 1:7; 6:20–21). There are problems of charges being made or lawsuits being initiated (1 Cor 6:1–5/1 Tim 5:19–20). The letters also share problems involving sexuality and gender.[297] In each case, the statement must be made that women can or should have a husband (1 Cor 7:2/1 Tim 5:14) and that marrying is not a sin (1 Cor 7:36/1 Tim 4:3). In each church as well, the place of widows is uncertain (1 Cor 7:8, 39/1 Tim 5:3–16). The role of women in the assembly arises in both churches, revolving in part around the question of what women should wear (1 Cor 11:2–16/1 Tim 2:8–10) and in part around the question of whether they should speak in the assembly or keep silent—and both letters have Paul respond in part by an appeal to Torah (1 Cor 14:33–36/1 Tim 2:11–15). Both communities have disputes over the eating of certain foods (1 Cor 8:1–10:33/1 Tim 4:3). Finally, in each church the issue of the financial support of ministers is broached (1 Cor 9:1–14/1 Tim 5:17–18).

---

296. Meeks, *First Urban Christians*.

297. S. H. Gritz sees some of these as arising from the influence of the Artemis cult in Ephesus in *Paul, Women Teachers, and the Mother Goddess at Ephesus: A Study of 1 Tim. 2:9–15 in Light of the Religious and Cultural Milieu of the First Century* (New York: University Press of America, 1991).

By listing these parallels between 1 Corinthians and 1 Timothy, I by no means want to suggest that the situations are exactly alike, much less that Paul's responses to them are identical.[298] Among other things, even the listing of verses makes clear that the proportionate weight of each item within the respective writings is different. But the listing of parallels is instructive on several counts:

1. It suggests that the kinds of problems addressed by 1 Timothy are not necessarily those of a generation later than Paul's own, but fit within the frame of first-generation Pauline communities.
2. It suggests that 1 Corinthians is the appropriate composition with which 1 Timothy should be compared within the Pauline corpus, just as 2 Timothy finds its best parallel in Philippians.
3. It suggests that 1 Timothy might usefully be read for the evidence it gives about the social setting of early Christianity in the way 1 Corinthians has been read.
4. It raises the question of why these suggestions have not been made before now. The answer, obviously, is that by being constantly grouped with 2 Timothy and Titus and read with them as a composite called the "Pastoral Letters," 1 Timothy has not seriously been read as a real letter.

THE PROBLEM OF FALSE TEACHING

Some of the difficulties in the Ephesian church are generated by false teachers.[299] The names Hymenaios and Alexander occur in 1:20 in combination as ones who have "spurned a good conscience. They have suffered shipwreck concerning the faith" (1:19), and Paul has handed them over "to Satan" for pedagogic effect (1:20). In 2 Timothy, the same names occur, but in different contexts: Hymenaios is joined to Philetos as a teacher (2 Tim 2:17–18), and Alexander is the coppersmith who opposed Paul (2 Tim 4:14). There is no way to sort out the plausibility of any of these names. Certainly, Alexander is a common enough name to belong to many people. All we can say is that according to this letter, Hymenaios and Alexander are linked. Since Paul can discipline them, it appears that they are members of the community, but we are told nothing about their teaching. Apart from these names, Paul refers to only "certain ones" (*tines*, 1:3, 6; 4:1; 5:15; 6:10, 21), as he frequently does elsewhere when speaking about opponents (2 Cor 3:1; 10:12; 11:20; Gal 1:7; 2:12; Phil 1:15; 2 Thess 3:11).

Timothy is to charge these certain people not to teach "other doctrines" or, more literally, "teach otherly" (*heterodidaskalein*, 1:3). What these deviant doc-

---

298. A similar set of observations has been made in P. H. Towner, "Gnosis and Realized Eschatology in Ephesus (of the Pastoral Epistles) and the Corinthian Enthusiasm," *JSNT* 31 (1987): 95–124, although he uses all the Pastorals rather than just 1 Timothy, as I do.

299. The General Introduction points to various attempts at identifying the "opponents in the Pastorals." I restrict myself here to 1 Timothy, which means starting the task from scratch.

trines might be is not clear. Some wanted to be considered "teachers of law" (*nomo-didaskaloi*, 1:7) and are preoccupied with "endless myths and genealogies" (1:4). Some "liars whose consciences are seared" are against marriage and advocate dietary restrictions (4:2–3) and possibly other forms of physical asceticism (4:7–8). Some may teach out of desire for gain (6:5), although this charge is so frequent in ancient polemic that it is difficult to know how to evaluate it. (Dio Chrysostom, *Oration* 32:9, 11; 35:1; Epictetus, *Discourses* 1.9.19–20; 1.29.45–47; Lucian of Samosata, *The Runaways* 14; *Philosophies for Sale* 24; *The Double Indictment* 31). Paul's final characterization is that they are involved with "godless chatter and contradictions of what is falsely called knowledge" (*gnōsis*, 6:20).

It is important to observe that the profile of the opponents in 1 Timothy is distinctive. We find here no reference to the teaching that the resurrection has already happened, as in 2 Timothy (2:18). We find no indication of a concern for circumcision or purity regulations or "Jewish myths," as in Titus (1:10, 14, 15). If we put together the pieces presented only by 1 Timothy and then peel away the characterizations that probably derive from conventional slander, we can posit an opposition that represents an intellectual elite that demands performance measured by law and asceticism rather than by grace and conscience.

The profile of the false teachers in 1 Timothy can be distinguished from those in 2 Timothy and Titus on several other points as well:

1. In contrast to both 2 Timothy and Titus, this letter makes no point of the progress being made by the opponents, particularly their success in upsetting households (2 Tim 3:6; Tit 1:11).
2. In contrast to Titus—in which the opposition is clearly "from the circumcision party" (Tit 1:10) and it is not clear whether they are Christian—the rivals in 1 Timothy are ambitious and elitist members of the Ephesian church.
3. In contrast to 2 Timothy, this letter does not call for the correction of the opposition (2 Tim 2:25; 4:2) and, in contrast to Titus, for the rebuke and silencing of the opposition (Tit 1:13; 3:10). In 1 Timothy, the false teachers are simply commanded to cease their ways (1:3).
4. In contrast to 2 Timothy, this letter does not hold out any hope for the conversion of the opposition (2 Tim 2:25–26).
5. In contrast to 2 Timothy, but like Titus, this letter does more than dismiss the opposition by means of polemic. The theological positions proposed by the opponents are engaged and refuted (1:8–10; 4:3–5, 7–8; 6:5–10).

In the course of the commentary, I will ask whether there is a direct connection between some of the positions espoused by the opponents and the disruptions they are creating, and Paul's personal directives to Timothy. That some connections can be made is clear. The emphasis on certain qualities in the supervisors and helpers correlates with problems, such as quarreling in worship and bringing charges against elders. In particular, it is worth pondering whether Paul's worry about young women becoming gadabouts and gossips (5:13) and his sharp rejection of a teaching role for women (2:11–15) are linked to the positions or practices of the opponents. Certainly it is possible to detect some connection between this composition's wholehearted affirmation of the order of creation—against the opponents' attitudes toward marriage and certain foods—and its deeply conservative stance on the "natural" roles of the genders.

THEOLOGICAL PERSPECTIVES

Approaching the theological texture of any composition is more than a matter of cataloguing its theological propositions, as impressive as these may be, or even of searching out the logic embedded in its statements, as necessary as that also may be. It means more than demonstrating the similarities or dissimilarities between the composition (on any of these points) and other compositions or collections of compositions. In the case of 1 Timothy, such a process would involve measuring its statements about God, Christ, and church against the norm presumably present in the "undisputed" Pauline letters in order to test the character of its "Pauline theology."

That such a process is futile quickly becomes apparent once it is seriously attempted. On one side, 1 Timothy has emphases that one intuitively associates with Paul, such as God's salvific will for all humans (1:15–16; 2:3–6; 4:9–10; 6:13–16). On the other side, 1 Timothy lacks entirely other themes that one also intuitively thinks of as characteristically Pauline, such as reconciliation and the cross. At least we *think* of them as characteristically Pauline until a more careful look reveals that language about the cross is utterly absent from Romans and 1 and 2 Thessalonians (although it does occur in the disputed Ephesians and Colossians!), and that reconciliation language is restricted to Romans and 1 and 2 Corinthians. Such measurings camouflaged as comparisons inevitably beg the question of what *is* Pauline, after all.

Thus, pointing out that 1 Timothy has a first-person account of Paul's conversion experience (1:12–16) has led to the objection that the "real Paul" does not describe his "call" in terms of a "conversion"—that is, in the other abbreviated allusions we have (Gal 1:11–16; 1 Cor 9:1; 15:8–9). It is never asked whether those allusions might also have been shaped by Paul for specific rhetorical ends, or whether Paul may have been capable of drawing out different aspects of an experience that clearly had considerable significance in his life and thought. Likewise, observing the fact that 1 Timothy combines a reference to a saying of Jesus and a text of Torah as warrants for the financial support of ministers (5:18) in precisely the way Paul also does in 1 Cor 9:9, 14—and it is not always observed—leads inevitably to the assertion that the use of a direct citation that appears also in the Synoptic Gospels demonstrates pseudonymity in the case of 1 Timothy, even though the same rhetorical move does not lead to such an inference in the case of 1 Cor 11:23–25. And so on.

Such comparisons are flawed above all because they fail to take into account the importance of the occasion and literary genre of the respective writings. By no means are all letters simply letters. The epistolary form was an astonishingly elastic one, able to include a variety of different rhetorical expressions. That Philippians contains a higher percentage of *syn* words and *koinōnia* expressions than any other Pauline letter owes a great deal to the fact that it is a friendship letter.[300] That 2 Timothy uses language about memory and imitation and moral virtue more than other Pauline letters is due to the fact that it is a paraenetic/protreptic letter to an individual. That Paul uses language of the cross and of the Law and of freedom more frequently in Galatians than elsewhere owes much to the fact that the relationship among those symbols is at issue in the Galatian churches to which Paul writes. That the Thessalonian correspondence has a specificity and intricacy of eschatological language beyond that of virtually any other Pauline letter is because the end-time is the issue forced on Paul by the Thessalonian church. Paul is not, in short, a systematic theologian, but a pastor whose practical theology responds to the situations he faces and the rhetorical instruments he chooses for response.

It is important, therefore, to start an examination of the theological texture — or the theological perspectives — of 1 Timothy from its character as a *mandata principis* letter. We are thus prepared from the start to recognize that the dominant elements in the letter are going to be practical instructions within the context of moral exhortation, with its "healthy teaching" (1:10; 6:3) and "training in godliness" (4:7), and with a contrast between a "good conscience" (1:5, 19; 3:9) and a "cauterized conscience" (4:2). Paul responds to the crisis posed by the challenge to weak local leadership in the Ephesian church by a twofold strategy. In contrast to his method in 2 Timothy, he engages the theological position of the opponents, an important rhetorical strategy for a letter that is meant to be "overheard" by the community. He also seeks to strengthen community structures, especially those pertaining to leadership. These two elements can be subsumed under Paul's overall understanding of *oikonomia theou en pistei* — which, for the moment, I deliberately leave untranslated.

This key expression occurs at the very beginning of the letter. Timothy is to forbid alternative doctrines that generate controversies instead of *oikonomia theou en pistei* (1:4). The placement and form of the statement indicate its importance, particularly since Paul then proceeds to spell out the *telos* (goal) of the commandment (*parangelia*) in terms of love, faith, and a good conscience, in opposition to the empty words of those who want to be teachers of Law (1:5–7). As the NOTE on 1:4 shows, however, the precise understanding of this key expression has escaped translators. A close consideration of each part of the phrase is required in order to understand it as expressing the theological perspective of 1 Timothy.

The noun *oikonomia* has as its first meaning "household management," but can be extended from that root meaning to notions of "ordering" or "dispensation" in larger spheres than the strictly domestic, without thereby losing its basic point of reference in the *oikos* (household). The genitive of the noun "God" (*theou*), in turn, can be read subjectively or objectively: Is this God's way of ordering things, or is the management of the household done with reference to

---

300. Johnson, *Writings of the New Testament*, 338–349.

God? Finally, the prepositional phrase *en pistei* stands in a detached fashion, making it unclear what it modifies. Does it specify a mode of management/ordering? Or does it refer to the sphere within which the ordering takes place? Or does it mean a manner of relating oneself to the management/ordering? Since all these decisions must be made simultaneously and without a great deal of guidance from the context, it is understandable that simple translation, much less a sense of the statement's thematic role, has largely been missed by interpreters.

But if we begin to take with full seriousness the metaphorical implications of *oikonomia*, we may find a way forward and see how this expression organizes much of the composition. I have translated the phrase as "faithful attention to God's way of ordering things." At an earlier stage of my reflection, I rendered the expression somewhat less elegantly, but perhaps more precisely: "God's way of ordering reality as it is apprehended by faith." The NOTES on 1:4 will provide support for the decisions leading to my translation. The problem with the opponents, says Paul in 1:4, is that they are not paying attention to God's activity, which structures reality itself and must be perceived and responded to by faith. Beginning with such a working translation, we can let this statement draw us into the theological perspectives of the composition.

First, then, the metaphorical implications of *oikonomia*. For the most part— or at least in the surviving literature—the Greco-Roman world did not divide the natural and the social worlds in the way that all heirs to Rousseau and the Age of Revolution instinctively do. The ordering of society, beginning with its basic unit, the *oikos*, was not perceived in terms of "the social construction of reality"—that is, as a reflection in equal parts of human need and calculation— but as a manifestation of human nature itself. The order of society should be *kata physin* (according to nature), which was understood in terms of the innate characteristics of humans in their respective races, genders, and ages. The assignment of complementary roles to the genders in the management of the household was based on the qualifications assigned by nature (Xenophon, *Oecumenicus* 3:10–15; 7:5–43; 9:15–10:5; Aristotle, *Politics* 1252b; 1253b; 1254b; 1259a–1260b; 1277b; 1334b–1337a; Plato, *Republic* 455C–457E; 459C–461E; 540C; *Laws* 781A–D; 783E–785B; 802E–803C; 804E–807D; 813C–814B; 833D). From a contemporary perspective, we can recognize the ideological— that is, the interested—character of some or much of this discourse. But being interested does not mean either that it was insincere or that it did not have a genuine and deep cultural effect. And for those who attributed nature itself to a creating God, it would not be much of a step to perceive social arrangements as well as the natural order of things as the *oikonomia theou*.

Just such a perception dominates 1 Timothy. In this composition, there is no radical discontinuity between the will of God and the structures of society. The structures of the *oikos* (household) and the *ekklēsia* (church) are not only continuous with each other, but both are parts of the dispensation of God in the world. Timothy's work to stabilize and secure such structures is therefore to be in service of the *oikonomia theou* and itself an expression of *pistis* (faith).

Because of the tendency to create a composite out of the three letters to Paul's delegates, it is important to repeat that the directives in 1 Timothy do not concern the *oikos* as such, but the *ekklēsia*—not the household, but the intentional community of the church. 1 Timothy distinguishes the two social arrangements. Indeed, it is because the supervisor and helper are good managers of their own households that they hold promise as leaders of the church (3:1–12). When discussing support of the widows (5:3–16), likewise, Paul makes a sharp distinction between the obligations of the household and those of the assembly. Children and grandchildren of a widow have a religious duty to support their own family members (5:4); failure to fulfill this duty is to "disown the faith" and become worse than an unbeliever (5:8). Note the force of this language: part of "faithful attention" to the *oikonomia theou* is to assume the responsibilities incumbent on households. In similar fashion, a believing woman with widowed relatives should support them (5:16)—we assume that such a woman is the head of a household and able to administer its financial resources. Such is also the case with the younger women Paul mentions in 5:14, whom he thinks should marry, bear children, and "rule their households." In these cases, we observe, care for widows within the *oikos* is specifically to relieve the *ekklēsia* of a burden it cannot bear, so that it is free to take care of "real widows" who have no other recourse (5:16).

Paul recognizes also a case where there is an obvious tension between the social obligations inherent in the arrangements of the *oikos* and the social ethos of the *ekklēsia* (6:1–2). The need to tell slaves of "believing masters" (*pistous despotas*) that they should not despise them because they are brothers, but should serve them as an act of benefaction, clearly arises from the dissonance between the community code of egalitarianism ("they are brothers") and the household reality of slavery ("they are masters"). Paul does not resolve the tension structurally ("masters, release your slaves"), but attitudinally ("slaves, act as though you were patrons")—testimony enough to the social conservatism embedded in the perception of society as part of the *oikonomia theou*.

When Paul refers to the "assembly of the living God," then, as the *oikos theou* (3:15), we fully expect any instructions concerning "how one ought to behave" to tend in the same conservative direction. Reading the final phrase of 3:15 as a delayed apposition to "how to behave" enables us to see an immediate application: a person who knows how to behave properly is a "pillar and support for the truth" (for support of this reading, see the NOTE on 3:15). The essential point is that the assembly of the living God, as an institution, is continuous with those social arrangements that are assumed to be set by creation, rather than discontinuous with them. Both can be apprehended "in faith," and the proper modes of behavior in one are transferable to the other.

The same theological perspective guides Paul's response to the "so-called *gnōsis*" of the opponents. In 4:2–3, we see that their "forbidding marriage [and enjoining] abstinence from certain foods" is attributed to having "cauterized consciences." Paul presents in response the perception of those who "have faith and have come to know truth" (4:3): that God has created all things to be received with thanksgiving. Note the implications for the broader understanding of *oikonomia theou* in Paul's inclusive statement: "every creature of God is good. Nothing is to be rejected that is received with thanksgiving" (4:4). Once more, the "sanctification" of the created order by "the word of God and prayer" confirms the goodness inherent in creation itself (4:5).

Similarly, Paul's response to those who seek profit in piety (6:5) is framed in terms of an attack on *philargyria* as a root of every sort of evil (6:10). It is easy to recognize the Hellenistic *topos* on "love of money" (*peri philargyrias*) in Paul's statements that those who seek to become rich fall into a temptation and a trap, while their senseless and hurtful passions drive them to ruin (6:9). He offers as remedy typical exhortations from the Hellenistic *topos* on "contentment" (*peri autarkeias*): they should be satisfied with food and clothing (6:6, 8). But Paul also characterizes such craving for wealth as a "wandering from the faith" (6:10). And he spells out *autarkeia* in terms of the nakedness of the human condition: "for we brought nothing into the world because neither can we take anything out of it" (6:7). The verbal echo of LXX Job 1:21 is clear, but so is the deeper resonance with the biblical creation story, in which humans stand naked before God (Gen 3:7, 11) and the need to wear clothing and to work for food are signs of disobedience to God (Gen 3:18–24). The rejection of acquisitiveness, in short, is connected to a claim about the human condition as created by God. Contentment with the meager food and covering required for survival is to affirm the *oikonomia theou* in faith.

Seeing the *oikonomia theou* as encompassing both natural and social orders helps account for Paul's views on women in 1 Timothy, which are discussed in detail in the NOTES and COMMENT on 2:8–15 and which legitimately create serious hermeneutical concerns. It is entirely consistent with the understanding that social roles should follow on natural or created capacities to state that young women should marry and bear children and rule their own households (5:14). It is consistent with the view that *philargyria* is opposed to faith to urge women not to wear braided hair, gold or pearls, or costly attire in the assembly, but to "adorn themselves in appropriate dress with modesty and discretion" and "in a way fitting to women dedicated to the service of God, through good works" (2:9–10). It is consistent with the view of gender roles as complementary to see women working as "helpers" (*diakonoi*) within the community if they are "faithful in every respect" (3:11), but not to see them filling the role of supervisor (*episkopos*), which is analogous to that of the head of the household, a male prerogative (3:4).

Finally, it is consistent with such a creationist perspective that the subordinate role of women within the *oikos* be carried over to the *ekklēsia*, so that Paul refuses them authority over a man or the ability to teach, but restricts their role to the domestic one of bearing and rearing children in the faith (2:11–15). As in the case of *autarkeia*, furthermore, the order of the household and assembly is buttressed by the specifically biblical accounts of the creation and fall (Gen 1:27; 2:22–23; 3:6, 13). In short, the position on the role of women adopted by Paul in 1 Timothy represents what would today be called the "downside" of the same perception of the order of creation and of society that has as its "upside" the rejection of a world-renouncing asceticism.

I have so far suggested how the theme of *oikonomia theou* works to support the perception of a continuity between creation and society as well as a continuity between them and the church of the living God. It is therefore equally important to note the ways in which 1 Timothy places as much or even greater emphasis on the One doing the creating and the ordering: the "living God." The phrase "living God" occurs first in 3:15 to specify the character of the *ekklēsia*, and is found once more in 4:10, when, in contrast to the value of physical training for the present life, Paul proposes the training in godliness, which "holds promise for the present life and also for the life to come" (4:8), adding as a reliable warrant for this assertion, "because we have come to hope in a living God who is the savior of all human beings, above all of those who are faithful" (4:10). The explicit affirmation of *theos* (God) as "living" expands the understanding of *oikonomia theou* beyond the order of creation to the order of salvation, and points to the ways in which the good news not only is continuous with the structures of society, but also transcends them.

Paul exhorts the community to pray for all people, for "this is a noble thing to do, and acceptable in the sight of our savior God, who wants all human beings to be saved and to come to the recognition of truth" (2:1, 3–4). God's desire to save humans—all humans—is the distinctive element in the "glorious good news from the blessed God" (1:11), just as the revelation of Jesus as the one "mediator between God and humans" (2:5) is the distinctive *mystērion tēs eusebeias* (mystery of piety) that is confessed by the household of God as the "assembly of the living God" (3:15–16). God's *oikonomia* of salvation is grounded in particularity—it is the human person Jesus who is the one mediator—yet in scope it is universal.

It is particular: Jesus "appeared in the flesh" (3:16); the "healthy words of our Lord Jesus Christ" (6:3) are remembered and applied to the life of the community, as in the matter of payment for elders (5:18; see Luke 10:7); his noble confession before Pontius Pilate (6:13) is the model for the "noble profession before many witnesses" of the delegate Timothy (6:12); and, Jesus' act of giving himself as a ransom for many is his *martyrion* (witness) for the appropriate seasons (2:6). It is also universal: the God who "gives life to all things" (6:13) raised Jesus from the dead, so that he was "made righteous by spirit, appeared to messengers, preached among nations, believed in by the world" (3:16). Note how the resurrection and glorification of Jesus are directly linked to his "being preached among nations."

Jesus' resurrection, then, establishes him as more than a single nation's messiah. He is the revelation of a "hope" (1:1) for all peoples, rooted in the power of the living God, that they might ultimately share in God's own life. We remember how Paul's rejoinder to physical asceticism was training for life to come, "for we have come to hope in a living God who is the savior of all human beings" (4:10). Likewise, the "genuine widow" is one who is aged and left alone, who has "put her hope in God and continues to make prayers and petitions night and day" (5:5). Finally, those who are "rich in this world" are warned "not to put their hope on the uncertainty of wealth, but rather upon God who sup-plies us with all things richly for our enjoyment" (6:17). If they expend their wealth in good deeds and generosity, in contrast, they will store up "for them-selves a noble foundation for the future, so that they can lay hold of real life (*tēs ontōs zōēs*, 6:19).

The God who "orders reality," in short, is a living God who encounters hu-mans and calls them beyond the frame of nature and the structures of society to a "real life" that can come only from God. This brings us, again, to the open-ing sequence in 1 Tim 1:3–17, where Paul asserts against those who want to govern life by Law that only the empowerment coming from "Christ Jesus our Lord" (1:12) was able to change him from a blasphemer and sinner to an apos-tle (1:12–17). He is the living proof that "Christ Jesus came into the world to save sinners" (1:15). The *oikonomia theou* to which faith attends, then, is not simply the work of God revealed in the natural order, but, above all, the work of God in the salvation extended to all humans through the death and resur-rection of Jesus. This is an *oikonomia* that only the living God can accomplish. Human wit and work cannot effect it, not by Law or by asceticism, for human effort serves for only this present life, whereas God's *oikonomia* extends beyond this world: "I was shown mercy for this reason, that Christ Jesus might demon-strate all possible patience in me first, as an example for those who would come to have faith in him unto eternal life" (1:16).

Understanding this, we are in a position to appreciate why 1 Timothy places such constant emphasis on "faith" (1:2, 4, 5, 11, 14, 16, 19; 2:7, 15; 3:9, 13, 16; 4:1, 6, 12; 5:8, 12; 6:10, 11, 12, 21), and characterizes the false teachers as having swerved from the faith (1:19; 6:10, 21), and why Paul places such emphasis on conscience (1:5, 19; 3:9) and accuses the false teachers as having corrupted con-sciences (4:2). Paul calls for a living response to the living God that is a matter of attitude even before it is of action. Thus as the gift of the Lord Jesus was abun-dantly given to Paul "with faith and love" (1:14), so is the goal of the command-ment "love from a pure heart, and a good conscience, and sincere faith" (1:5). The living God cannot be comprehended by human reason. God alone "possesses immortality. He dwells in unapproachable light. No human being has ever seen him. No one ever can see him" (6:16). It follows that neither can the human re-sponse to the living God be constrained by the dictates of Law, which can define only what is past and precedent. Living faith and love are responses to the faith and love shown humans—continuing to be shown humans—through the human person Jesus, who shows forth the living God. Only the flexibility of a living faith and the discernment of a healthy conscience can respond in this fashion.

Much careful work needs to be done in order to see how these perspectives might relate to those found elsewhere in Paul's letters. But it is at least worth noting that the letter that has drawn our attention already, 1 Corinthians, also touches, at least in passing, on the metaphor that I have been exploring. In that letter, Paul calls the church *theou oikodomē* (house of God, 1 Cor 3:9), speaks of the ministry of Apollos and himself as *oikonomoi mystērion theou* (household managers of the mysteries of God, 4:7), and says that what is asked of such man-agers is that they be *pistos* (faithful, 4:1–2). And he refers to his own work of proclaiming the good news as *oikonomian pepisteumai* (I have been entrusted with a household ordering, 9:17).

HEARING THE VOICE OF 1 TIMOTHY

It is much easier to describe the theological voice of 1 Timothy than it is to enter into conversation with it. For such a conversation to take place, after all, the reader must be willing to grant this voice from the past at least enough authority to be heard and to deserve a response. I think that we are most loyal to the voice of Paul in 1 Timothy when we are also most critical with respect to not only the text, but also our own standpoint. The point of engaging the writings of the New Testament theologically is not to take over their thoughts and impose them on our own; still less is it to suppress them in favor of our own. The point is to grow into deeper wisdom concerning God's ordering of reality through thinking with the text and thinking through the text.

Specifically, 1 Timothy offers readers today a range of rich resources for thinking about life before God: 1:4 itself provides a construal of the world as God's ordering that enables an appreciation at once of the gifts of creation and the grace of the new creation. Nowhere in the New Testament do we find so explicit a statement as in 1 Timothy of God's desire to save all humans, or so emphatic an assertion of the goodness of all that God creates. 1 Timothy invites us to consider the faith of Jesus as the mediator between God and humans who "gave himself," who bore witness before Pontius Pilate, and whose empowering grace can transform even the most arrogant person into a humble servant of God. Most of all, 1 Timothy helps us think about dimensions of the moral life—above all, the moral life in community—that no other NT writing does in the same way. We may not like what it says about male and female, but what it says should help force us to recognize how deep and intractable issues of gender are in our moral lives. We may not like the way 1 Timothy deals with church structure, but 1 Timothy also reminds us that we cannot think of church apart from structure. We may dislike some of what Paul says in this letter about the household, but we have learned, to our regret, what happens to civilization when the household is neglected. We also may not like what Paul says about the use of possessions, but what he says reminds us how our disposal of possessions is always and unavoidably a symbol of our self-disposal. And nowhere else in the New Testament do we find so sober and full a discussion of a fundamental moral dilemma as in Paul's consideration of the widows: here he brings together the reality of human need, the tension between household and church, and the tendency of humans to abuse their freedom and avoid their responsibilities, with the demand of faith in the most practical and pressing of circumstances. If everything else in 1 Timothy is abandoned, the church today should not turn its back on 5:3–16, which is all the more valuable a witness because it forces us to struggle to recognize the challenge it poses us beneath the surface tones that may repel us.

FIRST TIMOTHY:
TRANSLATION, NOTES,
AND COMMENTS

◆

I. THE GREETING (1:1–2)

◆

1 ¹From Paul, an apostle of Christ Jesus by the command of God our savior and of Christ Jesus our hope, ²to Timothy, my genuine child in faith: grace, mercy, and peace from God Father and from Christ Jesus our Lord.

NOTES

1. *From Paul, an apostle of Christ Jesus*: The greeting follows the basic form found in Hellenistic letters, and all the terms occur in Paul's undisputed letters. The same phrasing appears in 2 Tim 1:1. Paul similarly designates himself as *apostolos* (apostle) in Rom 1:1; 1 Cor 1:1; 2 Cor 1:1; Gal 1:1; Eph 1:1; Col 1:1; 2 Tim 1:1; Tit 1:1. He uses no self-designation in 1 and 2 Thessalonians. In Romans, Philippians, and Titus, he designates himself as *doulos* (slave), and in Philemon as *desmios* (prisoner). Concerning the name of Jesus and the title of *Christos*, Paul uses the same order of the words in the greetings of Philippians, Philemon, Colossians, 2 Corinthians and (possibly) Ephesians, but uses the order *Iēsous Christos* in Galatians and 1 and 2 Thessalonians. The textual evidence for the sequence of the words in Romans and 1 Corinthians is mixed.

by the command of God our savior: Codex Sinaiticus has *epangelian* (promise) rather than *epitagēn* (command), clearly under the influence of 2 Tim 1:1. The expression *kat' epitagēn* (literally, "according to the command," Polybius, *Histories* 21.6.1) is particularly appropriate for a *mandata principis* (commandments of a ruler) letter (see also Tit 1:3): as Timothy is under authority, so also is Paul. For the expression *kat' epitagēn* elsewhere in Paul, see 1 Cor 7:6 and, especially, Rom 16:26. Paul uses the designation *sōtēr* for Jesus in Phil 3:20; Eph 5:23; 2 Tim 1:10; Tit 1:4; 2:13. In addition to the present case, Paul applies the title to God in 1 Tim 2:3 and 4:10 (see also Tit 1:3; 2:10; 3:4), which fits the theological emphasis in 1 Timothy on salvation (1:15; 2:4, 15; 4:16).

and of Christ Jesus our hope: For Jesus as "our hope," see Col 1:27: "our hope of glory." The theme of hope is prominent in Titus (1:2; 2:13; 3:7), but is of particular theological significance in 1 Timothy. In three places, "hoping" (*elpizein*) in the living God is opposed to a hope placed in human means (4:10; 5:5; 6:17). It is therefore the more noteworthy that hope is here attached so simply and directly to Christ Jesus. For Paul's usage elsewhere, see Phil 2:19, 1 Thess 1:3, and especially 1 Cor 15:19, "we have hoped in Christ."

2. *to Timothy, my genuine child*: The sobriquet "genuine child" is found here and in Tit 1:4; see the use of *gnēsiōs* in 2 Cor 8:8. Paul calls Timothy *agapētos* (beloved) in 2 Tim 1:2. The difference may be due to the difference between

157

a personal paraenetic letter and a *mandata principis* letter. The designation, in any case, fits Paul's description of Timothy when writing to the Philippians, 2:20: "For I have no one of like spirit [*isopsychon*], who so genuinely [*gnēsiōs*] concerns himself in the things pertaining to you."

in faith: Note again the slight and perhaps telling distinction from 2 Tim 1:2, which lacks both this phrase and the phrase "common faith" found in Tit 1:4. The expression is appropriate in this semipublic letter as an indicator, to those readers "overhearing" it, of the basis of the relationship between Paul and Timothy. The contrast between *pistis* and its distortions is also thematic in 1 Timothy (e.g., 1:4, 5, 14, 19; 2:7, 15; 3:9, 13; 4:1, 6, 12; 6:10, 11, 12, 21). The importance of a theme cannot be determined simply from the number of times a word is used, but it is perhaps worth observing that these eighteen occurrences of *pistis* within the six chapters of 1 Timothy represent a proportionately greater occurrence than in any Pauline letter except Galatians (twenty-two uses in six chapters) and Romans (thirty-seven occurrences in sixteen chapters).

grace, mercy, and peace: The "and" in the translation is supplied to make the sentence read more smoothly. As in other Pauline letters, "grace" (*charis*) replaces the "greeting" (*chairein*) of the typical Hellenistic letter (1 Macc 10:18, 25; 11:30; 12:6, 20; 13:36; 14:20; 15:2, 16; 2 Macc 1:1; 9:19; 11:16; 3 Macc 3:12; 7:1; *Letter of Aristeas* 41; James 1:1). "Peace" (*eirēnē*) appropriates the traditional Jewish greeting of *shalom* (LXX Judg 6:23; 18:6; 19:20; 1 Sam 1:17; 20:42; Jdt 8:35), which appears as an epistolary salutation in 2 Macc 1:1 (compare Rom 1:7; 1 Cor 1:3; 2 Cor 1:2; Gal 1:3; Eph 1:2; Phil 1:2; Col 1:2; 1 Thess 1:1; 2 Thess 1:2; Tit 1:4). Although *eleos* (mercy) appears in other Pauline letters (Rom 9:23; 11:31; Gal 6:16), it forms part of the greeting only here and in 2 Tim 1:2. In both letters, it is inserted between "grace" and "peace."

from God Father: This asyndetic sequence represents the harder reading. It is found in the original hand of Sinaiticus, Alexandrinus, the original hand of Bezae, and other uncials, minuscules, and versions. The MSS that supply *hēmōn* (our), including the correctors of Sinaiticus and Bezae as well as the Koine textual tradition, clearly intend to relieve the grammatical awkwardness and conform the greeting to the common Pauline usage. The translator is, like the ancient scribes, tempted at least to supply something like, "God who is Father."

and from Christ Jesus our Lord: The prayer for the benefits of grace and peace from God and from Jesus as Lord are standard in Pauline greetings. As in 1:1, however, the placement of the titular *Christos* before the name of Jesus is unusual and characteristic of these letters to Paul's delegates.

COMMENT

The range of compositions in the ancient world that could be considered as letters is a wide one, extending from private notes scribbled on ostraca to philosophical treatises such as Seneca's *Moral Epistles* and the *Letter of Aristeas*. The most significant indicator that an implied author wanted a composition to be read as a letter—that is, as part of a conversational exchange between a real or fictive writer (sender) and a real or fictive reader (receiver)—was the greeting. Often, it was the only epistolary element in compositions that otherwise might have been read simply as treatises or sermons (e.g., the Letter of James). Whether or not the writing ever was sent and read by distinct parties, the greeting establishes such an interactive context for all subsequent reading. It also serves to signal the social relationships obtaining between sender and receiver, and even some of the social functions intended by the form of the composition.[301]

In 1 Timothy, as in his other letters, Paul follows the basic form of Hellenistic letter greeting. His frequent small variations within the form often suggest something of the character of the specific letter. When writing to the Corinthian community, for example, Paul greatly expands the part of the greeting dealing with the addressees, indicating that the attitudes and behavior of the Corinthians themselves were much on his mind. In contrast, when writing to the Romans and Galatians, it is Paul's authority as an apostle and the character of his gospel that are elaborated, and these themes are subsequently developed in the respective letters.

In 1 Timothy, the social relationship between sender and receiver is that of an implied sonship, since Timothy is designated as *teknos*. That this is a fictive filial relationship is known to us for three reasons. The first and most obvious is that we are aware that Timothy had natural parents (Acts 16:1–2). The second is that fictive-kinship language was widely practiced in Pauline churches as a way of establishing and strengthening community bonds.[302] Note in this letter how Paul prescribes certain attitudes for Timothy toward groups in the church along the lines of familial relationships (5:1–2). The third is that Paul characterizes Timothy as his son *en pistei* (in faith), indicating the nature of the bond between them as one of shared commitment to the same Lord, Jesus (1:2). The thematic importance of *pistis* will be noted repeatedly as we read through the letter.

The social function of the letter is suggested by two small details. The first is Paul's use of the phrase *kat' epitagēn theou* (by the command of God) with reference to his own apostleship. It is equivalent to the phrase *dia thelēmatos theou* (through the will of God), found in five of his letters at this point (1 Cor 1:1; 2 Cor 1:1; Eph 1:1; Col 1:1; 2 Tim 1:1), but is particularly fitting to a composition in which Paul is writing to a delegate with a commission to represent him: the ultimate authorization for the *entolē* (commandment) entrusted to Timothy is God. The second detail is the use of *gnēsios teknos* (genuine child) to describe Timothy. The difference from the *agapētos teknos* (beloved child) in 2 Tim 1:2 is not extreme, since Paul can use both terms for fellow workers (*gnēsios*, Phil 4:3; *agapētos*, Rom 16:5, 8, 9, 12). But it is at least worth noting that this does

---

301. Stowers, "Social Typification and the Classification of Ancient Letters."
302. Meeks, *First Urban Christians*, 87–89.

match the characterization of Timothy as Paul's delegate in Phil 2:20, and that *gnēsios* is used also for greeting Titus in the other *mandata principis* letter that Paul wrote to a delegate (Tit 1:4), in contrast to the personal paraenetic letter we find in 2 Timothy. My point is simply that these small touches are appropriate to the nature of the communication such as it appears in the rest of the composition.

The greeting anticipates two major theological themes of 1 Timothy. Paul calls God "our savior" and calls Jesus "our hope." The passages where these themes occur and intertwine are indicated in the NOTES on 1:1. Paul works to show that it is not human knowledge or asceticism that saves, but God, just as it is not human effort or riches that form the basis for authentic hope, but only the living God. The place in the letter that most explicitly grounds these convictions in Paul's own experience is the account of his calling/conversion, which he characterizes in terms of being shown mercy (*eleos*, 1:13, 16); it is perhaps therefore not entirely a casual matter that Paul here inserts "mercy" (*eleos*) among the benefits he wishes for Timothy from God and the Lord, Christ Jesus. That Paul strikes these dominant notes already in his greeting indicates that this *mandata principis* letter is more than a loose collection of commandments, but has a coherent and consistent theological perspective.

II. THE OPENING COMMISSION
(1:3–11)

◆

1 ³As I exhorted you when I left for Macedonia: stay in Ephesus so that you can command certain people not to teach different doctrine ⁴or devote themselves to myths and endless genealogies. These encourage speculations rather than faithful attention to God's way of ordering things. ⁵But the aim of the commandment is love that comes from a pure heart and a good conscience, and a sincere faith. ⁶Missing out on these, some people have turned aside to foolish chatter. ⁷They want to be teachers of law without understanding either the things about which they are speaking or the things concerning which they insist. ⁸But we know that the law is good if anyone uses it appropriately. ⁹We understand this: law is not laid down for a righteous person, but for the lawless and the reckless, the godless and the sinners, the unholy and the profane: people who kill fathers, who kill mothers, ¹⁰who are murderers; people who are fornicators, sexual perverts, slave dealers; people who are liars, perjurers, and who do whatever else is opposed to the healthy teaching ¹¹that accords with the glorious good news from the blessed God, with which I have been entrusted.

NOTES

3. *As I exhorted*: The sentence is anacolouthic, with two dependent clauses but no real independent clause to control them; it opens with an adverbial clause and leads into a purpose clause. The semantic range of *parakalein* is considerable, extending from "summoning" and "demanding" to "appealing" and even "encouraging," with the particular nuance being provided by the specific context. Here, the element of command is uppermost. Among Paul's frequent uses of the verb (e.g., Rom 16:17; 1 Cor 4:16), those involving the movements of his associate Apollos (1 Cor 16:12) and his delegate Titus (2 Cor 8:6; 12:18) should especially be noted.

when I left for Macedonia: For Macedonia and Paul's frequent contacts with the area where two of his most important foundations, Thessalonica and Philippi, were located, see the INTRODUCTION to 1 Timothy. As also discussed there, the best window of opportunity provided by Acts for the situation suggested here is 20:1–3. But by no means can we assume that Acts provides an adequate account of Paul's movements. Paul offers no reason for his absence, and there is every reason to suppose that his movements are unhindered.

161

stay in Ephesus: I have rendered the accusative with infinitive construction (*se prosmeinai*) as the equivalent of a direct command: "stay in Ephesus." The prefix *pros* intensifies the verb *menein* (to remain, LXX Jdg 3:25; Wis 3:9; Josephus, *Life* 62, 63; *Sibylline Oracles* 5:131; Mt 15:32; Mk 8:2). In Acts 18:18, it is used for Paul's continuing on in Corinth after the hearing before Gallio. In Acts 11:23 and 13:43, as well as 1 Tim 5:5, the verb is used for persistence in piety. For the city of Ephesus and its role in Paul's ministry, see the INTRODUCTION.

command certain people: Even though this order is given specific content, the purpose clause also conveys from the very beginning Timothy's entire mission, that of conveying Paul's commands, or mandates, to the Ephesian community. The verb *parangelein* (to command) is used in similar contexts by Paul in 1 Cor 7:10; 11:17; 1 Thess 4:11; 2 Thess 3:4–12. In 1 Timothy, see 4:11; 5:7; 6:13, 17. Note also how the verb is picked up by the noun, *parangelia*, in the thematic sentence of 1:5. The expression "certain people" (*tines*) is common in Paul as a way of designating persons in the community (1 Cor 6:1, 11; 8:7; 11:16) and especially those who are opponents or troublemakers (1 Cor 15:12; 2 Cor 10:12; Gal 1:7; 2:12; Phil 1:15; 2 Thess 3:10). It is used exclusively for troublemakers in 1 Tim 1:6, 19; 4:1; 5:15; 2 Tim 2:18.

not to teach different doctrine: The verb *heterodidaskalein* here and in 1 Tim 6:3 is a NT *hapax legomenon*, but appears in Ignatius, *Polycarp* 3:1. Other such *hetero-* combinations also appear in the Apostolic Fathers; see *heterognōmōn* (*1 Clement* 11:2), *heterodoxein* (Ignatius, *Smyrneans* 6:2), and *heterodoxein* (Ignatius, *Magnesians* 8:1). These observations formed the basis for Schleiermacher's original linguistic challenge to the authenticity of 1 Timothy. It should also be observed, however, that all three of the *hetero-* combinations also appear in literature prior to the second century (for *heterognōmōn*, see Josephus, *Antiquities* 10:281; for *heterodoxein*, see Josephus, *Jewish War* 2:129 Plato *Thaetetus* 190E; Epictetus, *Discourses* 2.9, 19; for *heterodoxia*, see Plato, *Thaetetus*, 193D). As his use of *heteroglōssos* (other tongue, 1 Cor 14:21) and *heterozygein* (mismatched, 2 Cor 6:14) shows, Paul is not averse to such constructions, and as 2 Cor 11:4 and Gal 1:6 indicate, he is capable of accusing his adversaries of preaching "another Gospel" (*heteron euangelion*).

4. *myths and endless genealogies*: The verb "devote themselves to" (*prosechein*) is a Pauline *hapax*, but occurs frequently in Koine for a "turning to" in the sense of "paying attention to" someone or something (Xenophon, *Cyropaedia* 5.5.40; Plato, *Symposium* 174D). The entire phrase "myths and endless genealogies" (*mythoi kai genealogiai aperantoi*) is easier to translate than to pinpoint with respect to reference. The noun *genealogia* refers simply to a pedigree or genealogy (Plato, *Cratylus* 396C; Josephus, *Antiquities* 11:71; *Against Apion* 1:16), and the verb form means to "trace a pedigree" (Xenophon, *Symposium* 4:51; Theophrastus, *Character-Types* 28:2; Plato, *Timaeus* 23B; LXX 1 Chron 5:1; Heb 7:6). The noun occurs only here in 1 Timothy. In Tit 3:9, it appears in connection with disputes over the Law. It is by no means clear what is intended by "endless genealogies," although the polemical tone is obvious. Paul here links endless genealogies with "myths." Once more, the language of myth has a noble ancestry, but fairly early takes on the

meaning of falsehood or tall tale, as opposed to truth (Herodotus, *Persian War* 2:45; Plato, *Republic* 330D; 377A; *Laws* 636C; *Timaeus* 26E; *Phaedo* 61B; Epictetus, *Discourses* 3.24.18; Josephus, *Against Apion* 2:256). In 1 Tim 4:7, Paul uses the expression "old-women myths" (*graōdeis mythous*), which finds parallel in Plato, *Gorgias* 527A, and Lucian, *Lover of Lies* 9. In 2 Tim 4:4, the term describes what people turn aside from the truth toward. In Tit 1:14, the author explicitly refers to "Jewish myths" (*mythois Ioudaikois*). The combination of "myths and genealogies" is found in Polybius *Histories* 9.2.4, and Julian, *Oration* 7:205C. The basic interpretive question is whether Paul means anything specific beneath his use of conventional rhetoric. Does Paul mean to equate such "myths and endless genealogies" with "foolish chatter" without particular content, in the way that present-day sterotypical language dismisses certain types of experts as people with "their charts and graphs"? Or does he have something more specific in mind, and, if so, what? The history of scholarship traced in the General Introduction shows some of the (more or less) educated guesses. The commentary of Cornelius à Lapide gives full citations for all the options suggested, including the two most popular: the speculations of proto-Gnostics concerning the pleroma, and Jewish preoccupations with *haggadoth* and chains of tradition.[303] Both are possible; neither is necessary.[304] Least likely is the suggestion that Paul is here objecting to the practice of constructing genealogies for Jesus, such as are found in the Matthean infancy account.[305]

encourage speculations: The verb *parechein* means to "produce or supply" something (Homer, *Odyssey* 18:317; Herodotus, *Persian War* 4:83). What is here produced or encouraged? Most MSS have *zētēsis* (dispute) rather than *ekzētēsis* (investigation/inquiry, LXX 2 Kgs 4:11). I take the harder reading, *ekzētēsis*, since the reading of "dispute" can be seen as an effort to make sense within this context as a whole.[306] And although *ekzētēsis* points to the intellectual ambition of the opponents, Paul regards such investigations as worth noticing because they lead to disputes within the community.

faithful attention: Verses 4 and 5 are both cryptic and thematic, which makes the difficulty in translating them both understandable and frustrating; see the extended discussion in the INTRODUCTION. The prepositional phrase *en pistei* (literally, "in faith") comes at the end of the verse. The critical question is deciding what it modifies. Translations vary considerably, as they do with respect to the phrase *oikonomia theou* itself. Because of my decision concerning the latter phrase, I take *en pistei* as referring to Paul's recommended way of receiving God's way of ordering reality: "in faith" or "faithfully." And since such faith is here contrasted with the speculative vagaries of the would-be teachers who "devote themselves" to myths and genealogies, I supply the English word "atten-

---

303. For Cornelius à Lapide, see Introduction, p. 40. For more recent discussion, see: G. Kittel,"*Genealogia* des Pastoralbriefe," *ZNW* 20 (1921): 49–69; Dibelius and Conzelmann, *Pastoral Epistles*, 16–17.

304. Colson, " 'Myths and Genealogies.' "

305. B. T. Viviano, "The Genre of Matt. 1–2: Light from I Tim. 1:4," *RB* 97 (1990): 31–53.

306. Elliott, *Greek Text*, 18.

tion" to make that intended contrast plain. The expression "in faith" could also, however, refer to the ordering of God itself and so be rendered as "that dispensation of God that consists in faith" or even "God's faithful ordering."

God's way of ordering things: A handful of MSS (such as the original hand of Bezae, the Old Latin, Irenaeus, and Origen) have *oikodomē* (edification) rather than *oikonomia* (the ordering/management of a household). *Oikodomē* would be a more familiar Pauline term (compare *oikodomein*, 1 Cor 8:1, 10; 10:23; 14:4, 17; Gal 2:18; 1 Thess 5:11; *oikodomē*, 1 Cor 3:9; 14:3, 5, 12, 26; 2 Cor 5:1; 10:8; 12:19; 13:10; Eph 2:21; 4:12, 16, 29), and it is preferred by Elliott.[307] Besides having overwhelming textual support, however, the reading of *oikonomia* fits the understanding of the community as *oikos tou theou* (household of God, 3:15). *Oikonomia* basically refers to the ordering or management of a household (Xenophon, *Oecumenicus* 1:1; Aristotle, *Politics* 1253B). Among the undisputed letters, Paul can speak of having been entrusted with an *oikonomia* in 1 Cor 9:17, and refers to Apollos and himself as *oikonomoi mystēriōn theou* (household managers of the mysteries of God, 1 Cor 4:1). It is not a great step from there to Col 1:25: "I have become a helper [*diakonos*] of the church according to the management of God's household [*kata tēn oikonomian tou theou*] that has been given to me in order to fulfill the word of God among you." Nor is the sense in 1 Tim 1:4 that far from the way *oikonomia* is used in Eph 1:10 for the divine plan. The right ordering of the community would certainly be included in Paul's understanding of the divine order, but 1 Timothy's understanding of what is to be received "in faith" above all includes God's way of creating and saving the world. A brief review of standard translations indicates the problems posed by the phrase: "godly edifying which is in faith" (KJV); "the divine order which belongs to faith" (Moffat); "the divine system that operates through faith" (Goodspeed); "the design of God which are [*sic*] revealed in faith" (JB); "God's plan for us, which works through faith" (NEB); "God's work—which is by faith" (NIV). The most widely used scholarly translations are divided. The RSV has "divine training that is in faith," but offers, in a note, "or: 'stewardship that is in faith,' or 'order that is in faith.'" The NRSV has "divine training that is known by faith" or "divine plan that is known by faith." The NAB provides, as a first option, "plan of God that is received by faith," with a second option: "God's trustworthy plan," or "the training in faith that God requires." If 1:4 is critical for understanding the theological perspective of this letter, such a range of translations does not inspire confidence that the perspective has widely been apprehended.

5. *aim of the commandment*: The term *parangelia* here serves as shorthand for Timothy's entire commission. For similar usage, see, for example, Diodorus Siculus *Library of History*, 4.12.3; Philo, *Against Flaccus* 141; Josephus, *Antiquities* 16:241. See also 1 Thess 4:2: "For you know what sorts of commandments [*tinas parangelias*] we gave you through the Lord Jesus." The word *telos* can mean "end"

---

307. Elliott, *Greek Text*, 19.

or "cessation" (as in 1 Pet 4:7), "conclusion" (as in Rom 6:22), or, as here, a *goal* (Epictetus, *Discourses* 1.30.4; Josephus, *Antiquities* 9:73; *Testament of Asher* 1:3). The meaning of the term in Rom 10:4 is a classic interpretive difficulty.[308] The usage here finds a particularly close parallel in Epictetus, *Discourses* 1.20.15; 4.8.11–12, and Diogenes Laertius, *Lives of Eminent Philosophers* 2:87.

is love: The goal of Paul's *parangelia* is not mere conformity to a set of behavioral norms, but the deep internal attitude and disposition of the human spirit, particularly in relation to other people. Chief among such attitudes for Paul is *agapē*, the kind of disinterested and self-donative love that builds community (Rom 12:9; 13:10; 14:15; 1 Cor 8:1; 13:1–13; 14:1; Gal 5:6, 13, 22; Phil 2:1–2; Phm 9; Col 2:2; 3:14; Eph 4:2; 1 Thess 5:13; 2 Thess 1:3; 2 Tim 1:7; 2:22).[309]

that comes from a pure heart: Paul lists three terms (heart, conscience, faith) for the sources of *agapē*, with a modifier attached to each. The first is the heart (*kardia*), which is the common biblical designation for the seat of human reflection and decision (LXX Gen 6:5; Exod 4:21; Deut 8:2), although the idea of a "pure character" is also found in Greco-Roman texts (Lucian, *Nigrinus* 14). Already in the LXX, the language of purity that originally attached itself to objects and then to ritual conditions (LXX Lev 16:19–20) is connected to interior dispositions. The "pure heart" is therefore a symbol for being rightly related to God (esp. LXX Ps 50:1–12). Although Paul frequently uses *kardia* as the seat of intentionality (e.g., Rom 1:21, 24; 2:29; 6:17; 2 Cor 1:22), he does not elsewhere use purity language in this connection (he uses *katharos* only in connection with things, as in Rom 14:20); the only adjective he uses with *kardia* is "fleshly" in 2 Cor 3:3. In contrast, the letters to Paul's delegates use *katharos* in connection with interior dispositions with some frequency (1 Tim 3:9; 2 Tim 1:3; Tit 1:15), although 2 Tim 2:22 is the only other time "pure heart" occurs in the Pauline literature.

a good conscience: The term *syneidēsis* can be used generally for any kind of consciousness (Diogenes Laertius, *Lives of Eminent Philosophers* 7:85). It refers more specifically to moral consciousness or self-awareness in Chrysippus, *Stoic Fragments* 3:43; Wis 17:11; Lucian, *Affairs of the Heart* 49. In three of his undisputed letters, Paul uses *syneidēsis* with some frequency (Rom 2:15; 9:1; 13:5; 1 Cor 8:7, 10, 12; 10:25, 27, 28, 29; 2 Cor 1:12; 4:2; 5:11), but otherwise the expression occurs in only the three letters to Paul's delegates (1 Tim 1:5, 19; 3:9; 4:2; 2 Tim 1:3; Tit 1:15). The usage is similar in both sets of letters, with Paul making a contrast between one's "own" conscience and that of others (1 Cor 10:29; 1 Tim 4:2). The main difference is that in the undisputed letters Paul uses only one modifier for conscience, "weak" (*asthenēs*, 1 Cor 8:7, 10, 12), whereas 2 Tim 1:3 and 1 Tim 3:9 use "pure conscience" and 1 Tim 1:5, 19 have "good conscience." Within the medical imagery of these letters, having a

---

308. See, for example, G. E. Howard, "Christ the End of the Law: The Meaning of Romans 10:4ff," *JBL* 88 (1969): 331–337.

309. C. Spicq, *Agape in the New Testament*, trans. M. A. McNamara and M. H. Richter (St. Louis: Herder, 1963, 1965, 1966).

good conscience stands in contrast to having a "seared/cauterized" conscience (1 Tim 4:2).

sincere faith: The use of "faith" here corresponds to the phrase *en pistei* (in faith) in 1:4. The modifier *anupokritos* (literally, "unhypocritical") emphasizes the quality of genuineness. The term occurs in Iamblichus, *Life of Pythagoras* 69, and Wis 5:18; 18:15. In Rom 12:9 and 2 Cor 6:6, Paul speaks of "unhypocritical love" (*agapē anupokritos*), while the same "sincere faith" is ascribed to the delegate himself in 2 Tim 1:5. For other early Christian uses of *anupokritos*, see James 3:17 and 1 Pet 1:22. That the expression "sincere faith" is not merely conventional here is indicated by 1 Tim 4:2, where the cauterized conscience is connected to insincere, lying speech (*en hypokrisei pseudologōn*).

6. *Missing out on these*: The personal internal qualities that produce *agapē* are what the would-be teachers have "missed the mark" on. For *astochein* (miss the mark), compare Plutarch, *On the Obsolescence of Oracles* 414F; Josephus, *Jewish War* 4:116; LXX Sir 7:19; 8:9. The word choice is particularly appropriate, since Paul has spoken of the "goal" (*telos*) of the commandment, and *astochein* suggests "missing a target." In 6:21, Paul will similarly speak of their missing the mark *peri tēn pistin* (concerning the faith; see also 2 Tim 2:18).

turned aside to foolish chatter: The verb *trepein* is used for any sort of turning (Josephus, *Antiquities* 18:87; *Letter of Aristeas* 245). The compound verb *ektrepein*, used here, has the metaphorical sense of turning away from something toward something else (Epictetus, *Discourses* 1.6.42; Philo, *Special Laws* 2:23). In this case, it is a turning aside *eis tēn mataiologian* (toward foolish speech). The noun *mataiologia* is found only here in Paul, although it is attested in Plutarch, *The Education of Children* 9 (*Mor.* 6F). Paul is clearly comfortable, though, with other language involving "foolishness" (Rom 1:21; 8:20; 1 Cor 3:20; 15:17). The characterization of opponents' speech as empty chatter is fairly standard in the polemic used by ancient philosophers (e.g., Lucian, *Zeus Rants* 27; *Timon* 9; *Hermotimus* 79; *Icaromenippus* 11; *Philosophies for Sale* 20–23; Epictetus, *Discourses* 2.1.31; 17.26).

7. *They want to be teachers of law*: The use of *thelein* (wish to be) is important: they want to be something they are not. They are therefore identified as intellectual imposters. The term *nomodidaskalos* is attested otherwise in the NT only by Luke, who uses it as equivalent to a scribe in Luke 5:17, and for a leader of the Pharisees (Gamaliel) in Acts 5:34. This is the sort of coincidence of diction that supports theories of Lukan involvement in the writing of these letters.[310] It is by no means clear, however, that Paul has in view Jewish teachers within the community or Jewish rivals outside the community. It is important to keep the portrait of the opponents in each of the letters separate. In Titus, it is clear that the opponents are "from the circumcision party" and that they advance a purity program based in Torah (Tit 1:10, 14–16; 3:9). The portrayal in 1 Timothy is less sharp. Nevertheless, the absolute construction *ho nomos* in 1:8 would

---

310. Wilson, *Luke and the Pastoral Letters*.

seem to suggest that the Law of Moses is meant (compare Rom 2:14–15, 20; 3:19; 7:7; 1 Cor 9:8; 14:21; Gal 3:10, 12).

understanding . . . speaking: It is good form in ancient polemic to insist on the ignorance of the teachers one is opposing (e.g., Dio Chrysostom, *Oration* 4:33, 37; 6:21; 70:8; Julian, *Oration* 6:181B; 7:225A). Here their ignorance includes both the things they say and the matters under discussion; the would-be teachers know neither the language nor the substance of the Law.

concerning which they insist: The verb *bebaioun* is found neither in the LXX nor in any other NT writing apart from Tit 3:8. It is an example of the diction that appears at first to be unique to the letters to Paul's delegates, but is actually comfortably at home in wider Koine usage. In the active voice, it means to "confirm something" (Diogenes Laertius, *Lives of Eminent Philosophers* 8:70). In the middle voice—as here—it means to "affirm or assert strongly" (Aristotle, *Rhetoric* 1389B; *Letter to Aristeas* 99; Sextus Empiricus, *Outlines of Pyrrhonism* 1:191; Josephus, *Against Apion* 2:14). It is also used by Polybius in the sense of being positive *peri tinos* (about something, *Histories* 12.12.6). The usage in Tit 3:8, "concerning these things I want you to insist," confirms the translation given here.

8. *We know that the law is good*: Nothing is more characteristic of Paul than such corrective cognitive language (for *oidamen*, "we know," see Rom 2:2; 3:19; 7:14; 8:22, 28; 1 Cor 8:1, 4; 2 Cor 5:1 [with *gar*]). The contrast with the ignorance of the would-be teachers is deliberate and emphatic, but the apparent wordplay in 1:8–10 makes a precise rendering difficult. Punning on the word *nomos* is something of a habit with Paul (e.g., Rom 2:14; 3:27, 31; 7:23; 8:2). This first part of the statement is, in any case, thoroughly Pauline in character. Paul says in Rom 7:12: "the law [*nomos*] is holy [*hagia*] and the commandment [*entolē*] is holy [*hagia*] and righteous [*dikaia*] and good [*agathē*]." In Rom 7:14, he says further: "the law [*nomos*] is spiritual [*pneumatikos*]." And in a statement virtually identical to this one, he says in Rom 7:16: "I agree that the law [*nomos*] is good [*kalos*]." As always, the adjective *kalos* has resonances beyond the merely moral good (*agathos*), including a range of possible nuances from beautiful to noble. In this case, the approbation of the Law is not absolute, for its quality as *kalos* is dependent on its right employment.

if anyone uses it appropriately: The conditional clause sets limits on how the *nomos* is good. But what does the clause say? The phrase "if anyone uses it" is itself difficult: *chraomai* has as wide a range of meanings as the English word "use." See, for example, Sextus Empiricus, *Outline of Pyrrhonism* 1:191, for "use" in the linguistic sense, and 1 Tim 5:23, where Paul's advice to "use a little wine" is equivalent to "drink" (for the range of NT usage, compare Acts 27:3, 17; 1 Cor 7:21, 31; 9:12, 15; 2 Cor 1:17; 3:12; 13:10). Paul could mean "if anyone follows it (as a guide to behavior)" or "if anyone applies it (as a measure of behavior)." That leaves the problem of what he means by the term *nomimōs*. The adverb has the literal sense of "lawfully," but it appears nowhere else in the NT apart from 2 Tim 2:5, where it clearly means "by the rules." In Plato, *Symposium* 182A, the adverb has the sense of "naturally" or "appropriately." In this verse, Paul objects to those who seek to make the Law replace conscience as a guide to behavior. It fits, therefore, to translate as "appropriately," with the following verses spelling out what Paul means by "appropriately."

9. *We understand this*: The perfect/present participle *eidōs* is adverbial, functioning as an explanatory clause to the statement "we know . . .": the reason we know that the Law is good if it is used appropriately is *touto* (this fact). I seek the equivalent effect in English by the use of an independent sentence. Although Paul uses the participle *eidotes* very frequently in just this kind of explanatory clause (Rom 5:3; 6:9; 1 Cor 15:58; 2 Cor 1:7; 4:14; 5:6, 11; Gal 2:16; Eph 6:8, 9; Phil 1:16; Col 3:24; 1 Thess 1:4), the form *eidōs* is found in only the letters to his delegates (2 Tim 2:23; 3:14; Tit 3:11). Paul appeals to an understanding shared with his reader.

not laid down: Here is another wordplay. Paul contrasts *keimai* in this verse and *antikeimai* in verse 10. The verb in verse 10 (*antikeitai*) clearly means "oppose/stand against," so that Paul can contrast the sickness of the wicked people and the health presented by the good news. The translation of *keitai* in this verse, however, is more difficult. The verb *keimai* means literally "to be laid down/lie" (Homer, *Odyssey* 11:577), and from that usage comes to mean "to be situated" (Herodotus, *Persian War* 5:49). The verb is also used specifically for "established laws" (Euripides, *Hecuba* 292; Xenophon, *Memorabilia* 4.4.21). In the NT, the verb has its literal sense in Matt 3:10, 28:6, and Luke 2:12, but is used metaphorically in 1 Cor 3:11; 2 Cor 3:15; Phil 1:16; 1 Thess 3:3. The COMMENT takes up further what Paul means by stating that Law is not "established for/laid against" a righteous person.

for a righteous person: The term *dikaios* is an adjective used substantively, as are so many other words in this passage. It occurs only here in 1 Timothy. Does Paul use it in its general meaning of "just" (Josephus, *Antiquities* 15:106; Acts 4:19) or "innocent" (Luke 23:47), as he does in Rom 5:7; Phil 1:7; 4:8; 2 Tim 4:8; Tit 1:8? Or, since the topic concerns law (*nomos*), should we read *dikaios* within the framework of Paul's forensic language on righteousness (*dikaiosynē*) before God (e.g., Rom 1:17; 3:21; 4:5; 5:17; 6:13; 8:10; 10:3, 5; Gal 2:21; 3:21; Phil 3:6; Tit 3:5), in which "righteousness in law" (Phil 3:6) is contrasted to "righteousness through faith" (Rom 1:17)? See the COMMENT.

lawless and . . . reckless: With these words, Paul begins a vice-list, a common instrument of the rhetoric of moral instruction in antiquity.[311] Compare the vice-list in Rom 1:29–31, which has twenty-two items, including seven NT and one Pauline *hapax*. This one has fourteen terms, of which five are NT and three are Pauline *hapax*, and one term found only in the letters to Paul's delegates. One might compare also the vice-list in 1 Cor 6:9, which has ten terms, only one of which also appears in Rom 1:29–31, but two of which (*pornoi, arsenokoitoi*) are found also in the list in this verse. The principle of selection of the terms in-

---

311. N. J. McEleny, "The Vice-Lists of the Pastoral Epistles," *CBQ* 36 (1974): 203–219; J. T. Fitzgerald, "Virtue/Vice Lists," in *The Anchor Bible Dictionary* (New York: Doubleday, 1992), 6:857–859.

cluded in some lists is more obvious than that in others. In this case, the first two terms are, in effect, synonyms for not being controlled by moral norms. The rest of the terms follow the basic lines of the Ten Commandments (Exod 20:2–17; Deut 5:6–21), in the sequence of the MT ("kill, adultery, steal") rather than that of the LXX ("adultery, steal, kill"). The "lawless" (*anomoi*) are literally "without law," but the designation suggests someone unconstrained by moral norms (Herodotus, *Persian War* 1:144, 162). The usage here is similar to that in 2 Thess 2:8 and to the employment of *anomia* (lawlessness) in Rom 6:19; 2 Cor 6:14; Tit 2:14, rather than the sense of being literally "outside the law" (as Gentiles are) in 1 Cor 9:21. The moral sense is frequent in the LXX (e.g., Pss 50:3; 64:3; 72:3; 103:35; Isa 53:12). Similarly, *anupotaktos* means literally "not in submission/not in order" (Heb 2:8). It can be used positively, as when Epictetus uses it for the independent person (*Discourses* 2.10.1; 4.1.161; see also Philo, *Who Is the Heir* 4; Josephus, *Antiquities* 11:217). But it also means "undisciplined/rebellious," as here and twice in Titus (1:6, 10).

godless and . . . sinners: The translation of *asebēs* as "godless" must be understood not as meaning someone who is "without god," but as indicating someone who acts impiously or blasphemously toward a god (Xenophon, *Memorabilia* 1.1.16; Xenophon, *Cyropaedia* 8.8.27; Josephus, *Antiquities* 8:251; Philo, *Who Is the Heir* 90). It appears frequently in the LXX with reference to those opposed to the righteous (Ps 1:1, 4, 5, 6; Prov 1:7, 10, 22, 32). The adjective is used substantively (as here) also by Paul in Rom 4:5 and 5:6. In 2 Tim 2:16, the noun *asebeia* characterizes false teachers, and in Tit 2:12, it indicates the condition or state from which people convert. Both instances match rather well Paul's use of *asebeia* in Rom 1:18 and 11:26. The term "sinner" (*hamartōlos*) appears in Greco-Roman literature for someone who errs (Aristotle, *Nicomachean Ethics* 1109A; Philodemus, *On Anger* 73; Plutarch, *On the Study of Poetry* 7 [*Mor.* 25C]). It is used frequently in the LXX and in the NT for those who do wrong in the sight of God or who fit into the category of those who so act (LXX Gen 13:13; Pss 3:7; 7:9; 9:17; 36:12, 14; Sir 1:24). Note, in particular, the combination of *hamartōloi* and *asebeis* in LXX Ps 1:1, 5. In the NT, see Luke 5:32; 13:2; 24:7. Apart from this chapter of 1 Timothy (see the NOTE on 1:15), Paul uses the term sparingly (Rom 3:7; 5:19; 7:13; Gal 2:15, 17). But note the important combination of the words "sinner" and "godless" in Rom 5:6, 8.

unholy and . . . profane: The second two terms of this vice-list, "godless" and "sinners," correspond to the first commandments of the Decalogue. These two may well fit the commandments dealing with taking the name of the Lord in vain and keeping holy the sabbath (Exod 20:7–8; Deut. 5:11–15). "Unholy" (*anosios*) can be found in contrast to *dikaios* (see Aeschylus, *Seven Against Thebes* 605–611; Josephus, *Jewish War* 6:399; *Against Apion* 2:201; 2 Macc 7:34; 8:32; 4 Macc 12:11; *Letter to Aristeas* 289; *Wis* 12:4). In the NT, the combination of *anosios* and *adikos* appears only here and in 2 Tim 3:2. "Profane" (*bebēlos*) is found in Greco-Roman texts in the sense of common or not holy, as in Philo Mechanicus, *Belopoieca* 2:165 (fragments), which combines *anosios* and *bebēlos*; in the NT, see also Heb 12:16. In LXX Lev 10:10, *hoi bebēloi* are contrasted to *hoi hagioi* (see also 1 Sam 21:4; 2 Macc 5:16). In Ezek 21:25, *bebēlos* is synoymous with *anomos*. In 3 Macc 2:2, *anosios* and *bebēlos* are used to characterize the king who persecutes the Jews. The connection with sabbath observance is established by the verb form *bebelooun* in Exod 31:14, used explicitly for "profaning the sabbath day," a usage echoed by Matt 12:5. The term is not found in the Pauline literature apart from 2 Tim 2:16 and 1 Timothy (1:9; 4:7 [with reference to myths]; 6:20 [with reference to empty speech]).

kill fathers, . . . mothers . . . murderers: Each of these words represents an extreme violation of the commandment not to kill; none of them occurs elsewhere in Paul or the NT, but each fits within the wider Koine. Spelled *patraloias*, the first term appears in Aristophanes, *The Clouds* 911, 1327; Plato, *Phaedo* 114A; Josephus, *Antiquities* 16:356. Marcus Aurelius lists the parricide among the worst of possible moral offenders (*Meditations* 6:34). The mother-killer (*matralōas* = Attic, *matraloias*) appears in Aristophanes, *Eumenides* 153, 210; is given recognition and definition in Plato, *Laws* 881A; and is found also in Lucian, *Assembly of the Gods* 12. The two terms appear together in Plato, *Phaedo* 114A. The noun *androphonia* (manslaying) occurs in Aristotle, *Nicomachean Ethics* 1107A. In Pindar, *Pythian Odes* 4:252, it is a term applied to women who kill their husbands. In Plato, *Phaedo* 114A, it refers to simply a murderer. It should be noted that in 2 Macc 9:28, the wicked king Antiochus is termed *androphonos* and blasphemer, and in 4 Macc 9:15, the word is combined with "godless."

10. *fornicators, sexual perverts*: These sexual offenses correspond to the commandment of the Decalogue not to commit adultery. If *pornos* is accented on the second syllable, it frequently refers to a brothel keeper (Aristotle, *Nicomachean Ethics* 1121B); when accented on the first syllable (Nestle–Aland), it can refer to homosexual activity (Xenophon, *Memorabilia* 1.6.13; Demosthenes, *Epistle* 4:11). In the LXX and in the NT, the term is used for the sexually immoral without specific reference to homosexuality (LXX Sir 23:16–18; 1 Cor 5:9–11; 6:9; Eph 5:5). The translation "sexual pervert" for *arsenokoitos* is not particularly appealing, but there is no reasonable alternative for a term that means literally "one who sleeps with [=has sexual congress with] men." The verbal form is found in *Sibylline Oracles* 2:73, and the substantive in *The Greek Anthology* 9:686. In 1 Cor 6:9, Paul combines this word with *malakoi*, which generally means "soft" and is used by Aristotle for one who lacks moral self-control (*Nicomachean Ethics* 1150A). There is no need to belabor the obvious point that the classification of same-sex intercourse among vices is characteristic of the Paul of the undisputed letters as well (Rom 1:24–27; 1 Cor 6:9–11). The issue in regard to such texts and the present-day struggle of communities with homosexuality is not so much an exegetical as a hermeneutical one.[312]

slave dealers: The term "slave dealer" (*andrapodistēs*) has the specific sense of "selling into slavery" free men who are captured in war (Herodotus, *Persian War*

---

312. L. T. Johnson, *Scripture and Discernment: Decision Making in the Church* (Nashville, Tenn.: Abingdon Press, 1996).

1:151; Plato, *Republic* 344B). It can also be used for a kidnapper (Xenophon, *Memorabilia* 4.2.14). It is a dramatic example of breaking the commandment of the Decalogue against stealing, since it is the very freedom of a person that is taken away.

liars, perjurers: The inclusion of these specific vices is best explained by reference to the Decalogue, which forbids bearing false witness: *ou pseudomartyrēseis kata tēn plēsion sou martyrian pseudē* (you shall not give false testimony against your neighbor, LXX Exod 20:16; Deut 5:20). The term "liar" (*pseustēs*) applies to one speaking untruth in any circumstance (Homer, *Iliad* 24:261; Herodotus, *Persian War* 7:209; Aristotle, *Nicomachean Ethics* 1127B; LXX Sir 15:8; 25:2; Ps 115:2; *Sibylline Oracles* 2:257); Paul uses the word again in Rom 3:4 and Tit 1:12. The perjurer lies under oath; the verb *epiorkein* means to "swear falsely" (Plato, *Laws* 948D). Note that Matt 5:33, *ouk epiorkēseis* (you shall not swear falsely), cites LXX Lev 19:12. The substantive often refers to that which has falsely been sworn (Homer, *Iliad* 3:279). When used of persons, it applies to the one who has committed perjury (Aristophanes, *The Clouds* 399; Philo, *On the Decalogue* 88; LXX Zach 5:3; *Wis* 14:25 [also in a vice-list]).

whatever else is opposed to: The summative phrase *ei ti heteron* (literally, "if anything else") is a shift to the impersonal, and reminds us that this has been less a vice-list than a catalogue of persons who act according to various vices. The verb *antikeimai* corresponds to the use of *keimai* in 1:9: the Law was "not established for/laid against," and these vices "oppose/lie against" the healthy teaching of the gospel. Generally, *antikeimai* is used to contrast two things (Plato, *Sophist* 258B; Aristotle, *Metaphysics* 1055A; Josephus, *Jewish War* 4:454). The participle can also have the more active sense of "opposing/being an enemy" (LXX Exod 23:22; 2 Macc 10:26; Luke 13:17; 21:15) and is used this way by Paul in 1 Cor 16:9; Phil 1:28; 2 Thess 2:4, as well as in 1 Tim 5:14. The use here is closer to that in Gal 5:17, where Paul says of the flesh and the spirit: *tauta gar allēlois antikeitai* (for these things lie opposed to each other).

the healthy teaching: As so often in the Pauline correspondence, diction concerning teaching is unevenly distributed. The three letters to Paul's delegates display a rich use of such language: *didaskalos* (teacher) in 1 Tim 2:7; 2 Tim 1:11; 4:3; *didaskein* (to teach) in 1 Tim 2:12; 4:11; 6:2; 2 Tim 2:2; Tit 1:11; *didachē* (teaching) in 2 Tim 4:2; Tit 1:9; *didaskalia* (teaching) in 1 Tim 1:10; 4:1, 6, 13, 16; 5:17; 6:1, 3; 2 Tim 3:10, 16; 4:3; Tit 1:9; 2:1, 7, 10. In all, there are twenty-five instances in these three letters. Paul employs such language otherwise in only six other letters, amounting to twenty-two uses: *didaskalos* in Rom 2:20; 1 Cor 12:28, 29; *didaskein* in Rom 2:21; 12:7; 1 Cor 4:17; 11:14; Gal 1:12; 2 Thess 2:15; Col 1:28; 2:7; 3:16; Eph 4:21; *didachē* in Rom 6:17; 16:17; 1 Cor 14:6, 26; *didaskalia* in Rom 12:7; 15:4; Col 2:22; Eph 4:14. The fact that these letters are written to delegates whose main function is to represent Paul's teachings in the community (1 Cor 4:17) makes the proportionately higher use intelligible. More striking is the use of "healthy" as a modifier of teaching, something that is not found in any Pauline letters except the Pastorals: *hygiēs* appears in Tit 2:8, and the attributive participle of *hygiainein* in 1 Tim 1:10; 6:3; 2 Tim

1:13; 4:3; Tit 1:9, 13; 2:1, 2. Here is a case in which the medical metaphor dominating ancient moral discourse is abundantly evident.[313] The verb *hygiainein* referred first to physical conditions of well-being (Plato, *Gorgias* 495E; Aristotle, *Metaphysics* 1032B; Herodotus, *Persian War* 1:153). It extended to include soundness of mind (Aristophanes, *The Clouds* 1275) and political affairs (Herodotus, *Persian War* 7:157). But by the time of Paul, it was used widely both for conditions of virtue and for the teaching that cultivated such conditions, among both Greco-Roman moral teachers (Plutarch, *On the Study of Poetry* 4 [*Mor.* 20F]; Herodotus, *Persian War* 1:153; Maximus of Tyre, *Discourses* 36:5a; Epictetus, *Discourses* 1.12.4; 12.5; 3.9.5) and Hellenistic Jewish moralists (Philo, *On Abraham* 223; *Special Laws* 2:164; *Letter of Aristeas* 250; Josephus, *Against Apion* 1:222).

11. *accords with the glorious good news*: This is the only time *euangelion* occurs in 1 Timothy, but it appears in 2 Tim 1:8, 10; 2:8. The preposition *kata* + the accusative means "according to" and can suggest both "as deriving from" and "as measured by"; the translation tries to capture something of both possibilities. That the gospel is both the source of and the norm for Christian teaching is not foreign to the Paul of the other letters (e.g., Rom 15:16; 1 Cor 9:14; 2 Cor 9:13; Gal 2:7), and the expression "according to my gospel" (*kata to euangelion mou*) occurs in Rom 2:16 and 16:25. The attachment of *tēs doxēs* is, however, unusual. The closest parallel construction is James 2:1, which presents the same problems for translation. Here, as there, the genitive should probably be taken as adjectival, thus rendering "glorious gospel." Although the *doxa* of God and of the Messiah is pervasively attested in Paul (e.g., Rom 1:23; 3:23; 1 Cor 2:8; 2 Cor 3:18; 4:6), he never elsewhere connects *doxa* to the gospel itself. The employment of *doxa* in 1 Tim 1:17 and 3:16 is closer to other Pauline usage.

from the blessed God: As in other places where *euangelion tou theou* appears, the genitive may be read both subjectively and objectively (e.g., Rom 1:1; 15:16; 1 Thess 2:2, 8, 9). It is at once good news from God and good news about or concerning God that Paul announces. The epithet *makarios* (blessed/happy) is used frequently by Greco-Roman authors for the gods (Aristotle, *Nicomachean Ethics* 1178B; Diogenes Laertius, *Lives of Eminent Philosophers* 10:123) and is even applied to God by Hellenistic Jewish writers (Philo, *On the Cherubim* 86; *On the Immutability of God* 26; Josephus, *Against Apion* 2:190). It is not found elsewhere in Paul or the other NT writings, apart from its reappearance in 1 Tim 6:15.

with which I have been entrusted: The phrase *ho episteuthēn egō* may seem at first typical of the letters to Paul's delegates, since it appears also in Tit 1:3. But compare Rom 3:2, where Paul says of the Jews: "they have been entrusted with the oracles of God" (*episteuthēsan ta logia tou theou*). Even more strikingly, in Gal 2:7, he says that the Jerusalem leadership recognized that "I had been entrusted with the gospel of the uncircumcision" (*pepisteumai to euangelion tēs akrobustias*), and most strikingly in 1 Cor 9:17: "I have been entrusted with a management/ordering" (*oikonomian pepisteumai*).

COMMENT

If, in fact, 1 Timothy is a *mandata principis* letter that provides Paul's delegates with his "marching orders" during his absence from the Ephesian church, then this first section of the composition—which seems so jumbled in comparison with some other Pauline letters—appears in a new light and with clearer purpose. Without pausing for a thanksgiving (compare Galatians), Paul addresses immediately the most pressing issue facing the community: the presence of elitist and intellectual members who seek to impose heteronomous norms on the community of faith. Each part of the section addresses that issue, in slightly different ways:

1. 1:3–4a characterizes the "other teaching" of the opponents in terms of intellectual inquisitiveness.
2. 1:4b–5 establishes the "goal of the commandment" in terms of interior dispositions.
3. 1:6–7 more fully identifies the opponents as those seeking to be teachers of Law.
4. 1:8–11 clarifies the role of Law from the perspective of the good news.
5. 1:12–17 expresses through personal thanksgiving the basis of life as gift rather than accomplishment, an example for all who have faith.
6. 1:18–19a restates the commission of the delegate in terms of interior dispositions.
7. 1:19b–20 refers to excommunication of specific troublemakers "for their education."

This analysis suggests that the central part of the section—the discussion of Law and the account of Paul's conversion (1:8–17)—be seen as the conceptual issue implicit in the political struggle reflected in the passages preceding and following it. Paul and his delegate are engaged in a "noble battle" (*kalē strateia*, 1:18) that involves real human persons, but also the fundamental principles by which this community lives.

Two Measures of Life

As always in situations in which Paul characterizes opponents, it is important to distinguish, as far as we are able, between the conventions of ancient rhetoric and the actual attitudes or practices of the persons with whom he is dealing. Since stereotypical slander is even more prevalent in 2 Timothy than 1 Timothy, a fuller discussion of it can be found there. For understanding this passage, we can take it as likely that Paul's references to "myths and genealogies" (1:4), "foolish chatter" (1:6), and speaking of things without understanding them (1:7) fall into the category of such standard polemical language. Certainly, it can be demonstrated that these are typical polemical *topoi* (see the NOTES). While it is possible that Paul himself—or his opponents—had something definite in mind by "myths and genealogies," it is safer not to build too much on such suppositions.

Characterizations that combine to form a consistent portrait are that they "teach otherly" (*heterodidaskalein*, 1:3), that they give themselves to speculations or investigations (*ekzēteseis*, 1:4), and that they "want to be teachers of law" (*nomodidaskaloi,* 1:7). Although the expression "teaching otherly" may appear at once obvious and unilluminating, it is helpful to remember that it enables us to locate the point of Paul's own position/doctrine. We can take it that the opponents' desire to teach Law to Christian communities is the central point of contention, for that is the issue taken up for specific refutation in 1:8–11. If we can determine more clearly what is problematic for Paul about that ambition, we shall have better access to his own position; likewise, the more sharply we can delineate Paul's understanding, the better we can grasp his objection to the Law as he perceives them advocating it.

We can begin with Paul's position. He complains that the opponents encourage speculations (or perhaps, disputes) rather than "faithful attention to God's way of ordering things" (1:4). I have gone into this thematic statement at some length in the INTRODUCTION and refer the reader to that discussion. For the present, I simply emphasize the point that the activity in question is God's. The *oikonomia* with which Paul is concerned is not a matter of "human management," but of divine economy. In addition, I point to the important role played by the phrase *en pistei*; whether it refers to the ordering itself or, as my translation suggests, to the way of perceiving and appropriating that ordering, it establishes *faith* as the fundamental principle for the community's existence.

Paul then elaborates the "aim of the commandment" in 1:5. Once more, careful attention is required to grasp the import. The *parangelia* (commandment) Paul refers to is the same divine ordering, considered as mandate. It is, in short, the position that Paul represents, which is that of the gospel. Note that the phrase *kata to euangelion tēs doxēs tou makariou theou* (according to the glorious good news from the blessed God) in 1:11 forms an interpretive bracket with the *parangelia* (commandment) in 1:5. What, then, is its *telos*? It is not mental inquiry or intellectual elitism or moral monitoring—all of which are conjured by the desire to be "teachers of law" (we can hear echoes of Paul's quick sketch of the boasting available to those who are the propagators of Torah in Rom 2:17–21). The *telos* of Paul's commandment is, simply, love (*agapē*, 1:5). We have now two oppositions: on one side, law and elitism; on the other, faith and love. With very short and deft strokes, Paul has in effect established the same contrast that dominates his Letter to the Galatians (Gal 2:15–21; 5:13–24). If we were allowed to read this passage in light of other Pauline statements on *agapē*, we would be able to see here an allusion to the ideal of self-donative service for others that Paul consistently advances as the antidote to divisive and elitist attitudes (Gal 5:6, 13; 5:21–6:2; 1 Cor 8:1–3; 13:1–13; Phil 2:1–3).

When in Galatians Paul lists the fruit of the spirit, he begins with *agapē* and then continues with other qualities, such as peace, long-suffering, sweetness, goodness, and faith. And he concludes, "against things such as these there is no law" (Gal 5:22–23). The reason is that all these qualities are internal dispositions that are expressed in actions in regard to others; they are both autonomous (deriving from within the self) and relational (expressed with and toward other humans). And because of the constantly shifting and complex character of human interactions, it is impossible to fix appropriate interpersonal responses within the frame of a law. It is of the essence of love to function by way of discernment—that is, inductively and responsively—rather than by way of law—that is, deductively and by a priori.

That Paul here understands *agapē* in the same fashion is underscored by the qualifying phrases he adds. This love is to derive from "a pure heart, and a good conscience, and a sincere faith" (1:5). These are all internal dispositions. Paul proposes a guide to behavior, then, that is based in a certain kind of character. It is faith and conscience and the heart that lead to the moral expressions of love, but only if they are sincere and good and pure. A person living this way is "a righteous person" (*dikaios*, 1:9), is one who lives by "the healthy teaching that accords with the glorious good news" (1:11). Note that Paul says it is because certain people are "missing out on these" that they have turned aside to their investigations and pretensions concerning the Law (1:6). It is fundamental to his understanding that "the law is not laid down for a righteous person" (1:9). As Paul said concerning the fruit of the spirit: "against such things as this there is no law" (Gal 5:22–23). Christian moral life is essentially autonomous rather than heteronomous, is measured by internal rather than external norms, is a character rather than a rule ethic.

The Law Used Lawfully

It is from such a perspective that we must try to understand Paul's punning comment that "the law [*nomos*] is good if anyone uses it *nomimōs* [literally, "lawfully"]. I have translated the adverb *nomimōs* as "appropriately" because Paul seems to mean that the use of the Law must be placed precisely within the framework I have just sketched. It would be used "inappropriately" or "not according to the rules" if it were to be "laid down for a righteous person" as an adequate guide to behavior. Paul has already excluded that, by showing how *agapē* derives from internal resources and criteria. It remains to see what its "appropriate" use might be.

We can begin by trying to define what is included by the term *nomos* in this instance. Paul, as we know, is not always clear on this important point; his use of *nomos* language is notoriously fluid and frequently confusing. In one circumstance, *nomos* can appear to refer specifically to commandment (*entolē*,

Rom 7:8); at another time, it can mean the entire narrative texture of Torah (Rom 3:31; 10:4); at still another time, it can mean something like "principle" (Rom 3:27). In this case—the only time in the Pastorals that *nomos* occurs—Paul seems to be thinking of Law in the sense of moral commandments rather than the entire spectrum of biblical legislation or of the biblical story.[314] Thus all the characteristics listed are moral vices. As the NOTES indicate in detail, there is also strong reason to think that the organizing principle of the vice-list in 1:9–10 is the Decalogue (Exod 20:2–17; Deut 5:6–21) according to the sequence in the Hebrew (MT) rather than in the Greek (LXX) translation: thus "kill, adultery, steal," rather than "adultery, steal, kill."

The vice-list is fascinating most of all for two things: its extravagance, and its listing of types of persons rather than of sins. First, it almost appears as though Paul wanted to cite the most extreme example of lawlessness he could find in each category. Thus under "You shall not kill," he has "people who kill fathers, who kill mothers, who are murderers"; rather than the straightforward "adultery," he lists "people who are fornicators, sexual perverts"; rather than simple stealing, he has "slave dealers." Second, the listing of vice-filled persons indicates that Paul is thinking consistently in terms of a character-ethic; the shift to "whatever else" at the end of the list is an awkward transition from people to categories.

These two clues enable us to approach the sense of the passage, although its full function becomes apparent only when read together with 1:12–17. The basic sense, I think, is that the Law—particularly the moral code embedded in the Decalogue—has a limited usefulness, and therefore must be used "appropriately." It can identify behaviors that are "against healthy teaching" (1:10), by leading to personal and social destruction. But it cannot adequately encompass the behaviors that express *agapē* as a positive response to God and other persons. And it certainly cannot empower such responses; those must come from interior dispositions (1:5), and such dispositions—Paul will argue next—are empowered by God's gift of mercy (1:12–17).

It is useless to ask whether this statement on *nomos* is genuinely Pauline, for the simple reason that Paul's range of expressions concerning the Law elsewhere is so broad. The sentiments here given expression, however, are certainly within Paul's repertoire: the conviction that the Law can prescribe but cannot empower is at the heart of Paul's discussion in Rom 7:7–8:5, and the position that *agapē* toward the neighbor is the ultimate norm that "summarizes" the entire *nomos* is expressed clearly in Rom 13:8–10. The reader will also remember that both Augustine and Luther found in this passage the heart of Paul's understanding on the subject.

---

314. Note that he cites Deut 25:4 as authoritative *graphē* in 1 Tim 5:18 and alludes to Deut 19:15 in 1 Tim 5:19.

III. Thanks For Empowering
Mercy (1:12–17)

◆

1 ¹²I give thanks to the one who has empowered me, Christ Jesus our Lord, for he has considered me faithful by putting me into service. ¹³I was earlier a blasphemer. I was a persecutor. I was an insolent person. But I was shown mercy because in ignorance I acted with faithlessness. ¹⁴And the gift of our Lord with the faith and love that are in Christ Jesus was extravagant. ¹⁵This saying is reliable and worthy of all acceptance, that Christ Jesus came into the world to save sinners. I am the first among them! ¹⁶But I was shown mercy for this reason, that Christ Jesus might demonstrate all possible forbearance in me first, as an example for those who would come to believe in him unto eternal life. ¹⁷To the king of the ages, to the immortal, invisible, only God, be honor and glory for ever and ever. Amen.

NOTES

12. *I give thanks*: The construction *charin echō* (I give thanks) is a common idiom in Greco-Roman literature. It is used for thanks between people, as in Plato, *Philebus* 54D, and Epictetus, *Discourse* 3.5.10; it can be used also to express thanks to the gods, as in Josephus, *Antiquities* 4:316; 7:208, and Epictetus, *Discourse* 4.7.9. Only here and in 2 Tim 1:3 does it appear as part of a Pauline thanksgiving period. The closest equivalent in the undisputed letters is Paul's expostulation "Thanks be to God" (*tō de theō charis*) in Rom 6:17; 7:25; 1 Cor 15:57. Some MSS (Codex Bezae and the Koine MS tradition) add the conjunction *kai* in the beginning of this sentence, thereby establishing a closer connection to the previous sentence.

the one who has empowered me: The verb *endynamoun* is found in some MSS of Judg 6:34 and 1 Chron 12:19, but is not widely attested outside the NT, where it is clearly a favorite Pauline term (Rom 4:20; Eph 6:10; Phil 4:13; 2 Tim 2:1; 4:17). Some MSS have the present tense of the participle (*endounamounti*) here (see the original hand of Sinaiticus, 33, a few more Greek witnesses, and the Sahidic), rather than the aorist tense (*endounamōsanti*), which is translated here and is found in the vast majority of Greek MSS and versions. The difference would be to put an emphasis on the resurrected Christ's *continuing* empowerment of Paul rather than a past strengthening. Perhaps the variant derived from

177

the strikingly similar Phil 4:13; "I am able to do all things in the one who empowers me" (*panta ischuō en tō endunamounti me*).[315]

considered me faithful: For *hēgēsthai* as a calculation or reckoning—another Pauline favorite—see 2 Cor 9:5; Phil 2:3, 6, 25; 3:7, 8; 1 Thess 5:13; 2 Thess 3:15. It reappears in 1 Tim 6:1. For Paul's self-designation as *pistos* (faithful), see, especially, 1 Cor 4:2 and 7:25.

putting me into service: The translation takes the predicative participle as specifying *how* Christ has empowered Paul. The participle *themenos* (from *tithemi*) is used here for a commissioning precisely as it is in 2 Cor 5:19. Paul refers to his ministry as a service (*diakonia*) also in Rom 11:13; 15:31; 2 Cor 3:7–9; 4:1; 5:18, and calls himself a *diakonos* in 1 Cor 3:5; 2 Cor 3:6; 6:4; Col 1:23. Note how Paul speaks of his experience here as the equivalent of a "call"—that is, being put into ministry or service, like the prophets of the OT.

13. *I was earlier a blasphemer*: The neuter comparative adjective *proteros* with the definite article means "once" or "formerly" (Xenophon, *Memorabilia* 3.8.1). The substantive adjective *blasphēmos* (blasphemer) is a Pauline *hapax*, although he does use the verb form *blasphēmein* in Rom 2:24; 3:8; 14:16; 1 Cor 10:30. The verb *blasphēmein* means to "slander or revile someone" (Philo, *Special Laws* 4:197; Josephus, *Life* 232). When such reviling is directed at a divine being, then it is "blasphemy" in the commonly understood sense (Diodorus Siculus, *Library of History* 2.21.7; Josephus, *Antiquities* 4:207). For the use of *blasphēmos*, see Dio Chrysostom, *Oration* 3:53; LXX Wis. 1:6; Sir. 3:16. The usage in 2 Macc 9:28 is particularly instructive since it is applied to Antiochus IV, the persecutor of the people; see also the epithet applied to all the enemies of the Jews in 2 Macc 10:36.

I was a persecutor: Paul does not otherwise use the substantive *diōktēs*, and it does not appear in secular literature either. It does appear in Symmachus's translation of Hos 6:8. We find "persecutor of the good" in *Didache* 5:2 and *Barnabas* 20:2. Paul does, however, use the verb *diōkein* for his persecution of the church before his encounter with Jesus (1 Cor 15:9; Phil 3:6; Gal 1:13), as does Acts (9:4, 5; 22:4, 7–8; 26:11, 14, 15). The depth of Paul's feelings about his past life—reflected also in this passage—can be gained from 1 Cor 15:9: "For I am the least of the apostles. I am not worthy to be called apostle, because I persecuted the church of God."

an insolent person: The word *hybris* refers to an attitude that combines insolence and arrogance, causing a person to overreach even into God's business (Philo, *Special Laws* 3:186; Josephus, *Antiquities* 6:61). The combination of *hybristēs* and *hyperēphanos* (arrogant person) is found in Diodorus Siculus, *Library of History* 5.55.6; Aristotle, *Rhetoric* 1390B; Rom 1:30.

I was shown mercy: The importance of this statement is indicated by the repeated use of *eleēthēn* in 1:16. The showing of mercy or pity has a note of condescension that reflects the power imbalance between a master and a servant (Achilles Tatius, *Leucippe and Clitophon* 3.5.4; Mark 5:19; 10:47), or a judge

---

315. My decision to go with the aorist rather than the present tense agrees with Metzger, *Textual Commentary*, 639, but disagrees with Elliott, *Greek Text*, 25.

and a wrongdoer (Luke 16:24). Thus a ruler may "show mercy" to the citizens of a city (Diodorus Siculus, *Library of History* 12.30.4; 20.4.6). Paul, therefore, speaks of the mercy that God can choose to show as God pleases to the earth's peoples (Rom 9:15, 16, 18; 11:30, 31): God "shut them all up in disobedience in order that he might show mercy to them all" (Rom 11:32). Paul also speaks of a much more individual granting of mercy to persons (2 Cor 4:1; Phil 2:27). The most striking parallel to this passage is 1 Cor 7:25: "I give advice as one who has been shown mercy by the Lord to be faithful" (*hos eleēmenos hypo kyriou pistos einai*).

in ignorance I acted with faithlessness: This statement is particularly important to construe correctly. At the superficial level, it seems to be an intrusion of Lukan theology, for Luke emphasizes the "ignorance" of those who put Jesus to death (Luke 23:34; Acts 3:17), while Paul appears to emphasize his moral uprightness in the time before his call to be an apostle (Gal 1:14; Phil 3:6). But, in fact, the statement is thoroughly Pauline in tone and meaning. First, the verb *apistein* and the noun *apistia* are used elsewhere by Paul as they are here — not like the adjective *apistos* as a pointer to a general state of "being an unbeliever" (compare 1 Cor 6:6; 7:12; 2 Cor 4:4; 1 Tim 5:8), but as representing an active state of "disbelief" or "failure to have faith" (Rom 3:3; 4:20; 11:20, 23). Second, Paul invokes "ignorance" (*agnoōn*) precisely with respect to that zeal for God held by Jews who cannot come to faith in the Messiah (Rom 10:3). This was his condition before his encounter with the Living Jesus.

14. *the gift of our Lord*: If *charis* generally refers to the favor or goodwill shown by someone — often superiors, sometimes the gods (Dio Chrysostom, *Oration* 30:41) — toward others, it can also mean the expression of such benevolence through benefaction or gift (Xenophon, *Symposium* 8:36; Dionysius of Halicarnassus, *Roman Antiquities* 2.15.4). The "gift of our Lord" here corresponds to "was shown mercy" in 1:13. For "the gift of our Lord," see also Rom 16:20, 24; 1 Cor 16:23; 2 Cor 8:9; 13:13; Gal 6;18; Phil 4:23; 1 Thess 5:28.

with the faith and love that are in Christ Jesus: This is awkwardly stated, but makes a critical point in Paul's argument. The awkwardness comes about because "Christ Jesus" seems to occur tautologously so soon after "gift of our Lord" (which has as its antecedent "Christ Jesus our Lord" in 1:12). But the point is that these qualities of faith (*pistis*) and love (*agapē*) — the very qualities that are associated with Paul's *parangelia* (1:5) — are the personal qualities also of Jesus; they are "in Christ Jesus." It follows that they are also his to give as a gift.

was extravagant: The verb *hyperpleonazein* is a NT *hapax*. However, Paul uses *pleonazein* several times (Rom 5:20; 6:1; 2 Cor 4:15; 8:15) and is fond of *hyper-*constructions (1 Thess 3:10; 4:6; 2 Cor 3:10; 10:14; Rom 7:13; 8:26, 37). Most pertinently, see Rom 5:20: "where sin abounded, the gift superabounded" (*hou de epleonasen hē hamartia hypereperisseusen hē charis*), and 2 Cor 4:15; "in order that the gift might abound . . . increasing to the glory of God" (*hina hē charis pleonasasa . . . perisseusē eis tēn doxan tou theou*).

15. *reliable and worthy of all acceptance*: The phrase *pistos ho logos* is distinctive of Paul's letters to the delegates (see also 3:1; 4:9; 2 Tim 2:11; Tit 3:8). The

use of *pistos* to characterize God is typical of Paul (1 Cor 1:9; 10:13; 2 Cor 1:18; 1 Thess 5:24; 2 Thess 3:3). A few Latin manuscripts, possibly operating under the influence of 3:1—where the reading also occurs—have *anthrōpinos* (human) rather than *pistos* (faithful). Paul uses *anthrōpinon legō* ("I speak in human terms") in Rom 6:19. The various possibilities concerning the phrase will be discussed for each occurrence. Overall, the issues involve the basic meaning and function of the expression, its reference (does it point forward or backward), and its connection to earlier traditions. The meaning and function are the least in dispute. The adjective *pistos* (faithful) is more or less the equivalent of *amen* in Hebrew. The phrase functions much like that in the Gospels placed in the mouth of Jesus: "Amen I say to you"; that is, it serves as a warrant or certification concerning another statement.[316] The other issues are much in debate. Ascertaining the meaning of the phrase in this verse is fairly easy, since it clearly points forward to the dictum that follows, and that dictum has roots in the gospel tradition.[317]

came into the world to save sinners: This piece of tradition echoes some passages in the Gospels, most specifically the conviction found in Luke 19:10: "The Son of Man came to seek out and find that which was lost" (see also Luke 5:32). 1 Tim 5:18 will echo even more closely another Lukan passage (10:7). And although Paul does not often use the language of "sinner" (*hamartōlos*), one instance is worth citing: "God shows his love for us in that while we were still sinners Christ died for us" (Rom 5:8). For other places where Paul connects the death of Jesus to "our" sins—including himself with the personal pronoun *hēmōn*—see 1 Cor 15:3; 2 Cor 5:21; Gal 1:4.

I am the first among them: The adjective *prōtos* does not here mean "first in a sequence," but "chief" or "foremost." Paul is not loath to make such self-deprecating remarks (e.g., 1 Cor 4:9). The most compelling example is 1 Cor 15:9; corresponding to his self-designation here as "first" among sinners is his confession there that he is "least among apostles" (*elachistos tōn apostolōn*)—and for the same reason: he persecuted the church. The extremity of Paul's sinfulness is important for the demonstration of the power of God's mercy to transform a life.

16. *shown mercy for this reason*: The *dia touto* (on account of this thing) sets up the following purpose clause; Paul draws the moral lesson from his personal experience. Note how "I was shown mercy" picks up directly from 1:13.

demonstrate all possible forbearance: The verb *endeiknumi* means to "present as a demonstration" (Xenophon, *Anabasis* 6.1.19; Plato, *Laws* 966B). Paul uses it in much the same way that he does here in Rom 2:15; 9:17; 2 Cor 8:24; see also his use of *deixis* (demonstration) in 2 Cor 8:24; Phil 1:28; and, above all, Rom 3:25: "as a demonstration of his righteousness" (*endeixis tēs dikaiosynēs*

---

316. Johnson, *Writings of the New Testament*, 124.

317. For further discussion, see G. W. Knight, III, *The Faithful Sayings in the Pastoral Letters* (Grand Rapids, Mich.: Baker Book House, 1979); J. M. A. Bover, "*Fidelis Sermo*," *Bib* 19 (1938): 74–79; J. G. Duncan, "*Pistos ho Logos*," *ExpT* 35 (1923–1924): 124; and R. A. Campbell, "Identifying the Faithful Sayings in the Pastoral Epistles," *JSNT* 54 (1994): 73–86.

autou). The word translated as "forbearance" (*makrothymia*) is particularly appropriate in this context, for it suggests that attitude of "large-mindedness" found in human judges who show leniency toward miscreants (LXX Sir 18:11; 35:19; 2 Macc 6:14; Jer 15:15; Matt 18:26, 29; Luke 18:7). For *makrothymia* as describing God's attitude toward erring humans, see, especially, Rom 2:4 and 9:22.

in me first: The *prōtos* here corresponds exactly with being the first among sinners. The greatness of the mercy is revealed best of all when shown to the most heinous of sinners.

as an example: The construction *pros hypotypōsin* expresses the goal of the demonstration of "forbearance" and mercy: Paul is to stand as an example. The term *hypotypōsis* is found in the NT only here and in 2 Tim 1:13. It is used in the sense of "sketch or outline" in Diogenes Laertius, *Lives of Eminent Philosophers* 9:78, and Sextus Empiricus, *Outlines of Pyrrhonism* 2:79—indeed, it is the title of Sextus Empiricus's work! The same meaning appears in Philo, *On Abraham* 71: a sense of the greater can be gained by seeing it "in small."[318] While unattested outside 1 and 2 Timothy, the meaning in these two instances can only be "example."

for those who would come to believe in him: The translation decision here is between "example to" and "example for." The first would make Paul a model to be imitated. The second would represent in Paul how God's mercy can work in others. I think that Paul clearly intends to say that it is God's power and grace that are exemplary, rather than any action of Paul's. Readers should be cautioned against taking "believe" in the narrow sense of confession; a stricter rendering of *pisteuein* would be "having faith." Similarly, the Greek phrase *ep' autō* is not "believe in him" in a confessional sense, but "having faith based on him" in a relational sense. The human response of obedience and trust (what Paul basically means by "faith") is the appropriate response to the gift of God shown in Christ Jesus.

unto eternal life: Although the phrase *zoē aiōnios* is relatively frequent in the letters to Paul's delegates (6:12; Tit 1:2; 3:7), it is an idiom that is well attested in Paul's other letters as well (Rom 2:7; 5:21; 6:22, 23; Gal 6:8). Its occurrence in this statement is particularly significant because of 1 Timothy's theme of "real life" (6:19) that can come from only the "living God" (3:15; 4:10) and because Paul argues that "eternal life" is available from only God, rather than from such human effort as observing laws.

17. *To the king of the ages*: The title *basileus* refers functionally to the one holding highest power in any sphere, and thus can easily be applied to God (e.g., Dio Chrysostom, *Oration* 2:75; Plutarch, *Isis and Osiris* 78 [*Mor.* 383A]). Paul uses *basileus* with reference to a human ruler in 2 Cor 11:32 and in this letter (1 Tim 2:2), but does not in other letters speak of God as king, despite employing the phrase *basileia tou theou* (kingdom of God), which bears the same import (Rom 14:17; 1 Cor 4:20; 6:9; 15:50; Gal 5:21; 2 Thess 1:5). It is a frequent

---

318. E. K. Lee, "Words Denoting 'Pattern' in the New Testament," *NTS* 8 (1962–1963): 167–173.

epithet for God in Jewish prayer, as is demonstrated by the Psalms (LXX Pss 5:2; 23:7–10; 43:5; 46:3; 94:3). See also the phrase "king of kings" in 1 Tim 6:15.

immortal, invisible, only God: Some MSS (the original hand of Bezae and some Latin witnesses) read "deathless" (*athanatos*) rather than "immortal/incorruptible" (*aphthartos*), possibly under liturgical influence. A large number of witnesses (including the second corrector of Sinaiticus and Bezae, and the Koine tradition) add *sophos* before *theos*, creating the phrase "only wise God." The second variant has impressive numerical support, but it is offset by the authority of the witnesses supporting the shorter reading—generally to be preferred in such cases (see the original hand of Sinaiticus, Alexandrinus, Bezae, and others).[319] The epithet "only God" (*monos theos*) echoes the *shema Israel* (God is one), which will be picked up immediately in 2:5. The phrase "invisible God" (*aphthartou theou*) is used by Paul in Rom 1:23. Likewise, Paul speaks—with reference to God—of "his invisible things" (*ta aorata autou*) in Rom 1:20 and, in Col 1:15, refers to Jesus as the image of the invisible God (*aoratou theou*).

honor and glory for ever and ever: In a culture that had honor (*timē*) and glory (*doxa*) as its highest coinage, those who considered the one God to be "king" were obliged to ascribe these qualities to God "eternally." For *timē* and *doxa* as associated with God, see Rom 2:7, 10; for a similar conclusion to prayer, see Rom 11:36 and 16:27.

COMMENT

The "Pauline thanksgiving" is not a single or uniform phenomenon.[320] In this case, Paul's initial instruction replaces the opening prayer, which, as a result and without doubt intentionally, thereby becomes part of the letter's argument. The thanksgiving is here self-referential, recounting Paul's turn from persecutor to believer in Christ Jesus, one to whom the good news had been entrusted. In its focus on his own experience and mission, it resembles the thanksgivings in Rom 1:8–15 and 2 Cor 1:3–7, rather than those that focus on the experience of the addressees (e.g., 1 Cor 1:4–9; Phil 1:3–11; Col 1:3–8).

The specific rhetorical effect of the thanksgiving can be discerned by reading it as part of Paul's opening argument against the opponents. Paul's own experience confirms his statement concerning the goal of the commandment and confutes the position of the false teachers concerning the Law. In Paul's former life, he demonstrated just such outrageous attributes as are found in the vice-list of 1:8–10: he was arrogant and a blasphemer, precisely because he was a persecutor of the church. Although he was a defender of the Law, in a word, he was

---

319. See also Metzger, *Textual Commentary*, 639.

320. P. Schubert, *The Form and Function of the Pauline Thanksgiving* (Berlin: Töpelmann, 1939); P. T. O'Brien, *Introductory Thanksgivings in the Letters of Paul* (Leiden: Brill, 1977).

not *dikaios*: he was ignorant of the way faith was to express itself in *agapē*, and his internal disposition of *apistia* (disbelief) drove him to rage and murder. The *nomos* could identify such characteristics in him, but it could do nothing to change them. Such profound change required a gift (*charis*) from God, through Jesus Christ, a gift of empowerment to change (1:12). The mercy shown to Paul by Jesus was an overwhelming gift that transformed him by giving him the same qualities of *pistis* and *agapē* that are "in Christ Jesus" (1:14) and are the goal of the commandment that Paul now advocates.

What happened in Paul is an example for all those who come to faith. Their relationship with God is enabled by the gift that comes from—and in some deep sense also *is*—Jesus. Because they are empowered by the gift, they can have and can display in behavior the interior dispositions that reveal the righteous person (*dikaios*). This is the "healthy teaching that accords with the good news from God" (1:10–11). In this light, the proposal that the Law function within the Christian community as a heteronomous guide to behavior becomes, startlingly, a manifestation of the same arrogance and blasphemy shown earlier in his life by Paul the persecutor. It reveals an ignorance of how God really is at work to transform the community through an empowerment and internal transformation. It is, indeed, an expression of *apistia* (1:13), a refusal to acknowledge "with faithful attention" the *oikonomia theou* (1:4), the way God has chosen to order reality through the gift of Jesus the Messiah. The Law is "good," therefore, and can be used "appropriately" as a way to locate behaviors dramatically opposed to healthy teaching; it is misused when it is applied as a norm for life in place of *agapē*. How God worked in Paul is the model for how God works in all believers. The final words of the thanksgiving remind readers by means of a doxology that no human norm or performance, but solely the "only God," can shape a life leading to "eternal life" (1:16–17).

IV. THE CHARGE REPEATED
(1:18–20)

◆

1 ¹⁸My child Timothy, I entrust this commandment to you according to the earlier prophecies made concerning you, so that you might continue fighting the noble battle by means of them, ¹⁹having faith and a good conscience, which some people have spurned and have suffered shipwreck concerning the faith! ²⁰Among such are Hymenaios and Alexander. I have handed them over to Satan, so that they may be taught not to blaspheme.

NOTES

18. *I entrust this commandment to you*: The phrase "this commandment" (*tautēn tēn parangelian*) refers explicitly to the commandment stated in 1:5, and forms an *inclusio* with it as well as with "that you command" in 1:3. Thus the contrast between false teaching and right understanding in 1:4–10 and 1:18–20 brackets Paul's presentation of himself as a model of the sinner saved by Jesus Christ (1:12–17). Similarly, the verb *paratithemi*, here in its meaning of "entrust," picks up from the participle *themenos* for Paul's commission for service in 1:12: Paul entrusts to Timothy just as he was entrusted by Christ Jesus. The phrase "My child Timothy" simply gives added weight to the exhortation, as does the use of the vocative in the similar charge at the end of the letter (6:20).

according to the earlier prophecies: The verb *proagein* can be used intransitively in the sense of "precede" in time or space, and appears rhetorically with reference to a "preceding discourse" (Plato, *Laws* 719A) or "earlier writings [*graphai*]" (Josephus, *Antiquities* 19:6.2). The main question here is whether Paul means prophecies from Torah or prophecies pronounced over Timothy (*epi se*) as he embarked on his mission. The latter better fits the usages attached to the *mandata principis* letter, which served as a memorandum for instructions delivered orally before taking up a position. For a picture of such a commissioning involving prophecy, see Acts 13:1–4. Such an understanding also makes better sense of *en autais* in the next clause, for Timothy can do battle "by means of them" if the prophecies are words empowering him with authority.

continue fighting the noble battle: It is difficult to decide between the present tense of *strateuein* (found in the corrected version of Sinaiticus, Bezae, and Alexandrinus, and in the majority of witnesses) and the aorist (found in the original hand of Sinaiticus and Bezae, and in other MSS). Together with Nestle–Aland, I accept the present tense, both because of its weightier external testimony and because it captures the sense of "continuing on" in the struggle. A *strateia* is literally a military campaign or expedition (Herodotus, *Persian War* 1:71; Xenophon, *Cyropaedia* 5.2.19); in the plural, it means "warfare" (Plato, *Republic* 404A). As shown also by 2 Tim 2:4, the rigors of military life form a neat analogy to those of the moral life; Epictetus refers to the life of each person as a *strateia* (*Discourse* 3.24.34), and Julian can speak of the true Cynic as a *stratēgos* (general, *Oration* 6:192C). For the combination *strateuein strateian* in the figurative sense of moral effort, see Plutarch, *Sayings of Romans* 6 [*Mor.* 204A]; Epictetus, *Discourse* 2.14.17; LXX 4 Macc 9:24. See also the extended use of military metaphors by Paul in 2 Cor 10:2–6. As here, the context there is that of opposing false teaching.[321]

19. *faith and a good conscience*: These are the very qualities that are said to be the basis of the love that is the *telos* of the commandment in 1:5; as always, the delegate is to embody the personal qualities that are taught to others. Note how the three sections 1:3–11, 1:12–17, and 1:18–20 become mutually interpretative.

which some people have spurned and have suffered shipwreck: The term translated "spurned" is the middle aorist participle of *apotheō* (to push away, reject, LXX Pss 42:2; 59:1; 107:11; esp. Rom 11:1). Note the emphasis on conscience. It is by spurning this internal norm in favor of heteronomy that the opponents have shipwrecked; for the figurative uses of *nauagein* (shipwreck), see *Tablet of Cebes* 24:2; Philo, *On the Change of Names* 215; *On Dreams* 2:147. For the construction *peri pistin* (concerning faith), compare *peri tēn alētheian* (concerning the truth) in 2 Tim 2:18.

20. *Hymenaios and Alexander*: Both names are found also in 2 Timothy, but separately: Hymenaios is teamed with Philetos in 2 Tim 2:17 as one of those claiming that the resurrection had already occurred (2:18); in 2 Tim 4:14, Alexander "the coppersmith" is named as one who has done Paul considerable harm. Why should names linked here appear separately in 2 Timothy? And who were these people? There is an Alexander in Acts 19:33 who appears momentarily during the Ephesian riot, but plays no active role. Did the author of 2 Timothy get this name from Acts, yet also confuse his identity with that of Demetrius "the craftsman in silver" (Acts 19:24), thus getting both his trade and his function in the narrative confused? Given the lack of any real evidence, it is useless to pursue the matter further, here. For further discussion of personal names, see the commentary on 2 Timothy.

handed them over to Satan: The language here, *paredōka tō satanā*, is remarkably close to that used by Paul in 1 Cor 5:5 for the procedure to exclude the brother committing incest in the Corinthian community: *paradounai ton toiouton tō satanā* (hand over such a one to Satan). The background for the ex-

---

321. A. J. Malherbe, "Antisthenes and Odysseus, and Paul at War," in *Paul and the Popular Philosophers* (Minneapolis: Fortress Press, 1989), 91–119.

pression is undoubtedly LXX Job 2:6: *eipen de ho kyrios tō diabolō, idou para-didomi soi auton monon tēn psychēn autou diaphylaxon* (The Lord said to the devil, "Behold I am handing him over to you; only preserve his life"). For Paul's general willingness to handle severe deviance with such rough measures, compare Gal 4:30 and 2 Thess 3:10–14.

be taught not to blaspheme: For the same purpose construction, see 1 Cor 5:6. The verb *paideuein* can mean both to "discipline" and to "educate" (e.g., Euripides, *Suppliants* 917; Plato, *Apology* 24E; *Laws* 741A; Xenophon, *Memorabilia* 1.3.5; Aristotle, *Rhetoric* 1389B); in the ancient world, the two went together (e.g., 1 Cor 11:32; 2 Cor 6:9; 2 Tim 2:25; Tit 2:12; Heb 12:6, 7, 10). Paul's excommunication in 1 Cor 5:1–5 was also intended to be salutary: "that his spirit might be saved in the day of the Lord" (1 Cor 5:5). The "divine passive" here suggested to patristic interpreters that Paul meant that God, not humans, should do the disciplining/educating. The object, "not to blaspheme," connects to Paul's self-characterization as "fomerly a blasphemer" in 1:13.

COMMENT

The opening section of the letter concludes with a renewed call to Paul's delegate to engage the opponents in a sustained "campaign" (*strateia*). As the NOTE on 1:18 indicates, the puzzling comment on the "earlier prophecies" may well be a reference not to ancient prophecies in Torah, but to the instructions given to Timothy as he took up his service in the Ephesian church. Everything in this opening section has fit within the genre of the *mandata principis* letter: Paul needs, above all, to authorize his delegate and identify the basic issue before turning to the specific points of behavior he wishes Timothy to address.

From the beginning, then, the reader understands the basic conflict as one between an intellectual elite seeking to impose an external, legal framework for community behavior, and Paul's own convictions concerning the sort of attitudes and actions that best respond to the work of the living God. In this letter, Paul does not present himself as a model of moral behavior to be imitated. He is, instead, the paradigm of how God's gift of empowering mercy through Christ can transform a despicable character into one considered faithful and placed into service (1:12). Thus in his renewed charge, we see that on one side Paul places *pistis* (faith) and *agathē synēdeisis* (a good conscience) as internal guides to behavior and, on the other, those who spurn conscience and shipwreck their faith (1:19).

As in other communities where deviance in teaching or practice has threatened the stability or moral integrity of the church, Paul engages in some straightforward social engineering. In Thessalonica, Paul says that those who have stopped working cannot share the community meal (2 Thess 3:10) and that others should not associate with those who resist his instructions (3:14–15). An even stronger parallel can be found in 1 Cor 5:1–6, where the community member living in (at least legal) incest with his mother-in-law is, as here, "handed over to Satan" for a time, in order that he might ultimately be saved. From Paul's willingness likewise to excommunicate Hymenaios and Alexander, we deduce the seriousness with which he saw the issue facing Timothy in Ephesus. We cannot be sure that they are the ones who "wish to be teachers of law" (1:7), but the logic of the passage certainly supports such a supposition. If so, then Paul's use of "be taught" might have a slight edge of sarcasm: those who want to be teachers must themselves be instructed in the strictest fashion, especially when their doctrines so fundamentally challenge the church's identity as a place where God's merciful grace transforms. They must be taught "not to blaspheme" by God, because their preference for Law over grace places them in the same position formerly occupied by Paul, when, in defense of the Law, he also was "a blasphemer" (1:13).

V. INSTRUCTIONS ON PRAYER
(2:1–7)

◆

2   ¹I am requesting first of all, therefore, that entreaties, prayers, petitions, and thanksgivings be made in behalf of all people, ²for kings and all those who are in positions of authority, so that we might lead a peaceful and quiet life in complete piety and dignity. ³This is a noble thing to do, and pleasing in the sight of our savior God, ⁴who wants all people to be saved and to come to the recognition of truth. ⁵For God is one. One also is the mediator between God and humans, the human being Christ Jesus. ⁶He gave himself as a ransom in behalf of all. The testimony was given at the right time. ⁷I have been appointed its herald and apostle—I speak the truth and do not lie—a teacher of Gentiles in faith and truth.

NOTES

1. *I am requesting first of all*: The Western text tradition (the original hand of Bezae and a number of Latin witnesses) reads the imperative *parakalei* (you exhort), rather than the first-person *parakalō* (I am requesting). The reading is less well attested and shows an effort to correct the text in order to make Timothy (who is, after all, the bearer of the *parangelia*) the one who expresses Paul's wishes. Analysis of Paul's letters shows that the transition to the body of the composition is frequently marked by such a *parakalō*-period (1 Cor 1:10; 2 Cor 2:8; 6:1; Eph 4:1; Phil 4:2; 1 Thess 4:1; Phm 10).[322] While the verb itself ranges in meaning from "comfort" to "exhort," the translation in the present progressive, "I am requesting," fits the context of this verse. Patristic commentators regularly point out that the use of this term shows Paul's humility. Paul uses the inferential particle *oun* (therefore) to indicate that his request/command builds on what precedes; the reader is invited to remember 1:3, where Paul also used *parakalein* (As I exhorted you), and 1:4, where he speaks of the *oikonomia theou en pistei*, aspects of which he now addresses. The phrase *prōton pantōn* (first of all) means here simply the first in a series, not necessarily that which is most important (compare 1 Cor 15:3; James 5:12).

---

322. C. J. Bjerkland, *Parakalo: Form, Funktion, und Sinn der Parakalo-saetze in den paulinischen Briefen*, Biblioteca Theologica Norvegica 1 (Oslo: Universitetsverlag, 1967).

entreaties, prayers, petitions, . . . thanksgivings: The four words probably do not describe a liturgical menu, but merely categorize modes of prayer; three of them occur together in similar fashion in Phil 4:6. "Entreaties" (*deēseis*) can refer to beseeching between humans (1 Macc 11:49), but is used generally for forms of petitionary prayer addressed to God (Josephus, *Against Apion* 2:197), as in Rom 10:1; 2 Cor 1:11; 9:14; Phil 1:4, 19; 4:6. "Prayers" (*proseuchai*) is the most inclusive category for prayer in the list; Paul enjoins "prayers" on his readers in Rom 12:12; 15:30; 1 Cor 7:5; Col 4:12; 1 Thess 1:2; Phm 4. "Thanksgivings" (*eucharistiai*) are obviously expressions of gratitude (Wis 16:28; Philo, *Special Laws* 1:224) and are recommended by Paul in 1 Cor 14:16; 2 Cor 4:15; 9:11–12; Phil 4:6; 1 Thess 3:9. The only term unattested in Paul, or anywhere else in the NT, is *enteuxeis* (petitions), which is used for requests between humans in Polybius, *Histories* 5.35.4, and *Letter of Aristeas* 252. It occurs with some frequency as a term for prayer in the *Shepherd of Hermas* (*Mandates* 5.1.6; 10.3.2; *Similitudes* 5.4.3).

in behalf of all people: The request that prayers be said in behalf of "all people" (*pantōn anthrōpōn*) is the first of several remarkable universalizing statements in 2:1–7: God wills the salvation "of all people"(2:4), Jesus is the mediator between God and "people" (2:5), he gave himself as a ransom "for all" (2:6), and Paul proclaims him to the "nations/Gentiles" (2:7).

2. *for kings*: The title *basileus* was used by Alexander the Great's successors (1 Macc 6:1–2; 8:6; 11:8), and in Paul's time could apply to a variety of regional leaders, such as Herod Antipas (Josephus, *Antiquities* 17:188; Mark 6:14), Herod Agrippa I (Josephus, *Antiquities* 18:273; Acts 12:1), Herod Agrippa II (Josephus, *Jewish War* 2:20; Acts 25:13), and Aretas, king of the Nabateans (2 Cor 11:32). The title was also appropriated by the Roman emperors, and the plural form could stand for the succession of Roman rulers (Josephus, *Jewish War* 3:351; 4:596; 5:563; *Life* 34). Within Judaism, sacrifices and prayers for kings are attested as early as Ezra 6:9 (see also Bar 1:10–12), and sacrifices for rulers are regularly mentioned in Hellenistic Jewish literature (*Letter of Aristeas* 45; 1 Macc 7:33; Josephus, *Jewish War* 2:197; 2:409–410; Philo, *Legation to Gaius* 157, 317; see also *Pirke Aboth* 3:2). Specific evidence that prayers were offered in synagogues for rulers is less diffuse; the best witness is Philo, *Against Flaccus* 49. The tradition is continued in early Christian literature (Polycarp, *Letter to the Philippians* 12:3; Justin, *Apology* 1:17), with an example of such a prayer given in *1 Clement* 60:2; 61:1–3. In Theophilus, *To Autolycus* 1:11, and Athenagoras, *Legation* 37:1, mention of the prayers offered for the emperor is accompanied by the motivation given by 1 Tim 2:2, "that we may lead a quiet and peaceful life," which may well reflect awareness of the Pauline dictum or even possibly of this passage.

and all those who are in positions of authority: The phrase is periphrastic: for those who are in a high place (*en hyperochē*), see Aristotle, *Politics* 1296A; for officials, see Polybius, *Histories* 5.41.3; 2 Macc 3:11; Josephus, *Antiquities* 9:3. Paul's language in Rom 13:1 is not greatly dissimilar: *pasa psychē exousiais hyperechousais hypotassesthō* (Let everyone be subject to those who have authority).

peaceful and quiet life: The adjective *ēremos* is a genuinely rare word, with only a few extant examples of its use. The noun *ēremia* is better attested. Aristotle makes it the opposite of *kinēsis*, so that it signifies "at rest" (*Physics* 202A; *On the Soul* 406A). An extant inscription reads, "of those leading a still [*ēremon*] and calm [*galēnon*] life" (BAGD, s.v.). The adjective *hēsychios* is better attested (Herodotus, *Persian War* 1:107; Plato, *Republic* 604E); Josephus speaks of "leading a peaceful and quiet life" (*Antiquities* 13:407; see also Philo, *Life of Moses* 2:235; *On the Confusion of Tongues* 43; *Who Is the Heir* 285). Although Paul does not use the word *hēsychia* elsewhere, the use of its cognates in 1 Thess 4:11 and 2 Thess 3:12 points to the same ideal of a quiet life, removed from public turmoil.

in complete piety and dignity: Within the NT, these two nouns are found in only the letters to Paul's delegates. With its cognates, "piety" (*eusebeia*, Plato, *Republic* 615C; Xenophon, *Cyropaedia* 8.1.25) is a favorite word in this correspondence (1 Tim 3:16; 4:7, 8; 5:4; 6:3, 5, 6, 11; 2 Tim 3:5; Tit 1:1).[323] Paul does use the cognate term "godlessness" (*asebeia*) in Rom 1:18 and 11:26, as well as the adjective *asebēs* in Rom 4:5 and 5:6. The noun "dignity" (*semnotēs*, Josephus, *Life* 258) occurs also in 3:4 and Tit 2:7, while the adjective "dignified" (*semnos*) appears in 3:8, 11, and Tit 2:2. Paul also uses *semnos* in Phil 4:8.

3. *a noble thing to do*: A large number of MSS (the corrector of Sinaiticus, Bezae, F, G, H, and the Koine tradition) improves the phrase by adding the particle *gar* (for), making its explanatory character clearer: "for this is a noble thing to do." The shorter text is read by the original hand of Sinaiticus, Alexandrinus, and a few other witnesses, but has the advantage of being the shorter and harder reading.[324] As always in these letters, the decision exactly how to translate *kalos* is difficult, given the range of possibilities. Considering the overall sensibilities of 1 Timothy (as shown, especially, by 6:1–2), I have with some trepidation chosen "noble" most often, since it contains the notion of "moral good," but also suggests the implicit dimension of the honorable as opposed to the shameful.

pleasing in the sight of our savior God: The adjective *apodektos* is formed from the verb *apodechomai* (to welcome, Acts 2:41; 24:3). Accented as it is here (and in 5:4), the nuance "pleasing" is preferred to "acceptable," found in other contexts (compare Plutarch, *On Common Conceptions*, 6 [*Mor.* 1061A]). For *enōpion tou theou* (before God) elsewhere in Paul, see Rom 14:22; 1 Cor 1:29; 2 Cor 4:2; Gal 1:20. The attributive construction *tou sōtēros hēmōn theou* can be translated either as "God our Savior" (RSV) or as "Our Savior God"; the meaning is much the same in either case. The title *sōtēr* as applied to God is found among Paul's letters only in the three letters to his delegates (1 Tim 1:1; 4:10; Tit 1:3; 2:10; 3:4),[325] but is implicit in all of Paul's language about God's power to save (e.g., Rom 1:16; 10:1; 1 Thess 5:9; 2 Thess 2:13).

---

323. Foerster, "EUSEBEIA *in den Pastoralbriefen.*"

324. See also Elliott, *Greek Text*, 35.

325. See the discussions in Dibelius and Conzelmann, *Pastoral Epistles*, 100–103 (with bibliography); Stettler, *Christologie der Pastoralbriefe*, 28–33; and P. Berge, " 'Our Great God and Savior': A Study of *Soter* as a Christological Title in Titus 2:11–14" (Ph.D. diss., Union Theological Seminary, 1974).

4. *all people to be saved*: This ranks with Rom 3:27–31 and 11:26–32 as the most inclusive and universal of Paul's statements concerning God's effective "will" (*thelei*) for the world.[326] If, however, 1 Timothy is read in line with Paul's undisputed letters, then *sōtēria* language is less about a future destiny ("eternal life"), than about present location. Salvation has a specific sociological referent: God wills all people to belong to the people God is forming in the world.[327] Taken in that sense—which does not preclude its broader theological appropriation—the statement coheres historically with the next phrase and with the idea of mission embedded in Paul's statement about his apostleship specifically to the Gentiles.[328]

come to the recognition of truth: The phrase *epignōsis alētheias* (recognition of truth) is exclusive to the Pastorals (see also 2 Tim 2:4; 3:7; Tit 1:1). The idea of "recognition" is, however, important to Paul elsewhere (Rom 1:28; 3:20; 10:2; Phil 1:9).[329] The true understanding of the good news is precisely what Paul considers to be under siege in Ephesus, so the emphasis here could be either on the "true version" of the good news associated with Paul and his delegate as opposed to the rivals, or on the "truth of the good news" that he has expressed in 1:12–17 as the gift of God's empowering mercy as opposed to the heteronomous norm of law. In effect, the two in this case go together.

5. *God is one*: Nestle–Aland indents 2:5–6, thus indicating an editorial judgment that the words are poetic or hymnic and/or traditional. The same indication is made in passages such as Phil 2:5–11 and Col 1:15–20. In 1 Timothy, however, such indentation also occurs in 2:5–6; 3:16; 6:6–8, 11–12, 15–16. Apart from the question of the appositeness of such judgments, the procedure exacerbates the impression that the letters to Paul's delegates are simply a rough pastiche of traditional materials. In this verse, there is no reason to consider Paul's statement as either hymnic/poetic or "traditional," in the sense that it preceded the writing of the passage. It is, however, one of Paul's typically compressed Christological-soteriological statements, as found also in Rom 3:21–26; 5:8–10; 1 Cor 8:6; 2 Cor 5:19–21; Gal 1:4; 2:20; Eph 5:2; Phil 2:5–11; Col 1:15–20; 1 Thess 5:9–10. For Paul's declaration that "God is one"—hearkening to the *shema Israel* of Deut 6:4—see, especially, Rom 3:30; Gal 3:20; 1 Cor 8:6.

the mediator between God and humans: As the term suggests, a mediator (*mesitēs*) is one who acts as a go-between or negotiator between two parties (Josephus, *Antiquities* 7:8). The word is used for the relationship between God and humans in LXX Job 9:33 and *Testament of Dan* 6:2. It is used for the role of Christ in Heb 8:6; 9:15; 12:24. Paul does not speak of Jesus as a mediator else-

---

326. Oberlinner, "*Epiphaneia* des Heilswillens Gottes in Christus Jesus."

327. Johnson, "Social Dimensions of *Sōtēria* in Luke–Acts and Paul."

328. The history of interpretation of this important theologoumenon is sketched in J. Turmel, "Histoire de l'intérpretation de I Tim. II, 4," *Revue d'histoire et de littérature religieuses* 5 (1900): 385–415.

329. M. Dibelius, "*epignōsis alētheias*," in *Neutestamentlich Studien Georg Heinrici* (Leipzig: Hinrichs'sche Buchhandlung, 1914), 176–189. Dibelius seeks to emphasize the difference in usage in the Pastorals.

where. Indeed, in Gal 3:19–20, he speaks of the Law being delivered through angels "by the hand of a mediator" (*en cheiri mesitou*) as a way of asserting that the Law was not given directly by God, since "a mediator is not for one person, and God is one" (*ho de theos heis estin*). It is striking that the affirmation "God is one" occurs also in this verse, but is joined to a very positive view of the mediatorship of Jesus.[330] Here it is not the case of lesser powers below God that diminishes God's unity, but rather "the human being Christ Jesus" who serves as *mesitēs*.

the human being Christ Jesus: The noun *anthrōpos* must be translated here as "human being" or "human person" not only because it is the humanity of Jesus, rather than his maleness, that defines him as mediator, but also because translating *anthrōpos* as "man" invites confusion with verse 12, where Paul does mean a male and uses *anēr*. For "the human being Christ Jesus," see, especially, Phil 2:7 and Rom 5:12–21. The humanity of Jesus is critical to the understanding of him as mediator.[331]

6. *gave himself as a ransom*: The word *antilytron* (ransom) is a NT *hapax*, but Paul uses *apolytron* in much the same sense in Rom 3:24; 8:23; 1 Cor 1:30; Col 1:14. The expression "the one who gave himself" (*ho dous heauton*) to define the essence of Jesus' gift to humans is thoroughly Pauline. Compare Gal 1:4 (*tou dontos heauton*), Gal 2:20 (*paradontos heauton hyper emou*), Eph 5:2 (*paredōken heauton hyper hēmōn*).

The testimony was given at the right time: The phrase *to martyrion kairois idiois* is problematic with respect to both its meaning and its connection to the phrases before and after it. Variant readings in MSS show how scribes were moved to ingenuity by recognition of the same problems. The noun *martyrion* means "that which stands as evidence or proof" (Herodotus, *Persian War* 2:22; 8:120; Plato, *Laws* 943C). It can, therefore, refer to a fact or a statement (Aristotle, *Rhetoric* 1376A). In the Gospels, for example, a healing "stands as evidence" to the priests (Matt 8:4; Mark 1:44; Luke 5:14). In Paul, the term can be used loosely, as roughly equivalent to "witness" (1 Cor 2:1 [variant reading]; 2 Cor 1:12; 2 Thess 1:10), and it is used in that way in 2 Tim 1:8, where Paul tells Timothy, "Do not be ashamed of the *martyrion* of/to our Lord," which means "the witness given by our Lord." The phrase *kairois idiois* is also difficult. The idiom *chronis idiois* appears in Diodorus Siculus with the meaning "the proper time" (*Roman History* 1.50.7; see also Josephus, *Antiquities* 11:5). But how do the phrases go together and make sense in context? Scribes struggled with the lapidary and asyndetic construction. Codex Sinaiticus adds the word *kai* (and), which has the effect of making the witness part of what Christ gave. Other MSS add a relative pronoun and a verb to make a full clause that com-

---

330. The contrast between the passages is emphasized in D. R. de Lacey, "Jesus as Mediator," *JSNT* 29 (1987): 101–121; a more positive reading is provided in A. T. Hanson, "The Mediator: 1 Timothy 2:5–6," in *Studies in the Pastoral Epistles* (London: SPCK, 1968), 56–77.

331. On the role of Jesus' humanity in this passage, see Towner, *Goal of our Instruction*, 54–56, 82–87.

ments on Christ's giving of himself as a ransom: "to which testimony was given at the proper time" (esp. the original hand of Bezae, F, and G). The scribal corrections indicate the sort of adjustments that must be made in order to make sense of the statement. Although I accept the shorter and harder reading adopted by Nestle–Aland, for example, my translation in effect approaches the solution offered by the textual variant: "the testimony was given at the right time." By no means, however, does this resolve the problem! The presence of the same idiom in Tit 1:3 confirms that this rendering moves in the right direction. But the precise significance remains ambiguous. Paul elsewhere uses the singular *kairǭ idiǭ* to mean "in the appropriate season" (Gal 6:9). But what "right time" does Paul mean? Does it point back to evidence provided by Jesus (the human person who is *mesitēs*), or does it point to present evidence given by Paul (the human *apostolos*)?

7. *appointed its herald and apostle*: Paul uses the passive of the verb *tithemi* in its sense of "set in place/establish/appoint," as he did in 1:12 (Xenophon, *Cyropaedia* 4.6.3; Josephus, *Antiquities* 9.3.3); compare 1 Cor 12:28 and 2 Cor 5:19. A philosopher could be designated as a *kēryx* (herald) of the gods (Epictetus, *Discourse* 3.22.70). Although Paul often uses *kēryssein/kērygma* language for his proclamation (Rom 16:25; 1 Cor 1:21; 15:14; Gal 2:2), he does not designate himself as *kēryx* in the undisputed letters. The self-designation of *apostolos*, though, is everywhere (e.g., 1 Cor 9:1). The same phrase occurs also in 2 Tim 1:11.

speak the truth and do not lie: The addition of the phrase "in Christ" in the majority of MSS (including the original hand of Sinaiticus, the corrector of Bezae, and the Koine tradition) is probably influenced by the clause in Rom 9:1: "I am telling the truth in Christ, I am not lying."[332] The shorter reading is attested by the second hand of Sinaiticus and Alexandrinus, and the original hand of Bezae. The expression *ou pseudomai* (I am not lying) occurs with perhaps disconcerting frequency in Paul's letters; in addition to Rom 9:1, see 2 Cor 11:31 and Gal 1:20. If the inauthenticity of the Pastorals is assumed, then the phrase is simply imitative.[333] But the question of why Paul may need to emphasize his truth telling is taken up in the COMMENT.

a teacher of Gentiles: When to translate *ethnoi* as "nations/peoples" and when as "Gentiles" is almost always difficult. I have chosen "Gentiles" here because of the specific issue being faced by the letter: whether a program of Law observance such as that forwarded by the would-be teachers (1:7) is efficacious and appropriate. This is also what makes the self-designation of *didaskalos*—found elsewhere in Paul only in 2 Tim 1:11—so appropriate, for it is Paul's teachings that Timothy is to represent in opposition to the rival program.

in faith and truth: Some MSS (notably Sinaiticus) replace the word "faith"

---

332. Metzger, *Textual Commentary*, 639.

333. J. L. North offers the intriguing suggestion—and not a little evidence in support of it—that Paul's statements are affected by the notorious reputation of Cilicians for lying, in "Paul's Protest that He Does Not Lie in the Light of His Cilician Origin," *JTS* 47 (1996): 439–463.

(*pistis*) with "knowledge" (*gnōsis*), possibly influenced by the phrase "recognition of the truth" in 2:4. Another MS (Alexandrinus) replaces "faith" with "spirit" (*pneuma*), again probably influenced by the Johannine combination "spirit and truth" (John 4:24). That Paul teaches the Gentiles truthfully the path of *pistis* (faith) is critical to the dispute with false teachers, and "faith and truth" are read by the great majority of manuscripts.

COMMENT

It is appropriate that Paul turns his attention first to matters concerning worship, for it is when the community gathers itself physically as *ekklēsia* that it truly realizes itself as church. Because of this, tensions and conflicts that might otherwise remain dormant within the life of the community take on a more acute form, as Paul reveals in his extended discussion of the problems generated by worship in the Corinthian church (1 Cor 11–14). The gathered assembly is consequently also the most dangerous manifestation of a nascent community; behaviors that might be disruptive or subversive of the social order will become visible to outsiders.[334] When the church is most powerfully and visibly an *ekklēsia* is also when the church can be most weakened and vulnerable. Whereas the Roman Empire was generous in its accommodation of foreign religions (Pliny the Elder, *Natural History* 28:4; Minucius Felix, *Octavius* 6:1–7:6), it was also swift to punish any religious gatherings that could be perceived as a threat to the social order (Livy, *History of Rome* 39:8–19; Pliny the Younger, *Letters* 10:34; 10:96).

Prayer for rulers, then, was the Jewish and Christian way of combining the refusal to acknowledge earthly princes as divine—no matter what they claimed for themselves—and the duties of good citizenship within the given political order. Those living in the fragile and fragmented social worlds resulting from Enlightenment and revolution find it difficult to appreciate the sheer facticity of the ancient social order. Nature and society were part of the same *oikonomia* governed by the divine. Deviation from the social order meant challenging God's *oikonomia*. Integral to the ordering of society in Paul's time was the fact of empire. The emperor could be considered as the chief patriarch of the household of the known world (*oikoumenē*). It would have been as unlikely for Paul to have imagined a Jeffersonian democracy as it would have been for him to conceive of a nuclear family. His instructions were aimed at a world different from the present-day one not only in structure, but, more important, in conception. Fundamental to the contemporary "symbolic world" of the West, after all, is the understanding that society can be changed. Such a fantasy had not actively been entertained in the Greco-Roman world since the utopian constructions of Plato; there may be good emperors or bad emperors, but there would surely always be emperors! Moralists of Paul's time tended to confirm this ordering of society by

---

334. Johnson, *Religious Experience in Early Christianity*, 163–172.

viewing it as "natural" and asking only what were the "duties" (*ta kathēkonta*) of each member within the given hierarchical structure.[335]

No more than Paul's discussion of problems in the Corinthian assembly enables us to reconstruct the order or even the contents of the Corinthian worship, can his brief remarks in 1 Tim 2 support a reconstruction of worship in the Ephesian *ekklēsia*. We can deduce only that it involved public prayers and readings and preaching (4:13), and probably some teaching. The surest sign that 1 Timothy is surely not in this respect a church order is that it gives us so little idea what order of worship it envisages. Instead, Paul addresses matters of potential or actual trouble: prayers for all people, including rulers (2:1–7); behavior of men at prayer (2:8); dress and adornment of women in the assembly (2:9–10); and women's teaching and authority (2:11–15). This COMMENT deals with only the first topic; the other issues are dealt with in NOTES and COMMENT on 2:8–15. Throughout the discussion, however, it is important to realize that Paul's concern for a "peaceful and quiet life" is persistent, as is his conviction that accomplishing that goal is dependent on people living "in complete piety and dignity" (2:2).

Prayer for Kings and Rulers

The place where this concern is made most explicit is in connection with the prayers offered for kings and others in authority. We see here another expression of Paul's strong affirmation of the Roman order in Rom 13:1–7, although with a slightly more subversive twist. As the NOTES on 2:2 indicate, prayers and sacrifices offered in behalf of rulers—sometimes even sponsored by kings (Philo, *Against Flaccus* 49)—were a feature of Jewish life for centuries before Paul.

Such prayer represents a survival strategy for a monotheistic cult in a polytheistic empire. At least since the time of Alexander the Great, Hellenistic kings had claimed for themselves various forms of religious *douleia* (service).[336] Jews who confessed that "God is one" (2:5) could acknowledge only that one God as *basileus*, as Paul also does in the prayer of 1:17. Indeed, 1 Tim 6:15 expresses the sovereignty of God over all other claimants: he is "King of those who exercise kingship, Lord of those exercising lordship." We have scant evidence for the formal growth of an imperial cult in Paul's time, but by the end of the first century, cities in Asia, such as Ephesus, were eager to become the *neōkoros* (keeper) of the imperial cult.[337] The narrative of Acts shows how a city like Thessalonica could be thrown into uproar by the charge that wandering preachers were subversive: "These people have been subverting the empire and now they

---

335. See, for example, Hierocles, *On Duties* 3.39.34–36, and Arius Didymus, *Epitome*, in A. J. Malherbe, *Moral Exhortation: A Greco-Roman Handbook*, Library of Early Christianity (Philadelphia: Westminster Press, 1986), 89–90, 145–147.

336. S. R. F. Price, *Rituals and Power: The Roman Imperial Cult in Asia Minor* (Cambridge: University Press, 1984): 23–40.

337. S. J. Friesen, *Twice Neokoros: Ephesus, Asia, and the Flavian Imperial Family* (Leiden: Brill, 1993).

are here! . . . These people are acting contrary to Caesar's decrees by saying there is another king, Jesus" (Acts 17:6–7).[338]

Practicing and making known that one was practicing all sorts of prayer in behalf of the rulers was even more important when other aspects of a community's life might make it appear suspect in the eyes of authorities. Such prayer is actually subversive of any claim to ultimate authority on the part of human rulers, for it turns to a still higher power with the request to bless the king. Indeed, by asking God to extend benefaction to the emperor, the human potentate's true status as creature is most sharply revealed.

As time went by, the subterfuge wore thin. The more forcefully Christians pressed the single and ultimate power of the one God, the more the strategy of prayer for would-be gods was exposed as a form of accommodation, as the frank declaration of Tertullian's *Apology* 30 makes clear: "Go to it, my good magistrates, rack out the soul that prays to God for the emperor. Here lies the crime — where God's truth is, where devotion to God is." With Paul, we are still far away from so direct a conflict. But his statements in 1 Tim 2:1–2 set the stage for it. If readers are reminded by this passage of Tit 3:1–2, with its exhortation to be submissive to rulers and authorities, then they should remember as well the even more profoundly conservative exhortation in Rom 13:1–7.

God's Will to Save All Humans

The most striking and original statement in this section is Paul's instruction to pray "in behalf of all human beings" (2:1), a request that he then supports theologically in 2:3. Avoidance of an androcentric translation of *anthrōpos* is particularly important here. The RSV, for example, has Paul ask for prayers for "all men" (2:1), says that God wills the salvation of "all men" (2:4), and has as mediator "the one man" Jesus (2:5). Such renderings (avoided by the NRSV) are misleading as well as inaccurate, for *anthrōpos* in each case really refers to all human beings, rather than just males (*andres*). It is not Jesus' maleness but his humanity that makes him mediator! Gender-exclusive translations of this passage are all the more unfortunate because Paul will proceed to make distinctions precisely on the basis of gender in the following verses (2:9–15).

Paul's extension of the community's prayer to "all people" is distinctive among early Christian compositions. Almost exclusively, the NT writings restrict the range of their concern to intra-community relations, expressed succinctly as "love of the brethren" (1 Thess 4:9). Reaching beyond the community was limited: "so then, as we have opportunity, let us do good to all [people], and especially to those who are of the household of the faith" (Gal 6:10). But in this composition, which is sometimes thought to signal a retrenchment within Pauline Christianity, we actually discover a more expansive vision: the community is to pray for all people, not simply for its own welfare — the motivation for the prayers for kings — because God "wants all people to be saved and to come to recognition of truth" (2:4).

---

338. Johnson, *Acts of the Apostles*, 304.

In as radical a fashion as Rom 3:29–30, furthermore, Paul grounds this salvific will in the *oneness* of God: "God is one" (2:5). If God is to be more than a tribal deity, then God must be one for all humans; and if God is to be righteous (fair), then there must be some principle by which all humans can respond to God: faith.[339] It is as a witness to this truth that Paul declares that he has been made a herald and apostle and teacher of the *Gentiles* (2:7). This is one of those "obvious" statements in the Pastorals that critics have delighted in using as evidence that the author was at best clumsy in his composition: Why should Paul be telling Timothy something he already knew? Such critics fail to see that in a letter like this the point is not information given to the delegate, but rhetoric to shape the perceptions of those readers meant to "overhear" the conversation between apostle and delegate.

Paul's insistence on the title "teacher" (*didaskalos*) here, then, and his placing it in direct connection with "Gentiles"—as well as his insistence that he is telling the truth—draws our attention to the probable polemic function of his self-designation in this specific situation. Against those would-be teachers of Law who seek to impose it on Gentile Christians, Paul teaches the primacy of God's grace, which empowers humans to have faith. If he were to teach otherwise, he would indeed be a liar, disavowing the truth of his own experience as he has reported it in 1:12–17.

One God, One Mediator

To the principle of God's universal will for salvation, Paul adds another and more paradoxical claim: "One also is the mediator between God and humans, the human being Christ Jesus" (2:5). At first, this may seem to contradict the earlier proposition, for it introduces an element of particularity. That is why it is important to observe that—as in Paul's argument of Rom 5:12–21—Jesus is mediator not through his deeds or words, or even as an object of belief, but on the basis of his very humanity. Jesus is the representative human before the one God, in whom "every promise of God was yes" (2 Cor 1:20). In this passage, Paul expresses this through the succinct narrative summary: "He gave himself as a ransom in behalf of all" (2:6). The phrase "he gave himself" is, as the NOTE on 2:6 shows, a thoroughly Pauline manner of summarizing the self-donative pattern of Jesus' existence. As the one God wills the salvation of all, the one mediator gives himself for all.

Certainly an element of particularity remains. Paul is convinced that it is through the gift of Christ Jesus that humans can be saved and come to a recognition of truth (2:4). Otherwise, he would not be a herald and an apostle of this message. But this particularity, it should be noted, is not rooted in an ethnic or a cultic difference, but in a shared humanity through which God seeks to reach all people. Nowhere in the New Testament is such an inclusive hope for humanity comparably expressed. The presence of such a statement in this place is especially noteworthy because the passage following it moves in such a different direction.

---

339. L. T. Johnson, *Reading Romans: A Literary and Theological Commentary* (New York: Crossroad, 1996).

VI. GENDER ROLES
IN WORSHIP (2:8–15)

◆

2 ⁸Therefore I want the men in every place to pray with their hands lifted up with piety, removed from anger and argument. ⁹Likewise also women should adorn themselves in appropriate dress with modesty and discretion, not in braids or gold or pearls or costly apparel, ¹⁰but in a way fitting to women dedicated to the service of God, through good works. ¹¹Let a woman learn quietly in complete subordination. ¹²I do not entrust teaching to a woman, nor authority over a man. She is to stay quiet. ¹³For Adam was made first, then Eve. ¹⁴Also, Adam was not deceived, but the woman, once she was deceived, fell into transgression. ¹⁵Yet she will be saved through childbearing, if they remain in faith and love and holiness with moral discretion. This is a reliable opinion.

NOTES

8. *I want the men in every place to pray*: The tone of command permeates this part of the letter: *parakalō* (I am requesting) in 2:1, *boulomai* (I desire/will) here, and *ouk epitrepō* (I do not allow) in 2:12. Note also the use of antithesis in 2:9–10, 12, 14. The term for "men" is gendered: *andres* (males). The word for "pray" is the verb form (*proseuchesthai*), corresponding to "prayers" (*proseuchai*) in 2:1. The phrase "in every place" (*en panti topō*) is somewhat odd, unless we think of the Ephesian church as consisting of several meetings or assemblies; note that in 1 Cor 16:19, Paul—writing from Ephesus—refers to the *"ekklēsiai* in Asia" as well as the *ekklēsia* that meets in the house of Aquila and Priscilla.

with their hands lifted up with piety: We learn something here of the posture of prayer: for lifting the hands in prayer (using this verb, *epairein*), see Neh 8:6; LXX Ps 133:2; using *ektenein*, see 4 Macc 4:11; Josephus, *Against Apion* 1:209. We find the gesture also in *1 Clement* 2:3 and *Barnabas* 12:2. I have separated the adjective *hosios* from the literal phrase "holy hands" in order to communicate the idea behind the metonymy. The phrase can also be rendered as "pure hands" with the same sense of approaching God in an appropriate and pious fashion; see, for example, "to raise pure hands to heaven" (Seneca, *Natural Questions* 3, Preface 14), "uplifting pure hands" (Josephus, *Jewish War* 5:380), "let us approach him in holiness of soul, raising pure and undefiled hands to him" (*1 Clement* 29:1), and "we raise holy hands to God" (Athenagoras, *Legation* 13:2).

198

removed from anger and argument: The proper attitude expressed by "pure/holy hands" is "apart from" attitudes that are all too profane. The choice of terms may reflect the concrete situation. Anger (*orgē*) in the ancient literature refers not simply to a feeling or passion (Herodotus, *Persian War* 3:25; 6:83) but to the active expression of that feeling in speech or gesture. Although Plutarch remarks that anger is more typical of women than men (*On the Control of Anger* 8 [*Mor.* 457B]), the vice is associated most often with men, as the rest of his tractate indicates. The lack of self-control found in anger is particularly connected to incontinence in speech (e.g., Prov 29:11; Qoh 7:9; Sir 1:22–24; Diogenes Laertius, *Lives of Eminent Philosophers* 1:70; 8:23; Lucian, *Demonax* 51; James 1:20), and therapy for one frequently involves the other (Seneca, *On Anger*, Plutarch, *On the Control of Anger*). The majority of MSS have the plural *dialogismōn* (e.g., the second hand of Sinaiticus and the Koine tradition), rather than the singular *dialogismou* (the original hand of Sinaiticus, Alexandrinus, and Bezae), perhaps out of confusion at the intended meaning of *dialogismos*: in the NT, it sometimes has the connotation of thought or design, even of evil designs (Matt 15:19); other times, it can refer to doubts (Luke 24:38); still other times, it means a dispute (Luke 9:46). Some scribes were probably thinking of "doubts in prayer" and considered the plural appropriate (compare James 1:6). Or they may have been influenced by Phil 2:14: "Do everything apart from grumbling [*gongusmōn*] and disputes [*dialogismōn*]." But the singular in the sense I have translated fits the context better.

9. *Likewise also women*: The *hōsautōs* (likewise) links sets of directions in 2:9 and 3:8, 11. Nestle–Aland places *kai* (also) in brackets; some MSS may have added it to relieve the awkwardness of the syntax. Although *hōsautōs* seems to begin an independent clause, the use of the accusative + infinitive (*gynaikes . . . kosmein*) construction suggests that this clause, too, is controlled by the verb *bouloumai* (I want).

should adorn themselves in appropriate dress: The noun *katastolē* can refer either to external appearance (Josephus, *Jewish War* 2:126) or to demeanor (Epictetus, *Discourse* 2.10.15). The verb *kosmein* is commonly used of self-adornment by women (Xenophon, *The Ephesians* 1.2.2; Achilles Tatius, *Leucippe and Clitophon* 3.7.5; Josephus, *Jewish War* 2:444). The adjective *kosmios* is cognate with *kosmein*, but is used in moral literature for modest adornment (Epictetus, *Encheiridion* 40; Philo, *Special Laws* 1:102). The insistence that women dress modestly and perform good deeds, rather than wear expensive finery, is a commonplace in both Greco-Roman and Jewish moralists (Phyntis, *On the Temperance of a Woman* 153:15–28; Perictione, *On the Harmony of a Woman* 143:26–28; Philo, *Special Laws* 1:102; 3:51, 169–71). 1 Pet 3:1–7 offers a particularly good parallel.[340] Dibelius and Conzelmann also cite regulations for the clothing of "holy women" dedicated to the Greco-Roman mysteries.[341]

---

340. D. L. Balch, *Let Wives Be Submissive: The Domestic Code in 1 Peter*, SBLMS 26 (Chico, Calif.: Scholars Press, 1981).

341. Dibelius and Conzelmann, *Pastoral Epistles*, 46.

with modesty and discretion: The noun *aidōs* can mean "religious awe" (Josephus, *Antiquities* 6:262; Philo, *Legation to Gaius* 352), but the context demands that it be translated as that combination of self-respect and sense of shame that is included in the word "modesty" (Diodorus Siculus, *Library of History* 13.55.4; Josephus, *Antiquities* 2:52). The translation of *sōphrosynē* is always difficult, for as one of the cardinal virtues its range of applications is so vast. Taking its basic sense as "right moral thinking" with an emphasis on "self-control" (Plato, *Republic* 430E; Aristotle, *Rhetoric* 1.9.9), the best rendering in the context of clothing and decorum would seem to be "discretion."

braids or gold or pearls or costly apparel: In contrast to the two moral qualities of modesty and discretion, we have four modes of self-adornment. Presumably, the problem with *plegma* (braid) is its complexity and artifice; the objection to gold (*chrysos*) and pearls (*margarita*) is their rarity and cost; the criticism of "costly apparel" (*himatismos polytelēs*) lies in both cost and showiness. Compare the description of the wealthy man in James 2:2 and, especially, 1 Pet 3:1–3, which also contrasts hairdos, gold rings, and costly raiment with internal moral qualities.

10. *a way fitting to women*: The construction is impersonal: "but that which is proper [*prepei*]." It is also anacoluthic, since the previous clause would lead one to expect something on the order of "but [adorn themselves] with good works such as are fitting to women."

dedicated to the service of God: The participle *epangellomenais* can equally be translated, as "who profess service of God" (for *epangellomai* in this meaning, see Xenophon, *Memorabilia* 1.2.7; Philo, *On the Virtues* 54; Paul otherwise uses it in the sense of "promise," as in Rom 4:21; Gal 3:19). The noun *theosebeia* finds its only NT use here; it means literally "reverence for God" and can be used generally to refer to piety or religion (e.g., Xenophon, *Anabasis*, 2.6.26; LXX Gen 20:11; Job 28:28; Sir 1:25).

through good works: As mentioned earlier, the construction with *di' ergōn agathōn* (through good works) is unexpected. The idea is that these are the practices that reveal the internal moral dispositions of the women. "Good works" (*kala erga*) are expected of a woman who is to be supported as a widow (5:10), of elders (5:25), and of the wealthy (6:18). These added uses indicate, at the least, that "good works" is not a trivializing phrase, but points to a life of productive virtue. Language about "good works" (either *erga agatha* or *erga kala*) is found throughout the NT (Matt 5:16; Heb 13:21 [variant reading]; 1 Pet 2:12), but most often in Paul—whether in the singular or the plural (Rom 2:7; 13:3; 2 Cor 9:8; Eph 2:10; Phil 1:6; 2 Thess 2:17; 2 Tim 2:21; 3:17; Tit 1:16; 2:7, 14; 3:8).

11. *learn quietly in complete subordination*: The most noteworthy parallel to this command is found in 1 Cor 14:33b–35, which reads (my translation): "As in all the churches of the saints, let women be silent [*sigatōsan*] in the assemblies. For it is not allowed for them to speak; rather, let them remain subordinate just as the law also says. But if any wish to learn, let them ask their own husbands within the household. For it is shameful to a woman to speak in an assembly." This verse carries over three elements: that a woman should learn (*manthanetō*), that she should do so "quietly" (*en hēsychia*, note *hēsychios* in 2:2), and that she should do so in "complete subordination" (*en pasē hypotagē*).

There can be no softening of *hypotagē*, which suggests not simply an attitude, but a structural placement of one person below another (Dionysius of Halicarnassus, *Roman Antiquities* 3.66.3; 2 Cor 9:13; Gal 2:5). The same demand will be made of the children of a household in 1 Tim 3:4 (compare Tit 2:5, 9; 3:1).

12. *I do not entrust teaching to a woman*: This can be rendered more literally as "I do not allow [*epitrepō*] to a woman to teach." For the strength of *epitrepō*, compare Epictetus, *Discourses* 1.10.10; 2.7.12; 4 Macc 4:18; Josephus, *Antiquities* 8:202; 1 Cor 16:7. This is also the word used by Paul in 1 Cor 14:34. Note that in this passage, the kind of speaking in the assembly is identified: teaching. Culturally, this was a role assigned to males, particularly in public settings.

nor authority over a man: The phrase *oude authentein andros* continues to be governed by "I do not entrust/allow to a woman." The verb *authentein* is not widely attested in the meaning of "dominate/have full authority over"; this is its only use in the NT. Its sense can be gained by its opposition to *hypotagē*: such a woman would have reversed the power structure.[342] The main question here is whether Paul means by *anēr* her husband or any man in the community. It would be pleasant for those who seek relief from the stringent patriarchalism of the passage to report that it refers to only the woman's husband, but in fact Paul's other usage (e.g., Rom 7:2–3; 11:3–4; Eph 5:22–23; Col 3:18–19) and, above all, the use of *anēr* immediately before this in 2:8 make it more likely that Paul means any man in the assembly (see also 1 Tim 3:2, 12; 5:9).

stay quiet: The phrase *einai en hēsychia* means literally "to be in quiet," which is different in tone, if not in meaning, from the "let them keep silent [*sigatōsan*]" of 1 Cor 14:34. I take the *einai* as expressing something of a continuing state of being. The noun *hēsychia* (quiet) echoes 2:2.

13. *For Adam was made first, then Eve*: Although "male" precedes "female" also in the first creation account (Gen 1:27), the *gar* (for) here probably refers to the second creation account—in which Adam is formed from the earth (Gen 2:7), and then Eve is formed from Adam's side (2:22)—as the scriptural (and therefore authoritative) warrant for Paul's directive. For this passage, it is equivalent to the statement in 1 Cor 14:34: "just as the law also says." The order of creation as expressed in the biblical account is used to support the ordering of the social unit of the family. As discussed in the INTRODUCTION, this is a corollary of Paul's strong emphasis on the *oikonomia theou* in terms of creation. The verb *plassein* (to make) is the same verb used in Gen 2:7 (see also 2 Macc 7:23; Philo, *On the Creation of the World* 137; Josephus, *Antiquities* 1:32). That the idea of such subordination grounded in the creation account is natural to Paul is shown by 1 Cor 11:8–9.

14. *Adam was not deceived*: The second argument is from Gen 3:1–13. By us-

---

342. Further research into the term has been made available in G. W. Knight, III, "*AUTHENTEŌ* in Reference to Women in 1 Tim. 2:12," *NTS* 30 (1984): 143–157; L. E. Wilshire, "The TLG Computer and Further Reference to *AUTHENTEŌ* in 1 Timothy 2:12," *NTS* 34 (1988): 120–134; and H. S. Baldwin, "*authenteō* in Ancient Greek Literature," in *Women in the Church*, ed. A. J. Koestenberger, T. R. Schreiner, and H. S. Baldwin (Grand Rapids, Mich.: Baker Book House, 1995), 269–306.

ing the verb *exapatan* (read by the original hand of Sinaiticus and Alexandrinus, and the original scribe of Bezae), Paul alludes to Eve's report to God in Gen 3:13: "The serpent deceived me [*ēpatēsen me*] and I ate." Once more, the story of the first parents is taken as inscribing essential qualities: women are more easily deceived than men are. The reading of *apatan* by some witnesses (the correctors of Sinaiticus and Bezae, and the Koine tradition) probably represents an even closer assimilation to the Genesis account. Paul also refers to Eve's being deceived in 2 Cor 11:3, using *exapatan*. It is perhaps not by accident that the verb *apatan* takes on the sense of "seduction" as well as "deception" in some LXX passages (e.g., Jdt 9:3; 12:16; 13:16).

once she was deceived, fell into transgression: The noun *parabasis* means literally "crossing of boundaries" and is used metaphorically to mean "stepping over" limits (Plutarch, *Advice About Keeping Well* 1 [*Mor.* 122E]) and laws (Philo, *On Dreams* 2:123; Rom 2:23; 4:15; Gal 3:19). Wis 14:31 uses it of Adam's trespass, as does Paul in Rom 5:14. The additional comment suggests that greater moral weakness accompanies a lower rank in the order of creation and therefore greater susceptibility to suggestion.

15. *saved through childbearing*: Grammatically, "she will be saved [*sōthēsetai*]" is singular, while the next clause, "if they remain" (*ean meinōsin*) is plural. Does the first clause refer to women in general (note the collective sense of *hē gynē* in 2:14), and the second simply make the implied plural explicit: "women will be saved through childbearing, if they [the women] remain in faith"? Or is there a shift in subject from the woman/women to their children (picking up from *teknogonia*): "she [the woman] will be saved through childbearing, if they [the children] remain in faith"? These options take "being saved" as referring to salvation—that is, being in a right relationship with God. The first option makes the woman's own faith response the critical element in her vocation of child rearing. The second makes her success in keeping her children within the faith the criterion for her own salvation! Another possiblity is to take *teknogonia* as the act of bearing children, and read "salvation" as the literal survival of that dangerous passage. Taken this way, the curse of Gen 3:16, "I will greatly multiply your pain in childbearing, in pain you shall bring forth children," is very much in the background. This reading demands, to be sure, a shift from the meaning of "salvation" in 2:4. That this is one of the great exegetical puzzles in 1 Timothy is obvious from the many different readings of the passage in the history of interpretation, which I have tried to trace through the various figures discussed in the General Introduction.[343]

if they remain: This phrase can also be rendered as "if they continue." The most likely subject for the verb is "women," even though *gynē* is singular in its earlier uses. The conditional clause elevates the importance of moral character

---

343. It should be pointed out that D. Doriani provides some valuable information in the "History of Interpretation of 1 Tim. 2" in *Women in the Church*, ed. A. J. Koestenberger, T. R. Schreiner, and H. S. Baldwin (Grand Rapids, Mich.: Baker Book House, 1995), 213–267, but also omits some valuable counterbalancing tendencies such as have been noted in the General Introduction. On the verse, see S. E. Porter, "What Does It Mean to Be 'Saved by Childbirth' (1 Timothy 2:15)?" *JSNT* 49 (1993): 87–102.

developed over time above the act of bearing children as an aspect of "being saved," which, in this perspective, might be seen as "living within the saved community" (see the NOTE on 2:4).

in faith and love and holiness: The designations of "faith and love" pick up the "aim of the commandment" as stated in 1:5. Women (or, alternatively, their children) are to live as members of the community defined by these internal norms of behavior. The additional attribute of "holiness" (*hagiasmos*) once more points to the distinctive character of the Christian community as "different" from the world and in allegiance with the Holy God (e.g., Rom 6:19, 22; 1 Cor 1:30; 1 Thess 4:3–4, 7; 2 Thess 2:13). The noun may also echo Paul's concern that the relationship between husband and wife "sanctify" them and their children (1 Cor 7:14; Eph 5:26).

with moral discretion: The phrase *meta sōphrosynēs* modifies all the qualities listed and forms a bracket with 2:9. It is possible to read it more negatively as "self-control," with specific reference to sexual conduct within the marriage relationship. But in light of its earlier occurrence and the positive character of the other virtues listed, it is best to read *sōphrosynē* here also in the broad sense of "moral discretion/prudence."

a reliable opinion: This is the second occurrence of *pistos ho logos* (1:15). An interesting textual variant in the Western tradition (e.g., the original hand of Bezae) replaces *pistos* with *anthrōpinos*, making the phrase read, "This is a [merely] human opinion," rather than "This is a reliable opinion." It is surely not the original text.[344] I have chosen to attach the slogan to 2:15, although it could conceivably also go with 3:1–2.[345] In 1 Tim 1:15, the faithful saying follows the rubric. But in Tit 3:8, it seems to follow the saying in question. In 1 Tim 4:9 and 2 Tim 2:11, the rubric could point either way, as it could here. All the other instances involve statements concerning salvation: 2:15 is such a statement; 3:1 is not. With Nestle–Aland, then, I take it as a comment on 2:15. It is not clear to which statement the scribes were referring when they reduced it to a merely human opinion!

COMMENT

Since the *Women's Bible* generated by such nineteenth-century feminists as Elizabeth Cady Stanton,[346] the hermeneutical issue—what contemporary Christians should do or think about the text—has colored the reading of 1 Tim 2:9–15,

---

344. Metzger, *Textual Commentary*, 640.

345. In "Identifying the Faithful Sayings in the Pastoral Epistles," Campbell insists that the saying must always follow the slogan, and therefore tries to identify 3:16 as the "faithful saying." J. L. North takes the "human speech" as the correct reading and seeks to understand it in terms of Paul's caution about the value of human discourse, in " 'Human Speech' in Paul and the Pastorals: The Investigation of the Meaning of *anthrōpinos ho logos* (1 Tim. 3:1)," *NovT* 37 (1995): 56–67.

346. E. C. Stanton, *Women's Bible* (New York: European, 1895, 1898).

making a clean exegesis of it difficult. In this comment, I will first address the exegetical issues, and then turn to some of the hermeneutical options.

After issuing the request that prayers be said for all people, including rulers, since God wills the salvation of all humans, Paul issues directives concerning the behavior of people at worship. In contrast to the inclusive statements about salvation and the one mediator Jesus, these directions are gender-specific. Although the things said respectively to men and women differ, the point is the same: worship is to exemplify the "peaceful and quiet life" (2:2), which is the goal of a people dedicated to God. In the eyes of the author, the behavior singled out in each case is disruptive of such tranquillity. We remember that in the circumstances of ecstatic speech and its divisive and disturbing manifestations, Paul also declared: "God is not a God of confusion [*akatastasia*] but of peace [*eirēnē*]" and "all things should be done decently [*euschēmonos*] and in order [*kata taxin*]" (1 Cor 14:33, 40).

Men's Competition and Women's Adornment

The first set of instructions is well balanced and even handed: the command to the males is linked (*hōsautōs*) to that of the females. And in each case, the behavior is typically—even stereotypically—associated with the respective genders. In a cultural context in which men are the public speakers in any assembly (*ekklēsia*), and in a tradition in which the saying of prayers and the interpretation of Torah merge easily one into the other, particularly when some of the men have set themselves up as "teachers of law" (1:7) without the whole-hearted agreement of others, we can easily understand how "anger and argument" (2:8) could break out to such an extent as to disrupt worship. It is precisely in the context of the "assembly" (*ekklēsia*) that differences about the community's moral norms would come under discussion and spill over into the act of prayer. Paul's response is simple and direct: the men are to pray with piety and without rancorous debate. The pertinence of this response not only for the ancient Ephesian community, but for any worship assembly is obvious and unproblematic.

Similarly, in a world in which women who dressed extravagantly could be perceived by moral rigorists as disreputable (see the NOTES on 2:9), and in a tradition in which women's roles were defined in terms of the domestic sphere rather than the public forum, Paul's instruction against elaborate hairdos and ostentatious clothing seems unexceptionable. Such self-adornment can also be disruptive of worship by causing excessive attention to personal appearance rather than goodness of character. It is, indeed, most unfortunate that the negative reaction by readers to the verses that follow also tends to color everything in this chapter, for Paul's statements here have important implications not only for a Christian appreciation of simplicity in the face of cultures that define and value in terms of appearance (above all, in the case of women!), but also for a way of addressing the issues of economic and ecological oppression implicit (both then and now) in the production of luxurious clothing and adornment.

Women's Speech and Authority in Assembly

The third instruction—concerning the speech and authority of women—breaks the balance found in 2:8–10. It is also more elaborate than the preceding instructions, consisting not only of a repeated command ("Let a woman learn quietly in complete subordination [*hypotagē*]" [2:11], and "She is to stay quiet" [2:12]), but also of a generalized statement of opinion ("I do not entrust teaching to a woman, nor authority over a man" [2:12]) and two theological warrants drawn from Scripture: the first from the order of creation (2:13) and the second from women's greater susceptibility to deception and moral failure (2:14). The instruction ends in 2:15 with a conditional clause that appears to define a woman's social/ecclesial role through either her biological function of childbearing or, at best, the domestic role of rearing her children, albeit with good moral character as the condition in either case.

The explicitness, fullness, and impact of Paul's statements raises the question of his motivation. Do these statements arise automatically out of an instinctive patriarchal bias? Or is Paul responding to some specific issue that gives his words additional edge? Here is a case where the operative hypothesis concerning authorship (and therefore dating) makes a difference.[347] Those who argue that the Pastoral Letters are pseudonymous productions of the second century sometimes also take the position that the pseudepigrapher is consciously and deliberately trying to stifle the sort of nascent women's movement that some detect in the apocryphal acts of the Apostles—above all, the *Acts of Paul and Thecla*. These readers take Paul's discussion of the widows in 5:6–15 as addressed not to a crisis in the community welfare system, but to a crisis concerning women's ministry, expressed by those who preach in households (5:13). In their reading, 2:11–15 deliberately targets such ministry and ruthlessly suppresses it.[348]

Even if 5:3–16 is read as a crisis concerning the community welfare system—as I argue it should be read—Paul's language in that passage explicitly finds fault with "younger widows" who are "learning in idleness" and have turned to "speaking things they ought not" (5:13). Paul's language undoubtedly tends to sexualize and discredit their behavior. But we should remember that Paul was also capable of precisely such sexualization in his torturous discussion of women

---

347. For exegetical soundings from several different perspectives in works not cited in this discussion, see H. Windisch, "Sinn und Geltung des apostolischen Mulier Taceat in ecclesia," *Die Christliche Welt* 9 (1930): 411–425; Hanson, "Eve's Transgression: 1 Timothy 2:13–15," in *Studies in the Pastoral Epistles*, 65–77; T. R. Schreiner, "An Interpretation of 1 Timothy 2:9–15: A Dialogue with Scholarship," in *Women in the Church*, ed. A. J. Koestenberger, T. R. Schreiner, and H. S. Baldwin (Grand Rapids, Mich.: Baker Book House, 1995), 105–154; and Gritz, *Paul, Women Teachers, and the Mother Goddess at Ephesus.*

348. See, for example, Bassler, "Widow's Tale"; J. Dewey, "1 Timothy," in *The Women's Bible Commentary*, ed. C. A. Newsom and S. H. Ringe (Louisville, Ky.: Westminster/John Knox Press, 1992), 355–357; and J. M. Ford, "A Note on Protomontanism in the Pastoral Epistles," *NTS* 17 (1970–1971): 338–346.

praying and prophesying without veils in 1 Cor 11:2–16.[349] What is no longer available to us is the perception of the women themselves who were thus prophesying or thus going from house to house. Paul's perceptions by no means can be taken as neutral reportage in such cases. It is certainly possible that during Paul's lifetime he should be irritated or worried, in Ephesus as he was in Corinth, with expressions of freedom among women that pushed past the cultural norms he finds comfortable, especially when such expressions are found among women with sufficient wealth and relative independence to be free of the harsher domestic restraints imposed on the poor by economic deprivation.[350] And it is plausible that here, as in 1 Corinthians, Paul defends male prerogatives and perspectives out of patriarchal reflex, especially when his sense of orderliness and proper decency is threatened.

Even more than in the parallel passage of 1 Cor 14:34–35, the social setting of teaching and learning in the assembly is here definitive. Furthermore, in this passage, teaching in the assembly is explicitly connected to having authority over a man. Paul proceeds to define gender roles in each case according to public and domestic spaces. In public, the woman is to be en pasē hypotagē (in all subordination) and is to be a learner, not a teacher. The passivity of her public role is expressed by her posture of silence or quiet (hēsychia here has a broader connotation than the sigē in 1 Cor 14:34). And the reference to her childbearing and child rearing locates her squarely in the private place of the oikos, rather than in the public space of the ekklēsia.

To this point, the passage is entirely consistent with that found in 1 Cor 14:34–35. It is important to add that it is also consistent with the overall attitude toward women in Paul's undisputed letters. Paul stood firmly for the fundamental equality of women in terms of membership and identity en Christō (in Christ, Gal 3:28) and resisted the desire for circumcision, which would have established a permanent "males-only" level of initiation within Christianity.[351] Paul could also see women working "for the Lord" beyond the bounds of biologically defined roles (1 Cor 7:25–35) and appreciate the services of women working in the field with him, such as Phoebe (Rom 16:1), Prisca (1 Cor 16:19; Rom 16:3), and Junia (Rom 16:7). Paul recognized that the power of the Spirit could be at work in women to pray and prophesy (1 Cor 11:5).

But precisely where the gifts of the Lord in the ekklēsia came up against the culturally defined gender roles of the oikos, Paul grew nervous. Thus we see him sexualize the situation of women prophesying without veils and call it shameful (aischron, 1 Cor 11:10–15, esp. 11:6). Thus we see him resist women assuming

---

349. Johnson, "Glossolalia and the Embarrassments of Experience," in *Religious Experience in Early Christianity* 124–136.

350. A. Padgett, "Wealthy Women at Ephesus: 1 Timothy 2:8–15 in Context," *Int* 41 (1987): 19–31.

351. Johnson, "Ritual Imprinting and the Politics of Perfection," in *Religious Experience in Early Christianity*, 69–103.

the male prerogative of teaching in the assembly (*aischron gynaiki*, "shame to a woman," 1 Cor 14:35). Thus we see him use (with slight modifications) the patriarchal tables of household ethics for relations between the genders within the *oikos* (Col 3:18–19). It is not particularly shocking to find such limits to Paul's egalitarianism, given his own cultural conservatism (Rom 13:1–7) and that of his overall social context, wherein the submission of women to men was the basic cultural assumption (Xenophon, *Oecumenicus*; Aristotle, *Politics*; Josephus, *Against Apion* 2:200; Philo, *Apology for the Jews* 7.3, 5)[352] and efforts to break free of domestic roles was rudely resisted by many males (Juvenal, *Satires* 6). In Rom 7:2, Paul alludes casually to that premise when he states, "A married woman [literally, "an under-a-man-woman" *gynē hypandros*] is bound by law to her man while she is alive" (see also 1 Cor 7:39).

Paul's Pharisaic background would only have exacerbated such bias.[353] Not only was the study of Torah an exclusively male prerogative in rabbinic circles, but women were routinely dismissed as distractions and temptations to the true sage (*Pirke Aboth* 1.5; *Aboth de Rabbi Nathan* 2). And the most enlightened of Stoic philosophers, Musonius Rufus, who recognized the equal intellectual and moral gifts of women and advocated their full education in philosophy, did so in order that they might better fulfill their domestic roles (*Oration III: That Women Too Should Study Philosophy* 10:2–4, 11–14).

The distinctively difficult aspect of 1 Tim 2:11–15 is Paul's use of theological warrants. In 1 Cor 14:34, he appeals to the authority of Torah for women being in submission. The obvious text supporting such a position would be Gen 3:16, where the woman is told, "Your desire shall be for your husband, and he shall rule over you." The immediately preceding words in Gen 3:16, it will be remembered, are "I will greatly multiply your pain in childbearing; in pain you shall bring forth children," which, I have suggested, lies in the background of the statement concerning being saved through childbirth (2:15). The Genesis account is here again clearly the basis for Paul's assertions. No surprise in this either, for Paul refers to the story of Adam when speaking of Jesus in 1 Cor 15:22, 45, and Rom 5:14–21. In those passages, he plays on the conviction that Adam is a "type" of the "man from heaven," and he contrasts the obedience of the human person Jesus with the disobedience of Adam. But Paul also makes a negative allusion to Eve in 2 Cor 11:3: "As the serpent deceived/seduced Eve by his cleverness"—using the same term (*exapatan*) as he does in 1 Tim 2:14.[354] In this passage, such a negative characterization of Eve dominates.

---

352. For a thorough review of the question, see G. E. Sterling, "Women in the Hellenistic and Roman Worlds (323 B.C.E.–138 C.E.)," in *Essays on Women in Early Christianity*, ed. C. D. Osburn (Joplin, Mo.: College Press, 1995), 1:41–92.

353. R. D. Chesnutt, "Jewish Women in the Greco-Roman Era," in *Essays on Women in Early Christianity*, ed. C. D. Osburn (Joplin, Mo.: College Press, 1995), 1:93–130.

354. T. C. Greer, "Admonitions to Women in 1 Tim. 2:8–15," in *Essays on Women in Early Christianity*, ed. C. D. Osburn (Joplin, Mo.: College Press, 1995), 1:281–302.

Paul's first argument is from the order of creation: Adam was made first, and then Eve (2:13). Paul tried the same line of argument in 1 Cor 11:8–9: "For man was not made from woman but woman from man; neither was man created for woman but woman for man." But in that letter, the perspective of the *new* creation in the resurrection led to his immediately qualifying such a flat reading of creation: "Nevertheless in the Lord woman is not independent of man nor man of woman; for as woman was made from man so man is now born of woman. And all things are from God" (1 Cor 11:11–12). There is no such qualification of the order of creation here, no perception of how "in the Lord" all are from God.

Paul's second argument is drawn from the account of the temptation and transgression of God's instructions concerning the Garden in Gen 3:1–7. As in 2 Cor 11:3, Paul plays on the fact that the serpent deceived Eve rather than Adam. Presumably, this is to show that women are less capable of distinguishing truth from error, or are too driven by their appetites to be reliable teachers and leaders. But the logic is flawed. The woman, after all, was deceived by "the most subtle creature that the Lord God had made" (Gen 3:1), but all the woman had to do was offer the fruit to the man and he ate it (3:6)! We can also note that in Gen 3:17 it is not the woman who is blamed for eating the fruit, but the man. Such corrections of Paul's exegesis of Genesis are beside the point, except to make clear that Paul was not in this case engaging in sober exegesis of Genesis, but supporting his culturally conservative position on the basis of texts that in his eyes demonstrate the greater dignity and intelligence of men and, therefore, the need for women to be silent and subordinate to men.

Hermeneutical Options

It is not inappropriate, in light of the way in which 1 Timothy as a whole has suffered in reputation and use within the church—above all, because of this passage—to give some attention to the hermeneutical options for contemporary Christian readers. I should make plain from the start of this discussion that I share with others many of the difficulties in regard to both the tone and the substance of the passage. I recognize, above all, that the uses to which this text have been put within the tradition to support patriarchal power arrangements, to suppress the leadership of women, and even to legitimate patterns of abuse against women (both within the assembly and within society as a whole) need to be acknowledged candidly and as emphatically disavowed. With other contemporary readers, furthermore, I find the statements here to be in sharp tension with other Pauline declarations of a more egalitarian character, above all Gal 3:28: "In Christ there is neither Jew nor Greek, slave nor free, male nor female; for you are all one in Christ Jesus." I agree that our growth in understanding of the human person, partly guided by the Holy Spirit, and partly driven by the resistance of brave women to these strictures, makes it impossible to regard the statements disqualifying women from public speech and roles of leadership as either true or normative.[355] What, then, is to be done with the passage?

One option seeks to remove the scandal posed by the passage by the denial of Pauline authorship. The authentic Paul, this position maintains, was the champion of egalitarianism and of the "eschatological woman" in the community.[356] It is only the author of the Pastorals who represents a repressive (and regressive) stance toward women. This solution is, in fact, no solution at all. In the first place, as I have shown, the evidence in the undisputed letters shows that Paul is fully capable of making the statements in 1 Tim 2:11–15. The strongest, although not only, evidence is 1 Cor 14:33–36. It so decisively agrees with the position in 1 Timothy that some scholars have argued that this passage is in reality an interpolation into 1 Cor 14 by the author/editor of the Pastorals, who thereby was able to "find" in the authentic letters the same sexist position advanced a hundred years later by 1 Timothy.[357] The fact that some Western MSS place 1 Cor 14:34–35 after 1 Cor 14:40 seems to them to support such an interpolation hypothesis.[358]

The textual evidence, however, is overwhelmingly in favor of regarding 14:34–35 as part of the original letter written by Paul.[359] Not only does the statement on women accord with the other cultural perceptions of Paul that I listed earlier, but the specific support offered for the regulation matches Paul's rhetorical strategy in other parts of 1 Corinthians. For the normative force of *nomos*, see 1 Cor 4:6; 9:8–9; 10:1–11. For an appeal to the broader custom of the churches, see 1 Cor 1:2; 4:17; 11:16.[360] And if 1 Cor 14:33b–36 is authentically Pauline, then there is no statement closer to the one we find in 1 Tim 2:11–15. The details are different, but the perspective and the mode of argument are the same.

There is another reason why a decision on the un-Pauline character of 1 Tim 2:11–15 is of no real hermeneutical help. Whether by Paul or by a pseudepigrapher, 1 Timothy is still part of the canon of the New Testament. This means

---

355. In this regard, I do not share the outlook of R. W. Yarbrough, "The Hermeneutics of 1 Tim. 2:9–15," in *Women in the Church*, ed. A. J. Koestenberger, T. R. Schreiner, and H. S. Baldwin (Grand Rapids, Mich.: Baker Book House, 1995), 155–196, whose essay, in my view, represents the exact wrong approach to the whole question.

356. R. Scroggs, "Paul and the Eschatological Woman," *JAAR* 40 (1972): 283–303.

357. H. Conzelmann, *A Commentary on First Corinthians*, trans. J. W. Leitch, Hermeneia (Philadelphia: Fortress Press, 1975), 246.

358. G. Fee, *The First Epistle to the Corinthians* (Grand Rapids, Mich.: Eerdmans, 1987), 699–702. On such theories generally, see J. Murphy-O'Connor, "Interpolations in 1 Corinthians," *CBQ* 48 (1986): 81–96.

359. A. Wire, *The Corinthian Women Prophets* (Minneapolis: Fortress Press, 1990), 149–152.

360. C. D. Osburn, "The Interpretation of 1 Cor. 14:34–35," in *Essays on Women in Early Christianity*, ed. C. D. Osburn (Joplin, Mo.: College Press, 1995), 1:219–242. For the contrary view, see R. W. Allison, "Let Women Be Silent in the Churches (1 Cor. 14:33b–36): What Did Paul Really Say, and What Did It Mean?" *JSNT* 31 (1987): 27–60.

that it gains its normative force not from its authorship, but from its canonical status. Proving the passage to be non-Pauline would help those who dislike it only if that demonstration would remove 1 Timothy from the canon. Now it is true that the effect of the 150-year challenge to 1 Timothy's authenticity has had the effect of removing it from the scholar's effective Pauline collection—and, therefore, largely from serious theological engagement—but this scholarly perception has not yet affected the church's official collection as such.

The second option also seeks to suppress the passage by negating its authority. This position draws a distinction between canonical and authoritative. It takes as a principle that only those parts of Scripture that lead to the liberation of women are truly authoritative—that is, are truly Scripture.[361] And since 1 Tim 2:11–15 does not liberate women in any discernible fashion—is, indeed, the classic NT example of a "text of terror" for women[362]—it thereby loses its authority for the church or, at the very least, for women. Whether or not editors of recent lectionaries explicitly adhere to this principle, their practice of eliminating this troublesome passage from the texts of Scripture read in the assembly to the people and serving as the basis for preaching to God's people is a clear example of its application.

The option of censorship, however, also has its problems. First, the assumption that the church should hear from Scripture only those texts that confirm contemporary perceptions and practices is one that is fraught with peril. There are few texts of Scripture that, examined closely enough, do not contain at least as much ambiguity as this one. Where does the process of purgation stop? The possibility must also be entertained that the salutary character of the Scripture consists at least as much in its ability to challenge us as it does in its capacity to comfort us. Not only should present-day readers be willing to state how and why they stand over against texts that conflict with their own practices, but they should be willing in principle to learn something important precisely from the theological dissonances caused by such disparities in practice. Just as it is a mistake to give the ancient text absolute authority, so is it an error to assume that a contemporary ethos or outlook has absolute validity.

A second reason why censorship is a bad hermeneutical option is that it does not have any effect on the harmful influence of the text; indeed, it may exaggerate it. Preventing texts from being read in the public assembly does not remove them from all reading. They continue to be read and used outside the framework of critical engagement through study and preaching and, in the hands of those already deeply prejudiced and violent, continue to help shape discriminatory and sometimes violent policy and practice. Only if texts that have scandalous and even harmful possibilities are confronted and engaged by pub-

---

361. R. R. Reuther, "The Feminist Critique in Religious Studies," Soundings 64 (1981): 388–402; E. Schuessler-Fiorenza, Bread Not Stone: The Challenge of Feminist Biblical Interpretation (Boston: Beacon Press, 1984), 23–63.

362. The phrase is from P. Trible, Texts of Terror: Literary-Feminist Readings of Biblical Narratives (Philadelphia: Fortress, 1984).

lic discourse within the assembly can their harmful potential be exorcised and their remaining positive features be safely considered.

This leads to the final and—as the previous sentences have suggested—only truly viable hermeneutical option, which is to engage the words of Paul in a dialectical process of criticism within the public discourse of the church, both academic and liturgical. Such readings should note the peculiar features of the text that make it problematic as normative: that it is gratuitous in context, going beyond what is required for the situation; that it is based solely on Paul's individual authority (*ouk epitrepō*, "I do not allow"), rather than on a principle intrinsic to the good news; and that the warrant for the injunction is, in fact, a faulty reading of Torah. They should also acknowledge the history of harm done to women within the church (exclusion from leadership functions, silencing of voices, restriction to domestic roles) based on this passage.

Such engagement, however, will also recognize that contemporary assumptions concerning family structures and power relationships are not themselves absolute, but are relative and culturally conditioned in a way not unlike Paul's own assumptions. We may prefer them; we may regard them as superior to Paul's; we may even hope that they represent growth toward God's will for the relations between the genders. But we cannot be so parochial as to think that further growth is not possible or even necessary. Finally, as we think about that growth, we might even be grateful to this passage as well as others in the Pauline corpus for reminding us that the noblest Christian ideals ("in Christ there is neither male nor female" or "God wills the salvation of all") must always be negotiated within the hard and resistent circumstances of cultural contexts in which the power and privilege—as well as the complex and ambiguous embodiments—of difference are always present.

VII. QUALIFICATIONS
OF THE SUPERVISOR (3:1–7)

◆

3 ¹If anyone seeks to be a supervisor, it is a noble role that he desires. ²The supervisor must therefore be blameless, the husband of one wife, sober, prudent, respectable, hospitable, an apt teacher. ³He must not be addicted to wine, nor be violent, but should be gentle, neither given to battle nor a lover of money. ⁴He should be ruling well over his own household, with his children in subordination with complete reverence. ⁵For if someone does not know how to rule his own household, how can he take charge of God's assembly? ⁶He should not be a recent convert in order that he not get a false sense of his own importance and fall into the judgment reserved for the devil. ⁷And he should also have the commendation of outsiders, so that he does not fall into disgrace and the trap of the devil.

NOTES

1. *seeks to be a supervisor*: The verb *oregomai* means to "strive after or aspire to" (Xenophon, *Memorabilia* 1.2.15; Plato, *Republic* 485D; Epictetus, *Discourses* 2.1.10). The sentence supposes that the position is attainable through some process other than direct divine appointment. The translation of *episkopos* is difficult, not because the Greek is unclear, but because English equivalents can be misleading. The usual translation of "bishop" is inadvisable because of the later accretions of meaning attached to that word. Present-day readers cannot see the word "bishop" without associating aspects of pomp and ceremony (and authority) that are inappropriate in the case of the supervisor of a relatively small *collegium* in the first-century Roman Empire. As the etymology suggests, the verb *episkopein* means simpy to "oversee, supervise" (e.g., Plato, *Republic* 506A; Philo, *On the Decalogue* 98). One who fulfills that role for a group, be it club or cult or community, is an *episkopos*, a "supervisor/superintendent/overseer" (Josephus, *Antiquities* 10.4). The office of the supervisor, therefore, is *episkopē* (LXX Num 4:16: "the *episkopos* is to have the office of *episkopē*). In 1 Tim 3:1, it is the office of *episkopē* (position of supervisor) that one seeks, and in 3:2, the *episkopos* is to be blameless. The larger issue has to do with the presence and character of such an office in the nascent Christian movement. This is the only place in the NT where *episkopē* appears with reference to a position within the community. The term *episkopos*, in turn, occurs among the undisputed letters

in Phil 1:1, where it appears, as here (but in the plural), in combination with *diakanoi*. Otherwise, it appears in the NT only here, in Tit 1:7, and in Acts 20:28. In these last three passages, the term *episkopos* occurs in combination with elder (*presbyteros*) or board of elders (*presbyterion*, 4:14).[363] My translation of *episkopos* as "supervisor" in 1 Timothy respects two features of this text: its remarkably simple structure of leadership, and its complete lack of any theological legitimation.

noble role that he desires: I have translated *ergon* (literally, "work") as "role" because *episkopē* is an office.[364] It is striking that this discussion begins with such a recommendation of the task itself. Would this not be self-evident to the readers? Note likewise the recommendation of the helper's role as a *bathmos kalos* (good position). The need to describe these offices as *kalos* (noble/good) may be a way of asserting that positions that demand much of the holder also represent a gain. Something else may also be at work here: the troubles experienced in the leadership ranks of this community (5:17–22) may have had the result of making such positions less attractive to occupy.

2. *must therefore be blameless*: We find here the sort of list typical of Greco-Roman moral discourse, found in inventories of virtues and vices, in catalogues of hardships, and in polemic.[365] There is really no parallel in the undisputed letters to the sort of list of qualities presented in this passage. This is undoubtedly due, in part, to the fact that Paul nowhere else addresses the same circumstances. The most striking parallel within early Christian literature is Polycarp, *Philippians* 4:2–6:1, which describes the moral characteristics desired in wives, widows, deacons, younger men, and elders. Dibelius and Conzelmann note the resemblance to Onasander's *De Imperatoris Officio*, written under Claudius (41–54), which contains a similar catalogue of qualities sought in officials and provide a detailed comparison of the lists in 1 Tim 3:1–7 and Tit 1:7–9.[366] The ideal of being "blameless" (*enepilēmptos*, see Philo, *Special Laws* 3:24; Dio Chrysostom, *Oration* 12:66) covers the entire catalogue and forms a bracket with the final recommendation concerning a good reputation (3:7).

the husband of one wife: The phrase *mias gynaikos anēr* (literally, "a man of one woman") is capable of several meanings. It could mean that the man was married once and, if widowed, did not remarry. It could mean monogamous rather than polygamous. It could mean faithful to a wife and without a mistress. It could also be taken as prescribing a married overseer rather than a celibate

---

363. R. E. Brown, "*Episkopē* and *Episkopos*: The New Testament Evidence," *TS* 41 (1980): 322–338.

364. Since the time of Chrysostom, commentators have spoken of the need to desire the "work" (*ergon*) and not the "honor" (*kalon*) of the office. By the time of Chrysostom, ambition could be confused on that point. For a history of interpretation of the passage, see U. Holzmeister, "Si Quis Episcopum Desiderat, Bonum Opus Desiderat," *Bib* 12 (1931): 41–69.

365. For discussion, see A. Charue, "L'Appel aux ordres dans les épîtres pastorales," *Collationes Namurcenses* 33 (1939): 323–334, and C. Spicq, " 'Si Quis Episcopum Desiderat' (I Tim. 3, 1)," *RSPT* 29 (1940): 316–325.

366. For the Greek text of Onasander, see Dibelius and Conzelmann, *Pastoral Epistles*, 158–160.

one.[367] All these definitions are possible. The decision matters mainly if communities seek normative guidance from the directive. Preceded as it is by the adjective "blameless," the main point of the requirement would seem to be first the avoidance of any appearance of immorality.[368] A second consideration may be the desire for the supervisor himself to be in charge of a stable household (as 3:4 makes explicit).

sober, prudent, respectable: The virtue of sobriety (*nēphalios*) is recommended also to the women deacons in 3:11 and older women in Tit 2:2. Paul may have in mind here the literal sense of being temperate in the use of wine (Philo, *On Sobriety* 2; Josephus, *Antiquities* 3:279), although he uses the verb *nephein* in 1 Thess 5:6–8 and 2 Tim 4:5 in its moral sense of being well possessed and reasonable (Plutarch, *Precepts of Statecraft* 3 [*Mor.* 800A]; Lucian, *Nigrinus* 5). In light of the phrase *mē paroinon* (not given to wine) in the same list (3:3), the broader moral meaning is likely here. The second quality is to be *sōphron*, which here is probably best translated as "prudent/self-controlled" (Herodotus, *Persian War* 1:4). The entire range of *sōphron*-terms, so central to Greco-Roman moral discourse, is found only lightly in the undisputed letters (Rom 12:3; 2 Cor 5:13), but heavily in the Pastorals (Tit 1:8; 2:2, 4, 5, 6, 12; 2 Tim 1:7). It is at least worth noting that the moral qualities desired in women are also prescribed here for the supervisor (1 Tim 2:9, 15), suggesting that despite the distinct privileges assigned by gender with respect to leadership, Paul requires the same responsibility of both genders on the plane of moral endeavor. The adjective *kosmios* is also familar from the recommendation that women "adorn themselves" (*kosmein*) with virtue, for it is cognate to that term and identical to *kosmios*, which is used in the same verse (2:9). As applied without qualification to a person, it suggests a respectable and honorable demeanor (see it combined with *sōphron* in Philo, *Special Laws* 3:89; Lucian, *Twice-Accused* 17). Present-day readers who may think this recommendation super-ficial should remember how much authority was associated in antiquity with an appearance and sense of dignity. It is a perception that persisted until very recently.

hospitable: The virtue of being hospitable (*philoxenos*, Homer, *Odyssey* 6:121; 8:576; Epictetus, *Discourses* 1.28.23; Philo, *On Abraham* 114; Josephus, *Life* 142) may well point to some of the duties of the supervisor and be one of the reasons why heads of households were expected to play the role of supervisors: the sending and receiving of guests was an important feature of earliest Christian life (Luke 9:4–6; 10:1–16: Rom 16:1–2; 1 Cor 16:5–12; Col 4:7–10; 2 John 10–11; 3 John 5–10) and, no doubt, an expensive one. Those who were able to "refresh the hearts of the saints" financially (1 Cor 16:18; Phm 7) were in the

---

367. A. D'Ales, "La Signification des termes *monandros* et *univera*: Coup d'oeil sur la famille romaine aux premiers siècles de notre ère," *RSR* 20 (1930): 48–60; W. A. Schulze, " 'Ein Bischof sei eines Weiber Mann,' zur Exegese von 1. Tim 3,2 und Tit. 1,6," *Kerygma und Dogma* 41 (1958): 287–300.

368. S. Page, "Marital Expectations of Church Leaders in the Pastoral Epistles," *JSNT* 50 (1993): 105–120.

best position to provide it. For the attitude of hospitality, see Rom 12:13; Heb 13:2; 1 Pet 4:9.[369] The theme is even more explicitly developed in writings of the second century (*Didache* 11–13; *1 Clement* 10–12; *Shepherd of Hermas, Similitudes* 9.27.2).

an apt teacher: The adjective *didaktikos* is found only here and in 2 Tim 2:24; it appears also in Philo, *Rewards and Punishments* 27; *On Preliminary Studies* 35. Including this quality may—as in the case of "hospitable"—point to the function of the supervisor as teacher. Note that in 5:17, Paul stipulates that elders who labor in speech and *didaskalia* (teaching) are to receive double pay (*diplē timē*).

3. *not be addicted to wine*: In contrast to the term "sober" earlier in the passage, *paroinos* can only refer to a literal indulgence in wine to the point of addiction (Diogenes Laertius, *Lives of Eminent Philosophers* 1:92; Lucian, *Timon* 55; *Testament of Judah* 14:4). The cognate verb *paroinein* also has the connotation of acting violently or rudely as a result of drunkenness (Plato, *Euthyphro* 4C; Plutarch, *Alcibiades* 38.2). The prohibition is found also in Tit 1:7.

nor be violent, but should be gentle: After "violent" (*plēktēs*), some later MSS (326, 365, 614, 630) add *aiskrokerdē* (fond of dishonest gain). It has clearly been added under the influence of Tit 1:7, and would make *aphilargyros* (not a lover of money) a few words later redundant.[370] The adjective *plēktēs* means a "pugnacious or bullying person" (Diogenes Laertius, *Lives of Eminent Philosophers* 6:38; Aristotle, *Eudemian Ethics* 1221B; see also Tit 1:7). Paul ascribes the quality of being kind and gentle (*epieikēs*, Josephus, *Against Apion* 2:211; Philo, *On Dreams* 2:295; *Letter of Aristeas* 295) to Jesus in 2 Cor 10:1 and to the community in Phil 4:5 and Tit 3:2.

neither given to battle nor a lover of money: To be *a-machos* is to be one who does not engage in *machē* (battle) and, therefore, to be peaceful. The contentiousness of philosophical debates in antiquity was a standard cause for criticizing would-be sages (Dio Chrysostom, *Oration* 8:9; Lucian, *Timon* 9; *The Double Indictment* 11; *Dialogues of the Dead* 332); the desire for a kindly and peaceful supervisor may be connected to a disputatiousness among the opponents (1:4) that even leads to anger and quarreling in prayer (2:8). Love of money (*philargyria*) is one of the consistent temptations of teachers in antiquity (Philostratus, *Life of Apollonius of Tyana* 1:34; Dio Chrysostom, *Oration* 32:9, 11; 35:1; Epictetus, *Discourses* 1.9.19–20; 29.45–47; 2.16.3; 17.3; 3.24.78; 4.1.139; Lucian, *The Runaways* 14; *Philosophies for Sale* 24; *The Double Indictment* 31; *Timon* 56; *Hermotimus* 9–10). Although a warning against love of money would be expected in a *mandata principis* letter, as discussed in the INTRODUCTION, it may take on special meaning here because of the desire of some to make piety a source of gain (6:5).

---

369. For a review of the theme of hospitality in the New Testament, see J. Koenig, *New Testament Hospitality: Partnership with Strangers as Promise and Mission* (Minneapolis: Augsburg, 1985).

370. Metzger, *Textual Commentary*, 640–641.

4. *ruling well over his own household*: With this qualification, we reach the specifically administrative capacities of the potential supervisor. The participle "ruling well" comes from the verb *prohistēmi*, which means to "govern or administer" (Diodorus Siculus, *Library of History* 40.3.4; 1 Macc 5:19; Josephus, *Antiquities* 8:300; *Life* 168), and is the verb used for such leadership within the community in Rom 12:8 and 1 Thess 5:12. In this letter, the term is used with reference to supervisors (3:5), deacons (3:12), and elders (5:17). The verb has another meaning altogether in Tit 3:8, 14.

children in subordination: The noun *hypotagē* is the same as the one used for women in the assembly in 2:11. Note the assumption that the function of the leader of a household is primarily maintaining order and that this order is conceived of in terms of subordination. The supposition is universally shared in Greco-Roman and Jewish culture of the time and, indeed, in most civilizations prior to our own. This is not to suggest that they are correct, but only that Paul was unexceptional in holding them.

with complete reverence: The noun *semnotēs* is the same as the one used in 2:2. But whose reverence does Paul have in mind? The placement of the clause would make the children seem the intended reference, and thus indicate their reverence toward the parent. But the noun does not usually have a transitive quality, and in this letter Paul sometimes delays modifying clauses (see the NOTE on 3:5). It is possible, then, to think of the dignity and probity of the father/supervisor's own presence (compare Diodorus Siculus, *Library of History* 17.34.6; Josephus, *Life* 258). Note how in 3:2 the dignified appearance of the supervisor is also important.

5. *take charge of God's assembly*: With the objective genitive, *epimelesthai* means to "take charge" of something or "govern" it (Herodotus, *Persian War* 1:98; Thucydides, *Peloponnesian Wars* 3:25; Plato, *Republic* 331D; Josephus, *Antiquities* 8:297). The usage in Luke 10:34–35 is different. Paul's question is rhetorical, with the answer assumed to be self-evident: the ability to rule the church presupposes at least the ability to govern one's own household.

6. *not be a recent convert*: The adjective *neophytos* means literally "newly planted" (LXX Pss 127:3; 143:12; Isa 5:7; Job 14:9). Here is the first instance of a figurative usage that will become standard in the Christian lexicon as "neophyte." This is one of the indications in 1 Timothy suggesting that the community has been in existence for some time, although a period of two years would be more than long enough to enable such comparative criteria. Note that this criterion is missing from the matching list of Tit 1:6–9, since the delegate is there in the process of managing new communities, and every supervisor would presumably be a "new growth."

false sense of his own importance: Here and in 3:7, Paul attaches a purpose clause to the instruction: "so that he not" (*hina mē*). That which is to be avoided has as its literal sense "to become puffed up" (*typhōtheis*), a term that is used frequently in moral discourse figuratively for the sort of arrogance that derives from a sense of superior station, whether political or moral (Strabo, *Geography* 15.1.5; Plutarch, *How to Tell a Flatterer* 16 [*Mor.* 59A]; Diogenes Laertius, *Lives of Eminent Philosophers* 6:7; Dio Chrysostom, *Oration* 6:21; Josephus, *Life* 53). See also 1 Tim 6:4 and 2 Tim 3:4.

judgment reserved for the devil: The difficulty in translation is twofold. Should the genitive construction *tou diabolou* be considered subjective or objective? If subjective, then the devil is active and delivers the *krima* (judgment in the sense of condemnation), and the verb *empesē* would mean "fall under." This is possible, but in the context is strained. More likely, the genitive should be taken as objective: the devil is the one who is condemned, and the supervisor needs to beware falling into the same condemnation. This interpretation also fits the tradition of the devil as one who is punished because of the arrogance he showed toward God (Jude 9).

7. *commendation of outsiders*: "Commendation" is literally "good witness" (*kalē martyria*), which is sometimes found as the testimony borne by humans concerning the moral worth of others (Aristotle, *Politics* 1338A; Dio Chrysostom, *Oration* 45:9; Josephus, *Antiquities* 6:346). "Outsiders" is literally "those from the outside" (*apo tōn exōthen*), which is used by Paul only here and (partially) in 2 Cor 7:5, although he speaks of "those outside" (*hoi exō*) in 1 Cor 5:12; Col 4:5; 1 Thess 4:12. The use of such phrases shows a consistent awareness by Paul of the boundaries between the *ekklēsia* and the *kosmos*.

fall into disgrace: We find the same verb (*empiptein*) as in 3:6. In this case, however, the supervisor falls into "reviling" (*oneidismon*). Here the meaning must be the sort of condemning speech that would be directed toward an immoral supervisor—to his shame—rather than any reproach that he might direct to others (Josephus, *Antiquities* 19:319; Rom 15:3; Heb 10:33; 11:26; 13:13).

the trap of the devil: The same set of difficulties is found here as in 3:6: the supervisor must beware of "falling into" two things. The first is reviling, and the second is *pagida tou diabolou*. In this case, despite the parallelism with verse 6, it is better to understand the latter phrase as "the trap set by the devil" (1QS 2:11, 17; CD 4:15). See the analogous situation in 2 Tim 2:26 and, above all, the author's connection in 5:14–15 between giving an opportunity for reviling (*loidoria*) and going off after Satan.

COMMENT

It may be well to begin a consideration of Paul's instructions concerning the supervisor by restating two basic points. The first is that the designation "church order in the Pastorals" is misleading. Titus has only a handful of verses that appear to meld the position of elder and supervisor (Tit 1:5–9). 2 Timothy gives no attention to church organization. A better designation, then, is "church order in Ephesus as it can be inferred from 1 Timothy." The second point is that the position holding that the earliest Pauline churches lacked any local structure[371] must be rejected as a misreading of the evidence that derives more from theological convictions than from a fair assessment of the data. The best recent study of institutionalization in Pauline churches within the conventional de-

---

371. Classically expressed by Campenhausen, *Ecclesiastical Authority and Spiritual Power*.

velopmental framework reveals how little there is to support the picture of institutional development, once those theological underpinnings are removed and the data are read fairly.[372] Analyses grounded in a better appreciation of Paul's placement within the organizational options provided by his Greco-Roman and Hellenistic Jewish environment offer a more balanced appreciation of the structural elements in Paul's churches from the beginning.[373]

The structure suggested by 1 Timothy is simple. I mention first several key Greek terms that will recur in the discussion. The leadership is exercised by an *episkopos* who functions as part of a "board of elders" (*presbyterion*, 4:14). The most important clue to the overall duties of this board is provided by 5:17: "Elders who govern well [*kalōs proestōtes*] should be considered worthy of double compensation [*diplēs timēs*], especially those who labor [*kopiōntes*] in speech [*logō*] and in teaching [*didaskalia*]." The statement suggests first of all that the basic job of the *presbyterion* was to govern and that further duties might or might not be involved, depending on gifts and needs.[374] Note, for example, how "governing well" (*kalōs proistamenoi*) is the same phrase used of the role of supervisors and helpers over their respective households (3:4, 12). The office of supervisor might well have been a revolving one, according to abilities. Apparently, not all elders "labor in speech and in teaching"—that is, preach and teach. Yet the supervisor should have among his moral qualities the capacity to be "an apt teacher"(*didaktikos*, 3:2).

The Collegial Structure of Ancient Communities

Such a collegial leadership, with a single figure serving as supervisor or coordinator, is the basic structure for intentional groups in the first-century Mediterranean world. Among the sectarians at Qumran, for example, we find a "council of holiness" (1QS 8:6–8; 9:3–11) as well as an officer called the *mebaqqer*, whose title and duties seem purely administrative and similar to those envisaged for the *episkopos* in 1 Timothy (1QS 6:12, 20; CD 9:18–19, 22; 13:6–7).[375] Cults and *collegia* in the Roman Empire had boards whose main functions were administrative, including the raising and distributing of group funds. Various cultic activities could be added to the basic administrative ones.[376] The most obvi-

372. MacDonald, *Pauline Churches*.

373. R. A. Campbell, *The Elders: Seniority Within Earliest Christianity* (Edinburgh: Clark, 1994); J. T. Burtchaell, *From Synagogue to Church: Public Services and Offices in the Earliest Christian Communities* (Cambridge: Cambridge University Press, 1992).

374. J. P. Meier, "*presbyteros* in the Pastoral Epistles," CBQ 35 (1973): 325–345.

375. Reicke, "Constitution of the Early Church in the Light of Jewish Documents."

376. J. Kloppenborg, "Edwin Hatch, Churches, and *Collegia*," in *Origins and Method: Towards a New Understanding of Judaism and Christianity: Essays in Honour of John C. Hurd* ed. B. H. McLean, JSNTS 86 (Sheffield: Sheffield Academic Press, 1993), 212–238; B. H. McLean, "The Agrippinilla Inscription: Religious Associations and Early Christian Formation," in *Origins and Method: Towards a New Understanding of Judaism and Christianity: Essays in Honour of John C. Hurd*, ed. B. H. McLean, JSNTS 86 (Sheffield: Sheffield Academic Press, 1993), 239–270.

ous example is the consulship in relation to the Roman Senate. The office
of consul was rotated among members of the larger *collegium* that was the
Senate.[377]

We do not know nearly what we would like to about the structure of the diaspora synagogue. We are able to reconstruct some of the basic lines of its organization.[378] Its leadership was provided by a board of male elders (*gerousia*).[379]
This board oversaw financial affairs, including the administration of the community charity, (Josephus, *Antiquities* 4:214–218; *Life* 294–302; Philo, *Life of
Moses* 2:216; *Special Laws* 2:62; *b. Ber.* 6a, 64a; *b. Ket.* 5a; *b. B.M.* 28b; *b. Pes.*
101a) and settled disputes (Josephus, *Antiquities* 14:110–118; Philo, *Embassy to
Gaius* 229; 2 Macc 1:10; 11:27). The *archisynagogos*, sometimes in the singular and sometimes in the plural, appears as the "head of the synagogue." Inscriptional evidence suggests that such persons were often heads of households—
in some cases, women[380]—who served as wealthy patrons of the community. It
is entirely plausible to suppose that in many cases a *gerousia* would consist of
males with property who were also heads of households. The synagogue also had
an officer known as the *chazzan* (Greek, *hypēretēs*, "server"), to carry out practical functions, including those in worship.[381]

In 1 Timothy, we have the board of elders, a leadership position called the
supervisor, and subordinate officials—probably both male and female (3:11)—
called literally "helpers" (*diakonoi*). The correlation of offices to functions is not
revealed. But we learn that the community carries out certain activities that
match those we know about in the diaspora synagogue. It performs public prayer
together with reading and exhortation (4:13; 2:1–3). It makes charity distribution to widows (5:3–16). It exercises hospitality (3:2). It hears and settles disputes
(5:19–20).

Organizational Elements in Early-Second-Century Writings

The same titles of supervisor, elder, and helper appear in the second-century
writings with which the Pastoral Letters are so frequently compared. We find
the combination *episkopos/diakonos* in *Didache* 15:1. In *1 Clement* 42:4–5, there
are *episkopoi* and *diakonoi*, together with *presbyteroi* in 44:5; 47:6; 54:2; 57:1.
Perhaps suprisingly, Polycarp's *Letter to the Philippians* does not speak of
episkopoi and mentions only *presbyteroi* (in the Greeting; see also 6:1; 11:1) and

377. Campbell, *Elders*, 67–96.

378. S. Appelbaum, "The Organization of the Jewish Communities in the Diaspora," in *The
Jewish People in the First Century: Historical Geography, Political History, Social, Cultural and Religious Life and Institutions*, ed. S. Safrai and M. Stern, CRINT 1 (Philadelphia: Fortress Press,
1974), 1:464–503; Safrai, "Synagogue."

379. A. E. Harvey, correctly notes the paucity of the occurrence of the actual term "elder" in
our evidence concerning the synagogue in "Elders," *JTS* 25 (1974): 318–322.

380. B. J. Brooten, "Inscriptional Evidence for Women as Leaders of the Ancient Synagogue"
(Ph.D. diss., Harvard University, 1982).

381. For the evidence, see Burtchaell, *From Synagogue to Church*, 180–271.

diakonoi (5:2). Even less is said in these writings about the respective responsibilities of the offices than in 1 Timothy, but the basic structure seems to be much the same. The threefold combination is found everywhere in the letters of Ignatius (e.g., *Eph* 1:3; 2:1–2; 4:1). In the case of Ignatius, however, the *episkopos* is singular and is definitely elevated to a position above that of the elders, a distinction impossible to detect in either 1 Timothy or Titus. Even more important, 1 Timothy lacks entirely the theological legitimation for the hierarchy that we find so prominently displayed in the writings of Ignatius (Eph 3:2; 4:1–2; 5:1–2; 6:1; *Magn.* 3:1–2; 6:1; 7:1; *Tral.* 2:1–2; 3:1; *Phil.* 3:2; 4:1; *Smyr.* 8:1–2; 9:1). The structure is both simple and functional.

Local Leadership in the Undisputed Pauline Letters

Evidence for local leadership roles and functions in Paul's communities is not overwhelming, but neither is it insignificant.[382] Indeed, the picture that 1 Timothy gives of the community organization in Ephesus, with its typical activities of worship, hospitality, sharing possessions, teaching, and settling disputes, accords remarkably well with the data concerning local leadership in the undisputed letters. At no point does it contradict that evidence or present a more elaborate structure. Only a theological conviction that Paul's communities necessarily were solely charismatic and, in principle, opposed to structure could account for the way in which the plain evidence presented by these letters is systematically underplayed by scholars.[383]

1 Thessalonians is generally acknowledged as Paul's earliest extant letter. It was written to a community that had been in existence for only a short time and was surviving under circumstances of considerable duress. After exhorting the community members as a whole to build one another up (5:11), Paul instructs them: "We beseech you brethren, to respect [literally, "know" (*eidenai*)] those who are laboring [*kopiōntes*] among you, and are ruling over you [*proistamenous hymōn*] in the Lord and admonishing [*nouthetountas*] you. Esteem them very highly in love because of their work." I note first that Paul assumes that there *are* persons in leadership roles even in this community, which had existed for only a short time (perhaps a matter of months). Second, we see that he uses the same expression, "ruling over" (*proistamenoi*), for this leadership that he uses in 1 Tim 3:4 and 5:17. Third, we observe that such leadership is designated as "labor" (*kopiōntes*), as in 1 Tim 5:17. Fourth, we learn that such labor involves ver-

---

382. Weizsäcker, "Kirchenverfassung des apostolischer Zeitalter"; J. Reumann, "Church Office in Paul, Especially in Philippians," in *Origins and Method: Towards a New Understanding of Judaism and Christianity: Essays in Honour of John C. Hurd*, ed. B. H. McLean, JSNTS 86 (Sheffield: Sheffield Academic Press), 82–91; B. Holmberg, *Paul and Power: The Structure of Authority in the Primitive Church as Reflected in the Pauline Epistles* (Lund: CWK Gleerup, 1978), tries to avoid the theological tendentiousness of von Campenhausen, but his analysis remains primarily within the realm of the charismatic gifts, rather than practical functions.

383. As in Sohm, *Kirchenrecht*, vol. 1, *Die Geschichtliche Grundlagen*.

bal admonition, which we may plausibly consider to be either a form of teaching or preaching. Finally, we find that the members of the community are to recognize and highly esteem such leaders among them. If this passage is taken as seriously as it should be, it demolishes all by itself the supposition that Paul's local communities had no leadership structure during his lifetime.

1 Corinthians is the supreme example of not only a letter that was written to a church founded by Paul himself and nurtured for some time by him, but also one in which Paul's stress on his own authority to teach (e.g., 4:14–21; 7:40; 14:37–38) and the spiritual gifts bestowed on the church (1:5; 12:4–31) might lead to the idea that Paul had no concern for local authority structures. In fact, however, Paul assumes in 1 Cor 6:1–6 that the *ekklēsia* should have a structure *epi tōn hagiōn* (before the saints) for settling disputes (*kritēria*). He rebukes the members of the church for appointing (*kathizete*, "sitting") in such positions those in the community who are not respected (*tous exouthenēmenous*). He asks by way of rebuke whether they do not have "any one wise enough among you who is capable of making a judgment between brothers" (6:5). Because of their failure to establish an effective court in the community, members are suing one another "before unbelievers" (*epi apistōn*)—that is, presumably, in Greco-Roman small-claims courts.[384] Two of the spiritual gifts listed by Paul in 12:28 point to such quotidian administrative tasks: *antilēmpsis* (doing helpful deeds) and *kybernēsis* (governing).

Finally, Paul provides in 1 Cor 16:15–18 a sketch of the sort of men he would like to see settling disputes in the Corinthian congregation. His readers are told to "recognize" (*oidate*) the household of Stephanas, which performed service (*diakonia*) for the saints (16:15). They are to "submit themselves [*hypotassesthe*] to such as these and to each one who is a fellow worker [*synergounti*] and laborer [*kopiōnti*]" (16:16). His language suggests that Stephanas and Fortunatus and Achaicus provided financial support—"they have refreshed my spirit and yours" (16:18)—and he tells the community to "recognize [*epiginōskete*] therefore people such as these" (16:18). As in Thessalonica, Paul clearly expects the Corinthian assemblies to have local leadership. The three wealthy men—may we add Crispus and Gaius (1:14)?—who serve as heads of households and as patrons of the community, would qualify as candidates for the *presbyterion/ gerousia* that we would expect to find in the diaspora synagogue, and do find in 1 Tim 3:4–5. In the latter, being an effective "head of household" is a positive criterion for serving as a supervisor (*episkopos*).[385]

---

384. A. C. Mitchell, "1 Cor. 6:1–11: Group Boundaries and the Courts of Corinth" (Ph.D. diss., Yale University, 1986).

385. Another way to approach this question is by observing the number and kinds of practical tasks that Paul expects the Corinthian *ekklesia* to perform, which would be virtually impossible were there not administrative structures in place to accomplish them. They are to (1) gather in assemblies; (2) receive and read letters; (3) receive guests and emissaries; (4) take up collections of money; (5) share meals; (6) practice prophecy and teaching in assembly; (7) excommunicate a member; and (8) settle disputes. Such things do not happen spontaneously within groups, but require coordination and decision making.

Paul's list of *charismata* in Rom 12:7–8 is also revealing. We find there *diakonia* (service), *didaskalia* (teaching), and *paraklēsis* (consolation; compare 1 Thess 5:12). Even more striking are the final three gifts. Two of them concern the sharing of possessions, which, as I have suggested, was a standard feature of the diaspora synagogue: *ho metadidous* (the one who shares) and *ho eleōn* (the one who shows mercy/gives alms). The third is the gift of presiding or ruling (*ho proistamenos*), using the same term that I have already noted in 1 Thess 5:12 and 1 Tim 5:17. In Rom 16:1, Paul identifies Phoebe as a "deacon [*diakonos*] of the church at Cenchrae" (a suburb of Corinth), and in 16:3 as a financial patron (*prostatis*) of many, including Paul himself. It is the context that makes the rendering of *prostatis* as "financial patron" certain; note, however, that it is etymologically related to *proistēmi*, the verb we have seen repeatedly used for leadership positions. Paul's reference to Phoebe is important for showing how he used *diakonos* for a title in churches other than Philippi (see the NOTE on 3:8) and for demonstrating that in the Corinthian church (broadly considered) there was at least one woman who served as such a "helper" (*diakonos*; see also the NOTE on 3:11).

Evidence from two other undisputed letters is pertinent. In Gal 6:6, Paul advises that "the one who is instructed [*katechoumenos*] should share in all good things with the one who is instructing the word [*ton logon katechounti*]." This confirms the presence of a teaching role that was financially supported in the Galatian churches, as well as Paul's general position concerning the financial support of those who labor in the word (1 Cor 9:3–18). Finally, we note Phil 1:1, which, to the embarrassment of all who seek to remove any such contrary evidence from the "authentic" Paul, sends greetings to "the saints who are in Philippi, together with [their] supervisors [*episkopois*] and helpers [*diakonois*]." The greeting plainly shows that at least in one Pauline church addressed by an "authentic" letter, there were leaders recognizable by the titles used also in the letters to Paul's delegates. The only discrepant note is Philippians' use of the plural and anarthous "supervisors" and "helpers," rather than the singular and articular forms found in 1 Tim 3:2 and Tit 1:7. One might want to argue that such precision represents a development from generic to specific and, therefore, from "several bishops" to "a single bishop." But it is equally possible to argue for a certain fluidity in offices and titles (suggested by Tit 1:5–7), as well as local variations.

Please note the precise claim that this review of evidence supports. It is impossible to reconstruct the "local authority structure of the Pauline church." The evidence is insufficient for that task, both in the undisputed letters and in 1 Timothy and Titus. Moreover, the assumption that exactly the same structure prevailed everywhere from the beginning is implausible. We should think rather of patterns of organization that share elements with diverse local expressions. The evidence I have adduced does, however, support the claim made earlier that the elements of stucture we are able to discern in both the undisputed letters and 1 Timothy are remarkably consonant in three ways:

1. With the exception of the title of elder, there are the same roles and functions, which fit within the collegial leadership structure of Greco-Roman associations and the Hellenistic synagogue.
2. In both sets of writings, the structure is simple and functional with no theological legitimation.
3. There is no discernible development in the direction of complexity or rationalization between 1 Corinthians and 1 Timothy.

The fairest way to deal with the evidence is to treat it as deriving from and addressing roughly the same circumstances. In short, analysis of the "church order" in 1 Timothy does not by any means demonstrate Pauline authorship of the letter, but it destroys the argument for inauthenticity on the grounds of a more developed church structure.

Qualities of the Supervisor

In order to assess and appreciate the qualities prescribed for the supervisor, it is important to note the way in which the *oikos* functions as a point of reference. Paul will later (3:15) speak of the *ekklēsia* itself as the *oikos tou theou* (household of God). But does this mean that the metaphor of the household has worked to dissolve the sociological boundaries between the *oikos* and the *ekklēsia*, so that there is little real distinction between the two realities? Some have made that argument.[386] But here and again in 5:3–16, the distinction between the two social realities is critical to Paul's argument. Precisely because the household is a distinct social institution different from the "assembly of the living God" (3:15) does an ability to manage well within it serve as a useful criterion for leadership within the assembly. The capacity to "preside/rule" (*proistamenos*) within an implied patriarchal arrangement of power is the constant: the social locations of *oikos* and *ekklēsia* are the variables.

The concept of "good management of a household" provides the best access to the particular virtues of the supervisor. We notice that only two of the specific qualities point to activities: that the supervisor be hospitable and an apt teacher. The function of teaching is touched on in 5:17 as one of the duties that might be taken on by a *presbyteros*. Providing hospitality is an obvious expectation of a householder in antiquity and is several times in the NT specifically connected to churches in households (1 Cor 16:10–12; Col 4:10; 2 John 10). Otherwise, it is the capacity to "preside well" over a household that is expected to be applied to the life of the church. What this means specifically is the ability to keep one's children behaviorally in good order (literally, in subordination) and attitudinally "in all reverence." Clearly, leadership here is envisaged as a

---

386. See, for example, D. C. Verner, *The Household of God: The Social World of the Pastoral Epistles* SBLDS 71 (Chico, Calif.: Scholars Press, 1983), esp. 128, 145–147.

much more directive and controlling role than is comfortable for contemporary readers who at best consider leaders as "enablers" or "facilitators."

Given the sort of authority assumed here, it is noteworthy that the other attributes expected in the supervisor are ameliorative moral qualities that mitigate against any hint of arbitrary or harsh uses of power. To be sober and not a lover of wine means that the supervisor is not corrupted by pleasure, and his judgments are not affected by crass addictions. To be nonviolent and not given to battle means that the leader is not corrupted by envy and vainglory and is able to cultivate cooperation rather than competition, foment peace rather than conflict. Not to be a lover of money means that the leader is not corrupted by avarice and thus is able to place the community's interests before his own. Likewise, the virtues of prudence and reasonableness point to a leader who applies the best qualities of mind and character to decision making.

Such characteristics are not terribly exciting, and when authentic faith is identified with sudden conversion or a single spasm of heroism, these virtues might be mistaken for that "bourgeois morality" often associated with the Pastorals. But Paul said in another letter, when speaking of himself and Apollos as "stewards of households" (oikonomoi), that "it is required of stewards that they be found trustworthy" (1 Cor 4:2). Fidelity to one spouse, sobriety, steadiness, and quiet sanity may seem negligible qualities to the romantically or erratically inclined, but those who are leaders within churches find that failure in such virtues does, in fact, erode and often destroy the fabric of trust that is essential for credible leadership. And for those who have found such qualities all too rarely in ecclesiastical leaders, this list of desiderata seems like pure gold.

It is, in fact, one of the sad consequences of the marginalization of these letters to Paul's delegates that the genuine wisdom concerning leadership that they contain speaks less convincingly to contemporary readers than it did to those readers of the past (like Augustine, On Christian Doctrine) who considered the instructions to come not only from Paul, but also from the Holy Spirit.

The final two qualifications can illustrate. In 3:6, Paul disqualifies from the supervisor's role one who is a recent convert (neophytos, "newly planted"). Such a limitation might offend present-day egalitarian instincts, especially when combined with a highly individualistic understanding of "vocation" to ecclesial leadership. Given the contemporary tendency to professionalize identity, a rapid movement toward leadership seems a natural ecclesial analogue to the competitive corporate world. But there is great wisdom in the insistence that persons grow to full maturity within a community identity before assuming leadership within it, and Paul's perception that a too rapid ascent to preeminence leads to arrogance has often enough been proved true. Indeed, precisely the failure to develop such maturity among leaders may have led in Ephesus to the sorts of leadership problems touched on in 5:17–23: note that Paul enjoins Timothy not to "lay hands on [that is, ordain] anyone quickly" (5:22).

Similarly, Paul's desire that the supervisor be "blameless" (3:2) and "should also have the commendation of outsiders" (3:7) may seem to modern readers as a capitulation to society's conventional standards, a failure in the church's prophetic stance, reflecting the process of the church "accommodating itself to the world." Such a view may make sense in the twenty-first century, after the church has existed for two millennia and accommodated itself all too often to a variety of outsiders. But taking the qualification in the historical context of Paul's efforts to found and sustain new communities allows a more sympathetic reading. First, it may be remembered that although Paul otherwise demanded a moral boundary between the saints and the world (2 Cor 6:14–18), he by no means considered it necessary to separate entirely from the world (1 Cor 5:9). Indeed, as in 1 Tim 5:8, he can use pagan morality as a baseline below which it is unthinkable that Christians should fall (1 Cor 5:1). Paul is sensitive to the perceptions that outsiders have of the community's worship practices (1 Cor 11:4–6; 14:23, 40). He advises meeting society's basic demands (Rom 13:7) and "doing good to all people" (Gal 6:10). In two places particularly, Paul shows an awareness of the community's reputation with outsiders. In Col 4:5, he advises readers to "walk in wisdom with regard to those outside, taking good advantage of the season," and in 1 Thess 4:12, after telling his readers to live quietly and work with their hands, he expresses the purpose: "so that you might walk becomingly toward those who are outsiders and may have no need." Second, we observe that a concern for reputation is especially necessary when the behavior of some leaders is bringing the community into disrepute. Paul's comments about troubled elders in 5:17–22 certainly points to a leadership crisis in the Ephesian community. And Paul's worry concerning younger widows who spend their time wandering from house to house gives a sharp edge to the issue of good reputation: if they observe their proper domestic roles, they are "giving no opportunity on the basis of reviling to the one who opposes us. For some have already turned aside after Satan" (5:14–15). To ask for a leader who has moral probity and is known by outsiders as having such virtue is to make a legitimate request at any time, but, above all, when the reputation of the community is threatened by leaders who lack such qualities.

VIII. BEHAVIOR IN THE
HOUSEHOLD OF GOD (3:8–16)

◆

3 ⁸Helpers likewise should be dignified. They should not be duplicitous, over-fond of wine, or willing to do anything for a profit. ⁹They should hold unto the mystery of faith with a pure conscience. ¹⁰They also should first be tested, and then, being blameless, they can carry out their service. ¹¹Women helpers like-wise should be dignified, should not be gossipers, should be sober, and should be faithful in every respect. ¹²Let the helpers be men who have one wife, who manage their children and their own household affairs well. ¹³Those who have served well have thereby gained a good position for themselves and much con-fidence in the faith that is in Christ Jesus. ¹⁴I am writing these things to you even though I hope to come to you shortly. ¹⁵But if I am delayed, you should know how it is necessary to behave in the household of God, which is the church of the living God, as a pillar and support for the truth. ¹⁶The mystery of godli-ness is—we confess—a great one: He was manifested in flesh, he was made righ-teous by spirit, he appeared to messengers, he was preached among nations, he was believed in by the world, he was taken up in glory.

NOTES

8. *Helpers likewise*: I have chosen to translate *diakonos* as "helper" to correspond to the lowercase rendering of *episkopos* as "supervisor." In this instance, we have a term that not only becomes a rank within the ecclesiastical hierarchy, but also served as a stage toward a still higher rank. Translating *diakonos* as "deacon" is therefore as potentially misleading as translating *episkopos* as "bishop." It is a common Pauline term. For the range of meanings in his letters, see Phil 1:1; Rom 13:4; 15:8; 16:1; 1 Cor 3:5; 2 Cor 3:6; 6:4; 11:15, 23; Gal 2:17; Col 1:7; 1 Thess 3:2 [variant reading]. The noun *diakonos* also appears together with *episkopos* in *Didache* 15:1, as well as in many writings of Ignatius of Antioch (e.g., *Eph* 1:3; 2:1). Qualities desired in a *diakonos* are listed in Polycarp, *Philip-pians* 5:2. A survey of the passages shows that the term can include a variety of specific activities that are linked primarily by their practical character. No spe-cific functions are assigned to the *diakonos* in 1 Timothy. As noted earlier, the *chazzan* (*hypēretēs*) in the diaspora synagogue helped in worship (Luke 4:20). No such liturgical function is mentioned in 1 Timothy. Burtchaell lists other

functions assigned to the *chazzan*.[387] We also know that synagogues appointed men as collectors and distributors of the community charity (*b. Meg.* 27a; *B. Bat.* 8a–b; *b. Rosh Hash.* 4a–5b; *Ta'an.* 24a; *b. Shab.* 118b). Although the title *diakonoi* is not given to them by Luke, the seven appointed by the Jerusalem church to oversee distribution to the Gentile widows (Acts 6:1–6) clearly fit into this category of helper. A number of times, moreover, the verb *diakonein* and the noun *diakonia* are used in connection with financial matters, such as Paul's collection (e.g., Acts 12:25; Rom 15:25, 31; 2 Cor 8:4; 9:1). It is possible that the *diakonoi* were involved also in the Ephesian welfare system for widows (5:3–16).

should be dignified: We have seen that the supervisor was to keep his children in subjection "with all reverence" (*semnotēs*); the adjectival form *semnos* is now applied to the helpers. It naturally has the same range of meaning as the substantive (e.g., Philo, *Decalogue* 136; *Embassy to Gaius* 163; *Sibylline Oracles* 5:262; *Letter of Aristeas* 31; Phil 4:8). I repeat the point that in antiquity authority was positively correlated with dignity in bearing.

not be duplicitous: I render *dilogos* as "duplicitous," taking the etymology ("double-worded") as justification. It is a NT *hapax legomenon* and is attested in this sense elsewhere in only Polycarp, *Philippians* 5:2, where it may well be dependent on this passage. Although such *di-* constructions are attested before the time of Paul, they multiply after it.[388] The vice of duplicity in speech is invariably disruptive within communities, but it is particularly destructive when practiced by those whose functions place them in the position of trusted go-betweens, as the office of *diakonos* apparently did. Honesty in such brokers is highly prized.

overfond of wine: The verb *prosechein* is the same one used of the devotion to speculations of the would-be teachers in 1:4. The effect of nighttime drink on sober-by-day philosophers is thoroughly observed by the critics of the profession (e.g., Lucian of Samosata, *Timon* 54; *The Carousal* 11; *Philosophies for Sale* 12; Philostratus, *Life of Apollonius of Tyana* 1:34).

do anything for a profit: My translation is unusually free, since the term *aischrokerdēs* is exceptionally rich in cultural associations that are no longer obvious to contemporary readers when it is translated as "eager for shameful gain." The basic idea is captured by "people who do anything for a profit," but it would be better to add the value judgment "they have no shame" (*aischros*). See, for example, Herodotus, *Persian War* 1:187; Plato, *Republic* 408C; Aristotle, *Nicomachean Ethics* 1122A; *Testament of Judah* 16:1 (see also the references for *philargyria* in 3:3). Lack of acquisitiveness is particularly important if the *diakonoi* were involved in the community's support for the widows (5:3–16). Such moral probity was also sought in those involved in synagogue charity collection and distribution (*m. Shek.* 5.2; *b. 'Abod. Zar.* 17b; *B. Bat.* 8b).

---

387. Burtchaell, *From Synagogue to Church*, 246–251.
388. See the note on James 1:8 (*dipsychos*) in Johnson, *Letter of James*, 180.

9. *hold unto the mystery of faith*: The phrase *mysterion tes pisteos* might also be translated as "the mystery that is faith"; it clearly anticipates the phrase *tes eusebeias mystērion* in 3:16. For Paul's understanding of God's plan as a *mystērion*—that which is revealed transcendently—see Rom 11:25; 16:25; 1 Cor 2:1, 7; 15:51; Eph 1:9; 3:3–4, 9; 6:19; Col 1:26–27; 2:2; 4:3; 2 Thess 2:7. The term has complex roots both in the Septuagint translation of the Hebrew/Aramaic *raz* by *mystērion* (Dan 2:18–47; Wis 2:22; 6:22) and in the religious traditions of Hellenism (Herodotus, *Persian War* 2:51; Diodorus Siculus, *Library of History* 1.29.3; Philo, *Special Laws* 1:319; 3:37–42). Of particular interest is the way that Paul characterizes himself and Apollos as *oikonomoi mystērion theou* (household managers of the mysteries of God), which comes close in both language and conception to the understanding of ministry in this passage. It is also striking how the *mystērion* is here defined simply as "faith," consistent with the emphasis on *pistis* throughout 1 Timothy (see the NOTES on 1:4–5). The concluding phrase, "with a pure conscience" (*en katharā syneidēsei*), recalls the "good conscience" of 1:5, with the added nuance of the probity asked of those serving the common good, especially in financial matters.

10. *first be tested*: No specific time or process of "testing" is specified, but the context of unworthiness among the ministers of the Ephesian church suggests the appropriateness of this step. The term *dokimazein* can be applied to the soundness of animals (Herodotus, *Persian War* 2:38; Luke 14:19) or persons for a specific task (*Letter of Aristeas* 276; Josephus, *Antiquities* 1:233; 1 Cor 11:28; 2 Cor 13:5; Gal 6:4).

being blameless, they can carry out their service: The adjective *anenklētos* (Epictetus, *Discourse* 1.28.10; Josephus, *Antiquities* 10:281; 3 Macc 5:31) is used by Paul also for Christians in 1 Cor 1:8 and Col 1:22 (see also Tit 1:6–7). I have translated the third-person imperative *diakoneitōsan* as "carry out their service," rather than "let them serve," to capture the sense of the present tense. The idea is that the helpers have proved worthy in the first phase of their service, so they can continue to do what they have begun.

11. *Women helpers likewise*: The basic difficulty here involves what is meant by "women." Does Paul mean "women in general," "wives of male helpers/ supervisors," or—as my translation indicates—"women helpers?"[389] I have chosen to translate as "women helpers" for the following reasons:

1. The connective *hōsautōs* seems to differentiate between men and women in the same function (compare 2:8–9).
2. Although 3:12 mentions that helpers should have one wife, 3:11 does not identify these women as *their* wives.
3. The characteristics sought in the *gynaikes* are strikingly similar to those desired in the male helper, with "not be gossipers" matching "not be du-

---

389. B. C. Blackburn, "The Identity of 'The Women' in 1 Tim. 3:11," in *Essays on Women in Early Christianity*, ed. C. D. Osburn (Joplin, Mo.: College Press, 1995), 1:303–319.

plicitous," "dignified" matching "dignified," and "faithful in every respect" matching "hold unto the mystery of faith."

4. In Rom 16:1, Paul names Phoebe as a *diakonos* of the church at Cenchrae, so we know that he had no difficulty with women holding such a position.[390]

Even if this is the case, of course, we have as little knowledge of what a woman helper would do as we have of the male helper. We do know that her functions would not include teaching in public or having authority over males (2:11–15).

dignified, . . . not be gossipers, . . . be sober: These qualities match those recommended to deacons: dignity (*semna*) matches dignity (*semnos*); not gossiping or slandering (*diabolous*, Thucydides, *Peloponnesian Wars* 6.15.2; Philo, *The Sacrifice of Abel and Cain* 32) matches not duplicitous (*dilogos*); and sober (*nēphalious*, 3:2) matches not devoted to wine in the case of deacons. The additional note for deacons is "not . . . willing to do anything for a profit" (*aischrokerdēs*), which may more properly apply to men who would be handling the community's financial resources.

faithful in every respect: The phrase *pistas en pasin* corresponds to the male deacons holding "unto the mystery of faith." The *pasin* could also be translated as "in all matters," with a more specific reference to her tasks than to her character. See also the "faithful woman" (*pistē*) in 5:16.

12. *men who have one wife*: The same range of options applies here as with the same criterion in the case of the supervisor (3:2). The most likely option is the same: that the man who has proved faithful in his marriage is the most likely both to have and to inspire trust within the covenanted community that is the *ekklēsia*.

manage their children and their own household affairs: The basic administrative ability is desired here as in the case of the supervisor (3:4), with only a slight difference. With the supervisor, it was only the managing (*proistamenos*) of the children that is in view. With the helper, it is both their children *and* their households. Does this suggest the sort of practical skill of management as well as of presiding that might be particularly pertinent to the helper?

13. *have . . . gained a good position*: There are three problems here. The first concerns the logical relationship (established by the connective *gar*, "for") between this sentence and the previous one. How does verse 13 illuminate or explain verse 12? The second problem is what is meant by a good or noble (*kalos*) position/rank/stage (*bathmos*), a NT *hapax legomenon* that literally means a "step" (Josephus, *Jewish War* 5:206), but is used figuratively to refer to a rank or grade (Philo, *On the Eternity of the World* 58). Does it imply a fixed hierarchical system whose stages one can progressively climb? Or is it simply an approval

---

390. See also the argument in J. H. Steifel, "Women Deacons in 1 Timothy: A Linguistic and Literary Look at 'Women likewise . . . ' (1 Tim. 3:11)," *NTS* 41 (1995): 442–457. K. Romaniuk argues rather oddly that whereas the women in 1 Tim 3:11 are deacons, Phoebe is not, in "Was Phoebe in Rom. 16:1 a Deaconess?" *ZNW* 81 (1990): 130–134.

of the present position? The decision depends to some extent on the solution to
the third problem, which concerns the final phrase. How is "much confidence"
connected to "in the faith that is in Christ Jesus," and how are both phrases connected to the previous clauses? None of this is clear. It is possible that Paul is
suggesting that the helper who has served well has a sort of career confidence —
that is, a hope for advancement through the ranks of the hierarchy. But nothing else in the letter suggests such a linkage between the offices. A second possibility follows.

much confidence in the faith: The expression "much confidence" (*pollē parrhēsia*) has a parallel in 2 Cor 3:12 and, especially, in Phm 8: *pollēn en Christō
parrhēsian echōn* (having much confidence in Christ). If we take "in the faith
that is in Christ Jesus" to be a general reference to the shared life of the community, then Paul's point may simply be that the one who has served well as a
helper has a secure place within the community of faith.[391] And, as in the case
of the role of the supervisor, the author may be seeking to rehabilitate services
within the community that recent troubles among the leaders (5:17–22) have
tarnished. But if we take "the faith that is in Christ Jesus" in a stronger sense,
as "sharing the faith that Jesus demonstrated in his humanity," then there is a
stronger link between the helpers' identity and their service: serving well in the
community is a strong and confident expression of their Christian faith.

14. *I am writing these things to you*: The phrase *tauta soi graphō* finds its exact parallel in 2 Cor 13:10: *dia touto tauta apōn graphō* (on this account because I am absent I am writing these things). If 1 Timothy is indeed a *mandata
principis* letter, Paul may well have discussed these *entolai* with his delegate before his departure and Timothy's taking up his duty. Such letters functioned not
as a source of new information, but as an aide-mémoire to instructions first delivered orally.

even though I hope to come: With 1 Tim 1:3 and 4:13, this verse and the next
sketch the mise-en-scène of the letter: Paul is away, hopes to return soon, but
delivers these instructions to his delegate (and, over the shoulder, to the community at Ephesus as well) in order to make his authority present. The judgment that this is all a fictional representation must deal with the fact that both
the words and the modus operandi are recognizably Pauline. In 1 Cor 4:17, Paul
sends Timothy to Corinth to remind that community "of my ways as I teach
them always in every church" while he is absent, even though he expects to
come to them shortly (1 Cor 4:19; see also 16:10–11). Paul sends Timothy to
the Philippians in order to learn how that church is doing (Phil 2:19), even
though, once more, he hopes to come to them quickly (Phil 2:24). When Paul
is not able to travel to Thessalonica, he sends Timothy as his delegate so that
the church might be "strengthened and comforted" in its tribulations (1 Thess
3:1–6). The sort of ad hoc directions we find in 1 Timothy are, in my view, per-

---

391. I confess to being mystified by Dibelius and Conzelmann's translation of *parrhēsia* as "true
cheerfulness" (*Pastoral Epistles*, 58–59).

fectly consonant with the functions of the delegate Timothy as touched on in Paul's other letters.[392] The alternative is to suppose that a pseudepigrapher has perfectly captured Paul's consistent practice as it was revealed in these scattered remarks across his correspondence.

15. *necessary to behave in the household of God*: This verse is often taken as expressing the central theme of 1 Timothy and, if taken in conjunction with 1:4–5, may fairly be understood as such. The phrase *pōs dei en oikō theou anastrephesthai* (how it is necessary to behave in the household of God) is similar to the one used by Paul in 1 Thess 4:1: *to pōs dei hymas peripatein kai areskein theō* (how it is necessary for you to walk and please God). The verb *anastraphesthai* is used in moral discourse not simply for "behavior" in the narrow sense, but for "manner of life" in accord with certain guiding principles (Polybius, *History of Rome* 1.9.7; Xenophon, *Anabasis* 2.5.14; Aristotle, *Nicomachean Ethics* 1103B; Josephus, *Antiquities* 15:190; in the NT, see Eph 2:3; 2 Cor 1:12; Heb 10:33; 2 Pet 2:18). Paul uses the expression *oikodomē theou* with reference to the assembly in 1 Cor 3:9 and Eph 2:21 and 4:12 (without *theou*). The translation of "household" here is important because of the theme of managing households in 3:4, 5, 12, but the imagery of the temple is not entirely absent in Paul's reference to the *stylos* (Rev 3:12).

the church of the living God: It is clear that the *ekklēsia* is the main point of reference here, with "household of God" serving as a prime metaphor, not least because Paul's instructions in 1 Timothy are directed to matters of public concern to the *ekklēsia*, not to matters of domestic economy. That this assembly is one gathered by "the living God" (*theou zōntos*) is of first importance thematically (4:10; 5:6) and theologically, for it means that the church does not contain or control God, but is only in service to the one who moves always ahead of humans in surprising yet faithful ways.

as a pillar and support for the truth: Both *stylos* and *hedraiōma* are architectural terms for "supports, stays, or pillars." For *stylos*, see Herodotus, *Persian War* 2:169; Sir 24:4; Exod 13:21; in the Temple, see Josephus, *Antiquities* 8:77; as applied to people, see Philo, *Migration of Abraham* 124. This is the only NT usage of *hedraiōma*. For the cognate adjective *hedraios*, see 1 Cor 7:37 and 15:58 and Col 1:23. The issue for the translator is not the meaning of the terms, but their referent. Are "pillar and support" to be read as in apposition to "church of the living God" or in delayed apposition to "how it is necessary to behave"? Such a delayed appositional phrase appears elsewhere in the letter (1:7). It also makes better sense of the metaphorical point: the community is the *oikos*, and the members should behave so as to be supports and pillars for it.[393] Such an understanding fits Paul's other use of *stylos* for leaders of the Jerusalem community

---

392. Mitchell, "New Testament Envoys in the Context of Greco-Roman Diplomatic and Epistolary Conventions."

393. For a more standard reading of the passage, see Hanson, "The Foundation of Truth: 1 Timothy 3:15," in *Studies in the Pastoral Epistles*, 5–20; Towner, *Goal of Our Instruction*, 131–135.

in Gal 2:9. Note also Paul's use of the adjective *hedraios* in a plea to his unstable readers in Corinth: "Become steady people (*hedraioi ginesthe*), not capable of being moved, abounding in the work of the Lord at all times, knowing that your labor in the Lord is not in vain" (1 Cor 15:58). See also the use of *stylos* with reference to an individual person in Rev 3:12, which functions within the Temple symbolism of that writing.[394]

16. *mystery of godliness*: The helpers are said to hold to the *mysterion tes pisteos* in 3:9. Paul's uses of *mystērion* are listed there. Also, as noted in 2:2, *eusebeia* is a term missing in the undisputed letters of Paul, but found in 2 Tim 3:5; Tit 1:1; and, above all, in this letter (1 Tim 2:2; 3:16; 4:7–8; 6:3, 5, 6, 11). It denotes the entire religious response of humans (Plato, *Republic* 615C; Xenophon, *Cyropaedia* 8.1.25; Epictetus, *Encheiridion* 31:1). It is used with particular frequency in 4 Maccabees (e.g., 5:18; 6:2; 15:1; 16:4); see also Philo, *On the Immutability of God* 17, 69, and Josephus, *Against Apion* 1:162. Used here to introduce a summary of Christian confession, it is virtually equivalent to "the mystery of faith."[395]

—*we confess*—: Some scribes considered the adverbial form *homologoumenōs* to be a mistaken contraction and corrected it to *homologoumen hōs* (we confess as great; see the original hand of Bezae and 1175). By seeking a more idiomatic rendering of the adverb, my translation (like the RSV) comes close to that scribal correction. For *homologoumenōs*, see Josephus, *Antiquities* 1:180; 2:229.[396]

is . . . a great one: The expression "this is a great mystery" (*to mystērion touto mega estin*) appears in Eph 5:32. A translation closer to the Greek would be "and confessedly great is the mystery of godliness." The term "great" (*megas*) here may well have a slightly polemical edge, since in Ephesus, the goddess Artemis was acclaimed as *megalē* (Acts 19:28, 34, 35; see also Xenophon, *The Ephesians* 1.11.5). The title is used of other gods as well (e.g., Philo, *On the Cherubim* 29; *Sibylline Oracles* 3:19; LXX Pss 47:2; 75:2; Dan 9:4 [especially Bel and Dragon 18]; Acts 8:10).

He was manifested in flesh: This section receives disproportionate attention from exegetes, since it is taken to represent the heart of the "Christology of the Pastorals."[397] It begins with the relative pronoun *hos* (who), which I translate as

---

394. G. Stevenson, "Power and Place: The Symbolism of the Temple in the Book of Revelation" (Ph.D. diss., Emory University, 1999).

395. See also Towner, *Goal of Our Instruction*, 87–89.

396. Hanson suggests that this is "an academic phrase" used to elevate the discourse showing that the author was familiar with 4 *Maccabees*, in "An Academic Phrase: 1 Timothy 3.16a," in *Studies in the Pastoral Epistles*, 21–28.

397. See, for example, D. A. Klopper, "Zur Christologie der Pastoralbriefe (1 Tim. 3, 16)," *ZWT* 45 (1902): 339–361; W. Stegner, "Der Christushymnus in 1 Tim. 3, 16," *Trierer theologischer Zeitschrift* 70 (1969): 33–49, and *Der Christushymnus 1 Tim. 3, 16: Eine strukturanalytische Untersuchung*, Regensburger Studien zur Theologie 6 (Bern: Lang, 1977); J. F. Strange, "A Critical and Exegetical Study of 1 Timothy 3:16: An Essay in Traditionsgeschichte" (Ph.D. diss., Drew University, 1970); and R. H. Gundry, "The Form, Meaning, and Background of the Hymn Quoted in 1 Tim. 3:16," in *Apostolic History and the Gospel*, ed. W. Gasque and R. P. Martin (Grand Rapids, Mich.: Eerdmans, 1970), 203–222.

"he," making a dependent clause into the beginning of a series of independent clauses. Part of the Western text tradition (the original hand of Bezae, 061, and the Old Latin) altered *hos* to the neuter pronoun *ho* (which), making it agree with the neuter substantive *mystērion* (mystery). Still other MSS, including the corrections made to several of the great uncials (Sinaiticus, Alexandrinus, Ephraemi, Bezae, and the Koine tradition) have *theos* (God) rather than *hos* (who). The correction represents a very high Christology, indeed. The reading translated here is found in the original hand of Sinaiticus, Alexandrinus, Ephraemi, F, G, and a few other witnesses, and it best explains the origin of the others.[398] Like other Pauline Christological passages that are often categorized as hymns (Phil 2:6–11; Col 1:15–20), 3:16 begins with the relative pronoun referring to Christ, has balanced clauses (only the phrase "appeared to messengers" breaks the consistent pattern), and contains elements of internal rhyme and assonance. The verb *phaneroun* in the passive has the sense of "being revealed/manifested" (Rom 3:21; 2 Cor 4:11; 5:10; Eph 5:13). In the sense of a mystery that "appears," see Rom 16:26 and Col 1:26.[399] The "flesh" is one of Paul's most frequently used "anthropological" terms, and its range of meaning has been extensively debated.[400] The simple phrase *en sarki* (in flesh) seems predominantly to signify ordinary human existence (Rom 2:28; 7:5, 18; 8:3; Gal 2:20; 4:14; Eph 2:11; Phil 1:22; 3:3; Col 1:24; Phm 16). This is the only use of *sarx* in the Pastorals.

made righteous by spirit: The contrast between Jesus' human appearance and his exaltation by resurrection seems to be the point here. The language, however, is typically dense. For *pneuma* as the power of Christ's resurrection, see Rom 1:4; 8:2; 15:19; 1 Cor 12:3; 15:45; 2 Cor 3:17. For *dikaioun* in the sense of "vindicated," see Rom 4:2, and for Christians "being justified" in Jesus' name through the Holy Spirit, see 1 Cor 6:11.

appeared to messengers: Most translations have "angels" instead of "messengers" for *angeloi*, so some discussion of the translation is necessary. The verb *horao* (appear) is used in the passive form (*ōphthē*) with some frequency with reference to resurrection appearances of Jesus to his followers (Luke 24:34; Acts 9:17; 1 Cor 15:5–8). But neither the Gospels nor other NT writings speak of appearances to "angels" as such, although that identification can be inferred from expressions like that in Luke 24:23. It may be better, then, to take *angeloi* here in its basic meaning of "messenger." Read this way, the phrase can apply naturally to those witnesses who became proclaimers of the word (Luke 1:2). This is, after all, the basic sense of the term (Herodotus, *Persian War* 5:92; Sophocles, *Antigone* 277; Euripides, *Suppliants* 203). We see Paul designating himself as an *angelos theou* in Gal 4:14, a self-designation thoroughly in the spirit of Epictetus, who says of the true Cynic philosopher that he "has been sent by

---

398. Metzger, *Textual Commentary*, 641.

399. M. N. A. Brockmuehl, "Das Verb *phaneroo* im Neuen Testament," *BZ* 32 (1988): 87–99.

400. Bultmann, *Theology of the New Testament*, 1:232–249; Dunn, *Theology of Paul the Apostle*, 62–72.

God as a messenger [*angelos*] to make demonstration to them concerning good things and evil things" (*Discourses* 3.22.23–24).

preached among nations: For the passive form of the verb *keryssein*, compare 2 Cor 1:19. As always, the noun *ethnoi* might also be understood as "Gentiles," and that understanding would establish an even firmer connection to Paul's self-designation in 2:7 as "herald, apostle, and teacher to the Gentiles."

believed in by the world: A similar use of the passive form of *pisteuein* (believe in) can be found in 2 Thess 1:10. The expression is among the most cryptic in this highly compressed summary, resisting easy translation. It is literally "believed on in the world," with *en kosmtō* being understood locatively. My translation at first blush appears to obscure the locative sense, but should be read along the lines of "believed in throughout the world," as the partner to "preached among nations." The implication is not that the whole world believes in the proclamation about Jesus.

taken up in glory: Although the verb *analambanein* is found in Eph 6:13, 16, it there means "take up" in the sense of "pick up" (see also 2 Tim 4:11). The use here is closer to that in Luke–Acts when it refers to Jesus' ascension (Acts 1:2, 11, 22; see also Mark 16:19). The word "glory" (*doxa*) expresses the presence and radiance of God (LXX Exod 16:7, 10; 24:16; 40:34; Lev 9:6; Deut 5:24; Ps 18:1) and is used in the NT as the fundamental symbol for the resurrection of Jesus (Rom 6:4; 1 Cor 2:8; 15:43; 2 Cor 3:18; 4:4, 6; Phil 2:11).

COMMENT

Taken as a whole, 1 Tim 3 comes as close to providing a "church order" as there is in the letters to Paul's delegates. We learn as much as we are going to about the Ephesian community structure in these few remarks on supervisors, helpers, and women helpers. Paul's allusion to the *presbyterion* (board of elders) in 4:14 and his comments on elders and widows in 5:1–25 clearly have an ad hoc and circumstantial character. It is possible at this point, therefore, to take stock.

How little, really, we learn. Paul's treatment of these two (or three) positions is spare. He devotes three sentences to the supervisor, one to female helpers, and four to male helpers. We learn nothing specific about their tasks. We are forced to rely on analogy and inference for the few surmises we have made concerning their functions. Neither do the instructions inform us of the relationship among the positions: How is the supervisor related to the board of elders or to the deacons? We are not told. Such as we are able to reconstruct it, we are impressed mainly by the simplicity of organization.

The role of the widows, which we will discuss in 5:3–16, offers some complication. For the most part, however, we see a simple collegial governance: older men form a board with a supervisor and have some helpers for practical assistance. We note again that none of these titles or roles is theologically legitimized. The leaders are not given religious titles and are granted no particular spiritual power; their tasks appear to be organizational, didactic, and practical, rather than cultic or liturgical. Finally, the author's concern is not to describe the respective duties of these offices so much as to recommend certain personal moral and managerial qualities desired in the holders of these positions.

A Crisis in the Local Leadership

The question therefore arises why the qualities listed are the ones desired, and how the attention to supervisors and helpers might be connected to the Christological hymn in 3:16. To readers who begin with the premise that the Pastorals are fictional and that the inclusion of materials has little to do with either real-life situations or theological argument, the question is not pressing; perhaps the odd juxtaposition of materials simply illustrates the literary incoherence of 1 Timothy.[401] But for readers who take the self-presentation of the letter seriously, there is a way of pursuing the question why Paul is writing *these things* (*tauta*) and not others (3:14). The point of entry is what the rest of the letter tells us about the state of leadership in the Ephesian church.

The letter suggests that the local leadership of the Ephesian community is troubled in two ways. First, some of the leaders appear to have demonstrated questionable moral character. In 5:19, we find that charges are being brought against some elders. And in 5:22, Paul's delegate is warned against appointing leaders hastily or getting caught up in their wrongdoing. Timothy, in fact, may want to rebuke "an older man/elder" harshly (*epiplēxēs*), but is told instead to exhort him as a father (5:1). Second, there is a competition for leadership among some whom Paul thinks unworthy and disruptive. They may well include the women who are going from house to house and saying what they should not (5:13) and perhaps even asserting in the assembly the right to teach and have authority over men (2:8–11). Included among the restive also may be those who "wish to be teachers of the law" (1:7) and who, in Paul's view, are "teaching different doctrines" (*heterodidaskalein*, 1:3), which doctrines Paul opposes throughout the letter.

Against the backdrop of such a leadership crisis, we can better appreciate the specific qualities that Paul desires in supervisors and deacons. If there is some question of sexual impropriety in worship or in the administration of community funds, the specification that supervisors and helpers be "men with one wife" seems more pertinent. The otherwise unexciting qualities of sanity, sobriety, and even dignity also take on new meaning when such qualities have been lacking among leaders. Seeking leaders who are not lovers of money and who will not "do anything for a profit" is particularly important when charges are being brought against leaders, perhaps precisely in connection with the handling of community funds (5:3–17), and when those seeking to be leaders are teaching that there is a profit to be made through piety (6:5).

---

401. As in Campbell, "Identifying the Faithful Sayings in the Pastoral Epistles," 73–86.

Similarly, attention to constancy and reliability in speech becomes more critical in the context thus envisaged. The supervisor, for example, is not to be like those wrangling over the law at worship, but is to be reasonable, not given to conflict, an apt teacher. Male helpers are not to speak out of both sides of their mouths, and female helpers are not to indulge in slander or gossip. And for all such leaders, the avoidance of drunkenness—which invariably leads to other forms of excess and rash behavior—is appropriately enjoined.

As I pointed out earlier, the quality of being blameless and enjoying a good reputation takes on a sharper edge of pertinence when the behavior of some in the community threatens its stability and safety. The need to "test" helpers in order to show that they are without fault is more intelligible if some already involved in ministry were ordained too quickly and are now open to charges. Finally, the ability to manage a household (*oikos*) well—maintaining its *oikonomia* of wife and children and slaves and funds (3:4, 12)—takes on an obvious importance when the disruption of God's assembly threatens the integrity of the *oikos theou* (3:15), because debates and divisions are cultivated, rather than the *oikonomia theou* that has to do with faith (1:4).

Holding on to the Great Mystery of Faith

These observations bring us to the question of the function of the Christological hymn in 3:16. The details of its content have been analyzed in the NOTES, including the basically Pauline character of its diction and of its conceptualization. The first stanza presents the revelational event: Jesus appeared in the flesh and was vindicated ("made righteous") in the spirit. The contrast is not unlike that drawn in Rom 1:3–4: "Concerning his son, who became according to the flesh from the seed of David, set apart as son of God in power according to the spirit of holiness from a resurrection from the dead, Jesus Christ our Lord."

The next two stanzas (or four lines) are more difficult to interpret. Are they meant to be taken in chronological sequence? That would not appear to work, since "preached among nations" would not temporally precede "taken up in glory." As discussed in the NOTES, it is also quite possible that "appeared to angels" should better be understood as "appeared to messengers"—that is, those who proclaimed the resurrected one. Read in this fashion, the last four verses do not represent a chronological sequence, but four *aspects* of Christ's being "made righteous by spirit," that is, four aspects of his resurrection: he appeared to witnesses, he was preached among nations, he was believed in by the world, and he was taken up in glory. Thus the four last lines form a chiasm, with appearance and ascension framing proclamation and belief. It is the mystery of the resurrected and powerful Lord who lives by the very life of God and who gives life to the community that makes this the "church of the living God" (*ekklēsia theou zōntos*, 3:15).

The content of the confession points, in turn, to its function in this part of the letter. This *oikos theou* is to ground all its activities in the work of the living God—that is, the *experience* of Jesus as the resurrected one—rather than in the lucubrations of human dialectic or the dictates of Law. I suggest that the rhetorical function of 3:14–16 is much the same as the one I have argued for 1:8–17. As Paul there opposed legalism by appealing to his own transforming experience of mercy, which came through the resurrected one, so here the community's confession of the risen Jesus shows it to be an assembly rooted in a revelation that is not simply verbal, but experiential. The great "mystery of godliness" for this community is nothing less than a living person, the resurrected Lord Jesus.

The leadership of this community, therefore, must hold *this* mystery as great and make *this* the principle for its *oikonomia*, or administration within the *oikos theou*. Note that Paul insists that the helpers are to "hold unto the mystery of faith [*mystērion tes pisteōs*] with a pure conscience" (3:9) and that the women helpers are also to be "faithful in every respect" (*pistas en pasin*, 3:11). The reason is that the *oikonomia theou*, as Paul stated in 1:4, is essentially and exclusively the "one that is in faith" (*en pistei*). The commitment of the leaders and helpers to this mystery is therefore essential.

This brings us to my fairly unusual translation of 3:15. If "pillar and foundation of truth" is taken in the usual way, as standing in apposition to "the church of the living God," there are two unfortunate results. The first is that Paul's metaphor is fractured. The church cannot logically be both the house *and* a pillar or foundation for the house. The second is the unhappy inference that some ecclesiologies have not been slow to draw: to equate the church with "the foundation of truth." The translation I have suggested, however, avoids both problems and makes better sense of the rhetorical function of the passage. If the helpers are holders of the mystery of the faith and are faithful in every respect, then they become also "pillars and supports for the truth" that is the "mystery of godliness" *within* the "household of God, which is the church of the living God." Thus they will be the sort of steady and stable leaders that can enable the community to survive its crisis of leadership without destroying the very mystery by which it lives.

IX. OPPOSITION TO HEALTHY
TEACHING (4:1–7a)

◆

4   ¹Now the spirit expressly declares that in later times some people will distance themselves from the faith. They will devote themselves to deceiving spirits and the teachings of demons. ²In hypocrisy they speak falsely, since their own consciences have been cauterized. ³They forbid marriage, forbid eating foods. These are things that God created to be shared with thanksgiving by those who are faithful and have come to a recognition of the truth, ⁴because every creature of God is good. Nothing is to be rejected if it is received with thanksgiving. ⁵For it is made holy by God's word and by prayer. ⁶If you propose these things to the brethren, you will be a good helper of Christ Jesus, nourished by the words of faith and by the noble teaching in which you have followed. ⁷But stay away from profane and old-women myths.

NOTES

1. *the spirit expressly declares*: All of 4:1–5 is one long sentence in Greek, whose syntactical connections are not entirely clear. To make good sense in English translation, smaller sentences must be formed, forcing decisions that could be finessed if the Greek were followed more slavishly. This is the only time the adverb *rhētōs* occurs in the NT (compare Diogenes Laertius, *Lives of Eminent Philosophers* 8:71; Philo, *Allegorical Laws* 1:60). The *pneuma* who declares must be the Holy Spirit, specifically the Spirit of prophecy. In the undisputed letters, Paul does not refer to the speech of the Spirit—although the charismatic activity in 1 Cor 14 would accommodate such a practice, and 2 Thess 2:2 suggests that it took place in his churches—but the idea is found in Heb 3:7; 9:8; 10:15, and is a dominant feature of the first section of Revelation (2:7, 11, 17, 29; 3:6, 13, 22).

   in later times: The portrayal of false teachers or false prophets as a feature of the last days (here the "latter days"; compare *en hysterois chronois* in Plato, *Laws* 865A) is common in apocalyptic literature (*Sibylline Oracles* 2:154–173; 7:120–138; *Testament of Judah* 23:1–5) and in NT eschatological discourse (Matt 24:24–28; Mark 13:22; 2 Thess 2:3–4; 2 Pet 2:1; 1 John 4:1–3; Rev 13:1–17).

   people will distance themselves from the faith: The verb used by Paul is *apostēsontai*, which forms the basis for the English word "apostasy," literally, "to stand apart from." Notice once more how the designation *pistis* (faith) stands for the entire Christian reality (1:5, 19). In this passage, it becomes clear that what Paul means by such faith involves more than religious profession; it encompasses an entire view of reality and way of life. The contrast to those who hold onto the "mystery of faith" in 3:9 and 3:11 is clear and deliberate.

devote themselves to deceiving spirits: The verb *prosechein* (devote themselves) is the same one used of those who "teach other doctrines" in 1:3–4, making it clear that the same people are again in view. The connection between false prophecy and a "spirit of falsehood" (*pneuma tēs planēs*) is found also in 1 John 4:6. Paul here uses the adjective *planos*, to make the phrase "deceiving spirits." The phraseology reminds one of the spirit-psychology of the *Testaments of the Twelve Patriarchs* (see *to pneuma tes planes* in the *Testament of Judah* 20:1). The most obvious parallel to this passage is 2 Tim 3:1–5, which lacks any mention of demonic spirits, but does combine "the last days," evil people, and false teachers.

the teachings of demons: Especially in the polemical rhetoric within first-century Judaism, the charge and countercharge of demonism was common.[402] It is a form of rhetorical hardball that is both dangerous and distressing to contemporary tastes.[403] It was, however, the common coinage of antiquity, and one that the Paul of the undisputed letters also employed vigorously (Rom 16:20; 1 Cor 10:20–21; 2 Cor 11:13–15; 2 Thess 2:9).

2. *In hypocrisy they speak falsely*: This expression can be translated literally as "in a hypocrisy of false words." The term *hypokrisis* originally meant to "play a role in a drama" (Aristotle, *Nicomachean Ethics* 1118A), but it also could mean to "feign something," to "put on a false show" (Polybius, *Roman History* 35.2.13; Luke 12:1; Mark 12:15; Matt 23:28). Thus Paul accuses Cephas of hypocrisy because of his behavior concerning table-fellowship in Antioch (Gal 2:13). Whether or not the term itself was used, the charge of teaching without doing is fundamental to the polemic between ancient teachers, since the essence of moral instruction in antiquity had precisely to do with "how one should conduct one's life" (*pōs dei anastrephesthai*, 3:15), and it was, reasonably, assumed that one needed to live virtuously in order to teach virtue (e.g., Philostratus, *Life of Apollonius* 2:29; Julian, *Oration* 7:223C, 225A; Dio Chrysostom, *Oration* 35:2, 3, 11; Epictetus, *Discourses* 2.8.23–26; 3.22.9; Lucian, *The Fisherman* 42).

their own consciences . . . cauterized: The verb *kaustēriazō* (to sear/brand) is rare (Strabo, *Geography* 5.1.9, has the form *kautēriazō*, from *kautērion*, "hot iron"), and some scribes did not recognize it in the form of a perfect passive participle, so they emended it either by replacing the reduplication *ke-* with *kai* (and, F and 0241) or by using the more familiar *kekautēriazomenon* (Ephraemi, Bezae, and many other witnesses). Nestle–Aland has the harder reading attested by Sinaiticus, Alexandrinus, L, and Origen.[404] We have seen the importance in 1 Timothy of a "good" and "healthy" conscience, the inner sense of moral dis-

---

402. L. T. Johnson, "The New Testament's Anti-Jewish Slander and the Conventions of Ancient Polemic," *JBL* 109 (1989): 419–441.

403. L. T. Johnson, "Religious Rights and Christian Texts," in *Religious Human Rights in Global Perspective*, ed. J. Witte, Jr., and J. D. van der Vyver (The Haguez Hijhoff, 1996), 1:65–95.

404. See also Elliott, *Greek Text*, 62.

crimination (1:5, 19; 3:9). To have one's conscience "seared" or "burned" is to have it desensitized; it is now covered over with scar tissue. Thus those who seek to impose laws and rules from without do so because they have no healthy inner guide. The metaphor is a typical appropriation of medical terminology for the moral life (see the commentary on 2 Timothy, passim).

3. *forbid marriage*: The two infinitives *gamein* and *apechesthai* without any linkage between them create an intolerable syntactic strain. The clause starts with the opponents "forbidding," but that verb cannot command "to abstain" as well. According to the textual apparatus in Nestle–Aland, one commentator (Toup) suggests an emendation, supplying "commanding that" before "abstaining from foods." In this translation, I create consistency in the English by ignoring the infinitive "to abstain" and repeating the verb "forbid." The opponents therefore forbid marriage and the eating of certain foods. The forbidding of marriage within Pauline Christianity would be to take the position of 1 Cor 7:1 literally, without any of the qualifications offered by the rest of that chapter. It is, however, a picture of Paul that is conveyed by the *Acts of Paul and Thecla* 5–6.

forbid eating foods: As just noted, the line is literally "to abstain from foods." The verb *apechesthai* means to "avoid or abstain," with the thing abstained from in the genitive case, as here (Wis 2:16; Josephus, *Antiquities* 11:101); Paul uses it in 1 Thess 4:3 and 5:22 for abstaining from evil. The noun *brōma* applies to food in general, but especially solid foods as distinct from drink (1 Cor 3:2), sometimes, as here, in the plural (Epictetus, *Encheiridion* 33:2; *Testament of Reuben* 2:7). There are two other Pauline passages in which the eating or not eating of certain foods threatens to divide the church. In each case, Paul steadfastly refuses to declare a rule about what can be eaten; in each case, Paul relativizes the importance of diet: "Do not destroy the work of God for the sake of food [*brōma*]" (Rom 14:20), and "Food [*brōma*] does not establish us before God" (1 Cor 8:8). In each case, he calls for the exercise of discernment to determine when it is appropriate to eat or not to eat, with the criterion being the upbuilding of the community.

These are things that God created: I take the neuter relative pronoun *ha* as including both marriage and food, even though, grammatically, it might refer back to only food. Paul uses the verb *ktizein* (Philo, *On the Decalogus* 97; *Sibylline Oracles* 3:20), as he does elsewhere when speaking of God's creative actions (Rom 1:25; 1 Cor 11:9; Eph 2:10; 3:9; Col 1:16). The order of reality (*oikonomia*) is from God (*theou*) because of God's gracious activity in creating the world (1:4).

to be shared with thanksgiving: The phrase *eis metalēmpsin* expresses purpose: they were created for this reason, that they could be shared. The noun *metalēmpsis* means to "take a part of" or "share" (Philo, *Noah's Work As a Planter* 74). The verb form *metalambanein* is used often in the context of sharing food (e.g., Josephus, *Jewish War* 2:143; Acts 2:46; 27:33); note the use also in 2 Tim 2:6. The communal dimension of the term *metalēmpsis* should not be missed. The tendency to avoid marriage and to avoid foods is a turn toward solipsism and control. The choice to share a life in marriage and to share food with others is to engage otherness and therefore complexity. The phrase *meta eucharistia* (with thanksgiving) does not refer solely to an attitude (gratefully), but to a mode of prayer. Paul himself frequently breaks into thanksgiving to God (Rom 1:8; 7:25; 1 Cor 1:4; 14:18; Phil 1:3), and he recommends *eucharistia* as a form of prayer to his readers (1 Cor 14:16; 2 Cor 9:11–12; Eph 5:4; Col 2:7; 4:2; Phil 4:6). It is one of the forms of prayer he commands in 1 Tim 2:1. It is worth observing that in his discussion of diet in Romans, Paul says that the one who eats "should give thanks to God," and the one who does not eat "should give thanks to God" (Rom 14:6).

faithful and have come to a recognition of the truth: The combination of terms in effect identifies those who are likely to give thanks to God for marriage and food. They are *pistoi* — that is, those who perceive the *oikonomia theou* "in faith" (*en pistei*, 1:4). And they are among "the saved," since they have "come to the recognition of the truth" (2:4). Such as these are not the only ones whom God blesses or who partake in the goods of creation, but they are the only ones who recognize them as God's creation and give thanks for them to the creator. Paul here states positively what he declared negatively in Rom 1:18–31, where those who refused to acknowledge the goodness of creation and to give God thanks for it distorted the very truth and in consequence also their lives.

4. *because every creature of God is good*: The precise function of the *hoti* clause is not clear, although the general sense is. I treat it as an explanatory clause, but it could also serve as a noun clause, supplying the content of "the truth" that has come to be known (4:3). The sentence would then read: "to be received with thanksgiving by faithful people and those who have come to recognize the truth that every creature of God is good." The conviction that every creature is good is not gained by empirical observation. Much evidence would seem to contradict it. It is derived from the very word of God that is Scripture, specifically, the narrative account of Genesis in which God declares the goodness of what had been made at every stage of creation and, above all, at its conclusion (Gen 1:31). Those who declare all creatures good, therefore, do so because they perceive them to be "creatures of God."

Nothing is to be rejected: It is possible also to translate this less prescriptively and more descriptively as "nothing is rejected" (that is, by God). The verbal adjective *apobletos* derives from the verb *apoballein* (to take off/reject). Paul uses the noun form *apobole* in Rom 11:15 when speaking of the rejection of the Jews (for *apobletos*, see Philo, *Special Laws* 2:169). There could hardly be a clearer statement of the conviction that evil is not to be found in the mere existence of things, but in their use. As such, Paul's sentiment militates equally against those forms of legalism that seek to establish categories of purity and impurity that taint humans by simple contact, and those forms of dualism that locate evil in sheer materiality. We are at the heart of the Paul that Marcion could not accept and therefore had, paradoxically, to "reject," for Marcion's entire view of salvation was based on the need for sectarian distinction rather than catholic embrace.

if it is received with thanksgiving: The predicative participle *lambanomenon* functions adverbially. Translating with a conditional clause ("if it is received") is only one possibility, and perhaps one that is too restrictive. It could also be rendered as "as it is received," "when it is received," or even "since it is received." The main thing to avoid is the implication that it is the prayer that makes marriage or food good; it is such, Paul says, by God's creation rather than human action. To read the phrase *met' eucharistias* (with thanksgiving) in terms of the eucharist is overly precise,[405] since common meals were customarily accompanied by blessings.[406]

5. *made holy by God's word*: Marriage and food not only are good by virtue of their creation by God, but also can be ingredient to the community life that is vivified by God's Holy Spirit. The verb *hagiazō* means to "make holy" in the sense of expressing contact with the holy God (Philo, *Special Laws* 1:67; *Allegorical Laws* 1:18). In regard to things, the term is often used for making them fit for ritual practices (LXX Exod 29:27; Matt 23:17–19); with respect to persons, the term signifies inclusion within the sphere of the holy (LXX Exod 28:41; Zeph 1:7). Thus Paul speaks of the Corinthians "having been made holy" by their baptism (1 Cor 6:11). More strikingly, he also speaks of spouses "sanctifying" each other and their children through their marriage relationship (1 Cor 7:14). The agent of sanctification here is twofold. The first is "the word of God" (*logos tou theou*). Paul could mean by this God's word as expressed in Scripture (Rom 3:4; 9:6). In this case, "the word of God" would refer to God's creative and approving word in Genesis. Much more frequently, however, Paul uses *logos tou theou* with specific reference to the Christian message (1 Cor 14:36; 2 Cor 2:17; 4:2; Col 1:25; 1 Thess 2:13; 2 Tim 2:9). If read this way, then "the word of God" that sanctifies could include even the words of Jesus declaring the goodness of all food (Mark 7:1–23) and the sanctity of marriage in God's eyes (Mark 10:2–9).

and by prayer: In 2:1, *enteuxeis* (prayers) were distinguished from *eucharistiai* (thanksgivings). In this passage, since *eucharistia* has twice been used (4:3–4), it would seem that the two terms are being used equivalently. The prayer of the community "sanctifies" food and sexual activity by bringing them within the world not only as created by God, but also as re-created by God's Holy Spirit.

6. *If you propose these things to the brethren*: Once more, the predicative participle *hypotithemenos* could also be translated as "when you propose" or "as you propose." In such contexts, the verb *hypotithēmi* connotes either "suggesting/proposing" (Herodotus, *Persian War* 1:90; Plato, *Charmides* 155D) or "enjoining/commanding" (Philo, *On the Posterity of Cain* 12); both elements are present in this passage. The "brethren" (*adelphoi*) is the common Pauline term for members of a church (e.g., 1 Thess 1:4; 2:1; 4:1; 5:1; 1 Cor 10:1; 12:1); in 1 Timothy it is used only here and in 6:2.

---

405. Hanson, "Eucharistic References in 1 and 2 Timothy," in *Studies in the Pastoral Epistles*, 96–109.

406. L. Bouyer, *Eucharist: Theology and Spirituality of the Ecuharistic Prayer*, trans. C. U. Quinn (Notre Dame, Ind.: University of Notre Dame Press, 1968).

a good helper: Paul uses the same term (*diakonos*) that he uses for the local helpers. He refers to Timothy as *diakonos* also in 1 Thess 3:2 [variant reading]. It is tempting to translate the word with another term such as "minister" in order to distinguish Paul's delegate from the local *diakonoi* discussed in 3:8–11. But I retain the term "helper" precisely because it appears that Paul is making a point about the continuity between Timothy's defense of right teaching and that expected of the local helpers.

nourished by the words of faith: The verb *entrephesthai* can be used for being nourished or reared, but in moral literature it can also be applied to the process of "training" in virtue (Plato, *Laws* 798A; Epictetus, *Discourses* 4.4.48). Paul calls Timothy a *diakonos* here, and we remember that the *diakonoi* were to "hold on to the *mysterion tes pisteos*" (mystery of faith, 3:9). So Timothy is to shape the community ethos according to the "words of faith" that come from the Scripture and the Gospel. Note how Philo can speak of being "trained by the holy writings" (*Legation to Gaius* 195; *Special Laws* 1:314).

noble teaching in which you have followed: The "noble teaching" (*kalē didaskalia*) is equivalent to the good news that Timothy has learned from Paul (1:10–11) and that gives articulation to the human response of faith (*pistis*). The verb *parakolouthein* means "to follow" in a figurative sense, as in "following an argument" (Polybius, *Roman History* 3.32.2; Epictetus, *Discourse* 1.6.13) or "following as a rule [of life]," as in Tebtunis Papyrus 124 line 4, and 2 Macc 9:27. See also the use of the verb in 2 Tim 3:10, where it refers to Timothy's careful attention to Paul's manner of teaching and life; there, as here, some MSS (C, F, G) think that the verb should be aorist, rather than perfect. Other MSS (Alexandrinus, 365, and a few more) also have the relative pronoun in the genitive, rather than the (somewhat surprising) dative case.

7a. *stay away from*: The verb *paraiteomai* has two distinct meanings: one is to make a request (Luke 14:18–19); the other is to decline a request or to refuse, for which the common meaning, "reject/avoid," which appears in philosophical discourse with reference to false teachings (Epictetus, *Discourse* 2.16.42; Philo, *On the Posterity of Cain* 2). It has that meaning here as well as in 2 Tim 2:23 and Tit 3:10. The usage with respect to the widows in 5:11 is more difficult.

profane and old-women myths: Apart from Heb 12:16, all the NT uses of *bebēlos* are in the Pastorals (1 Tim 1:9; 6:20; 2 Tim 2:16). The sense of "unholy/profane" (Philo, *Life of Moses* 2:158; Josephus, *Jewish War* 6:271) fits particularly well as a contrast to the community's sense of *eusebeia* (religious piety). For "myths," see the NOTE on 1:4. The translation of *graōdes* is difficult. "Old wives' tales" does not capture the seriousness of the warning. But how literally should we take the "old-women" aspect? Do we have here the casual sexism that we find also in the *gynaikaria* of 2 Tim 3:6? If this is the case, then the "endless myths and genealogies" of the male opponents in 1 Tim 1:4 are being trivialized by association with the stories told by old women. Or is there here a more specific reference to the social situation faced by Timothy? Some scholars have proposed that part of the teaching authority asserted by some women (among them, perhaps, the wandering widows of 5:13) consisted in the narration of folkloric tales, such as we find in the *Acts of Paul and Thecla*.[407] If the letter is written during Paul's ministry, such a reconstruction is less plausible, and Paul's language consequently more stereotypically dismissive.

COMMENT

It is typical of the *mandata principis* letter to alternate instructions concerning public order with personal exhortations to the delegate concerning his morals and manner of leadership. We are therefore not surprised to see Paul turn from his directions on public worship and on the qualities desired in supervisors and helpers to the attitudes that Timothy should have in the face of those opposing him. It is his delegate's task to represent and defend the noble teaching of the good news. As in 2 Tim 3:10–17, we note that the delegate's ability to meet this responsibility is connected to his having been nourished by the words of faith and has followed that noble teaching (4:6).

It is noteworthy that Paul designates Timothy also as a "helper of Christ Jesus" in 4:6. Although Paul uses *diakonos* language freely of himself and his associates, the word choice here seems particularly appropriate, for it links the attitudes and actions of Paul's delegate to those of local helpers. Timothy is to exemplify the behavior he enjoins on local leaders. The theme becomes explicit in 4:12, when Paul tells Timothy to "become a model [*typos*] for believers," but the point is subtly made already in 4:6. The two parts of 1 Tim 4 can be read, in fact, as paraenesis touching on two aspects of Timothy's presence in the Ephesian community: first, his defense of the noble teaching (4:1–7a), and, second, his own manner of life (4:7b–16). Within this paraenetic framework, we find the typical use of polemic against opponents as a foil to the positive ideal: just as Timothy presents the healthy teaching to the people, so he avoids the teaching of those with cauterized consciences. Little useful scholarship has been devoted to this section of 1 Timothy. Perhaps nowhere is the consequence of scholarship's historical fixation more obvious than in its disinterest or disability in engaging Paul's moral discourse. Yet in no section of the letter do the respective ideologies of Paul and the opponents come to a more concrete expression, and one, moreover, of singular importance for present-day readers.[408]

Labeling the Opposition

The background and function of polemic against opponents are discussed much more systematically in the commentary on 2 Timothy. Worth noting now is that

---

407. Davies, *Revolt of the Widows*, 95–129.

408. The discussions are equally distanced and detached in Redalié, *Paul après Paul*, 298–314, and Towner, *Goal of Our Instruction*, 237–241. Contrast the critically less sophisticated yet thoroughly engaged treatment in A. Charue, "Les Directives pastorales de Saint Paul à Timothee et à Tite," *Collationes Namurcenses* 34 (1940): 1–12.

Paul uses it in much the same way in 1 Timothy as in 2 Timothy, if less frequently: to provide a contrast to the good teacher. Thus the noble teaching (4:6) is identified with "godliness" (3:16), in contrast to "profane . . . myths" (*bebēlous mythous*, 4:7). Medical imagery also appears. In 2 Tim 2:17, the teaching of the opponents is compared to the spread of gangrene. Here, the opponents are said to have cauterized consciences (*kekaustēriasmenon syneidēsin*, 4:2). The term suggests branding with a hot iron, and we are meant to think of them as having a moral awareness (*syneidēsis*) that is scarred and insensitive. In 1:19, Paul had accused those seeking to impose Law on others as having abandoned faith and a good conscience. Consistent with that, he here accuses them of hypocrisy (4:2). We remember also that in 1:5 Paul had asked Timothy for a good conscience and sincere (literally, "unhypocritical") faith. Much of this might be sterotypical, but it also has a certain internal logic. Those lacking in genuine moral sensibility often seek a guide outside themselves in Law, just as those who rely overmuch on outside guides like the Law sometimes find themselves with consciences that are less than sensitive.

Another feature of this polemic deserves attention. As the NOTES show, it is not uncommon in ancient slander between schools to attribute the vices and bad teachings of opponents to spiritual forces such as demons. Thus here, the false teachers "devote themselves to deceiving spirits and the teachings of demons" (4:1). In this passage, however, the attribution is part of a more encompassing perception of the community as being under threat by Satan and evil spirits. We have already seen how the behavior of the supervisor must be such that he not fall into the judgment reserved for the devil (3:6) or himself fall into the trap set by the devil (3:7). And we saw in the beginning of the letter that Paul has already "handed over to Satan" two members of the community so that they may learn not to blaspheme (1:20). Finally, in 5:15, the apostasy of some of the younger widows is characterized as "turning aside after Satan." We find the same sense of a community ringed about by the power of demons in Paul's Corinthian correspondence. There, the cultic meals of the Gentiles are called by Paul sacrifices to demons, and eating at such meals is a fellowship with demons (1 Cor 10:20–21). Paul hands over an erring brother to Satan so that his soul might be saved in the day of the Lord (1 Cor 5:5). Married couples who remain apart may be tempted by Satan (1 Cor 7:5). Satan can outwit or gain the advantage over believers (2 Cor 2:11). Satan can change shape as an angel of light—like the super-apostles who are Paul's rivals (2 Cor 11:14). Satan is able to torment Paul (2 Cor 12:7). It is always difficult to know how literally to construe such language. At the very least, we can observe that both in 1 Timothy and in 1 and 2 Corinthians Paul places the battle for the integrity of the community within the framework of a cosmic—indeed, apocalyptic—battle.

Identifying the Opposition

In the manner distinctive to 1 Timothy among the letters to his delegates, Paul once more also engages the position of the opponents theologically. Earlier we saw that Paul seemed to connect the desire to be a "teacher of law" (1:7)—that is, the desire to impose moral structures on others from the outside—with the abandonment of a healthy conscience (1:19). With strong internal moral awareness, a person is able to make subtle and flexible discernments. Without such moral sensibility, an external norm such as the Law must give support. The same logic is visible here. People who have involved themselves with lying spirits and who have damaged (desensitized) moral sensibilities are now declaring limits to the extent to which believers can legitimately engage God's creation.

At the historical level, it is no simple matter to locate the source of an ascetic program that combines the forbidding of marriage and abstinence from at least certain foods. As the NOTES indicate, the prohibition of some foods on the grounds of impurity certainly fits within the classic observance of Torah in Judaism and within certain streams of earliest Christianity influenced by Jewish practice. Paul's own discussion of eating foods offered to idols in 1 Cor 8–10 shows the complexity of the issues involved. But how does abstention from certain foods connect to the forbidding of marriage? This is certainly not a dominant feature of Judaism, in most of whose manifestations marriage is considered one of life's essential blessings. The combination of Law, celibacy, and dietary regulations is a difficult and unexpected one, and complex efforts to identify the "opponents in the Pastorals" have not been lacking in scholarship. Unfortunately, such efforts have proceeded largely on the premise that evidence from all three letters should be used to create a composite picture. I take the opposite approach in this COMMENTARY, trying to consider only the evidence offered by each letter individually, and consider it within the broader context of our historical knowledge. This approach runs the risk of isolating each of the letters, but that risk is worth taking when the results of the other approach have generally been unilluminating.

Some help toward identification may be given by the bits of knowledge we have about groups of Jews—such as the Essenes and Therapeutae described by Philo—whose steadfast commitment to Torah was accompanied by ascetic practices, and Jewish mystics who were devoted to halakah yet practiced celibacy and fasting on a temporary basis in preparation for their vision-quests.[409] The closest thing elsewhere in the New Testament to the combination we find here is Paul's opposition in Colossae, whose practice of worship and devotion to circumcision and Law are connected to prohibitions (Col 2:21) such as "do not touch" (in a sexual manner) and "do not taste" (certain foods).[410] We must avoid false precision, however, particularly when we remember three important facts about the presentation of the opposition in 1 Timothy. First, we are to picture not outsiders, but members of the community, capable of being excommunicated or rebuked rather than simply resisted (1:19–20). Second, nothing is said in 1 Timothy about a program of Torah observance that includes circumcision

---

409. G. Scholem, *Major Trends in Jewish Mysticism* (New York: Schocken Books, 1941), 44.

410. F. O. Francis, "Humility and Angelic Worship in Col. 2:18," *ST* 16 (1963): 109–134; Johnson, *Religious Experience in Earliest Christianity*, 69–103. See also Goulder, "Pastor's Wolves."

or purity regulations. Third, Paul characterizes the opponents as "would-be" teachers of Law. They may not be Jews in any coherent sense, but only Gentile believers who seek to advance themselves within the community through an ascetic nomism with only a rough approximation to Jewish convictions or practices.

The practices here advocated, in fact, may have their roots in Pauline example taken further than Paul himself intended, in a fashion similar to the misunderstandings of his teachings with which he had to contend in Corinth, Thessalonica, and Galatia. Thus, although the slogan "It is good not to touch a woman" in 1 Cor 7:1 is immediately countered with a statement on the goodness and indissolubility of marriage (7:3–6, 10), Paul makes clear that in his view, celibacy is a preferred calling, especially in the present straitened circumstances (7:7–8). Likewise, Paul declared himself ready "never to eat meat again" if doing so should cause a fellow member of the community to stumble (1 Cor 8:13). Still, for Paul in 1 Corinthians, the choice for celibacy or marriage was a matter of gift, not of mandate (7:7), and the choice to eat food offered to idols also a matter of the discernment of one's conscience, rather than a matter of Law.

But we do find in the *Acts of Paul and Thecla* a form of (probably second-century) Christianity that takes Paul as its hero and professes just such an ascetic lifestyle as essential to that identity. Paul's preaching is effectively reduced in its content to "continence and the resurrection," as he proclaims, "Blessed are the bodies of the virgins" (*AP* 6). Paul fasts with Onesiphorus and his family (*AP* 23), and when he does take food, it consists of only bread, vegetables, and water (*AP* 25). Those who would like to place the Pastoral Letters in the second century as a repressive response to such an ascetic Paulinism connected to the free proclamation of the gospel by liberated women and their "tales" can make effective use of such connections.

Once more, however, not all the evidence fits. The *Acts of Paul and Thecla*, for example, draws no connection between such practices and the observance or teaching of Law. Neither is Thecla given free rein to preach by Paul, nor does she exercise authority over any man within the narrative (if we except her humiliating of Alexander). The issue of the use of money does not arise in *AP* the way it does in 1 Timothy. The fact that such ascetic tendencies were present already in some forms of Judaism, and that they manifested themselves early on in the communities of Colossae and Corinth, makes it more than possible that 1 Timothy is responding to a first-generation situation. In short, no more than in the case of the troubles at Galatia or Corinth are we able to adequately describe the profile of those riling the Ephesian community. What we have are only Paul's perceptions of the troublemakers and the responses he makes to them.

Paul's Theological Response

Paul's response is rooted entirely in his understanding of creation, specifically his reading of the creation account in Genesis. His categorical statement in 4:4, "every creature [*pan ktisma*] of God is good [*kalon*]," clearly echoes the LXX of Gen 1:31: "And God saw everything [*ta panta*] that he had made [*epoiēsen*], and behold, it was very good [*kala*]." Because God created all things good—in this case, the human body with all its marvels and miseries—then nothing pertaining to the body can be rejected as evil. To reject creation is to reject the creating God. It would be difficult to find a more powerful or comprehensive statement on the fundamental goodness of the created order. But its practical implications are pertinent to Paul's argument. A system of human law that proscribes some physical activities as evil necessarily tends toward a cosmological dualism that locates evil in the things/activities themselves. In sharp contrast, the "good conscience"—one not seared and scarred by hypocrisy, but transparent to God's way of ordering reality—can perceive that it is not the thing or action as such, but the use of the thing and the intention of the action, to which moral value should be attached. In this understanding, evil is a moral and not a cosmological category. It is, therefore, not sexual activity as such that must be proscribed, but the corrupt misuse of human sexuality. It is not food that must be avoided, but the evil disordering of human appetites.

Precisely because God created things good in the first place, furthermore, they can be received with thanksgiving or blessing (*eucharistia*). The appropriate human response to the living, creating, and gift-giving God is not a miserly selection among God's gifts (as though humans possessed a superior power of moral discernment than the very creator), but an openhearted and generous reception of all of them. Only "deceiving demons" say otherwise. Prayer and the word of God, then, do not *make* food and sex "good"—the unfortunate implication given by translations like the RSV—for they are already "good" (*kalos*) by virtue of having been created by the good God. Rather, prayer and the word of God "sanctify/ make holy" the creaturely activities of sexual love in marriage and the consumption of foods. Prayer and the word of God, that is, draw these good activities explicitly within the community that is itelf created and enlivened by the "Holy God" and can therefore affirm an otherwise ambiguous world as good and as God's creation.

This is now the third example of Paul's creation theology in 1 Timothy. The first grounded the necessity of praying for all human beings (2:1–2) in the truth that there is "one God" (2:5), understood as the creator of all humans: "God desires that all human beings be saved and come to the recognition of the truth" (2:4). The second occurs in 2:13, where Paul appeals to the order of creation to support his instruction that women be subordinate to men in the assembly. In this passage, finally, Paul grounds the acceptability of marriage and of all foods (4:3) in the goodness of all that God has created (4:4). For good and ill, the Paul of 1 Timothy is committed to an understanding of Christian life in which salvation and sanctification are fundamentally more continuous than discontinuous with God's creative activity—they are all moments in the *oikonomia theou*, "God's way of ordering reality" (1:4).

X. MODELING HEALTHY
TEACHING (4:7b–16)

◆

4 ⁷ᵇInstead, train yourself for godliness. ⁸Training the body is useful in a limited way. Godliness, however, is useful in every way. It bears a promise of life both now and in the future. ⁹The word is faithful and worthy of complete acceptance. ¹⁰For this is why we labor and struggle, because we have come to hope in a living God who is the savior of all human beings, above all those who are faithful. ¹¹Command these things. Teach them. ¹²Let no one despise your youth. Become, rather, a model to those who are faithful, in speech and in behavior, by love, by faith, by purity. ¹³Until I arrive, pay attention to the reading, to exhortation, and to teaching. ¹⁴Do not be careless with the special gift for service within you. It was given to you through prophecy with a laying on of hands by the board of elders. ¹⁵Pay attention to these things. Live by them, so that your moral progress is manifest to all. ¹⁶Be attentive to yourself and to the teaching, and remain steady in both. For if you do this, you will save both yourself and those who are listening to you.

NOTES

7b. *train yourself for godliness*: In Greco-Roman moral discourse, athletic imagery is as common as medical imagery.[411] It serves to emphasize the effort demanded for progress toward greater virtue. The term *gymnasia*, for example, refers in the first place to the training for athletic contests (Plato, *Laws* 648C), but is easily transferred to moral struggles (4 Macc 11:20). Here Paul distinguishes between physical training manifested in ascetic withdrawal from sex and food, and that training which involves moral behavior, here expressed as *eusebeia* (godliness). "Train yourself" (*gymnaze seauton*) occurs in the moral literature for just such mental and spiritual conditioning (Pseudo-Isocrates, *To Nicocles* 11; *To Demonicus* 21; Epictetus, *Discourse* 3.12.7).

8. *useful in a limited way*: The adjective *ōphelimos* (useful/worthwhile) is found in the NT in only the Pastorals (2 Tim 3:16; Tit 3:8), but its cognates are used more widely (e.g., Rom 2:25; 1 Cor 13:3; 14:6; 15:32; Gal 5:2; James 2:14,

---

411. A fine collection of such athletic metaphors in the service of moral instruction is provided in N. C. Croy, *Endurance in Suffering: Hebrews 12:1–13 in Its Rhetorical, Religious, and Philosophical Context*, SNTSMS 98 (Cambridge: Cambridge University Press, 1998).

16) and point to the basic concern of every moralist: the pragmatic effect of profession or practice (Plato, *Republic* 607D; Josephus, *Antiquities* 19:206). "In a limited way" translates the phrase *pros oligon*, understanding this with reference to a short human life, compared with God's eternal life.

bears a promise of life: The genitive *zōēs* should be taken as epexegetical: the promise that is life. The language of promise (*epangelia*) is thoroughly Pauline (Rom 4:13–20; 9:4–9; 15:8; 2 Cor 1:20; 7:1; Gal 3:14–29; 4:23, 28; Eph 1:13; 2:12; 3:6; 6:2), but only here and in 2 Tim 1:1 does the expression *epangelia zōēs* appear.

both now and in the future: Here is the fundamental contrast between human effort and divine power and, therefore, between the entire approach taken by the opponents and that taken by Paul. Physical exercise, at its best, can only extend this "little thing" that is human life. But training in *eusebeia* involves responding in faith to the one whose promise of life is both now and "to come" (*tēs mellousēs*). The same sense of future hope undergirds the teaching on possessions in 6:17–19.

9. *word is faithful and worthy of complete acceptance*: This formulaic expression occurs for the third and final time in 1 Timothy. As in 1:15, it asserts not only the faithfulness of the word (*pistos ho logos*), but its worthiness of acceptance as well (*pasēs apodochēs axios*). In 1:15, the formula clearly pointed forward, to the *hoti* clause stating that Christ came to save sinners. In 3:1, it is impossible to know in which direction to take the simple formula "the word is faithful." In this case, the *gar* in the following clause makes it unlikely to be the "worthy" statement, and more likely to be the explanation of it. The preceding statement concerning a promise of life both now and in the future, therefore, seems to be the best possibility, even though it does not have any recognizable sapiential pedigree.

10. *labor and struggle*: Some MSS (F, G, 1881, and the Koine tradition) add the word *kai* before the verb "labor," making the phrase read "both labor and struggle." More significantly, some important MSS (the corrector of Sinaiticus, Bezae, the Koine tradition, and some versions) contain the reading *oneidizometha* (we are being reviled), rather than *agōnizometha* (we struggle/wrestle). Despite its strong support, it must be considered the secondary reading to the one accepted here, read by the original hand of Sinaiticus and the other uncials besides Bezae. It would destroy the athletic imagery that runs through the passage as a whole.[412] The moral struggle is compared to the Olympic Games in Epictetus, *Discourse* 3.22.51–52. Paul's description of "labor and struggle" fits the same context. The *agon* is the athletic contest, classically a race or wrestling competition (Herodotus, *Persian War* 9:60; Epictetus, *Discourse* 3.25.3). Metaphorically, then, the struggle for virtue is just such a contest (Epictetus, *Discourses* 3.6.5–7; 4.4.29–32).

hope in a living God: Some texts (the original hand of Bezae and 33) replace the perfect tense, "we have come to hope" (*ēlpikamen*), with the simple aorist "we hoped" (*ēlpisamen*). The difference in only one letter between the two read-

---

412. Metzger, *Textual Commentary* 641–642; Elliott, *Greek Text*, 68.

ings suggests a mechanical scribal error, and the reading is not, in any case, well attested. I follow Nestle–Aland in reading the perfect.[413] That hope is directed to the "living God" (*theǭ zōnti*) is the reason why it has a promise for life now and in the future. Only God is able to give such life. The perception here is very close to that in 1 Thess 1:9–10; 4:13–14; 5:9.[414] For the "living God" as thematic in 1 Timothy, see the INTRODUCTION.

savior of all human beings: The statement makes even more explicit the identification of God as *sōtēr* in 1:1 and the conviction expressed in 2:4 that "God wants all human beings to be saved." For the title *sōtēr* applied to God, see LXX Pss 24:5; 26:1; 61:2; 64:5; 78:9; 94:1; Isa 12:2; 17:10; 45:15; Tit 1:3; 2:10; 3:4. The inclusivity of this statement of salvation matches the universality implied by the declaration that "everything created by God is good and nothing is to be rejected" (4:4).

above all those who are faithful: The translation of *malista* (above all) can easily give rise to misunderstanding. The superlative of the adverb *mala* denotes that whatever is true of one thing is "particularly" true of another (see the use in 5:17). But when the thing involved is God's saving of people, the English "above all those who are faithful" might be taken as indicating a special position for them. The point, rather, is that God's "desire that all human beings should be saved" (2:4) is "particularly" realized among the faithful, those who in fact have "come to the recognition of the truth" (2:4; see also 4:3).[415]

11. *Command . . . Teach*: Paul placed Timothy in Ephesus in order to "command" certain people (1:3), and reminders of Timothy's function are scattered throughout the letter (compare 5:7; 6:2). The exhortation to teach (*didaske*) establishes a connection between Timothy and Paul, the "teacher of the Gentiles" (2:7), and places both within the framework of ancient moral instructors, as the rhetoric of this passage in particular makes clear.

12. *despise your youth*: This is another of the biographical touches that so corresponds to the portrayal of Timothy in the undisputed letters as to allow only two reasonable hypotheses: either the author was drawing on those compositions in the construction of 1 and 2 Timothy, or the author who saw Timothy the way he is described in the undisputed letters also wrote 1 and 2 Timothy. The corresponding passage in this case is 1 Cor 16:10–11. Paul's desire that Timothy approach the Corinthian community "without fear" (*aphobos*) is echoed by his concern for Timothy's possible cowardice (*deilia*) in 2 Tim 1:7. This verse, in turn, is consistent with 1 Cor 16:11, in which Paul tells the Corinthians "let no one therefore scorn [*exouthenēsę*] him."

model to those who are faithful: That the moral teacher was to present himself as a "model" (*typos*) of the virtues he professed was a standard conviction among Hellenistic philosophers (Epictetus, *Discourses* 3.22.45–49; Dio Chrysos-

413. Against Elliott, *Greek Text*, 65–66.
414. M. J. Goodwin, "The Pauline Background of the Living God as Interpretive Context for 1 Tim. 4:10," *JSNT* 61 (1996): 65–85.
415. See the grammatical analysis in R. A. Campbell, "*kai malista oikeion*: A New Look at 1 Tim. 5:8," *NTS* 41 (1995): 157–160.

tom, *Oration* 77/78:40; Julian, *Oration* 7:214B–C; Lucian, *Demonax* 3; *Nigrinus* 25–27; *Sibylline Oracles* 1:380), just as failure to embody those virtues was the cause of reprobation (see the NOTE on 4:2).

in speech and in behavior: For ancient moral teachers, the two must go together: "In the first place, I require that the consistency of men's doctrines be observed in their way of living" (Plutarch, *On Stoic Self-Contradictions* 1 [*Mor.* 1033B]). See, similarly, Seneca, *Moral Epistles* 20:1; Diogenes Laertius, *Lives of Eminent Philosophers* 1:53; 9:37; Plutarch, *On Progress in Virtue* 14 [*Mor.* 84B]; Philo, *Life of Moses* 2:48; *Special Laws* 2:14; *The Sentences of Sextus* 177. For Paul's use of *anastrophē* as "behavior," see Gal 1:13.

by love, by faith, by purity: If *anastrophē* denotes behavior or way of life in general, these terms specify the qualities that Paul particularly wants to be modeled to the community. We are not in the least surprised to find *pistis* and *agapē*, for these attitudes are the "goal of the commandment" that Timothy is to proclaim (1:5). More startling is the inclusion of "purity" (*hagneia*), which in the moral literature is frequently narrowed to sexual purity, or chastity (e.g., Philo, *On Abraham* 98; *On the Contemplative Life* 68; Josephus, *Antiquities* 19:331). In Polycarp's *Philippians* 5:3, *hagneia* is among the first responsibilities of the young men. Is this another possible allusion to Timothy's youth? The question becomes more intriguing in light of the repetition of the term in 5:2. The Koine textual tradition adds *en pneumati* (by spirit) after *en agapē* (by love). The earlier and better witnesses (Sinaiticus, Alexandrinus, Ephraemi, Bezae, F, G, and many others) lack the phrase. It is not obvious why it should have been added, but following the principle that the shorter and better-attested reading should be followed, I side with Nestle–Aland in omitting it.[416]

13. *Until I arrive*: We are reminded again that Paul hopes to rejoin Timothy and the community quickly (3:14) and that Timothy is Paul's representative within the *ekklēsia* during Paul's absence. As a feature of the *mandata principis* letter, such reminders serve to bolster the teaching and commandments that the delegate delivers.

pay attention to the reading: Although the focus in this section has been on Timothy himself, it is less likely that Paul is reminding him of his personal reading habits, than that he is enjoining him to "devote himself" (*prosechein*, 1:4; 3:8; 4:1) to the public life of the community, beginning with the practice of reading within the *ekklēsia*. In this regard also, the church followed the long-standing practice of the synagogue (Neh 8:1–8; Luke 4:16, 20; Acts 13:15; 15:21). It was in the context of such public reading, in fact, that Paul's own letters were undoubtedly first read (2 Cor 7:8; Col 4:16; 1 Thess 5:27; 2 Thess 3:14).

to exhortation, and to teaching: The noun *paraklēsis*, like the verb *parakalein*, has so many nuances that its precise meaning in each case must be determined by context. From the way *parakalein* is used in the sense of "exhort" in 1 Timothy (1:3; 2:1; 5:1; 6:2), it is likely that *paraklēsis* (used only here) also has that meaning, rather than "comfort" (e.g., 2 Cor 1:3; 7:4). If "exhortation," then what sort? If the reading is the public reading of Scripture in the *ekklēsia*, then ex-

---

416. See also Metzger, *Textual Commentary*, 642.

hortation probably refers to preaching in the same context. For a "word of consolation" (*logos tēs paraklēseōs*) in the sense of "exhortatory discourse," see 2 Macc 7:24; 15:11; Heb 13:22; 1 Cor 14:3. Thus Paul is asked to deliver a "word of exhortation [*logos paraklēseōs*] to the people" after the reading of Scripture (Acts 13:15; see also Rom 12:8). The practice of preaching and of teaching may well have mingled, as was the case also in the worship of the synagogue (1 Cor 14:6, 26); this would in part explain the setting for Timothy's correction of those who wish to be teachers of the Law (1:7) and "teach otherwise" (1:3), and for the "anger and quarreling" that accompany the prayers of the men (2:8).

14. *Do not be careless*: The contrast between *amelein* (to be unconcerned with/neglect) and *meletan* (to practice/cultivate/take pains with) in 4:15 is also standard in Greco-Roman moral discourse. For *amelein*, see Epictetus, *Discourse* 3.24.113; for *meletan*, see *Discourse* 1.1.25; 2.1.29.

the special gift for service: I translate *charisma* here and in 2 Tim 1:6 as "special gift for service." Like *charis*, the term refers in the broadest sense, to a sign of favor or a gift (*Sibylline Oracles* 2:54; Philo, *Allegorical Laws* 3:78) and is sometimes used that way in the NT (e.g., Rom 1:11; 5:15; 11:29; 1 Cor 1:7; 2 Cor 1:11). Paul also uses the word for those gifts given to the community that are to be used for the common good—that is, to edify the church (Rom 12:6; 1 Cor 12:4, 9, 28, 30, 31). Such is the meaning here as well, as indicated by Paul's instruction "not to be careless."

through prophecy with a laying on of hands: For a similar combination of prophetic speech and laying on of hands, see the description of the commission of Saul and Barnabas by the Antiochian church in Acts 13:2–3: "While they were worshipping the Lord and fasting, the Holy Spirit said, 'Set apart for me Barnabas and Saul for the work to which I have called them.' Then after fasting and praying they laid their hands on them and sent them off'" (RSV). A similar sort of authorization of Paul's delegate is envisaged here and in 1 Tim 1:18. For the laying on of hands as a gesture symbolizing the transfer of power, see Exod 29:10; Lev 1:4; 4:15; 16:21; Num 8:10; 27:18–23; Deut 34:9; Acts 6:6; 13:3.

board of elders: The original hand of Codex Sinaiticus and one other MS (69) contain a variant of potential significance. Eliminating the iota, they read "by an elder" (*presbyterou*), rather than "by a board of elders" (*presbyteriou*). The omission of an iota is easy, and the scribes may have been affected by the fact that *presbyterion* is used much less frequently in the NT (Luke 22:66; Acts 22:5) than *presbyteros*, which, in fact, appears immediately after this in 5:1. If the variant were correct, we would have less confidence in defining the leadership structure of the Ephesian church as equivalent to the synagogal *gerousia*. But the reading *presbyteriou* is much better attested and makes more sense.[417] The "board of elders," as I have suggested, is the basic authority structure in the Ephesian church, corresponding to the *gerousia* of the Hellenistic synagogue or the *presbyterion* of the Greco-Roman *collegium*.[418]

---

417. See also Elliott, *Greek Text*, 71–72.

418. For the translation "Board of Elders," see J. Jeremias, "*presbyterion* ausserchristlich bezeugt," ZNW 48 (1957): 127.

15. *Pay attention to these things*: The imperative *meleta* corresponds to the *mē amelei* (do not be careless) in 4:14. The things (*tauta*) that Timothy is to give his attention to are the practices of the church and, especially, the moral qualities appropriate to his *anastrophē* (manner of behaving) as a person of faith.

Live by them: I have translated somewhat loosely. The phrase combines the imperative of *eimi*, "be" (*isthi*), with the dative neuter plural *en toutois* (literally, "in these things"). The question is whether the phrase adds anything to the previous one. Since the next clause picks up on Timothy's moral progress, I have chosen to translate in terms of his personal engagement with the values he teaches, so that "be in these things" becomes "live by them."

moral progress is manifest to all: Some MSS (the second hand of D, for example) have "in all things" (*en pasin*), rather than simply "to all" (*pasin*). This is undoubtedly a scribal correction owing to the natural impulse to include all the moral life in progress and to a misunderstanding of the point of 4:12, where Timothy is told to function as an example.[419] By using the term *prokopē* (progress), Paul aligns himself in the ancient dispute between philosophers concerning virtue: Was it possible to make progress in it—was it a matter of character development?—or did it come about all at once? The Cynics favored the view of instantaneous transformation. The great champion of moral growth is Plutarch (*On Progress in Virtue* [*Mor.* 75B–86A]; see also Epictetus, *Encheiridion* 12–13; *Discourse* 3.6). Compare Phil 1:25.

16. *attentive to yourself and to the teaching*: Used intransitively with the dative case, *epechein* has the sense of devoting mental attention to something (Polybius, *Roman History* 3.43.2; Sir 34:2; 2 Macc 9:25; Acts 3:5). Paul's usage in Phil 2:16 is slightly different, meaning "hold on to." Once more, notice how the person and the profession go together, how a teacher must attend not only to the content of instruction, but to the fit between what is taught and what is lived.

remain steady in both: The present imperative of *epimenein* suggests steady perseverance (Rom 6:1; 11:22, 23; 1 Cor 16:7; Phil 1:24). The plural pronoun *autois* presents a minor translation difficulty. Timothy is told to be attentive to himself and to the teaching, and the Greek continues, "remain steady *in them*," which makes grammatical but not logical sense. The RSV chooses to reduce the steadiness only to the teaching: thus "hold to *that* [emphasis added]." But to translate in that fashion is to miss Paul's focus throughout this section both on Timothy's personal character and on the quality of his instruction. The translation "remain steady in *both*" helps show how this final command, in effect, summarizes the point of the entire paraenesis.

save . . . yourself: Paul could not be plainer that God is savior of all. What can he mean, then, by saving oneself? Here we see the difference between theological discourse that may want to maintain a distinction between divine and human initiative, and moral discourse that always sees them together. The point is for Timothy to live as one whom God has called into the saved community;

---

419. Against Elliott, *Greek Text*, 72.

attention to himself and to the teaching of that community will enable him to grow in that identity and thus "save" himself.

and those who are listening to you: The focus of Paul and his delegate is not on themselves, but on the integrity of their own behavior for the sake of others. This is, in fact, a thoroughly Pauline sentiment. In Rom 11:14, Paul says that he magnifies his ministry to make his fellow Jews jealous, "that I might thus save [*sōsō*] some of them." In 1 Cor 9:22, Paul speaks of his own practice concerning Jews and Gentiles: "I became all things to all people, in order that I might above all save [*sōsō*] some of them." And, finally, in 1 Cor 10:33: "Just as I please everyone in all things not seeking my own advantage but that of the many, in order that they might be saved [*sōthōsin*]."

COMMENT

I have noted before that the way 1 Timothy alternates commandments concerning the community with personal instruction to the delegate fits the form and function of the *mandata principis* letter: the commands legitimate the mission of the representative, and the personal exhortation creates an expectation among the people concerning the attitudes and actions of the emissary. As in 2 Timothy, the use of short exhortations arranged antithetically, plus the themes of model and imitation, present the classic features of paraenesis. In contrast to 2 Timothy, however, it is not Paul who serves as the model of behavior to the delegate, but Timothy himself who is to play that role for the community (see also Tit 2:7). 1 Tim 4 as a whole works to show the delegate Timothy as an exemplar of devotion to the noble teaching and a life based on it. Timothy is to make himself a *typos* whose moral progress is manifest to all believers and whose dedication to good news can be emulated by them.

We are reminded of how seriously ancient philosophers regarded the responsibility of teachers to live in accord with what they professed. It was literally a matter of saving themselves and of saving others. Since philosophy in the Hellenistic period was considered to be essentially a matter of integrity of life, and since virtue was thought to be learned first and best by the imitation of living models, the teacher had no greater duty than to live in a manner consonant with the principles he enunciated. The strength of these convictions is what made the polemical attack on the hypocrisy and corrupt morals of opposing teachers effective. The focus in this section of the letter on Timothy's personal attitudes and actions is entirely consistent with the emphasis on moral character found in Paul's other letters.

The widespread unwillingness in contemporary Western culture to provide direct and unambiguous moral instruction or to assume responsibility for acting in a manner that can be exemplary for others would have been unintelligible in antiquity. If there are ways in which contemporary readers might legitimately consider themselves to occupy a higher plane of moral awareness than 1 Timothy, this passage provides a reminder that present-day sensibilities are not in every respect superior, and that a two-way conversation might be profitable.

Timothy's Relationship to the Ephesian Leadership

This passage also touches in critical fashion on the organization of the church at Ephesus and Timothy's relation to it. The entire self-presentation of the letter shows that Timothy is Paul's personal delegate to the Ephesian community and derives his authority from that commission. Yet in 4:14, Paul tells Timothy not to neglect the special gift for service (*charisma*) that was given to him. Two somewhat surprising aspects of that "giving" thereby come to light. The first is that the *charisma* came to Timothy "through prophecy" (*dia prophēteias*). This reminds us of Paul's reference in 1:18 to "the earlier prophecies concerning [or upon, *epi se*] you." Now we learn also that the setting for such prophetic speech was the *presbyterion* (board of elders) in the Ephesian church. The second unexpected thing is that this board of elders also "laid hands on" Timothy. The combination of the ritual imposition of hands with prophetic speech clearly suggests some sort of appointment or authorization, *through the leadership of the Ephesian community itself.*

Some readers find in this combination of data a logical and theological inconsistency. If Timothy is Paul's delegate and derives his authority from Paul, then how can his *charisma* be derived also from an appointment by local elders? This apparent inconsistency is then placed within the perspective holding that original Pauline Christianity had no concern for local offices and that there must be a rigid distinction between the charismatic and the institutional, between "faith" and "order." The same church could not therefore have both at once, and, if they had to follow sequentially, it is obvious that the true Pauline Christianity was prophetic and charismatic, whereas the developed Paulinism of the Pastorals was institutional and well on the way toward priesthood. The data thus assessed become evidence for the inauthenticity of 1 Timothy, the sure sign that it came from a period up to a hundred years after Paul's authentic letters. In this reading, "Timothy" is in reality only a cipher for the later ecclesiastical leaders who *are* so ordained by local boards of elders.

I have already suggested the ways in which theological presuppositions have dominated the study of church order in early Christianity, leading to conclusions that not only are sociologically implausible, but also fail to deal precisely with the evidence. In my discussion of 1 Tim 3, I have also shown the way in which Paul's concern for local leadership is found throughout his undisputed letters. At this point, we can also observe that interest in 1 Corinthians, when Paul sends Timothy as his delegate to remind the Corinthian church of Paul's ways as he teaches them in all the churches (4:17). Even though he himself plans to come to them quickly (4:19), he is concerned that Timothy be received by them and be shown respect (1 Cor 16:10–11). There is likewise no intrinsic reason why Timothy's service in the Ephesian church could not derive from the appointment of both Paul and the board of elders. The prophetic speech and the laying on of hands by this board would, indeed, serve to ratify Paul's delegation and confirm the local leader's approval of the leadership that Timothy is to exercise in this time of crisis within the community.

The mention of the *presbyterion* at this point also serves as a literary transition to the next part of the letter. Paul will immediately instruct Timothy on the proper way to exhort an older man (5:1), and after dealing with the issue of the support of the widows (in which service the elders likely had a key role), Paul will also direct Timothy on the means to handle serious problems in the presbytery (5:17–25). The need to carry out such a confrontational ministry places Timothy in an extraordinarily delicate situation. He must assert his authority over those who have had a role in appointing him, or at least ratifying his appointment. In such a situation, a reminder to Timothy and those elders that the voice of prophecy was involved in that process may serve to strengthen Timothy's hand. Paul also reminds Timothy not to let anyone hold his youthfulness in contempt. His authority is real, and he is to assert it. At the same time, Paul reminds him that the *presbyterion*'s support for his work is important. He should proceed with care. And his challenge to the elements of corruption within this church's leadership will have credibility only if his own virtue is unblemished and his moral progress is visible to all.

Hope in the Living God

The final aspect of this passage concerns the explanatory sentence following Paul's exhortation to "train yourself for godliness" (4:7b). The sentence actually continues Paul's response to the ascetic teaching advanced by the opponents in 4:3–5, and forms still another of 1 Timothy's distinctive theological arguments. The contrast drawn here is between the sort of physical training that pertains to only the present and the sort that is useful forever: "It bears a promise of life both now and in the future" (4:8). The promise, moreover, is grounded in that God in whom Paul and Timothy and other believers "have come to hope" (4:10). He means, we have seen, the "living God" (4:10; see also 1:16; 6:12). The use of the perfect tense ("we have come to hope") is intriguing, suggesting perhaps that a new level of understanding has been reached of how God is "living" in the light of the resurrection of Jesus (3:16), whom Paul designates in the greeting of the letter as "our hope" (1:1). Only because God is One and living can God be "savior of all human beings" (4:10; see also 2:4–5), by giving them a life beyond this present one, a life that Paul in 6:19 will call "life that is real" (*ontōs zōēs*).

Two distinct theological corollaries follow from the principle that Paul enunciates here: First, a focus on physical asceticism in the name of religion—the forbidding of marriage and the eating of certain foods—is exactly like the training that athletes undergo for the Olympic Games. The effort is physical, and the consequences are physical. The point is competition with other athletes, and that is the inevitable moral result: not a life of compassion and mercy, but one of competition and judgment. It does not lead to dispositions that build up others, but focuses on the building up of the self. Second, such training is naturally and deeply drawn to the keeping of rules as a set of dos and don'ts that provide a predictable and controllable outcome for each prescribed action. The link between legalism and physical training is deep and logical.

Such self-training is, however, entirely a this-worldly endeavor and does not pertain to the essence of faith, which is a response to the living God. Faith in the living God may demand a life less in self-control and less admirable for its symmetry and serenity, but it is the only response that can lead to a life greater than the one capable of being constructed by human effort alone, a share in the "real life" that is God's own. Once more, the pertinence of Paul's distinction for contemporary modes of spirituality that cultivate physical fitness and psychic serenity to a degree that can become obsessively narcissistic is clear. As Paul declares, we "labor and struggle" for something greater than mere survival and security and serenity in this life—a share in the promise of life that is both now and in the future (4:8).

An even more important theological corollary, in the light of our previous discussion, is that the *oikonomia theou en pistei* (1:4)—God's way of ordering reality as perceived by faith—is not entirely a matter of the order of creation, considered as "nature." The "mystery of faith," after all, concerns the one who was declared righteous in the Spirit and taken up in glory (3:16). God's self-revelation in Christ has shattered the previous understandings of God's way of working in the world and even of God's promises. The living God, who has exalted Jesus, does not restrict blessing to a long biological life, good health, many descendants, riches, or secure possession of the land. The resurrection makes it possible for humans to "take hold of eternal life" (6:12), and this changes everything. The living God opens up possibilities for life not defined by the continuity between creation and culture. If the living God gives not only life now, but also "real life" in the future, then living by the measure of this reality, and testifying to this noble teaching, may also mean reevaluating the ways in which the church's promise and cultural perceptions have—as even in 1 Timothy—tended to be identified. Here is the whisper of a more radical tone in this letter's theological voice.

XI. CRISIS IN THE CARE OF WIDOWS (5:1–16)

◆

5 ¹Do not castigate an older man. Instead, exhort him as if he were your father. Act toward younger men as toward brothers, ²toward older women as toward mothers, toward younger women as toward sisters, that is, in all purity. ³Provide financial support for widows who are truly widows. ⁴But if any widow has children or grandchildren, let them learn first of all to show godliness in their own household and to give back some repayment to those who gave them birth. For this is an acceptable thing before God. ⁵Now the real widow is one who, having been left alone, has put her hope in God and continues to make petitions and prayers night and day. ⁶In contrast, the woman who lives self-indulgently has already died even though she is alive. ⁷And you should command these things so that they can stay without reproach. ⁸But if people do not provide for their own relatives, especially if they are members of their household, they have denied the faith and are worse than unbelievers. ⁹A widow should be enrolled. She should not be less than sixty years old, married only once. ¹⁰She should have a reputation for good deeds, such as rearing her children, showing hospitality to strangers, washing the feet of the saints, helping those in trouble; in short, she has been dedicated to every sort of good deed. ¹¹But avoid younger widows. For they want to marry when they have grown wanton against Christ. ¹²They earn condemnation because they have put aside their first commitment. ¹³Moreover, they immediately learn to be idlers, going from house to house. They are not only idlers but also gossips and busybodies, saying things that they should not. ¹⁴I therefore want younger women to marry, to bear children, to run their households, giving no opportunity for reviling to the one who opposes us. ¹⁵For some women have already turned aside after Satan. ¹⁶If any faithful woman has relatives who are widows, she should provide for them. The church should not be burdened, in order that it might support those who are real widows.

NOTES

1. *castigate an older man*: The adjective used as substantive, *presbyteros* (comparative of *prebys*, "old"), is difficult to translate only because of its placement and our uncertainty about the structure of Ephesian leadership. Would it be better to translate as "elder?" Appearing so shortly after mention of the *presbyterion* (board of elders) in 4:14, that would be a natural assumption, especially

since further instructions concerning "elders" (in these cases, clearly members of the governing board) come up shortly in 5:17–22. Why else would Timothy be warned against "castigating" an older man (the verb *epiplēssein* suggests a very sharp rebuke, as in Plato, *Laws* 805B; *Protagoras* 327A; Philo, *Allegorical Laws* 2:46), if there were not some matter of conduct involved, such as is suggested by 5:19? We note, though, that this command is combined with parallel instructions concerning various age groups of both genders, so that the exhortation ends up being referred to the attitudes that Paul's delegate should have toward all members of the community in their respective stations in life. The issue is made still more complex by the likelihood that it was precisely "older men" who were heads of households who also served as the "elders" of the community. We face here, once more, our ignorance about the ways in which the structures of the intentional community designated as *ekklēsia* intersected with or overlapped those of the *oikos* (household). The same ambiguity is carried into the discussion of the widows in 5:3–16.

exhort him as if he were your father: As just noted, *epiplēssein* has the sense of a sharp rebuke—even of a physical striking at another (see also Epictetus, *Encheiridion* 33:16; Lucian, *Hermotimus* 20). In contrast, *parakalein*, as we have seen, has a range of nuances from "exhort" to "comfort"; it is by far a softer term (see also 6:2).

2. *as toward sisters . . . in all purity*: It is difficult to avoid the impression that the expansion of the two directives concerning elders and younger women is deliberate and part of the key to the passage that follows. Why the emphasis on "purity" (*hagneia*)? The noun occurs in the NT only here and in 4:12, where it is one of the characteristics that Timothy is to exemplify as a *typos*, despite his own youth. It is at the very least intriguing to discover the way in which the discussion concerning widows is bracketed on one side by the rebuke of older men and the call for purity concerning younger women, and on the other side by elders being brought up on charges.

3. *financial support*: The translation of *tima* is critical to the entire discussion of 5:3–16. The RSV and other translations have "Honor widows who are real widows," and the verb *timaō* definitely bears that meaning (e.g., Xenophon, *Memorabilia* 4.3.13; John 5:23; 8:49). But such honor could take the specific form of financial support (see *timē* in Diogenes Laertius, *Lives of Eminent Philosophers* 5:72; Sir 38:1). Indeed, the biblical commandment "Honor your father and mother" (Exod 20:12; Matt 15:4; 19:19; Mark 7:10; 10:19; Luke 18:20; Eph 6:2) bore with it the corollary of supporting one's parents in their old age. An allusion to that expectation appears in 5:4: the children who practice godliness by giving back to their parents do something that is pleasing to God. Compare Eph 6:2: "This is the first commandment with a promise, 'so that it might go well with you and you might live long on the land' " (quoting LXX Deut 5:16). Likewise, financial support for parents is the point at issue between Jesus and the Pharisees in Mark 7:9–13: he accuses them of voiding the commandment to honor parents by sequestering the funds they would have used to support them and declaring them *corban*. Notice, furthermore, that in 1 Tim 5:17,

the direction that elders who govern well should receive "double honor" (*diplēs times*) is clearly meant to be understood as financial support, as the two citations of Scripture adduced in its support makes obvious (5:18). Finally, the entire theme of the passage concerns which widows the *ekklēsia* should support financially (see, above all, verse 16). The translation, "Provide financial support," therefore is not only possible, but demanded.[420]

truly widows: This verse really sets the thesis of the discussion: it concerns financial support for widows, but only for those who are qualified to receive it. Paul begins with the (implied) distinction between "false" widows (developed in verses 6, 11, 13, 15) and "genuine" widows (*tas ontōs chēras*), whose credentials will be described in verses 5, 9–10. The term *ontōs* is an adverb from the participle *ōn* (to be) that Paul uses attributively here and in 6:19, in the phrase "real life" (*tēs ontōs zōēs*).

4. *learn first of all*: The singular "let him learn" (*manthenetō*) of some Western textual witnesses (e.g., 945, d, f, m, Vulgate, Ambrosiaster) is understandable, since the plural verb *mantanetōsan* (let them learn) in the apodosis does not agree with the singular subject *tis* in the protosis. But the overwhelming weight of the evidence and the fact that it is by far the harder reading make the plural preferable.[421]

godliness in their own household: The construction is extremely compact, with the infinitive of the verb *eusebein* and *ton idion oikon* directly linked. What is most significant here is that Paul's diction gives domestic relations a religious dimension. It is not simply social conventions that are at work, but religious piety. The term *oikos* here includes, naturally, human members of the family; thus the rhetorical force of the adjective *idios* (one's own). Note also how the distinction between the *oikos* and the *ekklēsia* as social realities is assumed and exploited throughout this discussion.

repayment to those who gave them birth: The phrase *amoibas apodidonai* is somewhat tautologous, since *amoibē* means a "return or recompense" (Homer, *Odyssey* 12:382; Aristotle, *Nicomachean Ethics* 1163B), and the verb *apodidonai* also means to "give back or return" (Philo, *Special Laws* 4:67; Josephus, *Life* 335). The combined phrase is found in Josephus, *Antiquities* 5:13. The phrase "those who gave them birth" is accurate if periphrastic for *progonoi* (2 Tim 1:3). Those holding that *timē* means "honor" must deal with this statement, which clearly implies a material recompense to parents on the part of children.

acceptable thing before God: Paul's comment resembles that in Eph 6:1–2. There he declares that obedience to parents (*goneis*) is a righteous thing: *touto gar estin dikaion*. And he goes on to cite the promise that accompanies the com-

---

420. Against my reading stands the tradition of exegesis represented by J. Mueller-Bardorff, "Zum Exegese von 1 Timotheus 5, 3–16," in *Gott und die Götter: Festgabe für Erich Fascher* (Berlin: Evangelische Verlag, 1958), 113–133, which takes *tima* in the opposite direction. For a reading in agreement with mine, see L. M. Maloney, "The Pastoral Epistles," in *Searching the Scriptures*, vol. 2, *A Feminist Commentary*, ed. E. Schuessler-Fiorenza (New York: Crossroad, 1994), 371.

421. See also Elliott, *Greek Text*, 74.

mand to "honor" (*tima*) mother and father in Scripture (Exod 20:12; Deut 5:16). The addition of *kalon kai* before the word "acceptable" in some Greek MSS and versions (3232, 365, Sahidic, Bohairic) is no doubt due to attraction from 2:3, where Paul had said of prayer for all people: "this is good and acceptable before God."

5. *Now the real widow . . . having been left alone*: After the (only apparent) digression concerning the responsibility of householders to support their own relatives (verse 4), Paul returns to the identification of the *ontōs chēra* (real widow). He begins with the fact that she has been left alone (*memonōmenē*): not only has her husband died, but she has been left with no other support; the verb *monoō* means to "be left solitary" (Thucydides, *Peloponnesian War* 2.81.5; 5.58.2; Josephus, *Antiquities* 5:280; *Life* 95). Thus she stands in contrast to those women who have adult children who, as householders, can support them. Such widows would not truly be "alone" and would therefore not be in need of support.

hope in God: In response to her state of desolation, the real widow has not taken advantage of others, but has *ēlpiken epi theon*; the perfect tense suggests a continuing and present orientation, rather than a single past action. She has done precisely what 1 Tim 4:10 states as the ideal of the entire community: "We have come to hope in a living God who is the savior of all human beings." She also lives within the piety of the Psalms, which speak frequently of "placing hope in the Lord" (e.g., LXX Pss 4:5; 7:1; 15:1; 20:7; 21:9; 30:1; 36:3; 37:15). This may, in fact, have influenced those scribes who wrote, "put her hope in the Lord" (*epi ton kyrion*, e.g., the original hand of Sinaiticus and Bezae).

petitions and prayers night and day: All of the language here suggests a serious and enduring commitment to the prayer life of the community. The verb *prosmenein* has just that sense of "staying with" something (Josephus, *Life* 62; *Sibylline Oracles* 5:131; Mark 8:2; Acts 11:23; 13:43); see 1 Tim 1:3. Her "petitions and prayers" (*deēsesin kai proseuchais*) echo the first kinds of prayers that Paul desires from the community as a whole (2:1). The phrase "night and day" is thoroughly Pauline (1 Thess 2:9; 3:10; 2 Thess 3:8; 2 Tim 1:3—and Acts 20:31!) and suggests unremitting application to something.

6. *lives self-indulgently*: With the RSV, I have translated the participle *spatalōsa* as "lives self-indulgently." The phrase bears implications for social location. It could also be rendered "luxuriously" or "ostentatiously," for a lifestyle enabled by wealth (Polybius, *Histories* 36.17.17). Note the use of the term in LXX Ezek 16:49 and Sir 21:15, and, in the NT, James 5:5. The contrast with the "real widows," in a word, is not only moral, but also social and economic. The women here described are not "left alone" economically, but can afford a life of luxury and idleness.

died even though . . . alive: A neat and ironic twist on Paul's declaration in 2 Cor 6:9 concerning those who live for others: *hōs apothnēskontes kai idou zōmen* (as those dying, and behold, we live!). This is a harsh judgment, yet consistent with the view elsewhere in 1 Timothy that regards excessive wealth as a mortal danger (6:6–10) and ostentatious display as a scandal (2:9). A life of self-indulgent luxury—particularly when others in the community are "left all alone" without resources—is not mildly reprehensible, but a death to that life by which the community claims to live by the one "who gave himself as a ransom for all" (2:6).

7. *command these things . . . stay without reproach*: The imperative *parangelle* picks up from 4:11: *parangelle tauta kai didaske* (command and teach these things). And the adjective *anepilēmptoi* (without reproach/blameless) echoes the desire expressed concerning the supervisor in 3:2 and signals the concern for community reputation that runs throughout this passage. What is less clear is the subject of "they can stay without reproach." It could refer to the true widows, the false widows, or the householders. The way that verse 8 picks up immediately from verse 4 makes the last of these options the most likely. Paul's concern here, in other words, is less the behavior of the women as such than the behavior of the responsible (or irresponsible) households in caring for their needy members.

8. *do not provide for their own relatives*: The Greek conditional (*ei tis ou pronoei*) is singular: "if anyone does not provide." I have made it plural for two reasons. The plural avoids the needless repetition of the grammatically demanded "he/his" in the remainder of the sentence. And, as the reference to "faithful woman" in 5:16 makes clear, Paul is thinking throughout the passage in terms of both genders. The generalized "people" therefore is appropriate. The verb *pronoein* means, first of all, to "perceive ahead of time" (Xenophon, *Cyropaedia* 8.1.13), which leads to the second meaning, to "provide for something beforehand" (Homer, *Odyssey* 5:364; Xenophon, *Cyropaedia* 8.1.1; Epictetus, *Discourse* 2.14.11). This is probably the meaning also in Rom 12:17 and 2 Cor 8:21, although translations obscure it. From *pronoein* comes the noun *pronoia* (providence), which has the same double meaning of pre-vision and pro-vision. Once more, it is extraordinarily difficult to suppose that anything else than financial support is under consideration.

members of their household: Note, again, the sociologically significant distinction between membership in a household and membership in the church. The term *hoi idioi* (literally, "one's own") undoubtedly refers to persons, rather than things, and therefore to family members or relatives (Vettius Valens, *Astrology* 70:5; Sir 11:34), a group that is often smaller than all those making up the *oikos*.[422]

denied the faith and are worse than unbelievers: No better evidence could be given concerning the understanding of *pistis* in this letter as involving an entire way of life. Making moral choices that are inconsistent with the standard of the community amounts to "denying" (*arnēsesthai*) that faith; the verb is most often used as the opposite of "confession" (Acts 3:13; 4:16; 7:35; 1 John 2:22, 23; 2 Tim 2:12–13), but Paul uses it in the letters to Timothy and Titus as a way of showing how practice can disconfirm profession (see also 2 Tim 3:5; Tit 1:16). As for the measure "worse than unbelievers" (*apistou*), the similarity to 1 Cor 5:1 is striking. In that passage, Paul refers to a case of *porneia* "such as is not

---

422. For those to be included under *oikeiōn*, see Campbell, *"kai malista oikeiōn."*

even among the Gentiles"; here it is a refusal of *pronoia* that is "worse than un-believers." In both verses, the rhetorical function of the comparison is to shock the reader into a recognition of how far short of the appropriate measure their behavior has fallen.

9. *A widow should be enrolled*: The verb *katalegesthai* (here in the third-person-singular imperative) is both important and ambiguous. It is a NT *hapax legomenon*. It means simply to "be included in a list" and is used widely in Hel-lenistic literature in a variety of contexts: the conscription of soldiers into the army (Herodotus, *Persian War* 1:59; 7:1), reception into the circle of the gods (Diodorus Siculus, *Library of History* 4:39.4), acceptance into the body of the Senate (Plutarch, *Life of Pompey* 13:7), and inclusion in a religious community (Oxyrhynchus Papyrus 416, line 4). It is obvious that Paul wants the Ephesian church to register certain persons as widows. The difficulty is exegetical: What does the enrollment signify? Is there an official *order* of widows, as there is a group called helpers (*diakonoi*)? Or is this enrollment to signify whom among the impoverished women in the community are to receive its resources in ex-change for their services to the church? Or is it some combination of those el-ements?

not be less than sixty years old: There is at least a superficial resemblance be-tween these criteria and those listed for the offices of supervisor and helper in 3:1–13. The main difference is that—apart from the criterion of age—this list focuses on what the women have done in the *past* (all the verbs are in the aorist tense), rather than on capacities for leadership or service in the *present*.[423] Al-though individual persons have always lived to considerable ages (as did re-markable prophetess Anna in Luke 2:36–37), sixty was certainly a much more advanced age for a woman in the first century than in the twenty-first century. By setting this limit, Paul automatically accomplishes two things: he eliminates widows of a marriagable and childbearing age, and he severely diminishes the number of those for whom the *ekklēsia* is financially responsible—not to men-tion the number of years for which it would thus be responsible!

married only once: Literally, "a woman of one man," this phrase has the same hypothetical possibilities that we have discussed with reference to supervisors and helpers in 3:2 and 3:12.[424] Two aspects of this requirement may be signifi-cant. The moral qualification is that the woman has demonstrated fidelity. The need qualification is that with her one husband dead, she is truly "alone in the world" and has no means of financial support.

10. *reputation for good deeds*: Turning to the earlier demonstration of the char-acter of the "real widow," Paul encloses a series of simple conditional clauses within a bracket formed by "good works" at the beginning and end. I have trans-lated rather freely, eliminating the "if" introductions and treating the clauses as examples ("such as"), with the final "every sort of good deed" then functioning

---

423. Dibelius and Conzelmann are quite wrong on this point, when they say that the author is here listing the responsibilities of the widows, in *Pastoral Epistles* 75.
424. Page, "Marital Expectations of Church Leaders."

resumptively. The phrase "reputation for" is literally "witnessed to" (*martyroumenē*, Acts 6:3; 10:22; Heb 11:4). The *kala erga* (good/noble deeds) are equivalent to the *agatha erga* recommended to the women in 2:10.

rearing her children: The verb *teknotrophein* means to "care for and nurture," as well as simply to "bear children" (Epictetus, *Discourse* 1.23.3). The widow has carried out the role of the wife as Paul envisages it in 2:15 and as he encourages it in 5:14.[425]

hospitality to strangers: For the verb *xenodochein* (to welcome a stranger), see Herodotus, *Persian War* 6:127, and Euripides, *Alcestis* 552; this is the only occurrence in the NT, even though the ideal of hospitality is an important one in the nascent Christian movement. See the NOTE on 3:2, which also demands hospitality of the supervisor. For hospitality as the special responsibility of the household (and nearly always the woman), see Xenophon, *Oecumenicus* 9:10, and Theophrastus, *Characters* 23:9. In the NT, see Luke 7:36–50; 8:1–3; 10:38–42; Acts 16:13–15; James 2:25–26.

washing the feet of the saints: Washing another's feet is a classic expression of hospitality in the biblical tradition (*nipsai podous*, LXX Gen 18:4; 19:2; 24:32; 43:24; Exod 30:19, 21; 38:27; Judg 19:21; 2 Sam 11:8). The sinful woman so welcomes Jesus by bathing his feet with her tears (Luke 7:36–50), and Jesus washes the feet of his disciples, instructing them to do the same for one another (John 13:5–14). This is the only time that the Pastoral Letters use the designation *hagioi* with reference to members of the community, a usage otherwise common in Paul's correspondence (e.g., Rom 15:25; 1 Cor 14:33; Phil 1:1). The term "washing the feet of the saints" may here be synecdoche for the entire posture of service shown to the *ekklēsia* by the woman who is now a widow.

helping those in trouble: Although the verb *eparkein* is a NT *hapax legomenon*, it is widely attested in the sense of giving aid or assistance to someone in need (Xenophon, *Memorabilia* 2.7.1; Polybius, *Roman History* 1.51.10; Lucian, *Nigrinus* 26; Josephus, *Antiquities* 1:247). In this case, the needy are identified as those "being afflicted" (*thliboumenous*, LXX Exod 3:9; Lev 19:33; 25:17; Deut 28:53), especially because of someone else's scheming (LXX Pss 12:4; 26:2; 30:9). She has helped others in the way that she needs help now; note the use of *eparkein* in 5:16. See also the definition of "true religion" in James 1:27 as involving "visiting orphans and widows in their affliction."

dedicated to every sort of good deed: The verb *epakolouthein* in this context suggests "following" in the sense of active pursuit or complete devotion to something (Plato, *Republic* 370C; LXX Josh 14:14; Josephus, *Against Apion* 1:6); compare 1 Pet 2:21. Paul will use the same verb in a different sense only a few verses later in 5:24. The phrase *panti ergō agathō* (in every sort of good deed) is resumptive, echoing the *erga kala* at the beginning of the list.

11. *avoid younger widows*: The decision made concerning the sense of *katalegesthai* affects the way *paraitou* is understood here. Does Paul mean "do

---

425. There is no reason to think here of the "orphans" belonging to the community, as Dibelius and Conzelmann imagine in *Pastoral Epistles*, 75.

not enroll," as the RSV has it? Or does he mean simply "stay away from," as the parallel passages in 1 Tim 4:7, 2 Tim 2:23; Tit 3:10 would seem to support? Since Paul is concerned with Timothy's *hagneia*, and since he has already somewhat sexualized the behavior of these younger women (*spatalōsa*) and will shortly do so even more, physical avoidance may be part of his point. But at the very least, he does not want them placed on the list of needy widows, as the subsequent discussion demonstrates. If we join *paraitou* to the verb *boulomai* in verse 14, we see that Paul is expressing his strong preference and advice rather than a command that he is confident of being enforceable.

grow wanton against Christ: This is very difficult in the Greek and demands choices by the translator. The first thing to observe is that the *gar* (for) makes this an explanatory clause for the delegate's refusal/avoidance of the younger widows. But the meaning of the explanation itself, while generally clear enough, has some obscurity. My translation reverses the sequence of the clauses in order to put the emphasis where I think Paul wanted it to fall: on the desire of the younger widows to marry. The *hotan* (when) clause indicates what precipitates that desire. The verb *katastrēnian* is difficult. By itself, *strēnian* appears in the works of some writers, especially dramatists, in the sense of "to live luxuriously/sensually" (Antiphanes *Fragment* 82; Sophilus *Fragment* 7; Lycophron, *Fragment* 1:2). Note that it is combined with *porneuein* (commit fornication) in Rev 18:7–9. The basic idea, then, is that the widows experience sexual desire and want to marry. But the prefix *kata-* (against) has "the Christ/Messiah" (*tou Christou*) as its object. The translation must therefore combine the element of their sensual itch and the result that this urge somehow turns them against Christ. But in what sense? Verse 12 provides the explanation.

12. *earn condemnation*: Literally, the phrase *echousai krima* is that they "have" or "bear" a condemnation; *krima* usually means the "negative verdict of condemnation by a court." In this case, it appears as the court of public reputation. Thus the phrase might fairly be rendered as "they earn disapproval."

put aside their first commitment: The phrase *ethetēsan tēn prōtēn pistin* explains why they deserve condemnation and why their wantonness is *kata tou Christou*. But each term also has some ambiguity. Should we translate *athetein* and *pistis* in the strongest manner possible, so Paul says that the young widows are denying their faith in the Messiah by wishing to marry? This is scarcely possible, especially since, in fact, he wants younger widows to marry and run households (5:14). Desire for marriage cannot therefore in itself be apostasy from the Christian movement. I have taken *pistis* in the broader sense of "commitment," and *athetein* in its literal sense of "putting aside/rejecting." Now Paul says that their desire represents a breaking of their prior commitment to pray for the community of the Messiah as widows in exchange for the community's financial support of them. Therefore, I have translated as "when they have grown wanton against Christ" and "they have put aside their first commitment." We find *pistin athetein* in just this sense of breaking a treaty in Polybius, *Roman History* 8.36.5. See also Gal 3:15.

13. *learn to be idlers*: The adverb *hama* joins with *de* and *kai* to form an elab-

orate transition to this clause: literally, "while at the same time they also." The verb "to be" (*einai*) must be supplied after *manthanousin* (they learn). The substantive *argai* is constructed from *a- ergos* (without work). It is used neutrally for the unemployed in the marketplace (Herodotus, *Persian War* 5:6; Matt 20:3, 6), but sometimes has the moral connotation of "lazy" (Aristophanes, *The Clouds* 53; Plato, *Republic* 572E; Aristotle, *Nicomachean Ethics* 1097B; Tit 1:12). It is picked up immediately in the next clause: "not only idlers [*argai*] but also." The capacity to do without work while not suffering economic consequences again points to the assumed social rank of the women in question.

going from house to house: The verb *perierchomai* means literally to "go around" (Herodotus, *Persian War* 7:225) and to "wander from one point to another," as a beggar seeking money (Xenophon, *Cyropaedia* 8.2.16) or as a tourist seeing one sight after another (Xenophon, *Oecumenicus* 10:10). With *tas oikias* here serving as the direct object, the connotation is one of going from one household to another. The impression given is one of instability and flightiness.

gossips and busybodies: The verb *phluarein* means to "bring unjustified charges against another" (Diogenes Laertius, *Lives of Eminent Philosophers* 7:173; Philo, *On Dreams* 2:291), as in 3 John 10. The adjective used as a substantive, *phlyaros*, therefore refers to a gossip of a serious and slanderous sort (Plutarch, *On Listening to Lectures* 3 Mor. 39A; Josephus, *Life* 150; 4 Macc 5:10). The adjective *periergos* (note the assonance with *perierchomai*) suggests someone curious to the point of being a meddler in the business of others (Xenophon, *Memorabilia* 1.3.1; Epictetus, *Discourse* 3.1.21; Josephus, *Against Apion* 1:16; *Testament of Issachar* 3:3). Compare, especially, Acts 19:19 and 2 Thess 3:11.

saying things that they should not: The phrase *ta mē deonta* is an attributive participle formed from the impersonal verb *dei* (must). It therefore means "what must not be said [*lalousai*]." The only issue here is whether Paul's point is that they should not be speaking publicly at all, or whether he disapproves of the content of their remarks. The construction of the sentence suggests the latter: they speak as gossips and busybodies speak, not to the benefit of others, but to their harm. Is this a fair judgment? Do the women see themselves as teachers, even if teachers who "teach other" than Paul and Timothy (1:3)? We cannot infer their perspective from the one Paul provides us.

14. *I . . . want younger women to marry*: The use of *boulomai* (I desire) is the same as in the instructions concerning worship in 2:8. Whatever we think of Paul's advice, it is important not to project contemporary mores onto the first-century world, in which "romantic love" was not necessarily the preeminent value among the factors in marriage. While at the explicit level the advice here certainly seems to be at odds with that given in 1 Cor 7:25–26, 40, it can also be stated that the behavior of "younger widows" depicted here may account for the difference in the advice Paul now gives.

bear children, . . . run their households: The verb *teknogonein* corresponds exactly to the noun *teknogonia* in 2:15. The verb *oikodespotein* appears here for the only time in such a context; the few other instances of its occurrence refer to the power of planetary influences (e.g. Oxyrhynchus Papyrus 235, line 16).

The noun *oikodespotēs* refers straightforwardly to the "ruler of a household" (Josephus, *Against Apion* 2:128; Matt 13:52) and is even used metaphorically of God as ruler (Epictetus, *Discourse* 3.22.4; Philo, *On Dreams* 1:149; Matt 13:27; 20:1). There is every reason, then, despite the theory of "complementary roles" undoubtedly lying behind it, to give full weight to the verb as "rule/run" the household (RSV), rather than "keep house" (NAB).

no opportunity for reviling: The phrase *charin loidorias* (on account of reviling) is meant to amplify "opportunity to the one who opposes us." Does Paul mean a human adversary who can revile the community because of the perceived immorality of its women? Or does he mean that Satan has the chance to do harm to the community because of the reviling that such behavior has brought to the community? In either case, Paul sees the behavior as both negative and serious in its consequences.

to the one who opposes us: The phrase *ho antikeimenos* has a more definite and formal feel to it than "someone who opposes" (Paul uses *antikeimenoi* in the plural for his opponents in 1 Cor 16:9 and Phil 1:28). The most striking parallel is 2 Thess 2:4, where Paul uses *ho antikeimenos* in apposition to "the son of lawlessness" of the last days. In this case, the mention of Satan in the very next verse strongly supports the position that "the opposer" of this community is Satan.

15. *already turned aside after Satan*: For the verb *ektrepomai* (turn away/aside) see 1:6 and 6:20; here it has much the same sense as *apostēnai* (to apostasize, 1 Tim 4:1; 2 Tim 2:19). The point is that the young women's behavior has already led them to a place outside the bounds of the community ethos. Whereas Paul had to "hand over to Satan" Hymenaios and Alexander (1:20), these women have gone willingly. Is this part of the basis of Paul's perception that women are more easily deceived than men, according to his interpretation of Genesis in 2:14?

16. *any faithful woman has relatives who are widows*: A number of MSS (e.g., Bezae and some of the Latin witnesses, plus the Koine tradition) add *pistos ē* to *pistē* to form the phrase "faithful man or faithful woman," presumably on the assumption that a woman would not be the head of a household.[426] The shorter and preferred reading is held by the strongest witnesses, including Sinaiticus, Alexandrinus, and Ephraemi. The New Testament, in fact, shows us a number of such wealthy women householders, among them Chloe (1 Cor 1:11), Phoebe (Rom 16:1–3), Prisca (1 Cor 16:19), Nympha (Col 4:15), and Lydia (Acts 16:14–15, 40). The presence of just such a wealthy cadre of women in the Ephesian church seems to be part of the complex situation facing Timothy.[427] The verb *eparkein* (come to the assistance) is used here and in the next verse, as it was for the care the real widows showed in their former lives toward those in trouble (5:10).

church should not be burdened: At the end of the passage we reach its real point, which is the gap between the resources of the *ekklēsia* and the potential

---

426. Metzger, *Textual Commentary* 642. There is a parallel in James 4:4, where some scribes added *moichoi kai* to the *moichalides* of the majority of MSS to create "adulterers and adulteresses" rather than simply "adultresses."

427. Padgett, "Wealthy Women at Ephesus."

number of people it may be called on to support. The need both to establish criteria for "real widows" and to encourage other sources of support from households point in this same direction. The *ekklēsia* has an obligation to meet the needs that cannot otherwise be met. But if it is "burdened" beyond its resources, it cannot respond. For *bareomai* in the sense of financial burden, see Dio Cassius, *Roman History* 46:32.1; for Paul's use elsewhere, see 2 Cor 1:8; 5:4.

support those who are real widows: The purpose clause provides a neat closure to the discussion—repeating "real widows" from 5:3—and by its use of *eparkein* (come to the assistance) demonstrates without a doubt that the "honor" (*tima*) recommended for the real widows in 5:3 was a matter not only of verbal or symbolic respect, but of community economic support.

COMMENT

Taken as a whole, the section appears at first more as a series of occasional instructions than as a single argument. The opening instruction against castigating an older man (5:1), for example, would seem to connect logically to those concerning elders in 5:17–22. The image of the older man as a "father," however, apparently triggers a miniature treatment of generational and gender relationships. We find again the ways in which early Christians applied kinship language to relationships within the *ekklēsia*. Here the kinship is recognized as fictive: the older man is to be regarded "as" (*hōs*) a father, and the younger woman "as" (*hōs*) a sister.

Such language functions to strengthen community bonds and helps regulate relations between potentially conflictual parties by transferring appropriate attitudes from the cultural to the fictive family. If the older man is regarded and treated "as" a real father, it would be unthinkable that he would be dealt with harshly; in the ancient Mediterranen world, respect would permeate every interaction between a younger and an older man. Such language also affects intergender relations. The young male delegate (4:12) Timothy, accordingly, is to treat younger women as sisters "in all purity" (5:2). It is worth noting that two of the relationships are left undeveloped: that with older women and other younger men. The development of the other two relationships may well have something to do with the problems discussed next concerning younger women and elders.[428]

The discussion of the widows in 5:3–16 is extended and far more complex than any other of Paul's instructions in this letter. This is at least partly due to the fact that "widows" in the Ephesian community is a problematic term, including not only those "older women" who can easily be regarded—in the fic-

---

428. Dibelius and Conzelmann, *Pastoral Epistles*, 72, rightly note parallels in Hellenistic moral literature advising the sage to relate to each member of a household appropriately. The standard character of such advice makes the specificity with respect to older and younger women in this case all the more interesting.

tive family scheme—"as" *mothers*, but also those "younger women" who, while technically widowed since their husbands have died, are nevertheless young and marriageable and sexually interested (5:11). Treating younger women as "sisters in all purity" takes on a whole new complexity for the delegate when the sisters in question are not young maidens within the shelter of the household, but young and liberated matrons who are themselves householders and able to visit other households at will.

The discussion of the widows has a discernible literary structure. Paul gives four apodictic commands: "Provide financial support for widows who are truly widows" (5:3); "A widow should be enrolled" (5:9); "avoid younger widows" (5:11); and "I therefore want younger women to marry" (5:14). The commands fairly summarize Paul's position. They mingle with two other kinds of statements. The first are conditional sentences ("if anyone") that appear as a kind of case law (5:4, 8, 16). Each of these places the burden of support for those who are not "real widows" on private households. The second are descriptions of the real and faux widows, respectively. They are arranged antithetically in 5:5–6, 9–23, 14–15.

The Passage as Patriarchal Suppression

The development of women's history and of feminist biblical scholarship has given this passage a prominence that it did not have earlier. For some scholars, the situation addressed in 5:3–16 is the key to the sociohistorical context of the Pastoral Letters considered as post-Pauline pseudonymous compositions. In this reading, the issue of women's place in the church is not one among several, but the most critical of those addressed by the fictive author. 1 Timothy is taken as a second-century patriarchal reaction to a protofeminist movement within early Christianity or, perhaps more accurately, as a rejection of Christianity's original egalitarian ethos.[429] In this view, the "widows" are not simply impoverished women cared for by the assembly. They are, instead, an order of women who practice an active ministry of preaching and teaching. At least some of these women, possibly those who are wealthy in their own right and therefore on the same social level as the householder "elders," are challenging their exclusive male leadership by carrying out an itinerant mission from house to house (5:13). These may well be the same wealthy women who assert the right to teach in the assembly and to have authority over men (2:12). Their refusal to stay at home, stay silent, and stay subordinate is, in this understanding, based on the women's claim to an authority for leadership given directly by God and consonant with the Spirit-led prophetic character of the Christian movement.

The author of 1 Timothy moves to suppress this movement by refusing women the right to speak in the assembly and by seeking to keep women in their traditional domestic roles. They are to marry, have children, and exercise only the

---

429. See, for example, Schuessler-Fiorenza, *In Memory of Her*, 284–342, and Bassler, "Widow's Tale."

limited authority that is theirs within the household (5:14). The author's argument is the classic patriarchal appeal to nature and complementary spheres of influence: the man's place of authority is the public forum; the woman's is the private household. But since, in this perspective, the only really important sphere is the public one, the result of this arrangement is the trivialization of women and their roles. By reducing the order of widows to old women who are poor and dependent, the author takes the wind out of the sails of this nascent yet powerful women's movement. The older men get to rule the church; the older women get to be cared for by the church. The real issue, this argument claims, is not that of sharing possessions and discerning resources. It is the sharing of power and the discerning of authority. The author's use of sexual innuendo toward the younger widows is seen as a disingenuous attempt to discredit an otherwise worthy effort by women to serve within the community.[430]

My own reading of the situation and the author's argument is different. But I want to acknowledge at once that the evidence is sufficiently ambiguous and difficult to allow honest disagreement and to provide some support to the case made by such scholars.[431] Certainly, there is some sort of unrest among the women in the Ephesian church. They are wearing expensive clothing and extravagant hairdos in the assembly (2:9–10) and are asserting the right to teach there (2:11–15). In this chapter, we see some of them charged with self-indulgence (5:6) and with being gossipers as they move from house to house, saying things they should not (5:13). Neither is there any doubt that Paul proposes that women generally should be in subordination (2:11) and that younger women should remain in domestic roles (2:15; 5:14).

My disagreement with the feminist interpretation begins with its neglect of what appears to be the most obvious and central concern in the passage: the effort to balance the needs of the poor and the resources of the intentional community. To suggest that this issue is fundamentally about power rather than possessions is, in my view, to misplace the emphasis established by the passage itself.[432] I also have trouble understanding the simple direction "A widow should be enrolled" as the designation for an official ministerial order, especially since the criteria given have to do with characteristics and actions of the candidates in the past, rather than with any activities they would be expected to carry out in the present. I see it as a straightforward directive that those receiving the

---

430. See, for example, Maloney, "Pastoral Epistles," 369–372, and L. A. Brown, "Asceticism and Ideology: The Language of Power in the Pastoral Epistles," in *Discursive Formations, Ascetic Piety, and the Interpretation of Early Christian Literature*, ed. V. L. Wimbush (Atlanta: Scholars Press, 1992), pt. 1:77–94.

431. See, for example, B. B. Thurston, *The Widows: A Women's Ministry in the Early Church* (Minneapolis: Fortress Press, 1989) 36–55, and C. Methuen, "The 'Virgin Widow': A Problematic Social Role for the Early Church?" *HTR* 90 (1997): 285–298.

432. I also agree that language about possessions is inevitably also language about power; in this case, however, the disputants over power (if that is the scenario) would appear to be equally matched in terms of possessions.

church's aid should be registered. Finally, I do not find the sexual innuendo to be a polemical ploy so much as a response to a very real situation.

Those better schooled in the hermeneutics of suspicion than I am may well observe that I am allowing myself to be misled by the author's own campaign of deflection and distraction: *of course* the surface argument is as I say, but that is beside the point; an ideological critique exposes the deeper structure of suppression at work beneath the author's ostensible concerns. But even though I grant that some rhetoric works in the way suggested, I find another sort of situation here to be more plausibly addressed by Paul's argument.

The Passage as a Call to Discernment

Two preliminary observations can help frame an alternative interpretation of the passage. The first concerns the care of widows in the synagogue contemporary to earliest Christianity. In a patriarchal, land-based economy like that of the ancient Near East, two groups within the population were chronically impoverished because they were fundamentally cut off from sustained support: orphans and widows. From the time of the earliest legislation found in Torah and continuing through the Prophets and wisdom writings, care for orphans and widows was shorthand for adherence to the covenant with the God who did justice for the oppressed.[433]

This tradition of "visiting orphans and widows in their distress" (James 1:27) found institutional expression in the structures of organized charity in each Jewish community.[434] Each synagogue was expected to provide a daily plate, or distribution of food, for the homeless, the vagrant, or the impoverished visitor. This straightforward form of aid helped in obvious cases, but did not meet all needs. For situations of long-term or chronic need, a second form of charity was provided: the community chest. Discernment in such cases was demanded in order to meet without abuse the real needs of the people in distress. The appointment of officials to collect money for this charity and to distribute it fairly was a difficult matter, for the task demanded a great deal of integrity (e.g., b. ʿAbod. Zar. 17b; B. Bat. 8b). That this tradition of sharing possessions was continued in early Christianity is suggested by the summary statements in Acts 2:41–47, and

---

433. L. T. Johnson, *Sharing Possessions: Mandate and Symbol of Faith*, Overtures to Biblical Theology (Philadelphia: Fortress Press, 1981), 88–100. For broader traditions within Greco-Roman culture, see A. R. Hands, *Charities and Social Aid in Greece and Rome* (Ithaca, N.Y.: Cornell University Press, 1968), and B. A. Pearson, "Philanthropy in the Greco-Roman World and in Early Christianity," in *The Emergence of the Christian Religion* (Harrisburg, Pa.: Trinity Press International, 1997), 186–213.

434. L. Frankel, "Charity and Charitable Institutions," in *The Jewish Encyclopedia*, ed. I. Singer (New York: Funk & Wagnall, 1903), 3:667–670; G. F. Moore, *Judaism in the First Three Centuries of the Christian Era* (1927–1930; reprint, New York: Schocken Books, 1971), 2:102–179; G. Hamel, *Poverty and Charity in Roman Palestine, First Three Centuries* C.E., Near Eastern Center Studies 23 (Berkeley: University of California Press, 1990).

4:32–37.[435] The conflict generated by the feeding of the widows of the Hebrews and the widows of the Hellenists in Acts 6:1–6 also shows the difficulties presented by any such welfare system, in which the needs and desires of those cared for require balancing with the limited resources of the caring community.

The second preliminary observation also helps contextualize this passage by attending to Paul's views on widows in the only other place he discusses them. In 1 Cor 7:8–9, Paul says to the "unmarried and widows" that for them to remain as he was would be a good thing. By this we are to understand that he prefers them to remain celibate. But then Paul adds a qualifying statement. If they are unable to exercise self-control, they should marry, for it is better to marry than to "burn" (presumably with uncontrolled passion). In 1 Cor 7:39, likewise, he declares that a woman whose husband has died is free to marry again, as long as she does so in the Lord—meaning within the community. Once more, however, Paul's preference is that she remain single. This discussion makes clear that Paul's preference in 1 Corinthians is for a life of celibacy dedicated to the Lord.

Paul recognizes, though, that not everyone has this particular gift. In such a case, marriage is preferable to *porneia*. In this passage, by contrast, Paul expresses no preference for celibacy. Rather, he recognizes that some younger women who had devoted themselves to celibacy after the death of their husbands now have grown wanton (5:11; for the problem in translation, see the NOTES). They want to back out of their commitment to spend their lives in prayer while being supported by the community. They seek to marry. And Paul clearly prefers this option to their becoming idlers and social butterflies (5:14). The Pauline perspective in the two passages is not identical, but neither is it fundamentally at odds. In both cases, marriage is considered superior to a life of sexual immorality, and inferior to a life dedicated solely to "the Lord."

The two preliminary observations help locate the passage within the social practice of Judaism and nascent Christianity in the first century with respect to the needy, and remind us that the place of unmarried women in at least one other Pauline community was not unambiguous. We are able now to see whether the passage can yield satisfactory sense as addressed to a first-century situation having to do primarily with the distribution of charity to widows.

As the NOTES suggest, the translation of *tima* as "provide financial support" is critical to my reading. The issue, as I see it, is not which women are worthy of respect or honor, but which ones are to receive the resources of the *ekklēsia*. As soon as the question is posed in this fashion, the other questions immediately occur: Who needs financial support? Among those in need, who has other available resources? And who among the needy is particularly deserving of the community's support? As Paul moves through these questions, he faces the classic problems confronting all welfare systems through the ages. What help should come from the community as such, and what help should be provided by private sources? And what sort of behavioral norms should be sought to determine

---

435. L. T. Johnson, *The Literary Function of Possessions in Luke–Acts*, SBLDS 49 (Missoula, Mont.: Scholars Press, 1977).

who ought to receive community help? As in the discussion of eating food offered to idols in 1 Cor 8–10, there is not a simple or single answer for every
case. Rather, discernment is necessary, above all because there is no limit to human need, but there are real limits to any community's disposable possessions.

Once the questions are stated so starkly, Paul's answers quickly emerge. He
basically wants individual households to support the widows who are part of that
oikos as relatives. This is an exercise of piety that is pleasing to God (5:4). More
than that, failure to provide for one's own relatives makes members of a household morally inferior to unbelievers (5:8). We recognize here the same sort of
shaming moral comparison that is used in 1 Cor 5:1, where Paul calls the *porneia*
among the Corinthians to be of a sort that is "not found even among the nations." The support offered to a relative by a household also relieves the *ekklēsia*
of a financial burden (5:16). As in his directions concerning supervisors and
helpers in 1 Tim 3, Paul's directives maintain a sharp distinction between the
social institutions of the *ekklēsia* as the *oikos theou* and the *oikos* as the basic
unit of society.

Paul begins to define the "real widow," consequently, in terms of her economic need and her lack of other support. She is one who has been "left alone"
(5:5). Since she has been the wife of one man (5:9), his death leaves her without resources of her own, if she does not have children or grandchildren with
means to help her. Since Paul makes a point of contrasting the condition of this
woman with that of a widow who does have children or grandchildren to support her, we are to picture the real widow as literally alone in the world. Her
lack of other resources is indicated as well by the phrase that she "has put her
hope in God" (5:5). Note that in 6:17, Paul establishes a contrast between hoping in riches and hoping in God. We assume in her case that there are no riches
on which she can rely. To use contemporary terms, this is a person who has
"fallen through the safety net" of society's ordinary structures of support. If the
ekklēsia does not come to her assistance, she will die.

The burden of such care on the resources of the community is reduced by
Paul's stipulation that the widow be no less than sixty years old (5:9). Life ex-
pectancy in the first-century Mediterranean world was shorter than it is today.
The list of widows in the Ephesian church who were sixty-plus years old cannot have been a long one. Care for them would have been manageable. The
age limit is significant in another respect. It suggests that the active work of such
widows is not before them, but in the past. What is now asked of them is only
that they devote themselves to an intensive life of prayer (5:5). We gain no impression of an order of women dedicated to an active ministry. Finally, Paul
calls for the community to support a widow of this age and this degree of need,
if she has a reputation for good deeds, both domestic (raising children, providing hospitality) and communitarian (washing the feet of the saints, helping the
afflicted). In short, Paul wants the church to provide its resources to those who
have devoted their own resources in the service of others (5:10).

It may be worth noting that we learn nothing more about the possible ministerial functions of widows in Polycarp's *Letter to the Philippians*. Besides being virtuous, the widows are simply asked to "pray without ceasing for all peo-

ple" (4:3). The widows are designated by Polycarp, however, as "the altar of God," another example of the sort of theological legitimation so signally lacking from Paul's practical disposition of financial resources in this passage.

We can turn now to those Paul does not want the church to support. When he tells his delegate to "avoid younger widows" (5:11), the warning may well be twofold. In light of 5:2, he may be cautioning Timothy against any contact that may be construed as something other than "pure." He also intends that such younger widows not be enrolled on the community support list. We have deduced that restricting the supported group to the oldest rank of widows works to relieve the community's resources. Other reasons connect to the actual behavior of some of the younger widows in Ephesus. Paul's comment in 5:6 about self-indulgence does not suggest someone who is destitute and dependent on the community dole.

If such women are placed on the church's welfare rolls, in fact, they present two kinds of problems. First, there is the possibility that they may grow restless and seek to marry (5:11). Paul can hardly object to this in principle, since this is what he wants younger widows to do in the first place (5:14). His difficulty seems to be based on the way in which they are positioning themselves for remarriage, and the fact that this desire represents a repudiation of their earlier commitment to serve the community through a life of prayer. Second, they might stay on the dole while indulging in a life of idleness (5:13) that finds expression in their wandering from house to house, gossiping, being busybodies, and saying things they should not say. This way of acting, indeed, may be what is leading to the desire (and the possibility) of remarrying. At the very least, such women needlessly and heedlessly strain the community's resources.

Their actions also create the possibility of scandal that can harm the entire *ekklēsia*. Paul says that some of them have already gone astray after Satan (5:15). He sees their behavior, therefore, as having serious implications for the very stability of the community (compare 1:20). The reason Paul wants such younger widows to marry is so that "the one who opposes us" may not be given an opportunity for reviling (5:14). The church would indeed be the object of severe reviling if it were perceived as a board of elderly men who financially supported a group of younger women who lived in public idleness and self-indulgence.

Such sexually suggestive behavior could bring a religious movement into serious disrepute and even danger. Dio Cassius reports how such suspicions brought troubles on the Isis cult (*Roman History* 47:15.4; 53:2.4). The element of sexual innuendo detectable in this discussion is not part of Paul's polemic against a legitimate missionary activity, I think, so much as a genuine (if culturally conditioned) worry about the possibility for scandal created by the combination of elderly male leaders supporting sexually interested younger women in socially offensive patterns of behavior. That such cultural sensibilities were alive and well—particularly for a Pharisee like Paul—is indicated by the warning given to the rabbinic scholar in *Aboth de Rabbi Nathan* 2:

Let no man be alone with any woman in an inn, even with his sister or his daughter or his mother-in-law, because of public opinion. Let no man chat with a woman in the market place, even if she is his wife, and needless to say, with another woman, because of public opinion. Let no man walk behind a woman in the market place, even behind his wife, and needless to say, another woman, because of public opinion.

Notice both the stringency of the behavior expected of the man with respect to all women and the repeated concern expressed for public opinion. Whether or not Paul's perspectives are considered appropriate, they are very much the perspectives of the ancient world, and his discussion cannot properly be assessed apart from this cultural context.

The interpretation given here leaves unresolved some important questions. The meaning of "grown wanton against Christ" in 5:11 remains obscure. Also troubling is the fact that Paul never seems to consider the case of younger widows who may also have been left without any resources of their own and without family. Are they simply to be abandoned if they cannot manage to find a spouse? It is less likely that Paul was deliberately callous toward such cases than that he did not know of them in the Ephesian church. Or perhaps he assumes that since they are still young, they would be under the responsibility of their parents' *oikos*. We cannot know, nor should we ask too much from a passage that, for all its gaps, provides a remarkable glimpse of the problems facing the ancient church as it sought to find its place in the world, asking its members to meet their social responsibilities even as it assumed the responsibilities it inherited from the tradition of the synagogue.

If Paul's discussion does not answer all our contemporary, historically motivated, questions, it nevertheless remains one of his most carefully crafted discussions of delicate social issues in the life of an intentional community. A genuinely tragic consequence of 1 Timothy's canonical marginalization is that 5:3–16 is not included with Rom 14 and 1 Cor 8–10 as one of Paul's splendid examples of moral reasoning within the complex cultural realities of the first-century Mediterranean world. It is equally unfortunate that a preoccupation with only one aspect of social inequity (that having to do with gender) has so dominated the analysis of the passage that its challenge to the contemporary church at other levels is obscured. Where else in the New Testament is the tradition of community support for the poor, and the mutual responsibility of households and of the *ekklēsia* for such support, as a manifestation in faith itself, so clearly stated? It is not Paul's success in solving the problems of the ancient Ephesian church that gives this text its perennial importance. It is that Paul witnesses to the prophetic demand of caring for those who have no other hope, and struggles with the deep ambiguities that any such commitment involves within every cultural context.

XII. MORE COMMUNITY
DIRECTIVES (5:17–6:2a)

◆

5 ¹⁷Elders who govern well should be considered worthy of double compensation, especially those who labor in speech and in teaching. ¹⁸For the Scripture says, "Do not muzzle an ox that is threshing," and, "The worker deserves his pay." ¹⁹Do not consider an accusation against an elder unless two or three witnesses support it. ²⁰Those who are sinning, rebuke in the presence of all, so that the rest might be afraid. ²¹I am charging you before God and before Jesus Christ and before the elect angels, that you observe these matters without favoritism. Do nothing on the basis of partiality. ²²Do not lay hands on anyone hastily. Do not associate yourself with other people's sins. Keep yourself pure. ²³Do not keep drinking only water. Use a little wine for the sake of digestion and for your frequent weakness. ²⁴The sins of some people are obvious, parading before them into judgment. The sins of some others trail behind. ²⁵In the same way, good deeds are also obvious, and deeds that are not cannot remain hidden.
6 ¹Let those who are slaves under a yoke regard their own masters as worthy of all respect, so that the name of God and the teaching not be blasphemed. ²ᵃAnd those who have believers as masters should not despise them because they are brothers. Rather they should serve them better because those who are receiving their benefaction are believers and beloved.

NOTES

17. *Elders who govern well*: The term here translated as "govern" (*prohistēmi*) is the same used in this letter for the running of households by supervisors and helpers (3:4, 12) and, in Paul's other letters, for leadership within the church (Rom 12:8; 1 Thess 5:12). Note that, in contrast, the same verb is used quite differently in Tit 3:8, 14. It is this phrase that supports the position that the basic responsibility of the *presbyterion* (4:14) was governance.

double compensation: The noun *timē* means, in the first place, "honor," but it often appears in the sense of "gifts" as an expression of respect (Homer, *Iliad* 9:155; *Odyssey* 20:129; Xenophon, *Anabasis* 1.9.14; Plato, *Republic* 347A; 361C) and even of "compensation" (Diogenes Laertius, *Lives of Eminent Philosophers* 5:72; Sir. 38:1). It must be translated as "compensation/payment" here for two reasons. First, it is difficult to conceive of a "doubling" of honor; second, the

277

scriptural citations adduced in favor of this proposition leave no alternative: they speak of payment, not of prestige.

labor in speech and in teaching: The use of a form of the verb *kopian* for work in the ministry is typical of Paul (Rom 16:6, 12; 1 Cor 15:10; 16:16; Gal 4:11; Phil 2:16; Col 1:29; 1 Thess 5:12). In this letter, compare 4:10. It is with some reluctance that I have translated *en logō* as "in speech," since it is obvious that *didaskalia* (teaching) also involves speaking. It is tempting to translate *logos* as "preaching" (compare 4:12 and, esp., 2 Tim 4:2), but in this case a more conservative rendering is appropriate since we really do not know the activities engaged in by the elders. Note, again, the use of the adverb *malista* in the sense of "above all" (compare 4:10; 5:8; Gal 6:10; Phil 4:22; Phm 16). It makes clear that the basic responsibility of the elder is governing, with other practices engaged according, perhaps, to need or gift.

18. *Scripture says*: The phrase *legei gar hē graphē* as a way of introducing a citation is exactly parallel to Rom 10:11. The letters to Paul's delegates do not cite Scripture often. Titus has no direct citation. 2 Tim 2:19 has a mixed citation from Num 16:5; Sir 17:26; Isa 26:13. 2 Tim 3:8 makes an allusion to the story of Moses in Exod 7:11, 22. In 1 Timothy, we have seen Paul touch on the creation story of Gen 1–3. In this section, we find one direct citation and two allusions.

muzzle an ox that is threshing: The citation from LXX Deut 25:4 has generated a number of textual variants. Some scribes (e.g., Alexandrinus and Ephraemi) were concerned to bring the citation into line with the Septuagint, and thus altered the word order. The original hand of Codex Bezae tried to make this citation agree with Paul's quotation of the same passage in 1 Cor 9:9, which uses the verb *kēmoun* rather than the one used here, *phimoun*. The similarity to 1 Cor 9:9 is striking and is discussed in the COMMENT. As in that letter, the argument is one from analogy: the care of beasts that labor for the family is a fortiori warrant for the support of humans who labor for the community. As Paul says in that passage: "Is God only concerned about oxen? Isn't he speaking above all in our behalf?"

worker deserves his pay: Undoubtedly influenced by Matt 10:10, a very few textual witnesses (notably the original hand of Sinaiticus) replace *tou misthou* (pay/reward) with *tēs trophēs* (food). As the margin of Nestle–Aland indicates, LXX Num 18:31 and 2 Chron 15:7 might be remote antecedents for this instruction, but the most obvious source for the principle Paul cites is a saying from Jesus. The precise wording of the statement is found in Luke 10:7 (with the noted different wording in Matt 10:10). The odd thing is that Paul seems to include this as falling under "scripture." Some suggest that this is a sign of the late dating of 1 Timothy, since a canonical Gospel is being cited as Scripture.[436] It may also be the case that the saying from Jesus has been added somewhat loosely to the scriptural passage as illustrating the same principle.

---

436. Dibelius and Conzelmann, *Pastoral Epistles*, 79.

19. *Do not consider*: The verb *paradechomai* means, in the broad sense, to "accept" and can be used in the sense of "admit/allow" (Plato, *Thaetetus* 155C; *Laws* 935D). The negative imperative in this verse may bear the nuance of "stop receiving," with the implication that Timothy had been allowing some. The other implication is that Paul's delegate has been put in the position of hearing such charges made against elders, as a "court of appeal" available when the *presbyterion* itself is corrupted.

an accusation against an elder: The noun *katēgoria* has the definite sense of a legal accusation (Herodotus, *Persian War* 6:50; Xenophon, *Anabasis* 5.8.1; Josephus, *Antiquities* 2:49; *Against Apion* 2:137). Rhetorically, Aristotle positions it epideictically opposite "praise" (*epainos*) and forensically opposite "defense" (*apologia*, *Rhetoric* 1358B). The position of this issue, so close to that of the need to pay elders and the problems in the care of widows, creates a complex but intriguing set of possibilities.

two or three witnesses: The charges can be considered only (*ektos*) when they are supported by more than a single witness. The allusion is to Deut 19:15, and ensures fairness in process for those accused. For Paul's allusion to this tradition elsewhere, see 2 Cor 13:1.[437]

20. *Those who are sinning*: Many MSS ease the awkward transition between verses 18–19 by supplying the connective *de* (but, and); see, for example, Alexandrinus and the original copyist of Bezae. The translation is complicated by uncertainty about how seriously to take the present participle *hamartanontes*. The RSV's "those who persist in sin" places a heavy stress on the continuous and perhaps recalcitrant character of the behavior, and reads the command against the backdrop of the charge being made against an elder. I have placed the emphasis on the making of the rebuke in the presence of all, without special attention to the note of persistence in sin. Another question concerns the subject implied by "those sinning." Is it those who charge the elders maliciously, or is it the erring elders?

rebuke in the presence of all: The verb *elenchein* has an unavoidable confrontational tone. What is less clear is the exact nuance in a place where the nuance is important. Three senses of the verb are possible. Does Paul mean that the sinners should be exposed and proved to be sinners (Josephus, *Life* 339)? Does he mean that they should be convicted (Philo, *On Joseph* 48; *Special Laws* 3:54)? Or does he intend the meaning of "reprove/correct"—or even "punish" (LXX Sir 18:13; 20:2; 31:31; Prov 9:7; Wis 1:8; 12:2)? The last is the most likely, but the forensic context may allow for the others. For the phrase *enōpion pantōn* (in the presence of all), compare Rom 12:17; Paul likewise rebuked Cephas in Antioch *emprosthen pantōn* (in the presence of all). Because of the phrase that follows, it may be that Paul is here taking a further page from the procedure recommended for charges by Deut 19, for that passage makes clear the public character of the proceeding (Deut 19:17–18).

---

437. And for the tradition's influence throughout the NT, see H. Van Vliet, *No Single Testimony: A Study on the Adaptation of the Law of Deut. 19:15 Par. into the New Testament* (Utrecht: Kreminck en Zoon, 1958).

the rest might be afraid: The effect of the public questioning/rebuke is to strike fear in the rest. One thing is certain: the influence of Deut 19 continues here. In the LXX, it reads: *kai hoi epiloipoi akousantes phobothēsontai kai ou prosthēsousin eti poiēsai kata to rhēma to ponēron touto en hymin* (and the rest having heard of it will be afraid, and they will not venture any more to do in this fashion the evil thing among you). What is not clear is the identity of *hoi loipoi*. Is it the rest of the community? Or, as seems likely, is it the other elders, who, seeing what happens when caught in error, mend their ways out of a healthy fear?

21. *I am charging you*: The solemnity of this charge, with its use of *diamartyromai* (compare 1 Thess 4:6; 2 Tim 2:14; 4:1) and its invocation of God, Jesus, and the angels, points in one of two directions. Either the statement is another example of 1 Timothy's supposed literary incoherence—an inappropriate solemnity at a pedestrian place—or the situation is not of ordinary, but unusual gravity. The argument I make in this commentary is that 1 Timothy is coherent at least in its logical connections. Therefore, the scenario that I have been suggesting concerning the elders and the charity fund may, indeed, loom very large among the matters with which Timothy must deal.

before God and before Jesus Christ: For the phrase *enōpion theou* (before God/in the presence of God), see Rom 14:22; 1 Cor 1:29; 2 Cor 4:2; Gal 1:20. Besides 2 Tim 4:1, this is the only time Paul adds "Jesus Christ." The phrase invokes their presence and their witness, adding weight to the statement about to be made, as in the English expression "as God is my witness."

before the elect angels: The phrase "elect" and "holy ones" occurs in *1 Enoch* 39:1, and "elect archangels" is found in the *Odes of Solomon* 4:8, but the precise meaning here is obscure. It is most likely that Paul combines the notion of the angels as God's heavenly court with the eschatological scenario of the angels accompanying the Son of Man in the final judgment (e.g., Matt 24:31, 36; 25:31; Mark 13:27; Luke 2:13–15; 9:26; 12:8–9; 15:10; 1 Cor 6:3; 11:10; 1 Thess 4:16; 2 Thess 1:7).

observe these matters: The use of *phylassein* (literally, "to keep/guard") in the sense of "observe" is the same as in Rom 2:26 and Gal 6:13. The *tauta* he has in mind are the matters involving the bringing and hearing of charges. The seriousness of the situation is indicated by the solemnity of the warning.

without favoritism: The diction in this phrase is particularly striking. Paul uses *prokrima* and *proklisis* to express acting without partiality. The idea of impartiality, or "not respecting persons" in judgment, is distinctively Pauline, but Paul otherwise uses some form of the NT neologism *prosōpolēmpsia* (Rom 2:11; Eph 6:9; Col 3:25). The term *prokrima* appears on some second-century Greek inscriptions—in addition to the much later Justinian Code (10.11.8.5)—as a legal expression meaning literally a "prejudgment."

on the basis of partiality: Some MSS (e.g., Alexandrinus and Bezae, and the Koine tradition) have *prosklēsis* rather than *prosklisis*. Orthographically, the difference is two letters, but the resulting text, "according to a summons/invitation," (see Plato, *Laws* 846C) does not appear to make sense in this setting.[438] The noun *prosklisis*, in contrast, suggests an "inclination" (Polybius, *Roman History* 6.10.11; Diogenes Laertius, *Lives of Eminent Philosophers* 1:20). In *1 Clement*, it is used specifically with reference to partisanship (21:7; 47:3; 50:2). Paul's point, then, is to allow the process to unfold without interference or discrimination.

22. *lay hands on anyone hastily*: It has been suggested that this gesture refers to a ritual of forgiveness of sins,[439] but it is more likely in this context that the ritual of admission to the board of elders is meant.[440] For the "laying on of hands" as a ritual for bestowing authority, see 4:14. The problem of consistency is more apparent than real. As observed in the NOTE on 4:14, there is plausibility to Timothy's having his authority confirmed by the agreement of the *presbyterion*. But in the present crisis situation, Paul's delegate is in the position of directing the affairs of the board of elders and, therefore, of approving its possible members. If charges of sufficient seriousness have been brought against an elder as to demand his expulsion from the board, then the present situation emerges. Taking the time to evaluate candidates beforehand, rather than rush to approve anyone put forward, is sound practice.

associate yourself with other people's sins: The adjective *allotrios* (belonging to another) is one that Paul uses in Rom 14:4; 15:20; and 2 Cor 10:15–16. The verb *koinōnein* means to "share in something" (Plato, *Laws* 947A; Xenophon, *Memorabilia* 2.6.23). With the dative, it can mean to "associate with" something.[441] In 2 John 11, we see that even greeting someone opposed to the correct teaching is to share in his or her evil deeds (*koinōnei tois ergois autou tois ponērois*). If Timothy keeps people in office who are sinning (5:20) or does not pay attention to the moral quality of those on the board, then Paul implies that he colludes in the corruption of the institution.

Keep yourself pure: For *hagnos* (pure), compare 2 Cor 7:11; 11:2; Phil 4:8. Above all, note the echo of "in purity" in 4:12 and 5:2. At an obvious level, staying pure means not associating with the corruption of the elders under charges. But the insistence on Timothy's staying pure, especially in the context of the situation with the younger widows, again raises the suspicion that both financial and sexual improprieties were the basis for charges against elders.

23. *drinking only water*: This sentence is altogether mystifying. First, it seems to break the sequence of thought between 5:22 and 5:24. Second, its meaning is not at all clear. If Paul is simply giving personal medical advice, then nothing much further can be said: Timothy had a weak stomach, and Paul recommends a little wine. But nothing else in this letter has been without rhetorical point, even the elements of personal paraenesis. Because the drinking of water alone was a sign of asceticism in antiquity (LXX Dan 1:12; *Pirke Aboth* 6:4;

---

438. Elliott, *Greek Text*, 85.

439. P. Galtier, "La Réconciliation des pécheurs dans la première épître à Timothee," *Mélange Jules Lebreton I*, RSR 39 (1951–1952): 317–320.

440. N. Adler, "Die Handauflegung im NT bereits ein Bussritus?" *Neutestamentliche Aufsaetze* (Regensburg: Pustet, 1963), 1–6.

441. J. Y. Campbell, "*Koinōnia* and Its Cognates in the New Testament," *JBL* 51 (1932): 352–380.

Epictetus, *Discourses* 3.13.21), it is sometimes thought that Paul may here be countering too close an association with the dietary regimen of the opponents (4:3). Note that in the *Acts of Paul and Thecla* 25, Paul and his companions share a meal of bread, vegetables, and water. Another possibility is that Paul is establishing a parable for the verses that follow: true character will emerge over time and need not be connected with obvious external signs. Timothy need not signal his purity by his drinking water.

for the sake of digestion: The phrase reads literally "on account of the stomach." Prov 31:6 recommends giving wine to those who are in distress, and it is possible to cite a number of sources offering the same basic advice for a variety of ailments, including dyspepsia (Juvenal, *Satires* 5:32, 49; Hippocrates *Ancient Medicine* 13:23; Pliny the Younger, *Letter* 7:21; Plutarch, *Advice About Keeping Well* 19 [Mor 133A–F]).

your frequent weakness: The term *astheneia* can also mean "illness." For Paul's range of usage, see Rom 6:19; 8:26; 1 Cor 2:3; 15:43; 2 Cor 11:30; 12:5, 9–10; 13:4; Gal 4:13. Once more, the small detail contributes to the overall impression of Timothy as a person of less than robust presence.

24. *parading before them into judgment*: Verses 24–25 are difficult both to translate and to place in context. If verse 23 has a certain parabolic character, as I tentatively suggest, then there has been consistent attention to the problems created by the charges brought against elders—or, better, by the misbehavior of the elders. The overall image here is of a courtroom in which things come to light. My translation tries to capture the nuance in *proagein* of "going before" someone (2 Macc 10:1; Josephus, *Jewish War* 1:673; *Antiquities* 14:388), as well as the sense of publicity suggested by the adjective *prodelos* (clear/evident/obvious, *Letter of Aristeas* 133; Philo, *On the Giants* 39; Josephus, *Life* 22; *Sibylline Oracles* 5:37). The author seems almost to suggest metaphorically that the people's sins march before them into the courtroom—as witnesses.

sins of . . . others trail behind: The translation here is made more difficult by a shift in syntax. Rather than use a genitive construction, "the sins of some people," Paul shifts to a dative of reference in this clause, *tisin* (with repect to some others). The verb *epakolouthein* means literally to "follow" (Philo, *Legation to Gaius* 185), even in someone's footsteps (Philo, *On the Virtues* 64); note the different (figurative) usage in 5:10. I have tried, then, to complete the image begun by *proagousa* in the previous clause by having other people's sins "trail along after." The people are visible before their sins are.

25. *good deeds are also obvious*: This verse tries to clarify the obscurity in the previous statement in terms of people's sins being obvious or hidden. The *erga kala* reminds us of the consistent emphasis on actions expressing convictions (2:10; 5:10; 6:18). The adjective *prodēla* (obvious) is the same as that used in verse 24.

cannot remain hidden: The use of the adverb *allōs* makes an accurate, literal translation almost impossible. The aorist passive infinitive *krybēnai* is not difficult, meaning "to be hidden" (LXX Gen 18:17; Matt 11:25; Luke 18:34; 19:42). The RSV has "so also good deeds are conspicuous; and even when they are not, they cannot remain hidden," translating the adverb *allōs* as "and even when they are not." That translation, however, could unfortunately be taken to mean that even when good deeds are not obvious, they cannot remain hidden. Such is definitely not Paul's thought here. He means, rather, that even deeds that are *not* good cannot remain hidden forever. My translation tries to make that point clearly.

6:1. *slaves under a yoke*: The phrase *hypo zygon* itself signifies "the yoke of slavery" (Plato, *Laws* 770E; Polybius, *Roman History* 4.82.2). The full phrase may be used here in order to make clear that no metaphorical sense is intended (as in Matt 11:29–30; Acts 15:10; Gal 5:1). For slaves (*douloi*) in the earliest Christian movement, see 1 Cor 7:21–23; 12:13; Gal 3:28; Eph 6:5–6; Col 3:11, 22; 4:1; Tit 2:9; Phm 16; 1 Pet 2:16.

regard their own masters: For *hēgeomai* (regard/reckon), see 2 Cor 9:5; Phil 2:3, 6; 3:7; 1 Thess 5:13. At issue is both a perception and a valuation. The same use of *idios* for "one's own" with respect to social relationships is found in 1 Cor 7:2; 14:35; Eph 5:22; 1 Thess 2:14; Tit 2:5, 9. The term *despotēs* is used explicitly for the owner/lord of slaves in Plato, *Parmenides* 133D; *Laws* 757A; Aristotle, *Politics* 1253B; 1 Pet 2:18. The attitude here advocated pertains to the slave's *own* masters who are believers, for that is where the problem lies. It does not inculcate a class consciousness toward *all* masters as a group.

as worthy of all respect: In contrast to 5:3 and 5:17, where the context demanded the translation of "financial support/payment," the term *timē* in this verse must be translated in its original sense as "honor/respect" (e.g., Xenophon, *Cyropaedia* 1.6.11), for two reasons: first, slaves ordinarily would not be in a position to recompense their owners financially (there were some exceptions); second, the term is used in combination with *kataphronein* (despise/hold in disrespect, Aristotle, *Rhetoric* 1378B). The language of honor/shame runs through this small segment. For *axios* (worthy), see Josephus, *Life* 250, and Lucian of Samosata, *Toxaris* 3.[442]

name of God and the teaching: For the "name" as bearing one's reputation for honor or shame, see, for example, Plato, *Apology* 38C, and 1 Macc 8:12. As everywhere in ancient moral discourse, we find here the assumption that bad behavior discredits the *didaskalia* represented by the teacher—and, in this case, the God of whom the teaching speaks.

not be blasphemed: Again, the verb *blasphēmein* means to "defame or injure the reputation of another" (Philo, *Special Laws* 4:197; Josephus, *Life* 232). Here, as in Rom 2:24, the LXX of Isa 52:5 probably lies in the background: *di hymas dia pantos to onoma mou blasphēmeitai en tois ethnesin* (because of you my name is everywhere slandered among the nations).

2. *believers as masters*: As throughout 1 Timothy, *hoi pistoi* stands for members of the believing community (4:3, 10, 12; 5:16). The situation here envis-

---

442. For the basic framework of such language, see J. B. Malina, *The New Testament World: Insights from Cultural Anthropology* (Louisville, Ky.: John Knox Press, 1981), 25–50, and D. De Silva, *The Hope of Glory: Honor Discourse and New Testament Interpretation* (Collegeville, Minn.: Liturgical Press, 1999).

aged is precisely that sketched by Paul's Letter to Philemon, in which the run-away slave Onesimus is being returned by Paul to his owner, Philemon. Paul is under a legal obligation to return the slave, who was regarded as property (Phm 18–19). Yet because Onesimus became a Christian through Paul's proclamation (Phm 10), Paul wants him to be received back not as a slave, but as a brother in the Lord (Phm 16). All this to one who was a "beloved brother" as well as a slave owner (Phm 1).

should not despise them because they are brothers: The verb *kataphronein* is quite strong; it means to "think contemptuously or show contempt toward another" (Herodotus, *Persian War* 4:134; Euripides, *Bacchae* 503; Plato, *Republic* 556D; Aristotle, *Rhetoric* 1378B). It is the precise opposite of "holding in honor." The *hoti* clause is somewhat ambiguous. Are they *not* to despise "because [the masters] are brothers" (thus, explaining the prohibition), or are they despising "because [the masters] are brothers" (thus, explaining the contempt). I take the second to be more likely, since the first option is taken up as the solution in the next *hoti* clause. The slaves despise the masters precisely because they are "brothers" in the *ekklēsia*, but they do not translate that egalitarianism into the domestic sphere of the *oikos*. Or the slaves use the egalitarian attitudes to erode the bonds of obligation that is theirs as slaves, presuming on the goodwill of the masters "because they are brothers." The first of these would be to think contemptuously; the second, to act contemptuously.

serve them better: This phrase is translated literally as "let them serve the more" (*mallon douleuetōsan*). For a similar use of the comparative adverb *mallon*, see 1 Cor 5:2; 6:7; 9:15; Gal 4:9; Eph 5:4; Phm 16. The most intriguing parallel is the infamously difficult advice to slaves in 1 Cor 7:21: *ei kai dynasai eleutheros genesthai mallon chrēsai* (And if you are able to become free, use it more).[443] The advice here is less ambiguous.

those who are receiving their benefaction: The noun *euergesia* (literally, "a good work") universally bears the sense of benefaction within the ancient system of patronage (Herodotus, *Persian War* 4:165; Xenophon, *Anabasis* 7.7.47; Plato, *Gorgias* 513E; *Laws* 850B; *Letter of Aristeas* 205). The key term here is *antilambanesthai*, which can mean either to "give" or to "receive" a benefit. This lexical slipperiness allows for the passage to be read either as the masters receiving a benefaction from slaves—as I read it—or as the masters giving a benefit. The overall context must determine the sense, and although it is a close call, I consider the weight of the evidence to fall in the direction reflected in my translation: the slaves are giving a benefaction to their masters.[444] If this is indeed correct, it is startling to see *euergsia* applied to any deed done by someone lower on the social scale for someone higher, most of all when it is a mat-

---

443. On this difficult passage, see S. S. Bartchey, MALLON CHRÉSAI: First Century Slavery and the Interpretation of 1 Corinthians 7:21, SBLDS 11 (Missoula, Mont.: Scholars Press, 1973).

444. See the fine discussion in Kidd, *Wealth and Beneficence in the Pastoral Epistles*, 140–156. Kidd reaches the opposite conclusion from the one I adopt here.

ter of a slave serving a master.[445] Paul is using conventional honor/shame language in a manner subversive of the system itself.[446]

believers and beloved: Although Paul can use the adjective *agapētos* (beloved) in the plural to refer simply to members of the community (e.g., Rom 1:7), he uses it mainly as a term of affection between himself and his readers (Rom 12:19; 16:5; 1 Cor 14:14, 17; 15:58; 2 Cor 12:19; Phil 2:12; 4:1; 1 Thess 2:8; see Phm 1!). Apart from the designation of his delegate as *agapētos* in 2 Tim 1:2, this is Paul's only use of the word in the Pastorals, making its appearance here seem all the more deliberate.

COMMENT

Whereas the discussion of the widows in 5:3–16 was well structured, the passage following it resembles more fully a loose collection of *mandata*, without any visible organizing principle apart from the need to address certain issues in the community—above all, those concerning elders. The center of attention is the pay of elders and the way to handle charges against (perhaps) unworthy members of the *presbyterion*. These are followed by another way in which the life of the *ekklēsia* intersects that of the Hellenistic *oikos*: the treatment of slaves by believers and the reciprocal attitudes toward their masters of those believers who are slaves. As suggested earlier, one possible reason for these topics being considered together is the repetition of the term *timē*, which in 5:3 and 5:17 clearly refers to financial support, but in 6:1 means "respect" or "honor."[447]

Another significant literary dimension of the passage is its concentration of scriptural citations and allusions. The letters to Paul's delegates do not cite Torah often. In Titus, there is no direct quotation. In 2 Tim 2:19, we find a mixed citation from Num 16:5; Sir 17:26; Isa 26:13. 2 Tim 3:8 makes an allusion to the story of Moses and the magicians of Pharaoh's court in Exod 7:11, 22. And we have seen Paul troping the Genesis creation story in 2:11–15. But in this section, we find a direct citation in 5:18 (as "Scripture") to the LXX of Deut 25:4 ("Do not muzzle an ox that is threshing"), a clear allusion in 5:19 to Deut 19:15 ("unless two or three witnesses support it."), and another nod in 6:1 to Isa 52:5 ("so that the name of God . . . not be blasphemed").

Paul also appears to make an allusion in 5:18 to a saying of Jesus: "The worker deserves his pay." The syntax of the Greek makes it possible to connect this

---

445. S. C. Mott, "The Power of Giving and Receiving: Reciprocity in Hellenistic Benevolence," in *Current Issues in Biblical and Patristic Interpretation*, ed. G. Hawthorne (Grand Rapids, Mich.: Eerdmans, 1975), 60–72.

446. For the use of benefaction language, see, above all, F. Danker, *Benefactor: Epigraphic Study of a Greco-Roman and New Testament Semantic Field* (St. Louis: Clayton, 1982).

447. For a fuller consideration of the literary structure and thematic unity of this section, see J. W. Fuller, "Of Elders and Triads in 1 Timothy 5:19–25," *NTS* 29 (1983): 258–263.

saying also to the introduction: "For the Scripture says. . . ." The margin of Nestle–Aland seeks a remote antecedent in Torah, such as Num 18:31 or 2 Chron 15:7. But the precise wording occurs in Luke 10:7 (with slight variation in Matt 10:10), and it seems most likely that it is Jesus' words that are being recalled. What are we to make of this? One possibility is to conclude that the author was actually quoting from a canonical Gospel and thought of it as Scripture. This would demand a late dating for 1 Timothy as well as its being a pseudonymous composition. It is also possible that Paul was recalling the words of Jesus as they were circulating in the oral tradition, but was careless in the shaping of his sentence: he did not think of Jesus' words as coming from Scripture, but his syntax makes it seem as though he did.

Of far more significance for placing 1 Timothy within the Pauline corpus is the observation that every element of this cluster of citations and allusions occurs elsewhere in Paul's undisputed letters. Paul recalls the tradition of Deut 19:15 concerning the need for testimony to be based on the evidence of two or three witnesses also in 2 Cor 13:1. He explicitly quotes the passage from Isa 52:5 concerning the blaspheming of God's name in Rom 2:14. Most impressively, in his discussion of the payment owed ministers of the gospel in 1 Corinthians, Paul explicitly quotes the same passage from Deut 25:4 as he does here: *ou komēseis boun aloōnta* (the version in 1 Cor 9:9 agrees with the textual variant in 1 Tim 5:18). Paul furthermore adds in 1 Cor 9:14, as additional authority in support of the position that ministers should be financially recompensed, a reference to a logion from Jesus: *houtōs kai ho kyrios dietaxen tois to euangelion katangellousin ek tou euangeliou zēn* (thus also the Lord commanded concerning those who preach the good news that they should live out of the good news). The combination of the same text from Deuteronomy and a saying of Jesus with reference to the same issue is all the more impressive because of the slight variation in the two passages. This web of intertextuality suggests one of two possibilities. Either it is the same author at work, instinctively citing identical authorities when addressing identical issues, or a later writer is consciously using both the Roman and the Corinthian correspondence to address an analogous (or fictional) situation.

Problems with Elders

In the COMMENT on 3:1–7, on the structure of the Ephesian *ekklēsia*, I presented what I considered to be a reasonable reconstruction of the makeup and responsibilities of the *presbyterion* (4:14), based on the meager evidence offered by 1 Timothy itself read against the backdrop of Paul's other letters and the structure of other *ekklēsiai* in antiquity—above all, the disapora synagogue with its *gerousia*. If my supposition is correct that one of the main obligations of the board of elders was handling the community finances, and that one of the main expenditures out of the community fund was for the care of orphans and widows, then the instructions in this section find an intelligible framework. It appears that the crisis of leadership that was implicit in the instructions concerning supervisors and helpers is explicit and serious in the case of the elders. The most obvious way to assess these mixed instructions on pay for the elders (5:17), charges being made against at least one of them (5:19), a warning not to ordain elders too quickly (5:22), and a reminder that some people's sins are slow to come to view (5:24–25) is to conclude that some of the elders of the Ephesian church—perhaps some who had been only recently appointed—were guilty of peculation with the community funds, perhaps precisely those earmarked for the care of the widows (5:3–16). This suspicion is made stronger when we note that Paul will return once more to those who consider "godliness a source of gain" (6:5).

Charges of some sort are definitely being made against at least one elder. This itself threatens the structure of the community, for it was probably one of the *presbyterion*'s functions to decide disputes within the community (1 Cor 6:1–6; see also COMMENT on 3:1–7). Dealing with a charge against one of the elders is obviously a responsibility that has fallen to Paul's delegate and requires considerable delicacy. Timothy, we see, is to consider such charges only if they are supported by more than one witness (5:19). He is to rebuke those who are sinning in the presence of everyone—presumably, either the full assembly or the full board of elders (5:20). The case is made more difficult by the circumstance that the charges may concern persons whose outward appearance is good (5:24). And Timothy himself is warned against getting involved in their practices (5:22). It is difficult to avoid the impression, if we take the sequence of the text seriously, that Paul's earlier deep concern to clarify who is a real widow and who is not is directly connected to the problems involving the elders.

It is unwise to step too far beyond the evidence, but analogous situations throughout the ages offer abundant reasons to think that some elders may well have been supplementing their own income at the expense of the community's shared possessions. Even worse, it is possible that some of them were using the assembly's funds to support those women whose flagrant behavior was bringing the church into disrepute and danger (5:14–15). Even though this cluster of mandates appears to be disjointed, they provide evidence that the crisis of leadership in Ephesus was real and was connected not only to the teaching of false doctrines, but also to the indulging in questionable moral behavior by some community leaders.

That my reconstruction of the situation is not without basis is shown by Polycarp's *Letter to the Philippians*, which suggests that elders may have been chronically exposed to such temptations. When he lists the qualities he desires in various officials, he singles out a number for the elders, who should

> care for all the weak, neglecting neither the orphan nor the widow nor poor, but ever providing that which is good before God and man, refraining from all wrath, respect of persons, unjust judgement, being far from the love of money, not quickly believing evil of anybody, not hasty in judgement, knowing that we all owe the debt of sin. (*Phil.* 6:1)

I have already stated that I think Polycarp may in fact be using 1 Timothy in his own composition, so I do not mean to suggest that his letter provides a full analogy. It is, however, instructive to note that the qualities desired center on two functions of the elders: the settling of cases, and the care of the needy. We see, furthermore, how personal vices connected to wrath, or the respecting of persons, or the desire for gain, typically will corrupt these functions. Toward the end of his letter, in fact, Polycarp takes up the case of Valens, a former elder in the Philippian church. Polycarp's comments make it abundantly clear that Valens's misdeeds had to do with avarice and the misuse of funds (*Phil.* 11:1–2). If, then, Ephesian elders were similarly misusing community funds and were being brought up on charges because of such practices, the church's structure would indeed be under threat from within.

Paul's response shows the wisdom of the experienced administrator. The only piece of advice that appears at this distance as odd is that concerning Timothy's diet. Would his abstinence from wine seem a lifestyle too close to that of the false teachers who forbade the eating of certain foods (4:3)? Perhaps, but that may be over-reading. It may also be that Paul was aware of the stress suffered by Timothy because of the situation he faced, and his advice simply represented the common-sense medical wisdom of the age, since wine was regarded as a help to digestion and a source of strength. The other pieces of advice can still be read with profit by anyone dealing with similar institutional problems: the need for patience, the importance of being fair-minded and without prejudice, and the insistence on due process. It is striking that as he frames his response, Paul reaches into the antecedents established by Torah, finding there the principle concerning payment of ministers, that concerning two or more witnesses, and that concerning impartiality in judgment. The first bit of advice is really the most critical because it addresses the structural roots of the problem; everything else is a symptom. Paul makes the straightforward recommendation that excellence in administration should be rewarded (5:17). If elders are paid sufficiently, they will be less tempted to cupidity. Finally, we are allowed to surmise that the emphatic "Keep yourself pure" in 5:22 may point us to the problem of the widows. We are certainly able to recognize that Timothy's own authority to deal with the crisis in Ephesus is directly dependent on his not being implicated in any fashion in similar vices.

Slaves and Masters

In 6:1–2a, Paul addresses another sort of problem. It appears at first glimpse to be a purely domestic situation, a matter of slaves not being submissive to their masters. But we find something other than a snippet from a typical household code, like those in Col 3:18–4:1 or Eph 6:5–9, which lay out the mutual responsibilities of slaves and their owners. In this passage, the focus is entirely on the slaves. The issue, furthermore, is one of attitude rather than behavior. The slaves are despising their masters rather than considering them worthy of respect or honor. In the ancient world, such attitudinal derogation was almost worse than open rebellion, for it more effectively subverted the social order. It is at this very point that we find that the life of the *oikos* and that of the *ekklēsia* intersect again, and catch a hint that the ideal of "in Christ there is neither slave nor free" (Gal 3:28) was perhaps as active among some members as "neither male nor female" among others. The basis for the lack of respect seems to have been the fact that, whereas in the assembly (*ekklēsia*), slaves and masters interacted simply as "brothers and sisters," this equality did not carry over into the life of the household (*oikos*). The clash between the ideal of equality in one sphere and the reality of social inequality in another created the same sort of difficulties as in the case of women.[448]

That such tensions between religious ideal and social reality were present even in the first generation is demonstrated vividly by Paul's letter to Philemon. Philemon's slave Onesimus had run away, joined Paul, and become a Christian. Paul is returning him to his master, as the social order demands. But he wants Philemon to regard Onesimus "no longer as a slave, but more than a slave, as a beloved brother, especially to me, but how much more to you, both in the flesh and in the Lord" (Phm 16). We note that, as in 1 Timothy, both master and slave are Christians. Paul addresses Philemon's attitudes toward Onesimus. And it is clear that he really wishes that the owner would release the slave so that he can join Paul as an assistant (Phm 12–14). But Paul does not fundamentally address the problem of slave owning and never suggests that the social order itself is wrong. Nor does he find it necessary to deal with the attitudes that Onesimus might have toward his master—they were at least sufficiently negative for him to have run away! The point is that the "authentic Paul" was no more in a position to adjudicate the overall social order in the case of slavery than he was in the case of gender roles. He had a notion of what equality in Christ might mean in the *ekklēsia*—although even there we have noted his limitations—but with respect to the social order as such he was far from a utopian thinker.

In the Ephesian church, it seems, we are finding expressed just those hostile attitudes toward masters that we might well have found also in Onesimus if he had been asked. They are "despising" their owners, who are also believers. Indeed, it is precisely the fact that their owners *are* believers that seems to occasion the slaves' contempt (6:2a). The slaves apparently think that the masters should be translating the egalitarian ideals of the assembly into the social realities of the household, but they have not done so. The tension might well have become more severe if the slaves themselves had considerable wealth—as was possible for slaves within the Roman order—and therefore within this affluent Ephesian community may have been separated from their masters only by the thin yet inexorable line established by legal ownership. We see here, then, still another threat to the stability of the Ephesian community because of the fer-

---

448. For an orientation to the subjects of slavery and patronage in the Roman Empire, see M. I. Finley, *Ancient Slavery and Modern Ideology* (New York: Penguin, 1980); R. Saller, *Personal Patronage Under the Early Empire* (Cambridge: Cambridge University Press, 1982); P. Garnsey and R. Saller, *The Roman Empire: Economy, Society, and Culture* (Berkeley: University of California Press, 1987); and R. MacMullen, *Roman Social Relations: 50 B.C. to A.D. 284* (New Haven, Conn.: Yale University Press, 1974).

ment of egalitarianism. Others than the board of elders want to be teachers; women want to speak and have authority over men; slaves want to have their spiritual equality made effective in the social order.

Nothing in Paul's response to this situation should surprise us if we have been reading carefully through the letter. He has consistently expressed his desire that households respect the socially defined subordination of ranks. His administrative criterion for supervisors and deacons, we recall, is that they can manage the children of their own household, keeping them in subordination (3:4, 12). His expectation of women is that they marry, govern their households, have children, and raise them in the faith (2:15; 5:14). Children are to care for their parents as an expression of godliness (5:4). The apostle's concern for the stability and order of households derives from both his appreciation of the Hellenistic *oikos* as part of the *oikonomia theou* (1:4) and his concern that a Christianity associated with social unrest and revolutionary ideas will bring the good news into discredit and even danger (3:6–7; 5:14). In this case as well, he makes clear that he fears that the disrespectful attitudes of Christian slaves toward Christian masters will lead to the name of God being blasphemed—that is, God's own reputation will be dishonored (6:1).[449]

What is most intriguing about Paul's response is not that he fails to meet the challenge of changing the social order—we could scarcely expect that—but that he uses language in such fashion as to enable another kind of subversion of that order. He makes an obvious and deliberate use of the language of honor and shame, which had its home in the ancient system of patronage. But he reverses it. In ancient patronage, only masters would be in the position to exercise benefaction, and it was because they were benefactors that they were considered to be worthy of honor. When he asks the slaves to serve their masters even better *because* they are fellow believers (*pistoi*), Paul uses two terms that are quite startling in this context. First, he designates such service as *euergesia* (6:2a). It is itself a benefaction! By so doing, Paul suggests that the slaves' service is given from a position of strength and nobility and brings honor on themselves, as well as on "the name of God and the teaching" (6:1). Second, he characterizes the masters as also "beloved" (*agapētoi*). The term suggests both that there are bonds of intimacy between master and slave that are positive, even affectionate, and that the slave is in the position of demonstrating toward the master attitudes that are distinctive to their shared commitment to the Lord Jesus. Without challenging the structure of the social system, Paul's language creates the possibility of envisaging the sort of reciprocity between master and slave that was at the heart of ancient *koinōnia*.

The Paul of 1 Timothy certainly falls far short of solving the "problem" of slavery, just as he failed to solve the problem of gender roles. But his failure is no greater than that of the Paul of the undisputed letters. Indeed, it is possible that the subtle use of language in 1 Tim 6:1–2a might well be more liberating, in the final analysis, than Paul's clever diplomacy in Philemon.

---

449. Verner correctly assesses the overall conservative tendency in 1 Timothy with respect to social roles in *Household of God*, 140–145, 182–183.

XIII. CRAVINGS FOR WEALTH

(6:2b–10)

♦

6 ^{2b}Teach and urge these things. ^{3}If anyone teaches otherwise and does not attend to the healthy words of our Lord Jesus Christ and the teaching that accords with godliness, ^{4}that person is deluded, understanding nothing. Instead he is sick from debates and controversies, from which come envy and strife and reviling speech, evil suspicions, ^{5}the constant wranglings of people with corrupted minds. And defrauded from the truth, they think that godliness is a means of financial gain. ^{6}Now godliness is a great source of gain, when it is accompanied by self-sufficiency. ^{7}For we brought nothing into the world, because neither can we take anything out of it. ^{8}But if we have food to eat and a covering, with these we shall be content. ^{9}Now those who want to be rich are falling into temptation and a trap, and into many senseless and harmful cravings that plunge people into ruin and destruction. ^{10}For the love of money is a root for every kind of wickedness. By pursuing it some people have been led astray from the faith and have tortured themselves with many agonies.

NOTES

6:2b *Teach and urge these things*: In the manner typical of this letter, Paul turns from the matters of community concern to the mission of his delegate to "teach and urge" (4:11) the very things (*tauta*) that Paul has given him as *mandata*. And as in 1:3–11 and 4:6–16, attention to Timothy means concern as well for the opponents and their teaching.

3. *If anyone teaches otherwise*: The verb *heterodidaskalein* remains almost as difficult to translate here as it did in 1:3, although my translation fits this context somewhat better. The term is found in Ignatius, *Letter to Polycarp* 3:1. Compare *heterognōmēs* (other minded) in *1 Clement* 11:2. Note the typical Pauline vagueness concerning the identity of the opposition: "if anyone" (*ei tis*).

does not attend: The original hand of Sinaiticus and some Old Latin MSS replace the difficult *proserchetai* (come to) with the more familiar *prosechetai* (pay attention to), found also in 1:4; 3:8; 4:1, 13; and Tit 1:14. The reading *proserchetai* must be retained because it is the best attested and by far the harder reading, and it is used in this sense also in Epictetus, *Discourse* 4.11.24.^{450} Trans-

---

450. See also Metzger, *Textual Commentary*, 642–643.

lations must, in any case, shade the meaning toward *prosechetai* (as my "attend to" does), simply to make sense.

to the healthy words of our Lord Jesus Christ: The idea of "healthy words/ teaching" (*hygiainousē didaskalia/logoi*) is characteristic of these letters to Paul's delegates (compare 1:10; 2 Tim 1:13; 4:3; Tit 1:9, 13; 2:1, 2). For teaching as "sound" or "healthy," see Plutach, *How to Study Poetry* 4 (*Mor.* 20F); Philo, *On Abraham* 223; Josephus, *Against Apion* 1:222. As so often, the genitive construction *tou kyriou hēmōn Iēsou Christou* is ambiguous. It could be an objective genitive, and therefore mean "healthy words concerning our Lord Jesus Christ," or it could be a subjective genitive, and mean "healthy words uttered by our Lord Jesus Christ." The translation does not decide between them. For further discussion, see the COMMENT.

teaching that accords with godliness: In 6:1, Paul linked the reputation of God and of the teaching (*didaskalia*). The description of the *didaskalia* as *kat' eusebeian* (according to godliness) makes the same connection. Note also the construction in 1:10–11, where Paul speaks of that which opposes the healthy *didaskalia kata to euangelion* (teaching according to the good news). All these terms, then, are roughly equivalent and go back to Paul's conviction that what he and his delegate teach is grounded in the *oikonomia theou* (1:4).

4. *deluded, understanding nothing*: In 2 Tim 3:4, I translate the passive of the verb *typhoun* as "crazed." It is a term that occurs frequently in polemic between rival teachers in antiquity, sometimes with the nuance of being "puffed up" (Diogenes Laertius, *Lives of Eminent Philosophers* 6:7), and sometimes—as here— with the sense of "deluded/ stupid" (Dio Chrysostom, *Oration* 6:21; Philo, *On the Confusion of Tongues* 106; Josephus, *Against Apion* 1:15). For "understanding nothing," compare the characterization of the would-be teachers of Law in 1:7, and the references given there.

sick from debates and controversies: We recognize here once more the use of medical terminology so frequent in ancient moral discourse.[451] The verb *nosein* means, first of all, to "be physically ill or sick" (Herodotus, *Persian War* 1:105), but is applied to mental states of unrest or instability (Xenophon, *Memorabilia* 3.5.18; Philo, *Allegorical Laws* 3:211). I translate the phrase *peri zētēseis kai logomachias* as "sick from debates and controversies," although the construction could also be rendered as "having a morbid fascination for debates and controversies" (Plutarch, *On Inoffensive Self-Praise* 20 [*Mor.* 546F]).

from which come envy and strife and reviling speech: The Western text tradition (represented most consistently in this case by Codex Bezae) makes a number of alterations, mainly turning the singular verb *ginetai* into the plural *gennōntai*, and then making "envy" and "strife" plural forms as well. The text used by this translation maintains the singular throughout. This miniature vice-list contains several of the items that are found also in Rom 1:29–31. Not only do envy (*phthonos*), strife (*eris*), reviling speech (*blasphēmiai*), and the other vices here listed share a misanthropic attitude—they are all intensely antisocial—but they appear together in much ancient moral discourse, especially that

---

451. Malherbe, "Medical Imagery in the Pastorals."

concerning envy, which tended to make that "comparative/competitive" vice the source of all social unrest and murderous impulse (e.g., Anacharsis, *Letter* 9:10–25; Plutarch, *On Tranquillity of Mind* [*Mor.* 473B]; *On Brotherly Love* [*Mor.* 487E–488C]; Epictetus, *Discourse* 3.22.61; Dio Chrysostom, *Oration* 77/78:17–29).

evil suspicions: The phrase *hyponoia ponēra* occurs also in LXX Sir 3:24. For *hyponoia* as "suspicion" or "conjecture," see *Letter of Aristeas* 316, and Josephus, *Jewish War* 1:227. Notice that Paul has shifted from mental incapacities to actual vices, these of a much more general sort than those in 1:8–10. To be suspicious of others is once more a function of envy, which bases itself on competitive measurement.

5. *constant wranglings*: This is the only occurrence in ancient literature of the term *diaparatribai*. It appears to function as an intensified form of *paratribai* (friction/irritation, Polybius, *Histories* 2.36.5).[452] Once more, we may see here some of the background to the "anger and argument" that are besetting the men at worship in the *ekklēsia* (2:8).

corrupted minds: More medical imagery for moral teaching. The false teachers are sick from controversies and have corrupted their minds (compare 2 Tim 3:8), so that they have nothing to do with the "healthy teaching" associated with Jesus. The phrase *ton noun* is in the accusative, indicating that with respect to which they are corrupted. For the use of the verb *diaphtherein* (literally, "to ruin") with morals and minds, see Aeschylus, *Agamemnon* 932; Diodorus Siculus, *Library of History* 16.54.4; Dio Chrysostom, *Oration* 43:10; Plato, *Laws* 888A; Josephus, *Antiquities* 9:222.

defrauded from the truth: Some scribes were confused by the participle *apesterēmenōn*, which means to "be defrauded" (Josephus, *Life* 128) and is found in that meaning in 1 Cor 6:8 and James 5:4. In this sentence, however, it struck a couple of copyists as odd; two of them (the original hand of Bezae and 365) offer separate corrections in the direction of "having turned away from" (compare 1 Tim 1:19). But to have those who seek wealth in the process find themselves "defrauded from the truth" is simply strong writing.

godliness is a means of financial gain: The noun *porismos* means a "source of gain," especially of money (Polybius, *Roman History* 3.112.2; Musonius Rufus, *Fragment* 11; Plutarch *On Love of Wealth* 4 [*Mor.* 524D]). It occurs both here and in the next verse; Paul plays with the term, giving it different applications in the two cases. In the first instance, I translate it as "means of financial gain," since that is what the context demands: some people are seeking to get rich through *eusebeia* (6:9). A large number of witnesses (including the second hand of Bezae and the Koine tradition) have "keep away from such as these" (*aphistaso apo tōn toioutōn*); the shorter reading is found in Sinaiticus, Alexandrinus, Bezae, and others. The addition may have resulted from the desire to relieve the awkward link between verses 5 and 6.[453]

---

452. For the relationship of envy to such social unrest, see the NOTE on verse 4 and L. T. Johnson, "James 3:13–4:10 and the *Topos* PERI PHTHONOU," *NovT* 25 (1983): 327–347.

453. Metzger calls it a "pious but banal gloss" (Textual Commentary, 643).

6. *great source of gain*: This second use of *porismos* I translate as "source of gain," since here Paul plainly does *not* mean a financial advantage, but a gain that might be called spiritual: the life of godliness itself. As always in this letter, *eusebeia* virtually stands for the entire life of the community shaped by *pistis* (3:9, 16).

accompanied by self-sufficiency: The translation "accompanied by" takes the preposition *meta* seriously: Paul's point is that *autarkeia* (self-sufficiency) itself cancels the materialistic meaning of gain, leaving *porismos* as only the spiritual sense of "advancement/advantage." Compare Paul's statements on physical training in 4:8. The *topos* PERI AUTARKEIAS (On Self-Sufficiency) is a standard in Hellenistic moral discourse, and one that Paul shows familiarity with elsewhere (2 Cor 9:8; Phil 4:11–12).[454] As the etymology suggests, *autarkeia* can be translated as "self-rule/self-sufficiency," which emphasizes its note of detachment and freedom from any claims made by possessions of any sort. More positively, it can be translated as "contentment," which emphasizes the willingness to be satisfied with what one has, rather than having that craving disease that always seeks more.

7. *For we brought nothing into the world*: The connective *gar* (for) suggests that Paul is alluding to well-known proverbial knowledge. The statement bears a thematic resemblance to Job 1:21: "I came naked from my mother's womb and naked I shall return." There is an even stronger resemblance to LXX Qoh 5:14: "As he came from his mother's womb he shall go again, naked as he came, and shall take nothing for his toil, which he may carry away in his hand." Such sentiments find parallels in other wisdom literature as well (*Greek Anthology* 10:58; Philo, *Special Laws* 1:294–295; Seneca, *Moral Epistles* 102:25).

because neither can we take anything out of it: Ancient copyists found the syntax of 6:7 as difficult as do present-day translators. We would expect syntax of this sort: "for since we brought nothing into the world, neither will we take anything out of it." The sapiential sentiment, as just noted, echoes Job 1:21 and Qoh 5:11–15. But, as my translation indicates, the presence of *hoti* at the beginning of the second clause is very awkward. Some scribes tried to alleviate the difficulty by supplying an additional phrase, either *alēthes hoti* (it is true that, e.g., the original hand of Bezae) or *dēlon estin* (it is clear that, e.g., the second corrector of Sinaiticus and Bezae). For the use of *dēlon estin*, compare Philo, *On the Eternity of the World* 75.[455]

8. *food to eat and a covering*: A large number of witnesses have the singular *diatrophēn* (Bezae, F, G, K, P, and a number of versions), rather than the plural *diatrophas* (Sinaiticus, Alexandrinus, and the Koine tradition). The difference is not great, and, in any case, I have translated both phrases (including the plural *skepesmata*) in a generalizing fashion, taking the plural as corresponding to the inclusive plural subject "we." The noun *diatrophē* means broadly "means of sustenance" (Epictetus, *Encheiridion* 12:1), and *skepasma* can mean either "clothing" (Aristotle, *Politics* 1336A) or "shelter" (Aristotle, *Metaphysics* 1043A). In the

---

454. For selections on the topic, see Malherbe, *Moral Exhortation*, 112–114, 120, 145.

455. See the discussion in Metzger, *Textual Commentary*, 643, and Eliott, *Greek Text*, 95.

Cynic tradition, which made so much of *autarkeia*, the translation "clothing" would be more likely, but I have tried to include both possibilities by translating as "a covering."

we shall be content: The verb *arkesesthai* (to be content/to be self-sufficient) again makes explicit Paul's topic that holds these discrete observations together: self-sufficiency (Herodotus, *Persian War* 9:33; Aristotle, *Nicomachean Ethics* 1107B; Josephus, *Antiquities* 12:294; 2 Macc 5:15; 4 Macc 6:28; 2 Cor 12:9). Paul has now established the perspective of faith on the *oikonomia theou*, to which he will contrast the vice of acquisitiveness.

9. *those who want to be rich*: The phrasing here is particularly intriguing. Paul speaks of those "wishing" (*bouloumenoi*) to be rich (*ploutein*, Herodotus, *Persian War* 1:32; Plato, *Republic* 421D). We are struck, first, by the resemblance to 1:7, where he speaks of those "wishing to be teachers of the law." There is a difference between being rich and wanting to be rich. Second, just as those who are not teachers of Law but want to be tend toward rigor and severity, it is not the truly wealthy who most demonstrate the vice of avarice so much as those whose lives are consumed by the *desire* to be wealthy. For the charge that Sophists teach *chremata porizein* (in order to gain wealth), see Dio Chrysostom, *Oration* 54:1.

falling into temptation and a trap: There is a stunning alliteration here: *ploutein, empiptousin, peirasmon, pagida, pollas*. The verb *empiptein* is used also in 3:6–7, but not otherwise in Paul (for *epipiptein*, see Rom 15:3, and compare *peripiptein peirasmois* in James 1:2). For "temptation," see 1 Cor 10:13 and Gal 4:14. Apparently influenced by 1 Tim 3:9, some MSS (e.g., the original hand of Bezae) add *tou diabolou* (of the devil) to *pagida*, forming the phrase "trap of the devil." It is probably not original, but there is a fascinating passage in the Qumran literature that associates avarice with "Satan's nets" (CD 4:14–5:10). See also the vivid picture in 2 Tim 2:26 of God snatching people alive *ek tēs diabolou pagidos* (out of the trap of the devil).

senseless and harmful cravings: Because this is a *topos* on self-sufficiency, I have rendered *epithymiai* as "cravings" in order to fit within the focus on acquisitiveness in this passage. For the range of (mostly negative) meanings of *epithymia* in Hellenistic moral discourse, see Plato, *Phaedo* 83B; *Phaedrus* 232B; Epictetus, *Discourse* 2.16.45; 18.8; 3.9.21; Wis. 4:12; 4 Macc 1:22; 3:2; Philo, *Special Laws* 4:93–94; *Contemplative Life* 74; *Preliminary Studies* 172; *Migration of Abraham* 60. For "senseless" (*anoētos*), see Dio Chrysostom, *Oration* 4:33; 70:8; Gal 3:1, 3; Tit 3:3. For "harmful" (*blaberos*), see Xenophon, *Memorabilia* 1.3.11; 5.3.

plunge people into ruin and destruction: The verb *bythizein* means to "sink something in the depths" (*bythoi*) and is used figuratively of moral decline (esp. Philostratus, *Life of Apollonius of Tyana* 4:32). The noun *olethros* occurs as early as Homer (*Odyssey* 4:489) and appears frequently in Hellenistic Jewish literature (LXX Wis 1:12; 18:13; Sir 39:30; 2 Macc 6:12; 4 Macc 10:15; Josephus, *Antiquities* 17:38; *Life* 264; *Sibylline Oracles* 3:327). Paul elsewhere uses it with reference to the excommunicated Corinthian (1 Cor 5:5) and as part of the eschatological scenario (1 Thess 5:3; 2 Thess 1:9). The noun *apōleia* is, if anything, even more extreme in its connotations (Aristotle, *Nicomachean Ethics* 1120A; *Letter of Aristeas* 167; Philo, *On the Eternity of the World* 20; *Testament of Dan* 4:5). The combination of terms could be translated as "utter ruin." It is possible, but unlikely, that Paul is thinking of economic collapse; he is thinking mainly of the corruption of the person.

10. *love of money is a root for every kind of wickedness*: The maxim finds parallels in other writings and is itself one of the most frequently quoted lines from 1 Timothy. My translation is more restrictive than the traditional: "for the love of money is the root of all evils" (e.g., RSV). In the first place, the anarthous character of *riza* should be respected. Paul does not say it is "the" (exclusive) root, but "a" root (among others). In the second place, the phrase *pantōn tōn kakōn* should be taken as generic: "for every kind of wickedness." Certainly no ancient moralist would confine the perils of *epithymia* to the love of money! For similar sentiments among Greco-Roman moralists, see Bion, "Love of money is the mother-city of all evils" *philargyria metropolin pantōn tōn kakōn*, cited in Diogenes Laertius, *Lives of Eminent Philosophers* 6:50. Other statements capturing the theme with less verbal resemblance are found in Diodorus Siculus, *Library of History* 21.1.4; *Sibylline Oracles* 8:17; *Sentences of Pseudo-Phocylides* 42; Philo, *Special Laws* 4:65. The love of money (*philargyria*) is one of the standard vices to which ancient sages were particularly prone and therefore repeatedly attacked (Philostratus, *Life of Apollonius of Tyana* 1:34; Julian, *Oration* 6:181C; 198B; 200C; Dio Chrysostom, *Oration* 32:9, 11; 35:1; 77/78:37; Epictetus, *Discourse* 1.9.19–20; 1.29.55–57; 2.16.3; 3.24.69–83; 4.1.139; Lucian, *The Runaways* 14; *Philosophies for Sale* 24; *Nigrinus* 25; *Zeus Rants* 27; *Timon* 56; *Hermotimus* 9–10).

By pursuing it some people have been led astray from the faith: Paul uses the same verb, *oregomai*, as for the ambition to be a supervisor (3:1). Such avarice, as with other forms of vice and false teaching opposed by Paul in this letter, is found among members of the community; thus their vice has "led them astray [*apoplanasthesai*, Epictetus, *Discourse* 4.6.38; Mark 13:22] from the faith" (*apo tēs pisteōs*). For the way in which *pistis*, like *eusebeia*, stands for the ethos of the entire community, compare 1:19; 4:1; 5:8; 6:21.

tortured themselves with many agonies: The original hand of Codex Bezae and H (015) have the adjective "various" (*poikilois*), rather than *pollois* (many), possibly influenced by James 1:2. The verb *periperein* means literally to "impale or pierce something" (Josephus, *Jewish War* 3:296). Here, the wound is self-inflicted: they have pierced themselves (*heautous*). The phrase *odynais pollais* is in the dative case, describing metaphorically the means or the manner of being pierced: they are impaling themselves with many agonies, or they experience agonies as they pierce themselves. The RSV has, "pierced their hearts with many pangs," which is literal (although "hearts" is not in the Greek) and unhelpful: What can it mean? In this translation, I have taken the liberty of rendering it as "tortured themselves with many agonies," understanding the point to be that a life driven by such constant craving is a form of self-torture.

COMMENT

As 1 Timothy nears its end, the theme that has been just below the surface throughout the letter now becomes explicit: the ways in which wealth and the craving for wealth are affecting the life of the Ephesian *ekklēsia*, threatening its identity as a community shaped by *pistis* and *eusebeia*. Paul confronts the issue in this section by addressing the attitudes of his delegate Timothy. Within the form of the *mandata principis* letter, as we have seen, the things said to the delegate also serve as exemplary to the wider readership. In the manner typical of polemic, Paul connects the mental errors of the false teachers to a moral sickness: the love of money (*philargyria*, 6:10). A sign that something more than stereotypical slander is at work here, however, is that the desire by some to find religious profession a source of financial gain (6:5) receives the most elaborate theological response in the letter. Positively, Paul responds to the vice of *philargyria* with the attitudes associated in antiquity with the virtue of *autarkeia* (self-sufficiency, 6:8). And after the final charge made to Timothy in 6:11–16, we will find Paul returning to the same theme one last time in 6:17–19.

Literary and Historical Connections

This passage provides a virtual test case for locating the letters to Paul's delegates within the early Christian movement. There is language here that points us in turn backward toward Jesus, forward toward Polycarp, and toward Paul's undisputed letters.

Paul refers to the "healthy words of our Lord Jesus Christ" in 6:3, which he combines with the "teaching that accords with godliness," which his opponents fail to appropriate. I point out in the NOTES that the genitive construction is ambiguous. Does Paul make what is, in effect, a generalized reference to tradition? In such a case, an argument could be made for the late dating of the composition, since the "words of Jesus" would have lost any real specificity. Or does Paul have in mind actual words spoken by Jesus and handed down orally in various Christian communities? It is widely appreciated that Paul in the undisputed letters does not make frequent use of such Jesus-sayings. But it is also clear that when he does use these traditions, he regards them as authoritative. The two clearest instances are his full recollection of the words of Jesus at the Last Supper (1 Cor 11:23–25) and his appeal to a commandment of the Lord with respect to divorce (1 Cor 7:10). In the discussion of 1 Tim 5:18 in the COMMENT on 5:17–6:2a, we have seen how the author quotes a saying of Jesus to the effect that preachers and teachers should be supported by the community and that this citation resembles the broader allusion made by Paul to the instructions of Jesus on the same point in 1 Cor 9:9. The practice of the author of 1 Timothy with respect to the sayings of Jesus, in short, is essentially the same as that of the Paul of the undisputed letters.

If, in fact, Paul also had certain sayings of Jesus in mind, there are any number of candidates for the subjects under discussion in this passage. Is the topic that of service to others under the rubric of benefaction (6:2)? There is at least one outstanding example of a Jesus-saying on that point, again from the Gospel of Luke:

> The kings of the Gentiles exercise lordship over them; and those in authority over them are called benefactors. But not so with you; rather let the greatest among you become as the youngest, and the leader as one who serves. For which is the greater, the one who sits at table, or the one who serves? Is it not the one who sits at table? But I am among you as one who serves. (22:25–27)

Or if the subject is the foolishness of seeking life in wealth, rather than in a relationship with God, the sayings of Jesus in the Gospel of Luke again offer several possibilities (e.g., 6:20, 24; 9:23–25; 12:22–34; 14:25–33; 16:13), the most succinct of which, framing the parable of the rich fool, could stand as commentary on this passage: "Take heed and beware of all covetousness; for a man's life does not consist in the abundance of his possessions . . . so is he who lays up treasure for himself and is not rich toward God" (12:15, 21). Readers have often been struck by the resemblances in diction and tone between the letters to Paul's delegates and the Gospel of Luke, some even finding the parallels sufficiently persuasive as to suggest shared authorship.[456] Is it also possible that Paul's own language and perceptions are being shaped by those of Jesus? As in all such cases, no real proof is possible in either direction, but it is at least good to keep alive an awareness of more than one possibility.

Does Polycarp Write or Use 1 Timothy?

A second intertextual question arises from the cluster of pronouncements in 6:6–10. As indicated in the NOTES, 6:7 has a thematic resemblance to Job 1:21 and an even stronger one to Qoh 5:14, as well as to a variety of statements that offer the same sentiment in Greco-Roman and Jewish writings. Similarly, Paul's declaration concerning money as a root of evils in 6:10 finds a variety of parallels within the same broad cultural world. Paul's statements, in short, represent a cultural commonplace. One must, therefore, be wary of two extremes when interpreting. One extreme is to recognize the proverbial nature of such statements and seek nothing further from them except another version of a cultural cliché. The other extreme is to overemphasize whatever small points of individuality in expression Paul's language might possess and consider them as demonstration of a freshness of appropriation or insight. It is difficult to maintain a healthy perspective on such common language, recognizing on one side that an author is relying on standard observations, while also recognizing on the other side that the reason such observations become common is because they contain widely recognized wisdom.

---

456. Wilson, *Luke and the Pastoral Epistles*; Quinn, "Last Volume of Luke."

These cautionary remarks are appropriate to keep in mind as we move to the next complication, which is presented by the fact that both 6:7 and 6:10 appear to find expression in Polycarp: "But the beginning of all evils is the love of money. Knowing therefore that we brought nothing into the world and we can take nothing out of it, let us arm ourselves with the armour of righteousness and let us teach ourselves first of all to walk in the commandment of the Lord." (*Letter to the Philippians* 4:1). How are we to evaluate this occurrence? One option is to insist on the importance of the parallels to 1 Timothy in order to suggest that 1 Timothy's language has nothing distinctive about it in the first place, so that both Polycarp and 1 Timothy are simply drawing from the great pool of Hellenistic paraenetic traditions.[457] In fact, however, a close comparison between 1 Tim 6:7, 10 and all the parallels adduced show that none has 1 Timothy's precise language; the closest is the statement attributed to Bion, quoted in the NOTE on 6:10. In other examples adduced as parallels, there is a sharing of sentiment, but not of language.

Another approach is to explain the resemblance between 1 Timothy and Polycarp by a shared authorship. The same sentiment appears in both writings because Polycarp, a second-century bishop in Smyrna, is the actual author of 1 Timothy.[458] Presumably, the only available options for this hypothesis are either that Polycarp echoed his own language unconsciously or that he cleverly salted the composition written under his own name with language that he himself employed in the composition he wrote pseudonymously: 1 Timothy. We must therefore think of Polycarp either as someone who can or as someone who cannot carry off a complicated literary scam.

Such a hypothesis is difficult to sustain on two preliminary counts: first, Polycarp's character—from what we know of it—scarcely comports with such manipulation; second, it is hard to determine what real profit he would gain from a subterfuge so subtle that only twentieth-century scholars could suspect it. More to the point, the literary evidence suggests that Polycarp himself thought that he was quoting lines from Paul. We see this best if we begin reading some sentences before the pertinent passage:

> These things, brethren, I write to you concerning righteousness, not at my own instance, but because you first invited me. For neither am I, nor is any other like me, able to follow the wisdom of the blessed and glorious Paul *who when he was among you in the presence of the men of that time taught accurately and steadfastly the word of truth.* (Polycarp, *Phil.* 3:1–2 [emphasis added]).

We notice that Polycarp clearly distinguishes himself and his authority from that of Paul, who is portrayed not only as a man of a previous generation, but as one whose ways are well known to the Philippians. If Polycarp authored the senti-

---

457. See, for example, Dibelius and Conzelmann, *Pastoral Epistles*, 85–86.
458. Campenhausen, *Polykarp von Smyrna und die Pastoralbriefe*.

ments he subsequently quotes, he could scarcely have been bolder in the act. But Polycarp then adds, "And also when he was absent *wrote letters to you from the study of which you will be able to build yourselves up into the faith given to you*" (Polycarp, *Phil.* 3:2 [emphasis added]). The sentence makes two things clear: first, the words that follow are understood by Polycarp as deriving from Paul's letters; second, since his readers have such letters in their possession, they could check on them if they wished. After a short transition sentence that contains an allusion to Gal 4:26, Polycarp writes *archē de pantōn chalepōn philargyria* (Love of money is the source of all hurtful things). This is possibly an echo or allusion to 1 Tim 6:10. Then he follows immediately with *ouden eisenēnkamen eis ton kosmon all' oude exenēnkein ti echomen* (We brought nothing into the world and neither do we have anything to bring out of it). Once more, the citation is not exact, yet the wording is closer to 1 Tim 6:7 than to any other parallel from antiquity. We see, therefore, that Polycarp writes lines that also appear in 1 Tim 6:7 and 6:10 but in reverse order. Polycarp next follows with further instructions that contain echoes, in turn, of 2 Cor 14:25; Gal 6:7; 1 Tim 3:8; 2 Tim 2:12; Gal 5:17; 1 Cor 6:9–10, and other Pauline texts. None of them is an exact citation; all are echoes or allusions. Yet Polycarp has left no doubt that he intends to remind his readers of things that they read in *Paul's letters*.

The evidence suggests two things:

1. Paul's language concerning possessions is sufficiently distinctive to be recognizable among other variations on the theme.
2. Polycarp echoes that language and not some other expression of the same sentiment.

If, as I argue, Polycarp not only knew and used 1 Timothy, but assumed that his readers would also recognize the words as those of Paul, then we can also conclude two further things:

1. At the very least, 1 Timothy was in existence and circulation before 130, thereby disallowing any theory positing its composition at around 150.
2. Polycarp thought that these letters were by Paul, and included them within a catena of Pauline allusions in order to illustrate the sort of wisdom that might be gained by a reading of the Pauline letters.

Is This Language Pauline?

Recognizing such complex patterns of intertextuality enables us, finally, to view the old issue of the diction in 1 Timothy with refreshed eyes. In addition to such measures as sentence length, syntax, and the use of connectives, it will be recalled, the criterion of style has been applied, above all, to the author's word choice. The standard way to employ this gauge has been through counting the number of *hapax legomena* used by a composition. The number of *hapax legomena* per page of Greek text in one of Paul's undisputed letters—let us say, Romans—is compared with the number found per page in 1 Timothy. As I point out in the INTRODUCTION, the entire stylistic analysis is based on flawed premises. Among them is the presumption that there is a stylistic consistency in the undisputed letters. This is patently not the case. Another is that Paul did not employ the rhetorical device called *prosōpopoiia* (writing in style). But that he did can be shown in his letters.

Even when such fundamental methodological disqualifications are bracketed, the practice of compiling statistics about vocabulary is misleading, above all, because it does not take into account the most obvious factor in all of Paul's correspondence: that it is occasional and responds to different circumstances by different means. In short, a writer's vocabulary is not a constant, but a shifting repertoire, affected by such basic facts as the subject matter being discussed.

In this passage, for example, the number of NT and Pauline *hapax legomena* places it at the far extreme of the continuum that might reasonably be called Pauline. There are fully ten words whose only occurrence in the NT is 1 Timothy: *heterodidaskalein, nosein, logomachia, hyponoiai, diaparatribai, porismos, diatrophē, skepasma, blabera, periperein,* and there are another nine terms found elsewhere in the NT, but nowhere else in the Pauline corpus: *proserchesthai, epistēmai, zētēsis, eispherein, ekpherein, empiptein, bathizein, oregesthai,* and *apoplanan.* Then there are three words found only in the Pastorals: *typhoun, hygiainein,* and *eusebeia.* If we paid attention to only the numbers, we might be impressed at how "different" this language is from the "normal" Pauline usage. But other considerations complicate matters.

First, we need to recognize those terms that are so common in Greek that Paul's failure to use them elsewhere is a statistical oddity. In this category can be included the verbs of movement *proserchesthai, eispherein,* and *ekpherein.* Second, we need to acknowledge those words whose cognates appear in Paul; he may not have used this *form* of the word elsewhere, but it must be included in his potential vocabulary. Under this head, we can list *eusebeia, empiptein,* and *apoplanan.* Third, we must note the use of terms that are appropriate to a specific subject matter and that may appear in one place but not in another. In this passage, we can single out words that are at home in polemic between rival teachers: *heterodidaskalein, nosein, logomachia, hyponoiai, blaberos, epistēmai, zētēsis, oregesthai,* and *typhoun.* Forms of such diction appear frequently in contexts of dispute between schools. In this passage as well, we recognize *philargyria, porismos, diatrophē, skepasma, arkesthai,* and *autarkeia* as vocabulary that is at home within the Greco-Roman moral topic of self-sufficiency or contentment (more on this later). When all these considerations are taken into account, the number of terms that are genuinely rare or unusual (e.g., *diaparatribai, periperein*) is remarkably reduced. Clearly, such discussions cannot serve to either make or break a case for Pauline authorship. What they can do is limit the number of methodologically weak arguments that are used for either position.

The Problem and Paul's Response

Hard evidence for the social situation of early Christians is difficult to come by, but the close analysis of the Pauline letters—above all, 1 and 2 Corinthians, which are so filled with social data—has enabled a better sense of at least some Pauline communities. Although dispute continues on a number of points,[459] it is possible to assert confidently that the sociological assumptions of an earlier generation—that the Christian movement was centered in the poorest of the poor—[460]must be adjusted considerably. Paul's urban converts were not exclusively from among the destitute or even the disadvantaged. At least some could be considered moderately, if not extravangantly, wealthy.[461] Among them were such members of the Corinthian congregation as Erastus, whom Paul identifies as the *oikonomos tēs poleōs* (treasurer of the city, Rom 16:23); Phoebe, the deacon of Cenchrae, whom Paul designates as his financial patron (Rom 16:3); Chloe, who was the owner of slaves (1 Cor 1:11); and such householders as Stephanus, Fortunatus, and Achaicus (1 Cor 16:15–17). Understanding that not all believers were of the same social rank or enjoyed the same degree of wealth (1 Cor 1:26) also enables a better grasp of certain problems in communities; in Corinth, for example, disparities in wealth may well have been a factor in creating the tensions found in the question of eating food offered to idols (1 Cor 8–10) or behavior at the Lord's Supper (1 Cor 11:17–22).[462] Similarly, the disruption of a community's sense of egalitarianism by ostentatious wealth can be seen in the condemnation of the favoritism shown to the rich by the Letter of James.[463] In short, the presence of wealthy members within a movement that stemmed from a founder who was intensely critical of wealth helped create severe tensions.[464]

It is possible to sense such tensions just below the surface throughout 1 Timothy.[465] As the next passage (6:17) will make explicit, there were those in the Ephesian *ekklēsia* who were "wealthy in this age." We have already seen that some believers were also slave owners (6:1–2). Some women were able at worship to make a display of their extravagant clothing, hairdos, and jewelry (2:9). Some families were in the position to support the poor widows of their households (5:4, 8, 16). I have already suggested that the presence of such visible

---

459. J. J. Meggitt, *Paul, Poverty, and Survival* (Edinburgh: Clark, 1998), challenges the dominant portrait constructed by Judge, "Early Christians as a Scholastic Community," Meeks, *First Urban Christians*, and G. Thiessen, *The Social Setting of Pauline Christianity: Essays on Corinth*, trans. J. Schuetz (Philadelphia: Fortress Press, 1982).

460. K. Kautsky, *Foundations of Christianity*, trans. H. F. Mins (New York: Russell, 1953); Deissmann, *Light from the Ancient East*.

461. Meeks, *First Urban Christians*, 51–73.

462. Theissen, *Social Setting of Pauline Christianity*, 145–174.

463. Johnson, *Letter of James*, 218–229.

464. L. W. Countryman, *The Rich Christian in the Church of the Early Empire: Contradictions and Accommodations*, Texts and Studies in Religion 7 (New York: Mellen, 1980).

465. Kidd, *Wealth and Beneficence in the Pastoral Epistles*, esp. 35–110.

wealth presented temptations to leaders. Charges have been made against elders (5:19–20) about matters that do not easily come to light (5:24–25). Elders envious of such pervasive wealth may have been taking advantage of their position to improve their own situations. The instruction that they be paid double if they teach (5:17) may have been directed against such a temptation. As we have seen as well, Paul takes pains to ensure that supervisors and helpers not be lovers of money (3:3) or do anything for a profit (3:8). All these elements now surface in Paul's charge that some are using godliness (*eusebeia*)—which here should probably be translated as "religious profession"—as a means of financial gain (*porismos*, 6:5). Lest this be too oblique, Paul charges that some "want to be rich" (*bouloumenoi ploutein*, 6:9) and have been led astray from the faith by this ambition (6:10).

Paul's own understanding of faith as something more than a set of convictions about reality becomes clear in his response, which is fascinating, above all, for the ways in which it embraces and extends the moral discourse of his culture. Much of his reply can be fitted within the standard views of Greco-Roman (and Hellenistic Jewish) moralists concerning material possessions. On one side, he emphasizes the danger and deceptiveness embedded in such cravings for wealth: people who pursue wealth have "senseless and harmful cravings" that both torture them—acquisitiveness is the vice that never says "enough"—and lead them to ruin and destruction (6:9). The deceptiveness is found in the claim of possessions to ensure life and security and worth; the danger lies in the fact that a life lived in pursuit of such false security can end up in utter destruction.

On the other side, Paul argues that *autarkeia* is an authentic expression of the Christian life of faith (6:6). As indicated in the NOTES, *autarkeia* is a central term for ancient discussions concerning the appropriate way to live within a world of material possessions, especially in the Cynic–Stoic philosophical tradition. It connotes both a detachment from possessions and a contentment with whatever things are available at the moment. By no means is it an attitude that derives from a dualistic pessimism about materiality. It is, rather, a sober assessment that pursuing possessions as an end in itself is ruinous. In contrast, a life in appropriate engagement with the world can be satisfying to the human spirit (thus "contentment" as another translation for *autarkeia*).

As we have found with some frequency in reading 1 Timothy, the same themes are expressed by Paul in his undisputed letters as well, if not so fully. As a means of encouraging the Corinthians to share their material possessions in the collection for the saints in Jerusalem, for example, Paul assures them that God "is able to make every gift abound for you, so that always, in every way, having *autarkeia*, you can yourselves abound in every good work" (2 Cor 9:8). We see in that case how Paul attaches their willingness to relinquish some of their own possessions for the sake of others to the perception that God is a giver of gifts that are always renewable, so that their self-dispossession will not lead to their ruin, but to their own abundance (2 Cor 9:6–15). This theological perception Paul comfortably designates as *autarkeia*. Similarly, Paul writes to the Philippian church, thanking them for a gift of money that they made to him: "Not

that I complain of want; for I have learned, in whatever state I am, to be content [*autarkēs*]. I know how to be abased and I know how to abound; in any and
all circumstances I have learned the secret of facing plenty and hunger, abundance and want" (Phil 4:11–12). Paul here supplies an almost perfect definition
of *autarkeia*. Ancient moralists—or some of them at least—would have caviled
only when Paul adds, "I can do all things in him who strengthens me" (Phil
4:13). For our present purposes, it is important to note how, once again, the
concept of *autarkeia* is given an explicitly theological dimension by Paul.

It is this sort of self-sufficiency that Paul urges on his delegate and, through
Timothy, on the believers in the Ephesian church. Paul counters an extravagance in clothing and adornment with an ideal close to that of Cynicism: food
and a covering are enough to satisfy a person (6:8). Such simplicity is really a
dimension of freedom. We note here also that Paul's advocacy of *autarkeia* is
connected to a certain theology of creation. In this case, it is the reality that humans are born with no possessions and die with no possessions; they *cannot* take
anything with them (6:7). Embedded in this simple yet profoundly true observation are at least three theological corollaries. The first is that true "godliness"
(*eusebeia*) must begin with precisely this recognition, that human existence is
itself a gift from God that cannot in any significant fashion be improved by material possessions. The second is that the insensate pursuit of possessions is a
flight from the truth of creation, which is that humans are at every moment dependent on the God who makes all things good and to be received with thanksgiving (4:3). The third is that to make religious profession itself a means of gain-
ing wealth is a peculiarly twisted perversion of the proper order of creation and
of the human realtionship with God. It ought to be the essence of true *eusebeia*
to testify to the nakedness and yet the giftedness of all human existence. A reli-
giosity that made the accumulation of wealth either the point of profession or
the proof of righteousness is deeply inimical to the spirit of Paul's teaching. Once
more, it may be worth noting the loss to theological and ethical reflection caused
by the marginalization of the letters to Paul's delegates.

XIV. CLOSING COMMISSION
(6:11–21)

◆

6 ¹¹But you, O Man of God, flee these things! Instead, pursue righteousness, godliness, faith, love, endurance, and a generous temper. ¹²Engage the noble athletic contest for the faith. Take hold of the eternal life. You were called to it. And you pronounced the noble profession before many witnesses. ¹³I command you before the God who gives life to all things, and before Jesus Christ who testified to the noble profession before Pontius Pilate, ¹⁴keep the commandment spotless and blameless until the appearance of our Lord Jesus Christ, ¹⁵which God will reveal at the proper season. He is the blessed and only ruler, the King of kings, and the Lord of lords. ¹⁶He alone possesses immortality. He dwells in unapproachable light. No human being has ever seen Him. No one can ever see Him. To Him be eternal honor and power. Amen. ¹⁷Tell the rich in this world not to be arrogant and not to put their hope upon the uncertainty of wealth, but rather upon God who supplies us with all things richly for our enjoyment. ¹⁸Tell them to do good work, to be wealthy in noble deeds, to be generous in giving, to be sharers of possessions, ¹⁹thereby storing up for themselves a noble foundation for the future, so that they can lay hold of real life. ²⁰O Timothy! Protect the tradition! Avoid the profane chattering and contradictions of so-called knowledge. ²¹Some have professed it. They have missed the mark concerning faith. Grace be with you.

NOTES

11. *O Man of God, flee these things*: The apostrophe "But you, O Man of God" here, combined with "O Timothy" in 6:20 gives a particular solemnity to this final exhortation. There is, however, no reason to suppose that it has an origin outside the letter.[466] The use of *pheugein* (flee) and *diōkein* (pursue) for moral responses, rather than physical ones, is the same here as in some of Paul's undisputed letters (1 Cor 6:18; 10:14; 14:1; Rom 9:30). For the turn of phrase *su de* (but you), see 2 Tim 3:10, 14 and 4:5.

pursue righteousness, godliness: This virtue-list of six members corresponds to the vice-list of 6:4–5. As in 2 Tim 2:22, the "pursuit" of *dikaiosynē* here is un-

---

466. E. Käsemann, "Das Formular einer neutestamentlichen Ordinationsparänese," in *Neutestamentliche Studien für Rudolf Bultmann* (Berlin: Töpelmann, 1954), 261–268.

encumbered by any of the weightier forensic associations of Galatians and Romans, and has to do with the living out of a righteous existence (compare 2 Cor 11:15; Phil 1:11; Eph 5:9; 6:14). As we have seen repeatedly, "godliness" (*eusebeia*) is shorthand in this letter for a life directed toward God's way of ordering reality.

faith, love, endurance: The virtue of *pistis* (faith, 1:4–5, 14, 19; 2:7, 15; 3:9, 13; 4:1, 6, 12; 5:8, 12) is by now familiar as the most consistent indicator of the ethos of the church. Here, in particular, the pursuit of it is in contrast to those who have been led astray from the faith in 6:10. Likewise, *agapē* (love), which was identified as the *telos* (goal) of the commandment in 1:5, has reappeared as a shared virtue in the church (2:15; 4:12). This is the only reference to *hypomonē* (endurance) in the letter, although it is a favorite theme in Paul (Rom 2:7; 5:3–4; 8:24–25; 12:12; 15:4–5; 1 Cor 13:7; 2 Cor 1:6; 6:4; 12:12; Col 1:11; 1 Thess 1:3; 2 Thess 1:4; 3:5; 2 Tim 3:10; Tit 2:2).

a generous temper: Some significant MSS (such as the second corrector of Sinaiticus and Codex Bezae, as well as the Koine tradition) understandably alter the rare *praupathia*; it is not found elsewhere in the NT. They replace it with the much more common *prautēs* (meekness); see, for example, 1 Cor 4:21; 2 Cor 10:1; Gal 5:23. The difference in meaning is negligible.[467] More significant is the same emphasis on the gentleness of his delegate as in 2 Tim 2:24–25.

12. *Engage the noble athletic contest*: For the use of *agon* and *agōnizesthai* (athletic contest/athletic struggle) for moral and spiritual effort, see Aristotle, *Nicomachean Ethics* 1104A; 3.9.3–4; Epictetus, *Discourse* 3.15.1–5; 22.51; 4.4.30; Seneca, *Epistle* 78:16; LXX Dan 6:14; 1 Macc 7:21; 2 Macc 8:16; Sir 4:28; 4 Macc 17:14; Philo, *Allegorical Laws* 2:108; *On Abraham*, 35, 48. For Paul's usage elsewhere, see 1 Cor 9:25; Col 4:12; Phil 1:30; 1 Thess 2:2. This verse challenges the translator because of the double occurrence of cognate constructions, especially since the substantive in each case is modified by the adjective *kalos*, which, when translated as "noble," rings falsely in contemporary ears. Yet the elevated tone of the Greek in this passage demands a more than casual level of diction in English.

Take hold of the eternal life: The verb *epilambanesthai* (used here in the aorist imperative) is found in Paul only here and in 6:19, both cases with reference to "eternal" life and "real" life. It refers to "taking hold" literally of things like horses (Herodotus, *Persian War* 6:114; Xenophon, *Anabasis* 4.7.12) or legal claims (Plato, *Laws* 954C); in the LXX, it can refer to "taking hold" of instruction (Prov 4:13) or wisdom (Sir 4:11). As observed in the NOTE on 1:16, the phrase "eternal life" is characteristically Pauline (Rom 2:7; 5:21; 6:22, 23; Gal 6:8).

called to it: Some few MSS try to relieve the difficult construction in 6:12 by adding *kai* (and) before "you were called" to create "you were both called and professed the noble profession." I have chosen not to relieve the severely asyn-

---

467. See the discussion of the text in Elliott, *Greek Text*, 99–100.

detic construction and retain some of its awkwardness. Compare the RSV: "to which you were called when you made the good confession." The passive indicates that the "calling" (*kalein*) is by God (compare Rom 4:17; 8:30; 9:24; 1 Cor 1:9; 7:15; 15:9; Gal 1:15; Eph 4:4; 1 Thess 2:12; 4:7; 5:24). In 2 Tim 1:9, Paul says that God "called us with a holy call."

you pronounced the noble profession: The use of "call" (*kalein*) and "profession" (*homologein/homologia*) for moral and spiritual commitments is common in Paul (e.g., 1 Cor 1:9; 7:18; Col 3:15; Rom 10:9; 2 Cor 9:13). The cognate phrase "profess profession" (*homologein homologian*) presents the same stylistic problems to the translator as does the other example, *agōnizesthai/agōn*, earlier in the verse.

before many witnesses: The public character of Timothy's profession corresponds to the quasi-public character of the *mandata principis* letter. Does Paul refer to Timothy's assumption of responsibility before the *presyterion* (4:14), or does he mean Timothy's baptismal confession? Either is possible; the second is the more likely. The phrase *enōpion pollōn martyrōn*, in any case, helps throw some light on the more difficult expression *dia pollōn martyrōn* in 2 Tim 2:2: we can picture in both cases a group of people around Timothy as he makes his profession.

13. *before the God who gives life*: Perhaps a desire to make the text seem more familiar accounts for the replacement of *zōogonountes* (life-generator, found also in Luke 17:33 and Acts 7:19) with the more obviously Pauline expression *zōopoiountos* (maker of life, Rom 4:17; 8:11; 1 Cor 15:22, 36, 45; 2 Cor 3:6; Gal 3:21) in Sinaiticus and the Koine tradition. The reading accepted here is found in Alexandrinus, Bezae, and a number of uncials and minuscules. The translation of 6:13–16 as a whole is challenging, above all, because it consists in Greek of a single extended sentence. As elsewhere, I have decided to construct shorter and more idiomatically English sentences in the translation, seeking thereby to capture some of the rhetorical effect of the long Greek sentence.

Jesus Christ who testified to the noble profession: The verb *martyrein* is straightfoward enough, meaning simply to "testify" or "bear witness." The difficulty in the phrase lies in *tēn homologian kalēn* in the accusative case. How does it relate to the verb? Is it simply to be identified with the act of testifying, as though an adverbial phrase: "he bore witness with a noble profession?" Or, as in my translation, does Paul mean that to which Jesus testified? In either case, I suspect that it is the act of testifying that is important to Paul here, rather than the content of the profession.

before Pontius Pilate: The use of both names for Pilate is particularly striking. Pontius Pilate was the Roman prefect of Palestine under whom Jesus was executed (Tacitus, *Annals* 15:44, 28). Although Paul alludes to "the Lord of glory" being killed by "the rulers of this age" in 1 Cor 2:8, the name of the Roman prefect does not occur in Paul's undisputed letters, and although *Pilatos* appears frequently in the Gospel passion accounts, the combination *Pontios Pilatos* occurs outside this passage only in Matt 27:2 (variant reading); Luke 3:1; Acts 4:27. The character of the· Roman prefect is developed in the *Acts of Pilate* and other apocryphal elaborations of the Passion account.[468] As with the citation of a saying of Jesus in 5:18 and the allusion to "the healthy words of our Lord Jesus Christ" in 6:3, the reference indicates an interest in the human Jesus roughly proportional to that found in Paul's undisputed letters. Note that the Synoptic Gospels do not have Jesus speaking before Pilate. This letter has awareness of either the Gospel of John 18:36–38 or, as is more likely, the tradition that found inclusion in that Gospel. The inclusion of the name helps give specificity to the exemplary function of the statement.[469] The explicit mention of Pilate also reminds us that the author was fully aware of the grimmer possibilities of dealing with the Roman Empire than are suggested by the positive commands in 2:1–7.

14. *the commandment spotless and blameless*: By this point, we recognize the *entolē* as the entire commission that Timothy has received from Paul, and whose *telos*, as we saw in 1:5, is *agapē* sprung from internal dispositions of faith and a good conscience. In 1:5, he spoke of a "pure heart" (*kardia kathara*) and a "unhypocritical conscience." Here he speaks even more succinctly of keeping the *entolē* itself "spotless" (*aspilos*, compare James 1:27; 1 Pet 1:19) and "blameless" (*anepilēmptos*, 3:2; 5:7).

until the appearance: Here the term *epiphaneia* clearly refers to the manifestation of "Our Lord Jesus Christ" at the end-time, as in 2 Thess 2:8; 2 Tim 4:1, 8; Tit 2:13. It is striking how often this unusually full title appears in eschatological contexts, as in 1 Thess 5:9, 23, 28; 2 Thess 2:1, 14; 3:18.

15. *will reveal at the proper season*: For the difficulties attendant on the phrase *kairois idiois*, see the NOTE on 2:6. I have supplied "God" as the subject, since he is implied as such by both the phrase *enōpion theou* in 6:13 and the doxology identifying him as *despotēs* in the verses that follow. Translating in shorter sentences demands some adaptation. This is the only use by Paul of *deiknymi* apart from 1 Cor 12:31; it is used here in its straightforward sense of "show forth" (Homer, *Iliad*, 3:452; Epitetus, *Discourse*, 3.24.75; Zech 3:1; Rev 1:1; 4:1).

He is the blessed and only ruler: In Nestle–Aland, 6:15b–16 is indented, indicating the editors' judgment that the author is quoting traditional hymnic material. It is possible: the clauses are well balanced, and there are elements of rhyme, such as occur frequently in hymns as well as in other forms of prayer. One must be careful, however, in making such judgments, for Paul is perfectly capable of constructing rhetorically balanced sentences of this sort. This is the only time in the NT that *dynastēs* (ruler/sovereign) is used as a title for God. Ordinarily it is applied to human rulers (Herodotus, *Persian War* 2:32; LXX Gen 49:24; Prov 1:21; Luke 1:52; Acts 8:27), although it is used of God by Sophocles, *Antigone* 608; 2 Macc 12:15; 15:3–5, 23, 29; 3 Macc 2:3; *Sibylline Oracles* 3:719. For *makarios* (blessed/happy) as an epithet for God, see the NOTE on 1:11; and for "only" (*monos*), compare 1 Tim 2:5.

King of kings, Lord of lords: This phrase is translated literally as "King of those exercising kingly rule" and "Lord of those exercising lordship." The title *basileus*

---

468. J. K. Elliott, *The Apocryphal New Testament* (Oxford: Clarendon Press, 1993), 164–225.
469. G. Baldersperger, "Il a rendue témoignage devant Ponce Pilate," *RHPR* 2 (1922): 1–25.

basileōn is found in Rev 17:14. It is striking that the designation appears in two compositions addressed to Asia Minor, where the cult of the Roman emperor was active early on. For the use in Judaism of such titles for God that serve to diminish the claims of earthly kings, see 2 Macc 13:4; 3 Macc 5:35; Dan 2:37; 2 Ezra 7:12; Philo, *Special Laws* 1:18; *On the Cherubim* 99. Precisely this sort of confession, and the political/social posture it revealed, made the necessity of "praying for kings and those in authority" politically necessary (2:1–3).

16. *He alone possesses immortality*: The quality of *athanasia* (literally, "death-lessness") is particularly associated with the divine life (*Sentences of Pseudo-Phocylides* 115; Philo, *On the Eternity of the World* 44; *Sibylline Oracles* 3:276). Paul thinks of the resurrection as a partaking in *athanasia* (1 Cor 15:53–54). Compare the attributes of God in 1 Tim 1:17.

dwells in unapproachable light: Some witnesses from the Western textual tradition (e.g., the original hand of Bezae) add a *kai* (and) before "dwells in unapproachable light." The support is too little to make it likely that this was the original reading. The image of God "dwelling in light" is remarkable; for *phōs* associated with God, see LXX Exod 27:20; 39:17; Num 4:16; Pss 4:6; 35:9; 42:3; 55:13; 88:15; Wis 7:26; 2 Cor 4:6; Eph 5:8; Col 1:12. The adjective *aprositos* makes clear the infinite distance between God and humans (Philo, *Life of Moses* 2:70; Josephus, *Jewish War* 7:280; *Antiquities* 3:76).

No human being has ever seen Him . . . can ever see Him: What the previous line implied this one makes explicit. The statement echoes LXX Exod 33:20, where God says, "You cannot see my face. For no human can see my face and live." The closest statement in the NT to this one is the ending of John's prologue: "No one has ever seen God at any time" (John 1:18).

17. *the rich in this world*: There is a deliberate wordplay at work in verses 16–17 using variations on "rich" (*plousiois, ploutou, plousios, ploutein*): the rich are not to rely on riches but on God, who gives richly, and they are to be rich in good deeds! The expression *en tǭ nyn aiōni* (literally, "in the now age") is distinctive to the Pastorals among Paul's letters (2 Tim 4:10; Tit 2:12); Paul ordinarily uses *tǭ aioni toutǭ* (in this age, Rom 12:2; 1 Cor 1:20; 2:6; 2 Cor 4:4; Eph 1:21). The phrasing here reminds slightly of the implied contrast in James 2:5.

not to be arrogant: Some MSS (e.g., Sinaiticus, I, 048) replace *hypsēlo-phronein*, meaning literally "to think high thoughts" (Plato, *Republic* 550B), which is found only here in the NT, with the combination *hypsēla phronein*, which is found twice in Romans (11:20; 12:16). The tendency of scribes to conform texts to more commonly known passages probably accounts for the variant. That arrogance accompanies wealth is such a truism that only its dreary manifestation day after day keeps it credible.

hope upon the uncertainty of wealth: This phrase can also be rendered as "upon uncertain [*adēlotēti*, Polybius, *Histories* 5.2.3] wealth." That human wealth is by nature transitory and unreliable is the constant witness of the biblical tradition (e.g., Luke 12:13–31; James 1:9–12; 4:13–17; 5:1–6).[470] Note that

---

470. Johnson, *Sharing Possessions*.

Paul once more speaks of placing one's *hope* in something other than God (compare 4:10; 5:5).

God who supplies us with all things richly: A substantial number of MSS (Codex Bezae and many Latin MSS, as well as the Koine tradition) supply the participle *zōnti* after the phrase *epi tō theō*, in order to create the phrase "upon the living God." The shorter reading is to be preferred here because of the natural tendency of scribes to conform this passage to the phrase "living God" in 3:15 and 4:10 as well as in Rom 9:26; 2 Cor 6:16; 1 Thess 1:9.[471] The verb *parechein*, which in 1:4 was used in its sense of "give rise to," here means to "grant/give" something to someone (Josephus, *Antiquities* 2:329; 11:2; Acts 17:31; 22:2). Three aspects of God's gift giving here (which reminds us of James 1:5, 17) deserve attention. The first is that God gives *panta* (all things), a statement of God's universal beneficence that stands with 4:4. The second is that God gives all things *hēmin* (to us), a statement of God's providential care for humans. The third is that God gives all things to us "richly" (*plousios*), a statement that God's beneficence will not run out and, unlike "uncertain riches of the now age," can be relied on.

for our enjoyment: The phrase *eis apolausin* expresses purpose, "for the very sake of giving them pleasure," which is the fourth and most remarkable statement made here about God's gifting humans with possessions: that they are for pleasure and enjoyment (Aristotle, *Nicomachean Ethics* 1148A; *Politics* 1314B; 3 Macc 7:16; Philo, *Life of Moses* 2:70). This is a dramatic turn to Paul's development of the *oikonomia theou*, that all of creation is for enjoyment. But since Paul does not specify *whose* enjoyment or pleasure, perhaps we can even entertain the idea that it is for God's own pleasure that God gives to the world so generously (compare Prov 8:30–31).

18. *do good work*: My translation provides a repetition of *parangelle* (tell them to . . .) that the Greek does not have, but is understood in the convoluted accusative + infinitive construction of the sentence: *plousious . . . agathoergein*. The "doing of good works" echoes previous similar statements (2:10; 5:10, 25) and probably provides the initial way of expressing the sharing of possessions by the wealthy.

wealthy in noble deeds: The verb *ploutein* (to be wealthy) has something of a transitive quality here: they are to exercise their wealth in the doing of *erga kala* (noble deeds, compare 2:10; 5:10). Among these would undoubtedly be the support of the needy among their relatives (5:4, 16), as well as support of the community welfare system.

generous in giving, . . . sharers of possessions: These two terms point to the attitudes that should accompany the sharing of possessions. The verb *metadidomi* means to "share something" (Luke 3:11; Rom 1:11; 12:8; Eph 4:28; 1 Thess 2:8). To do so "well" or "generously" is to be *eumetadotos* (Marcus Aurelius, *Meditations* 1.14.4). Similarly, the verb *koinōnein* means to "share possessions," and the adjective *koinōnikos* means to "be generous in such sharing,"

---

471. Metzger, *Textual Commentary*, 644.

a willing participant in sharing (Aristotle, *Rhetoric* 1401A; Lucian, *Timon* 56). Paul suggests that they enter as wholeheartedly into giving as God does in gifting.

19. *storing up for themselves*: The verb *apothēsaurizō* is a NT *hapax*, but the verb *thēsaurizein* is a familiar one (Rom 2:5; 1 Cor 16:2; 2 Cor 12:14; James 5:3) and points us toward the language in the Gospels about storing up treasures on earth and in heaven (Matt 6:19–20; 19:21; Luke 12:21, 33–34), which language, in turn, has a rich ancestry in Judaism (Prov 8:21; 13:22; Sir 29:11; *m. Peah* 1:1; *b. Shab.* 156b; *b. Rosh Hash.* 16b; *b. Gittin* 7a–b).

a noble foundation for the future: the idea of "storing up [*apothēsaurizein*] a foundation [*themelios*]" is somewhat odd and may be accounted for in part by the assonance afforded by the phrase: *themelion kalon eis to mellon*. Although the metaphor seems forced at best, *themelios* here stands for something firm on which something else can be built, as elsewhere in Paul (Rom 15:20; 1 Cor 3:10–12; Eph 2:20; 2 Tim 2:19). For the figurative use of *themelios* as that which is laid so that something else can be accomplished, see Dionysius of Halicarnassus, *Roman Antiquities* 3:69, and Josephus, *Antiquities* 11:93; 15:391.

lay hold of real life: This is a purpose clause: the reason they have laid a foundation is so that they can "lay hold" (*epilambanein*) of true life. For the nuances of *epilambanein*, see the NOTE on 6:12. The phrase *tēs ontōs zōēs* (real life) is exactly equivalent to *tas ontōs charas* (real widows) in 5:3. Since Paul has repeatedly made the point that God is the "living God," then "real life" and "eternal life" (6:12) must in fact be a share in God's own life. Some MSS (among them the third hand of Bezae, K, L, and P) have "eternal life" here, and others combine the versions into "true eternal life" (69, 296).[472]

20. *Protect the tradition*: The verb *phylassein* bears the sense of both "observe/keep" the tradition and "protect/guard" the tradition. Both are possible here, and both fit within the dual emphasis of the *mandata principis* letter. The *parathēkē* is that which has been entrusted (*paratithēmi*) to someone, such as a deposit (Herodotus, *Persian War* 6:86; 9:45; *Sentences of Pseudo-Phocylides* 135). The language of "deposit" is particularly intriguing in a section in which treasures, possessions, and laying claims have figured so prominently. What does Paul mean by *parathēkē* here? Surely the same thing he has meant throughout the letter by *entolē*, by *pistis*, and by *eusebeia*: the way of life found in the "healthy teaching" that accords with the good news.[473]

chattering and contradictions: The term *antithesis*, here translated as "contradiction," simply means "opposition" (Plato, *Sophist* 257E) and is used in logic for the opposition of propositions (Aristotle, *Topics* 113B) and in rhetoric for the presentation of the thesis by opposition (Aristotle, *Rhetoric* 1410A). Here it is combined with *kenophōnia* (literally, "empty sound") and *bebēlos* (profane, 1:9; 4:7); both terms are, as in 2 Tim 2:16, being used as generalized slander.

---

472. Metzger, *Textual Commentary*, 644.
473. See the rich display of learning in C. Spicq, "Saint Paul et la loi des dépôts," *RB* 40 (1931): 481–502.

so-called knowledge: The term "so-called" or "falsely named" (*pseudōnymos*) has a variety of uses, but no particular technical application (e.g., Plutarch, *On Brotherly Love* 4 [*Mor.* 479E]; Philo, *Life of Moses* 2:171). The noun *gnōsis*, likewise, is employed broadly. There is no need to take it as referring to a second-century Christian elitist movement; for Paul's uses elsewhere, see Rom 2:20; 11:33; 15:14; 1 Cor 1:5; 8:1; 7, 10, 11; 12:8; 13:2; 14:6; 2 Cor 2:14; 4:6; 6:6; 8:7; 10:5; 11:6; Eph 3:19; Phil 3:8; Col 2:3. From the beginning of the letter, the author has scorned the pretensions of those who want to be teachers of Law "without understanding what it is they are talking about" (1:7), in contrast to those who "have come to the recognition of the truth" (2:4; 4:3). The same contrast occurs here. Paul claims for his readers a true *gnōsis* in contrast to the "so-called *gnōsis*" of the pretenders.

21. *Some have professed it*: The verb *epangellomai* is the same one as that used for "women dedicated to the service of God" in 2:10 (Xenophon, *Memorabilia* 1.2.7; Philo, *On the Virtues* 54). Paul is typically circumspect about these "certain ones" (*tines*), giving no further information about them—and possibly not having any to give.

missed the mark concerning the faith: This last verse recapitulates 1:6, where Paul uses the same verb (*astochein*) for their error. But in this case, the phrase *peri tēn pistin* brings home the point of the letter: they have thought to add on to their profession by claims to knowledge and the imposition of legalism and asceticism; by so doing, Paul says, they have missed entirely the nature of this life, which is the response of the human person to the living God in *pistis*—faith, trust, obedience, commitment, love.

Grace be with you: The MSS (mainly of the Western tradition) that have the singular "with you" (*meta sou*) at the end of the prayer, rather than the plural *meta hymin*, probably reflect the concern of scribes with the literary self-presentation of the letter as one written to the individual Timothy (compare 2 Tim 4:22); the use of the plural here and in Tit 3:15 may, however, better fit the quasi-public character of the *mandata principis* letter.[474] Similarly, the MSS that add *amen* at the end of the prayer seek to conform the text to other Pauline letters (e.g., Rom 16:27; Gal 6:18).

COMMENT

1 Timothy concludes with what appears at first sight to be a series of disconnected remarks.[475] Closer examination, however, shows the passage to be a well-constructed exhortation, with the admonitions concerning the wealthy connected to those concerning Paul's delegate, with both rooted in the reality of God. We note first the elements of paraenesis. Paul makes the familiar transi-

---

474. Metzger, *Textual Commentary*, 644.
475. A view not unexpectedly found in Dibelius and Conzelmann, *Pastoral Epistles*, 87–92.

tion from the condemnation of false teachers to the positive instruction of his delegate: "but you" (*su de*, 6:11; compare 2 Tim 2:1; 3:10, 14; 4:5). Timothy is also portrayed as the example of the attitudes Paul desires to inculcate among the wealthy: his pursuit of virtue has as its goal that he "take hold of the eternal life" (6:12), just as the good works of the wealthy will enable them to "lay hold of real life" (6:19). Timothy finds his own model in the behavior of Jesus (compare 2 Tim 2:8): Timothy's pronouncing "the noble profession before many witnesses" (6:12) has as its exemplar Jesus' own witnessing to the noble profession before Pontius Pilate (6:13). Finally, we can note that the final exhortation to Timothy in 6:20–21 forms an *inclusio* with 1:3–7 and emphasizes the urgency of dealing with the threat posed by false teachers in Ephesus. The end of 1 Timothy has a structure not unlike its beginning. In 1:12–17, Paul presented his experience as part of his argument concerning faith and law. Here his delegate's teaching and example are part of Paul's argument concerning wealth and eternal life.

Hope in the Living God

In the analysis of the previous section (6:2b–10), we saw that pervasive and even ostentatious wealth among the members of the Ephesian *ekklēsia* underlies a number of the problems faced by Paul's delegate. In 6:17, Paul now turns not to those who "want to be rich" (6:9), but to those whom he explicitly designates as "rich in this world" (or age [*aiōn*]). His advice is brief, but completes the teaching on *autarkeia* that he initiated in 6:5, and touches on many of the themes common to the early Christian understanding of material possessions.

Paul first cautions the wealthy against arrogance. He does not use the term *hyperēphania*, which appears so commonly in discussions of envy and avarice,[476] but tells them "not to think high things" (*hypsēlaphronein*). We find the equivalent expression used twice by Paul in Romans. In the first instance, he warns Gentile believers not to "be arrogant" but to fear (Rom 11:20). In the second, he likewise warns members of the Roman community not to "be arrogant," but to be lowly minded (Rom 12:16). The possession of many material things leads easily to the assumption of greatness in other respects as well. And because great wealth not only wields power, but also gathers flattery to itself, arrogance is a constant temptation.

Most of all, wealth can lead to a false sense of security, expressed so vividly by the rich fool in Jesus' parable: "Soul, you have ample goods laid up for many years; take your ease, eat, drink, be merry" (Luke 12:19). But as the rich man is told in the parable, "You fool, this night your soul is required of you; and the things you have prepared, whose will they be?" (Luke 12:20), so here Paul warns the rich "not to put their hope upon the uncertainty of wealth, but rather upon God" (6:17). We are reminded of the poor widows who have been left all alone and

---

476. Johnson, *Letter of James*, 282–283.

have "put their hope in God" (5:5). Paul here repeats the constant contrast drawn by the entire biblical tradition—above all, by the Prophets—between the illusory promise offered by the idols of pleasure and possessions and power, and the promise of real life (*ontōs zoē*) offered by the one who alone can give it, the living God.

The distinction between the false offer of life from possessions and the offer of true life from God is supported by Paul's hymnic encomium of God in 6:15–16. The hymn is notable for its emphasis on the transcendence, uniqueness, and power of God. Transcendent: God dwells in unapproachable light; God is immortal; God is unable to be seen by any human. Uniqueness: God is "alone" (*monos*) in might (*dynastēs*), in immortality (*athanasia*). Power: God's might is greater than that of all others, since he is "King of kings, and the Lord of lords" (6:15). Appearing as it does in connection with human pretensions to greatness on the basis of possessions, and also in close proximity to the statement concerning Jesus' noble profession before Pontius Pilate, Paul's encomium naturally provides a subtle contrast between the sovereignty of God to which humans rightly submit and the claims of human rulers to ultimacy to which humans cannot ever assent.

It is appropriate, therefore, to ascribe honor and eternal power only to God (16:16), not to anything less than God. And because God "alone has immortality"—that is, life eternal—only God can give to humans "true life" (16:19). And this is what is most striking about Paul's description: God is virtually defined as the one "who gives life to all things" (6:13). God does not remain in lonely solitude removed from the realm of creation. God has acted in the witnessing of Jesus Christ before Pontius Pilate (6:13), and God will act again in showing forth the appearance of the Lord Jesus in the future (6:14). Paul emphasizes the otherness of God precisely in order to praise the astonishing reality that God has chosen to cross over the boundary and enter into relationship with humans.

The consequence of this conviction is that the way in which humans dispose of their possessions is itself intimately connected to their self-disposition before God.[477] Paul had in the previous section stressed the potential for possessions to deceive and entrap humans. Now he turns to their positive potential. Paul wants the rich to hope not in the uncertainty of riches, but in God, "who supplies us with all things richly for our enjoyment" (6:17). Two things should be noted in this remarkable statement. The first is the understanding of God as richly beneficent in every respect (*ta panta*) "to us." This affirmation of God's generosity and unstinting giving of gifts resembles the characterization of God in James 1:5 as the one who "gives to all generously and without grudging." Part of the proper perception of material possessions, therefore, is that they are all gifts from God. They have no power separate from God and can offer no life or security on their own. Like us, they are simply creatures. If we pursue them as the source of life, we destroy them and ourselves. But if we see them as gifts from God, then they become the occasion for thanksgiving.

This brings us to the second part of the statement: God has given us all things

---

477. P. Dschulnigg, "Warnung am Richtung und Ermahnung der Reichen. 1 Tim. 6:6–10, 17–19 im Rahmen des Schussteils 6:3–21," *BZ* 37 (1993): 60–77.

richly, "for our enjoyment" (*apolausis*). Paul here recognizes the inherent good-ness in all things that God gives through creation. We are reminded of the strong view of creation that runs through this letter, found, above all, in the declara-tion that God created things "to be received with thanksgiving" and that noth-ing created by God as good was to be rejected, but was to be received with thanksgiving (4:3–4). Although Paul will immediately turn to the fruitful use to which possessions can be put—thus shading *apolausis* in the direction of "fruit" or "benefit"—it is well to pause and appreciate one of the few places in the New Testament that approves of simple pleasure taken in things.

One aspect of *autarkeia* was the freedom it gave from the enticement and en-trapment of material possessions. But within Paul's theological understanding of creation, freedom is seen as the capacity to give away possessions to others with no diminishment to the self. Paul could scarcely be more emphatic in his desire that the rich use their possessions in just this way. He uses four separate and roughly equivalent terms in 6:18 to express the same point: they are to "do good work" (*agathoergein*), "be wealthy in noble deeds" (*ploutein en ergois kalois*), "be generous in giving" (*eumetadotous*), and "be sharers of possessions" (*koinōnikous*). This emphasis takes on particular force coming at the end of a letter which has dealt with the problems of misused wealth. The riches that God has given humans are not for their ostentatious display (2:9–10) or their selfish hoarding (5:4, 8), but are to be used for the common good.[478]

When Paul states the motivation for such sharing of possessions, we glimpse again his sense of possessions as expressing the human relationship with God. Sharing wealth will be "storing up for themselves" (6:19). The statement makes sense only within a transcendental, relational framework: God honors those who give away their possessions to others with still greater wealth in God's own pres-ence. The notion is one that is found frequently in Jewish and early Christian literature: possessions shared in this life lead to spiritual riches in the life to come. [479] Thus the mixed metaphor of "storing up treasure" and "laying a foun-dation." Doing good deeds now is the basis for the future reward. The reward, however, is not material, but a share in God's own life, "so that they can lay hold of real life [*ontōs zōē*]" (6:19).

Bearing Witness to the Truth

By having his final exhortations to his delegate bracket these instructions on the use of possessions, Paul has them apply also to Timothy. Thus the passage be-gins with the command that Timothy "flee these things" (6:11), the desires for

---

478. C. Spicq, "La Philanthropie hellénistique, vertu divine et royale," *ST* 12 (1958): 169–191; Pearson, "Philanthropy in the Greco-Roman World and in Early Christianity"; Kidd, *Wealth and Beneficence in the Pastoral Epistles*, 151–191.

479. It is, in particular, a Lukan theme, another point on which the outlook of Paul and the third evangelist meet. See L. T. Johnson, *The Gospel of Luke* Sacra Pagina 3 (Collegeville, Minn.: Liturgical Press, 1991), 243–249.

wealth that have led many to their destruction. Instead, he is to "pursue" those qualities associated with the "commandment" (1:4) delivered by Paul: righteousness, godliness, faith, love, endurance, and—especially needful in the circumstances Timothy faces—a generous temper (6:11). Thus living out the profession to which he was called and to which he committed himself, Timothy will "engage the noble athletic contest for the faith" (6:12), with the result not that he will gain a material crown, but that he will "take hold of the eternal life" (6:12).

Once more, Paul evokes the story of Jesus as guidance for his delegate, once more showing how his theology is not centered in creation alone, but includes the new creation through Jesus' death and resurrection. This time, he refers to the Passion narrative. The use of Jesus' suffering and death as exemplary for the Christian life is scarcely novel in Paul. We need recall only his use of Ps 69 in Rom 15:1–3, and his use of the Christ-hymn in Phil 2:1–11. The naming of Pontius Pilate is novel and somewhat startling, but the point of the reference is not: Timothy is to follow the example of Jesus, who before him "testified to the noble profession before Pontius Pilate" (6:13). Paul has no need here to spell out that Jesus' fidelity to God was answered by God's raising him from the dead as life-giving Spirit (Rom 1:4; 1 Cor 15:45); that conviction is surely embedded in his characterization of God as "the one who gives life to all things" (6:13), as the one who "will reveal the appearance of our Lord Jesus at the proper time" (6:14–15), and as the one who "alone possesses immortality" (6:16). Because this truly is "the living God" (3:15; 4:10), in other words, fidelity toward God and hope in God will find its reward in "true life," for the delegate and for the people he seeks to save (4:16).

Paul concludes the letter with a final appeal to Timothy to "keep" or "protect" the *parathēkē*. If our reading of 1 Timothy has been correct, Paul understands this "tradition" not as a set of prescriptions concerning the ordering of the community or as a body of beliefs, but as a certain way of life that is based in the *oikonomia theou*, the way that God has created and saved the world through gift, a way of life that is perceived and practiced not by rancorous debates or so-called knowledge, but by that response to God's gift that is faith. This was the goal of the commandment from the beginning (1:5). It is the point of the letter.

SECOND TIMOTHY:
AN INTRODUCTION

◆

INTRODUCTION

◆

Second Timothy presents itself to the reader as a letter written by Paul the Apostle to his delegate Timothy (2 Tim 1:1–2). Paul is in captivity (1:16; 2:9; 4:16). Although the place of his imprisonment is not stated explicitly, the fact that when Onesiphorus was "in Rome" he could visit Paul "in chains" makes Rome the obvious place from which Paul wrote. A Roman captivity lasting for at least two years is confirmed by Acts 28:16–31. The conditions of that captivity as described by Acts also fit the implied setting for this letter: Paul is under guard, but he is able to receive visitors and to engage in some fashion in the work of ministry (Acts 28:30–31). So in 2 Timothy we find Paul receiving guests (1:16; 4:21), engaging in study and correspondence (4:13), and arranging the movements of the delegates still associated with him (4:12). Paul has had an opportunity to present his defense a first time (4:16), but has not been released.

The letter does not specify where Timothy is at the time of writing. In view of Paul's concern that Timothy come to him "quickly" (2 Tim 4:9) and "before winter" (4:21), the location of the delegate may not be far distant from the writer, especially since Paul can request that Timothy bring with him the cloak that Paul had left with Carpus (4:13). Concern for warm clothing could indicate a period in the early fall—travel by water in the Mediterranean waters was dangerous between October and May.

In many respects, the setting of 2 Timothy is the same as that of Philippians, which happens to be co-sponsored by Timothy (Phil 1:1). There also, Paul is a prisoner, most likely in Rome (1:12–14; 4:22). There also, he sends delegates to the church, including Epaphroditus (2:28) and Timothy himself (2:19). There also, he is able to receive visitors bringing financial assistance (4:18), write letters, and direct community affairs (4:2–3). I will show that there is also a similarity in the mode of argumentation between 2 Tim 1:8–2:13 and Phil 2:1–3:17.

The main difference between the letters is one of tone and perspective. In Philippians, Paul retains optimism concerning the mission, despite his own captivity and despite some rivalry among his associates (Phil 1:12–18; 4:2–3). He is peremptory in his dismissal of rival teachers (if there actually are any in view; 1:28; 3:2–3, 18–19). He is certain that he will again be among his churches (1:19–26) and seeks news from them eagerly (2:19–24).

In 2 Timothy, the mood is much grimmer. Paul does not express any hope of this-life deliverance, but sees his death as imminent (4:6). His mission is under serious assault, both from opponents like Alexander the coppersmith (4:14) and from rival teachers like Hymenaios and Philetos (2:17–18), who are enjoying considerable success (3:1–5; 13; 4:3–4). At this critical juncture, furthermore, Paul feels himself abandoned by some of his key allies. He names among "all those in Asia" who abandoned him, Phygelos and Hermogenes (1:15); Demas likewise "fell in love with the world" and headed for Thessalonica, leaving Paul "in the lurch" (4:10). Paul complains that at his first defense, "no one took my part; all deserted me" (4:16). But the fact that Onesiphorus came to visit him in Rome (1:16) and that Paul continues to be supported by Luke (4:11), Eubulus, Pudens, Linus, Claudia, and "all the brethren" (4:21) suggests that Paul's abandonment is as much emotional as physical.

Finally, the letter clearly communicates a sense of urgency about his close associate Timothy's commitment to the cause. He is writing to "stir up to new fire" that commitment, speaking ominously of a "spirit of cowardice" that is incompatible with the spirit that empowers them (1:6–7). He suggests that Timothy may be fearful out of shame at Paul and the message he proclaims (1:8). He begs Timothy to "take a share of the suffering" for the good news (1:8). He solemnly enjoins him to "complete [his] ministry" (4:5). And he twice urges him to visit him at the first opportunity (4:9, 21).

Paul writes to Timothy, then, in order to encourage his delegate in his struggles and persuade him to stay the course. In so doing, the apostle also fights for the success of his own ministry and demonstrates that "the word of God is not chained" (2:9). The letter is distinctive for its unswerving attention to Timothy, his character and his qualities as a teacher. Only one verse (2:2) suggests that Timothy hand over to others who are equally faithful and able to teach. Otherwise, everything in the letter, including the attacks on opponents, bears on Timothy himself. It is critical to recognize that 2 Timothy has no element of church order and no discussion of any sort bearing on social roles either in the church or in the household. Only the final word of the letter (the plural personal pronoun in the phrase "grace be with you") breaks the consistent attention given to Timothy as an individual—and its textual status is questionable. The letter, then, is personal not only in its tone, but also in its focus.

LITERARY GENRE

2 Timothy inarguably has the form of a letter, and one that conforms rather well to the standard Pauline elements: greeting (1:1–2), thanksgiving (1:3–5), body (1:6–4:8), personal remarks and greetings (4:9–21), and final prayer (4:22). Scholars have nevertheless asked whether it is a real letter or another sort of literary genre that has simply been fitted to the standard letter form. The question is not in the least an inappropriate one, for the letter form was sufficiently elastic in the Hellenistic period to allow any number of genres to be fitted within it. One can think, for example, of the *Letter of Aristeas* or, for that matter, the Letter to the Hebrews in the NT, compositions that are, respectively an apologetic treatise and a homily, but pass as "letters."

Given such precedents, scholars have asked whether some of the elements in 2 Timothy might suggest a similar situation. The image of an aging—indeed, dying—religious leader who before his death instructs his follower on the struggles that lie ahead and warns of the necessity for perseverance in the face of opposition reminds many scholars of the literary genre known as the testament or farewell discourse.[480]

Although the rudiments of a testamentary form can be found in Greco-Roman literature (e.g., Farewell Letter of Epicurus), the full expression of the genre is found primarily in Second Temple Jewish literature.[481] Building on the biblical prototype provided by Gen 49 (the dying Jacob summons his sons and predicts their diverse futures), such compositions as *Testaments of the Twelve Patriarchs*, *Testament of Job*, and *Testament of Abraham* elaborated the elements: the death of the religious figure/patriarch, an autobiographical narrative revealing the character of the patriarch, predictions of future events (usually negative), and moral exhortations to avoid evil and do good—that is, keep God's commandments.

That a NT composition can accommodate such a genre within itself is demonstrated conclusively by Luke's presentation of Paul's farewell speech to the Ephesian elders at Miletus (Acts 20:17–35), which is a classic example of the type:[482] Paul faces his imminent death, relates elements of his life that have an exemplary value, warns of future troubles, and exhorts followers to follow in his path.[483] The presence of this farewell discourse within the narrative of Acts, it should be noted, is taken as one of the surest signs that Acts was composed after the death of Paul. Understandably, then, those who hold that 2 Timothy is a testament are also confident that it was written after Paul's death and is, therefore, necessarily a pseudonymous composition. This does not mean that the elements associated with the testament are not discernible in the letter. They are. Paul, as I have noted, faces death. He addresses his follower, Timothy. He warns of hard times to come that will involve apostasy from the truth. He encourages Timothy to persevere in Paul's way. The question is whether these elements add up in the way some scholars conclude they do.

The decision to regard 2 Timothy as a farewell discourse can be questioned on the basis of two considerations. The first is that some elements in 2 Timothy do not fit the genre as well as might be expected:

1. Paul's death, after all, is not made explicit, although it is surely intimated. But there is no sense that he is himself ceasing in his efforts for the mission.

---

480. Most extensively, S. C. Martin, *Pauli Testamentum: 2 Timothy and the Last Words of Moses* (Rome: Editrice Pontificie Universita Gregoriana, 1997). See also Wolter, *Die Pastoralbriefe als Paulustradition*, 222–241, and Redalié, *Paul après Paul*, 101–107.

481. J. Munck, "Discours d'adieu dans le Nouveau Testament et dans la littérature biblique," in *Aux sources des traditions chrétiennes* (Paris: Neuchatel, 1950), 155–170; A. B. Kolenkow, "The Genre Testament and Forecasts of the Future in the Hellenistic Jewish Milieu," *JSJ* 6 (1975): 57–71; W. Kurz, *Farewell Addresses in the New Testament* (Collegeville, Minn.: Liturgical Press, 1990).

482. W. Kurz has also shown the elements of the Farewell Discourse in Luke's version of the Last Supper, in "Luke 22:14–38 and Greco-Roman and Biblical Farewell Addresses," *JBL* 104 (1985): 251–268.

483. F. Prast, *Presbyter und Evangelium in nachapostolisher Zeit: Die Abschiedsrede Paulus in Milet (Apg 20, 17–38) im Rahmen der lukanischen Konzeption der Evangeliumsverkuendigung*, FzB 29 (Stuttgart: Katholisches Bibelwerk, 1979); Johnson, *Acts of the Apostles*, 359–368.

2. Nor is his commission to Timothy really a generational transition. Timothy may be younger than Paul, and may, in the language of fictive kinship be called "beloved child" by him, but he is, after all, his colleague and coworker. He is not of the next generation (even fictively), but of Paul's own generation.

3. The attention given to the opponents in this letter is far more explicit than in most testamentary literature, which specializes in vague characterizations. The degree of specific detail in 2 Timothy is impressive even when its use of stereotpyical polemic is taken into account.

4. The predictions of future woes are in reality statements about present circumstances, as can be seen in 3:1–6.

The second and even more substantial reason for doubting that 2 Timothy is a farewell discourse is that another literary genre fits its literary self-presentation better: the personal paraenetic letter. This is a letter type that was available to Paul during his lifetime and does not require that 2 Timothy be a pseudonymous composition. In the rhetorical handbooks of Pseudo-Demetrius and Pseudo-Libanius, we find the type called *epistolē parainetikē* (paraenetic letter). Pseudo-Libanius says that such a letter is written "to exhort someone, advising him to pursue something and to abstain from something."[484] We see, then, that the paraenetic letter is advice in the form of exhortation that encourages certain actions and discourages others. Pseudo-Libanius provides a sample letter that makes clear how such exhortation involved moral behavior in particular: "Always be an emulator, dear friend, of virtuous men. For it is better to be well spoken of when imitating good men, than to be reproached by all for following evil men."[485] This sample letter contains several of the elements of the moral exhortation that is broadly referred to as paraenetic.[486] It includes the imitation of a model, establishes an antithesis between pursuing good and avoiding evil, and makes explicit a concern for good reputation (honor/shame) in the eyes of others.

The best example of paraenesis in antiquity is Pseudo-Isocrates, *To Demonicus*. The uncle of Demonicus writes to him in place of the younger man's father, who had died. There is, then, something like a fictive father–son relationship present in the composition. The discourse takes a form very similar to that of a letter. The author explicitly identifies his missive as a paraenesis (*To Demonicus* 5). He begins by proposing the young man's father as the perfect model for his imitation and recalls that *paradeigma* to Demonicus's memory (9–12). Note here the elements of memory, model, and mimesis.

The author next amplifies the sketch of virtue presented by the father with a long series of moral maxims—often in the antithetical form, "Do this, don't do

---

484. For the text of both authors, see Malherbe, "Ancient Epistolary Theory."
485. Malherbe, "Ancient Epistolary Theory," 71.
486. Malherbe, *Moral Exhortation*, 122–124.

that"—offering advice to the young man on everything from the company he keeps to his piety (13–49). Throughout, there is a constant emphasis on the need for the young man to maintain a good reputation in the opinion of others. It is clear that honor and shame are strong motives for behavior. At the conclusion, the author proposes another series of models that the young Demonicus might imitate or avoid (50–51).

In 2 Timothy, likewise, we find Paul presenting himself to Timothy as fictive father to "beloved" fictive son. In the beginning of the composition, Paul repeatedly reminds Timothy of the models that he can imitate, especially the example set by Paul himself. Paul then explicates the model by means of a series of maxims. And at the end, he presents himself a final time as a model for imitation. 2 Timothy is the closest thing we possess in antiquity to the rhetorical handbook's ideal paraenetic letter and is remarkably close to *To Demonicus* in its way of arranging the elements of memory, model, mimesis, and maxims.

The dimension of 2 Timothy that does not obviously fit within the frame of the personal paraenetic letter is the polemic against false teachers. If the point of the letter is the reinforcement of moral behavior in Paul's delegate, why so much attention to the opponents? Doesn't Paul's attack on false teachers suggest that this letter's interest has a wider scope and perhaps even a wider audience? The results of two lines of research help clarify this difficult and appropriate question. The first is the recognition that much of the language used to characterize the opposition takes the form of conventional slander used in Hellenistic schools between rival teachers of every stripe,[487] including battles between rival Jewish schools.[488] The primary social function of such vituperation was the disparagement of opposing teachers in order to recommend one's own teaching as superior. The satirist Lucian of Samosata provides many unforgettable pictures of just this sort of verbal mudslinging between teachers (e.g., *The Eunuch, Philosophies For Sale*), and the literature of Hellenistic moral discourse is replete with such attacks against the words and behavior of rival sects. This is not, however, the function in 2 Timothy, for Paul does not direct his charges against the opponents themselves; instead, he alternates characterizations of them in third-person language—using largely conventional rhetoric—and direct exhortation of Timothy in second-person language: "but you. . . ." The false teachers become the negative model that Timothy is to avoid.

The same use of polemic as a negative foil is found in Hellenistic *protreptic* discourses, which encourage young men to pursue the life of philosophy or, for those already professing the philosophical life, to live up to the ideals of their profession. In such exhortations, the personal vices and the vicious practices of the "false philosophers" serve to highlight the positive ideal. In such compositions as Lucian's *Demonax* and *Nigrinus*, Epictetus's *Discourse* 3.22 ("On the Calling of the Cynic"), and Dio Chryostom's *Oration* 77/78, we find the same elements as in 2 Timothy: the memory of the respected teacher who is the model

---

487. Karris, "Background and Significance of the Polemic of the Pastoral Epistles."
488. Johnson, "New Testament's Anti-Jewish Slander."

that the aspirant can imitate and the presentations of maxims ("do this, avoid that") in antithetical fashion, using the polemic against false teachers in order to portray in vivid colors that which should be avoided.

2 Timothy, then, has the overall form of the paraenetic letter. Since Paul is concerned, however, not simply with his delegate's personal virtue, but, above all, with his character as a delegate—that is, as a teacher of churches—he uses polemic in the way it is used in protreptic discourses, as a negative foil to the ideal image presented by Paul himself. Leaving aside the greeting (1:1–2) and the final personal comments (4:19–22), the structure of the letter is consistent with this analysis:

1. The presentation of Paul as a model, together with other exemplars (1:3–2:13)
2. Maxims for Timothy as a teacher, presented in contrast to the false teachers (2:14–4:5)
3. The representation of Paul as a model (4:6–18)

THEOLOGICAL PERSPECTIVES

As a personal paraenetic/protreptic letter, 2 Timothy has a specific rhetorical goal: the strengthening of Paul's delegate in his commitment to his profession as "the Lord's Servant" (2:24). It should not be read, therefore, as a repository of theological propositions, Pauline or otherwise, but as an instrument of persuasion whose argument and topics are selected for their appropriateness to the situation addressed by the letter.[489] To ask about the theological perspectives of 2 Timothy is, in reality, to consider the theological texture of the composition's rhetoric: How does it help create or support an understanding of human existence before the living God? And as for all of Paul's letters—or, for that matter, all the writings of the New Testament—the manner of asking that question must fit itself to the literary shape of the writing.

In 2 Timothy, it is Paul's delegate's character and qualities as a teacher that provide focus for the composition's theological perspectives. In 1 Cor 4:17, Paul said that Timothy's mission to that church was to remind them of Paul's ways, "just as I teach them everywhere in every church." And although in contrast to 1 Timothy, Paul's delegate in this letter is not explicitly commanded to "teach" (1 Tim 4:11; 6:2), it is clear that his mission is precisely *to be* a teacher, for he

---

489. It is encouraging that studies of the theology of 2 Timothy in its own right are beginning to appear. See, for example, the three essays sponsored by the Society of Biblical Literature Seminar on the Theology of the Disputed Pauline Letters, all appearing in *The Society of Biblical Literature 1997 Seminar Papers* (Atlanta: Scholars Press, 1997): J. W. Aageson, "2 Timothy and Its Theology: In Search of a Theological Pattern," 692–714; L. R. Donelson, "Studying Paul: 2 Timothy as Remembrance," 715–731; G. D. Fee, "Toward a Theology of 2 Timothy—From a Pauline Perspective," 732–749.

is expected to be "an apt teacher" (*didaktikos*, 2 Tim 2:24), his training in Scripture is useful for teaching (*eis didaskalian*, 3:16), and his fickle audience "piles up teachers" according to their whims because they are no longer able to sustain "healthy teaching" (4:3). Timothy, in turn, is to find associates capable of also "teaching others" (2:2). If Timothy is to be a teacher, and if Paul is, as we have suggested, presented as his model, then Paul's own teaching would logically also receive attention—and it does. Timothy has found an example in Paul of both the content and the manner of the good teacher (3:10; 4:2). It is not accidental, then, that in both the letters to the delegate that Paul considered as a teacher, Paul designates himself also as *didaskalos* (2 Tim 1:11; 1 Tim 2:7).

Within the Greco-Roman culture shared by Paul and his delegates—according to Acts, we remember, both Paul and Timothy are diasporic Jews, and Timothy has a Gentile father—the teacher was, above all, a moral teacher—that is, a philosopher. Philosophy in the Hellenistic period was not a matter of theory so much as therapy, not a matter of knowing reality so much as knowing how to live well.[490] The rhetoric of 2 Timothy, and to a lesser extent of 1 Timothy as well, is that of Hellenistic moral philosophy. I have already touched on how 2 Timothy uses polemic in the manner of philosophical protreptic treatises. Even more significant is the recurrent metaphor of medicine that I will note throughout the commentary: vice as sickness, virtue as health, the teacher as physician. Most significant of all is the steady attention given to personal character, for ancient ethics is character ethics. And this brings us full circle, for it was a deep conviction in Greco-Roman culture that character is best learned by imitation. Thus for Paul to teach Timothy, he must exemplify the virtues he teaches, and for Timothy to teach virtue as Paul's delegate, he must also live them out. The character of the teacher, and that which is taught, coalesce.

Such moral instruction within Hellenistic philosophy was often placed within a specifically religious framework. Thus Epictetus says, "The man who lays his hand to so great a matter as this without God [*dicha theou*] is hateful to him [*theocholōtos esti*]" (*Discourses* 3.22.2), and, again, the true Cynic "must know that he has been sent by Zeus to men, partly as a messenger . . . and partly as a scout" (3.22.23–24). Likewise, Dio Chrysostom says, "In my own case, for instance, I feel that I have chosen that role, not of my own volition, but by the will of some deity [*daimoniou tinos*]" (*Oration* 32:12; see also 32:13, 21; 13:9–10). Not only the call but also the mission of the philosopher could be construed religiously. Julian can speak of the true Cynic as a general (*stratēgos*) appointed by God (*Oration* 6:192C; see also 7:225D). And in language remarkably close to that found in 2 Timothy, Epictetus calls the philosopher a "herald of the gods [*kēryka tōn theōn*]" (*Discourse* 3.22.70) and a "servant of Zeus [*hypērētes tou Dios*]" (3.22.82).

In similar fashion, 2 Timothy places the role of the teacher within an explicitly theological worldview, one shaped not by convictions concerning Zeus

490. Still a marvellous evocation of the spirit of philosophy in the empire is S. Dill, *Roman Society from Nero to Marcus Aurelius*, 2nd ed. (1904; reprint, New York: World, 1956), 287–440.

and the Olympic pantheon, but by the symbolic world of Torah and the experience of the death and resurrection of Jesus the Messiah. Within this world, the virtues of the teacher are those appropriate to life before God in light of a crucified Messiah, just as the vices are those that overturn "faith," the most fundamental apprehension and articulation of the symbolic world of Torah as reshaped by the one who "destroyed death and manifested life and immortality" (1:10).

The most fascinating dimension of 2 Timothy theologically is the way it pays attention to the character of the individual in a manner unparalleled in Paul's other letters (even 1 Timothy and Titus); they are aimed much more at building a community's character. A personal focus is no surprise in a personal paraenetic/protreptic letter. In antiquity, no worse charge could be brought against a philosopher/moral teacher than that his life did not conform to his words (Aelius Aristides, *Platonic Discourse* 2.307.6; Philostratus, *Life of Apollonius of Tyana* 2:29; Lucian, *Timon* 54). It is Paul's character that Timothy is to emulate, just as he is to look to the personal attitudes and actions of the soldier, the athlete, the farmer, Onesiphorus, and, above all, Jesus Christ (1:13–2:13)! It is all a matter of personal character. Timothy's ministry is not measured by its success, but by its fidelity to the one "who called us with a holy call" (1:9); it is not evaluated by his skills and techniques, but by his being "tested, an unashamed workman" (2:15).

The character of Paul's delegate is defined particularly by the self-disposition called faith (*pistis*). What is most impressive about the understanding of *pistis* in 2 Timothy is how it so completely fails to match the stereotypical perception of faith in the Pastorals as a matter of belief alone. In fact, faith is here an intensely personal quality, an internal disposition that can be sincere (1:5) or counterfeit (3:8). Sincere faith is one that comes from a pure heart (2:22), which is rightly aligned with God (*dikaiosynē*, 2:22) and expresses itself through love (*agapē*, 1:7, 13; 2:22). The life of faith is, moreover, interpersonal. Timothy has learned faith from his grandmother Lois and his mother, Eunice (1:5), and has learned it as well from Paul: "You have carefully followed my teaching, my practice, my purpose, faith, forbearance, love, and endurance" (3:10). Paul's distinctive language about "that which has been entrusted" (*paratithēmi/parathēkē*) points to this interpersonal dimension of faith: God has entrusted Paul (1:12), Paul entrusts Timothy (1:14), and Timothy is to entrust others (2:2), and what is "entrusted" in each case is precisely this manner of life defined by faith.

Because faith is a living reality that is entrusted person to person and is learned person to person, the church is truly an "intentional" community existing through the shared convictions and commitments of its members. For this reason, deviance in teaching or behavior must strenuously be resisted; it is a matter not simply of destabilizing institutions, but of corrupting and destroying persons (2:18; 3:2–5).

As the "Lord's servant" (*doulon kyriou*, 2:24) and "God's man" (*anthrōpos theou*, 3:17), Timothy is himself shaped by that which he proclaims. He has been called by God with a holy calling and has been saved through God's plan and gift (1:9). He is empowered by the Holy Spirit (1:7–8) and can guard the "noble deposit" through the Holy Spirit that dwells in him (1:14). This is the same Spirit that breathes through the Scripture in which Timothy has been instructed since youth and which instructs him in the salvation that comes through the faith of Jesus and equips him for every form of teaching (3:15–17). Timothy is also empowered by the grace that is given him in Christ Jesus (2:1).

In contrast to the false teachers who are corrupt in mind and have counterfeit faith (3:8), who are imposters both deceived and deceiving (3:13), whose words are chatter that does no one any good (2:14–16), who engage in endless controversies and quarrels (2:23), who prey on those hungry for learning but easily confused (3:6), and whose influence is like a sickness that corrupts others as gangrene does (2:17), Timothy must be committed to "accurately delineating the word of truth" (2:15) and proclaiming the word (4:2), knowing that the truth with which he has been entrusted is not simply a human word. It is good news from and about God (1:8, 10; 2:8); it is the very word of God (*logos tou theou*) that is faithful (2:11), that cannot be bound as humans can (2:9), and that works with the power of God (1:8) for salvation (1:9). Timothy, therefore, should teach with sincerity and genuineness (1:5, 13; 2:22); he should avoid cravings for novelty and stay steady (2:22; 3:14) and sober in every respect (4:5); he should aim at righteousness, faith, love, and peace (2:22); he should show kindness and forbearance (2:24); and he should hope for the conversion even of those who have fallen into the trap of the devil (2:25–26).

At the heart of Paul's conception of Timothy's ministry is a call to endurance and suffering. This note of hardship is not absent from Greco-Roman philosophers, who understand that a life spent in exhorting to virtue people who prefer vice will inevitably involve hardship. Epictetus says, "For this is a very pleasant strand woven into the Cynic's pattern of life; he must needs be flogged like an ass, and while he is being flogged, he must love the men who flog him, as though he were the father and brother of them all" (*Discourses* 3.22.54–55; see also 3.22.100; Julian, *Oration* 7:215A; Dio Chrysostom, *Oration* 32:11, 19; Lucian, *Demonax* 11).

So Paul calls on Timothy repeatedly to *endure* (2:13; 3:14; 4:15), convinced that suffering is a consequence of witnessing to the good news: "All those who wish to live piously in Christ Jesus will be persecuted" (3:12). The suffering of the teacher and preacher takes three forms. The easiest is that coming from the outside, as Paul suffered from Alexander the coppersmith (4:14) and now suffers an imprisonment shameful by worldly standards (1:12). But there is also the suffering caused by resistance from within by fellow believers who teach wrongly and deceive others (2:17–18). Worst, perhaps, is the suffering caused by the sheer indifference of the hearers or their tendency to prefer teachers who pander to their own sick desires (3:1–6; 4:3). In the case of Paul and Timothy, such suffering is especially acute, because their allies are leaving and their foes are making headway; when Paul declares, "They will not make more progress" (3:9), it is difficult to avoid the impression that he is engaging in wishful thinking. But because the conditions of receptivity are so variable, and perhaps getting worse

(3:1–5), preaching and teaching must take place in all seasons (4:2), not because of a hope for success, but in loyalty to the one who has called the minister with a holy call (1:9) and instilled in the minister a special gift for service (*charisma*, 1:6).

A commitment to being "the servant of the Lord" means, therefore, a willingness to overcome shame (1:8) and cowardice (1:6) to "take one's share of suffering" for the good news (1:8; 2:3, 13). This is the burden of the examples that Paul presents: the soldier who does everything to please his recruitment officer (2:4), the athlete who hopes for the crown because he has competed by the rules (2:5), the farmer who expects the reward of a harvest because he has labored (2:5). The same example is presented by Onesiphorus, who overcame his shame to share Paul's presence in chains and can therefore expect mercy from God (1:17–18).

It is, after all, the pattern of the gospel itself. Timothy is to "remember" (that is, imitate) Jesus himself: "Keep on remembering Jesus Christ. According to the good news I preach, he is raised from the dead, he is from the seed of David" (2:8). Like the opponents, Paul claims that the resurrection has already happened (2:18): Jesus is raised from the dead. He has, indeed, "abolished death. He has manifested life and immortality, and this through the good news" (1:10). The power of the resurrection at work in believers, however, does not prevent suffering, but enables it to be endured for the sake of others: "This is why I endure all things for the sake of the chosen ones, that they also might attain salvation with eternal glory that is found in Christ Jesus" (2:10). The pattern of "share his suffering now, share his glory later" is reinforced by that "faithful word" in 2:11, which binds together the endurance and death experienced with Jesus and the hope for a share in his life and kingdom.

Just as Paul models for Timothy a pattern of healthy teaching, so does he exemplify in his own attitudes this pattern of endurance and hope. At the point where he is facing both abandonment and death, both professional failure and personal shame, he declares, "I have fought the noble fight, finished the race, held tight to the faith. There is waiting for me now the crown given to the righteous, which the Lord, the righteous judge, will award me on that day, not only me but all those who have loved his coming" (4:7–8).

APPROACHING 2 TIMOTHY

Present-day readers have two basic options for approaching an ancient religious writing such as 2 Timothy: an engaged or a nonengaged reading. These two approaches are not the same as declaring for or against authenticity, although that issue may be involved. The distinction is, rather, that the nonengaged reading seeks to be informed, while the engaged reading seeks to be challenged as well.

The nonengaged reading is characteristic of the straightforward historical-critical method. In this approach, we are interested primarily in how to place and understand 2 Timothy historically. Perhaps it is authentically Pauline; perhaps not. In either case, the significance of the composition is restricted to what it can tell us about either the shape of Paul's ministry and thought or the shape of a Pauline Christianity in a later generation. A nonengaged reading need by no means be without energy or dedication or discipline. Nor is it without benefit. But in such a reading, the past stays past and only past. Whether the thought in the composition is Paul's or another's, it has no particular claim on us as readers.

A good portion of this commentary, like all critical commentaries, consists of such a nonengaged reading. It is obvious from the entire tenor of the commentary that I think that 2 Timothy has every right to be considered as an authentic Pauline letter. And in the NOTES and COMMENTS, I will show many of the ways in which it connects to the other Pauline letters. In so doing, I will also try to show the problems for such a placement that form the basis for the nonauthenticity position. I also adduce many examples from other philosophical and religious literature of antiquity in an effort to contextualize the language and perceptions of 2 Timothy within that world.

Most readers of 2 Timothy, however, do not want simply to be informed, but also to be challenged. They read this composition not as a distinct historical puzzle, but as part of a biblical witness. They must struggle, therefore, with the implicit authority it bears because of its canonical status. For such readers, the issue of Pauline authorship is not really paramount, any more than the actual authorship of the canonical Gospels is either an impediment or an encouragement to their reading them as witnesses to Jesus. Such readers are correctly less concerned with the consistency of "Pauline theology" than with the truthfulness—and, therefore, the reliability—of this biblical witness for the present-day struggle to live before God faithfully as disciples of Jesus.

For such readers, and for such questions, other sorts of critical engagements are necessary beyond historical inquiry. History can to some extent determine what something might have meant to readers in the past. History has little to say about what a text should mean to readers in the present. The best that historical analysis can do is make the voice of the past as clear and authentic as possible, so that a clean critical engagement is possible. In this case, the best the historical portion of the commentary can do is to allow the literary composition called 2 Timothy speak on its own terms, without being subsumed by theories of historical placement.

The text is truly engaged when readers begin to ask other sorts of critical questions, both those addressed to the text—in terms of its theological cogency, for example, or its moral adequacy—and those addressed to the readers of the text—how their cultural and ideological presuppositions are challenged.

It is incumbent on present-day readers, for instance, to ask whether the language of 2 Timothy concerning women is morally defensible, even if it is, as I have suggested, historically and culturally intelligible. And they must decide whether the characterization of certain women as always learning, yet not capable of reaching recognition of truth, or the characterization of other women as exemplifying the faith and instructing in the Scripture, should have more weight in present-day debates over the role of women in the church. Even more pertinent is the question whether the use of polemic in 2 Timothy, even when understood as a function of protreptic rhetoric, does not lead to the demonization of difference, so that even when we recognize the need for drawing boundaries and for dealing with deviance within the community, we must question whether the wholesale use of vituperation is morally acceptable.

2 Timothy also challenges present-day cultural and religious sensibilities in important ways. One of the misfortunes of the entire authenticity debate has been the way a decision concerning authorship has led to the marginalization of these writings in Christian life. So we can begin with the obvious: the way in which 2 Timothy focuses on the formation of individual character in a manner quite distinctive in the New Testament. And in order to talk about personal formation, the letter uses the language of virtue, together with the instruments of memory, modeling, mimesis, and maxims. Only very recently has the state of disarray in late-Enlightenment ethics led to a recovery of "character ethics" in some quarters. 2 Timothy is a precious resource precisely because, in a manner far more flexible and fresh than in the writings of Thomas Aquinas, it demonstrates the compatibility of faith and virtue in the Christian life, not to mention the necessity of becoming living exemplars for the teaching of values.

Particularly for those called to a life of ministry within the church, 2 Timothy poses some powerful challenges. It proposes that ministry is not a career choice, but a call from God to become holy. Neither is ministry a body of lore to communicate or a set of skills to exercise, but a matter of living in a certain manner that expresses one's deepest convictions in consistent patterns of behavior. Transformation of character or, if one prefers, continuing conversion is the very essence of ministry, as it is of discipleship. Carrying out acts of ministry without the corresponding affections is a form of counterfeiting, to "have the form of piety while denying its power" (3:5). Ministry, furthermore, is not measured by success, but by fidelity. Ministry demands witnessing to uncomfortable and unpopular truths in the face of indifference and disagreement. Ministry inevitably involves suffering if the gospel is truly lived and rightly proclaimed. The minister labors in a hope not of reward or recognition in this life, but in a hope of sharing in the resurrection life. Not one of these truths is supported by present-day culture. Few of them are supported by the church. The voice of 2 Timothy is not a voice that lulls Christians into a comfortable security, but one that speaks with the urgency of prophecy, calling for witnesses to truth in an age that prefers teachers who cater to its desires (4:3).

SECOND TIMOTHY:
TRANSLATION, NOTES,
AND COMMENTS

◆

I. GREETING (1:1–2)

◆

1 ¹From Paul, an apostle of Christ Jesus because God wills it and based on the promise of life found in Christ Jesus, ²to Timothy my beloved child. May you have grace, mercy, and peace from God who is Father and from Christ Jesus our Lord.

NOTES

1. *an apostle of Christ Jesus*: Paul's self-designation is the same as that in the greeting of 1 Timothy. He takes pains to identify himself as *apostolos* in Rom 1:1; 1 Cor 1:1; 2 Cor 1:1; Gal 1:1; Eph 1:1; Col 1:1. 1 and 2 Thessalonians lack any self-description. In Phil 1:1 and Phm 1, the title of *doulos* replaces that of *apostolos*, and in Tit 1:1, we find *doulos theou* (slave of God) and *apostolos de Iēsou Christou* (apostle of Jesus Christ).

because God wills it: The translation puts the phrase *dia thelēmatos theou* (literally, "through the will of God") in the active voice. The phrase occurs frequently, although not invariably, in Pauline greetings (1 Cor 1:1; 2 Cor 1:1; Gal 1:4; Eph 1:1; Col 1:1). It is not used in 1 Timothy or Titus.

based on the promise of life: The language of "promise" is prevalent in the NT literature (e.g., Luke 24:49; Acts 2:33; 7:17; 13:23; 23:21; 26:6; Rom 4:13–21; 9:4; 15:8; 2 Cor 1:20; Gal 3:14–29; 4:28; Eph 1:13; Heb 4:1; 6:13; James 1:12), but is largely absent from the OT (only LXX Ps 55:9; 2 Macc 2:18). The phrase *kat' epangelian zōēs* is pregnant and not easily translated. First, the anarthrous genitive noun *zōēs* could be understood as equivalent to an adjective, thus "living promise." Second, the prepositional phrase *kat' epangelian* (again, anarthrous) could be taken as "according to [or, with a view to] the promise of life." I have chosen to translate it as equivalent to "in virtue of" (compare Heb 7:16): Paul's apostleship is grounded in God's choice and the promise of life in Christ Jesus.

found in Christ Jesus: Once more, the precise translation is difficult, although the general idea is clear enough: the promise of life is associated with Jesus. But is it a promise enunciated by Jesus in his sayings? Or is it a promise established by the death and resurrection of Jesus, so that others could also hope for such a new resurrection life? Apart from 1 Pet 5:10, the phrase "in Christ Jesus" (*en Christō Iēsou*) is found in only the Pauline literature. The phrase does not occur in Titus, but is found in 2 Tim 1:1, 9, 13; 2:1; 3:12, 15, and 1 Tim 1:14 and 3:13. It is characteristic of 2 Timothy to have usage relatively closer to that found in the undisputed letters (compare Rom 3:24; 15:17; 1 Cor 1:4; 4:17; Gal 2:4; Phil 2:1; 3:14; Col 1:4; 1 Thess 5:18; Phm 8). The way in which the phrase is used in the Pastorals, however, has been contrasted to the use in the undisputed letters.[491] But although the *en christō* statements in 1 and 2 Timothy are frequently obscure in their exact denotation, it must also be said that Paul's usage in his other letters is not without ambiguity.

2. *my beloved child*: The sobriquet *agapētos* (beloved) is sometimes used by Paul simply for fellow believers (Rom 1:7; 1 Cor 10:14; 15:58; 2 Cor 7:1; Phil 2:12; 1 Tim 6:2; Phm 16) and sometimes for designated fellow workers (Rom 16:5, 8, 9, 12; Eph 6:21; Phil 4:1; Col 4:7, 9, 14; Phm 1). We cannot, therefore, make a great deal of the difference between Paul's use of *agapētos* here for Timothy and his use of *gnēsios* in 1 Tim 1:2. It is nevertheless striking that in this personal paraenetic letter, the designation of Timothy as *agapētos teknos* matches precisely the description of him used by Paul in 1 Cor 4:17.

grace, mercy, and peace: Grace (*charis*) and peace (*eirēnē*) are part of the standard Pauline greeting. Paul uses the term *eleos* (mercy) elsewhere (Rom 9:23; 11:31; Gal 6:16), but not as a part of a letter greeting except in 1 and 2 Timothy (compare *charis kai eirēnē*, Tit 1:4).

God who is Father: In his greetings, Paul ordinarily adds *hēmōn* (our) to the phrase "God who is father." The only exceptions are 1 Thessalonians (where many MSS contain the pronoun) and the Pastorals. Several MSS of 1 Timothy correct to the common practice, but, remarkably, no MSS of 2 Timothy or Titus appear to supply the pronoun.

Christ Jesus our Lord: There are some variant readings here affecting the word order: the original hand of Sinaiticus, for example, has "Lord Jesus Christ," and other MSS have "Jesus Christ our Lord." The variations are understandable, since Paul's usage elsewhere varies.[492] Each of the letters to his delegates has "Christ Jesus" in the greeting, as do 2 Corinthians, Philippians, Philemon, Colossians, and Ephesians. In Galatians, 1 Thessalonians, and 2 Thessalonians, Paul uses "Jesus Christ." In Romans and 1 Corinthians, we find the same textual uncertainty as here.

COMMENT

The main points to be made concerning the greeting in 2 Timothy are made in the NOTES and COMMENT on 1 Tim 1:1–2: the role of the greeting in establishing a writing as real or fictive correspondence, the social relations signaled by the respective designations of sender and receiver, and the significance of the modifications made by Paul to the standard elements in the Hellenistic letter greeting. Only two further observations require some elaboration.

---

491. J. A. Allen, "The 'In Christ' Formula in the Pastoral Epistles," *NTS* 10 (1963): 115–121.
492. Elliott, *Greek Text*, 17.

The first concerns the way in which, despite the personal nature of this parae-netic letter—the focus throughout is on the character and practice of Timothy—the greeting indicates that the personal relationship between Paul and his del-egate is entirely shaped by their shared religious convictions. Paul writes to his "beloved child" not as a surrogate father (as did the inscribed writer of the parae-netic letter *To Demonicus*) offering him advice for success in the world, but as an emissary of God (*apostolos tou theou*) and of the Messiah Jesus, who quite literally frame the greeting. It was not outside the range of a Greco-Roman philosopher to consider himself "God's scout to humanity" with a divinely approved mission of salvation that involved personal witness and authentic teaching (Epictetus, *Discourse* 3.22). And such a self-understanding was stan-dard for a Jewish Prophet. Such consciousness of divine commission requires an understanding of the world quite different from that constructed by post-Enlightenment cosmology; it supposes that the phenomenal world is both open to and suffused by divine power and agency. This claim to prophetic/apostolic authority grounded in divine commission alone distinguishes Paul's correspon-dence from the moral advice of a Seneca or a Plutarch, who, for all their piety, claimed no such commission.

What is even more startling about Paul's letter greeting, however, is that the direct commissioning agent is a person who, at the time of Paul's writing, had been dead for at least two decades: Jesus. The name Jesus can refer to only Je-sus of Nazareth, in whose name Paul preached. But it is of first importance to note that the implied characterization of Jesus is not as a historical figure of the past, but as a powerful presence in the present day of Paul and his readers. Mes-siah Jesus is the one who now "sends out" Paul (1:1), and Messiah Jesus is now named, together with "God who is Father," as the *kyrios* who can bestow grace, peace, and mercy on humans. By implication, Jesus is one sharing the fullness of the life and power of the creator God of Israel.

Second, it is within this context of Jesus as *kyrios* that we best understand Paul's distinctive way of grounding his apostleship. With respect to God who is Father, Paul uses an expression that he uses elsewhere: *dia thelēmatos theou* (through God's will). Paul's God is not a remote and uninvolved deity, but one who directs human affairs and who "desires" certain outcomes. The most dis-tinctive phrase in 2 Timothy's greeting, however, is the second one qualifying Paul's apostleship. It is grounded in God's will, but also *kat' epangelian zōēs tēs en Christō Iēsou* (based on the promise of life found in Christ Jesus, 1:1).

The NT's use of promise (*epangelia*) language is remarkable not only for its widespread incidence—despite little explicit grounding in Torah—but also on two further counts. First, by employing "promise" as a category, it provides de-finition for what in Torah was a variety of aspirations and declarations in a va-riety of forms: the narrative is given a specific focus. Second, by identifying that "promise" with the Holy Spirit, who enables humans to live with the resurrec-tion life of Jesus (esp. Acts 2:33; Gal 3:14–29), the NT writers fundamentally transformed the shape of God's blessing. What is hoped for from God is now not simply expectations concerning length of natural life, land, posterity, and property. What is anticipated is a share in God's own Spirit and, therefore, in God's own life. The specific phrase "promise of life" is found in the NT otherwise only in 1 Tim 4:8 ("a promise of life both now and in the future"), although the same combination of ideas is found also in Tit 1:2 ("eternal life that was promised by the truthful God") and James 1:12 ("the proven one will receive the crown that is life which he has promised to those who love him"). The way this greeting connects "the promise of life" with "in Christ Jesus" is developed thematically by 2 Tim 1:9–10.

II. THANKSGIVING (1:3–5)

◆

1 ³I thank the God whom I serve, as did my forebears, with a pure conscience. I hold you constantly in my memory as I pray night and day. ⁴I long to see you, as I remember your tears, that I might be filled with joy ⁵holding in memory your sincere faith, the same kind that dwelt in your grandmother Lois and in your mother Eunice before you. I trust it is in you as well.

NOTES

3. *I thank the God whom I serve*: Paul uses the expression *charis tǫ theǫ* (thanks be to God) elsewhere (Rom 6:17; 7:25; 1 Cor 15:57), but the combination *charin echō* is found only here and in 1 Tim 1:12. Here, Paul expresses thanks *tǫ theǫ*, and in 1 Tim 1:12 he directs thanks to "the one who empowers me, Jesus Christ our Lord." The verb *latreuein* has the specific sense of fulfilling religious duties (Euripides, *Ion* 152; Philo, *Special Laws* 1:300; Rom 1:25), so that the translation "whom I worship" would suit equally well. The expression "the God whom I serve" is attributed to Paul by the author of Acts (27:23; see also 24:14; 26:7). Paul elsewhere speaks of his ministry as a "religious service" (*latreuein*, Rom 1:9; Phil 3:3).

as did my forebears: The noun *progonos* originally referred to an older child or the firstborn (Homer, *Odyssey* 9:221), but is also used for an ancestor (Euripides, *Ion* 267; Herodotus, *Persian Wars* 7:150). In the LXX, it can be used of one's natural parents (Sir 8:4) or of ethnic ancestors (LXX Esther 4:17; 2 Macc 8:19; 3 Macc 5:31; 4 Macc 9:2), a usage found also in Hellenistic Jewish literature (*Letter to Aristeas* 19; Josephus, *Antiquities* 12:150; *Against Apion* 2:157). Paul uses the term only here and in 1 Tim 5:4. In that passage, it clearly refers to the natural parents of children who are heads of households. The phrase *apo tōn progonōn* is therefore more ambiguous than it may at first appear. Paul may be claiming that he worships God in a manner that he learned from the Jewish tradition ("from my ancestors")—and thus imitates those ancestors. He may also be claiming that he worships God in the manner he learned from his own parents, who are also, of course, Jewish. In light of the emphasis that Paul places on Timothy to continue the faith that was in *his* "forebears" and in light of the general emphasis on Paul as exemplar for Timothy in this section of the letter, the reference to Paul's own natural parents is quite possible. The translation, "as did my forebears," seeks to retain some of the ambiguity.

337

with a pure conscience: As the NOTES to 1 Tim 1:5 have shown, *syneidēsis* (conscience/ moral awareness) is a characteristic Pauline term (Acts 23:1; 24:16; Rom 2:15; 9:1; 13:5; 1 Cor 8:7, 10, 12; 10:25, 27, 28, 29; 2 Cor 1:12; 4:2; 5:11) found also in all three of the letters to his delegates (Tit 1:15; 1 Tim 1:5, 19; 3:9; 4:2). This is the only occurence in 2 Timothy. The qualification "pure" (*katharos*) is roughly equivalent to "sincere" (compare 1 Tim 3:9).

constantly in my memory: Paul does not elsewhere use this exact expression, but his language in Rom 1:9 comes very close: *hōs adialeiptōs mneiean hymōn poioumai* (as I constantly make memory of you). The memory of the other was a standard feature of letter writing in antiquity (e.g., Seneca, *Epistle* 40:1–2), but it was also an important element in paraenetic discourse (e.g., Seneca, *Moral Epistles* 94:21, 25–26; *On Clemency* 1.1.7; Plutarch, *On Listening to Lectures* 8 [*Mor.* 42A–B]; *Education of Children* 13 [*Mor.* 9D–F]; *Progress in Virtue* 15 [*Mor.* 85B]; Pseudo-Isocrates, *To Demonicus* 9–15; Philo, *Contemplative Life* 26, 78).

pray night and day: Paul uses much the same language in 1 Thess 3:10: "praying earnestly night and day," and in 1 Tim 5:5 wishes the widows to engage in prayer "night and day." The conventional character of the phrase is suggested by Paul's speaking in 1 Thess 2:9 and 2 Thess 3:8 of "working night and day." He means consistently and faithfully.

4. *I long to see you*: The sentiment is a common one in Hellenistic epistolography,[493] but the language is also thoroughly Paul's own. Compare Rom 1:11: "for I long to see you" (*epipothō gar idein hymas*; see also 2 Cor 9:14; Phil 1:8; 2:26; 1 Thess 3:6).

remember your tears: The perfect participle of *mimnēskomai* marks the second mention of memory, helping to shape the major theme of this first section of the letter. The "tear" (*dakryon*) is synechdoche for "weeping" (Lucian, *True Story* 1:21; Josephus, *Life* 420) and, in this letter, is metonymy for a state of sorrow, since it is opposed to the "joy" (*chara*) that would be fulfilled if they were to see each other again. What is more difficult to assess is the nature and cause of Timothy's sorrow. Is this conventional language for the natural response to the separation of friends? Possibly it is.[494] Or does Paul suggest a deeper spiritual state of depression and fear? His veiled comments later make a more precise application for "your tears" possible.

filled with joy: The diction is Pauline; see especially Paul's exhortation to the Philippians (2:2), *plērōsate mou tēn charan* (fill up my joy), by their mode of conduct (see also 2 Cor 7:4; Rom 15:13). Joy (*chara*) is a consistent Pauline theme: it is a state more than a feeling, the residue of the presence of the Spirit that is compatible even with conditions of suffering and affliction (Rom 14:17; 15:13, 32; 2 Cor 1:15, 24; 7:4, 13; 8:2; Gal 5:22; Phil 1:4, 25; 2:2, 29; 4:1; Col 1:11; 1 Thess 1:6; 2:19, 20; 3:9; Phm 7).

5. *holding in memory*: This is still a third way of expressing memory within one long sentence: *hypomnēsin labōn*. A few MSS (such as Codex Bezae and

---

493. Stowers, *Letter Writing in Greco-Roman Antiquity*, 60, 65, 68, 69, 76, 82, 159.
494. Stowers, *Letter Writing in Greco-Roman Antiquity*, 64.

the second hand of Sinaiticus) have the present participle of *lambanein*, rather than the aorist participle. The correction may have been made to establish consistency with the present and perfect tenses used in the two previous mentions of memory, but the difference in meaning is in any case slight.

your sincere faith: This is translated literally as "the unhypocritical faith within you" (*tēs en soi anypokritou pisteōs*). Compare *anypokritos agapē* in Rom 12:9 and 2 Cor 6:6, and, especially, *anypokritou pisteōs* in 1 Tim 1:5, with the references there. Timothy's faith is genuine.

dwelt in your grandmother Lois: The verb *enoikein* (to dwell in/among) originally designated a geographic or ethnic location (Xenophon, *Anabasis* 5.6.25), although Euripides could speak of the self's relationship to the body in this fashion: "we possess it not, save to dwell in [*enoikēsai*] during life" (*Suppliants* 535). In the LXX, the geographic meaning obtains in every usage (e.g., LXX Lev 26:32; Judg 6:10; Sir 25:16; Isa 5:3; 26:5; Jer 29:12; 1 Macc 5:5 [variant reading]). Apart from his citation of Isa 26:11–12 in 2 Cor 6:16, however, Paul uses the term to express qualities that are inwardly realized: thus "sin dwells in me" (Rom 7:17), "through the Holy Spirit dwelling in you" (Rom 8:11), and "let the word of Christ dwell richly within you" (Col 3:16). Paul uses the verb here for the "faith" that dwells in Timothy, and in 1:14 will use the same verb for the indwelling of the Holy Spirit. The term for "grandmother" (*mammē*) does not appear in the LXX except in 4 Macc 16:9, and the name Lois is also unattested in the Bible.

your mother Eunice: According to Acts 16:1, Timothy's mother was a "faithful Jewish woman" (*gynē Ioudaia pistē*), whereas his father was a Greek (*Hellēn*). The adjective *pistē* is ambiguous. Does Luke mean that, like Timothy, Eunice was a disciple, so that we should translate this phrase as "a Jewish woman who was a believer"? Or is she simply a faithful member of the Jewish people? Neither Luke nor the Paul of this letter seems terribly concerned about the differentiation. It is her character as a believer in God that is significant and exemplary.

I trust it is in you as well: Paul frequently uses the verb *peithein* in the sense of "having confidence" in something (e.g., Rom 2:19; 2 Cor 2:3; 5:11; 10:7; Gal 1:10; Phil 1:6, 14, 25; 2:24; 3:3; 2 Thess 3:4; Phm 21). In Gal 5:10, we find *egō pepoitha eis hymas en kyriō* (I have confidence toward you in the Lord), and in three places in Romans he uses precisely the perfect middle construction (*pepeismai*) that we find in this passage (Rom 8:38; 14:14; 15:14). He will use it again in 1:12 to express his confidence in the power of God. The precise nuance of the usage in this verse, however, is difficult, and will be discussed in the COMMENT. I have tried to capture the ambiguity by making the clause a separate, terse English sentence.

COMMENT

The short thanksgiving period of 1:3–5 appears in the classic Pauline position immediately following the greeting; in this respect, as in many others, 2 Timothy conforms more closely to the expected Pauline pattern than do 1 Timothy and Titus, making even clearer their special character as *mandata principis* letters. The three verses are a single long sentence in Greek. I have translated them into four more nearly normal-length English sentences while trying to preserve the sense of connectedness between the thoughts that is such a feature of the Greek.

Analysis of the other Pauline thanksgiving prayers shows that while they are undoubtedly genuine prayers—and demonstrate further just how relations between Paul and his readers were shaped by religious convictions—they also serve definite rhetorical purposes. Above all, they provide Paul the opportunity to anticipate themes that he will develop later in the letter and thereby already begin the process of persuasion.[495] Given the dominant assumption that the Pastoral Letters are neither by Paul nor genuine letters, it is not surprising that such analysis has not been systematically applied to them.

We can, nevertheless, see how in this short opening prayer Paul establishes three themes of the letter that are intimately connected to its character as a personal/paraenetic letter. Such letters seek to reinforce the moral character of the recipient through the creative invocation of memory, the presentation of models for imitation, and instruction through discrete moral maxims. The first theme is that Paul serves as Timothy's exemplar; thus we find mention of Paul's own prayer and worship of God, his loyalty to his ancestral traditions and to his colleagues in the faith, and his personal attributes of sincerity and affection. The second theme is that Timothy should imitate such qualities; thus we find stressed his own sincere faith and his own inherited tradition of piety. The third theme is the need for growth in character; thus we see Paul's implied concern—expressed mainly through "I trust it is in you as well"—that Timothy may be deficient in some of these qualities.

The thanksgiving is intensely personal, even intimate. We notice how the second-person pronoun is repeated seven times in one sentence: Paul holds in memory "concerning you" (*peri sou*); he longs *idein se* (to see you); he remembers *sou tōn dakruōn* (your tears); he remembers the sincere faith "in you" (*en soi*), as it was in "your" (*sou*) grandmother and "your" (*sou*) mother, and is confident it also is "in you" (*en soi*). The intimacy embraces Paul's *personal knowledge* of Timothy's parentage and grandparentage as well as his present sorrow, and it includes Paul's *personal feelings* expressed by his constant memory of his delegate, his desire to see him, his diligence in prayer for him, his expected "filling up" of joy at seeing him, and his explicit statement of confidence in him.

The personal character of the thanksgiving is precisely to the point for Paul's paraenetic rhetoric, for moral instruction in the Hellenistic world was very much a matter of imitating the personal qualities of others, and memory was the mode by which such models were summoned. Here we see the significance of the otherwise inexplicable threefold emphasis on *memory* in these few verses: Paul re-

---

495. Schubert, *Form and Function of the Pauline Thanksgiving*; O'Brien, *Introductory Thanksgivings in the Letters of Paul*.

members Timothy in his prayers, he remembers his tears, and he remembers his sincere faith. Paul remembers because he wants Timothy also to remember (1:6; 2:8) and, by remembering, not only renew his commitment to his call, but also be able to remind others (2:14). It is likewise not accidental that Paul expresses his intense longing to see Timothy in person, for the letter later makes clear that he wants Timothy to visit him as soon as possible (4:21), and he will shortly offer Onesiphorus as a model for such diligence in visiting (1:16–17).

We see the same sort of rhetorical function in Paul's mention of his worship in the tradition of his ancestors (or parents [*progonoi*]). The picture of Paul as faithful to his Jewish identity not only corresponds to his presentation in Acts (26:4–21) and his undisputed letters (Rom 9:1–5; 11:1; 2 Cor 3:4–5; 11:22), but also serves a hortatory purpose. Paul suggests that Timothy has a tradition of faith as well, one that comes to him from his (presumably) Jewish grandmother and mother (1:5). Paul will later make a point to remind Timothy to persevere in the things he learned from childhood, including instruction in the Scripture, since he knows from whom he learned them (3:14–15). Paul's "pure conscience," likewise, is to be matched by Timothy's "sincere [literally, "unhypocritical"] faith," for Paul will later in the letter encourage Timothy to place himself among the "purified vessels" of the household (2:21) and to "pursue faith" (2:22), in contrast to those who are "unsound in faith" (3:8) and are "upsetting the faith of some" (2:18).

The thanksgiving also suggests—as so often in Paul's other letters—something of the reason why the apostle finds it necessary to write. His memory of Timothy is scarcely casual, but is sustained in prayers "night and day." It is the expectation that Timothy will overcome his reluctance and visit him that enables Paul to anticipate joy. What accounts for such intensity of feeling and expression? The clue is to be found, I think, in the final (and emphatic!) Greek clause of the thanksgiving, which I have translated as a separate sentence: "I trust it is in you as well." As indicated in the NOTE on 1:5, the perfect tense of *peithein* has the straightforward sense of "I am confident" or "I am persuaded." It is, however, difficult to avoid the impression in this context that such a statement, coming as it does at the very end of the thanksgiving, also expresses some doubt and concern. Paul will continue in the next sentence: "For this reason I remind you" (1.6).

But if everything were fine, why would such a reminder be necessary? And when we look at the content of the reminder, which is to revivify his commitment because God has given "us" a spirit of power, *rather than a spirit of cowardice* (*deilias*, 1:7), then we have reason to pose the question concerning the last clause of 1:5. Paul's language suggests that although these qualities of faith dwell in Timothy, as in his maternal forebears, there is reason for real concern and the need to exhort him to bring those qualities to a fresh commitment. Paul's invocation of this personal network, then, is critical to his moral exhortation. He appeals to that sense of personal loyalty lying dormant within Timothy that perhaps has been suppressed by his fear and depression (see the "tears") generated by the bleak circumstances of the Pauline mission.

Finally, the thanksgiving tells readers something of Paul's understanding of faith in this letter and the role played by women in its transmission. First, the concept of faith in the Pastorals has sometimes been unfavorably compared with the "authentic" Pauline understanding. Paul supposedly thinks of faith in terms of a personal and existential decision in response to the gospel that involves both trust and obedience, whereas in the Pastorals, faith is "reduced" to an intellectual assent to doctrine, a general designation for the community's life, or a personal virtue. The comparison is flawed from the start by its failure to recognize how, even in the undisputed letters, Paul can speak of faith in ways that by no means fit the composite category. He can speak of *pistis* as the content of belief (1 Cor 15:14, 17; 2 Cor 13:5), the general ethos of the community (Gal 6:10), or even a virtue to be developed (Gal 5:22; Phil 1:25). And our analysis of 1 Timothy has shown some of the richness and complexity of *pistis* in that letter. That being said, it is certainly the case that in 2 Timothy, *pistis* stands mainly (there is one great exception in 3:15) as the belief and commitment of the delegate (2:18; 3:8; 4:7) and as a personal virtue that combines elements of loyalty and endurance (1:5, 13; 2:22; 3:10).

What positive insight might we gain from Paul's particular emphasis on faith in 2 Timothy? Three dimensions should draw our attention. The first is how Paul makes no distinction between the faith of his Jewish ancestors (and Timothy's) and that shared by Timothy and himself (as "Christians"). This sense of continuity is deeply consonant with Paul's own emphasis on faith, especially in Romans, which argues that the fundamental human response is always toward or away from the living God, so that the faith of Abraham, the faith of Jesus, and the faith of Christians is much more continuous than it is discontinuous (Rom 3–4). In light of the crypto-Marcionism that afflicts so much Christian theology that bases itself on Paul, 2 Timothy highlights an important aspect of Paul's understanding in the undisputed letters that often is overlooked.

The second dimension is another way of stressing continuity, this time between faith as human loyalty and faith as a theological virtue. The way Paul intertwines Timothy's loyalty to himself and to his ancestral tradition with his fidelity to the worship of the living God that they share makes this point subtly but effectively. The third dimension also is linked to continuity: that faith is not solely or even essentially an existential decision so much as it is an ongoing process of response toward God—a quality of character, indeed—that can be implanted and nurtured by human relationships and passed down from parent to child; thus the fidelity shown by parents and teachers toward the young, and emulated by the young in the formation of their own character, is a critical part of the formation of the theological virtue. Faith is not a momentary decision that occurs at a moment of crisis or conversion. It is a virtue that can grow through the stages of a person's life.

This last aspect of faith, finally, points us toward Paul's distinctive outlook on women in this letter. Attention is usually drawn to his characterization in 3:6–7 of certain "silly women" as "always learning but never capable of reaching a recognition of truth." The statement is indeed difficult and requires consideration in its place. In the thanksgiving of this letter, however, we see the other side, which is Paul's gratitude for the gift of faith given to Timothy by women. Lois and Eunice are portrayed as the source and model for Timothy's own faith. In 3:14, Paul will return to the point when he reminds Timothy of the tutelage in the Scripture he had received from infancy. The teaching activity of Lois and Eunice took place in the domestic sphere, rather than in the assembly, but Paul certainly recognizes them as women who could and did "reach recognition of truth" (3:7) and who could teach the faith to others.

I make this observation not to add support to communities that persist in excluding women from full public leadership roles in the church, based—it is claimed—on the words of Paul. Just the opposite. I want Paul's other point to be heard clearly: if women are indeed capable of transmitting the faith in a truthful and competent fashion within the most important realm of the home through the raising of children, then the burden of proof is on those who would restrict women's role only to that domestic sphere. My larger point is a positive one that does not touch directly on gender roles as such, which is to value what Paul says here about the key role of personal witness and nurture in the forming of faithful persons. If churches face any crisis today, it is that they are expected to bear the burden of primary socializing in the faith that should have been carried out in households and families. Indeed, by focusing only on the public and ecclesial ways of shaping faith, the church has colluded in neglecting the most important—because most formative—influences of grandparents and parents in the transmission of faith. It does not matter whether men or women model and teach faith as a human and theological virtue from the earliest days of a child's life within the home. What matters is that someone does it.

III. PAUL AS A MODEL OF PATIENT SUFFERING (1:6–14)

◆

1 ⁶For this reason, I remind you to revivify that special gift for service that God gave you through the laying on of my hands. ⁷God did not give us a spirit of cowardice. He gave us a spirit of power, of love, and of self-control. ⁸Do not be ashamed, therefore, of the witness of our Lord or of me, a prisoner for him. But as God gives you power, take your share of suffering for the good news. ⁹God saved us and called us by a holy calling. He did this, not on the basis of our own accomplishments, but on the basis of his own purpose and gift. The gift was given to us before the ages in Christ Jesus. ¹⁰But it has been revealed now through the appearance of our savior, Christ Jesus. He has abolished death. He has manifested life and incorruptibility, and this through the good news ¹¹whose proclaimer, apostle, and teacher I have been appointed. ¹²For this reason I suffer even these things. But I am not ashamed, for I know the one I have trusted. I am positive he is able to preserve that which has been entrusted to me until that day. ¹³Keep holding to the example of healthy teaching that you heard from me. In the faith and love that are in Christ Jesus, ¹⁴protect the precious deposit through the Holy Spirit that dwells in us.

NOTES

6. *For this reason*: The phrase *di' hēn aitian* (literally, "for which cause") is here used as a causal conjunction linking the thanksgiving to the body of the letter (2 Macc 4:28; Philo, *On the Creation of the World* 100; for the construction, see Josephus, *Antiquities* 3:279). In effect, remembering the spirit given Timothy prompts Paul to write to him concerning it. See also 1:12 and Tit 1:13.

I remind you: A few MSS (Bezae and 365) have *hypomimnēskō* for "I remind," rather than *anamimnēskō*, a verb that occurs elsewhere in Paul (1 Cor 4:17; 2 Cor 7:15; see also 1 Cor 11:24–25). Scribes who put *hypomimnēskō* could easily have been influenced by the presence of the noun *hypomnēsis* in the preceding verse.[496]

revivify that special gift for service: The verb I translate as "revivify" (*anazōpyrein*) means literally to "set on flame again" (Aristotle, *On Spirit* 484A; Josephus, *An-*

---

496. Against Elliott, *Greek Text*, 116.

tiquities 8:234). It appears in some MSS of 1 Macc 13:7, but its occurrence here is the only one in the NT. I have translated the noun *charisma* pleonastically as "special gift for service," in order to better capture the virtually technical meaning of the term as it is used by Paul in Rom 1:11; 12:6, and 1 Cor 1:7; 7:7; 12:4, 9, 28, 30–31. Apart from the single instance of 1 Pet 4:10, the word *charisma* is exclusively Pauline within the NT, appearing also in 1 Tim 4:14.

that God gave you: I have translated the genitive *tou theou* (of God) as subjective—God is the one who gave it—and have added the "to you," which is implicit in the Greek. Codex Alexandrinus alone has *tou Christou* (of Christ) as a variant. The meaning of the genitive is made explicit in the next verse when Paul says, "God did not give us. . . ."

laying on of my hands: For the significance of this ritual gesture for the transmission of power and the bestowal of authority, see the NOTE on 1 Tim 4:14. In that verse, Timothy has hands laid on him by the *presbyterion* of the Ephesian assembly. It is not clear what event Paul here refers to, although it could mean Timothy's initial enrollment as a worker in the Pauline mission (Acts 16:3).

7. *a spirit of cowardice:* The genitival phrase *pneuma deilias* is difficult; it could as easily be translated adjectivally as "cowardly spirit." Paul is contrasting the spirit that God has given (in 1:14 identified as the Holy Spirit) with a hypothetical "spirit"; in each case, the "spirit" leads to certain attitudes and behaviors. The psychology is much like that in the *Testaments of the Twelve Patriarchs*, which envisages a variety of *pneumata* influencing human freedom (*Testament of Reuben* 2:1; 3:5; *Testament of Levi* 3:3; 9:9; *Testament of Judah* 13:3; 16:1–3; *Testament of Gad* 1:9; *Testament of Dan* 1:6, 8). A "spirit of cowardice" is one that reveals itself in attitudes of fear, timidity, and the refusal to face challenges. In Plato, *Laws* 648B, it is opposed to *andreia* (courage; see also Herodotus, *Persian War* 1:37; 8:26; LXX Lev 26:36; Ps 54:4; Prov 19:15; Josephus, *Life* 172). In 3 Macc 6:19, it is joined to terror (*tarachē*), and in LXX Sir 4:17, it is linked to fear (*phobos*).

of power: Again, the Greek genitive case is richly ambiguous. On one side, power, love, and self-control can describe the spirit that God has given; on the other side, this spirit leads to or expresses itself in power, love, and self-control. Power (*dynamis*) is a term that in Paul's undisputed letters is very much associated with the resurrection of Jesus (Rom 1:4; 1 Cor 1:24; 5:4; 6:14; 2 Cor 13:4; Eph 3:7; Phil 3:10; Col 1:11, 29), the gospel (Rom 1:16; 1 Cor 1:18; 4:20; 2 Cor 6:7; 1 Thess 1:5), and the Holy Spirit (Rom 15:13, 19; 1 Cor 2:4; 12:10; Gal 3:5; Eph 3:16). The noun is absent from 1 Timothy and Titus, but in 2 Timothy, we find it repeated immediately in 1:8 and again in 3:5. The close conjunction of "as God gives you power" in 1:8 and the "Holy Spirit that dwells in us" in 1:14 make it clear that the power of which Paul speaks in 1:7 is that of the Holy Spirit expressing itself in courage.[497]

---

497. P. J. Graebbe does a good job of showing how power and Holy Spirit are connected in the undisputed letters, in "*Dynamis* (in the Sense of Power) in the Main Pauline Letters," *BZ* 36 (1992): 226–235. His analysis could have included 2 Timothy, for the same is true in this letter.

of love: The term *agapē* occurs as frequently in the letters to Paul's delegates as it does in his undisputed letters. Its distinctive aspect is that rather than being used as a singular expression of response, it tends to appear among other virtues of the Christian life. It occurs five times in 1 Timothy (1:5, 14; 2:15; 4:12; 6:11) and twice in Titus (2:2, 10 [variant reading]). In 1 Timothy, it is the *telos* of the commandment (1 Tim 1:5). In 2 Timothy, *agapē* always appears as a virtue that Paul displays (1:13; 3:10) or that Timothy should pursue (1:7; 2:22).

and of self-control: The noun *sōphronismos* is a NT *hapax legomenon*, and its precise meaning here is debatable. My translation of "self-control" is cautious and traditional, placing it in the semantic field of the *sōphron-* terms that appear so frequently in the Pastorals: *sōphronein* (Tit 2:6), *sōphronos* (Tit 2:12), *sōphronizein* (Tit 2:4), *sōphrosynē* (1 Tim 2:9, 15), and *sōphrōn* (1 Tim 3:2; Tit 1:8; 2:2, 5). Of these terms, only *sōphronein* is used by Paul in his undisputed letters (Rom 12:3; 2 Cor 5:13). The entire range of words is, however, commonplace in Greek moral philosophy, referring in the broadest sense to "moral right thinking," including among its nuances prudence, temperance, self-control, sobriety, and moderation. The translation I adopt here, then, makes *sōphronismos* equivalent to *sōphrosynē*. There is precedent: note that the Vulgate translates it as *sobrietas*. It is nevertheless tempting to follow the lead of the Syriac version, which translates *sōphronismos* as "moral teaching," actually the more common meaning of the term in Hellenistic moral discourse (e.g., Plutarch, *Table-Talk* 3.6 [*Mor.* 653C]; Strabo, *Geography* 1.2.3; Philo, *Allegorical Laws* 3:193). The translation "moral teaching" would also nicely fit the program of the letter.

8. *Do not be ashamed*: With the term *epaischynomai*, we meet one of the most pervasive and important social realities of Paul's milieu. Honor and shame are the sociopsychological categories that function as measures of worth in the stratified world of the Roman Empire. As honor is ascribed to that which is noble in stature or deed, so shame is attached to that which is ignoble in behavior or rank. Here Paul uses the accusative case to indicate the objects of Timothy's shame: the *martyrion* of Jesus and *eme* (that is, Paul); compare the use of *epaischynomai* in Plato, *Sophist* 247C, and Diodorus Siculus, *Library of History* 1.83.4. Note how Paul in Romans contrasts the deeds that his readers formerly did, "of which you are now ashamed" (Rom 6:21), and the good news that he preaches, "of which I am not ashamed" (Rom 1:16).

the witness of our Lord: Two interpretive decisions are required by the phrase *to martyrion tou kyriou*. The first is the meaning of *martyrion* in a place where we would expect *martyria*. The noun *martyrion* ordinarily means "something that serves as evidence" (Plato, *Laws* 943C; Josephus, *Antiquities* 6:66; Luke 5:14), whereas *martyria* can refer the act of giving evidence/witness (Plato, *Laws* 937A; Epictetus, *Discourse* 3.22.86). Yet both Luke and Paul can use *martyrion* in ways that come close to meaning "bearing witness" (Luke 21:13; Acts 4:33; 1 Cor 1:6; 2 Cor 1:12; 2 Thess 1:10). The second decision concerns taking the genitive *tou kyriou* as subjective or objective. If subjective, then it is the evidence/testimony borne by Jesus himself of which Timothy is ashamed, and such an interpretation can be supported by both the use of *martyrion* in 1 Tim 2:6 with reference to the work of Jesus and the allusion in 1 Tim 6:13 to the "noble profession" that Jesus made before Pontius Pilate. If the genitive is taken as objective, then Timothy would be ashamed of bearing witness *to* the Lord. The major objection to this interpretation is that the second object of *epaischynthēs* is *eme* (me; that is, Paul) in the accusative. Finally, Timothy could be ashamed of the *evidence* concerning the Lord. All these possibilities remain open, and the translation allows room for each suggestion except the last.

or of me, a prisoner for him: Paul uses a common designation for a prisoner: *desmios*, or "one in chains or bonds" (*desmoi*, 2 Tim 2:9). Compare Josephus, *Antiquities* 13:203; 17:145; Acts 16:25; 23:18; Heb 10:34; 13:3. Paul refers to himself as a *desmios Xristou Iēsou* in Phm 1 and 9 (see also Eph 3:1; 4:1). Two things are noteworthy here. One is the relatively late point in the letter that this identification is made, suggesting that the motivation is rhetorical. The second is the obvious way in which imprisonment would be a cause for Timothy's being ashamed of Paul (compare Heb 10:32–35).

as God gives you the power: I have taken *kata dynamin theou* (according to God's power) as the enabler of Timothy's overcoming his shame and taking on suffering. I have therefore rendered the prepositional phrase in active verbal form, and have changed its position from the end to the beginning of the sentence. The theme of empowerment will be made even more explicit in 2:1 (see also 1 Tim 1:12).

take your share of suffering: Here is a characteristic Pauline emphasis expressed in diction not otherwise found in Paul's letters: the point of the power given by the resurrected Christ is not self-aggrandizement, but the capacity and willingness to follow in the path of the crucified Messiah (e.g., Gal 5:25–6:2; 2 Cor 3:12–4:5). The verb *synkakopathein* (literally, "share the suffering of hard things with") is a NT *hapax legomenon*. The closest parallel is *kakopathein* (suffer hardship, Xenophon, *Memorabilia* 1.4.11; *Letter of Aristeas* 241; Philo, *On Dreams* 2:181) in 2 Tim 2:9 and 4:5 (see also James 5:13).

the good news: The "good news" (*to euangelion*) frames the following kerygmatic statement, being repeated also in 1:10. The term is characteristically Pauline (Rom 1:1, 9; 2:16; 15:19; 1 Cor 4:15; 15:1; 2 Cor 2:12; 4:3; Gal 1:7, 11; Eph 1:13; Phil 1:5; 2:22; Col 1:5; 1 Thess 1:5; 2:2; 2 Thess 1:8; 1 Tim 1:11). Paul will use it again in 2:8. For the connection between the proclamation of the good news and God's power, see, especially, Rom 1:16; 16:25 and 1 Thess 1:5.

9. *God saved us*: Nestle–Aland indents verses 9–10, thereby indicating the kerygmatic character of the verses; the same caution should be exercised by the reader as in the case of other such passages in the Pastorals—no inference should be drawn about the "traditional" nature of the indented materials. Note that the well-balanced phrases in the kerygmatic statement of 1 Cor 15:3–8 are not similarly indented by Nestle–Aland. My translation supplies the word "God" as the subject of "saved us," since in the previous clause I had rearranged the sequence of the words. This is the first "salvation" statement in 2 Timothy (see also 1:10;

2:10; 3:15; 4:18), and much like the declaration in 1 Tim 1:15, this one seems intensely personal and experiential. Whoever else is included by the *hēmas* (us), Paul and his delegate are certainly in view. For further discussion, see the COMMENT.

called us by a holy calling: There is little in this apparently simple expression that is simple or straightforward. The first question is construing the dative; it apparently indicates means, but the cognate construction (*kalein/klēsis*) makes it difficult to determine what this would mean. The second question is the meaning of "holy" (*hagia*): it modifies "calling," but how? Does it characterize the holy God who did the calling, does it indicate the nature of the Christian life as calling, or does it characterize the specific vocation to which the apostle and delegate have been called? The third question is really at the heart of the first two: the question of reference. Does Paul mean God's call to all humans to repent and be saved in response to the good news, or does he mean a specific way of life or ministry? Unfortunately, Paul's other uses of *kalein* and *klēsis* do not exclude any of these possibilities (e.g., Rom 8:30; 1 Cor 1:9, 26; 7:17, 20; 15:9; Gal 1:6, 15; Phil 3:14; 1 Thess 4:7; 2 Thess 1:11). Given the following contrast between human effort and God's gift, it is probable that the wider sense of "calling to God's people" is intended.

not on the basis of our own accomplishments: In the contrast between *charis* and *erga* in this verse, I have translated the first as "gift" and the second as "accomplishments," trying on one side to capture the sense of unmotivated bestowal in the term often translated as "grace" (*charis*), and, on the other side, to avoid the more technical sense of "works" that Paul sometimes employs (Gal 2:16) in favor of the broader sense of "human deeds" that he uses more frequently (e.g., Rom 2:6–7; 15:18; 1 Cor 3:13–15; 9:1; 2 Cor 11:15; Gal 5:19; 6:4; Phil 1:22).[498]

own purpose and gift: The verb *protithēmi* means to "lay out/present," and from that the noun gains its further sense of a plan or intention ("that which is set forth," Josephus, *Antiquities* 18:272; Plutarch, *The Cleverness of Animals* 3 Mor. 960F; Polybius, *Histories* 4.73.2; Acts 11:23). The sense of human intentionality is present in 2 Tim 3:10. It is distinctive of Paul in the NT to use the noun for God's plan or purpose for humans (Rom 8:28; 9:11; Eph 1:11; 3:11), such as we find it here. As for Paul's understanding of God's benevolent plan toward humans as "gift" (*charis*), see Rom 3:24; 4:4, 16; 5:2, 15, 17, 20, 21.

given to us before the ages: The phrase *pro chronōn aiōniōn* (literally, "before times of ages") signifies "from eternity" or, perhaps better, "beyond time." Puzzling here is the exact significance of the passive participle *dotheisan* (which has been given), especially in relation to "in Christ Jesus." If the plan and gift were already given "before time," how could they be given "in Christ Jesus"? One possibility is that the phrase "before the ages" is a delayed modifier for *prothesis*. Then it would be the plan that was made from eternity, and the gift that was given in Christ Jesus. But if the phrase modifies both *prothesis* and *charis*—as

---

498. I. H. Marshall, "Salvation, Grace, and Works in the Later Writings in the Pauline Corpus," *NTS* 42 (1996): 339–358.

it seems it must—then we see here the notion of Jesus as God's plan for the world from the beginning. The sequence of ideas in this passage is not far from that in Rom 8:28–30:

> We know that all things are working together with those who love God for the sake of good, those who are called [*klētois*] according to (God's) plan [*prothesis*]. Because those whom he foreknew, he also selected to be shaped into the image of his son, so that he might be the firstborn of many brothers. Those whom he selected ahead of time, these he also called [*ekalēsen*], and those whom he called [*ekalēsen*], these he also made righteous, and those he made righteous he also glorified.

10. *revealed now*: The plan and the gift that were "given" already before time have been revealed now. In the passive voice, the verb *phaneroun* (to make visible/known, Herodotus, *Persian War* 6:122; Josephus, *Antiquities* 20:76) connotes God's revealing something ("the divine passive"), as in Rom 3:21; 16:26; Col 1:26; 3:4; 1 Tim 3:16.

through the appearance: The noun *epiphaneia* (appearance) occurs frequently in the letters to Paul's delegates (1 Tim 6:14; 2 Tim 4:1, 8; Tit 2:13), referring either to the past/present manifestation of Jesus or to one in the future—determining which is an exegetical challenge. In this case, the appearance is modified by the adverb *nyn* (now) and clearly refers to the life, death, and resurrection of Jesus, rather than to his future coming. Paul uses *epiphaneia* only once otherwise in 2 Thess 2:8, with reference to the *parousia tou kyriou* (coming of the Lord).[499]

our savior, Christ Jesus: A rather large number of witnesses (Codex Ephraemi and the correctors of Sinaiticus and Bezae, as well as the Koine tradition) have "Jesus Christ" here, rather than "Christ Jesus." This is all the more fascinating because there seem to be no such variants for the occurrence of the same phrase in 1:9. Since the sequence of these words is so irregular both in the letters to Paul's delegates and in the undisputed correspondence, scribal confusion is understandable. The use of the title *sōtēr* (savior) is applied to both Jesus and God in the Pastorals (1 Tim 1:1; 2:3; 4:10; Tit 1:3, 4; 2:10, 13; 3:4, 6). Paul elsewhere uses the title of Jesus (Phil 3:20; Eph 5:23). Here we see that God's saving us is through (*dia*) the appearance of the savior Jesus. The source of salvation is God; the instrument is Jesus.

abolished death: The verb *katargein* means literally to "work against something" to the effect that it is nullified, diminished, or even destroyed. It is a thoroughly Pauline term, used in Romans alone, for example, in connection with "canceling" obligation to Law (Rom 7:2, 6), "nullifying" the Law (Rom 3:31) or promise (Rom 4:14) or faith (Rom 3:3), and "destroying" the sinful body (Rom 6:6). Passages reminiscent of this one are Eph 2:15, where Christ destroys/nullifies the Law through his death, and, above all, 1 Cor 15:24–26, where all God's

---

499. For a very positive appreciation of this emphasis, see Lau, *Manifest in the Flesh*.

enemies will be destroyed and the last of them to be destroyed is death. What is anticipated in that passage as an eschatological destruction is stated here as a soteriological nullification.

manifested life and incorruptibility: Paul uses the verb *phōtizein*, which literally means to "shine a light on something" (Diodorus Siculus, *Library of History* 3.48.4) and is used here in its sense of "bringing to light/manifesting" (Polybius, *Roman History* 22.5.10; Epictetus, *Discourses* 1.4.31). Notice how Paul uses it in 1 Cor 4:5, "bringing to light the hidden things of the darkness," and Eph 3:9, "has shone on the eyes of your hearts." The "life" (*zōē*) that has been brought to light is God's life through the resurrection; see 1:1: "according to the hope of life that is in Christ Jesus." That this is so is clear also from the noun "incorruptibility" (*aphtharsia*), which is equivalent to "immortality" (Wis 2:23; 6:19; 4 Macc 9:22; 17:12; Philo, *On the Eternity of the World* 27). Paul associates it with God and the resurrected Christ (Rom 2:7; 1 Cor 15:42, 50, 53, 54; Eph 6:24).

through the good news: Here, *to euangelion* stands first of all for the content of the "good news": what God did through Jesus for the salvation of humans. Then, it stands for the "good news" as proclamation, for it is what "makes manifest" or "brings to light" (*phōtizein*) for humans what in fact God has done.

11. *proclaimer, apostle, and teacher*: A great many MSS (the second hand of Sinaiticus, Ephraemi, Bezae, F, G, and the Koine tradition) have "teacher of the Gentiles" (*didaskalos ethnōn*), rather than simply "teacher" (*didaskalos*). Alexandrinus and the original version of Sinaiticus are the strongest witnesses for omitting "of the Gentiles." Even though the external evidence supports the longer reading, the shorter is to be preferred, especially since the longer reading can be explained by assimilation from 1 Tim 2:7 (note that both lack the definite article before *ethnon*).[500] A still stranger reading is that in 33, which has *kai diakonos* (and a minister) in place of *didaskalos*. The self-designation as *apostolos* is Paul's most common (e.g., Rom 1:1; 1 Cor 1:1; 9:1; 15:9; Gal 1:1; Col 1:1); for "apostle of nations," see Rom 11:13. In contrast, while the act of preaching/proclaiming (*kēryssein*) and the content of preaching (*kērygma*) appear frequently in the undisputed letters (for *kērygma*, see Rom 16:25; 1 Cor 1:21; 2:4; 15:14; Tit 1:3; 2 Tim 4:17; for *kēryssein*, see Rom 2:21; 10:8; 1 Cor 1:23; 9:27; 15:11, 12; 2 Cor 1:19; 4:5; 11:4; Gal 2:2; 5:11; Phil 1:15; Col 1:23; 1 Thess 2:9; 1 Tim 3:16; 2 Tim 4:2), only here and in 1 Tim 2:7 does Paul refer to himself as "proclaimer" (*kēryx*). It is a designation that would not be unwelcome to some Greco-Roman moral philosophers (Epictetus, *Discourse* 3.22.69; 3.21.13).

I have been appointed: For *tithēmi* in this sense, see Xenophon, *Cyropaedia* 4.6.3; Josephus, *Antiquities* 11:39; LXX Lev 26:31; Isa 5:20; Wis 10:21; 1 Cor 12:18, 28. The phrase is precisely the same as that in 1 Tim 2:7. The point is that Paul has been appointed to the task of preaching the good news, just as he insists Timothy has; as Paul accepts the burdens of that office, so also should his delegate. The usage should be taken into account when assessing the meaning of *parathēkē* in this letter.

---

500. Metzger, *Textual Commentary*, 647.

12. *I suffer even these things*: A few MSS and Versions (e.g., the original hand of Sinaiticus, some MSS of the Vulgate, and the Peshitta) lack the emphatic *kai* before *tauta*, which would yield "I suffer these things" rather than "I suffer even these things/these things also." In this case, the longer text is preferable, since the shorter version can be explained more easily as an attempt to reduce the awkwardness of the Greek.[501] What is pertinent here is not simply that Paul "suffers even these things," meaning his chains and the other griefs he will shortly catalogue, but that he suffers them *di' hēn aitian* (for this very reason): his commitment to the task of preaching the good news (for the same phrase, see 1:6).

But I am not ashamed: The adversative *alla* (but) is deliberately strong here, for it opposes Paul's attitude to the one he projects of Timothy: a spirit of cowardice and shame (1:7–8). Paul's words echo the thesis statement of Rom 1:16: *ou gar epaischynomai to euangelion* (for I am not ashamed of the good news).

I know the one I have trusted: Paul works complex variations on the basic notion of trust: he has "placed his trust" (*pepisteuka*) in the one whom he knows (God). He is "confident" (*pepeismai*) that God can protect the "what has been entrusted to him/deposit" (*parathēkē*). It should be clear that Paul is here speaking of the personal relationship of trust between God and himself, rather than some external set of teachings or practices.

able to preserve that which has been entrusted: The adjective *dynatos* again points to the theme of power (1:7–8). The phrase "that which has been entrusted" translates the noun *parathēkē*, which occurs here, again in 1:14, and in 1 Tim 6:20. As the form of the word (from the verb *paratithēmi*) suggests, it refers to anything put in trust, such as a deposit (e.g., Herodotus, *Persian War* 6:86; LXX Lev 5:21; *Sentences of Pseudo-Phocylides* 135).[502] The verb *phylassein* can mean to "guard," "protect," or even "observe" in the sense of "keep." Here the sense of preserve seemed the point of emphasis because of the future orientation in the phrase "until that day."

until that day: The phrase *eis tēn hēmeran* could be understood as "for that day," as in a trust that would come due on a certain date. When Paul uses "the day" absolutely, he usually refers to the future time of judgment (Rom 2:16; 13:12; 1 Cor 1:8; 3:13; 5:5; 2 Cor 1:14; Phil 2:16; 1 Thess 5:4; 2 Thess 1:10; see also 2 Tim 1:18; 4:8).

13. *Keep holding to the example*: The noun *hypotypōsis* (example/model) is found in the NT only here and in 1 Tim 1:16, although it occurs often enough in Hellenistic moral discourse (Diogenes Laertius, *Lives of Eminent Philosophers* 9:78; Sextus Empiricus *Outlines of Pyrrhonism* 2:79; Philo, *On Abraham*, 71). Paul expresses the same idea in Phil 3:17: "You have an example [*typos*] in us." I translate the present singular imperative in a progressive sense, for it is the danger of Timothy's *ceasing* to hold to that example that Paul fears.

healthy teaching that you heard from me: Timothy can look to Paul for both appropriate teaching/ speech (*logoi*) and the corresponding moral attitudes (*pis-*

---

501. Elliott, *Greek Text*, 209.
502. Spicq, "Saint Paul et la loi des dépôts."

tis and *agapē*). Precisely the coherence of this combination is what made the advice of the ancient philosopher "healthy" (*hygiainontōn*)—that is, both sound in themselves and able to give health to others. The pervasiveness of medical imagery in ancient moral discourse is noted more fully throughout this commentary. At this point, Paul emphasizes that Timothy "heard" (*ēkousas*) such teaching; later, he will note how Timothy has "followed" it (*parēklouthēsas*, 3:10).

faith and love that are in Christ Jesus: The emphasis on faith and love is as constant in this letter as in 1 Timothy (2:22; 3:10, 15). Note that Timothy has observed these qualities in Paul, and Paul is able to say at the end of the letter: "I have kept *tēn pistin*" (4:7). In contrast, the false teachers are those who have affected the faith of some people (2:18) and are themselves "untested in regard to the faith" (3:8). The example of Paul is particularly pertinent at this point because he seeks to evoke that "sincere faith" that he remembers being "in you" (1:5). Note also that the spirit given to Timothy is one of power, *agapē*, and self-control (1:7). The prepositional phrase *en Christō Iēsou* is not incidental, for it is attributive, meaning that it modifies the faith and love to which Paul has just referred. It is the faith and love "that are in Christ Jesus" that Timothy has learned from Paul. As in 3:15, it is very difficult to avoid the conclusion that Paul is speaking about the human qualities of Jesus himself.

14. *protect the precious deposit*: The link with 1:12 is obvious: just as Paul has been entrusted by God, so has Timothy. As the next line makes clear, however, it is in both cases the power of God that enables the *parathēkē* to be preserved.

the Holy Spirit that dwells in us: The indwelling of the Holy Spirit is a common theme in Paul's letters (Rom 5:5; 8:9, 11, 14, 16; 1 Cor 2:12; 3:16; 6:19; 12:13; Gal 3:14; 4:6). Paul here makes clear the identity of the "spirit" (*pneuma*) that God gave "us" (*hēmin*) in 1:7. Note the *hēmin* in both verses.

COMMENT

Although the thanksgiving already implicitly presented Paul as a model for Timothy's imitation, this section of the letter makes that motif explicit. The rhetorical function of the theme is also clear. It is "for this very reason" that Paul writes: to stir into new life Timothy's calling and commitment by activating his memory of his mentor and model, Paul. We find the same paraenetic motive in *To Demonicus*: the author presents to the young man his father as the model of the virtues he should emulate. Paul is, in fact, the first of the examples presented for Timothy's imitation. In 1:15–2:13, other models will be brought forward, climaxing in the example of Jesus himself.

Literary Structure

Although the elliptical character of the Greek syntax provides a number of exegetical challenges and the precise import of some phrases is ambiguous, the passage has been carefully constructed. Paul weaves together three things: the good news that both Paul and Timothy were called to proclaim, Paul's willingness to bear the suffering ingredient to his role as a teacher, and his exhortation to Timothy to claim his own "special gift for service" with its attendant suffering. The extended kerygmatic statement in 1:9–10 is bracketed on one side by the commands "do not be ashamed" and "take your share of suffering" for the good news (1:8) and on the other side by the declaration that although Paul "suffers even these things" for the good news, he is "not ashamed" (1:12). Similarly, Paul's confidence in preserving what was entrusted to him (1:12) corresponds to his desire that Timothy guard what was entrusted to him (1:14).

Finally, the kerygmatic statement itself has carefully balanced clauses, with a clear contrast drawn between God's determination "before the ages" (1:9) and the revelation of salvation "now" through Christ Jesus (1:10). The same contrast is found in Rom 16:25–27 and bears the marks of a standard formulation in Paul.[503]

The Importance of Context for Interpretation

The historical context in which one places this passage profoundly affects its interpretation. If 2 Timothy is pseudonymous, as the majority of scholars hold, then this entire section is fictional, the product of the creative imagination of an author writing between thirty and ninety years after Paul's death. There is, therefore, no real "Timothy" about whose courage and loyalty Paul is concerned. There is only a "fictive Timothy"—perhaps the general believer of a later generation?—whom the pseudonymous author wishes to influence in some fashion. But in what fashion and to what end? Here is the fundamental problem of the majority position on the Pastorals. It works far better at the level of generalization than it does at the level of particular details as they are found in these specific letters as distinct and integral literary compositions.

If the purpose of this fictional correspondence is basically to rehabilitate Paul or to mediate his teaching to a later generation, then it is difficult to grasp the subtle appropriateness of the specific language to another context: that of an imprisoned and abandoned apostle who fears that his most reliable delegate lacks the courage to continue his ministry. When read within the context of its literary self-presentation, in contrast, every single detail rings true. We may still struggle with the issues of diction or sentence structure—why they are both so like the undisputed letters and yet so distinctive—but the overall function of the rhetoric and each of its turns make excellent sense.

For those challenging Paul's authorship, the reference to Timothy's "special gift for service" (*charisma*), which was given to him through the laying on of Paul's hands, provides two opportunities. First, 1:6 seems to demonstrate how charism was routinized in the post-Pauline church, since the "authentic" Paul

---

503. N. A. Dahl, "Form-Critical Observations on Early Christian Preaching," in *Jesus in the Memory of the Early Church* (Minneapolis: Augsburg, 1976), 30–36.

never mentions such laying on of hands in his undisputed letters and since the ritual is mentioned repeatedly in Acts (6:6; 8:18; 13:3; 19:6), a book that is considered generally untrustworthy in matters pertaining to Paul's thought and practice, and in the case of the elders is reading back into Paul's time a practice of its (late first or early second century) author. Second, 1:6 appears to conflict with 1 Tim 4:14, which says that Timothy received ordination from the whole board of elders (already in Schleiermacher). Again, the supposition is that this is all fiction and that the practices of ordination from a later time (reflected in 1 Tim 4:14) are clumsily adapted to Paul's own practice (2 Tim 1:6).

In response to the first point, we can observe that the ritual of laying on hands to signify the bestowal of authority was an ancient practice within Judaism (e.g., Num 8:10). Early Christianity no more had to invent such a ritual after the first generation than it needed to invent an institutional structure. Just as the synagogue was available in the first generation as a model for community structure, so were its practices. In response to the second point, we can observe that the conflict between 1 Tim 4:14 and 2 Tim 1:6 is more apparent than real. There is no reason why Timothy could not have received authority from Paul personally, and then had that authority confirmed or legitimated by a local assembly. Finally, concerning the supposed fictional character of the Pastorals, it is more the mark of fiction to be consistent than it is the mark of occasional correspondence written by real humans in response to real situations. Anyone who has struggled with Pauline eschatology in any three of his undisputed letters will readily grant the point. If there is some inconsistency in the two passages, it is more likely to be the result of life than of design.

More significantly, overattention to the detail that is supposed to indicate inauthenticity leads to a misapprehension of the real point of the passage. There is no hint of any "routinization of charism" in this passage. The charging of Timothy is direct and personal. The emphasis, furthermore, is not on some ecclesiastical office, but precisely on spiritual—charismatic, if you will—*power*. Note how Paul repeats that the spirit that God gave "to us" is not one of cowardice, but of *dynamis* (power, 1:7), that Timothy is able to take his share of suffering for the good news "as God gives *dynamis* (power, 1:8), and that God is *dynatos* (able/powerful enough) to preserve what was entrusted to him (1:12). And the source of this power—as of the *charisma* given to Timothy in the first place— is the "Holy Spirit that dwells in us" (1:14). It would be difficult, perhaps impossible, to find a passage in Paul's other letters in which the connection between the spirit and charismatic power was more emphatically or explicitly established.

The Power of God

Recognizing the divine *dynamis* as the point of emphasis helps us better appreciate the rest of the passage. It makes more intelligible, for example, why Paul expands his statement about suffering for the good news "as God gives you power" (1:8) into a full-blown kerygmatic summary of that good news (1:9–10). His rhetorical logic is the same as that in other instances in which he does the same thing (Rom 1:2–5; 2 Cor 5:11–21; Col 1:9–23): to show that the power at work in the ministry is not simply that of humans alone, but comes from God. Just as Paul states in Rom 1:16 that he is "not ashamed of the good news" precisely because it was "the power of God for salvation," so in this passage he connects lack of shame in ministry to God's power to save, revealed in the good news (1:8–9). Paul and Timothy are not the elected leaders of a Hellenistic *collegium*. Nor do they hold their positions because of their own accomplishments (*erga*). They have, instead, been "called . . . by a holy calling" (1:9) from a God who by "his own will" (*prothesis*) and "gift" (*charis*)—even before their own age (1:9; compare Gal 1:15–16)—entrusted them with the work of the gospel.

God's power is for human salvation (1:9), which has been brought to light now (*nyn*) through "the appearance of our Savior, Christ Jesus" (1:10). Here we find ourselves at another passage that has served to fuel suspicions concerning the authenticity of 2 Timothy. Scholars tend to focus in this case on the combination of the terms *epiphaneia* and *sōtēr*, arguing that in the Pastorals we find a new development within Christianity that is not found in Paul: the infiltration of influence from Greco-Roman savior cults.[504] Also innovative, in this view, is the emphasis on a realized salvation—indicated by the "now" (*nyn*)—that stands in tension with Paul's conviction that "salvation" is a future reality for which we now hope (Rom 5:9–10; 8:24; 11:26; 1 Thess 1:10).

Such judgments, unfortunately, are based on a narrow (and, I fear, prejudicial) reading of the evidence. As the NOTES indicate, Paul calls Jesus *sōtēr* in Phil 3:20. He also applies this designation to Jesus in Eph 5:23, although most contemporary scholars reject this usage because Ephesians, also, is considered an inauthentic letter. But Paul certainly uses the title for Jesus once. And like his single use of *episkopos* and *diakonos* for leaders of local churches in Phil 1:1, once is enough! A single use shows that Paul is capable and willing to consider Jesus as *sōtēr*, a fact that all of his other "salvation" language already should have made clear. That the letters to Paul's delegates use the title with greater frequency proves nothing. In fact, however, 2 Timothy uses the title for Jesus in only this passage.

As for saying that God "saved us"—using the aorist tense to indicate action in the past—the evidence in the larger Pauline corpus is again more mixed than sometimes proposed. Even if we leave aside the two instances in Ephesians that use the perfect tense for being saved (2:5, 8), we find that Paul speaks of "being saved" as a present progressive reality (1 Cor 1:18, 21; 2 Cor 2:15) and the opportunity to be saved as a present one (2 Thess 2:10; 1 Cor 15:2). Finally, 2 Tim 4:18 also speaks of God saving in the future! The use of the word "now" (*nyn*) in the undisputed Pauline letters, furthermore, closes rather than opens any perceived gap between them and 2 Timothy, even if we leave aside the kerygmatic statement in Rom 16:25–26 that so closely parallels 2 Tim 1:9–10; see, for example, Rom 5:9, 11; 13:11; 1 Thess 3:8. It is the Paul of 2 Cor 6:2, after all, who declares, "Behold, now is the day of your salvation [*sōtēria*]!"

---

504. See, for example, the argument in Redalié, *Paul après Paul*, 157–174.

Much more to the point is that this passage is thoroughly Pauline in the way that it specifies the manner in which God saved us through the death and resurrection of Jesus: "He destroyed death [compare 1 Cor 15:26], and [literally] exposed to light life [compare Rom 5:10; 6:23; 2 Cor 4:11] and immortality [compare Rom 2:7; 1 Cor 15:42–54]." And by closing this statement with the summative "through the gospel" (*dia tou euangeliou*), Paul effectively frames the kerygma (1:8) and makes the same connection between the power of God for salvation and the gospel that he makes in Rom 1:16.

The Deposit that Has Been Entrusted

Focusing on the elements of personal agency and divine power in this passage also helps clarify the meaning of the term *parathēkē*, used in 1:12 and 1:14, and translated slightly differently each time. In 1:12, I render it "that which has been entrusted to me," and in 1:14, "the precious deposit." The noun is found only here and in 1 Tim 6:20 among the Pauline writings, and scholars who question the authenticity of the Pastorals make two points with respect to the term. First, they stress its "static" character, in contrast to the "dynamic" sense of tradition (using the verb *paradidōmi*) found in the genuine Paul (e.g., 11:2, 23; 15:3). Second, they identify the deposit with a set body of teachings that the pseudonymous author wishes to be kept intact rather than developed in the later Pauline churches, thus demonstrating that the letters are addressed to a later, stabilized form of Christianity, rather than a more fluid and creative stage such as we find in the authentic letters.[505]

There are three objections that should be made to this evaluation. First, we note the theological tendentiousness of characterizations such as "static" and "dynamic." The terms are not merely descriptive, but also evaluative. Dynamic stands for life, movement, and change; static connotes immobility, rigidity, and lack of spirit. The contrast, therefore, corresponds exactly to the classic reconstruction of Christian origins as beginning in "spiritual authority" and ending in "ecclesiastical power," a development that is always viewed in terms of a decline rather than an improvement.

Second, the argument is linguistically simplistic, resembling those appeals to the "dynamic" character of Hebrew thought (based on the verb) and the "static" character of Greek (based on the noun) so prevalent in the last generation and so thoroughly discredited as being based on faulty linguistics.[506] The fact that "handing over" is a verb and "deposit" is a noun does not make the reality involved either dynamic or static. A deposit, after all is handed over, and the act of handing over must involve something. It is quite clear, for example, that the

---

505. For this sort of argument, see Wolter, *Pastoralbriefe als Paulustradition*, 114–130, and Trummer, *Paulustradition der Pastoralbriefe*, 219–222.

506. The classic work is J. Barr, *The Semantics of Biblical Language* (London: Oxford University Press, 1961).

Paul of the undisputed letters is capable of demanding conformity to a set body of teaching (in Rom 6:17; 16:17, and, for that matter, 1 Cor 15:3–8), and is willing to expel from the community those who "teach another gospel" (Gal 1:8–9; see also 2 Cor 11:4).

Third, the argument is flawed because it interprets 2 Tim 1:12–14 through the lens of 1 Tim 6:20, rather than reading it cleanly within its own context. Even in 1 Tim 6:20, furthermore, the "deposit" includes the entire manner of life ordered by *pistis* and not simply true teaching as opposed to false teaching. But the same meaning cannot be assumed in 2 Timothy. Once more, the assumption that the Pastorals are not real and discrete letters, but a single literary composition, enables the scholar to discard the rhetoric of specific passages in favor of an appeal to the "overall concept" found in the composite of all three letters.

It would be disingenous to deny that "sound teaching" is a part of what is meant by the deposit in 2 Tim 1:1–12, for the text explicitly states that Timothy has a model of "healthy words" in the ones he heard from Paul (1:13). But is the emphasis simply on a body of teaching? Two aspects of the passage suggest not. First, Paul follows the words on healthy teaching in 1:13 with "in the faith and love that are in Christ Jesus." Whether these words serve to modify Paul as an example or Timothy's mode of imitation (they could refer to either or both), the qualities in question denote characterological traits rather than doctrinal content. Paul presents and Timothy is to imitate a *way of living*, not a package of teaching. Second, the use of *parathēkē* in 1:12 cannot be separated from Paul's personal loyalty to the one who called him to be an apostle. Paul expresses confidence that what has been entrusted to him (literally, "deposit") will be preserved "until that day"—the eschatological judgment. His confidence is grounded in the fact that God is "strong enough" (*dynatos*) to enable this endurance. This language is recast in 4:8, where Paul declares that "in that day the righteous judge" will give the crown of righteousness to him and to all who love his coming. And both passages express the same conviction that Paul states in 1 Cor 1:7–9: "as you wait for the revealing of our Lord Jesus Christ; who will sustain you to the end, guiltless in the day of our Lord Jesus Christ. God is faithful." When Paul exhorts Timothy two verses later to "preserve the deposit" through the power of the Holy Spirit, then, it means more than keeping intact Paul's teaching. It means staying loyal to his way of life; it means specifically accepting the suffering that comes as a consequence of proclaiming the gospel faithfully, as Paul does. And because the deposit given to Timothy is the same as that entrusted to Paul, it means remaining loyal to the God who has saved them and called them with a holy calling.

Shame and Cowardice / Taking a Share of Suffering

Paul's use of shame language in this passage deserves closer attention. Research into ancient Greco-Roman culture has shown how pervasive the categories of honor and shame were as measures of value and as motivators of behavior.[507] To act in a way that earned the honor of others was an unquestioned good, just as earning the contempt of others was an unmitigated evil. Classical rhetoric, in turn, inculcated, manipulated, and reinforced such measures: an entire branch of oratory consisted in displaying subjects for praise or blame. The human court of opinion meant everything within the larger culture.[508] Those who chose to belong to groups that in one way or another were in tension with the larger society's values—philosophers, for example, or Jews—did not thereby abandon honor and shame as measures of worth. Instead, they attached them to different behaviors and appealed to a different court of opinion. A philosopher choosing to live outside the ordinary range of honorable activities could claim that "countercultural" clothing, diet, and practices were *more* honorable than those praised in the majority culture, and appealed to the "higher court of opinion" that was his conscience. Jews whose beliefs and practices were scorned by outsiders as shameful could claim that they were more honorable in the sight of the God who had chosen them and revealed to them these ways.[509]

Research has also shown how much the rhetoric of the NT compositions themselves functions within such an alternative honor/shame framework.[510] Nothing could be more shameful in the eyes of the world than the death by execution that Jesus had undergone, or the suffering of contempt and rejection experienced by those who gathered in his name and proclaimed him as their Lord. One of the ways in which the NT writers comforted and stabilized their congregations was by appealing to the higher court of opinion that was God's and by transvaluing suffering and death as an honorable participation in the *basileia* (kingdom) revealed in Jesus. Notice, for example, how Paul in 1 Cor 1:18–31 turns the tables on the "wisdom of the world," which sees the cross of Jesus as foolishness, with the "wisdom of the cross," which sees Jesus' death and resurrection as life-giving, and challenges his readers: "Let the one who boasts, boast in the Lord" (1 Cor 1:31). And as we have already noted, Paul in Rom 1:16 uses litotes to express his "boast" in the Lord: "I am not ashamed of the gospel." He contrasts those who boast of their own accomplishments (Rom 2:17, 23; 3:27) with those whose boast is in what God has done in Jesus Christ (5:2, 11), a boasting that is possible even in the midst of afflictions (Rom 5:3).

Grasping some of this cultural context helps us appreciate both the real-life seriousness of Timothy's situation and the force of Paul's rhetoric in response. The letter gives us ample insight into why Timothy should feel shame. He is as-

---

507. Malina, *New Testament World*; B. Malina and J. H. Neyrey, "Honor and Shame in Luke–Acts: Pivotal Values of the Mediterranean World," in *The Social World of Luke–Acts: Models for Interpretation*, ed. J. H. Neyrey (Peabody, Mass.: Hendrickson, 1991), 25–65.

508. V. K. Robbins, *The Tapestry of Early Christian Discourse: Rhetoric, Society, and Ideology* (London: Routledge, 1996), 144–191.

509. De Silva, *Despising Shame: Honor Discourse and Community Maintenance in the Epistle to the Hebrews*, SBLDS 152 (Atlanta: Scholars Press, 1995).

510. D. A. DeSilva, *The Hope of Glory: Honor Discourse and New Testament Interpretation* (Collegeville: Liturgical Press, 1999).

sociated with a Messiah whose "witness" (*martyrion*) ended in antiquity's most shameful form of death.[511] He is the junior colleague of an apostle who is himself in chains for proclaiming the message about Jesus: "I am suffering even to the point of imprisonment, and this as a criminal [*kakourgos*]" (2:9). That apostle's mission is further discredited by the fact that no one is willing to come to his defense (4:16), and many of his associates have abandoned him completely (1:15; 4:10). Finally, Timothy himself is facing opposition from Paul's opponents (4:15). The letter also suggests the effect that such shame is having on Timothy: he is in danger of giving way to cowardice (1:7) and letting his commitment to the gospel die out (1:6). This cowardice is shown by avoidance of the suffering being experienced by Paul (1:8). The most specific sign of this avoidance is the refusal to come to Paul in his final and shameful moments (1:4; 4:9, 21).

The entire rhetoric of 2 Timothy specifically addresses the personal situation of Paul's delegate, but since the language of shame and cowardice occurs most frequently in this passage, it is helpful to note how Paul's response helps recast the categories. We observe first how Paul's invocation of the tradition of ancestral faith, both his own and Timothy's maternal forebears, serves to provide an alternative human court of opinion. If Timothy is tempted to cowardice in the face of actual or possible suffering and its attendant shame, Paul's rhetoric reminds him that within their shared culture, there is also deep shame consequent on abandoning one's ancestral traditions and, above all, one's friends.

Paul places the situation in which he and Timothy find themselves within an even greater court of opinion, that of God. It is God who called him, God who gifted him, God who "entrusted to him" this tradition, God who saved him. Timothy is answerable not only to Paul and his own maternal ancestors, but to God. His response to God, however, is mediated by his response to "our Lord Christ Jesus." Paul reminds Timothy that the "witness of our Lord" (1:8) is not a cause for shame, because through his death, he destroyed death and brought to light life and immortality (1:10)—there are no higher benefits than these!

Finally, Paul evokes the power of that spirit that has been given to Timothy (1:7, 14). Timothy will be able to "keep the deposit" because it is not only his own strength on which he must rely. It is the power of the God who was "strong enough" to destroy death and reveal life, and who is "strong enough" to sustain the preachers of the gospel. Filled with such power, Timothy can demonstrate those same qualities of faith and love that he sees exemplified in Paul—qualities that are "in Christ Jesus" as well. Active faith and active love are covenantal qualities that involve bonds of loyalty and commitment to his network of family and friends as well as to God. Finally, this Holy Spirit can give Timothy the *sōphronismos*, the self-control (1:7), that will enable him to overcome his temptation to cowardice and take his share of suffering for the gospel at the side of Paul.

---

511. M. Hengel, *Crucifixion in the Ancient World and the Message of the Cross*. Trans. J. Bowden (London: Sem Press, 1977).

IV. THE EXAMPLE SET BY ONESIPHORUS (1:15–18)

◆

1   ¹⁵You know this fact: that all those in Asia, among them Phygelos and Hermogenes, have abandoned me. ¹⁶May the Lord grant mercy to Onesiphorus's household! Many times he refreshed me. He was not ashamed of my chains! ¹⁷Rather, once in Rome, he sought me eagerly and he found me. ¹⁸May the Lord grant him to find mercy in that day. And you know well how many services he rendered in Ephesus.

NOTES

15. *You know this fact*: Two verbs of knowing bracket this section concerning Onesiphorus, providing a clue to its literary function. Timothy knows (*oidas*) the fact (*touto*, literally, "this thing")—what has happened in Asia (1:15)—and he knows (*ginōskeis*) what service Onesiphorus has done (1:17). Why, then, does Paul tell him what he already knows? As a reminder and as an example that he should imitate.

all those in Asia: The statement is hyperbolic (4:11, 21), but Paul and his reader undoubtedly know who are included in the designation "those in Asia" beyond Phygelos and Hermogenes (members of the mission scattered throughout the Roman province of Asia? members of the community in Ephesus?), and how many are included by the word "all" (*pantes*). However inaccurate literally, the statement apparently expresses an emotional truth about Paul's sense of abandonment.

have abandoned me: The verb *apostrephein* denotes a turning away from something, and figuratively connotes a rejection or disaffection (Xenophon, *Cyropaedia* 5.5.36; 3 Macc 3:23; 4 Macc 5:9; Josephus, *Antiquities* 4:135). Paul will use the verb again in 4:4 of those who are turning away from the hearing of the truth. In this case, there may be a combination of physical abandonment (thus the significance of Onesiphorus's gesture) and spiritual disaffection. See also the statement in 4:16 that nobody stood by him at his first defense.

Phygelos and Hermogenes: Phygelos does not appear anywhere else in our literature. Hermogenes appears as a character in the *Acts of Paul and Thecla*, but as "Hermogenes the coppersmith," who opposes Paul (AP 1). Note the resemblance to "Alexander the coppersmith" in 2 Tim 4:14. An "Alexander" also appears in *Acts of Paul and Thecla* 26 as a would-be suitor of Thecla. Paul does not here connect Phygelos and Hermogenes to the false teachers, and it may be that they, like Demas in 4:10, had simply left the mission.

16. *May the Lord grant mercy*: Here and in 1:18, Paul uses the optative of *didōmi* to express a wish. As noted in 1 Timothy, there is an unusual concentration of *eleos* (mercy) language in the letters to Paul's delegates (1 Tim 1:2, 13, 16; 2 Tim 1:2, 16, 18; Tit 3:5), although it is not absent from Paul's other letters (Rom 9:23, 15, 16, 18; 11:30–31, 32; 12:8; 15:9; 1 Cor 7:25; 2 Cor 4:1; Phil 2:27; Eph 2:4). Of special interest is the prayer for *eleos* in Gal 6:16.

to Onesiphorus's household: Onesiphorus does not appear elsewhere in the canonical writings, but he (and his household!) reappear in 2 Tim 4:19. He is also a character in the *Acts of Paul and Thecla* as a householder and helper of Paul. See the discussion in the COMMENT.

Many times he refreshed me: The verb *anapsychein*, as its etymology suggests, means to "re-vive" or "re-fresh" someone (Josephus, *Antiquities* 15:54; in the noun form, see Philo, *On Abraham* 152; Acts 3:20). In this verse, it is likely that Paul uses the term the way he does the similar verb *anapauō*, to indicate financial support or assistance (1 Cor 16:18; 2 Cor 7:13; Phm 7, 20). This may well be why the household of Onesiphorus is included in Paul's blessing, because it provided him with hospitality during his active ministry.

not ashamed of my chains: The phrase "my chains" (*halysis mou*) is synecdoche for Paul's captivity. In contrast to Paul's delegate, whose shame at Paul's imprisonment makes him cowardly and keeps him from visiting, Onesiphorus is not ashamed, just as Paul himself is not ashamed to suffer for the sake of the good news (1:12).

17. *once in Rome*: Literally, "being in Rome" (*genomenos en rhōmē*), but the aorist participle suggests that he arrived and then sought and found the apostle. This verse is the main reason, together with the reference to Paul's "first defense" in 4:16, for considering Rome as the place from which Paul writes, since that city also agrees with Acts 28:30–31 concerning Paul's captivity there at the end of his career. The convoluted exegesis of this verse in service of making Caesarea the place of captivity and composition is unconvincing.[512]

sought me eagerly and he found me: Many MSS have the comparative of the adverb *spoudaiōs*: *spoudaioteron/ōs* (Codex Alexandrinus, the corrector of Bezae, and the Koine tradition). The plain *spoudaiōs* is read by Sinaiticus, Ephraemi, and the original hand of Bezae. The comparative "more eagerly" would make an even sharper contrast between Onesiphorus and the reluctant Timothy. Note that in 4:9, Paul tells Timothy to "be eager" (*spoudason*) to come to him quickly.

18. *find mercy in that day*: The phrase "in that day" clearly echoes 1:12, and like the previous usage, refers to the day of judgment and of reward. That Onesiphorus "find" (*heurein*) mercy at that time deliberately picks up his "seeking and finding" Paul in Rome.

you know well: The neuter comparative adjective *beltion* is used adverbially and can mean either "you know better than me" or, as I have translated it, "you

---

512. Robinson, *Redating the New Testament*, 67–85.

know well." The flat statement *ginōskeis* (you know) forms a bracket around the section dealing with Onesiphorus and makes clear its paraenetic function.

how many services: The relative adjective *hosos* is here in the neuter plural, and the verb *diakonein* is aorist, so the phrase is literally "how many things he provided service." As with *anapsychein*, the verb *diakonein* in all likelihood — as in other significant Pauline contexts — refers to financial services or assistance (Rom 15:25, 31; 2 Cor 8:4, 19–20; 9:1, 12, 13; 11:8).

he rendered in Ephesus: Some textual witnesses (e.g., 104, 365, the Old Latin, the Clementine Vulgate, and the Syriac) have *emoi* (to me), which would once more emphasize the personal character of Onesiphorus's service in contrast to Timothy's. These texts may have been influenced by Paul's statement concerning the service of Onesimus "to me" (*moi*) in Phm 13.

COMMENT

The appearance of the personal names Phygelos, Hermogenes, and Onesiphorus in 1:15–18 sets up two interrelated literary questions. The first concerns the historical context for the names themselves. As mentioned in the NOTE on 1:15, Hermogenes and Onesiphorus, plus Titus and Demas — but not Timothy! — appear also in the apocryphal *Acts of Paul and Thecla*, a composition that is usually dated in the second half of the second century. And they interact with Paul in Iconium after his flight from Antioch (*AP* 1), place-names also mentioned in 2 Tim 3:11. In *De Baptismo* 17, Tertullian claims that *Paul and Thecla* was written by a presbyter of Asia Minor, but we cannot be certain about this attribution. In the Commentary on 1 Timothy, I touched on the way *Paul and Thecla* has figured into hypotheses concerning 1 Tim 5:3–16 and the possibility of a nascent women's ministry in second-century Christianity.

In 2 Timothy, all these characters, except Onesiphorus, are associates of Paul who have in one way or another left him. Phygelos and Hermogenes "abandoned" him; Demas went to Thessalonica because he was "in love with this world" (4:10). Titus, though, simply went to Dalmatia, presumably on a mission (4:10). In the *Acts of Paul and Thecla*, Titus and Onesiphorus are loyal to Paul. Indeed, Onesiphorus provides hospitality to Paul in his household in Iconium (*AP* 3–5). Demas and Hermogenes, in contrast, are jealous of Paul's success in Iconium and seek to destroy him. They are, in fact, identified as the opponents who say that "the resurrection has already taken place" (*AP* 14; compare 2 Tim 2:17–18, where the statement is attributed to Hymenaios and Philetos). Each writing also has characters (the *AP* many more of them, including the names of Onesiphorus's wife and children) not found in the other.

The question, therefore, is what to make of this overlapping of dramatis personae. There can be no question of literary dependence in the strict sense: the compositions are in different genres, have totally different outlooks, and share only the few verbal echoes I have named. It is possible that the author of the

Acts of Paul and Thecla simply mined 2 Timothy for some of these biographical details and wove them into a novelistic account for his own purposes—mainly the glorification of Thecla and the advancement of an ascetic form of Christian life (esp. *AP* 5–6). Logically, if we were to suppose a very late dating for the Pastorals and think Tertullian's dating of *AP* too late, we could also imagine that the *Acts of Paul and Thecla* were written first. In this case, the Pastorals would be pseudonymous compositions that lifted the names and places from *AP* in order to present a very different sort of Paul. He would not be the sponsor of asceticism, but a critic of it; not be someone who cooperated (even if reluctantly) with free-spirited women evangelists, but who worried about susceptible women who "were always learning but were never capable of reaching recognition of truth." Finally, there is the theory that both 2 Timothy and *AP* drew independently from local or regional folk stories concerning Paul and Thecla, with each composition not responding to the other, but independently advancing competitive versions of Pauline Christianity in second-century Asia.[513] Lacking any firm external controls, scholarly judgments must rest on which construal of the evidence seems most reasonable, and readers can legitimately disagree in their conclusions. The position I adopt concerning the authenticity of 2 Timothy on a variety of other grounds obviously affects my judgment on this matter as well. But the further elaboration of secondary and tertiary characters is such a standard feature of fictional apocrypha (compare, e.g., *The Acts of Pilate*), that the most plausible hypothesis is that *AP* lifted some details from 2 Timothy and used them creatively.

The Paraenetic Function of Onesiphorus

Discussions about the literary relationships between 2 Timothy and the *Acts of Paul and Thecla* should not distract from the important literary function of these three verses in 2 Timothy. Paul has already responded to his perception that Timothy is fearful and ashamed to share in the suffering entailed by the proclamation of the good news by offering his own example of unashamed suffering for the gospel. Onesiphorus clearly serves to provide another example.

In contrast to all those who abandoned Paul—and, by implication, Timothy's reluctance to visit him can also be so construed—Onesiphorus showed no shame at Paul's chains. He came to Rome. He sought Paul out. He found him. Such eagerness, courage, and generosity with his own resources were consistent with the constant service that Onesiphorus had already shown to Paul in Ephesus. The point is plain. Timothy is also to imitate the unashamed courage of Onesiphorus and, by visiting Paul, take his share of the suffering for the good news. Further examples follow, but this one is particularly poignant, for Onesiphorus is someone just like Timothy who has done what Timothy is apparently afraid to do.

---

513. The three positions are enunciated, respectively, in Rohde "Pastoralbriefe und *Acta Pauli*"; Mayer, *Über die Pastoralbriefe*; and MacDonald, *Legend and the Apostle*.

V. MORE EXAMPLES FOR
IMITATION (2:1–7)

◆

2 ¹Be strengthened therefore, my child, by the gift that is in Christ Jesus. ²The things that you heard me say in the presence of many witnesses you must entrust to men who are faithful and will be competent enough to teach others as well. ³Take your share of suffering as a good soldier of Christ Jesus. ⁴No one serving military duty allows himself to become entangled in everyday matters — so that he might please his recruiter. ⁵And also, if any one competes in an athletic contest he won't be crowned unless he competes by the rules. ⁶The hardworking farmer ought to share first in the fruits of the harvest. ⁷Grasp what I am telling you. For the Lord will give you quickness of understanding in all these matters.

NOTES

1. *Be strengthened*: The connective *oun* (therefore) indicates that this exhortation is based on what has preceded, as discussed in the COMMENT. The verb *endynamoun* means "to strengthen" someone or something (LXX Judg 6:34 [in some mss]) and is used in the active voice in Phil 4:13 ("I can do all things in the one who strengthens me") and 1 Tim 1:12 ("I give thanks to the one who has strengthened me, Christ Jesus"). Here it appears in the passive voice, as in Rom 4:20 (where Paul speaks of Abraham "being strengthened in faith"), and Eph 6:10 (where Paul tells his readers to "be strengthened in the Lord"). Paul will use the same verb at the end of this letter (2 Tim 4:17): "But the Lord stood by me and strengthened me." We are clearly still in the realm of that "power" (*dynamis*) of the Holy Spirit established by 1:7–8, 12.

the gift that is in Christ Jesus: Here, as in other places, the the articular prepositional phrase *tē chariti tē en Christō Iēsou* intrigues because of its polyvalent potential. Clearly, God is the source of Timothy's empowerment. But if the grace/gift is "in Christ Jesus," does he mean the Holy Spirit that comes through Jesus' agency, or does he mean those qualities of existence that were Jesus' own (1:13)?

2. *The things that you heard me say*: This phrase also echoes 1:13, where Paul speaks of the healthy words "which you heard from me" (*hōn par' emou ēkousas*). The process of communication is direct and personal, rather than institutional.

in the presence of many witnesses: The phrase *dia tōn pollōn martyrōn* can also be translated as "through many witnesses," but "in the presence of" is also possible.[514] Paul gathers even more figures into the network of those *martyroi* before whose eyes Timothy is invited to perceive his own attitude and behavior. The reminder of the public character of Timothy's participation as a student hearing Paul's words serves rhetorically to renew that profession.

entrust to men who are faithful: The verb *paratithēmi* is the verb cognate to *parathēkē* (that which is entrusted/deposit) in 1:12, 14. The verb occurs in 1 Cor 10:27, but only in its sense of "setting at table." The phrase *pistois anthrōpois* could be translated as "faithful people," since *anthrōpos* is inclusive for all humans, in contrast to *anēr*, which can mean only males. I translate "faithful men," however, because that is clearly what the text means. In the case of the Pastorals, an attempt to create a gender-inclusive translation only camouflages the pervasive androcentrism of the composition. For better or worse, the assumptions of the author's culture (or place within his culture) should be accepted by the translation. It is the task of hermeneutics to decide what to do about those assumptions. More critical to exegesis is the recognition that the quality of being *pistos* (faithful) is precisely the one most desired (1:5, 12, 13). We are reminded of 1 Cor 4:2, where Paul makes the same point with respect to Apollos and himself: stewards of God's mysteries are expected first of all to be *pistoi*.

competent enough to teach others: The translation tries to capture the adjectival quality of *hoitines hikanoi esontai*. The adjective *hikanos* basically has a quantitative sense of "large enough" (Plato, *Laws* 736C; Rom 15:23), but also can have the qualitative sense of "qualified" (Plato, *Protagoras* 322B; *Letter to Aristeas* 211), as used by Paul in 1 Cor 15:9 and 2 Cor 2:16; 3:5; see also the cognates in 2 Cor 3:6, and Col 1:12. The use of the future *esontai* makes clear that the personal character of being faithful is not the same as the skill to teach others; for that task, these people need to become *hikanos* (competent). The phrasing neatly combines the classic Hellenistic convictions concerning the teacher: the truth is witnessed to both through deeds and in words.

3. *Take your share of suffering:* The second-person-singular imperative of this rare verb points us to two other places in the letter, back to 1:8 and forward to 4:5, reminding us that this is the central commitment that Paul is trying to encourage in his delegate. The imperative also sets up the next sequence of examples by establishing their common theme.

as a good soldier of Christ Jesus: The soldier is a standard example in Hellenistic moral discourse (e.g., Plato, *Apology* 28; Epictetus, *Discourse* 3.24.34–36; 3.26.27) for the reasons that Paul's elaboration makes clear: the soldier's dedication, effort, and willingness to suffer in order to accomplish a goal are morally transferable qualities. Paul uses the metaphor also in 1 Cor 9:7 (see the COMMENT) and employs the military metaphor for the work of the mission in 2 Cor 10:3–4 as well as in 1 Tim 1:18. The literalization of the metaphor that has led

---

514. C. F. D. Moule, *An Idiom-Book of New Testament Greek*, 2nd ed. (Cambridge: Cambridge University Press, 1959), 57.

to such unfortunate distortions in Christian behavior—through crusades and holy wars of every stripe—is not to be blamed on Paul. The phrase "of Christ Jesus" therefore does not mean that Timothy is to fight as a soldier for Christ, but is to demonstrate the same attitudes toward the service of Jesus that the soldier does toward the one who recruited him. For the image of God as a military general, see Philo, *On Providence* 2:61; Maximus of Tyre, *Discourse* 10:9; Epictetus, *Discourse* 3.24.35.

4. *No one serving military duty*: Some MSS (F, G, and Latin witnesses) add the words *tō theō* (for God) here, clearly missing the intended analogy, but instead carrying forward the notion of being a "good soldier for Christ" in the previous verse.

allows himself to become entangled: The verb *emplekomai* has almost the same sense as the English word "implicated"; literally it means to "get entangled" (as in thorns, see *Shepherd of Hermas*, *Similitudes* 6.2.6), and figuratively to "get involved" (Epictetus, *Discourse* 3.22.69; Polybius, *Histories* 24.11.3). It is the distracting quality of such involvement that is problematic (compare 1 Cor 7:28–35).

in everyday matters: The noun *pragmateia* can mean simply an "occupation" (Josephus, *Antiquities* 1:5), but here it has the sense of business affairs or undertakings that concern material existence (*tou biou*). Compare Philo, *Special Laws* 2:65, and Paul's slighting allusion to *ta biotika* in 1 Cor 6:3.

to please his recruiter: The verb *stratologein* means to "assemble soldiers" or "recruit" (Diodorus Siculus, *Library of History* 12.67.5; Dionysius of Halicarnassus, *Roman Antiquities* 11:24; Josephus, *Jewish War* 5:380). Paul uses here the attributive participle in the aorist: "the one who had recruited him." The analogy works particularly well because Paul has established that Timothy and he have been "called . . . by a holy calling" (1:9).

5. *competes in an athletic contest*: The athlete is again one of the most widely used exemplars for moral effort in Hellenistic philosophy (Epictetus, *Discourses* 3.24.34–35). Paul makes an extended use of the image in 1 Cor 9:14–27.

be crowned: The *stephanos* is the garland wreath that is placed on the heads of winners of athletic contests, and the sign of the honor they have won by their exploits (Herodotus, *Persian War* 8:59; Diodorus Siculus, *Library of History* 20.84.3). By extension, it becomes metaphorical for all forms of being honored or rewarded (1 Cor 9:25; Phil 4:1; 1 Thess 2:19; 1 Pet 5:4; Rev 2:10; James 1:12). See, especially, the *stephanos tēs dikaiosynēs* in 4:8.

competes by the rules: The adverb *nomimōs* is found also in 1 Tim 1:8. Unlike its obscure use in that verse, here it clearly has the straightforward meaning suggested by the translation (4 Macc 6:18; Josephus, *Against Apion* 2:152; *Sibylline Oracles* 11:82; for the athletic analogy, see Epictetus, *Discourse* 3.10.8).

6. *hardworking farmer*: As the soldier and the athlete, so also the farmer (*geōrgos*) is a stock example for moral learning in the Greco-Roman world (Epictetus, *Discourses* 4.8.35–40; James 5:7). In 1 Cor 9:7, Paul attaches the examples of the vine-grower and shepherd to that of the soldier. The verb *kopiaō* denotes hard labor even to the point of exhaustion (Josephus, *Antiquities* 2:321;

Philo, *On Change of Names* 254; *On the Cherubim* 41; 1 Cor 4:12). Paul uses it frequently for "laboring" in the mission (Rom 16:6, 12; 1 Cor 15:10; 16:16; Gal 4:11; Phil 2:16; 1 Thess 5:12); see, especially, 1 Tim 4:10 and 5:17. The placement of the phrase *ton kopiōnta geōrgon* puts the emphasis on the laboring more than on the reward.

share first in the fruits of the harvest: The phrase "of the harvest" are supplied by my translation; the Greek reads literally "must first of the fruits take a share." The original hand of Sinaiticus has the comparative *proteron* (earlier), rather than *prōton* (first). The verb *metalambanein* ordinarily takes the genitive of the thing shared (Josephus, *Jewish War* 2:143).

7. *Grasp what I am telling you*: This is literally "know what I am saying"; I have added "you." Rather than the singular neuter relative pronoun *ho*, a great many MSS have *ha* (neuter plural relative pronoun), in order to make the clause refer to all the points that Paul had been making. Since the sentence ends with *en pasin* (in all things), this can be seen as a fairly obvious correction.

the Lord will give you: A significant number of textual witnesses (e.g., the third hand of Ephraemi Rescriptus and the Koine tradition) have the subjunctive optative *dōē* (may the Lord give), rather than the future indicative *dōsei*. The variant is probably due to the influence of the repetition of *dōē* in 1:16, 18.

quickness of understanding: My translation tries to capture the nuance of "putting things together" implicit in the noun *synesis* (Plato, *Cratylus* 412A; *Philebus* 19D). The function of this verse is to alert Timothy to the metaphorical or analogical mode of argument that Paul has been following by listing these examples in such succinct fashion: without having to spell it out, he expects Timothy to get the point.

COMMENT

The literary unfolding of 2 Timothy continues to follow the classic lines of a personal paraenetic letter. The theme of memory was struck immediately and insistently in 1:3–6, and, with it, the theme of the imitation of models. Timothy is to maintain the same ancestral faith as his mother and grandmother (1:5) and to imitate the example of healthy teaching and suffering for the gospel that he saw in Paul (1:8–14). The mention of Onesiphorus in 1:15–17 is by no means haphazard, either: he provides the most pointed example of how Timothy can prove loyal in the present circumstances, by risking danger and visiting Paul in prison. Now Paul follows with three rapid-fire and extremely cryptic moral exemplars, which are standard for Greco-Roman moral instruction: the soldier (2:3–4), the athlete (2:5), and the farmer (2:8–13). This series of examples will reach its climax in the next section, where Paul will tell Timothy to "keep on remembering Jesus Christ."

I will take up these specific examples for discussion later in the COMMENT, with an interest particularly in the way they resemble and differ from the use of the same three examples by Paul in 1 Cor 9. But it is also noteworthy that the identical pattern of exemplification is found in one of Paul's undisputed letters, the Letter to the Philippians. In the INTRODUCTION to 2 Timothy, I touched on the many resemblances between these two captivity letters. But their shared form of argument—especially as applied to two different subjects—is most striking.

Examples in Philippians and 2 Timothy

In Philippians, Paul is seeking to turn a community from attitudes of envy and rivalry to attitudes of fellowship and cooperation[515] by advising them to look to others' interests and not merely their own (Phil 2:1–4). The lesson is to live in service to others, rather than only to oneself. Paul then illustrates the attitude he wants them to have by a series of examples:

1. He begins by exhorting the Philippians to have "the mind of Christ," which is demonstrated by Jesus' self-emptying obedience to God (Phil 2:5–11).
2. Paul then presents himself as one who has poured himself out as a libation for them (Phil 2:14–18).
3. Then Timothy is portrayed as one who is "genuinely anxious for your welfare" in contrast to those who "look after their own interests" (Phil 2:19–24).
4. Epaphroditus is next mentioned as one who has been longing to see the Philippians and who "nearly died for the work of Christ, risking his life to complete your service to me" (Phil 2:25–30).
5. In an extended presentation of himself as an example, Paul shows how he did not cling to his privileges as a Jew, but "counted them as nothing" in order to "share in the sufferings" of Christ (Phil 3:1–16).

Paul concludes this series of examples by saying, "Brethren, join in imitating me, and mark those who so live as you have an example in us" (Phil 3:17). In Philippians, then, we have a statement of principle; a series of five examples that in various ways illustrate that principle, including such real people as Timothy, Epahroditus, Paul himself, and, above all, Jesus; and a final call to imitation.

In 2 Timothy, Paul is trying to convince his delegate to take courage and share in suffering for the gospel. The lesson is that it is necessary to suffer in order to participate in the good news. And he once more presents a series of examples for imitation:

1. Paul himself, who suffers in chains for the good news (1:8–14)
2. Onesiphorus, who was not ashamed and shared Paul's chains (1:15–18)
3. The soldier who avoids distraction to serve his recruiter well (2:3–4)

---

515. Johnson, *Writings of the New Testament*, 338–349. See also W. Kurz, "Kenotic Imitation of Paul and Christ in Phil. 2 and 3," in *Discipleship in the New Testament*, ed. F. Segovia (Philadelphia: Fortress Press, 1985), 103–126.

4. The athlete who competes by the rules to win a crown (2:5)
5. The farmer who works hard to get a share of the harvest (2:6)
6. Jesus, who suffered and then entered into life (2:8–13)

The similarity in argumentation is unmistakable and, together with the frequently noted resemblances between the letters in terms of style and situation, suggest either a very close imitation of this specific undisputed letter by a skilled pseudepigrapher or the argumentative instincts of the same rhetorician.

Institutional Strategy or Charismatic Power?

This section of 2 Timothy provides another opportunity to test reading strategies found in diverse approaches to the Pastorals. From the perspective of the conventional view, in which all the Pastorals are a single, pseudonymous composition, 1:15–2:13 appears as an ill-coordinated series of statements that mix instructional and autobiographical elements without any real logic or argumentation.[516] The mention of personal names in 1:15–18 appears as intrusive, perhaps at best a fictional embellishment without any real hortatory function. The analogies of 2:3–7, likewise, are scrambled adaptations of Pauline analogies. All these elements are, in this reading, simply the accoutrements of pseudepigraphy. The real key to the passage is 2:1–2. Indeed, it is the key to the function of the Pastorals as a whole: Timothy is instructed to "entrust" (*paratithēmi* is cognate with *parathēkē* in 1:12, 14) the things he heard from Paul to other faithful men who, in turn, can teach them to others.

What this passage is about, in short, is the transmission of the Pauline tradition from one generation to the next. 2 Timothy—specifically 2:1–2—functions as the (pseudo)-biographical legitimation for a conservative Paulinism that is found in the mandates of both 1 Timothy and Titus. The phrase *dia pollōn martyrōn* in 2:2 appears to such readers as providing strong support for this interpretation, for it is read as meaning "through many witnesses." The pseudonymous author has inadvertently revealed his real situation: the author stands chronologically at some distance from the historical Paul, and the tradition has been handed from one generation of witnesses to the next.[517]

The author of 2 Timothy, in other words, is in reality one of those "faithful men" who is "competent enough to teach others as well." The readers of 2 Timothy are those "others" of a later generation who are being taught the things that Paul said. In fact, however, Paul's tradition has undergone a fairly substantial change in the direction of domestication, so that the fiction is not entirely innocent.

---

516. It is instructive, I think, that contemporary studies of the Pastorals do not read the letters *as* letters, but cut sections out of them according to a topical arrangement. The specific kinds of arguments being made by the sentences and sections in sequence are ignored.

517. See, for example, P. Trummer, *Paulustradition der Pastoralbriefe*, 189–190.

Another reading of the passage is, however, available and appealing. What happens if readers take seriously the context suggested by the letter's self-presentation (with Paul as a captive experiencing abandonment by his co-workers) and the rhetoric of personal paraenesis (which teaches character through the imitation of models)? The autobiographical elements now appear not as incidental ornamentation for an institutional strategy, but as the essential argument. We remind ourselves of the point made by the preceding section (1:6–14):

1. Timothy should not give in to cowardice, but should take hold of the *power* that is his by gift.
2. He should not be ashamed of the witness of Jesus or of Paul because of his chains.
3. He should preserve the teaching and character of Paul as he saw them displayed in Paul's own behavior.
4. He should take his share of suffering for the gospel, for suffering is intrinsic to the good news.

The same four elements are now elaborated through the use of examples in 1:15–2:7. The personal names in 1:15–18 function as part of the argument. Phygelos and Hermogenes are antithetically opposed to Onesiphorus, as differing ways of responding to Paul's situation. The first two have abandoned him, together with "all those in Asia." In contrast, Onesiphorus stands as an example of fidelity to Paul. The subtle note in 1:16 that "he was not ashamed of my chains" is the all-important clue to Paul's rhetorical aim. Onesiphorus was willing eagerly to seek Paul out and find him (1:17). He thereby took upon himself the danger of suffering with the apostle. Paul expects Timothy to take the same risk (4:9, 21). Onesiphorus also exemplifies the pattern of "suffer now, reward later." Paul prays that his loyalty and that of his household will be rewarded with mercy "in that day" (1:18).

Onesiphorus's example of strength in loyalty immediately precedes Paul's direct exhortation to Timothy: "Be strengthened therefore, my child" (2:1). The connective "therefore" is scarcely incidental, but shows that the exhortation builds directly on what preceded. Timothy is to be empowered, we note, by that "gift" (*charis*) in Christ Jesus that Paul spoke of in 1:9 as having been given to them, and echoes the "special gift for service" (*charisma*) in 1:6 that Paul characterized in terms of power (*dynamis*). Timothy's empowerment here must be understood, in other words, as an actualization of that gift bestowed by the Holy Spirit dwelling in him (1:14). Paul wants Timothy to claim and use that gift by exhibiting attitudes of loyalty and courage.

It is in this connection that we are to understand the instruction in 2:2. Paul is being abandoned by some, although not all, of his followers. Others, we shall see, are becoming or are following false teachers. Before coming to Paul personally, therefore, Timothy is to express his loyalty and courage in the first place by extending the influence of Paul and building the network of "faithful people" committed to the same message. Timothy is asked to remain loyal himself and to build up a cadre of those loyal to Paul. In this reading, the problematic phrase *dia pollōn martyrōn* is read not in terms of a succession of generations, but in its possible sense of "in the presence of many witnesses." The phrase stands as another reminder to Timothy of the living network of believers of which he is a part and which he is now called on to extend and strengthen. Timothy is to act now to extend the "healthy teaching" by recruiting more teachers. As he has benefited from the human network of faith and loyalty, so he is to take responsibility now for extending it to and through others.

The Necessity of Suffering

For Timothy to accept this responsibility for leadership in the Pauline mission will inevitably mean effort, struggle, and perhaps even personal suffering. Paul therefore lays before him in remarkably compressed fashion three standard exemplars of Hellenistic moral teaching: the soldier, the athlete, and the farmer. The reason these were such pervasive and popular examples is that each represented the active, strenuous life, fitting in particular the Stoic–Cynic understanding of moral progress as a kind of struggle for self-mastery.

As noted, Paul uses the same examples in 1 Cor 9. It will be remembered that the overall function of 1 Cor 9 within the context of 1 Cor 8–10 is to present Paul himself as an example to the Corinthians of behavior that gives up legitimate rights in order to serve others.[518] In that letter, Paul emphasizes the reward side of the examples, since the point he is making there is that preachers have the right to financial support. So, he argues, the soldier does not serve "at his own expense" (1 Cor 9:7), while those who plant vines and tend herds also expect recompense (1 Cor 9:7). The plowman, he says, "should plow in hope, and the thresher in hope of a share in the crop" (1 Cor 9:10). Likewise, he later invokes the athlete, partly to note the need for self-discipline, but mostly to emphasize that athletes compete for a prize (1 Cor 9:24), a "perishable wreath" (1 Cor 9:25).

In 2 Timothy, Paul uses the same examples to stress a different point. Paul here wants to emphasize the necessity of doing one's job and putting up with what it requires (its "suffering") as the basis for the expectation of a reward. Thus the example of the soldier is turned in the direction of discipline: he seeks to please his recruiting officer and, therefore, must not get involved in the distractions offered by everyday matters (2:4). Timothy should be that sort of "noble soldier" for Christ Jesus (2:3). Likewise, the athlete must play by the rules if he hopes to be crowned, and these rules inevitably involve discipline and hardship (2:5). Finally, and most cryptically, Paul says it is the hard-working farmer who can expect to have a first share in the crop (2:6). The examples are tossed

---

518. For Paul's use of analogies in 1 Cor 9, see Robbins, "Intertexture: Every Comparison has Boundaries," in *Tapestry of Early Christian Discourse*, 96–143.

off quickly. Paul expects Timothy to "get them"; he is, after all, himself a teacher. Paul expects him to understand the point of all this: one needs to be willing to suffer if one wants to gain a reward.

It remains to ask which angle of vision on this passage yields the better reading. Those who consider the Pastorals pseudonymous can make something of a case for the function of 2:1–2, but give no account of the rest of the passage. The reading that takes the self-presentation and rhetoric of the letter seriously can make sense of everything.

VI. JESUS AS
EXEMPLAR (2:8–13)

◆

2 ⁸Keep on remembering Jesus Christ. According to the good news I preach, he is raised from the dead, he is from the seed of David. ⁹For this good news I am suffering even to the point of being enchained as a criminal. But the word of God is not enchained. ¹⁰This is why I endure all things for the sake of the chosen ones, that they also might attain salvation with eternal glory, which is found in Christ Jesus. ¹¹The word is faithful! For if we have died together, then we shall also live together. ¹²If we endure, we shall reign together. If we deny him, he will deny us. ¹³If we are unfaithful, he still remains faithful, for he is not able to deny himself.

NOTES

8. *Keep on remembering Jesus Christ*: I translate the present imperative *mnēmoneue* with full force as expressing continual action (compare 1 Thess 2:9), since the point for paraenesis is not a momentary recall, but a persistent and formative recollection. Paul uses the verb *mnēmoneuein* also in Gal 2:10; Eph 2:11; Col 4:18. It is striking that there are no textual variants for the sequence "Jesus Christ," and given the preponderant use of "Christ Jesus" in this letter (1:1–2, 9–10, 13; 2:1, 3, 10; 3:12, 15; 4:1), we may be justified in seeing in this case a special emphasis on the human person, Jesus. A similar alternation is observable in Paul's undisputed letters (e.g., Rom 3:22, 26; 5:1, in contrast to Rom 6:3, 11, 23; 8:1–2).

According to the good news I preach: For the phrase *kata to euangelion mou* (literally, "according to my gospel"), see Rom 2:16. This is now the third use of the term *euangelion* (see also 1:8, 10).

he is raised from the dead: The verb *egeirein* (to raise) is here in the form of the perfect passive participle. The tense strictly suggests past action with continuing consequences: he was raised and is still raised.[519] Since the participle lacks the definite article, it could be either attributive ("who was raised from the dead") or predicative (e.g., "as he has been raised from the dead"). The second

---

519. E. D. Burton, *Syntax of the Moods and Tenses in New Testament Greek*, 3rd ed. (Edinburgh: Clark, 1898), 37–39.

would put more emphasis on Jesus' present state; the first would serve as an identity marker (*"that* is the Jesus I mean"). For the use of the perfect passive with this verb, compare 1 Cor 15:4: *hoti egēgertai* (that he has been raised) and 1 Cor 15:14: *ei de christos ouk egēgertai* (but if Christ has not been raised). The phrase *ek nekrōn* means literally "from among the dead ones [*nekroi*]" and is commonplace in the NT (e.g., Mark 12:25; Luke 9:7; 20:35; John 2:22; Acts 3:15; Rom 4:24; Gal 1:1; Eph 1:20; Phil 3:11; 1 Thess 1:10; 1 Pet 1:3).

from the seed of David: Apart from two attributions of the Psalms to their author, in Rom 4:6 and 11:9, Paul refers to David only twice in all his letters, this in sharp contrast to the Gospels, which make the connection between Jesus and David with some frequency (e.g., Matt 1:1, 6, 17, 20; Luke 1:32; 2:4). More striking is the similarity of the two instances. As in the kerygmatic summary of Rom 1:1–4, Paul here combines the resurrection with descent from the seed of David, but does so in reverse order. The sequence in Romans seems the more natural because it is the more chronological, contrasting the (earlier earthly) Jesus to the (now raised) Lord. The order here, however, may have its own logic, as discussed in the COMMENT.

9. *For this good news I am suffering:* The translation supplies "good news" in order to make clear the antecedent for the relative pronoun *en hǭ* (in which) and to compensate for the awkward word order in English. For the verb *kakopathein* (lacking in the undisputed letters), see the NOTE on 1:8. Paul links the *martyrion tou kyriou* (witness/testimony of the Lord) and *eme ton desmion autou* (me his prisoner) as closely as possible.

even to the point of being enchained: The phrase *mechri desmōn* is literally "as far as chains," with the preposition *mechri* governing the genitive case and expressing a measure of degree (Josephus, *Antiquities* 11:81). In the neuter plural, *desmos* is used for bonds or fetters that keep someone captive (e.g., Luke 8:29; Acts 16:26; 26:29). Paul elsewhere uses *ta desma* as synecdoche for "imprisonment" (Phil 1:7, 13, 14, 17; Col 4:18; Phm 10, 13), which is also the meaning here. I retain the literal "chains" in order to signal the literary link with "word of God enchained" (*dedetai*) in the next line.

as a criminal: The term "criminal" (*kakourgos*) is not found in the undisputed letters. It refers generally to a malefactor or an evildoer (*kakos* + *ergon*); see, for example, Herodotus, *Persian War* 1:41; LXX Prov 21:15; Sir 11:33. It can be used of one who stands as a criminal in the eyes of the Law (Josephus, *Antiquities* 2:59; Philo, *Against Flaccus* 75; *Sentences of Pseudo-Phocylides* 133). Apart from this passage, the term appears in the NT only in Luke, applied to the men who were crucified with Jesus (23:32, 33, 39). The last phrase is not therefore incidental or unimportant. For Paul to suffer as a criminal is a far more shameful thing than to be imprisoned as the *martyr* (witness) or *apostolos* (designated representative) of a deity. Note the distinction made by 1 Pet 4:15–16: "But let none of you suffer as a murderer, or a thief, or a wrongdoer [*kakopoios*], or a mischief-maker; yet if one suffers as a Christian, let him not be ashamed, but under that name let him glorify God."

the word of God is not enchained: Although "enchained" is not a common term, I use it to capture the verbal link between Paul's chains (*desmos*), in the preceding line, and the unboundedness of the word of God (*ou dedetai*). The confidence that Paul expresses here is not unlike that in Rom 9:6: *ouch de hoti hoion ekpeptōken ho logos tou theou* (It is not as though the word of God has fallen). Note that in Romans also, Paul puts the verb "fallen" into play with the "falling" of the unbelievers (Rom 11:11, 22).

10. *I endure all things*: For *panta hypomenō* (I endure all things), compare Rom 8:24 and 12:12, and, especially, 1 Cor 13:7, where Paul declares of *agapē* that it "hopes all things, endures all things" (*panta hypomenei*). Paul's declaration here prepares for the statement in 1:12.

for the sake of the chosen ones: The concept of the "elect" or "chosen ones" (*hoi eklektoi*) is found in Torah (1 Chron 16:13; Pss 88:3; 104:6; Isa 65:9, 15), is carried into the NT (Matt 20:16 [variant reading]; 22:14; Luke 18:7), and is used by Paul in Rom 8:33; 16:13 and Col 3:12. In 1 Tim 5:21, Paul speaks of the "elect angels," and in Tit 1:1 of the "elect of God." Paul's description of himself as "living for others" is strikingly similar to those found in 1 Cor 8:13; 9:19–23; 10:33; 2 Cor 4:5–6, 14–15; Phil 1:21–26; Col 1:24.

they also might attain salvation: See the very similar statement in 1 Cor 9:22–23: "I became all things to everyone, so that I might in every way save some of them; and I am doing everything on account of the good news, in order that I might become a sharer in it." See also 1 Tim 4:16: "By doing this you will save yourself and those who are hearing you." Paul's understanding of himself as a "delegate" of Christ involves living out his life according to the same pattern as that enacted by Jesus. Thus his "living for the sake of others" extends the salvific work of the Messiah.

with eternal glory: The phrase comes at the end, but without any clear antecedent or referent in the Greek. I have connected it to salvation, as the expected *telos* expressed by Paul elsewhere (Rom 2:7, 10; 5:2; 8:30; Eph 3:13; 1 Thess 2:12).

which is found in Christ Jesus: As in all these attributive prepositional phrases, evaluating the precise significance is difficult. Is this merely a stylistic flourish, meaning "Christian salvation," or does it have a more specific sense of "the salvation that comes to us through the faith of Jesus the Messiah"? As in the other instances, I am inclined to think that these expressions have more rather than less specific meaning. This is especially so here, because of the way "Christ Jesus" is the only alternative antecedent to the "word of God" for the entire set of statements that follow: *ekeinos* (that one) in 2:12–13 can best be understood as referring to Jesus himself.

11. *The word is faithful*: Although the construction *pistos ho logos* is distinctive of these letters to Paul's delegates (1 Tim 1:15; 3:1; 4:9; Tit 3:8), the use of *pistos* (faithful) to characterize God is typical of Paul (e.g., 1 Cor 1:9; 2 Cor 1:18; 1 Thess 5:24; 2 Thess 3:3) and is applied in 2:13 to Jesus as well. The interpretive issue posed by this phrase is whether to treat it merely as a stereotyped

introduction to a fragment of tradition (this is the option indicated by the editors of Nestle–Aland) or as an independent statement whose antecedent is "the word of God" in 2:9.

if we have died together, . . . we shall also live together: I have translated these balanced clauses without supplying the (implied) referent of the *syn-* constructions—that is, "with him." I do not dispute that such association with Christ seems logically to be intended. The construction is thoroughly Pauline. In Rom 6:8, Paul says *pisteuomen hoti kai syzēsomen autō* (We believe that we shall also live together with him). Even more striking a parallel expression is found in 2 Cor 7:3: *en tais kardiais hēmōn este eis to synapothanein kai syzēn* (You are in our hearts to die together and to live together). This is the basic, deep pattern of Christian existence, imprinted on believers through their initiation into Christ in baptism (Rom 6:1–11).

endure, we shall reign together: The construction "ruling together" (in God's reign) is found ironically in 1 Cor 4:8: *hina kai hēmeis hymin synbasileusomen* (in order that we also might reign together with you). For "endurance" (*hypomenein/hypomonē*) as thematic in Paul, see Rom 2:7; 5:3; 8:24; 12:12; 1 Thess 1:3; 2 Thess 1:4; 3:5; Col 1:11; 1 Tim 6:11; Tit 2:2. Endurance (*hypomonē*) is one of the qualities singled out for Timothy's imitation in 3:10. The fundamental pattern of death/life is now spelled out in terms of power: on one side, enduring what is imposed from without; on the other side, sharing in the power of God's rule.

12. *If we deny him*: The MSS evidence is almost evenly divided between the present tense of the verb "deny" (*arnoumetha*, the second hand of Sinaiticus, Bezae, and the Koine tradition) and the future tense (*arnēsometha*, the original hand of Sinaiticus, Alexandrinus, Ephraemi). Nestle–Aland contains the future tense because it is clearly the harder reading. It interrupts the sequence, since the protasis of the other three conditional sentences is in either the aorist or the present tense. Scribes would therefore be tempted to "correct" the future to the present tense for the sake of consistency. The meaning is not greatly affected either way. The verb *arneomai* means to "deny, refuse, or disdain" (e.g., Diogenes Laertius, *Lives of Eminent Philosophers* 6:40; Josephus, *Antiquities* 6:151); it is not used by Paul elsewhere, but appears with some frequency in the Gospels (e.g., Matt 26:70; Luke 8:45; John 13:38; Acts 3:13) and the Pastorals (2 Tim 3:5; 1 Tim 5:8; Tit 1:16; 2:12).

he will deny us: The statement falls into the pattern that has been identified as "Sentences of Holy Law," which posit an equal reaction from God to an action by humans. Examples in Paul include 1 Cor 3:17 (*ei tis ton naon tou theou phtherei, ptherei touton ho theos*, "If anyone destroy the temple of God, God will destroy this one") and 1 Cor 14:38 (*ei de tis agnoiei, agnoieitai*, "if anyone ignores [this], he is ignored").[520] The content of this particular statement resembles the logion in Luke 12:9: *ho de arnēsamenos me enōpion tōn anthrōpōn*

---

520. E. Käsemann, "Sätze heiligen Rechts im Neuen Testament," *NTS* 1 (1954–1955): 248–260.

aparnēthesetai enōpion tōn angelōn tou theou (The one who has denied me before humans will be denied before the angels of God).

13. *If we are unfaithful*: The construction is similar to that in Rom 3:3: *ti gar; ei ēpistēsan tines* (what then, if some of them were faithless). The quality of *apistia* is active for Paul; it is not simply "lack of belief," but connotes resistance to God's word (Rom 4:20; 11:20, 23; 1 Tim 1:13).

he still remains faithful: The demonstrative pronoun *ekeinos* (that one) is here translated as "he," and refers to Jesus. The repetition of *pistos* is particularly striking because of the *pistos ho logos* that precedes this rhythmic set of statements. And in light of the overall emphasis on *pistis* (faith) in this writing (1:5, 13; 2:18, 22; 3:8, 10, 15; 4:7), the conviction that Christ Jesus remains faithful no matter the response of humans grounds the expectation that the *parathēkē* entrusted to humans will indeed be preserved (1:12).

for he is not able to deny himself: There is rather remarkable disagreement among MSS on whether or not to read *gar* (for). The original hand of Sinaiticus, for example, has it, but it is omitted by the second hand; most fascinating is the disagreement even within manuscripts of the ancient versions—thus the Harclean Syriac lacks the conjunction, while the Peshitta has it; the majority of Bohairic Coptic MSS have it, while some lack it. Since the explanatory nature of the final clause is to be inferred in either case, the presence or absence of *gar* makes little real difference. The statement itself is remarkable for virtually defining fidelity as the essential quality of Jesus. To be unfaithful (to God, to his word, to humans) would be to deny, to repudiate, his very being.

COMMENT

The passage concludes the first section of 2 Timothy, in which memory and the imitation of models give shape to the paraenesis. The dramatic "keep on remembering Jesus Christ" in 2:8 shows that Paul's series of examples is reaching its climax. Each example has made the same point with some variations: in order to share in a reward, one must also share in suffering. Now that point is made explicitly: one must share in Jesus' death in order to share his life; one must endure now to share in the future kingdom (2:11–13). Within this final example is entwined once more the implicit reminder that Timothy's mentor is exhibiting just that sort of endurance in his captivity (2:9–10).

Literary Considerations

The fundamental literary problem here concerns determining the relationship between tradition and redaction, and the implications of such determinations for interpretation. Take, for example, the phrase *pistos ho logos* (the word is faithful) in 2:11. In the NOTE on 1 Tim 1:15, I discussed the basic issues surrounding this phrase, which is distinctive of the letters to Paul's delegates.[521] In 1 Timothy and Titus, the phrase is definitely formulaic; the only real questions are whether it refers backward or forward, and whether it must always be attached to quoted material. The usage in Tit 3:8 definitely refers backward, but it is impossible to determine whether 3:3–7 is a tradition quoted by Paul (or the pseudepigrapher). In 1 Tim 1:15, the phrase points forward and introduces what appears to be a quoted saying. 1 Tim 3:1 is impossible to decide on either count, as is 1 Tim 4:9.

The usage in this passage is particularly difficult, since it occurs in a passage that makes both the fidelity and the word of God thematic. Should the phrase be taken as the formulaic introduction to an implied citation, or should it be read primarily with reference to *ho logos tou theou* (the word of God) in 2:9? Methodologically, the question involves the degree to which the usage in the other Pastorals determines interpretation here. If the intrinsic ambiguity in the passage is denied and the decision is made to treat the phrase as a reference to a citation—simply because that is the way it (presumably) functions in 1 Timothy and Titus—then the pseudonymity of 2 Timothy is implicitly asserted, the literary logic of the specific passage is slighted, and the Pastorals are assumed to be entirely self-referential. Another option, however, is available, which is to treat *pistos ho logos* contextually in the argument of this passage within 2 Timothy, and hold open the possibility that the phrase functions otherwise in the other letters.[522]

We can look next at the form of 2:11–13. Taken individually, we find a series of statements that resemble a number of balanced or antithetical statements found elsewhere in Paul. The exception is *ei arnēsometha, kakeinos arnēsetai hēmas* (if we [will] deny, that one will deny us). This sentiment is not found elsewhere in Paul. But the form resembles the statements that have been identified form-critically as "sentences of holy law," which propose that a human action is answered by an identical divine reaction (see the NOTES). The closest parallel to the statement here is found in the Synoptics: "The one who denies me before humans will be denied before the angels of God" (Luke 12:9), which, as indicated in the NOTES, uses forms of the verb *arneomai*. The other three statements made here, however, do not fit that form.

But why should we think of 2:11–13 as a unit in the first place? Two factors affect our reading. The first is the assumption that the phrase *pistos ho logos* has a clear meaning and function in the Pastorals. The second is the effect of decisions made by the editors of critical editions of the Greek text. Nestle–Aland, for example, indents 2:11b–13, thereby implying that the material is traditional and at least quasi-poetic. It is but a short step to designating the verses *hymnic* and considering this "hymn" as a crystallization of some Pauline themes that

---

521. See, for example, Duncan, *"Pistos ho Logos"*; Knight, *Faithful Sayings in the Pastoral Letters*; and Campbell, "Identifying the Faithful Sayings in the Pastoral Epistles."

522. Another possibility is to suggest that 2 Timothy itself became the source for the "tradition introduction" function to which the phrase is put in 1 Timothy and Titus.

the author included in his composition to lend it additional Pauline coloration. It is patent that such editing both derives from and reinforces for other readers conventional views of 2 Timothy and its authorship.

There is no question that the four balanced conditional sentences in sequence, with the last providing an extended reversal of the third, have rhetorical power. But by no means are such extended series of balanced clauses unfamiliar in the undisputed letters. Sometimes, such passages are also designated as hymns by scholars (e.g., Phil 2:4–11; Col 1:15–20), although it is not clear whether in fact they ever existed as hymns of any sort, or what is gained by the designation. Other passages in Paul have at least the same poetic form and force, but are not termed hymnic or considered traditional. I have in mind such passages as 1 Cor 13:1–3; Rom 8:31–39; 2 Cor 4:8–10; 6:3–10. Perhaps the most impressive parallel to this passage—because of the subject matter and the use of conditional sentences—is 1 Cor 15:12–19 (RSV):

> [12]Now if Christ is preached as raised from the dead,
> how can some of you say that there is no resurrection of the dead?
> [13]But if there is no resurrection of the dead,
> then Christ has not been raised;
> [14]if Christ has not been raised,
> then our preaching is in vain and your faith is in vain. . . .
> [16]For if the dead are not raised,
> then Christ has not been raised.
> [17]If Christ has not been raised,
> your faith is futile and you are still in your sins. . . .
> [19]If for this life only we have hoped in Christ
> we are of all men most to be pitied.

By indenting the lines to show their balance and repetitive character, I have in effect created a "hymnic fragment." Yet in the case of 1 Corinthians, no one would suggest either that this was such a hymn or that it was not Paul's own composition. And such is its tone of affirmation that Paul could well have prefaced it also with the words *pistos ho logos*. I remind the reader of the point made in the General Introduction about the "power of construal": the ways we have become accustomed to "seeing" the letters to Paul's delegates has a great impact on the way we subsequently interpret them.

The Faithfulness of Christ

No one would want to deny that 2 Timothy has elements that make it distinctive among Paul's letters, yet it is also difficult to deny that there is something particularly Pauline about this delegate letter. This passage exemplifies the combination of similarity and difference. What is distinctive is not the content or even the diction, which is remarkably Pauline throughout (as in the threefold repetition of *to euangelion*), but the extremely compressed, almost telegraphic, form in which Paul's ideas are expressed. It is as though Paul could write in shorthand knowing that his reader was utterly familiar with his perceptions and could "put things together" without a great deal of elaboration.

Paul offers Jesus as the final example he wants Timothy to "keep on remembering" and, in remembering, to imitate. It is typical of Paul to offer Jesus as the supreme example for his readers' behavior while also placing himself as a model for imitation.[523] After his long discussion in 1 Cor 8:1–10:31 concerning the legitimacy or usefulness of eating food offered to idols, Paul concludes, "Give no offense to Jews or Greeks or to the church of God, just as I try to please all men in everything I do, not seeking my own advantage, but that of many, that they may be saved. Be imitators of me as I am of Christ" (RSV 1 Cor 10:32–11:1). In the prior discussion, Paul made it clear that Jesus was an example because he "died for the brother" (1 Cor 8:11)—that is, gave his life in service to others rather than himself. Paul imitated that example by "making myself a slave to all, that I might win the more" (1 Cor 9:19). And he instructs the Corinthians to imitate Jesus and himself by seeking to build up one another in love: "Let each one seek not his own good, but the good of his neighbor" (1 Cor 10:24). The same sort of appropriation of the Jesus story—in its basic pattern of service to the death for others—is put to hortatory use by Paul in Rom 15:1–13 and Phil 2:1–11.

What makes 2 Tim 2:8–13 distinctive, then, is not the content or goal of the argument, but the cryptic manner of its presentation. When Paul summarizes his gospel as "raised from the dead, . . . from the seed of David," his point is not immediately clear. Why these elements and why in this sequence—reversed from that in Rom 1:3–4, where the same two elements occur? Then Paul seems to shift abruptly to his own experience of suffering "as a criminal." This all seems haphazard and disorganized.

But perhaps the juxtaposition, however awkward, is the most important clue to Paul's intended meaning. Paul begins his gospel summary with the resurrection of Jesus, for that is the source of the power of life that he and Timothy share (1:10). The rapid turn to Jesus' human origins, and the immediate connection to Paul's imprisonment, in contrast, point Timothy to the reality that the delegate's present call—as is Paul's own—is to share the human suffering of Jesus that preceded his resurrection. Making a preemptive argument against those who claim that the resurrection is already (2:18)—that is, Christian existence is all about power and not about suffering—Paul insists that the present time is one in which the transformative power of the Holy Spirit (1:14) manifests itself in enabling humans to follow the messianic power of suffering in behalf of others (Gal 5:25–6:2). Paul, we see, continues to be an example: he endures his shame and suffering "for the sake of the chosen ones, that they might be saved" (2:10).

---

523. See, for example, the rhetorical function of his personal *exemplum* in 1 Cor 13 (located between 12 and 14), which is analogous to the function in 1 Cor 9 (between 8 and 10). See C. R. Holladay, "1 Corinthians 13: Paul as Apostolic Paradigm," in *Greeks, Romans, and Christians*, ed. D. L. Balch, E. Ferguson, W. A. Meeks (Minneapolis: Fortress Press, 1990), 80–98.

The messianic pattern is one of life for others, inevitably involving the necessity of endurance rather than glory.

Paul therefore wants Timothy to grasp two apparently contradictory realities as parts of a larger truth. Paul himself is a prisoner in chains, but the word of God is not enchained (2:9)! The power of God that has been put to work in the world through the resurrection of Jesus is paradoxical. It accomplishes its effects through circumstances that in appearance absolutely contradict the plausibility of that power. Here we find, in a highly compressed fashion, precisely the theme argued by Paul in 2 Cor 4:7–12: God's glory shines through cracked clay pots; life is given to others by those carrying about in their bodies the death of Jesus.

When Paul next turns to the cadenced clauses that remind Timothy of this truth, the phrase *pistos ho logos* (2:11) does not appear to be simply a formal introduction to a traditional fragment, for the immediate antecedent to *logos* is the *logos tou theou* (word of God) in 2:9! Paul is saying that the word of God is faithful! Paul and his delegate can trust the pattern of suffering now, glory later, because it is confirmed in the story of Jesus. Jesus was born of the seed of David, a human among others: he endured; he suffered; he died. But he was raised from the dead. And his gift, the Holy Spirit, now indwells and strengthens his followers (1:14; 2:1) as they undergo experiences of shame and suffering for the sake of that same good news.

The next four statements elaborate in carefully constructed sentences— whether or not they are "hymnic"—the point that Paul has made through personal reference to Jesus and himself. First is the affirmation: "If we have died together [with him], we will live together [with him]" (2 Tim 2:11b). I have noted the remarkable resemblance to Paul's statement in Rom 6:8: "If we have died with Christ, we believe that we shall also live with him." Paul goes on to elaborate: "Since we know that Christ, having been raised from the dead, will die no more: death no longer has any power over him" (Rom 6:9). In Romans, Paul turns this conviction to a slightly different hortatory end. They are to live their (moral) lives now as though dead to sin but alive to God in Christ Jesus (Rom 6:11). In 2 Timothy, as we shall see in the next line, Paul turns the conviction in the direction of endurance in the present life. In each case, though, there is the shared understanding that identification with Christ in his death leads to an identification with him in his resurrection life (see also Phil 3:10–11).

The life empowered by the Holy Spirit dwelling within believers (1:14) is not one of present glory but is defined by endurance: "If we endure, then we will also rule together [with him]" (2:12a). The saying has some resemblance to a logion of Jesus found in Mark 13:13/Matt 10:22 and 24:13: *ho de hypomeinas eis telos houtos sōthēsetai* (The one who has endured to the end, this one will be saved). For the theme of endurance elsewhere in Paul, see the NOTE on 2:12. The most pertinent point of reference, however, is found in this passage itself, for Paul has presented himself immediately before this (2:10) precisely as exemplifying this pattern: "This is why I endure [*hypomenō*] all things for the sake of the chosen ones." That the full rule of God is a future and not a present reality conforms to Paul's perception also in 1 Cor 4:6–10: some of the Corinthians considered themselves already to be ruling, and Paul responds sarcastically, "Would that you were ruling, so that we could rule together with you" (1 Cor 4:8); he then shames such arrogance by reciting the sorts of humiliations that the apostles endure (1 Cor 4:9–10).

As in other "sentences of holy law" in Paul, the statement in 2:12b posits a direct relationship between human action and divine reaction: "If we deny him, he [literally, "that one"] will deny us." Leaving moot whether the saying is traditional, it is again most pertinent within the context of the letter. Paul is facing abandonment by some of his followers and opposition from others. Worse, he fears that Timothy's shame will also lead him to cowardice and denial. Timothy, after all, must face the popular success of charlatans who "have the form of piety but deny its power" (3:5). This statement asserts the supreme importance of choice. Denial itself generates denial.

What is most striking about this set of statements is the way in which the final sentence reverses the one before it: "If we are unfaithful, he still remains faithful, for he is not able to deny himself." This is a truly remarkable affirmation and one deeply consonant with the theme of the divine fidelity found elsewhere in Paul (1 Cor 1:9; 10:13; 2 Cor 1:18; 1 Thess 5:24). But in this verse, it is Jesus himself who extends fidelity even to those who are not faithful to him. Humans may deny him, but he cannot deny himself, and since his very identity is defined by faith (2 Tim 1:13; 3:15), he remains faithful. The power at work in this good news is not one that is circumscribed by human possibilities, but is one that comes from God's own design and gift "that has been given to us in Christ Jesus" (1:10). This triumphant note of fidelity and mercy dominates 2 Timothy and extends even to those who are opposing Paul and his delegate (2:24–25).

This passage concludes the first major section of 2 Timothy. Paul has presented himself to his delegate as a model to be imitated, both in his healthy teaching and in his willingness to suffer for the sake of the good news to which he was appointed as a preacher and teacher. In order to encourage Timothy, who is in danger of allowing shame to drive him to a cowardly withdrawal from the work of the gospel, Paul adduces many examples of those who have suffered for a goal. By so doing, he seeks to reignite that special gift for service that is Timothy's. With the partial exception of 2:1–2, everything in the letter to this point has been directed toward this basic summoning of a courageous spirit within his delegate. In the next section, Paul turns to the positive qualities that Timothy should exhibit as he carries out his work as a teacher, in contrast to the negative practices of the opposition.

VII. THE DELEGATE AS
PROVEN WORKMAN (2:14–21)

◆

2 ¹⁴Remember these things as you admonish before God. Do not engage in polemics that are of no profit but lead to the destruction of those hearing them. ¹⁵Be eager to present yourself as a proven workman to God, one with no reason for shame, as you accurately delineate the word of truth. ¹⁶But keep avoiding profane chatter. Those people are going to make ever greater progress in impiety ¹⁷and their teaching will spread like gangrene. Hymenaios and Philetos are among those ¹⁸who have missed the mark concerning the truth by saying that the resurrection has already happened. They are upsetting some people's faith. ¹⁹Nevertheless, God's firm foundation still stands, bearing this seal: "The Lord has known his own," and, "Everyone who names the Lord's name should depart from wickedness." ²⁰In a great household there are not only gold and silver utensils, but also wooden ones and clay. Some are for noble use, some for ignoble. ²¹If then one cleanses oneself from these, one will be a vessel ready for noble use, consecrated, useful to the master, prepared for every good work.

NOTES

14. *Remember these things*: The second-person-singular imperative of *hypomimnēskein* would ordinarily be considered transitive and be translated as "remind," followed by a direct object (Xenophon, *Cyropaedia* 3.3.37; Plato, *Philebus* 67B; 2 Pet 1:12). Thus in Tit 3:1, Paul tells his delegate: *hypomimnēske autous hypotassesthai* (remind them to be subject). In this case, however, there is no direct object. It is supplied by modern translations that read "remind them of these things" (RSV, NRSV). The verb can, however, also bear a reflexive, intransitive meaning, as "I recall" or "I remember" (e.g., Plato, *Phaedrus* 241A; Herodotus, *Persian War* 7:171). Thus in Wis 18:22, the author says of Moses: "By his word he subdued the punisher, calling to mind [*hypomnēsas*] the oaths and covenants of the fathers)." For a combination of reasons, this is the meaning adopted in this translation. For further discussion, see the COMMENT.

admonish before God: In a section relatively free of textual variants, this verse has several, perhaps because of the awkwardness of the transition to a new section. Some few MSS, for example, have *christou* (before Christ) instead of *theou* (before God). Many more witnesses have *kyriou* (before the Lord); see, for example, Alexandrinus, Bezae, the Koine tradition, and several versions. Although the evidence is fairly well divided, Nestle–Aland chooses *theou*, which in this case is the easier reading, since the expression "before God" occurs frequently in Paul (Rom 14:22; 1 Cor 1:29; 2 Cor 4:2; 7:12; Gal 1:20), whereas "before the Lord" occurs only once (2 Cor 8:21). Also, *enōpion theou* is constant in 1 and 2 Timothy (1 Tim 2:3; 5:4, 21; 6:13; 2 Tim 4:1). For *diamartyromai* (admonish), see 1 Thess 4:6.

Do not engage in polemics: Some witnesses have *mē logomachei* instead of the infinitival construction *mē logomachein*, taking it as a present imperative (the contract verb *logomacheō* yields *ei* rather, than *e* in that form), agreeing with *anamimnēske*, and introducing a new sentence. I have accepted this variant as the correct reading. It is supported by the original hand of Ephraemi and Alexandrinus, some Old Latin MSS, and the fifth-century 048. The reading accepted by Nestle–Aland (and most modern translations) is found in the third corrector of Ephraemi, Sinaiticus, the Syriac, and the majority Koine manuscript tradition. One way to account for the dominant reading, despite its intrinsic problems, is that the scribes (like modern translators) took *anamimnēske* in only its transitive sense, thereby requiring some sort of object clause.

that are of no profit: The term for "profit" or "usefulness" here is *chrēsimos*, a NT *hapax*. There is some indecision among scribes whether to read *ep' ouden* (literally, "upon nothing"), which is one of the common constructions following *chrēsimos* (Plato, *Gorgias* 480B; *Laws* 796A), or *eis ouden* (to nothing) as a way of expressing result. The reading *ep' ouden* followed by Nestle–Aland is found in the original hand of Sinaiticus, Alexandrinus, Ephraemi, and some other uncials. The meaning is unaffected either way. Among ancient moralists, it was usefulness (*chrēsimos*) or profit (*ōphelimos*) for life that served as the measure for the value of a teaching (e.g., Plato, *Gorgias* 504E; 513E; *Republic*, 607D; Epictetus, *Discourse* 1.4.16; 6.33; 3.24.51; Philo, *Migration of Abraham* 55; *The Worse Attacks the Better* 21).

lead to the destruction: The verb *katastrephein* means to "overturn or tear down" (Diogenes Laertius, *Lives of Eminent Philosophers* 5:82; Matt 21:12; Acts 15:16), and the noun *katastrophē* has the sense of destruction (Josephus, *Antiquities* 15:287; 2 Pet 2:6). Note how the "destruction of the hearers" in 2 Tim 2:14 corresponds to the "saving of the hearers" in 1 Tim 4:16.

15. *present yourself as a proven workman*: The language here is thoroughly Pauline: for *parastēsai* (present oneself), see Rom 12:1; 14:10; 1 Cor 8:8; Col 1:22, 28; for "approved" (*dokimos*), see Rom 14:18; 1 Cor 11:19; 2 Cor 10:18; for "workman" (*ergatēs*), see 2 Cor 11:13 and Phil 3:2, as well as the "hardworking farmer" in 2 Tim 2:6. The thought here is pervasive in ancient moral teaching: unless character is tested and proved, it cannot be considered fully formed (e.g., Seneca, *On Providence* 2:1–6; Epictetus, *Fragments* 28b, 112; Prov 27:21; Sir 2:1; Wis 3:5–6; *Pirke Aboth* 5:3; 4 Macc 7:22; 1QH 4:22; *Testament of Job* 4:2–11; *Testament of Joseph* 2:6–7; *Book of Jubilees* 17:17–18; 19:8–9; *Sentences of Sextus* 7a).

no reason for shame: The note of shame here continues the theme that was established by Paul's warning not to be ashamed in 1:8, his declaration that he was not ashamed in 1:12, and the statement that Onesiphorus was not ashamed of Paul's chains in 1:16. If Timothy is *dokimos* (proven worthy), then he has no need to be ashamed (the privative *an* + *epaischyntos*). See the use of the same adjective in Josephus, *Antiquities* 18:243.

accurately delineate the word of truth: For *logos tēs alētheias* as equivalent to the gospel, see Col 1:5 and Eph 1:13. See also 2 Tim 1:13; 2:9, 11; 4:2. The contrast will immediately be drawn with *ho logos autōn* (their word). The participle *orthotomounta* is unattested in this construction elsewhere. It is derived from *ortho-* (rightly/correctly) and the verb *tomein/temnein* (cut). The verb is used in LXX Prov 3:6 and 11:5 for "cutting a path in the right direction" (see also Thucydides, *Peloponnesian War* 2.100.2; Plato, *Laws* 810E). How one could "cut a way" for the word of truth is not clear, which leads to the possibility that medical imagery is once more in play. The verb may suggest "cutting straight," as in the act of surgery. Philo speaks of dealing with passions that cannot be handled with drugs and must be excised by means of "sharp reason" (*logō tomei to kat' epistēmēn temnetai*.[524] The imagery works in context because it is a gangrene that is being opposed. My translation picks an English verb that is appropriate to how a "word" might be rightly cut.

16. *keep avoiding profane chatter*: I translate the second-person singular imperative of the verb *periistēmi* in its continuous sense. For the use of the verb, which literally means to "stand around" in the sense of avoid or shun, see Lucian, *Hermotimus* 86; Philo, *On Drunkenness* 205; Josephus, *Jewish War* 2:135. The same verb is used for the avoidance of legal wrangles in Tit 3:9. For "profane" (*bebēlos*) and "chatter" (*kenophōnia*), see the NOTES on 1 Tim 1:9 and 6:20.

greater progress in impiety: This is the first of three times in which Paul uses, with reference to the opponents, the verb *prokoptein* (see also 3:9, 13, and compare Rom 13:12; Gal 1:14). Here, it is making progress in *asebeia*, the direct opposite of *eusebeia*; he will later say that they have the form of *eusebeia*, but deny it with their deeds (3:5). The use of *prokoptein* is somewhat sardonic, since such "advancement" can often refer to moral progress (Epictetus, *Discourse* 2.17.4; Lucian, *Hermotimus* 63). The verb can, it is true, also be used for the process of moral degradation (Josephus, *Antiquities* 4:59; 18:34; 20:205; *Testament of Judah* 21). The next verse makes clear that their progress is to be seen in terms of convincing others as well.

17. *teaching will spread like gangrene*: For the use of medical terminology in Hellenistic moral teaching, see the COMMENT. Paul makes it clear that Timothy is opposed by people not only with bad character, but also with a message (*logos*) that is having an injurious effect on others. The phrase *nomēn echei* means literally to "have pasturage," but is used metaphorically for the spreading of a disaster or a disease, such as an ulcer (Polybius, *Histories* 1.48.5; 81.6; Galen, *On Simple Medicine* 9). The ultimate "spreading disease" is gangrene

---

524. Malherbe, "Medical Imagery in the Pastorals," 127–128.

(*gangraina*, Hippocrates, *On Joints* 63). Plutarch uses the image of gangrene for the spreading effect of a bad reputation, in *How to Tell a Flatterer* 24 (*Mor.* 65D). Paul's image is unforgettable and devastating: the spread of this moral disease will consume and destroy.

Hymenaios and Philetos: The name Hymenaios appears also in 1 Tim 1:20 as one of those whom Paul has handed over to Satan in order to learn not to blaspheme; there he is linked to Alexander. Philetos is not otherwise attested. The puzzle presented by these personal names is the same that perplexes every reader of the Pastorals: we do not know how the pieces fit together. If the letters are authentically Pauline, these could be different people or people in changed circumstances. If the letters are pseudonymous, the mystery actually deepens, for why would a pseudepigrapher not make the data fit together better?

18. *missed the mark concerning the truth*: For the verb *astochein*, see 1 Tim 1:6, and for the construction *peri* + the accusative, see 1 Tim 6:21. In that passage, the false teachers miss the mark concerning *pistis*, meaning the entire response to God, and here concerning *alētheia*; the content of their error is then stated.

the resurrection has already happened: The presence or absence of the definite article *tēn* before *anastasin* could be significant. It is lacking in Sinaiticus, F, G, and a few other Greek witnesses. It is present in Alexandrinus, Ephraemi, Bezae, and the Koine tradition. The evidence is fairly well balanced, with no corrections in either direction, making the decision difficult.[525] Nestle–Aland contains it within brackets, indicating a degree of doubt concerning its inclusion. What difference does it make? That between "a resurrection" happening already and "the" resurrection already happening. For further discussion, see the COMMENT.

upset some peoples' faith: The verb *anatrepein* means literally to "overturn" (John 2:15) and figuratively to "upset or throw into commotion" (Diodorus Siculus, *Library of History* 1.77.2; *Testament of Asher* 1:7). In Tit 1:11, the opponents are "upsetting entire households." It is probable that in this verse, *pistis* refers to people's entire understanding of the Christian *alētheia*; having their grasp of this most fundamental mystery disturbed will have, in Paul's view, attitudinal and behavioral corollaries that are not yet spelled out.

19. *God's firm foundation still stands*: For "foundation" (*themelios*) in household imagery, see 1 Cor 3:10 and Rom 15:20.[526] The term here prepares for the metaphor of the *oikia* in 2:20. I have translated the perfect *hestēka* strictly, as "still standing," since the particle *mentoi* (nevertheless) sets up a direct opposition (however awkward) between the "upsetting of some's faith" and the stability of the house.

---

525. Metzger, *Textual Commentary*, 647–648.

526. For a reading of the entire passage, see Hanson, "The Apostates: 2 Timothy 2:19–21," in *Studies in the Pastoral Epistles*, 29–41.

bearing this seal: The *sphragis* is a seal or signet belonging to one in authority that is used to make a mark of ownership (Herodotus, *Persian War* 1:195). Thus it is also a seal of state by which official documents could be certified (Aristotle, *Athenian Constitution* 44:1). Secondarily, the *sphragis* is the mark or impression made by such a seal (Thucydides, *Peloponnesian War* 1:129) and, as such, could be found, for example, on property owned by the state (Tebtunis Papyrus 105 line 13).

The Lord has known his own: Paul has two statements joined by the simple conjunction *kai* (and), suggesting that these are the statements printed on the *sphragis*. The phrase *egnō kyrios tous ontas autou* (the Lord has known his own) echoes part of LXX Num 16:5: *egnō ho theos tous ontas autou*, replacing only *theos* (God) with *kyrios* (Lord); the MT of the Hebrew has YHWH (Lord) rather than Elohim (God). This has the effect of having "Lord" in both parts of the complex statement, and prepares for the identification of Timothy in 2:24 as "servant of the Lord." The addition of "all those" (*pantas*) is found in only the original hand of Sinaiticus.

Everyone who names the Lord's name: Detecting the scriptural echo in this statement is more difficult; *onomazōn to onoma kyriou* is perhaps an allusion to LXX Isa 26:13: *kyrie, ektos sou allon ouk oidamen, to onoma sou onomazomen* (Lord, apart from you we know no other, we name your name). The phrase also resembles "calling on the name of the Lord" (LXX Joel 3:5), allusions to which are found in Acts 2:21; Rom 10:13; 1 Cor 1:2, and which appears soon after in 2 Timothy (2:22). The use of "the Lord" in both lines has the effect of signaling that the *oikia* in question belongs to him as master: it is his property.

depart from wickedness: The third-person imperative of *aphistēmi* is *aposteto*, meaning literally to "withdraw from something" (Herodotus, *Persian War* 3:15; Epictetus, *Discourse* 2.13.26) and figuratively to "keep away from or avoid" in the moral sense (Josephus, *Life* 261; Sir 7:2; 35:3; Tob 4:21); see also 2 Cor 12:8 and 1 Tim 4:1. The noun *adikia* denotes wrongdoing in the broadest sense, being the logical opposite of *dikaiosynē* (Herodotus, *Persian War* 1:130; Plato, *Gorgias* 477C). The statement may echo LXX Sir 17:26: *apostrephe apo adikias* (turn aside from wickedness). More likely is that Isa 52:11 lies in the background: *apostēte apostēte exelthate ekeithen kai akathartou mē haptesthe, exelthate ek mesou autēs aphoristhete, hoi pherontes ta skeuē kyriou* (Turn aside, turn aside, come out from there and do not touch the unclean thing. Come out from the midst of her, separate yourselves, you bearers of the vessels of the Lord). Two things are particularly interesting in this possibility. The first is that Paul also cites this verse in the passage spiritually closest to this one in 2 Cor 6:17. The second is that the connection between separation and vessels in this passage is anticipated by the Isaian prophecy.

20. *In a great household*: It is important neither to force the logic of Paul's metaphors in this section nor to read them through the lens of his other household images in the Pastorals. The *oikia* does not really become thematic here. It simply has a foundation (*themelios*) with an inscription (*sphragis*), and within are various vessels. But the personification (allegorization) of the vessels in 2:21

makes it clear that it is not the "household as community" that is the main point here, but the "community member's moral response."

gold and silver utensils: The sentence is structured oddly to make its point. It is, after all, only in a *megalē oikia* (great household) that there would be silver and gold utensils at all! Lowlier habitations would not have such richly fashioned vessels. The *ou monon . . . alla kai* (not only . . . but also) construction, therefore, points to the full range of vessels that a large household would have.

noble use . . . ignoble: The *men . . . de* construction makes the obvious contrast. The clay and wood utensils would be used primarily for food preparation; such menial tasks are characterized as *eis atimian* (lacking honor). The costlier vessels, in contrast, would be employed for ornamentation and service at table; thus they are *eis timian* (for honorable use). Paul uses the same metaphor to a different end in Rom 9:21. For more on this, see the COMMENT.

21. *cleanses oneself from these*: For the use of *ekkatharein*, compare 1 Cor 5:7. The phrase *ean oun tis* (if anyone therefore) shifts the discourse from metaphor to allegory by means of personification. Now it is a matter of human persons "cleansing themselves" from these (*apo toutōn*), the dishonorable persons who are standing in (implicitly) for those vessels that are used *eis atimian* in 2:20. The verb *ekkathairein* does not actually have a ritual background in Torah (LXX Deut 26:13; Josh 17:15, 18; Judg 7:4; Isa 4:4), but is found in the sense of moral purification in Hellenistic moral philosophy (Philostratus, *Life of Apollonius of Tyana* 5:7; Epictetus, *Discourses* 2.23.40, esp. 2.21.15).

a vessel ready for noble use: Embedded in this imagery is the notion of conversion, that one can, through a process of cleansing, change from dishonorable to honorable status within the community. Remarkably, the one to whom this assurance is addressed is Paul's delegate, who is to "present [himself] as a proven workman to God, one with no reason for shame" (2:15). Thus the language of honor and shame not only continues from the previous section, but helps shape this complex metaphorical argument.

consecrated: The introduction of *hēgiasmenos* (sanctified, 1 Cor 1:2) introduces still a further complexity into Paul's metaphoric/allegorical trope on the *oikia*, for it turns the notion of cleansing toward the ritual language associated with Temple worship and enables the reader to draw the conclusion that this "great house" is, in fact, the *oikos theou* that is the community and the living Temple of God. Compare 1 Cor 3:9–17 and, especially, 1 Cor 6:19: "Do you not know that your body [the body that is the community] is the temple of the Holy Spirit among you, which you have from God, and you are not your own," which follows 6:11: "You have been washed [*apelousasthe*], you have been sanctified [*hēgiasthēte*]."

useful to the master: MSS are divided over putting *kai* (and) before this phrase. Nothing significant rests on the decision. The adjective "useful" (*euchrēstos*) appears also in Phm 11, and is there a pun on the title *christos*. Onesimus had been "useless" as well as "not a Christian" (*achrēstos*), but since hearing the good news, he is *euchrēstos*, both a "good Christian" and "useful." If Paul committed the pun once, he was capable of repeating it. For *despotēs* (master) as a title appropriate to the head of a great house, see the NOTE on 1 Tim 6:1.

prepared for every good work: The phrase *eis pan ergon agathon* (for every good work) is used by Paul also in 2 Cor 9:8 and Rom 13:3. The perfect passive participle of the verb *hetoimazein* (to be prepared, ready) fits beautifully the dual sense of a vessel that has been "set out" for the master (3 Macc 6:31) ready for any good use, and a person who is "prepared" to serve the master usefully. Note the similar phrase concerning "The man of God" in 3:17.

COMMENT

In a manner similar to that of the classic paraenetic treatise *To Demonicus*, Paul shifts in this section (2:14–4:5) from the memory and imitation of models to a more direct form of moral instruction through maxims. In paraenesis, maxims were intended to fill out the model sketched by living (or dead) exemplars (Seneca, *Moral Epistles* 94). They usually take the form of short direct commands, but are sometimes expanded by explanation or illustration. All the imperatives are in the second-person singular: the focus is on the character and practice of Paul's delegate, and only indirectly (if at all) on those "faithful men" he is to recruit and instruct (2:1–2).

This realization helps us grasp the interpretive difficulty in 2:14, reflected in the textual variants. As a transition, it is confusing. According to the majority of modern translations, Paul says simply "remind" (*hypomimneske*), in the singular. It is clearly meant for Timothy, his implied reader. The verb is transitive, but the object is unexpressed. So is Timothy to remind the "faithful men," or is he to remind the opponents? What makes this command even more obscure is that Timothy's audience never again comes into view. Everything else in the section is either a command to Timothy himself or a description of the opponents. Nowhere else is Timothy to tell something to anyone else. Thus immediately in 2:15, we find, "Be eager to present yourself." It is perhaps more understandable, therefore, that some manuscripts do not read, "Remind them . . . not to engage in polemics," but "Remind . . . do not you engage in polemics." The scribes were confused by the same thing we are. What has happened to those Timothy is supposed to remind? In fact, they have had to be imported from 2:2. These obscurities are removed, however, if we read *hypomimnēskō* as "recall/remember these things" and accept the variant reading, "do not engage in polemics." Now the passage is internally consistent, with the focus remaining on Timothy's character and practice as Paul's delegate.

In this section of the letter, Timothy's positive dispositions are constantly contrasted with the attitudes and actions of the opponents. It is here that we see the influence of Hellenistic protreptic discourses. As suggested in the INTRODUCTION, such protreptic writings also use the themes of memory, model, and imitation as they encourage someone to pursue or fulfill certain professed ideals. They also use maxims to spell out the requirements of a certain mode of life, such as that of the philosopher. It is in this connection that protreptic uses the stereotyped forms of polemic that had developed in disputes among Sophists and philosophers, and among various schools of philosophy.[527] Now, however, the slander is not found in direct attack, but as a negative image to provide contrast to the ideal portrait of the authentic sage/teacher. In Epictetus, *Discourse* 3.22 ("On the Calling of the Cynic"), which is a classic example of such protreptic, we find precisely this sort of contrast, employing elements of slander:

> So do you also think about the matter carefully; it is not what you think it is. "I wear a rough cloak even as it is, and I shall have one then. . . . I shall take to myself a wallet and staff, and I shall begin to walk around and beg from those I meet and revile them. . . ." If you fancy the affair to be something like this, give it a wide berth; don't come near it, it is nothing for you. (3.22.9–13)

In similar fashion, we find in this section of the letter that descriptions of what the opponents are doing are contrasted with the positive instruction of Timothy. Time after time, Paul turns to his reader and addresses him, "But you. . . ." The pattern continues in such antithetical fashion until Paul returns once more to the presentation of himself as a model in 4:6.

Since Paul places his instruction of Timothy within the conventions of Hellenistic moral instruction, and, above all, because the contrast between the ideal teacher and false teachers assumes a range of implicit convictions concerning the moral life in the Greco-Roman context, it is appropriate to consider four aspects of this cultural context, suggesting in the process some of the ways in which 2 Timothy fits within it and some of the ways in which Paul's instructions may have a distinctive touch. This discussion serves as the background and framework for discussion of polemic in 1 Timothy as well.

Slander and the Identity of Opponents

Identifying the opponents in the Pauline letters has been one of the enduring preoccupations of scholars working within the historical-critical paradigm. The motivation is straightfoward. If Paul's opponents can be connected to some specific group in antiquity about which we have complementary evidence, then his all-too-oblique responses may gain greater intelligibility and the character of the struggles in which he was engaged may become clearer. The methodology used for determining opponents has often left much to be desired, but such considerations have not prevented repeated and repetitive efforts.

There has been no lack of efforts to determine the opponents in the Pastoral Letters either, as the General Introduction has indicated. Such efforts reveal three consistent features. The first is that descriptions of rival teachers in the Pastorals are taken denotatively rather than connotatively; that is, they are taken as descriptive of who they were and what their teachings were, rather than as a conventional form of slander. The second is that, as in other matters, the Pas-

527. Johnson, "II Timothy and the Polemic Against False Teachers."

torals were treated as a single literary expression; that is, traits of the opponents in each of the letters have been brought together to form a composite portrait. The third is that scholars sought a match between this composite and some previously known (or thought to be known) group in the ancient world. The candidates have ranged from Essenes[528] to Gnostics[529] to Jewish mystics.[530] Given the complexity of the traits found in all three letters, it is not surprising that no such effort has found universal approval.

In order to make better sense of the language of the Pastorals about opponents, two basic steps are required. The first is to sort out which elements of the language are conventional rhetoric and which ones might genuinely be denotative and provide information about the specific opponents; here research into disputes between ancient sages has established how pervasive was the use of certain consistent kinds of vituperation.[531] The second is to treat each of the letters separately and to take into account its perception of the rival teachers, without moving to an overall composite derived from all three letters.[532] Just as Paul's attention in the letter is constantly on Timothy, so our attention will be directed solely to 2 Timothy.

Certain standard charges were leveled against opponents on either side of the debates between ancient teachers and members of ancient rival traditions. Epicureans attacked Stoics, and Platonists reviled Epicureans; Gentiles and Jews criticized each other with scathing language; Pharisees scorned the Sadducees; and the Essenes vituperated against the Pharisees.[533] These conventional attacks were used in protreptic discourse to provide a foil for the ideal teacher. Just as it is possible to sketch the "best of all philosophers" (e.g., Lucian, *Demonax*; Julian the Apostate, *Orations* 6 and 7; Epictetus, *Discourse* 3.22), so are there standard elements in the depiction of the "false philosopher." The rival is often characterized as a "sophist" (*sophistēs*) or "charlatan" (*goes*) whose speech is filled with quarrels over words, quibbles, and contentious wranglings, using obscure jargon (Lucian, *Timon* 9; *Zeus Rants* 27; Epictetus, *Discourses* 2.1.31; 17.26). Sometimes, however, the opposite charge is leveled: the false teacher is one who seduces in order to win adherents, flattering listeners by telling them what they want to hear and pandering to their vices (Dio Chrysostom, *Oration* 32:11).

False teachers are often accused of hypocrisy—that is, of preaching virtue in public, but practicing vice in private (Philostratus, *Life of Apollonius of Tyana* 2:29; Julian, *Oration* 7:225A; Lucian, *Timon* 54). These vices, in turn, fall into standard categories, the most noteworthy being love of pleasure (*philedonē*, Julian, *Oration* 6:198B; Dio Chrysostom, *Oration* 33:13; Epictetus, *Discourse* 3.22.39), love of money (*philargyria*, Philostratus, *Life of Apollonius of Tyana*

528. Michaelis, *Introduction to the New Testament.*
529. Baur, Die Sogennanten Pastoralbriefe; Lütgert, *Irrlehrer der Pastoralbriefe.*
530. Gouldner, "Pastor's Wolves."
531. Karris, "Background and Significance of the Polemic of the Pastoral Epistles."
532. Johnson, "II Timothy and the Polemic Against False Teachers."
533. Johnson, "New Testament's Anti-Jewish Slander."

1:34; Julian, *Oration* 6:181C; Lucian, *The Runaways* 14), and love of glory (*philodoxia*, Dio Chrysostom, *Oration* 32:10; Julian, *Oration* 6:190D; Epictetus, *Discourse* 1.21.3–4; Lucian, *Peregrinus* 38). When the opponents in 2 Timothy are charged with "word-chopping" (2:14, 24), "vain and uninstructed debates" (2:23), "profane chatter" (2:16), or even "having the form of godliness while denying its power" (3:5), we recognize the elements standard in polemic and do not conclude that these were necessarily the actual characteristics of the people who were opposing Paul and Timothy.

Some of the charges are less easy to categorize as part of the conventional rhetoric. And it must always be remembered that even conventions—like clichés—have some basis. We can, therefore, identify some of this language as stereotyped and connotative (and thus not to be taken as reliable description), but must be careful not to go to the opposite extreme of denying any possibility that Timothy's rival teachers could in fact have had some of these characteristics. The accusation that some "are sneaking into homes" in order to influence women (3:6), for example, may or may not point to an actual practice. Certainly, the similar complaint about women going from house to house in 1 Tim 5:13 suggests a pattern of social behavior.

The claim that Hymenaios and Philetos are saying that the resurrection already happened (2:18) may likewise have some basis in fact. The charge clearly identifies the opponents as Christian, since a "realized resurrection" is scarcely conceivable among any group other than the Christian at this time. Determining the precise meaning of their claim is more difficult. All Christians would agree that *Jesus'* resurrection had already taken place—although even that confession could have its variations (1 Cor 15:1–58). The opponents must, therefore, be referring to the general resurrection of *believers*, which Paul elsewhere clearly understands as a future event (1 Cor 6:14; 15:23, 49; 1 Thess 4:14–17). What could it mean to say of this event, "It has already happened?"

Certainly the oddest version appears in the apocryphal *Acts of Paul and Thecla*. In that second-century composition, Paul proclaims a future resurrection that is dependent on physical asceticism, specifically virginity, in the present life. He proclaimed "the word of God concerning continence and the resurrection" (AP 5), including, "Blessed are the bodies of the virgins, for they shall be well-pleasing to God and shall not lose the reward of their purity . . . they shall have rest forever and ever" (AP 6). In contrast, his opponents teach that the resurrection has already happened—the position supposedly advanced by Hymenaios and Philetos in 2 Timothy. But what they mean by their position is that "it has already taken place in the children whom we have, and that we are risen again in that we have come to know the true God" (AP 14). The first part of their statement is a simple reduction of resurrection to biological descent, but the second part suggests that they have been "resurrected" by coming to a spiritual knowledge of God. Resurrection, in any case, is not something that happens after human death, but is available now through progeny and gnosis.

It is at least plausible that Hymenaios and Philetos were professing some form of acute realized eschatology—that is, an understanding of existence as in a real sense participating in eternal life, so that future eschatology is implicitly either denied or denigrated. The clearest statement of such conviction is found in some of the writings in the library discovered at Nag-Hammadi, such as the *Treatise on the Resurrection* 49, and *The Gospel of Philip* 56. A dualistic view of reality that considered the body as evil made such a purely spiritual interpretation of the resurrection logical. Such views did not need to wait for the second century to find expression within Christianity. The canonical Gospel of John, for example, while acknowledging a future eschatology (3:18–21; 5:24–29), certainly emphasizes the possibility of experiencing eternal life in the here and now.[534]

Paul's criticism in 1 Cor 15:12 of those who "say there is no resurrection of the dead," furthermore, may actually be directed against a denial of a bodily resurrection based on the certainty that the power of new life already enjoyed by believers was already the realized end-time, the full *basileia* of God: they were already filled, already rich, already ruling (1 Cor 4:8)—as Paul sardonically observes. In Corinth, this acute realized eschatology is connected to a view of moral behavior that was so "strong"—that is, so liberal and individualistic—that it verged on actual immorality and social disruption.[535] Paul reins in members of the Corinthian community who disregard basic moral standards (1 Cor 15:32–34), practicing incest (5:1–5) and frequenting prostitutes (6:12–20).

A similar combination of realized eschatology and immoral practice appears possible in 2 Timothy. Paul's comments suggest that the teaching on the resurrection is connected to "youthful passions" (or, possibly, "revolutionary passions," 2 Tim 2:22). And the opponents notoriously disrupt households by the seduction of women driven by impulses (3:6). In short, the few clues we can gain about the rivals' teaching concerning the resurrection have it resembling not the spiritual knowledge derived from an ascetic regimen (as at Nag-Hammadi), or the biological descent that sought conventional bonds of marriage (as in *Paul and Thecla*), but the license for disruptive behavior (as in 1 Corinthians).

Metaphor, Medicine, and Morals

One of the structural metaphors for moral discourse in the Hellenistic world was the practice of medicine.[536] Structural metaphors are called such because they give rise to and organize a variety of other metaphors.[537] In this case, the metaphor derives from a perception of human behavior in terms of health and sickness. The person who practices vice is ill, and the person who practices virtue is healthy (Plutarch, *On Virtue and Vice* 1–4 [*Mor.* 100B–101C]). Moral in-

---

534. For a useful summation of this basic point, see R. Kysar, *John: The Maverick Gospel*, 2nd ed. (Louisville, Ky.: Westminster/John Knox Press, 1996), 97–127.

535. A. C. Thiselton, "Realized Eschatology in Corinth," *NTS* 24 (1977–1978): 520–526.

536. M. C. Nussbaum, *The Therapy of Desire: Theory and Practice in Hellenistic Ethics* (Princeton, N. J.: Princeton University Press, 1994).

537. G. Lakoff and M. Johnson, *Metaphors We Live By* (Chicago: University of Chicago Press, 1980), 7–32.

struction, therefore, had as its aim to make someone "well" in the fullest sense of the term. In Plutarch's *Advice About Keeping Well*, the fields of medicine and philosophy are deliberately merged; it is inconceivable to talk about one without the other (*Mor.* 122B–137E). Epictetus calls his philosophical lecture hall a hospital: "Men, the lecture room of the philosopher is a hospital; you ought not to walk out of it in pleasure, but in pain" (*Discourse* 3.23.30). The philosopher or moral teacher was therefore a "physician of the soul" (Dio Chrysostom, *Orations* 32:10; 77/78:43–45; Epictetus, *Discourses* 3.22.72–73; Lucian, *Demonax* 7, 10; *Nigrinus* 38).

I have suggested that 2 Timothy is a personal paraenetic letter with a protreptic element. Rather than focusing on only Timothy's personal virtue and vice (which is the business of paraenesis), Paul places them within the framework of Timothy's profession as a moral teacher, especially in this section of the letter. His goal is to encourage Timothy to live up to his calling, which is the business of protreptic discourse. It is no real shock, then, to find generous use of medicine as a metaphor.[538] In 1:13, we have seen Paul present himself to Timothy as a model of "healthy words" (*hygiainontōn logōn*). In this passage, in contrast, the opponents' teaching is characterized as "gangrene" (*gangraina*) that—in a decidedly medical usage—will "spread" (*nomēn hexei*, 2:17). Finally, Timothy's own teaching practice is compared to the work of a skilled surgeon (2:15). The metaphor is camouflaged by most translations, since *orthotemnein* (literally, "to cut right") is difficult to combine with "word of truth." I have translated, "rightly delineate the word of truth"—but the medical allusion is clearly present. Its application is particularly suggestive when the "surgeon" Timothy is facing false teaching that is "gangrenous and spreading"! It should be emphasized, however, that Timothy is not urged to practice surgery on the opponents as such, but to "rightly cut" the word of truth. This leads to another consideration.

Teaching Styles

Although ancient moral teachers agreed that the goal of philosophy was not the accumulation of knowledge, but the transformation of life, they also disagreed in significant ways on the best way to reach that goal—thus the many disputes among philsophers and schools, and the development of the stereotyped polemic we have recognized also in 2 Timothy. One of the common charges made against philosophers by others, in fact, was that they all promised the truth but could not agree on what it was (Lucian, *The Parasite* 27; *Hermotimus* 15–16). Some differences were doctrinal, concerning the nature of the self and therefore the character of a healthy person. Thus the Platonist Plutarch considered the teachings of the Epicureans positively destructive of the self and, especially, the state (e.g., *Reply to Colotes* 22, 27 [*Mor.* 1119F, 1123A]). Other differences concerned

---

538. Malherbe, "Medical Imagery in the Pastorals."

practices. Should philosophers charge money for their services, or should they provide them freely?[539]

Still other differences concerned style of teaching. What degree of severity was appropriate in correcting the vices of others? What amount of encouragement was effective in leading them to virtue? Clearly, flattery of those living in vice was itself corrupting of the moral teacher (Epictetus, *Discourses* 1.21.3–4). Dio Chrysostom declared of such flattery and display: "It is as if a physician when visiting patients should disregard their treatment and their restoration to health, and should bring them flowers and courtesans and perfumes" (*Oration* 32:10). Some form of encounter was therefore necessary (Epictetus, *Discourses* 3.22.26–30), and some amount of severity: "A good prince is marked by compassion, a bad philosopher by lack of severity" (Dio Chrysostom, *Oration* 32:18). But how much severity? Within the Cynic tradition, there developed two different approaches, each of which could be expressed through a medical metaphor.[540] The first emphasized the need for rebuke and abuse, the rough treatment expected from a surgeon (Dio Chrysostom, *Oration* 77/78:45). The second put its emphasis on encouragement, the gentle healing approach of the nurse (Epictetus, *Discourse* 3.22.90; Dio Chrysostom, *Oration* 4:19; Lucian, *Demonax* 12–67). In 2 Tim 2:23, we find the opponents' teaching characterized in terms of its harshness and disputatiousness. In contrast, Timothy is to conduct himself without polemics (2:14) and with gentleness (2:24–25). This is also the style adopted by Paul himself, when in a passage redolent of the language of moral philosophy, he says, "We were gentle among you, like a nurse taking care of her children" (1 Thess 2:7).[541] Note also how Paul tells Timothy in 2:24 to instruct those who are in opposition "with meekness" (*en prautēti*), just as he himself exhorted the Corinthians "through the meekness [*prautētos*] and the gentleness [*epieikeias*] of Christ" (2 Cor 10:1).

Images of Conversion

The decision to follow the philosophical way of life was phenomenologically a form of conversion.[542] At the end of Lucian's encomium of the philosopher Nigrinus, the recitation of the teacher's teaching so moves the listener that he wants to go at once to join the philosopher (*Nigrinus* 38). The philosopher himself was expected to be someone who was of proven virtue. Thus Timothy is to "present [himself] as a proven workman" to the Lord (2:15). As Epictetus's discourse on the calling of the Cynic makes clear, the philosopher was not to be governed

---

539. Hock, *Social Context of Paul's Ministry.*

540. A. J. Malherbe, "Self Definition Among the Cynics," in *Paul and the Popular Philosophers* (Minneapolis: Fortress Press, 1989), 11–24.

541. A. J. Malherbe, "Gentle as a Nurse: The Cynic Background of 1 Thess 2," in *Paul and the Popular Philosophers* (Minneapolis: Fortress Press, 1989), 35–48.

542. A. D. Nock, *Conversion: The Old and the New in Religion from Alexander the Great to Augustine of Hippo* (Oxford: Clarendon Press, 1933).

by love of pleasure (*Discourses* 3.22.13) or love of money (3.22.26–30) or love of reputation (3.22.83–86). The philosopher's concern, however, was not simply with his own virtue. He was like a scout sent by God to help others (Epictetus, *Discourses* 3.22.24–25, 38). His behavior was to serve as a model for other people (Epictetus, *Discourses* 3.22.45–49), and his speech was to be directed to their healing, "in the hope that he may thereby rescue somebody from folly" (Dio Chrystostom, *Oration* 77/78:38). In this section, we see the first emphasis: the need for Timothy himself to "cleanse himself" from anything unworthy (2:21). In the next section, we will see the hope for the conversion of others (2:25–26).

Household/Temple/Vessel

Paul's concern for Timothy's own moral purity is here entangled with a particularly complex development of the metaphor "the assembly is a household/temple." We are reminded at once of the designation of the *ekklēsia* of the living God in 1 Tim 3:15 as the *oikos theou* (house of God). Elements of the metaphor, however, are also found elsewhere in Paul. The "house" or "household" as metaphor for the community is worked out most elaborately in 1 Cor 3:9–4:2, where Paul discusses the cooperative ministries of Apollos and himself. In that passage, as in this one, there is mention of the *themelios* (foundation) of the building. There it is laid by the apostle (1 Cor 3:10), being none other than Jesus Christ (1 Cor 3:11). Others may build on that foundation with materials made of gold, silver, precious stones, wood, hay, or straw (1 Cor 3:12). Within the household, the ministers of the gospel are "stewards" who "dispense the mysteries of God" (1 Cor 4:1). Paul extends the metaphor even further by calling the community the temple of God: "God's temple is holy, and that temple you are" (1 Cor 3:17).

The metaphor "people are household utensils," in turn, is deployed briefly in Rom 9:20–23 as a development of the metaphor "God is a potter" (Rom 9:20). Paul uses the potter image to support God's absolute sovereignty over creation (what he has made), expressed by whom God chooses to "call" into God's people at various times in history (Rom 9:6–16, 24–32): "Has the potter no right over the clay, to make out of the same lump one vessel for honor [*timē*] and another for shame [*atimia*, Rom 9:21]"? It would be possible to understand the cryptic phrases as suggesting the honorable or dishonorable uses to which the vessels would be put and/or the manner in which they would be treated. In line with the latter suggestion, Paul shifts in Rom 9:22 to a "vessel of wrath prepared for destruction [*apōleia*]" and a "vessel of mercy prepared for honor/glory [*doxa*] (9.23)." The point here is not that either of these elaborate and complex metaphors corresponds exactly to the one we find in 2 Tim 2:19–21. The point is rather that Paul is capable of creating such fully complex metaphors and that he does so by employing the same elements as in this one.

In order to understand the shape of the household metaphor in this passage, it is useful to remember the context: Timothy is to be a "proven workman" who can rightly delineate the word of truth, in contrast to those whose teaching is like sickness, who miss the mark concerning the truth, and who are upsetting people's faith. The metaphor is brought to bear on the distinction. Paul begins therefore by pointing to the *themelios* (foundation) of the building—an immediately identifiable image of solidity—in order to indicate two things. First, this household's foundation is *stereos* (firm); no challenge has ultimately threatened it, even though the "faith of some" is being shaken. Second, there is a *sphragis* (seal or sign, possibly referring to an identifying inscription on a building's cornerstone) that clarifies who truly is master of the household and who truly belongs in it.

The allusions to Scripture contained in the two statements are discussed in the NOTES. Here it can be observed that together they stress two aspects of membership. The first is that it is God's call of God's own that is sovereign: "The Lord has known those who are his own." It is possible that *kyrios* both in these clauses and in 2:24 refers to Jesus as Lord—and Paul may have had that in mind—but we remember that earlier Paul had emphasized to Timothy the power of God that saved them and called them (1:8). Paul's point is that it is God who will sort out truth and falsehood in the final judgment, when "God judges the secrets of men" (Rom 2:16). The second aspect of membership is that God's call demands of humans a moral response, or conversion of life: "Everyone who names the Lord's name should depart from wickedness" (compare 1 Cor 5:1–8; 2 Cor 6:14–18).

To make the point about moral conversion, Paul moves from the foundation of "a great house" to the vessels within it (2:20). What is fascinating about this use of the metaphor is the construction. Such a house contains "not only" vessels of gold and silver, "but also" those of wood and clay. The point seems to be the inevitability of less worthy instruments involved in the household's work. We recognize the same realism in Paul's discussion of the various building materials used for the construction of a house in 1 Cor 3:13–15, where he acknowledges that the worth of the material used by each builder will become clear only when tested by fire. In 2:20, the vessels made from different materials suit different uses. Here the phrase *eis timēn* and *eis atimian* clearly refer not to the honor ascribed to the vessels, but to the sort of tasks in which they are employed. Thus it is possible to become a "vessel ready for noble use" (2:21), if "one cleanses oneself from these." The metaphor here breaks down and reveals itself as an allegory for Timothy's situation, for a vessel cannot "cleanse itself," only humans can. Yet even here, we see how metaphor pervades, for humans are not to "cleanse" themselves from physical dirt by washing, but rather to "purify" their moral intentions and attitudes.

The movement of conversion is therefore a movement of self-cleansing. But who or what is meant by "from these"? Presumably, Paul could be referring to the opponents themselves, as unclean vessels. But since the one who calls on the name of the Lord is to separate from "wickedness" (*adikia*, 2:19), Paul may mean the teachings and practices of the opponents. This option is supported by the following commandment, which tells Timothy to "flee" not the false teachers, but certain attitudes and practices (2:22–23). It is striking that Paul uses the verb *ekkathairein* (cleanse from) otherwise only in 1 Cor 5:7, in a passage demanding a similar sort of separation from those who behave immorally within the assembly of believers (1 Cor 5:9). Such purification language echoes the temple aspect of the household metaphor in 1 Cor 3:16–17. We note that Timothy can "cleanse/purify himself" and thereby become "consecrated/sanctified" (*hēgiasmenon*).

The section is internally consistent. It begins with the desire that Timothy show himself to be "tested" before the Lord, an "unashamed worker" (2:15). The notion of "unashamed" (*anepaischynton*) continues the theme of "shame" that recurred in 1:8, 12, 16. The image of the "worker" fits the functional character of Timothy's ministry. The passage ends with Timothy cleansing himself by moral conversion from everything that is unworthy and is to be used shamefully (*eis atimian*). He is then an instrument fit for "honorable/noble" uses (*eis timēn*), a workman "useful to the master, prepared for every good work" (2:21).

VIII. THE CHARACTER OF THE LORD'S SERVANT (2:22–3:9)

◆

2 ²²Flee cravings for novelty. Instead pursue righteousness, faithfulness, love, and peace, with all those who call on the Lord's name with a pure heart. ²³Avoid foolish and uneducated disputes. You know that they generate conflicts. ²⁴The Lord's servant, in contrast, must not engage in conflicts, but must be gentle toward all, an apt teacher and long-suffering. ²⁵He must teach with mildness those who oppose him. Perhaps God will give them a change of heart so that they recognize truth. ²⁶And perhaps they will regain their senses, once they have been snatched alive by God from the devil's snare, so that they can do God's will.

3 ¹But know this: difficult times are approaching in the last days. ²People will be selfish, greedy, boastful, arrogant, blasphemers. They will not be obedient to their parents. They will be ungrateful, unholy, ³unaffectionate, intractable. They will be slanderers, out of control, wild. They will not care about doing good. ⁴They will be traitors, rash and crazed. They will love pleasure more than they love God. ⁵They will have the appearance of piety while denying its power. Avoid these people especially. ⁶Now from among them are the ones who are sneaking into households and capturing silly women who are beset by sins and driven by various passions, ⁷women who are always learning but never capable of reaching a recognition of truth. ⁸In the very way that Jannes and Jambres opposed Moses, so also these men oppose the truth. They are corrupted in mind, untested concerning the faith. ⁹But they will not progress much further, for just as it happened with those men, their stupidity will become obvious to everyone.

NOTES

22. *Flee cravings for novelty*: The phrase *neōterikas epithymias* is difficult to translate. The noun *epithymia* itself, which we have seen in 1 Tim 6:9 and which will reappear in 2 Tim 3:6 and 4:3, has the meaning of "a desire," with the specific content filled in by the context.[543] The adjective *neōterikos* usually means "pertaining to youth" (Polybius, *Histories* 10.21.7). Thus the phrase can be translated as "youthful desires," and for those seeking biographical verisimilitude, the phrase would support the portrait of Timothy as Paul's younger colleague. A sec-

---

543. Johnson, *Letter of James*, 193–194.

ond meaning, attested in some papyri, is "modern in style" or "novel." The cognate verb, *neōterizein*, is stronger, having the sense of "making innovations," sometimes with a nuance of violence or revolution (Isocrates, *Letter* 7:9; see also Josephus, *Against Apion* 1:28). Josephus combines *neōterikos* with *authadeia* (boldness/rashness) in *Antiquities* 16:399. I have shaded the translation away from the biographical and toward Timothy's possible attraction to the "novel teachings" generated by the opposition. In an even stronger reading, Timothy would be warned once more away from the violent toward the gentle.

pursue righteousness, faithfulness, love, and peace: Greco-Roman moral teaching listed virtues as it did vices. A series of four or five such qualities is common in this sort of instruction. See, for example, Lucian's listing of philosophy's companions as virtue (*arētē*), temperance (*sōphrosynē*), righteousness (*dikaiosynē*), culture (*paideia*), and truth (*alētheia*) in *The Dead Come Back to Life* 16; Epictetus's listing of the qualities of the genuine philosopher as tranquillity (*ataraxia*), fearlessness (*aphobia*), and freedom (*eleutheria*) in *Discourse* 3.1.21 (compare 3.26.13); and Epictetus's reward for the genuine philosopher: "The prize is a kingdom [*basileia*], freedom [*eleutheria*], serenity [*eupoia*], peace [*ataraxia*]" (*Discourse* 2.18.29). For "pursue" (*diōke*) as figurative for dedication to the moral life, see Plato, *Gorgias* 482E; Dio Chrysostom, *Oration* 77/78:26; Rom 9:30, and for the phrase "pursue righteousness," see 1 Tim 6:11. As for the individual virtues here listed, *dikaiosynē* reappears in 3:16 and 4:8; *pistis* in 1:5, 13; 3:10, 15; 4:7; and *agapē* in 1:7, 13 and 3:10. But *eirēnē* appears in only the greeting (1:2). Its reappearance here may again be a way of signaling a contrast to the harsh characteristics of the opponents.

call on the Lord's name: Some MSS add the adjective "all" to the phrase "those who call on the Lord's name" (e.g., Ephraemi Rescriptus, F, G, other Greek witnesses, and some variants, such as the Harclean Syriac). This longer reading is probably influenced by the text of LXX Joel 3:5, which is the passage here being alluded to and which reads "all who call." The adjective "all" is present also in other Pauline passages making the same allusion (Rom 10:13; 1 Cor 1:2). A much stranger version is offered by Alexandrinus: "all those who love the Lord" (*pantōn tōn agapantōn ton kyrion*). This is one of several idiosyncratic readings in Alexandrinus for this passage (see also the NOTES on 3:1, 3:6, and 3:9). The reading of Nestle–Aland, which is accepted here, is extremely well attested (Sinaiticus, Bezae, the Koine tradition, and several versions such as the Peshitta), and is both the shorter and the harder reading.[544] The incidence of the phrase (1 Cor 1:2; Rom 10:13; Acts 2:21) and its employment suggest that it may have been a mode of self-designation among some believers.

with a pure heart: The Greek is actually "from" (*ek*) a pure heart (*kathara kardia*), with the heart being understood, as so often in the biblical tradition, as the seat of intentionality (LXX Gen 6:5; Exod 4:21; Deut 6:6; Ps 11:2). For "pure heart," see also 1 Tim 1:5. That Timothy is to pursue virtue "with" those who call on the name of the Lord with a pure heart means that he is to associate

---

544. See also Elliott, *Greek Text*, 144.

himself with companions that strengthen his resolve (compare 2:2). Although Paul focuses in this letter on his delegate, such subtle touches indicate that his constant concern for the building of communities is by no means absent.

23. *Avoid foolish and uneducated disputes*: The characterization "foolish" (*mōros*) is used of both persons (Epictetus, *Discourse* 3.24.86) and things (*Sibylline Oracles* 3:226). In this case, the foolish activity points to and reveals foolish people. The adjective I translate as "uneducated" is *apaideutos*, which can also bear the connotation of "rude" or "boorish" (Plato, *Gorgias* 510B). With that coloration, the harshness of the opposition would once more be intensified. For the imperative *paraitou* (avoid), see 1 Tim 4:7 and 5:11.

they generate conflicts: My translation is quite literal, since *gannaō* means precisely to "give birth to" something (*Letter of Aristeas* 208; LXX Isa 66:9; 4 Macc 10:2) and is found elsewhere in this sense of "producing" (Josephus, *Antiquities* 6:144). For the way in which debates between philosophers could degenerate into battles (*machai*), see Lucian, *Timon* 9; *Dialogues of the Dead* 332; *The Double Indictment* 11; *The Eunuch* 1–13.

24. *The Lord's servant*: Although human slavery is a form of degradation, being the slave of God is a mark of great honor, since one is serving the ultimate power over the world.[545] Thus the designation of God's agents in Scripture (Josh 14:7; 24:29; Judg 2:8; 1 Sam 22:8; Ps 77:71; Isa 48:20; 49:3; Dan 3:85 [A]). Thus also the self-designation of Paul as *doulos* (Rom 1:1; 2 Cor 4:5; Gal 1:10; Tit 1:1). In Phil 1:1, Paul includes Timothy with him as *douloi Christou Iēsou* (slaves of Christ Jesus). The identification of Timothy as *doulos kyriou* here brings to a satisfying conclusion Paul's elaborate metaphor of the *oikia*, which he began in 2:19, since the two "seals" on the house both employed the term "the Lord." Like Moses (servant over God's house, LXX Josh 1:2; Heb 3:5), Timothy's position is one of great authority and requires equal gentleness.

must not engage in conflicts: The verb *machesthai* means literally to "do battle" (Josephus, *Jewish War* 3:365; Herodotus, *Persian War* 1:18; James 4:2) and includes verbal wrangling (Josephus, *Against Apion* 1:38; Lucian *Timon* 9; Philo, *Allegorical Laws* 2:106). It deliberately echoes *machas* (conflicts) in the previous verse.

gentle toward all: There is surprisingly strong evidence for *nēpios* (child/ minor) rather than *ēpios* (gentle). It is found in the original hand of Codex Bezae, as well as F and G. I say surprising because of the difficulty of making sense of *nēpios* in this passage. It is possible that some scribes were influenced by 1 Thess 2:7, where the same variants occur. In this case, not only is *ēpios* better attested (Sinaiticus, Alexandrinus, the second hand of Bezae, and the Koine tradition), but it fits precisely within the framework of moral discourse concerning modes of teaching. The only way *nēpios* would work is if it were thought to represent Timothy's youth.[546]

---

545. D. Martin, *Slavery as Salvation: The Metaphor of Slavery in Pauline Christianity* (New Haven: Yale University Press, 1990).

546. See also Elliott, *Greek Text*, 144.

an apt teacher: The ideal of being *didaktikos* (Philo, *Rewards and Punishments* 27) is desired of the supervisor also in 1 Tim 3:2. Note how—in accord with the social construction of the philosopher in antiquity—Paul's delegate is to have the qualities of the teacher, rather than those of the priest or prophet or ruler.

long-suffering: The adjective *anexikakos* is a NT *hapax legomenon*, but as its component elements suggest, it refers to putting up with evil without recrimination (Lucian, *The Consonants at Law*; Josephus, *Jewish War* 1:624; Wis 2:19). We remember the exhortation to Timothy to "take a share in suffering" (*kakopathein*) in 1:8.

25. *teach with mildness those who oppose*: The precise translation of *paideuein* is difficult, for the verb can mean to "correct" or "discipline" in the sense of "punish" (Xenophon, *Memorabilia* 1.3.5; LXX Hos 7:12; Pss 6:1; 37:1; 1 Cor 11:32; 2 Cor 6:9). The entire context, however, supports the sense here of "teach" or "instruct" (Euripides, *Suppliants* 917; Plato, *Apology* 24E; *Laws* 741A; Aristotle, *Politics* 1260B); compare Tit 2:12 and 1 Tim 1:20. This is particularly clear from the phrase "with mildness" (*en prautēti*), a characteristic that combines humility, considerateness, and meekness (Josephus, *Antiquities* 19:330) and that is cherished by Paul (1 Cor 4:21; 2 Cor 10:1; Gal 5:23; 6:1; Eph 4:2; Col 3:12; Tit 3:2). The phrase "those who oppose" translates the present middle participle of the verb *antidiatithēmi* (those who put themselves against, Diodorus Siculus, *Library of History* 34:12).

God will give them a change of heart: MSS evidence is divided between the subjunctive *dǭ* and the optative *dǭē* for the verb "give." The optative better expresses the tentative tone of the statement and is used also in 1:16, 18. This consistent use also makes it the "easier" reading, but the fact that the optative is found in the original hand of Sinaiticus and Bezae, and is "corrected" to the subjunctive by the second hand in each MS, is another point in its favor. The phrase "change of heart" translates *metanoia*, which literally means a "change of mind" (Polybius, *Histories* 4.66.7; Josephus, *Against Apion* 1:274), but in the NT literature has the sense of repentance. The use of the noun "heart" aims at the same sense of moral as well as mental turning (Rom 2:4; 2 Cor 7:9–10).

they recognize truth: The construction *eis* + the accusative expresses the desired result. The precise phrase "recognition of truth" (*epignōsis alētheias*) is peculiar to the Pastorals (see also 1 Tim 2:4; 2 Tim 3:7; Tit 1:1),[547] although in Paul's other letters, he uses *epignosis* in several combinations (Rom 1:28; 3:20; 10:2; Eph 1:17; 4:13; Phil 1:9; Col 1:9–10; 2:2; 3:10).

26. *they will regain their senses*: The verb *ananēphein* means literally to "become sober [*nēphō*] again [*ana*-]." It is used here in the moral sense of conversion, a meaning attested elsewhere in Hellenistic moral discourse (*Tablet of Cebes* 9:3; Dio Chrysostom, *Oration* 4:77; Josephus, *Antiquities* 6:241). In *Allegorical Laws* 2:60, Philo defines it just so: *ananēphei, touto d' esti metanoei* (to regain the senses, that is, to convert). See *metanoia* in the previous clause.

snatched alive by God: The translation here is very difficult, depending on

---

547. Dibelius, "*epignosis aletheia*."

who is thought to be the subject of "snatching alive." Is it the devil, or is it God? God is the main subject preceding this verse, in the phrase "perhaps God will give." But the Greek has here only *hyp' autou* (by him), which could also point to the devil. Many translations make the devil the one who has captured the sinners alive in his trap in order to do the devil's will: "They may escape from the snare of the devil, after being captured by him to do his will" (RSV). At issue is both who snatches alive and whose will gets done. The verb *zōgrein* (here in the perfect passive participle) means literally "to capture alive," as one does in fishing (Luke 5:10). Note that in LXX Josh 2:13 and 6:25, this verb is used for the rescuing of Rahab and her family from Jericho before its destruction. It seems better, then, despite the awkward word order, to take the "capturing alive" as God's action: God plucks them from the trap of the devil.

from the devil's snare: See 1 Tim 3:6–7 for the phrase "snare of the devil" as something lying just outside the community as a danger and a temptation. It would make sense, then, that those who were in the community, but took up a position opposing the healthy teaching of Paul and his delegate, could be thought of as trapped by the devil (see also 1 Tim 5:15).

they can do God's will: The translation supplies "God's will" for the much more obscure *to ekeinou thelēma* (literally, "the will of that one"), which in principle could have as its antecedent either the devil or God. The devil is syntactically closer, but God is logically more consistent with the intended sense. The topic, after all, is conversion (*metanoia*); it follows that they are rescued alive from a trap so that they can do God's will. For *thelēma tou theou* in Paul, see Rom 1:10; 12:2; 15:32; 1 Cor 1:1; 2 Cor 1:1; 8:5; Gal 1:4; Eph 1:1, 5, 9, 11; 6:6; Col 1:1, 9; 4:12; 1 Thess 4:3; 5:18.

3:1. *But know this*: Typical of its idiosyncratic path in this section of the letter, Codex Alexandrinus (together with F, G, and 33) has the plural *ginōskete* rather than the singular *ginōske*, which is found in all other witnesses. The singular is undoubtedly correct, since it is Timothy who is addressed throughout the letter. A few (mainly Latin) witnesses have the third-person-singular imperative *ginōsketō*, which would make the person saved from the devil in 2:25 the implied subject.

difficult times are approaching: The verb *enistēmi* (to be present/have come, Josephus, *Antiquities* 12:175; 2 Thess 2:2) is here in the future tense, thus "approaching." Paul uses the future *esontai* in the next verse as well, but 3:6 makes it clear that the opponents are already bringing on these times. This is not so much a prediction of the future as a diagnosis of the present. The adjective *chalepos* has the nuance of "harsh" or "hard" (Josephus, *Antiquities* 4:1; 13:422; *Letter of Aristeas* 289; Matt 8:28); the noun *kairoi* might almost be rendered here as "period/season," thus "in the last days a hard season approaches."

in the last days: A phrase with prophetic roots (Isa 2:2; Hos 3:5; Mic 4:1; Jer 23:20; 25:19), this is the only occurrence of *eschatais hemērais* in the Pauline corpus. Paul speaks of the "last" (*eschatos*) enemy and trumpet (1 Cor 15:26, 52), but not of time. Phrases similar to this one do occur in James 5:3; 1 Pet 1:5; 2 Pet 2:20; 3:3; 1 John 2:18; Jude 18.

2. *selfish, greedy, boastful*: The vice-list contains a large number of *hapax legomena*. Among the nineteen items in verses 2–3 are seven NT and five Pauline *hapax legomena*. Four of the terms are found in the undisputed letters, and two appear in only the Pastorals. Compare the vice-list in Rom 1:29–31: among its twenty-two items are seven NT *hapax legomena* (same as 2 Timothy), one Pauline *hapax legomenon* (four fewer than 2 Timothy), and fourteen terms found elsewhere in the undisputed letters (only four in 2 Timothy). The translation of long Greek sentences into more idiomatically English sentences is always a challenge, never greater than in such vice-lists, in which the Greek rhetorical effect is achieved in a manner quite different from the English. "Selfish" translates the Greek *philautoi* (literally, "lovers of self") is a NT *hapax legomenon*; it can be used in a positive sense (Aristotle, *Nicomachean Ethics* 1169A), but also, as here, to refer to an inordinate self-regard (Epictetus, *Discourse* 1.19.11; Philo, *Allegorical Laws* 1:49). "Lovers of money" (*philargyroi*) is one of the classic charges placed against philosophers by rivals (Luke 16:14; for references, see the NOTES on 1 Tim 6:10). Similarly, the *alazōn* is a standard figure of ridicule in such polemic, designating someone who is self-important and boastful—and therefore foolish (Herodotus, *Persian War* 6:12; Dio Chrysostom, *Oration* 4:33; 55:7; 70:8, 10; Philo, *Life of Moses* 2:240; Josephus, *Antiquities* 8:264; Rom 1:30).

arrogant, blasphemers: Like the person with *hybris* who overreaches toward the gods, the *hyperēphanos* is arrogant and haughty toward other humans, assuming toward them a superior status; the adjective appears together with *alazōn* in Josephus, *Jewish War* 6:172 (see also *Epistle of Heraclitus* 2:7; *Letter of Aristeas* 263; Xenophon, *The Ephesians* 1.2.1; *Testament of Reuben* 3:5; LXX Exod 18:21; Pss 30:19; 100:7; Prov 8:13; Tob 4:13; Wis 5:8; esp., Sir 10:7: "hateful to God and humans is arrogance"). The term also appears in the vice-list of Rom 1:31. For *blasphēmoi*, see the NOTE on 1 Tim 1:13.

not be obedient to their parents: We might find it odd to find such a domestic failing in a list filled with otherwise dramatic vices, but this would be to read anachronistically. Lack of piety toward parents was a shameful failing in both Greco-Roman and Jewish cultures. For Paul, in particular, *apeitheia* toward parents was a grievous offense. He includes the same phrase in the vice-list of Rom 1:30. Note further his comments concerning the duties owed parents in Eph 6:1–2; Col 3:20; 1 Tim 5:4, 8, 16, as well as the vice-list in 1 Tim 1:9, not to mention his comments on parents and grandparents in 2 Tim 1:3–5 and 3:15.

ungrateful, unholy: A few MSS (the original hand of Ephraemi and K) have *achrēstoi* (worthless) rather than *acharistoi*, probably through a mechanical error or the influence of Luke 6:35; *chrēstos estin epi tous acharistous* (He is gracious to the ungrateful)—the only other NT use of the word. The adjective *acharistos* fits within the generally hostile vices listed here, denoting, as its etymology suggests, lack of gratitude (Epictetus, *Discourse* 2.23.5; Wis 16:29; Sir 20:16; 4 Macc 9:10; Philo, *On Joseph* 99). The adjective *anosios*, likewise, suggests its meaning by its construction: they are without holiness (*a* + *hosios*) and are, in fact, wicked (2 Macc 7:34; 8:32; 4 Macc 12:11; *Letter of Aristeas* 289;

Josephus, *Against Apion* 2:201). The only other appearance in the NT is in the list of 1 Tim 1:9.

3. *unaffectionate, intractable*: Codex Bezae and a few other witnesses reverse the sequence of these two vices; it makes no difference either way. As in the previous pair, the alpha-privative construction indicates the lack of a positive quality. To be *astorgos* is to be unloving or without affection (see also its appearance in Rom 1:30). The adjective *aspondos* is a NT *hapax* and means to have an attitude of nonreconciliation (Polybius, *Histories* 1.65.6; Philo, *Life of Moses* 1:242).

slanderers: As in 1 Tim 3:11 and Tit 2:3 alone, the adjective *diabolos* is used in its original sense of being a slanderer (Thucydides, *Peloponnesian War* 6.15.2; Philo, *Sacrifice of Abel and Cain* 32).

out of control, wild: Two adjectives with alpha-privative prefixes: the person who is *akratēs* is dissolute and without self-control (LXX Prov 27:20; *Letter of Aristeas* 277; Josephus, *Antiquities* 16:399); the term is found only here in the NT, although Paul uses the noun *akrasia* in 1 Cor 7:5. A person who is *anēmeros* lacks any gentleness and is brutal, even savage (Epictetus, *Discourse* 1.3.7; Dio Chrysostom, *Oration* 12:51; *Letter of Aristeas* 289). This word also is a NT *hapax legomenon*.

not care about doing good: My translation is slightly periphrastic for a "not loving good" (*aphilagathos*) person. Another NT *hapax legomenon*, and in fact unattested anywhere else, it is perhaps a Pauline construction generated in the spirit of creating alpha-privative vices. The noun *aphilagathia* and the adjective *philagathos* are attested in the second-century Oxyrhynchus Papyrus 33, II, 11, and 13.

4. *traitors, rash and crazed*: The noun *prodotēs* refers to one who betrays another (from the verb *prodidōmi*, used by Paul in Rom 11:35), as in *Letter of Aristeas* 270; Josephus, *Jewish War* 3:354; *Life* 133; Philo, *Special Laws* 3:164. It is found also in Luke 6:16 and Acts 7:52 with reference to the betrayal of Jesus. Similarly, Acts 19:36 uses the neuter of the adjective *propetēs* as an adverb; it means to "be reckless and thoughtless" (LXX Prov 10:14; 13:3; Sir 9:18; Josephus, *Antiquities* 5:106; *Life* 171). Although the last term in our triad, the perfect passive participle of *typhoō* (*tetyphōmenoi*) used as an adjective, can mean to "be puffed up or conceited" (e.g., 1 Tim 3:6), here it probably has the sense of being deluded, which is also well attested (Polybius, *Roman History* 3.81.1, combining it with ignorance, as does Dio Chrysostom, *Oration* 6:21; see also Philo, *On the Confusion of Tongues* 106; Josephus, *Against Apion* 1:15; 2:255, as well as the usage in 1 Tim 6:4).

love pleasure more than they love God: Although the adjective *philēdonos* is a NT *hapax legomenon*, the "love of pleasure" (*philēdonia*) is a standard charge against rival teachers (Aelius Aristides, *On the Four* 307:15; Julian, *Oration* 6:182B, 198B; 7:225A; Philostratus, *Life of Apollonius of Tyana* 1:7; 2:29; Dio Chrysostom, *Oration* 33:13; Epictetus, *Discourses* 1.9.19–21; 2.4.1–11; 3.22.93; 24.38–39; Lucian, *Icaromenippus* 21; *Nigrinus* 25; *Carousal* 11; *Timon* 54; *Philosophies for Sale* 12; *The Parasite* 53; *Dialogues of the Dead* 369–370;

Hermotimus 11). In philosophical circles, the charge would be that they loved pleasure more than wisdom or virtue; for these teachers within a religous philosophy, the contrast is with "love of God" (*philotheos*, another NT *hapax*, but attested in Aristotle, *Rhetoric* 2.17.6; Lucian, *Slander* 14; Philo, *On Husbandry* 88).

5. *the appearance of piety*: Paul uses the noun *morphōsis* (form, *Testament of Benjamin* 10:1) also in Rom 2:20, but there more in the sense of "formulation," whereas here the term refers to an outward form that is denied by actions. For *eusebeia* (piety), see the NOTE on 1 Tim 2:2. The contrast between outer profession of virtue and inner vice is constant in the polemic used between rival teachers in antiquity (Aelius Aristides, *On the Four* 307:6, 10; Epictetus, *Discourses* 4.8.5–9; Julian, *Orations* 6:197C; 7:223C). See also the NOTE on 1 Tim 4:2.

denying its power: It is unlikely that "denying" (*ērnēmenoi*) is confessional; it is rather a denial in the form of behavior (compare 2:13). Once more, we see the importance of the "power" (*dynamis*) of the *eusebeia* shared by Paul and his delegate (1:7, 8, 12; 2:1); as in the undisputed letters, it is the power of the message to transform lives that is its most convincing feature.

Avoid these people especially: The phrase is *kai toutous apotrepou*. It could be rendered as "and avoid these," but I have taken the *kai* in the first position—after such a long vice-list—as signaling emphasis. Note how the *gar* in the next line picks up from this one. The verb *apotrepein* in the middle voice means to "turn away from" (Josephus, *Jewish War* 3:500; 4 Macc 1:33) and is a NT *hapax legomenon*.

6. *Now from among them*: The translation may not be sufficiently emphatic: the connective *gar* establishes a strong link to the *toutous* whom Timothy is to avoid and who have all the characteristics listed in the vice-catalogue. Notice further that this connection also makes their practices the sign that the "hard seasons" of the last days are truly approaching and perhaps even present.

sneaking into households: The verb *endynō* means to "enter," as by creeping (Aelian, *Various Histories* 4:22; Greek Magical Papyrus 7:271), and the translation "sneaking" seems appropriate here. In 1:16 and 4:19, Paul uses *oikos* for the household of Onesiphorus, but elsewhere he makes no real distinction between *oikos* and the term used here (*oikia*) when referring to houses or households (e.g., 1 Cor 11:22; 16:15). Apart from the references to the very real household of Onesiphorus, and the metaphor of the "great *oikia*" in 2:20, this is the only case of household language in 2 Timothy.

capturing silly women: There is no real difference in meaning between the *aichmalotueontes* read by the second hand of Bezae and the Koine tradition, and the *aichmalotizontes* read by Sinaiticus, Alexandrinus, F, G, P, and many other witnesses. Both forms are found in other Pauline texts (see Eph 4:8 for the first and Rom 7:23; 2 Cor 10:5 for the second, which is also adopted by Nestle–Aland). The verb means literally to "take a prisoner in war" (Diodorus Siculus, *Library of History* 14:37; Plutarch, *Mor. Sayings of Spartans* 21 233C; Epictetus, *Discourse* 1.28.26) and can be used, as here, for a more figurative capturing (Dio Chrysostom, *Oration* 32:90). So Paul in Rom 7:23 uses it of the Law and, in 2 Cor 10:5, of capturing thoughts. In this passage, there may be an element of "misleading," as in LXX Jdt 16:9 and *Testament of Reuben* 5:3. For *gynaikaria* (one or two MSS have the definite article *ta*), see Epictetus, *Encheiridion* 7; Marcus Aurelius, *Meditations* 5:11; and the COMMENT.

beset by sins: The verb *soreuein*, here in the perfect passive participle, means to "heap or pile something up" (Josephus, *Antiquities* 12:211; *Jewish War* 4:380) and is used that way by Paul in Rom 12:20; it can also mean to "fill up something" (Polybius, *Histories* 16.8.9). The sense here is that they are overwhelmed by sins. The letters to Timothy actually speak very little about sin (*hamartia*). In addition to this passage, see only 1 Tim 1:9, 15; 5:20, 22, 24.

driven by various passions: As noted earlier, Codex Alexandrinus tends to go its own way in this section. With a very few other witnesses (notably the Harclean Syriac), it adds the words *kai hēdonais* (and pleasures) to "various passions." The effect would be to further deprecate the women. There is insufficient evidence to support this longer reading. The adjective *poikilos* (various) already adds to the sense of confusion among such people, as does the participial form of the verb *soreuein*. Finally, the passive participle *agomena* (being driven) reminds us of Paul's usage in Rom 8:14, but especially in 1 Cor 12:2. For the negative (and usually sexual) associations of *epithymia* (desire) among Hellenistic moralists, see the NOTE on 1 Tim 6:9.

7. *always learning*: The present participle of *manthanein* might even make legitimate the translation "always in the process of learning" in the sense of receiving instruction from another (Xenophon, *Cyropaedia* 2.2.6; *Memorabilia* 1.2.17), or even, given the context, "always becoming someone's disciple."

never capable of reaching: Here the theme of power is again expressed negatively. The false teachers deny the power of piety, and those they teach are "never with the power" (*mēdepote dynamena*) to reach what they seek. In view of the striving implicit in the description, I translate the infinitive *elthein* (coming) as "reaching."

a recognition of truth: The phrase *epignōsin alētheias* (recognition of truth) is virtually a technical term in the Pastorals (1 Tim 2:4; 2 Tim 2:25; Tit 1:1). As in 2:25, it here means that kind of spiritual acknowledgment that constitutes *metanoia*. There is a perfect fit between the teachers who have the form, but not the power, of piety and their followers who always are learning, but never have the power of reaching the truth. All this is the language of polemic.

8. *In the very way*: The accusative relative construction *hon tropon* is an abbreviated way of expressing *kata hon tropon* (literally, "according to the manner," Xenopohon, *Memorabilia*, 1.2.59; *Anabasis* 1.1.9; Plato, *Republic* 466E). Although Paul elsewhere uses several kinds of construction with *tropos* (Rom 3:2; Phil 1:18; 2 Thess 2:3; 3:16), this specific construction is lacking in his other letters, while present in Matt 23:37; Luke 13:34; Acts 1:11; 7:28; 15:11; 27:25.

Jannes and Jambres opposed Moses: A few witnesses (F, G, the Old Latin, and Cyprian) have Mambrēs for one of Moses' opponents, rather than the Iambrēs read by most MSS. Neither of the names occurs in the biblical account of the "wise men, sorcerers, and magicians" in Pharaoh's court. In Exod 7:12, the magicians match Aaron's trick of turning a rod into a serpent, even though Aaron's turns and eats theirs! The magicians also are able to equal the feat of turning the water of the Nile into blood (Exod 7:22). They do not reenter the story for the later wonders worked by Moses and Aaron. Perhaps this is one way in which they anticipate Paul's assurance concerning the current opponents: "They will not progress much further" (3:9). The names Jannes and Jambres seem to derive from Jewish haggadic tradition. According to Eusebius, *Preparation for the Gospel* 9.8.1, their names appear in the work of the second-century B.C.E. writer Numenius of Apamea, and there may have been an apocalyptic work (no longer extant) that contained their names (CD 5:18). See also Pliny the Elder, *Natural History* 30.2.11, and Apuleius, *Apology* 90. The presence of the names in *Targum Pseudo-Jonathan* may or may not offer further evidence for the pre-Christian Jewish tradition concerning the magicians.[548]

so also these men oppose the truth: The phrase *houtōs kai houtoi* (so also these) establishes the link to "in the same manner." The phrase "thus also" is frequent in Paul (Rom 5:18, 19, 21; 6:4, 11; 11:31). The same verb (*anthistemi*, "to stand against") is used here as for opposing Moses, and recurs in 4:15 for the resistance to Paul's teaching. The reason why the women cannot reach recognition of truth is that these charlatans are actively opposing it!

corrupted in mind: The verb *kataphtheirein* (here in the aorist participle passive) is a NT *hapax* (unless the Textus Receptus of 2 Pet 2:12 is correct), meaning to "destroy or ruin" (Polybius, *Histories* 2.64.3; Lev 26:39; 2 Macc 5:14). The accusative *ton noun* expresses that with reference to which they have been ruined: their minds. They cannot teach truth, for their minds themselves cannot contain it, so ruined are they.

untested concerning the faith: As so often in protreptic discourse addressed to teachers, the positive qualities of the ideal philosopher are negated in the case of the opponents. Timothy was told in 2:15 to present himself to God as "tested" (*dokimos*) and as someone who "rightly delineated the word of truth." In contrast, the false teachers resist the truth and are "untested" (*adokimoi*) with respect to faith (*peri tēn pistin*).

9. *not progress much further*: This is now the second use of *prokoptein* (to make progress). In 2:16, Paul said that the opponents were making "ever greater progress in ungodliness." He will return to the same point in 3:13: "they progress from bad to worse." The distinction is between their moral progression, which is in fact a regression, and their external success. This statement deals with the latter. It contains some ambiguity. If they are not going to progress "much further" (*epi pleion*), that itself is an admission that they have made significant inroads.

---

548. L. L. Grabbe, "The Jannes/Jambres Tradition in Targum Pseudo-Jonathan and Its Date," *JBL* 98 (1979): 393–401; S. Gero, "Parerga to the Book of Jannes and Jambres," *Journal for the Study of Pseudepigrapha* 9 (1991): 67–85; K. Koch, "Das Lamm, das Ägypten vernichtet: Ein Fragment aus Jannes und Jambres und sein geschichtlichen Hintergrund," *ZNW* 57 (1966): 79–93.

stupidity will become obvious to everyone: Once more, Codex Alexandrinus (this time standing alone) provides a distinctive and ingenious reading: rather than *anoia* (lack of mind/stupidity), it has *dianoia*, so that the opponents' "purpose" will become obvious to everyone. The analogy with the Moses situation is complete: the eventual triumph of Moses and Aaron over the charlatans of the past provides assurance that Paul and Timothy's opponents also will be exposed.

COMMENT

Although for purposes of interpretation it is necessary to divide the text into manageable portions, it is also important to remember that this section (and, for that matter, the next) are part of the second major unit of Paul's personal paraenetic-protreptic letter to Timothy, in which Timothy's character and practice are developed by means of positive maxims and through contrast to the opponents. The most obvious literary observation about this section, therefore, is that the basic antithetical pattern of instruction continues. Paul alternates positive and negative commands to his delegate in the second-person singular (2:22, 23, 24; 3:1, 5) and juxtaposes them to descriptions of the practices of the opponents in the third-person plural (2:23, 25; 3:2–5, 6, 8–9).

Characterizing the Opponents

The portrayal of the opponents is enriched by the use of a vice-list in 3:2–5. The vice-list is a regular feature of a Hellenistic moral discourse that was particularly enamored of catalogues and lists of every sort—vices, virtues, hardships, pedigrees.[549] The specific elements in this list are discussed in the NOTES. The point of such catalogues is not found in their specific contents, however, so much as in their overall rhetorical effect. The lists are based on the premise that just as virtuous people practice good in a variety of ways, so bad people exhibit all imaginable vices. Some lists are so extensive as to make one wonder whether the point is simply the rhetorical skill of the writer. Philo, for example, constructed a vice-list with 140 elements (*Sacrifices of Cain and Abel* 32).

The rhetorical effect of catalogues is achieved in part by length and in part by the internal rhymes and rhythms created by the separate elements put into certain combinations. It is important to remember that all reading in antiquity was done out loud rather than silently; all public reading therefore was in some sense a rhetorical performance. Lists like these do not appeal to the eye. But through oral delivery, they can have considerable impact. In the list in this passage, note the repetition of the *ph* sound (almost a sibilant rhythm) in *philautoi philargyroi . . . hyperēphanoi blasphēmoi*. Note also the effect of the *oi* end-

---

549. Fitzgerald, "Virtue/Vice Lists"; N J. McEleny, "Vice-Lists of the Pastoral Epistles."

ings in the same sequence. Similarly, a stylistic effect is achieved by the series of words beginning with the alpha-privative: *acharistoi anosioi astorgoi aspondoi*, an effect that is accomplished in English by the repetition of "without" time after time.

The rhetorical function of the list is accomplished by the transition statement in 3:6: "Now from among them are the ones. . . ." Although 3:1 alerts Timothy to the characteristics of "people" in the last days, it turns out that the collection of vices actually serves to identify Timothy's opponents and to place the struggle with the false teachers within the framework of the eschatological battle. Just as strongly as in 1 John 2:18–19, the presence of opposition from within the community is taken as evidence that the "difficult times" of the last days are in process (compare 1 Tim 4:1).

The brief allusion to the magicians of Pharaoh's court who opposed Moses and Aaron (3:8–9) is of interest not because of the puzzle of their names, but because the use of such a scriptural *exemplum* is so typically Pauline. We see in 1 Cor 10:1–11 how Paul uses part of the Exodus story—more precisely, the Exodus and Wilderness accounts—as an example for the fractious Corinthian congregation: "These things happened to them as a warning [*typikos*] but they were written down for our instruction, upon whom the end of the ages has come" (RSV 1 Cor 10:11). Paul uses Exodus as an example—really, an analogy—for those who are "in the last days"! Elsewhere, Paul implies that he plays the same role for the present age that Moses played in the story of the Exodus (Rom 9:3; 2 Cor 3:12–18).

It should not be shocking, then, to see the Exodus story yield one more lesson for his delegate, and a particularly pertinent one. Timothy, after all, is to Paul what Aaron was to Moses. So Paul draws the analogy: the fact that the LXX designates them as "sophists, magicians, and sorcerers" fits perfectly the polemic of Paul's culture, in which charges and countercharges of being "charlatans" and "magicians" could be exchanged by those wearing the solemn mantle of philosophers (esp. *Letters of Apollonius of Tyana* 1–2, 5, 8, 16–17). Then, as now, the opponents seem the more spectacular and enjoy greater success. But then they simply disappear from the narrative, while Moses and Aaron prove triumphant as the servants of the Lord! Paul therefore holds out the hope that these charlatans also "will not progress much further" because "their stupidity will become obvious to everyone" (3:9). The way Paul here uses Scripture as a source for exhortation is of particular importance because of his statement concerning the didactic functions of Scripture in the next section (3:15–16).[550]

The portrait of the opponents is relentlessly negative. They reveal in their character and actions all the negative traits that Timothy is to avoid. As in the previous section, much of this is the standard rhetoric of polemic: in addition to exemplifying all the vices listed in 3:2–3, they are stupid (3:9) and foolish

---

550. Although I am reluctant to follow his thesis concerning 2 Timothy as a whole, in *Pauli Testamentum*, Martin throws light on much of this section of the text by exploiting the Moses connection, particularly the designation of Timothy as "Servant of the Lord."

(2:23), engage in uneducated debates (2:23), and seek after novelty (2:22). They oppose the truth (3:8) and are corrupted in mind (3:8). All such charges can readily be found in virtually any of Lucian's attacks on phony philosophers (e.g., *Philosophies for Sale; The Eunuch; Menippus*).

More distinctive of polemic between adherents of a religious movement is the charge in 3:8 that the opponents are "untested [*dokimos*] with regard to the faith" and that they "overturn the faith of some people" (2:18). This is particularly significant because of Paul's desire that Timothy present himself as "tested" (*dokimos*) before God (2:15), that he "pursue faith" (2:22), and that he be an "unashamed workman" (2:15) who is "prepared for every good work" (2:21). Similarly, the Hellenistic commonplace that false philosophers preach but do not practice (Lucian, *Hermotimus* 79; Epictetus, *Discourse* 3.5.17; Philostratus, *Life of Apollonius of Tyana* 2:29) is given a specifically religious turn in 3:5: the opponents have the form of piety (*morphē eusebeias*), but they deny its power (*dynamin autēs arnēmenoi*). Once more, the contrast with the *dynamis* (power) operating through Paul and his delegate (1:7–8, 12; 2:1) is deliberate and emphatic.

The Treatment of Women

As with the preaching about the resurrection in 2:18, it may be possible to cut beneath the rhetoric on one point of actual practice: the charge in 3:6 that the opponents "sneak into" or "insinuate themselves" into households and make captives of *gynaikaria*. Charges of this sort are not entirely absent in the literature. Lucian, a consistent critic of all pretentiousness, touches on instances in *Alexander the False Prophet* 6, and in *The Runaways* 18:

> The thing would not be so dreadful if they offended against us only by being what they are. But although outwardly and in public they appear very reverend and stern [*semnoi kai skythpropoi*], if they get a handsome boy or a pretty woman in their clutches or hope to, it is best to veil their conduct in silence. Some even carry off [*apagousi*] the wives of their hosts, to seduce them [*moicheusontes*] after the pattern of that young Trojan, pretending that the women are going to become philosophers [*hōs philosophoiein de kai autai*].

This charge of seducing members of a household under the cover of philosophy or religion is not a standard part of the rhetoric, however, even though we will see it again as applied to Paul in the *Acts of Paul and Thecla* and to the heretic Marcus in Irenaeus, *Against Heresies* 1.13.1. And as I have mentioned, even stereotypical polemic can occasionally hit the mark. It is entirely possible that Paul here describes an actual proselytizing practice of the opposition, casting it in negative terms.

The translation of *gynaikaria* as "silly women" or "weak women" is not linguistically off-base, for the term bears the connotation of male condescension embedded in the English expression "little woman." Because the Pastorals are so regularly charged with sexism—and this commentary has shown the ways in which 1 Timothy must be considered, at the very least, androcentric and patriarchal—it may be worthwhile to give closer attention to this passage, which is in tension with the other statements in 2 Timothy concerning women. It is abundantly clear, first of all, that the Paul of this letter is not sexist in the full sense of that term. In the beginning of the letter, Timothy's mother and grandmother stand as examples of faith that he is to imitate (1:5). They have shown the capacity to "recognize truth." Then, in 3:14–15, we shall see Paul reminding Timothy to remain within what he has learned and of "those from whom" (in the plural) he learned it, since from his childhood he had been schooled in the Scripture. The natural, if implicit, referents for this allusion are Eunice and Lois, the maternal forebears who taught Timothy in the faith of Judaism and in Torah. They therefore had the capacity not only to "learn" and "come to recognition of truth," but also to teach the faith and the Scriptures, if only within the realm of the household. Finally, the greetings at the end of the letter include Paul's co-workers Priscilla, Pudens, and Claudia (4:19–21). Given these notices, it would appear that the author of the letter would not consider women *as such* to be silly or incapable of learning and reaching recognition of truth. And it is within that perspective that this passage is most constructively interpreted.

The author's description of these particular women in 3:6–7—that they are "beset by sins and driven by various passions . . . always learning but never capable of reaching a recognition of truth"—is not applied to the nature of women as a class of humans, but to the dilemma of women within a certain societal class in the Greco-Roman world. It is the dilemma posed, on the one hand, by the privileges of wealth, status, and the opportunity for education, and, on the other hand, by a lack of significant opportunities for expression in the larger world.[551] The closest (near-) contemporary analogy is provided by the gentle parodies of "women of a certain class" in the *New Yorker* cartoons of Helen Hokinson: they are women of means and mobility, but without a disciplined education or access to real power in the world. Their lives are a round of study-groups and projects, but however seriously they take themselves and their endeavors, they always appear to male observers as somewhat "silly." It should be observed, with relief, that Hokinson's cartoons from the 1940s and 1950s now appear quaint rather than pointed, for the social situation of women in Western culture has changed dramatically.

But it should also be observed that Hokinson's cartoons (like Lucian's satires) provide valuable insight into a cultural reality. In Paul's era, the most enlightened champion of women's ability to think philosophically as well as men was

---

551. There has been an explosion of literature on the topic of women in the Greco-Roman world. Among many others, see A. Cameron and A. Kuhrt, *Images of Women in Antiquity*, rev. ed. (London: Routledge, 1993); M. R. Lefkowitz and M. B. Fant, *Women's Life in Greece and Rome*, 2nd ed. (Baltimore: Johns Hopkins University Press, 1992); J. F. Gardner, *Women in Roman Law and Society* (Bloomington: Indiana University Press, 1986); and J. P.V. D. Balsdon, *Roman Women: Their History and Habits* (New York: Barnes and Noble, 1962).

the Stoic philosopher Musonius Rufus, the teacher of Epictetus. He insisted that women were fully the equal of men in mental and moral capacities and therefore should be taught philosophy. But to what end? That they should be a help to their husbands and manage their households well. They should not become arrogant and leave their households to join the public debates of men: "The teachings of philosophy exhort the woman to be content with her lot and to work with her own hands" (Musonius Rufus, *That Women Too Should Study Philosophy*, frag. 3). Within such a male-defined culture, women with intelligence and ambition would easily be attracted to intellectual leaders who paid attention to either.

We meet in 2 Tim 3:6–7, I think, just such wealthy women—within households, we notice—who have the leisure for the pursuit of philosophy, but are prevented by societal norms from more than an amateur's engagement with it, making them as a consequence also less able to distinguish the authentic from the counterfeit. Paul's comments are not so much sexist as they are acute social observation. Such women are the "perpetual students" of antiquity, available for the suasions of charlatans who go from house to house with an impressive appearance and a compelling message.

Women of position and means have often been seduced in just this fashion within patriarchal structures. In the twentieth century, the place and power of the monk Rasputin in the court of the czar owed everything to his capacity to "captivate" the czarina with his manner and message. The problem is obviously not the natural defects of women, but the artificial and culturally induced deficiencies of a society that systematically keeps certain categories of persons in a chronically undereducated and disempowered position, and therefore chronically in the posture of victims of unscrupulous manipulators of desperate human need.

If my analysis is sound up to this point, and I recognize the inevitable speculation it involves, perhaps I can push one step further. If, indeed, there is a real situation being addressed in the letter, and the stereotyped polemic enables us to disentangle three probable facts about the opposition—that it uses harshness in its teaching, that it proclaims a realized resurrection life, and that it aims at women within households—then we are allowed to ask what appeal such a message and such a style of teaching might have for women of the sort I have depicted.

I have already suggested that an acute realized eschatology could lead logically either to sexual promiscuity (since "we" are already in the kingdom and are not subject to rules restricting the use of our bodies) or to sexual rigor (since "we" are already leading the life of the angels and should share their purely spiritual conditions of being). Thus while some in Corinth asserted the freedom to consort with prostitutes, using the slogan "Food for the belly, the belly for food" (1 Cor 6:13)—that is, sexual behavior has nothing to do with spiritual status—others also had a slogan, "It is good not to touch a woman" (1 Cor 7:1), apparently out of the conviction that a devotion to God precluded the entanglements of sex. Paul absolutely forbids sexual promiscuity (1 Cor 6:18–20), but he also carefully qualified his approval of celibacy. He encouraged it insofar as it gave freedom for service "in the Lord," while also insisting that marriage was preferable to sexual immorality and was indissoluble except under special conditions (1 Cor 7:1–11).

Could either option have particular appeal for the leisured women of households who were always seeking wisdom? Paul's characterization that they are "driven by various passions" in 3:6 can be taken as suggesting sexual impulses; on this basis, we might imagine something more than spiritual seduction taking place. But he adds that they are also "beset [or burdened] by sins." An acute realized eschatology that combined a harsh and demanding regimen with celibacy could have an enormous appeal to women whose lives within the household were defined by biology and social bias. The history of female religious orders and of such charismatic movements as the Shakers demonstrates how in a context where women's lives are often short, defined by childbearing and child rearing, and sometimes also characterized by abuse, the option of celibacy within the framework of an ascetic discipline has much to offer. It could provide them with freedom from the ambiguities of sexual life—both its passions and its guilts—and from household obligations.

It is fascinating that just this combination of elements is met in the second-century *Acts of Paul and Thecla*. The young woman Thecla is seduced by the teachings of a visiting preacher who proclaims that the resurrection is dependent on virginity. She abandons her intended spouse and creates a societal uproar, especially when she seeks to follow the charismatic teacher in a public career of preaching. She is prepared to cut her hair, wear men's clothes, and take part in the larger world. No wonder her family and friends and city officials alike are aghast. What is most fascinating of all in this account is that it is Paul who is the seducer and the upsetter of households!

Timothy's Character and Practice

The point of this section of the letter is not the description of the false teachers or of their victims, but the shaping of Timothy's character and practice. As Paul's delegate, he must carry out the delicate role of moral teacher in the communities to which he is sent (1 Cor 4:17). Two things in particular stand out in this portion of Paul's portrait of the "servant of the Lord" (2:24). The first is the focus on Timothy's personal virtue. The second is the attention paid to his manner of instruction.

Fundamental to the character ethics of the Hellenistic world—an ethics that shows itself so pervasively in 1 and 2 Timothy—is the conviction that the teacher of morality must first of all have the highest standard of morality. The true philosopher is true because of a personal conversion from vice to virtue. Attention to one's own moral purpose is particularly necessary because of the vulnerability of the one who proclaims to others. Emperor Julian says, "Then let him who wishes to be a cynic, earnest and sincere, first take himself in hand like Diogenes and Crates, and expel from his own soul and from every part of it all passions and desires, and entrust all his affairs to reason and intelligence and steer his course by them" (*Oration* 6:201D). The same sentiments are everywhere expressed (Epictetus, *Discourse* 3.22.93–96; Dio Chrysostom, *Orations* 33:13–15; 77/78:40, 45; Julian, *Orations* 6:196C; 7:225D). The philosopher must be able to be utterly transparent to the gaze of others (Epictetus, *Discourse* 3.22.160), governed by his own commitment to reason and virtue. Lucian says of Demonax,

> Even from his boyhood he felt the stirring of an individual impulse toward the higher life and an inborn love for philosophy, so that he despised all that men count good, and, committing himself unreservedly to liberty and free-speech, was steadfast in leading a straight, sane, irreproachable life, and in setting an example to all who saw and heard him by his good judgment and the honesty of his philosophy. (*Demonax* 3)

In the previous section, Paul suggested the need for anyone wishing to be a noble vessel useful to the master to "cleanse himself" from vices (2:21). Now in an antithesis typical of paraenesis, Paul tells him to "flee" cravings for novelty and to "pursue" righteousness, faithfulness, love, and peace (2:23). The concatenation of qualities is another typical feature of Hellenistic moral discourse. Just as vices are strung together, so are virtues. Paul will quickly provide a similar listing for Timothy's imitation in 3:10 (compare 1 Tim 1:5 and 4:12; 6:11). It would be a mistake to read such lists as mindless. They present in compressed form the ideals toward which this particular form of moral endeavor strives. As the NOTES indicate, each of these qualities is generously attested in the undisputed Pauline letters as a "virtue" as well.

Timothy's personal qualities are to translate themselves into a teaching practice that is remarkable for its gentleness. Being himself a person of righteousness and peace, Timothy can be "gentle [*ēpios*] toward all" and "long-suffering" (*anexikakos*), a term that suggests the hardships that are endemic to being an "apt teacher" (*didaktikos*, 2:24). He is not to fall into the harsh methods of the opponents and get into wrangles with them. He is, instead, to instruct them with mildness (*prautēs*, 2:25). This positive and irenic teaching style is the more to be noted because it is distinctive of 2 Timothy among the Pastorals; the approach in 1 Timothy and Titus is much more severe (1 Tim 1:3; 6:20; Tit 1:11; 3:9–11).

Paul connects such gentleness in teaching to an optimism about the consequences. He holds out the hope—even if expressed as a velleity—that "perhaps" God will give even such opponents as these a change of mind (*metanoia*) so that they can gain recognition of truth (2:25). The teacher, then, assists God in "snatching them alive" from the trap of the devil in which they were caught. And the result? They are now able also to do God's will (2:26). This hope for repentance among the false teachers is, like the gentleness and mildness recommended to the delegate, a distinctive trait of 2 Timothy among the Pastorals. In this letter, moral teaching is medicine that really heals. The point is not cutting off a sick member. The point is making the community well.

IX. THE LIVING TRADITION
(3:10–17)

◆

3 [10]But you have followed closely my teaching, my way of life, my purpose, my faith, my patience, my love, my endurance, [11]my persecutions, and my sufferings, such as befell me in Antioch, in Iconium, and in Lystra. I endured such persecutions, and the Lord delivered me from them all. [12]And indeed all those who choose to live piously in Christ Jesus will be persecuted. [13]Evil men and charlatans will get even worse. They are deceivers and are themselves deceived. [14]But you, remain in those things that you learned and about which you have become convinced. You are aware of the ones from whom you learned them. [15]And you have known the sacred writings since you were a child. They are capable of making you wise concerning salvation through the faith that is in Christ Jesus. [16]Every scripture is God-inspired and useful for teaching, reproving, correcting, toward an education in righteousness, [17]in order that the man of God might be fit, prepared for every good work.

NOTES

10. *followed closely*: The translation of the aorist verb *parēkolouthēsas* is particularly important for understanding Paul's point. Some MSS (notably Bezae and the Koine tradition) have the perfect tense *parēkolouthēkas*, probably under the influence of 1 Tim 4:6. The verb is based on *akolouthein*, which means simply to "follow" in the literal sense (e.g., Mark 1:18), but can also be used in the sense of "following as a disciple" (e.g., Mark 2:14; Luke 9:23). The form *parakolouthein* has a similar range, from the act of literally walking behind someone, to "following with the mind," as in the case of an argument (Epictetus, *Discourse* 1.6.13). This seems to be the sense in Luke 1:3, where the author does not claim to have been personally present at events, but to have "observed them." Translations like "you have observed" (RSV) in this passage are accurate, therefore, but are inadequate on two counts. First, the translation might give rise to the notion that Timothy actually was present at the events. At the point of this composition, from captivity, that would require another trip of Paul to the region of Antioch, Iconium, and Lystra for that to be possible. Second, the expression misses the implication that Timothy has paid close attention to what he has learned of Paul's experiences and the manner in which he had en-

dured them. The motif of imitation lies just below the surface, as the next verse demonstrates.

my teaching, . . . way of life, . . . purpose: Paul joins three interrelated aspects of the philosopher's mission: what he teaches, how he lives it, and his intentions. For the noun *agogē* as indicating "way of life," see Polybius, *Histories* 4.74.1; Marcus Aurelius, *Meditations* 1:6; LXX Esther 2:20; 2 Macc 11:24. For the convergence in the true philosopher of "teaching" (*didaskalia*) and "manner of life," (*agogē*), so that both are open to the observation (and imitation) of all, see Epictetus, *Discourse* 3.22.16; 22.45–49; Dio Chrysostom, *Oration* 35:5; Lucian, *Demonax* 6–8. For *prothesis* as a plan of action, or resolve, see Polybius, *Histories* 1.26.1; Josephus, *Antiquities* 18:272; Acts 11:23; 27:13.

my faith, . . . patience, . . . love, . . . endurance: In contrast to the vices characterizing the false teachers, Paul himself exemplifies inner qualities appropriate to the "Lord's servant." For *pistis* and *agapē* as qualities demonstrated by Paul, see 1:13; as qualities to be pursued by his delegate, see 2:22. The terms *makrothymia* and *hypomone* both denote "endurance" in the broad sense (Plato, *Thaetetus* 177B; *Testament of Dan* 2:1; *Testament of Joseph* 2:7), with *makrothymia* having the additional nuance of enduring with a certain "large-mindedness" or "patience" in the positive sense (LXX Prov 16:32; 19:11; 25:15; Sir 29:8; 1 Macc 8:4).[552]

11. *my persecutions, . . . sufferings*: The entire sequence of nouns in this litany is in the dative case, governed by the verb "you have followed closely," but it is possible that the plural dative in the case of these last two terms might better be taken as "in my persecutions and sufferings." They show the circumstances, in other words, in which the truth of Paul's teaching and character has been demonstrated. Note how Paul speaks elsewhere of his positive attitude in the midst of straitened circumstances and "persecutions" (*en diōgmois*) in 2 Cor 12:10, and of the "sufferings" (*pathēmata*) that he endures for the sake of others in Col 1:24.

in Antioch, in Iconium, and in Lystra: The events mentioned here are those that occurred, according to Acts, in the period before the recruitment of Timothy (Acts 16:1–3), during Paul's first missionary trip with Barnabas through Antioch of Pisidia (Acts 13:49–52), Iconium (14:4–6), and Lystra (14:19–22). Iconium is also the setting for Paul's activities in the *Acts of Paul and Thecla* 1–2, immediately after his departure from Antioch. Some MSS (K, 181, and the Harclean Syriac) contain a marginal gloss of an explanatory character after the words "in Antioch": they add, "That is, the things he suffered on account of Thecla from Jews who had come to believe in Christ." The gloss is of interest primarily for showing familiarity among some copyists with the apocryphal writing the *Acts of Paul and Thecla* and their willingness to use it as a supplementary historical source.

I endured: The verb *hypopherō* means literally to "put up with" or "submit to" (Plato, *Thaetetus* 173A; *Laws* 879C; 2 Macc 7:36). Paul uses the same term in 1 Cor 10:13 for the endurance of testings by believers.

---

552. For a fuller discussion, see Johnson, *Letter of James*, 312–313.

the Lord delivered me from them all: The deponent verb *rhyomai* means to "save or rescue something" (Herodotus, *Persian War* 1:86–87; Euripides, *Orestes* 1563). It is a favorite Pauline term for God's action toward the faithful (Rom 7:24; 11:26; 15:31; 2 Cor 1:10; Col 1:13; 1 Thess 1:10; 2 Thess 3:2; 2 Tim 4:17). Paul will return to the hope for such deliverance again in the future in 4:18.

12. *choose to live piously*: The verb *thelein* can be translated as "wish," but in this case, the implied sense of real choice demands a stronger rendering (compare Rom 7:15; 1 Cor 7:36; Gal 4:9; 5:17; 1 Thess 2:18; Col 1:27). Some MSS reverse the order of the Greek words in the phrase "live piously," which has no effect on the meaning. The phrase puts in verbal form the ideal expressed frequently in 1 Tim (2:2; 4:7–8; 5:4; 6:3, 5, 6, 11). In this letter, the ideal has been found up to now only by way of negation, in the deeds of the opponents (3:5). More significant for Paul's point here are the phrases on either side of this one. It is living piously "in Christ Jesus" that will bring on persecution, and— the paraenetic point—it will happen to "all those" who choose it (see the COMMENT).

will be persecuted: Paul returns in this passage to the theme of suffering for the sake of the good news that he established in 1:6–2:13. For Paul's other statements concerning the *diōgmoi* (persecutions) that come to those committed to Jesus as Messiah, see Rom 8:35; 1 Cor 4:12; 2 Cor 4:9; 12:10; Gal 4:29; 5:11; 2 Thess 1:4.

13. *Evil men and charlatans*: The adjective *ponēros* (evil) is sometimes used substantively for "evil people" (Lucian, *Timon* 48; Deut 21:21; Esther 7:6; Philo, *On Rewards and Punishment* 3; Josephus, *Antiquities* 6:307), but here it qualifies the noun "men" (*anthrōpoi*). For the full phrase, see also 2 Thess 3:2. The noun "charlatan" (*goēs*) is a NT *hapax legomenon*, but is common in Hellenistic moral discourse, being used especially in just this sort of polemical context, to dismiss an opponent (e.g., Dio Chrysostom, *Oration* 32:11; Plato, *Symposium* 203D; Demosthenes, *Orations* 18:276; 19:109; Polybius, *Histories* 4.20.5; Lucian, *Nigrinus* 15; Philo, *Special Laws* 1:315; *Who Is the Heir* 302; Josephus, *Jewish War* 4:85; *Antiquities* 20:97; *Against Apion* 2:145, 161).

will get even worse: In 3:9, Paul assured Timothy that the opponents would not "progress much further," in the sense of having greater success in their efforts to persuade others. There is some sarcasm built into this statement, since the verb *prokoptein* (to make progress) can be used of progress in moral effort (Epictetus, *Discourse* 2.17.4; Lucian, *Hermotimus* 63; Marcus Aurelius, *Meditations* 1.17.8; Gal 1:14). Here, however, it is progress *epi to cheiron* (toward the worse), a phrase that occurs also in Plato, *Republic* 381B; Strabo, *Geography* 16.2.39; Josephus, *Antiquities* 16:207.

deceivers . . . themselves deceived: This is another standard charge against opponents in the polemic of antiquity (Dio Chrysostom, *Oration* 4:33, 37; 33:14, 15; 48:10; 54:1; of those who boast of being philosophers without demonstrating the character of philosophers, he says, *kai auton exapatēsai kai tous allous*, "he both deceives himself and others," 70:10); see also Philo, *Migration of Abra-*

ham 83, and Porphyry, *Life of Plotinus* 16.[553] In this case, Paul already charged the opponents with having "corrupted minds" (3:8), and their disputes as being "foolish and uneducated" (2:23).

14. *remain in those things that you learned*: In contrast to those who are "progressing," even if it is toward the worse, Timothy is to remain (*mene*), and in contrast to their false novelty, Timothy is to stay within the tradition. Note how the attention of this letter stays consistently on Timothy and his attitudes and practices.

about which you have become convinced: The verb *pistoō* is rare: in the active, it is attested in Thucydides, *Peloponnesian War* 4:88; LXX 2 Sam 7:25; 1 Chron 17:14; 2 Macc 7:24; in the middle voice, see *Letter of Aristeas* 91. This is the only use in the NT, and it appears in the passive voice (compare *1 Clement* 15:4; 42:3), expressing a state of confidence or conviction. The issue has never been Timothy's being persuaded by the good news, but his courage to stand by it in the face of suffering. This phrase may, then, be another subtle reminder of how one thing should connect with another.

from whom you learned them: Some witnesses (notably the third hand of Ephraemi and the first hand of Bezae, as well as the Koine tradition) have the singular *para tinos* rather than the plural *para tinon*, which is found in Sinaiticus, Alexandrinus, the first hand of Ephraemi, and a variety of other MSS. The plural is the preferred reading on two counts: it is attested by a better and wider range of independent witnesses, and it is the harder reading. The plural points back to Timothy's maternal forebears (1:5), as well as Paul. The singular can attach to only Paul. The tendency of scribes would be to make Paul the sole source for Timothy's learning of the Scriptures and to connect this exhortation to Paul's example sketched in 3:10–11.

15. *the sacred writings*: Paul uses a phrase (*hiera grammata*) widely employed by Greek-speaking Jews to designate the Scriptures (Philo, *Life of Moses* 2:290–292; *On Rewards and Punishment* 79; *Legation to Gaius* 195; Josephus, *Antiquities* 1:13; 10:210; *Against Apion* 1:54). He uses *gramma* with reference to Scripture elsewhere, but never so positively (Rom 2:27, 29; 7:6; 2 Cor 3:6, 7).

since you were a child: The noun *brephos* refers to the earliest stage of human development, even back to an embryo (*Sentences of Pseudo-Phocylides* 184; Josephus, *Antiquities* 20:18). Here it means "infancy" or "very early childhood," which demands that we understand Eunice and Lois as Timothy's instructors in the Scriptures. For the phrase *apo* [or *ek*] *brephous* as indicating "from earliest childhood," see Philo, *Special Laws* 2:33 and *On Dreams* 1:192.

capable of making you wise: With the participle *dynamena* applied to the sacred writings, we once more see Paul's contrast between the power of God—at work in the Scripture and in the good news—and the powerlessness of the false teachers: they deny the power of godliness (3:5), and their students are "powerless" (*me dy-*

---

namena) to learn (3:7; see also 1:7, 8, 12; 2:1). The verb *sōphizein* here means to "make wise" in the sense of providing instruction (Hesiod, *Works and Days* 649; Diogenes Laertius, *Lives of Eminent Philosophers* 5:90). Paul seems to be echoing what LXX Ps 18:8 says about Torah: *ho nomos tou kyriou amōmos, epistrephōn psychas, hē martyria kyriou pistē, sophizousa nēpia* (the law of the Lord is blameless, converting the soul, the witness of the Lord is faithful, making wise the babes).

salvation through the faith that is in Christ Jesus: The construction of the phrase demands attention. The linkage of *sōtēria* and *pistis* (faith, salvation) is familiar from Rom 1:16–17 and 10:1–4. In Romans, furthermore, it is more than likely that Paul is arguing that it is Jesus' faith that saves.[554] The phrase in this passage, "that is in Christ Jesus" (*tēs en Christō Iēsou*), cannot mean the Christian's faith in Jesus (that would be *eis Christon*), but probably refers to the faith shown by the human person Jesus toward God.

16. *Every Scripture is God-inspired*: This is a classic *crux interpretum*. The adjective *theopneustos*, as its etymology suggests, means simply "breathed by a god," or "divinely inspired" (*Sentences of Pseudo-Phocylides* 121; *Sibylline Oracles* 308, 406). That's clear enough. The debate concerns the attributive or predicative character of the adjective. Should we understand "every God-inspired Scripture is. . . ." or "every Scripture is God inspired and . . ."? (The omission of the *kai* before the adjective *ōphelimos* in some Latin MSS [a, f, m, t, and others] cannot be considered original and should not affect the discussion.) The debate is not central to Paul's point, which concerns the function rather than the origin of Scripture, and is generated by theological concerns about the inspiration of Scripture that are driven by an anachronistic literalism. For further discussion, see the COMMENT.

useful for teaching: Here is Paul's emphasis, on the "usefulness" of Scripture (for *ōphelimos*, see Plato, *Republic* 607D; 1 Tim 4:8; Tit 3:8; for Paul's use of the verb *ōphelein*, see Rom 2:25; 1 Cor 13:3; 14:6; Gal 5:2). For ancient philosophers, it was the usefulness of doctrine for the transformation of life that measured its value: the question *ti ophelos* (what use is it) is raised frequently as a criticism of arcane and useless teaching or teaching without a corresponding practice (Plato, *Gorgias* 504E; Epictetus, *Discourse* 1.4.26; 6.33; 2.32.24, 51; 32.24.51; LXX Job 15:3; Sir 20:30; 41:14; Josephus, *Antiquities* 17:154; Philo, *Migration of Abraham* 55; *Posterity and Exile of Cain* 86). The adjective *ōphelimos* governs four identical prepositional phrases with *pros* + the accusative construction. The first, "for teaching" (*didaskalia*), is the most comprehensive, encompassing the role of the delegate, and is recapitulated in the conclusion of the final phrase (1:11; 2:2; 3:10; 4:2, 3).

reproving, correcting: Codex Bezae and the Koine tradition read *elenchon* here rather than the *elegmon* found in Alexandrinus, Sinaiticus, C, F, G, and many other witnesses. There is a slight difference in meaning: *elegmos* appears almost exclusively in the LXX in the sense of punishment or reproof (Num 5:18; Ps 149:7; Sir 21:6; 32:17; 48:7; Judith 2:10; 1 Macc 2:49), while *elenchos* is used widely in logic and rhetoric for a proof or the process of proving (Plato, *Gorgias*

471E; Epictetus, *Discourse* 3.10.11; Philo, *On Rewards and Punishment* 4; Josephus, *Against Apion* 2:17), although it can also refer to a correction or reproof (LXX Hab 2:1). As for "correcting" (*epanorthōsis*), it has less the sense of censure than of "improving" or "setting right" (1 Macc 14:34), especially in the moral sense (Polybius, *Histories* 1.35.1; Epictetus, *Discourse* 3.21.15; *Encheiridion* 51:1; *Letter of Aristeas* 130; Philo, *Allegorical Laws* 1:85). Scripture is here proposed as a guide to moral growth. Compare "rightly delineating [*orthotomounta*] the word of truth" in 2:15.

education in righteousness: The noun *paideia* can denote teaching or training in the broad sense (Plato, *Phaedo* 107D; *Philebus* 55D), or even discipline in the sense of chastisement (LXX Prov 22:15). But here, as frequently, it has the sense of "education" or even "culture" (Plato, *Protagoras* 327D; *Gorgias* 470E; Aristotle, *Politics* 1338A). This last term, then, corresponds to the "teaching" with which the series began: these modes of instruction lead to a certain culture, which is defined as—and consists in—"righteousness" (*diakaiosynē*), a term whose Pauline resonances are obvious (see only Rom 1:16–17), but as in the rest of the letter is here considered primarily in moral terms.

17. *man of God*: Especially in the narrative portions of Scripture, the title *anthrōpos [tou] theou* is given to special representatives of God like the Prophets and, preeminently, the prophet Moses (LXX Deut 33:1; Josh 10:14; 14:6; Judg 13:6; 1 Sam 2:27; 9:6–10; 1 Kings 13:5; 14:3; 2 Kings 1:9; 4:7; 1 Chron 23:14; 2 Chron 11:2; 30:16; Neh 12:24, 36). Given the analogy between Moses and the magicians in 3:8–9, it is a particularly apposite designation (compare *doulos kyriou* in 2:24).

might be fit: There are slight variants in the original hand of Codex Bezae, which replaces *artios* with *teleios* (perfect). That is actually one meaning of *artios*, and the Greek side of Bezae may have derived this rendering from the Latin translation. In the margin of 104 there is also the gloss *hygiēs teleios* (healthy/perfect), which appears to be an attempt to make precise the sense of *artios* that is to be understood. Actually, the meaning of "prepared/ready" seems to fit best here (Philostratus, *Lives of the Sophists* 1:9; Herodotus, *Persian War* 9:27; Epictetus, *Discourse* 1.28.3).

prepared for every good work: The verb *exartizein* is cognate with *artios*, and has the same range of meaning. Thus here, the sense could move in the direction of "finished/perfect" (Josephus, *Antiquities* 3:139) or, more likely, "prepared/ready" (Josephus, *Antiquities* 3:43). The phrase "for every good work" (*pros pan ergon agathon*) echoes 2:21, where the verb used is *hetoimasmenon* (made ready).

COMMENT

The pattern of antitheses continues into this section, with the focus entirely on Timothy himself; note the repetition of *su de* (but you) in 3:10, 14. We observe also the way verbs of movement create an effect. The opposition has been characterized in terms of movement and progress (2:16–17; 3:6, 9, 13). In contrast, Timothy's attitudes have largely been those of avoidance. He has been told to "shun," "avoid," "flee," and "turn away from" them and their practices (2:16, 22–23; 3:5). Only in 2:22 has Timothy been encouraged to move: he is to "pursue" (diokein) the virtues of righteousness, fidelity, love, and peace! Now Timothy is reminded that he has "followed" Paul's own way (3:10), and he is commanded to "remain" (menein) in what he has been taught (3:14). In contrast to progressive novelty that will "not go much further" (3:9), Timothy is to be as stable as "God's firm foundation" (2:19).

The theme of imitation appears again in this section as well, echoing the more explicit development of Paul as Timothy's model in 1:6–14. Here, as there, it is imitating Paul in his willingness to suffer for the good news that is the point of this paraenetic/protreptic exhortation. Thus the generalizing statement "And all those who wish to live piously in Christ Jesus will be persecuted" (3:12) serves to establish a link between the fact that Paul both endured sufferings and was rescued by the Lord, and the implication that Timothy likewise is "following closely" (3:10) in the same path.

The Uses of Scripture

One of several passages in the Pastorals that the interpreter would just as soon avoid, 3:16–17 has been systematically tortured by readers less interested in considering what Paul had to say to Timothy than in using these verses to support theological position taking. The verses have been caught up in controversies involving theologoumena about the divine inspiration of Scripture. Endless arguments have been constructed in support of reading the controverted phrase as "all Scripture is inspired by God" or "every God-inspired Scripture is. . . ." The controversies have been heated (especially in what has come to be called the modernist/fundamentalist struggle) because the proper translation was regarded as critical for convictions concerning the inspiration of the entire Bible and therefore the character of the Bible as the exclusive source of divine revelation and therefore the authority of the Bible for Christian life.[555]

The first thing that needs to be said in response to these premises is that they are all wrong, not only exegetically (more on that later) but also hermeneutically. The authority of the Bible does not rest on its inspiration, but on its canonicity, a status that each church confirms by the use of the Bible in every generation in liturgy and in decision making.[556] The Bible functions within the process of revelation not as an exclusive textual source, but as an essential and normative resource for discerning and measuring God's self-disclosure within human existence and activity.[557] Finally, the theological conviction that the Bible is di-

---

555. See, for example, B. Warfield, Biblical Foundations (Grand Rapids, Mich.: Eerdmans, 1958).

556. Johnson, Scripture and Discernment.

557. S. Schneiders, The Revelatory Text (San Francisco: HarperCollins, 1991).

vinely inspired rests not on the Bible's self-referential statements, but on the faith in Christians that through its very human and culturally conditioned words, God's word is also spoken and God's Spirit is at work, so that the historical meaning of any passage does not exhaust its significance or the uses to which God's Holy Spirit can put it.[558] And this leads us back to the exegetical question and Paul's concern.

It should be obvious that Paul cannot be making a statement about the Christian Bible, for the New Testament collection was not yet in existence. The term *graphē*, as everywhere else in Paul, refers to those compositions read and studied in the synagogue from the Law (*Torah*), Prophets (*Nebi' im*), and Writings (*Ketubim*), in whatever collection then existed in what we now call the Septuagint (LXX), the Greek translation of the Jewish Scriptures that was carried out in Alexandria around 250 B.C.E. Since the process of canonization of the Jewish Scriptures was not yet formalized, it was not possible—particularly because what Scriptures there were existed in separate scrolls rather than within the covers of a codex—to have *graphē* refer to a single anthology. Paul's reference was necessarily, then, to whatever collection of compositions he and the earliest churches used and regarded as authoritative.

Paul's purpose, moreover, was not to make an ontological or a doctrinal declaration concerning the status of those compositions. Insofar as they were *graphē*, Paul agreed with all his fellow Jews that they were inspired by God and authoritative, were indeed revelatory of God's very word. This is not arguable. But it must also be pointed out that Paul and his contemporaries did not confine "inspiration" to those literary compositions that are now found in the Bible. Other compositions could claim inspiration and could have inspiration ascribed to them. And it is clear that within some Pauline communities, various kinds of prayer and prophecy were regarded as inspired by God and containing revelation from God. Paul himself could claim to speak in the spirit of God. To say that all Scripture was inspired, in other words, was not in Paul's day to make a unique or an exclusive claim, even though it was to make an important one.

Paul's purpose in talking about Scripture is to make a point about its usefulness. Therefore 3:16–17 is not an ontological, but a functional statement. Paul makes similar declarations in other letters. He concludes an application of LXX Ps 68:9 to the sufferings of Jesus and to the present attitudes of the Roman Christians by stating, "Whatever was written in former times was written for our instruction, that by steadfastness and by the encouragement of the scriptures, we might have hope" (RSV Rom 15:3–4). The Scriptures, therefore, provide instruction (*didaskalia*) and encouragement/exhortation (*paraklēsis*). And it does this in Romans by presenting a text that was exemplified in the life of Jesus for the readers' imitation (Rom 15:1–3). Similarly, Paul concludes his application of the Wilderness story to the Corinthian congregation by asserting, "These things happened to them as a warning [*typikōs*], but they were written down for

---

558. K. Rahner, *Inspiration in the Bible*, QD (New York: Herder and Herder, 1961).

our instruction [*nouthesia*, "correction"], upon whom the end of the ages has come" (RSV 1 Cor 10:11).[559] It should come as no great surprise, then, that after again employing an example from the Exodus account—the opposition of Jannes and Jambres to Aaron and Moses (3:8–9)—Paul should make another such statement concerning the usefulness of Scripture for purposes of instruction. The difference here is that the statement is more general and inclusive, and, in keeping with the character of this paraenetic/protreptic letter, it focuses on the way in which it shapes the identity and practice of Timothy as a "person who belongs to God" (*ho tou theou anthrōpos*, 3:17).

The first thing that the Scripture can do is make Timothy wise (*sophisai*) unto salvation through the faith that is in Jesus Christ (3:15). This is the transformative function of Scripture with respect to Timothy himself. Most striking in this characterization is not the conviction that reading the Scripture can make one wise, for that is a widespread understanding connected to the study of Scripture in the Jewish tradition, within which, we are to understand, Timothy was raised (Acts 16:1–3; 2 Tim 1:5). No, it is the statement that Scripture helps Timothy understand the salvation that is through the faith in Jesus Christ. The phrase "salvation through faith" is certainly familiar from Paul's thesis statement in Rom 1:16, but more intriguing is the possibility that, as in Rom 1:16–17 and 3:21–26, Paul is here referring to the personal faith of the human person, Jesus. The "faith that is in Christ Jesus" can scarcely be rendered in this passage as a faith directed to the Messiah. Rather, the construction suggests a faith that belongs to Jesus. And if this is the case, then we have a very deep point of connection to Paul's distinctive convictions concerning the role of Jesus. The role of Scripture in the formation of Timothy, then, is much like the role of Scripture in Rom 15:3–4: the Scripture illuminates the story of Jesus in his faithful gift of himself for humans, and his story provides the *telos* for Scripture itself (Rom 10:4).

Paul's main emphasis here, however, is on Scripture's "usefulness" (*ōphelimos*), which in ancient moral teaching is the ultimate test of value in anything. The usefulness for the teacher is spelled out in terms of how Scripture can be used. The first three functions, we notice, correspond to the characterizations provided by Paul in the passages from 1 Corinthians and Romans discussed earlier. Teaching (*didaskalia*), for example, is stated as the function of Scripture in Rom 15:4. Rebuke or reproof (*elegmon*) and correction (*epanorthōsis*) point in the same direction as the *nouthesia* (admonition/instruction) found in 1 Cor 10:11. What these terms suggest is that Scripture serves as a source of moral and spiritual improvement. This is made clear by the final, summative statement of function: Scripture is useful for an entire education in righteousness (*paideia en dikaiosynē*). To take *paideia* at its full value in Greco-Roman discourse, this is equivalent to saying that Scripture draws its readers into the culture of divine and human righteousness.

---

559. Hanson also notices these parallels in "Inspired Scripture: 2 Timothy 3:14–17," in *Studies in the Pastoral Epistles*, 43–55. But (to my mind inexplicably) he tries to show how they are different from, rather than like, the usage in 2 Timothy.

The final *hina* clause serves as a result rather than a purpose clause, indicating the end result of *sophisai* (making wise) in 3:15. Paul shows the connection between personal and professional formation in a balanced clause that plays on the two meanings of *artios/exartizesthaai*. The result of Timothy's reading in Scripture will be that he is a "man of God" who both is personally "complete and capable" (*artios*) and "has been made complete/capable" as a teacher "for every good work" (3:17).

The Contrast Completed

As Paul approaches the climax of his exhortation in 4:1–8, the real contrast between Timothy and his adversaries is made clearer. The opponents, we have learned, are eager for novelty and engage in disputes precisely to generate controversy. In contrast, Paul urges Timothy to be a person situated within a tradition. He is to stand fast within that which he learned as a child (3:14–15) from his mother and grandmother, who had the same faith dwelling in them as Timothy now also has (1:4–5): the long heritage of Torah that can make one wise toward salvation through the faith of Jesus. The rivals engage in profane chatter just for show, but the words of Torah are "useful" for the correction and instruction of others, since they can create a genuine *paideia* of righteousness (3:16).

Whereas the opponents are charlatans, the effect of whose teaching is to make people sick, Timothy has learned "healthy words" to make people well. The false teachers enter into households in order to disrupt them. They make captives of women who are eager for novelty and are unable to discriminate between the counterfeit and the authentic. In contrast, Timothy offers the stability of the "firm foundation" of the community of faith, a network of those who nurture growth in truth, even in children. This is a community where women are not the weak or silly captives of charlatans, but are educators who transmit the wisdom of Torah and the faith of Jesus.

The opponents have the form of piety, but their actions deny its power, and their preaching of a present resurrection threatens to diminish the significance of the cross. Paul and Timothy, in contrast, claim the gift of power that has come from the one who has suffered and by his death has destroyed death and revealed immortality. It is this power that enables them to endure the suffering and persecution that accompanies a life truly dedicated to God. The vices demonstrated by the opponents are a sign that "the last days" are here. But Paul and Timothy pursue the virtues that will win a reward for all those who love God on "that day."

The antithetical pattern of exhortation that Paul has used from 2:14 to 3:17, then, demarcates two approaches to life and ministry within the faith. There can be no question that he gives positive approval to stability, continuity, tradition, peace, and the household, while discouraging insurrection, conflict, discontinuity, innovation, and disruption of households. But this part of the letter poses two questions to every reader. The first calls for a historical judgment: Are these emphases dependent on a "development" within Christianity in the direction of "domestication," or are they compatible with the Paul of 1 Corinthians who declared, in his discussion of charismatic gifts within the community, "God is a God not of confusion but of peace. As in all the churches of the saints . . . did the word of God originate with you or are you the only ones it reached? . . . [A]ll things should be done decently and in order" (1 Cor 14:33, 36, 40). The second question calls for theological discernment: Whether these emphases derive from Paul himself or from his followers, do they represent a set of values that diminish the good news, or do they challenge the church in every age concerning the conditions within which genuine *paideia* in righteousness can flourish?

X. FINAL EXHORTATION
(4:1–8)

◆

4 ¹I admonish you before God and before Christ Jesus, who is coming to judge the living and the dead, and in view of his appearance and his kingdom: ²Preach the word! Apply yourself to it in good times and in bad. Refute and rebuke! Give comfort with every sort of long-suffering and teaching. ³For there will be a time when, because they have itchy ears, they will not put up with healthy teaching, but will multiy teachers fashioned to their own passions. ⁴They will stop listening to the truth. They will turn aside to myths. ⁵But you, stay sober in all matters. Endure the hard things. Do the work of proclaiming good news. Fulfill your ministry. ⁶For I am already being offered up as a sacrifice, and the time for my death is near. ⁷I have fought the noble fight, finished the race, held tight to the faith. ⁸There is waiting for me now the crown given to the righteous, which the Lord, the righteous judge, will award me on that day, not only me but all those who have loved his coming.

NOTES

1. *I admonish you*: The beginning of Paul's final summons to his delegate is very solemn. Compare the use of *diamartyromai* in 2:14 and 1 Tim 5:21, as well as in Xenophon, *Cyropaedia* 7.1.17; Polybius, *Roman History* 3.110.4; Exod 19:10, 21. A number of MSS, including the Koine tradition, add one or more words: *oun* (therefore), *egō* (I), or *oun egō* (I therefore). The additions would make the charge even more solemn as well as more firmly attached to the previous verses, but for that very reason the shorter text (found in Sinaiticus, Alexandrinus, Ephraemi, and the original hand of Bezae) is to be preferred, since the alternatives can be explained by the helpful creativity of copyists.

before God and before Christ Jesus: Again, note the resemblance to 2:14, where Timothy is to exhort "in the presence of God." The addition of "Christ Jesus" is found also in 1 Tim 5:21. The expression serves to call God and Christ as witnesses in order to enhance the gravity of Paul's exhortation.

coming to judge the living and the dead: That Jesus will participate in the judgment of humans at the end-time is stated by Paul (Rom 2:16; 2 Cor 5:10), but never elsewhere so clearly as here. The form of the statement combines elements that appear to be traditional: for Jesus' coming to judge (*mellei krinein*) the world, see Acts 17:31; for Jesus as the one "set aside by God to be judge [*kritēs*] of the living and the dead," see Acts 10:42. Paul speaks of Jesus as "lord of the living and the dead" in Rom 14:9.

in view of his appearance and his kingdom: The precise function of this co-ordinated clause is difficult to grasp. After the verb *diamartyromai* the accusative stands for the thing sworn by: thus "by his appearance [*epiphaneia*]" or "in view of his appearance."[560] The second clause may have been put in the accusative as well in order to avoid a series of dependent genitives.[561] It could also, there-fore, be translated as "by the appearance of his kingdom." It is clear in that Je-sus' "appearance" refers to the parousia, as in 2 Thess 2:8 and 1 Tim 6:14.

2. *Preach the word*: This exhortation builds on what Paul has said earlier in the letter concerning "the word" (*logos*): the word of God is not bound (2:9), it is faith-ful (2:11), and Timothy is to "rightly delineate" it (2:15). Paul does not identify his own words with the word of God (1:15; 4:15). For similar language elsewhere in Paul, see 1 Cor 1:18; 14:36; 2 Cor 1:18; 6:7; Gal 5:14; 1 Thess 1:8; 2:13. Paul tells his delegate to "preach" (*kēryssein*), just as he himself is a "preacher to the nations" (1:11). Paul will later interpret God's preserving him as ensuring that his *kērygma* will be fulfilled to all nations (4:17). For such language elsewhere in Paul, see Rom 10:8; 1 Cor 1:23; 15:12; 2 Cor 1:19; Gal 2:2; 1 Thess 2:9.

Apply yourself to it: The verb *ephistēmi* is here in the aorist imperative. It means literally to "stand by something" or "take one's stand" on something (Acts 10:17; 12:7; 1 Thess 5:3). But the verb can also mean to "fix one's mind on" something or "pay attention to" it (Aristotle, *Metaphysics* 1090A; *Politics* 1335B). The translation tries to capture something of both senses; compare "be urgent" in the RSV.

in good times and in bad: The Greek phrase here is asyndetic, placing to-gether the two adverbs *eukairos akairos* (literally, "good season/without season"), which can be rendered in a variety of ways. With some variations, the sentiment is fairly widely attested and communicates the basic idea of "whatever the cir-cumstances."[562]

Refute and rebuke: In a manner similar to the earlier presentation of Paul's example in 3:10–11, the charge spells out three (or four) modes of discourse in-volved in the "preaching of the word," as well as an attitude. The first form of discourse is *elenchein*, which has the same range of possible meanings as its cog-nate *elenchos*, the variant reading with *elegmos* in 3:16. It could certainly have the more positive sense of "demonstrate" or "convince" here (Josephus, *Against Apion* 2:5; Wis 2:11; Philo, *On Joseph* 48; *Special Laws* 3:54), especially since the next two terms can be read, respectively, as "negative" and "positive" (see also 1 Cor 14:24; Eph 5:11, 13). But I have cautiously adopted the translation "refute," which maintains the meaning of "logical engagement," but empha-sizes a combative stance (Sir 20:2; 31:31) and perhaps even the sense of cor-

---

560. Zerwick and Grosvener, *Grammatical Analysis*, 2:644.

561. Blass and Debrunner, *Greek Grammar*, 446, par. 16).

562. A. J. Malherbe, " 'In Season and Out of Season': 2 Timothy 4:2," in *Paul and the Popular Philosophers* (Minneapolis: Fortress Press, 1989), 137–145.

rection (Matt 18:15; compare 1 Tim 5:20; Tit 1:9, 13; 2:15). The verb *epitiman*, in contrast, has the straightforward sense of rebuking (Thucydides, *Peloponnesian War* 4.28.1; Epictetus, *Discourse* 3.22.10; Josephus, *Antiquities* 5:105). This is the only use of the term in the Pauline corpus, although it is used frequently in the Gospels (Matt 8:26; 12:16).

Give comfort: Some MSS (the original hand of Sinaiticus, F, G, and some others) reverse the order of *epitimēson* and *parakaleson*. Once more, the widely used verb *parakalein* has a number of possible meanings that depend on the context, ranging from "inviting" (Josephus, *Antiquities* 12:172; Acts 8:31; 2 Cor 5:20) to "requesting" (Josephus, *Antiquities* 6:143; Phm 10; 1 Tim 2:1) to "exhorting" (*Testament of Naphtali* 9:1; 1 Cor 16:12; 1 Tim 5:1; 6:2) to "comforting" (*Testament of Reuben* 4:4; 2 Cor 1:4). My translation moves in the direction of "comforting" because of the attitude of *makrothymia* that Paul connects to it. But the other translations are also possible (see also Rom 12:8; 1 Cor 14:31; 2 Cor 7:6; Eph 6:22).

every sort of long-suffering and teaching: Paul asks his delegate to have the same attitude of "long-suffering" (*makrothymia*) that Paul had exhibited (see the NOTE on 3:10). I translate the adjective *pasa* as "every sort," rather than "all," in order to capture the responsive character of this virtue in the process of preaching and teaching. More difficult is deciding how to translate *didachē* (Rom 6:17; 1 Cor 14:6, 26; Tit 1:9), which is here simply connected to *makrothymia* with the conjunction *kai*. The problem is alleviated slightly if we take the noun *didachē* not as the content, but as the act of teaching (Herodotus, *Persian War* 3:134; Plato, *Phaedrus* 275A; Philo, *Special Laws* 2:3); then we can regard the adjective *makrothymia* almost as an adverb and translate the phrase as "in every sort of patient teaching."

3. *there will be a time*: The reason why *makrothymia* will need to characterize the teacher is now made clear. The noun *kairos* (season) echoes the slogan *eukairos akairos* (in good times and in bad) in the previous verse. Paul now proceeds to sketch the "unseasonable season" that faces his delegate. As in 3:1–6, however, the future times are, in reality, also the present times.

because they have itchy ears: I have added "because" in order to make clear the explanatory function of the predicative participle, which functions adverbially. The expression *knēthomenoi tēn akoēn* means, literally, "being itchy with respect to hearing," making the traditional translation "itchy ears" almost unavoidable. For the idiom, see Clement of Alexandria, *Stromateis* 1.3.22.5. The itchiness is a restlessness to hear new things, and not necessarily healthy ones. The metonymy also brings out the medical aspect of the metaphor.

not put up with healthy teaching: The phrase continues the medical imagery begun with "itchy ears." The hearers are unable to "bear with" (*anexontai*) healthy teaching (*hygiainousēs didaskalias*). For this sense of the verb *anechein* + the genitive, see Philo, *Every Good Man is Free* 36; Josephus, *Against Apion* 2:126; Heb 13:22. Since healthy teaching is precisely what Paul and Timothy have to offer (1:13), they face continuing rejection, and will require all the patience and long-suffering they can muster.

multiply teachers: The verb that I have translated as "multiply" is *episoreuein* (Epictetus, *Discourse* 1.10.5), which is an intensification of the verb *soreuein*, used by Paul in 3:6 for the "piling up" of sins among the ever-learning women in households. Unlike that verb, it is a NT *hapax*. Note that the disaffected hearers express their disaffection by multiplying *didaskaloi* (teachers). The self-understanding of the philosopher runs through 1 and 2 Timothy.

fashioned to their own passions: The translation "fashioned to" seeks to express the sense of the construction *kata* + the accusative. The Koine MS tradition reverses the word sequence from *kata tas idias epithymias* to *kata epithymias tas idias*; there is no difference in meaning. For the negative associations of *epithymia* in Hellenistic moral discourse, see the NOTE on 3:6. It is important to emphasize that "their own desires" (RSV) is too weak a rendering; just as the women in households are driven by passions, so will people seek teachers who cater to such drives. The adjective *idios* (own) adds an emphasis on the self-directedness or willfulness involved in such selection of teachers.

4. *stop listening to the truth*: Paul employs another dramatic metaphor for spiritual dispositions. Now the metaphor is truth = a path. Using the same verb as in 1:15 for those who abandoned him, Paul says that they "turn away from" (*apostrephein*) the hearing (*akoē*) of the truth (*alētheia*). Similar constructions with *akoē* are frequent in Paul's letters (Rom 10:16–17; 1 Cor 12:17; Gal 3:2, 5; 1 Thess 2:13). Paul makes a very strong claim. Truth (*alētheia*) is the defining characteristic of the message of Paul and Timothy, which implies that resistance to their message is opposing the truth (compare 2:15, 18, 25; 3:7, 8).

turn aside to myths: The verb *ektrepomai* is used in similar fashion in 1 Tim 1:6; 5:15; 6:20, but not in other Pauline letters. It continues the spatial metaphor, with the turning *away* from the truth being accompanied by a turn *toward* myths. The usual construction is *eis* + accusative (Epictetus, *Discourse* 1.6.42; Philo, *Special Laws* 2:23). Here it is *epi* + accusative. For *mythoi* as a typical term of slander between philosophers, see the NOTES on 1 Tim 1:4 and 4:7.

5. *stay sober in all matters*: The turn to personal exhortation is marked by *sy de* (but you), as in 3:10. Sobriety in the broadly moral, not only the literal, sense is widely recommended in Hellenistic moral discourse, which treasured rational responses to reality (e.g., Lucian, *Hermotimus* 47; *Nigrinus* 5; Marcus Aurelius, *Meditations* 1.16.3; *Letter of Aristeas* 209; *Sibylline Oracles* 1:154; Josephus, *Jewish War* 4:42). The attitude of sobriety is demanded of the supervisors and helpers in 1 Tim 3:2–3, 11, and also of the Thessalonians in their eschatological circumstances (1 Thess 5:6, 8).

Endure the hard things: The original hand of Sinaiticus and some MSS of the Vulgate lack the verb *kakopathein* altogether, while the consistently idiosyncratic Codex Alexandrinus adds "as a noble soldier of Christ Jesus." The verb is attested by all the rest of the witnesses, and the scribe of Alexandrinus was undoubtedly influenced by 2:3. The exhortation clearly echoes the opening plea to Paul's delegate to "take his share of suffering" for the good news (1:8), just as Paul suffers (1:12) and "suffers hard things" (*kakopathein*, 2:9).

Do the work of proclaiming good news: Literally, "do the work of an *euange-*

listēs," the term is used of Philip (one of the Seven) in Acts 21:8, but is otherwise not used in the NT. It later comes to be used of the Gospel writers. The translation of "evangelist" is possible, but I wanted to avoid confusion with those later writers.

Fulfill your ministry: The verb *plērophorein* means to "bring" (*phērō*) to fullness (*plēroō*). Alternatively, it can mean either to "finish and complete" (Luke 1:1; Rom 4:21; Col 4:12) or to "carry out in a complete and perfect manner" (Rom 14:5; see *plērophoria* in Col 2:2; 1 Thess 1:5). Here it refers to fullness of performance; in 4:17, Paul will use it in the sense of completion. Paul refers elsewhere to his own work as a *diakonia* (Rom 15:31; 2 Cor 5:18) and of Timothy as a *diakonos* (1 Thess 3:2 [variant reading]).

6. *offered up as a sacrifice*: The translation is fairly free, seeking to capture the precise sense of Paul's extremely compact language. The verb *spendomai*, for example, means literally to "pour out as a drink offering," and the cultic association is unavoidable (Homer, *Iliad* 9:177; Josephus, *Antiquities* 6:22; *Sibylline Oracles* 7:81; Philo, *On Drunkenness* 152). The verb here is in the passive, with the "pouring out" standing metaphorically for the offering of a person's life in dedication. The adverb *ēdē* (already) indicates that Paul sees his life of dedication reaching its end. He uses similar cultic language for his work also in Rom 15:16 and, especially, in Phil 2:17, where he uses *spendomai* in the same way as here.

time for my death is near: This phrase is translated literally as "the season [*kairos!*] of my dissolution." The noun *analysis* can mean a "deliverance," as from evils (Sophocles, *Electra* 142), or a "departure" (Josephus, *Antiquities* 19:240). The phrase "dissolution of the body" appears in *Sentences of Secundus* 19. It is therefore possible to argue that the author intended something other by the phrase than Paul's death,[563] but the context so strongly suggests this meaning that it seems the most natural translation. Note that in Phil 1:23, Paul's use of *analysis* can be understood only as a reference to the apostle's death, and here, the verb *ephistēmi* only strengthens that impression (compare Josephus, *Antiquities* 13:241 [in some mss]; *Life* 137; Philo, *Against Flaccus* 187).

7. *fought the noble fight, finished the race*: Paul picks up and applies to himself the image of the athlete first stated in 2:5, elaborating it in terms of the wrestler (*agōna ēgōnismai*) and the runner (*dromon teteleka*). Paul applies both metaphors directly to himself in 1 Cor 9:26. In addition to the references given for athletics as metaphor for the moral life in 2:5, see also Marcus Aurelius, *Meditations* 3.4.3; Epictetus, *Discourses* 3.22.57–58; 4.4.30; Seneca, *Epistle* 78:16; Philo, *On Husbandry* 111–121; 4 Macc 6:9–10; 17:11–16. What is most significant here is that Paul speaks of these efforts as reaching their end (using the perfect tense of both verbs): he is now bringing his efforts to a close.

held tight to the faith: This is the struggle that the metaphors of fighting and racing point to: Paul's moral effort to preserve *pistis* in three ways: by his own

---

loyalty to the good news and willingness to suffer for it, his resistance to the corruptions of the false teachers, and his preserving the tradition through his delegate (1:5, 13; 2:18, 22; 3:8, 10, 15).[564] Once more, the use of the perfect tense suggests a past effort that continues into the present.

8. *waiting for me now*: The adjective *loipos* in the neuter functions as an adverb of time: "from now on" or "henceforth." I have translated it lightly as "now." The verb *apokeimai* (to be stored up, put aside) is here impersonal: the crown has been reserved for him (compare Josephus, *Antiquities* 6:368; 2 Macc 12:45; esp. Col 1:5).[565]

the crown given to the righteous: The phrase *ho tēs dikaiosynēs stephanos* is, especially because of its attributive construction, open to several interpretations, and my translation is unusually free. The *stephanos* is the wreath awarded to the victor in athletic games (see the NOTE on 2:5). But how is the genitive to be understood? It could be epexegetical: the crown that is righteousness. I take it rather in the sense that the crown is given *for* righteousness and, therefore, "to the righteous." The contest has been about keeping the faith, and the wreath is awarded to those who have been righteous by faith.

the Lord, the righteous judge: Who is the "Lord" (*kyrios*) in this case? It would seem to be Jesus, since this section opens with Paul exhorting his delegate by Christ Jesus, "who is coming to judge the living and the dead." For *kritēs* applied to Jesus, see Acts 10:42 and James 5:9. The designation *dikaios* (righteous) is certainly ascribed to Jesus in Luke 23:47; Acts 3:14; 7:52; 22:14; 1 Pet 3:18; 1 John 1:9; 2:1; 3:7, and (I think) by implication in Rom 1:17 and Gal 3:11.

will award me on that day: The verb *apodidōmi* is used for the paying out of wages or awards (Xenophon, *Anabasis* 1.2.12; Dio Chrysostom, *Oration* 7:12; Philo, *On the Virtues* 88; Rom 13:7) and is used by Paul for God's rewarding and punishing in Rom 2:6. For the phrase "in that day" (*en ekeinē tē hemērą*), see the COMMENT.

all those who have loved his coming: The adjective *pasi* (to all) is missing in many of the MSS of the Western tradition, but although that makes for a shorter reading, the other major witnesses have it. The phrase "who have loved his coming" has as its closest parallel James 1:12, which states that "he will receive the crown of life which [God] has promised to those who love him [*tois agapōsin auton*]." Paul also can speak of those "who love God" (Rom 8:28; 1 Cor 2:9; Eph 6:24). I have translated *tēn epiphaneian autou* (literally, "his appearance") as referring to the parousia, since the use of *epiphaneia* in 4:1 and the entire context seems to demand that referent. It is theoretically possible to read *epiphaneia* here as referring to the incarnation, because of its use in 1:10 in that connection and because of Paul's use of the perfect tense. But this would be to ignore the immediate context.

---

564. My reading is not unlike that of J. M. T. Barton, "Bonum Certamen Certavi . . . Fidem Servavi," *Bib* 40 (1959): 878–884.

565. Some parallels are provided in F. Pfister, "Zur Wendung *apokeitai moi ho tes dikaiosynes stephanos*," *ZNW* 15 (1914): 84–86.

COMMENT

The paraenetic/protreptic argument of 2 Timothy reaches a satisfying rhetorical climax in this passage, even though the final personal comments in 4:9–22 are not without hortatory implication. With words that combine solemnity and urgency, Paul commissions his delegate in the work of ministry. His words take on greater depth because he faces death, so that, at this point, his charge truly does have the force of a testament. Until the end, Paul demonstrates to Timothy a model for his delegate's behavior.

Not only the end of Paul's life is in view. The passage is remarkably rich in language concerning another and greater turning. Paul says that Christ Jesus is coming to judge the living and the dead, and this judgment is connected to "his appearance [epiphaneia] and his kingdom [basileia]" (4:1). Paul himself is awaiting a crown of rightousness, "which the Lord, the righteous judge, will award me on that day"—not only to Paul, in fact, but to "all those who have loved his coming [epiphaneia]" (4:8). Such language invites us to consider the eschatology of 2 Timothy more closely. Does the letter present itself as responding to the situation of a delayed parousia in which there is a diminished expectation of Jesus' coming? Is its eschatology reduced to the private realm of individual reward and punishment after death? Is there here no longer a sense of apocalyptic battle between God and evil leading ultimately to God's triumph in history?

The Last Days

Before assessing the evidence provided by 2 Timothy, it is worth remembering that the eschatology in Paul's undisputed letters is less than totally consistent. Each letter has a slightly different perspective on the end-time. Nor is it possible to trace a linear development on this point. Rather, it seems that Paul's eschatological language is made up of several not entirely reconcilable elements that are put together in a variety of ways according to circumstances. They probably fitted together well enough for him, but since we never get a view of the entire picture he had in mind, we are less able to see the coherence. This is in part because Paul's letters are always addressed to a specific situation. As a pastor whose main concern is the construction of faith communities, he deploys aspects of eschatological expectation as it fits paraenetic needs, rather than as it fits within a system.

Take 1 and 2 Thessalonians, for example: it is patent that a future cosmic eschatology dominates the thinking of some in the Thessalonian church, but it is less clear how important such a view is to Paul himself. A fair reading of the letters, in fact, might suggest that Paul seeks to retard a too-vivid sense of expectation within those congregations (1 Thess 4:13–5:3; 2 Thess 2:1–12). Certainly his own interest is the maintenance of their community identity and attentiveness to their own lives, rather than the timing of the end. In 1 Corinthians, by contrast, Paul responds to certain members of the community who consider themselves already to be within the realized kingdom of God (1 Cor 4:8) by emphasizing the "not-yet" side of things: they need to be morally transformed in the present in order to participate in the future resurrection of the righteous and God's final triumph (1 Cor 7:29–31; 15:35–58).

In 2 Corinthians, we find something still different: Paul uses language that suggests an individual encounter with Jesus after one's death with no reference to a general resurrection or apocalyptic scenario. Thus Paul says that when our earthly dwelling is destroyed (he seems to be referring to death), then "we have a dwelling that comes from God, an eternal house not made by hands in the heavens, and for this reason we groan as we long to be clothed with our dwelling that is from heaven" (2 Cor 5:1–2). The language is complexly metaphorical, but it points toward what might be called a "vertical and individual" eschatology rather than a "horizontal and communal" one. It sounds more private and Platonic than we would have thought possible for the author of 1 Thessalonians, who emphasized that both the dead and the living would go to meet Christ at his coming (1 Thess 4:16–17). Paul adds that "all of us must appear before the judgment seat of Christ, in order that each one might be repaid for the things done through the body, whether good or bad" (2 Cor 5:10). In Philippians, finally, Paul combines both streams. On one side, he insists that "the Lord is near" (Phil 4:5), indicating a future expectation; on the other side, he speaks of "dying and being with Christ" as a possibility available to the individual (Phil 1:23).

This brief and incomplete survey of Pauline eschatology in the undisputed letters—I have not considered at all, for example, the image of cosmic labor pains in Rom 8:18–23—shows the complexity of Paul's notions about what lies ahead for the individual person and the world.[566] That complexity includes the sort of characterizations that Paul uses for the future event. He can speak in the undisputed letters of "that day" (*hēmera ekeinē*, 2 Thess 1:10), of "the day" (*hēmera*, Rom 2:16), of "the day of Christ Jesus" (*hēmera Christou Iēsou*, Phil 1:6), of the "day of Christ" (*hēmera Christou*, Phil 2:16), of "the day of the Lord" (*hēmera tou kyriou*, 1 Thess 5:2), and of "the day of our Lord Jesus Christ" (*hēmera tou kyriou hēmōn Iēsou Christou*, 1 Cor 1:8). Such designations make clear that in some very real way, Jesus will have a role as judge of humans at the end. Thus Paul says in Rom 2:16, "on that day, when, according to my gospel, God judges the secrets of men by Jesus Christ." Similarly in Rom 14:9–10: "for to this end, Christ died and lived again, that he might be Lord both of the dead and the living . . . for we shall all stand before the judgment seat of God."

Paul's apocalyptic perspective, in turn, involves not simply an expectation of the end, but the nature of the conflict preceding the end. Paul includes the future conquest of "every rule and authority and power" as an ingredient to the establishment of God's kingdom (1 Cor 15:23–25; 2 Thess 2:7–12). But he is

566. J. Dupont, *Syn Christē: L'Union avec le Christ suivant Saint Paul* (Paris: Desclee et Brouwer, 1952); J. Plevnik, *Paul and the Parousia: An Exegetical and Theological Investigation* (Peabody, Mass.: Hendrickson, 1997).

even more consistent in his emphasis on the presence of inimical spiritual powers that threaten the community at every turn. Demons inhabit places of idolatrous worship (1 Cor 10:20–21). Satan stands as a present threat and opponent who seeks to take advantage of the community's failures (Rom 16:20; 1 Cor 5:5; 7:5; 2 Cor 2:11; 12:7; 1 Thess 2:18; 2 Thess 2:9). Paul is by no means averse to comparing his human adversaries or rivals to agents of such cosmic enemies (2 Cor 11:12–15).

How does Paul's language about the end in 2 Timothy fit within this framework? We find in 2 Timothy that Paul uses the expression "that day" (*hēmera ekeinē*) three times. On each occasion, he refers to the judgment of humans by God that will lead to their punishment or reward. Thus God will preserve Paul's *parathēkē* until "that day" (1:12) and will reward Onesiphorus with mercy on "that day" (1:18). Finally, in this passage, "that day" is when Paul will receive the crown of righteousness from the "righteous judge" (4:8). The connection of "the day" in 2 Timothy with the parousia is unavoidable. Note that "appearance" (*epiphaneia*) in this case is explicitly connected both to Jesus' judging of the living and the dead and to his "kingdom." Note also that this reward is not private, but communal. The crown will also be given to "all those who have loved his coming." Finally, the future, communal sense of eschatology is affirmed by 2:11–12: "If we have died with him we shall live with him; if we endure, we shall also reign with him [*symbasileusomen*]."

The apocalyptic perspective of 2 Timothy is seen in the description of "the last days" (*en eschatais hēmerais*) in 3:1 as being ones of "hard times" populated by evil and malicious people (3:2–5). Paul uses the future tense, "there will be," it is true, but he then applies all these negative characteristics to the present-day opponents: "From among these are those" (*ek toutōn gar eisin hoi*). He collapses the horizon between the present day and the eschatological time of stress, giving the distinct impression that the present days are, incipiently at least, "the last days." The same perspective is found in this passage. When Paul says that "there will be a time when . . . they will not put up with healthy teaching" (4:3), his tense is future, but his diagnosis concerns the present. This is the audience Timothy can expect to face. Finally, as in the undisputed letters, we find in 2 Timothy a sense that the activity of human opponents is connected to cosmic powers, exemplified by "the trap of the devil" into which they have fallen (2:26).

Whether all this is from Paul's own perceptions or is due to the imagination of a pseudepigrapher, a fair reading of the eschatological dimensions of 2 Timothy must conclude that this letter combines the same elements as are found in the undisputed letters and in much the same way. 2 Timothy is also at least as future-oriented, communal, and apocalyptic in its eschatology as those undisputed letters we have surveyed. Certainly, taking 2 Timothy on its own terms and reading it against the backdrop of the other Pauline letters, there is nothing here to suggest a "diminished eschatological expectation."[567]

---

567. P. H. Towner, "The Present Age in the Eschatology of the Pastoral Epistles," *NTS* 32 (1986): 427–428.

The Challenge of the Last Days

The point of the perception of the last days as evil and the listeners as restless cravers after novelty is to emphasize the seriousness and the difficulty of the charge taken up by Paul's delegate Timothy. Just as Timothy was to "admonish them before God" (2:14), so does Paul now admonish "before God and before Christ Jesus" his representative (4:1).

The portrait of the audience is scathing. They have (literally) diseased hearing, so that they are unable to "bear" healthy teaching (4:3). Paul here shows the keen diagnostic ability of Hellenistic moral philosophers, who recognized the ways in which humans resist and repel what is good for them (e.g., Plutarch, *On Listening to Lectures* [*Mor.* 37C–48]). And when he says that people such as these "multiply teachers fashioned to their own passions" (4:3), he pursues the same topic: moral sickness is like those sorts of physical disorders that get worse because the disease keeps getting fed by the unhealthy desires. Just as the sick person repels the food that can cure, so the morally sick person rejects all teaching except that which caters to its corrupt desires.

In light of this depiction, it is the more impressive that Timothy's "preaching of the word" (4:2) is to be carried out in a manner that fits the true philosopher or moral teacher. First, he must demonstrate the personal moral qualities that are the opposite of those craved by the superficial and sensation-seeking crowd. He is to be consistent in all circumstances, in season and out of season (4:2), for he cannot rely on the crowd's popularity to sustain him. He is to be sober in every respect (4:5), precisely because the fickle crowd is so easily swayed and so easily seduced. He is to have "long-suffering" (*makrothyia*)—that is, the sort of largeness of spirit that enables him to endure in the face of resistance without retaliating or quitting in disgust (4:2). Second, Timothy must confront the moral diseases in his hearers, by verbal reproof and refutation, and, when appropriate, exhortation or comfort (*parakalēson*, 4:2). The final three statements in the charge (4:5) are mutually interpretive. To do the work of an evangelist in such a hostile and unwelcoming environment as Paul has described is, inevitably, to "endure the hard things" (*kakopathēson*). We remember how Paul had asked Timothy to "take his share of suffering" for the Gospel in the first section of the letter (1:8, 12; 2:9). And if Timothy endures in this fashion, he will also "fulfill his service/ministry" (*diakonia*).

Paul remains Timothy's model for imitation. In 2:5, he told his delegate that an athlete does not receive a crown unless he competes by the rules. Now Paul applies that metaphor to himself (4:7). He is the wrestler who has completed the "noble struggle." He is the runner who has completed running the track. And has he competed "by the rules"? Yes, for he has also "kept the faith" (*tēn pistin tetērēka*). Paul had earlier expressed his own lack of shame on the basis that he "knew the one in whom he had placed his trust" and was confident that he was powerful enough to protect what had been entrusted to Paul "until that day" (1:12). Now Paul sees the end as one in which God has indeed proved faithful. Paul had, in fact, taken his share of suffering for the gospel (1:9) and experienced his ministry as a process of being poured out as a sacrificial offering (4:6). All that remains (*loipon*) is to receive from the "just judge"—the one who established this as the rule for life in Christ through his own passion, death, and resurrection—the "crown of righteousness," which will also be given to all those (now including Timothy again) who have loved his coming (4:8). Since Paul has endured with him and is dying with him, he will also live with him and rule with him, wearing a crown (2:11–12). The implications for Timothy, as for all those who take up the work of this ministry, are clear.

XI. PAUL'S NETWORK OF
COMMUNICATION (4:9–22)

◆

4 ⁹Make an effort to come to me quickly, ¹⁰for Demas, having fallen in love with this world, has left me and gone to Thessalonica. Crescas has gone to Galatia, Titus to Dalmatia. ¹¹Only Luke is with me. When you have picked up Mark, bring him along with you, for he is useful to me in service. ¹²And I sent Tychichos to Ephesus. ¹³When you come, bring along the cloak I left behind at Carpus's place in Troas. Bring also the books and especially the parchments. ¹⁴The coppersmith Alexander has acted badly toward me in many ways. The Lord will repay him according to his deeds. ¹⁵You keep away from him also. He has greatly opposed our words. ¹⁶No one was beside me at my first defense presentation. Instead they all abandoned me. May it not be counted against them! ¹⁷The Lord, on the other hand, stood by me and gave me strength, so that through me the proclamation might be fulfilled and that all nations might hear. And I was delivered from the mouth of the lion. ¹⁸The Lord will deliver me from every evil deed, and he will save me for his heavenly kingdom. To Him be glory for ever and ever. Amen. ¹⁹Greet Prisca and Aquila and the household of Onesiphorus. ²⁰Erastus has remained in Corinth. But I left Trophimus ill in Miletus. ²¹Try to get here before winter. Eubulus and Pudens and Linus and Claudia, and all the brethren, greet you. ²²The Lord be with your spirit. Grace be with you.

NOTES

9. *Make an effort to come to me quickly*: I translate *spoudason* (literally, "be eager to," Gal 2:10; 2 Tim 1:17; 2:15) as "make an effort," because in this case there is the suggestion that Timothy must overcome a certain reluctance (4:21). The adverb *tacheōs* (quickly) is used in just this fashion by Paul in 1 Cor 4:19. Paul will repeat the plea in 4:21.

10. *Demas, having fallen in love with this world*: Paul mentions Demas together with Luke as among the "co-workers of mine" in Col 4:10. The phrase *agapēsas ton nyn aiōna* establishes a contrast with those who "love his coming" in the future and who will receive a crown greater than any available in Thessalonica. Demas also appears as a character in the *Acts of Paul and Thecla*. There, teamed with Hermogenes the coppersmith, he is pictured as "full of hypocrisy" and "flattered Paul" as though they loved him (AP 1). He turns out to be, in the course of that narrative, one of Paul's enemies (AP 14).

has left me . . . gone to Thessalonica: As in 4:13, 16, 20, one group of MSS consistently reads as imperfect, rather than aorist, the verbs with *leip/lip* stems. Thus in this verse, the imperfect is found in Alexandrinus, Ephraemi, the second hand of Bezae, F, G, L, and P. The aorist is read by the original hand of Bezae, Sinaiticus, and the majority of witnesses. Since there is a consistency in pattern, the shared testimony of the original of Bezae and Sinaiticus seems decisive. Two things are noteworthy in this brief phrase. The first is Paul's way of emphasizing that Demas had left *him*: it is a personal abandonment. And this is exacerbated by his word choice, for *enkataleipein* can bear the sense of "leave in the lurch" (Plato, *Symposium* 179A). His departure left Paul worse off than he had been. What the attraction was in Thessalonica is not stated, but although Paul wrote two letters to communities there, his slighting comment here does not make it likely that Demas is off to do pastoral work.

Crescas has gone to Galatia: This is the only mention of Crescas (*krēskēs*) in the NT. As with Titus in the next phrase, his "going" does not, as in the case of Demas, appear as an abandonment of Paul, but a stage in the mission. A significant number of witnesses read *Gallian* (to Gaul) here rather than *Galatian* (to Galatia); see Sinaiticus, Ephraemi, 81, 104, 326, and some versions. The implications are considerable. If Crescas goes to Galatia, it is to familiar Pauline territory; if to Gaul, then—as with Titus's trip to Dalmatia—to a place far beyond the reaches of the Pauline mission as we ordinarily construe it. If this were the original meaning, it could suggest that the pseudepigrapher anachronistically retrojected later mission developments into the time of Paul. If it is a scribal alteration, which most critical editions conclude, then it can be accounted for by an understandable desire to find a territory as important to the later church as Gaul was, within the Pauline mission field. Metzger suggests that the change may have been deliberate "by copyists who took it to mean Gaul, which in the early centuries of the Christian era was commonly called *Galatia*." [568]

Titus to Dalmatia: Titus plays an important role in Paul's ministry as a delegate (2 Cor 2:13; 7:6, 13–14; 8:6, 16, 23; 12:18; Gal 2:1, 3; Tit 1:4). No Pauline mission to Dalmatia (the coastal region above Macedonia) is mentioned in Acts or the other letters. Fascinatingly, however, in Rom 15:19 Paul characterizes his mission as extending "from Jerusalem to Illyricum," which is the same area.

11. *only Luke is with me*: A *Loukas* is identified as a physician (*iatros*) and as "beloved" (*agapētos*) to Paul in Col 4:14. In Philemon, a letter probably written at the same time as Colossians, Luke appears again, together with Demas, as among Paul's *synergoi* ("co-workers") who greet Philemon (Phm 24). The happenstance that Luke–Acts is also attributed to a Luke is serendipity to those who would like to regard the third evangelist as the author also of these letters;[569] the other alternative is to think of Luke as Paul's readily available amanuensis.[570]

568. Metzger, Textual Commentary, 649.
569. Wilson, Luke and the Pastoral Epistles; Quinn, "Last Volume of Luke."
570. Moule, "Problem of the Pastoral Epistles."

Mark . . . is useful to me in service: Some MSS change *age* (bring/lead) to *agage*, which has pretty much the same meaning. A John Mark appears in Acts 12:12, 25 and 15:37, 39 as a companion of Paul and Barnabas, holding roughly the same position that Timothy assumed after him (Acts 16:3) after Paul and Barnabas separated—according to Acts, again—over his desertion of them (Acts 15:38–39). A Mark is located in prison with Paul by Col 4:10. Someone named Mark is also identified as an associate of Peter in 1 Pet 5:13. The expression that Mark "is useful [*euchrēstos*; compare Phm 11] to me in service" is ambiguous. The term *diakonia* could mean "ministry," as in 4:5: "Fulfill your ministry." But it might also refer to the "personal service" that Mark could render to Paul as his assistant (compare Phm 13).

12. *I sent Tychichos to Ephesus*: Tychichos is mentioned together with Trophimos in Acts 20:4 as "Asians" who worked with Paul and accompanied him on his last journey to Jerusalem. In Col 4:7 and Eph 6:21, Tychichos is the delegate who brings news of Paul (as well as letters?) to communities in the region of the Lycus Valley. In Tit 3:12, Paul expresses his intention to send either "Artemas or Tychichos"—possibly as replacement delegates for Titus in Crete.

13. *bring along the cloak*: The noun *phailone* derives from *phainolē* (Epictetus, *Discourse* 4.8.34), apparently as a Latin loanword for a heavy outer cloak; variants of the spelling used here (especially *phelonē*) are found in papyri (Oxyrhynchus Papyrus 531:14; 736:4). The preoccupation with acquiring a cloak before the onset of winter (4:21) lends verisimilitude to the letter.

I left behind at Carpus's place in Troas: As in 4:10, some MSS (basically the same as those listed in the NOTE on 4:10) have the imperfect *apeleipon* rather than the aorist *apelipon*; once more, the difference in meaning is negligible. As the place in Asia from which easy access to Macedonia by sail was possible, Troas could have been Paul's frequent stopping place; Acts mentions his being there twice, once merely passing through (Acts 16:8, 11), and the other time spending a week and preaching a lengthy sermon (20:6–12). At the height of his Aegean ministry, Paul speaks of traveling to Troas for the sake of the good news and finding an opportunity opening for him there (2 Cor 2:12).

the books and especially the parchments: A handful of MSS (notably the original hand of Bezae) add the connective *de* (and/but); a single MS (1175) adds *kai* (and) between "books" and "manuscripts," recognizing the asyndeton that my translation also relieves by supplying the "and" that the best MSS lack. The sentence structure does not allow us to decide whether these materials also were left in Troas, or Timothy is simply to bring them. A *biblion* is a document (Herodotus, *Persian War* 1:123; Josephus, *Against Apion* 1:101) or a book (Plato, *Apology* 26D). In Judaism, the plural *ta biblia* was frequently used for the scrolls of Torah, often with some adjective attached, such as *biblia hiera* (sacred books, Josephus, *Life* 418), *biblia ta hagia* (1 Macc 12:9), or *ta biblia tou nomou* (books of the law, 1 Macc 1:56). While it is certainly possible, then, that Paul is requesting biblical scrolls for his study, it is not certain. There is similar ambiguity concerning *membrana*, which is another Latin loanword meaning "parchment." This could mean, therefore, materials on which Paul could write.

Alternatively, the plural *ta membrana* could refer to scrolls or even codices. In short, we know that Paul requested materials to read and probably also materials for writing, but nothing more than that.[571]

14. *the coppersmith Alexander*: An Alexander appears in 1 Tim 1:20 as one of two members of the community that Paul has handed over to Satan for disciplining. For further discussion, see the NOTE on 1 Tim and the COMMENT.

has acted badly toward me: The translation is difficult, although the basic meaning is clear. The Greek is literally "Alexander the coppersmith showed me many bad things [*kaka*]." The verb *endeiknymi* means to "show or demonstrate" (Xenophon, *Anabasis* 6.1.19; Wis 12:17); here it has the sense of "exhibited toward me." I try to capture the sense in appropriately clear English.

will repay him according to his deeds: For the verb *apodidōmi*, see 4:8. The phrase echoes LXX Ps 61:13: *hoti su apodōseis hekastǫ kata ta erga autou* (because you will repay each one according to his deeds; see also LXX Ps 27:4; Prov 24:12; *Psalms of Solomon* 9:5; Dionysius of Halicarnassus, *Roman Antiquities* 6.73.3). That Paul is familiar with this theologoumenon is clear from his use of it also in Rom 2:6: *hos apodōsei hekastǫ kata ta erga autou*. A substantial number of MSS (the second hand of Bezae, the Koine traditions, and some Latin witnesses) have the optative *dǫē* (may he give) here, but that reading is probably influenced by 1:16–17.

15. *keep away from him*: The middle of the verb *phylassō* has the sense of "protect yourself from," with the one presenting the threat in the accusative case (here the relative *hon*; see also Aeschylus, *Prometheus* 715; Josephus, *Jewish War* 4:572). The use of the personal pronoun *sy* (you) is emphatic.

greatly opposed our words: For *logoi* in the plural for Paul's teaching, compare 1:13. The plural possessive pronoun *hēmetera* would seem to include Timothy's teaching as well as Paul's, unless Paul is using the plural he sometimes does when speaking of the mission (see especially that section of 2 Corinthians beginning in 3:1). The verb *anthistēmi* (to stand against/oppose) is the same one used of the rivals in 3:8; for Paul's other uses, see Rom 9:19; 13:2; Gal 2:11; Eph 6:13. The adverb *lian* (not otherwise used by Paul) adds intensity to the opposition (compare Matt 2:16; Mark 9:3; Luke 23:8).

16. *No one was beside me*: The verb *paraginomai* means literally to "come or be present," and when used in that spatial sense usually has *eis* or *pros* with the accusative case (e.g., Philo, *Life of Moses* 1:86; Herodotuss, *Persian War* 3:32). Here Paul uses the dative *moi* without any preposition, and the sense is not simply that no one was present with him, but that no one assisted him (Thucydides, *Peloponnesian War* 3.54.4; Plato, *Republic* 368B). My translation seeks to capture that ambiguity. A large number of MSS (including the second hand of Sinaiticus and Bezae as well as the Koine tradition) use the verb *symparaginomai* rather than the simpler form translated here (*paraginomai*), which is found in the original hand of Sinaiticus, Alexandrinus, and a significant number of other witnesses.

---

571. T. C. Skeat, "'Especially the Parchments': A Note on 2 Timothy 4.13," *JTS* 30 (1979): 173–177; P. Trummer, "Mantel und Schriften," *BZ* 18 (1974): 193–207.

my first defense presentation: The term *apologia* corresponds to *katēgoria*, the statement of charges in a criminal or civil case; it enables the defense to make a statement of its position (Plato, *Apology* 28A; Xenophon, *Memorabilia* 4.8.5; Josephus, *Against Apion* 2:147; see also Acts 22:1; 25:16). By referring to his "first" (*prōtē*) defense presentation, Paul implies that he is awaiting another.

all abandoned me: In an odd scribal tic, the same group of MSS as cited in 4:10 and 4:13 have the imperfect *enkateleipen* rather than the aorist *enkatelipen*. For the strength of that verb, see the NOTE on 4:10. This may be another "abandonment" than the one mentioned in 1:15, for those people were specified as "in Asia," whereas presumably the people who abandoned Paul at his defense were in Rome. But this may be too fine. In any case, Paul's abandonment is not absolute, since he still has some companions with him (4:11, 21).

not be counted against them: The verb *logizomai* means to "reckon/calculate," as in "reckoning an account" for or against someone (Xenophon, *Cyropaedia* 3.1.33; Plato, *Timaeus* 34B; *Phaedrus* 246C; *Testament of Zebulon* 9:7). For Paul's use elsewhere, see Rom 2:26; 4:3, 5, 8, 10; 2 Cor 3:5; 12:6; Gal 3:6; Phil 4:8. Unless the negative wish be taken ironically (as in the use of "bless" in place of "curse" in passages like Job 1:5, 11; 2:5, 9), Paul shows himself a practitioner of *makrothymia* (compare 3:10; 4:2), once more setting an example for Timothy.

17. *stood by me*: As with *paraginomai* in the previous verse, the verb *paristēmi* (to stand by)—used in the sense of "presenting" in 2:15—is sometimes used to express coming to the aid of another (Xenophon, *Cyropaedia* 5.3.19; Josephus, *Jewish War* 2:245; *Antiquities* 1:341; *Sibylline Oracles* 3:705; 8:407). See Paul's use in Rom 16:2.

and gave me strength: Paul uses the same verb here (*endynamoō*) that he employed in 2:1, and deliberately: as the Lord strengthens him in his sufferings, so can Timothy expect the same power to work through him (see also 1:7, 8, 12; 3:15).

proclamation might be fulfilled: For the verb *plērophorein* (to fulfill), see the NOTE on 4:5. The meaning here is surely "bring to its full term/complete." The noun *kērygma* can be used by Paul for the content of his preaching (Rom 16:25; 1 Cor 2:4; 15:14), but here it has the sense of "mission of preaching" (1 Cor 1:21).

all nations might hear: This is the "fulfillment" that Paul has in mind, the extension of the good news to all the nations, an ideal expressed by Paul mainly in Romans (1:5, 13; 3:29; 4:18; 9:24; 11:11, 25; 15:9–12, 16, 18; 16:26); for a similar statement of hope concerning the mission, see Phil 1:12–18. The Koine text tradition has the singular *akousē*, rather than the plural *akousōsin*, for "might hear," which is grammatically possible; the plural is, however, read by the best witnesses. In 1 Timothy, because of the nature of the struggle faced there by Paul, I considered *ethnoi* translated best by "Gentiles"; here, "nations" seems appropriate.

delivered from the mouth of the lion: The passive *errhysthēn* suggests that it is God who has so delivered Paul. In Scripture, the lion is a creature of the wilds and fierce in reputation (LXX Pss 7:2; 9:30; Prov 22:13; 26:13). To be "delivered from the mouth of the lion" is therefore to be saved from extreme danger, as was Daniel from the den of lions (LXX Dan 6:20, 22; 4 Macc 18:13). Paul's wording here resembles that in LXX Ps 21:22: *sōson me ek stomatos leontos* (save me from the mouth of a lion), but comes even closer to the reference in 1 Macc 2:60 to the rescue of Daniel: *Daniel en tē̦ hapolotēti autou errhysthē ek stomatos leontōn* (Daniel in his simplicity was delivered from the mouth of the lion). In light of such obvious Scriptural intertextuality, it is not necessary to posit a connection between this lion and the "beasts" that Paul fought in Ephesus (1 Cor 15:32) or the "lion" that appears in the *Acts of Paul and Thecla* 7.

18. *deliver me from every evil deed*: Some MSS try to relieve the asyndetic character of these sentences by adding *kai* before this phrase (Bezae, G, F, and the Koine tradition; Sinaiticus, Alexandrinus, the original hand of Bezae, and Ephraemi lack the conjunction). Paul's confidence in future deliverance is based on his past (3:11) and present (4:17) experience; note that he uses the same verb in all three statements. It is difficult not to detect some echo here of the Matthean version of the Lord's Prayer, which reads in Matt 6:13: *alla rhysai apo tou ponērou*; Paul's statement simply adds "every work": *rhysētai me ho kyrios apo pantos ergou ponērou*.

save me for his heavenly kingdom: The precise meaning of *eis tēn basileian autou* is unclear. Is it simply elliptical, so that the full sentence would read, "He will save me [so that I can enter into] his heavenly kingdom"? Or does the construction of *eis* + accusative denote purpose: "he will save me [so that I can work for] his heavenly kingdom"? The adjective *epouranios* refers to the place where God dwells, and therefore to anything pertaining to the transcendent realm of God's life (Homer, *Odyssey* 17:484; *Iliad* 6:131; 3 Macc 6:28; *Sibylline Oracles* 4:51; Philo, *Allegorical Laws* 3:168). For Paul's use elsewhere, see 1 Cor 15:40, 48, 49; Phil 2:10; Eph 1:3, 20; 2:6; 3:10; 6:12. Although it would certainly make sense to see this statement as expressing Paul's hope for sharing God's life "in heaven" (see also 2 Cor 5:1–5; Phil 1:21–26), the possibility cannot be excluded that he is thinking of a continued work "for" God's kingdom (using "heavenly" in the manner Matthew does "kingdom of Heaven," Matt 3:2; 5:3).

glory for ever and ever. Amen: Such a turn to prayer in such an expressive moment is entirely typical of Paul (e.g., Rom 1:25; 9:5; 11:36; 16:27; Gal 1:5; Eph 3:21; Phil 4:20; 1 Thess 3:13; 1 Tim 1:17; 6:16) and reflects the forms of Jewish blessings that are part of the heritage of the early church as a whole (Heb 13:21; 1 Pet 4:11; 5:11; 2 Pet 3:18; Jude 25; Rev 1:6; 7:12).

19. *Greet Prisca and Aquila*: Prisca and Aquila are named as fellow workers of Paul. They arrived from Rome after the expulsion of the Jews under Claudius (Acts 18:2). They continue to be associated with Paul's mission (Acts 18:18, 26; 1 Cor 16:19; Rom 16:3). The same MS (181) that added a gloss from the *Acts of Paul and Thecla* in 3:11 contributes another here. After the name Aquila, it adds "Lectra his wife [presumably Aquila's?] and Zimmia and Zenon his children" (AP 2).

household of Onesiphorus: Although Onesiphorus appears in only this letter in the NT, he is an intriguing character, not least in the way he is associated with his household. In 1:16, Paul prayed that the Lord grant mercy to Onesiphorus's household (*oikos*) because of the many times Onesiphorus refreshed Paul and the way he sought him out. It is not clear whether Onesiphorus is the head of the household, although that is the most reasonable surmise. Now Timothy is expected to be able to greet Onesiphorus's "household"—presumably its members—but not Onesiphorus himself. Are we to conclude that he remains in service to Paul? Paul's greeting and gratitude are appropriate if Onesiphorus's family sacrifices his presence as an act of benefaction to Paul.

20. *Erastus has remained in Corinth*: Erastus is named in Acts 19:22—with Timothy—as one of those ministering to Paul and sent by him to Macedonia. In Rom 16:23, an Erastus is called the treasurer (*oikonomos*) of the city (presumably, Corinth). An inscription discovered at Corinth confirms that a certain Erastus served in a lesser financial office in that city.[572]

I left Trophimus ill in Miletus: For the final time, a somewhat smaller group of MSS that had the imperfect rather than the aorist for *leip/lip* verbs in 4:10, 13, 16, does the same thing in this case (esp. C, L, P). In addition to his listing with Tychichos as an "Asian" in Acts 20:4, Trophimus is mentioned in Acts 21:29 as "Trophimos the Ephesian" who had been spotted by the people as being in the city of Jerusalem with Paul, and whose presence in the Temple helped stir up a riot. Miletus is, in effect, a suburb of Ephesus, the place where, according to Acts 20:17, Paul met the Ephesian elders for a final discourse when on his way to Jerusalem. The English adjective "ill" translates the present participle *asthenounta*, which can mean anything from "illness" to "weakness," and as a predicative participle could express either concession ("despite his being ill") or cause ("because he is ill"). For the apparent conflict with the present passage, see the COMMENT.

21. *get here before winter*: The short command testifies to the difficulties of travel in the Mediterranean world during the winter, especially by sea. For vivid accounts of the dangers, see Thucydides, *Peloponnesian War* 2:25, 6:22, 104; 8.31, 34; Herodotus, *Persian War* 3:138; 7:188; Josephus, *Life* 15; *Jewish War* 1:279; Diogenes Laertius, *Lives of Eminent Philosophers* 7:3; Aelius Aristides, *Sacred Tales* 2:11–17, 65–68; 4:35–37; Chariton of Aphrodisias, *Chaeeas and Callirhoe* 3.5.1. Shipowners were paid bonuses if they risked their property to deliver the goods under such conditions (Suetonius, *Life of Claudius* 18:1).

Eubulus and Pudens and Linus and Claudia: Whether these names have more a Latin than a Greek origin, and whether this Linus was, as Irenaeus suggests, Peter's successor as bishop of Rome (*Against Heresies* 3.3.3), are less important than the evidence they provide that Paul was, in fact, in the company of fellow believers, and that his sense of abandonment was as much an emotional as a physical reality. The names do not appear elsewhere in the NT.

---

572. H. J. Cadbury, "Erastus of Corinth," *JBL* 50 (1931): 42–58.

all the brethren, greet you: A few MSS omit the adjective "all" (e.g., the original hand of Sinaiticus). We find the same greeting "from all the brothers" in 1 Cor 16:20 and Phil 4:21.

22. *Lord be with your spirit*: The "your" in this case is singular in the Greek: it is Timothy's spirit that is intended. As might be expected, scribes added to the prayer, making it either "Lord Jesus" (Alexandrinus and others) or "Lord Jesus Christ" (e.g., the second hand of Sinaiticus). Although the following phrase is found (with variations) in almost all of Paul's letters, this personal wish for Timothy is paralleled only by Phil 25.

Grace be with you: In various forms, a prayer for *charis* on the readers concludes the majority of Paul's letters (compare 1 Cor 16:23; 2 Cor 13:13; Gal 6:18; Eph 6:24; Phil 4:23; Col 4:18; 1 Thess 5:28; 2 Thess 3:18; 1 Tim 6:21; Tit 3:15; Phm 25). The final phrase has also given rise to many textual variants. Since all of these letters are written to groups of people (including Philemon), all of them also wish for grace to be with "you" in the plural (*meth' hymōn*). It is not surprising, then, that many scribes would harmonize 2 Timothy with that usage: we find "grace be with us," "grace be with you" (singular), and "be well in peace." Finally, some MSS also add *amen*. If the reading chosen by Nestle–Aland ("grace be with you [plural]") is correct, this would be the first time that the letter breaks its fixed attention on Timothy the individual. It is fascinating that the text read by three early commentators—Chrysostom, Theodoret of Cyr, and Theodore of Mopsuestia—all had *meth' hēmōn* (with us). Alternatively, it may be that at this point Paul himself greets all those he wants Timothy to greet as well.

COMMENT

Paul's undisputed letters often, although by no means always, end with such a set of greetings and messages (Rom 16:1–23; 1 Cor 16:1–23; Col 4:17–18).[573] The Pastorals are equally diverse in this respect: 2 Timothy has a lengthy personal section (4:9–22), Titus has only four verses (3:12–15), and 1 Timothy has nothing. The percentage of known to unknown personal names in this passage is relatively high. From other New Testament sources, we can account for nine of the people Paul mentions. Compare Philippians, which mentions Timothy, but whose four other personal names (not to mention the "members of Caesar's household") cannot be checked against any other source. In Rom 16, likewise, only six of the many names mentioned by Paul are attested elsewhere, while twenty-seven are completely unknown to us.

In the Pauline letters that contain this element, we can determine three functions for the messages and greetings. The first is simply to take care of the com-

---

573. K. Erbe, "Zeit und Ziel der Gruesse Rom. 16, 3–15 und der Mitteilungen 2 Tim. 4, 9–21," *ZNW* 10 (1901): 185–218, is basically an exercise in trying to fit the information of the passage into the framework of Acts.

plex business of the Pauline mission, which involved the movement, equipping, and lodging of large numbers of people. A cumulative count of all the names associated with Paul "in the field" by both Acts and the letters yields a missionary team of at least forty persons, male and female. Paul's "daily care for the churches" was not an insignificant, but a climactic element in his catalogue of hardships (2 Cor 11:28). And the management of the mission remained a constant pressure on him, even in prison. The second function is to reinforce the networks of communication essential to the success of the mission. This function is clearest in Romans. Despite addressing a community he has never met, Paul greets many in the community by name, thus helping to establish his own credibility by invoking their mutual recognition of him.[574] The third function is the reinforcement of points made earlier in the letter. Romans is again the best example: the identification of some in the community as Paul's "kinsmen" helps reinforce his point about the inclusion of both Jews and Gentiles in God's plan of salvation. In 1 Corinthians, Paul's request that his readers be submissive to household leaders like Stephanus (1 Cor 16:15–18) helps reinforce his plea for good order in the assembly, just as his news about Apollos supports his earlier argument that Apollos was a cooperative worker in his mission field rather than a rival (1 Cor 16:12).

The literary functions of 2 Timothy's final section are much the same. Paul touches on the movements of his delegates, communicates greetings, and reinforces his main argument. He does the last by continuing to present himself as a model for Timothy. Paul faced opposition from Alexander the coppersmith; Timothy, too, should beware of him (4:14). Paul was abandoned by all at his first defense, but the Lord empowered him (*endynamosen*, 4:16–17), just as Timothy is to be "empowered" (*endynamou*) by the grace of Christ Jesus to carry out his work (2:1). Paul was nevertheless rescued and saved for the heavenly kingdom (4:18), just as Timothy, if he endures, will also reign with Christ (2:12) and share the crown of righteousness given to all those who have loved his appearance (4:8).

Interpretive Perspectives

The final passage of 2 Timothy can, like so much of this letter, be read from two distinct perspectives: that of pseudonymity and that of authentic Pauline authorship. Like so much of 2 Timothy, a close examination of the two options shows that the evidence favors the second position more than the first.

The perspective of pseudepigraphy sees the passage as doing two things. First, the network of names and the remarks about personal business are the typical accoutrements of pseudonymity.[575] The author may have available to him some bits of information about Paul and his associates (from Acts and Philippians and

---

574. Johnson, Reading Romans.
575. Donelson, *Pseudepigraphy and Ethical Argument in the Pastoral Epistles*; Brox, "Zu den persönlichen Notizen der Pastoralbriefe."

Romans, perhaps), and combines these traditions with the elaboration of new characters (Crescas, Carpus, Alexander, Onesiphorus, Eubulus, Pudens, Linus, Claudia) to present a picture of Paul that is familiar, yet suggests a "new stage" in his life. The effect of such details as the apostle's abandonment at his first defense, his desire for company, and his wish for materials to study and a cloak to keep warm is the creation of a poignant, if fictional, portrait of an aging apostle facing death with discomfort yet dignity.

Second, the passage's stress on Paul's solitary struggle together with his expectation of human defeat and certain death serve the function of setting up the generational transition that the Pastoral Letters as a whole are intended to effect. Having Paul at the point of death, prescient about the continuation of opposition to his heritage into the future, is the classic mis-en-scène for the farewell discourse or testament. If Paul is now about to die, then his tradition, if it is to continue, must do so through his "delegates"—that is, those committed to this form of Christianity in the succeeding generations.

Such an interpretation demands that 2 Timothy not be read as a real, individual letter, even a pseudonymous one. The theory demands that all three letters be a single literary production, for without 1 Timothy and Titus, 2 Timothy could not accomplish the role assigned to it. As a separate pseudonymous letter, it could have been written simply as hagiography or for entertainment. But even as the "cover" for the other two letters—regarded in this view, we remember, as inchoate church orders—2 Timothy serves only the very narrow purpose of legitimating the domesticated form of Paulinism the other two letters are supposed to purvey. And if this reading is correct, then we learn nothing real about the Pauline mission or even the character of Paul from this exercise in pseudepigraphy.

Suppose, however, that this part of 2 Timothy is considered as part of a separate letter and compared with the appropriate parallels in the undisputed correspondence. If it is read within the context of Paul's ministry—including his Roman captivity—the information provided by the passage concerning the apostle's situation, his attitudes, and the movements of his associates appear both credible and instructive.

We can begin with the network of names, remembering that this is a common, although not invariable, feature of Paul's letters and that the proportion of new names is not unusually high when compared with the number in other letters. One name that has caused critics difficulties is that of Trophimus. As noted earlier, he is mentioned in the NT only here and in two passages of Acts. The first calls him an "Asian" (Acts 20:4), and the second refers to him as an "Ephesian" (Acts 21:29). I note parenthetically that Ephesus is near Miletus (Acts 20:17). By saying that "I left Trophimus ill in Miletus," 2 Timothy is thought to be making an error, since Acts 21:29 places Trophimus in Jerusalem with Paul after he passed through Miletus. Thus the conjectured emendation of *melite* (Malta) in 4:20 has been suggested in order to relieve the supposed inconsistency. But the problem is more imaginary than real. For there to be a real conflict, three conditions are required. First, Acts must be regarded as a complete account of the relations between Paul and Trophimus. Second, the (pseudonymous) author of 2 Timothy was using the Acts account as the basis of his knowledge of Trophimus (since we know of him nowhere else). Third, the author was also careless about the narrative sequence in Acts. But there is at least the possibility that Acts itself is mistaken in its statement about "Trophimus the Ephesian" being in Jerusalem with Paul. Or if Acts is correct, Trophimus could have returned to his home region to continue his work for the movement after Paul's arrest. It is conceivable, although the usage is not attested except in Tit 1:5, that Paul means that he has "left Trophimus" not in the sense of physical departure, but in the sense of "left in a position"; observe that this comment comes immediately after Paul's statement that "Erastus has remained in Corinth." We simply do not have enough information to conclude that the statement is an impossible one for Paul to have made.

Another difficult name is that of Alexander (4:14). A certain Alexander also plays a minor role in the narrative of Acts, his head almost literally appearing momentarily above the mob during the Ephesian riot (Acts 19:33). Did the author of 2 Timothy derive the name from this account, yet also confuse Alexander, whom he here calls a coppersmith, with Demetrius the silversmith, the instigator of the riot in Ephesus (Acts 19:24)? Another Alexander appears in the *Acts of Paul and Thecla*, but is explicitly called a Syrian, and his role is restricted to accosting Thecla on the street and being thoroughly humiliated by her (*AP* 26). Finally, to confuse matters even further, 1 Tim 1:20 names Alexander (with Hymenaios) as one of those in the Ephesian community whom Paul has consigned to Satan so that they will learn not to blaspheme! In a case like this, we must simply confess our inability to sort out the confused state of the evidence. Connections may be possible, but in the case of a common name such as Alexander (or Mark), it is a hazardous exercise.

Indeed, it is easy to apply the same critical eye to Paul's other letters with similar results. Take Rom 15: How can Paul claim that his mission has extended as far as Illyricum (15:19) when neither Acts nor any of this other letters offers any support for his being there? Or take Rom 16: How can Paul speak of Phoebe as a deacon when he nowhere else—in his "authentic" letters—speaks of women deacons? How can she be his financial patron in Cenchrae if he was being supported by the churches of Macedonia? How can Prisca and Aquila have a house church in Rome if, according to 1 Cor 16:19, they have a house church in Ephesus? How can Junia be a Jewish female apostle? Each of these questions can be pursued in the way that Trophimus and Alexander have been pursued in the case of 2 Timothy. But in the case of Romans, the authenticity of the letter is so generally accepted that at most the problems give rise to the hypothesis that Rom 16 may have been addressed (by Paul) to the Ephesian church rather than to the Roman church. The difficulties raised by the inconsistencies do not cause its overall authenticity to be challenged. Indeed, it is seldom in the case of Paul's "undisputed" letters that such critical questions any longer get addressed—or even asked.

But we must return to 2 Tim 4:9–10. Corresponding to the troublesome names of co-workers about whom we know just enough to be confused, or even suspect the author of 2 Timothy of being confused, there are other pieces of information embedded in the passage that are impressively if indirectly confirmed by other evidence. Take Demas as an example. In Col 4:14, he is listed with Luke as one of Paul's companions in the captivity from which he wrote Colossians. Not surprisingly, then, he is listed also in Phm 23 with Luke, Mark, and Aristarchos as "my fellow workers." In this passage, consequently, Demas's departure is described in terms that would be appropriate only for one who was a close collaborator and who has abandoned his post. He not only went to Thessalonica, but did so because he has "fallen in love with this world" (more than the coming kingdom of God) and, most pertinently, "has abandoned me": the verb *enkataleipein* here has the sense of leaving someone inconveniently and at a loss. The tone of anger or bitterness is appropriate, in short, only against the backdrop of Colossians and Philemon, in which alone we learn that Demas is not simply a casual acquaintance, but Paul's "fellow worker."

If we pursue this intertextual context further, we see also that the notice in 2 Tim 4:11 that "only Luke is with me" makes sense if we think of him associated with Aristarchos, Demas, and Mark (as reported by Colossians and Philemon). Demas has left, and Mark is to be picked up and taken back to Paul by Timothy when he comes (4:11). We see also how what is said of Mark, that he is "useful to me in service," reflects the same ambiguity in his role—part missionary, part personal assistant—that is found also in the brief account concerning him in Acts 12:25; 15:37–39.

In similar fashion, the remark that Titus has gone to Dalmatia corresponds well with the information provided to us only by Rom 15:19 that Paul conceived of his mission in terms of an arc extending from Jerusalem to Illyricum. If Titus could go on an embassy to Dalmatia, a territory about whose place in the Pauline mission we had no idea apart from these two isolated references, then it should also be conceivable that he was for a time Paul's delegate in Crete, about whose evangelization we are also (but no more profoundly) in ignorance. The link between Erastus and Corinth, likewise, can nicely be correlated to the note in Romans (probably written from Corinth) that Erastus was the "treasurer of the city" (Rom 16:23). Yet the author of 2 Timothy does not exploit any of the legendary possibilities of that connection, which he might have if his source for this information had been the Letter to the Romans itself. Prisca and Aquila are itinerant as always, with Prisca's name appearing with the spelling that Paul himself gives it, rather than as Acts does (Priscilla, Acts 18:2, 18, 26), and named in the order found in Rom 16:3 rather than in the order of 1 Cor 16:19. Finally, the mention of sending Tychichos to Ephesus corresponds with the mention of him in Ephesians 6:21 as Paul's messenger of personal news to the churches in Asia Minor.

The movements of delegates and the messages to colleagues have verisimilitude when compared with the information about them in other Pauline letters and what we know otherwise about the practices of first-generation Pauline Christians. More to the point, for a pseudepigrapher to have drawn precisely these connections would have required on one side a sufficient knowledge of

Acts, Philemon, Colossians, 1 Corinthians, Romans, and Ephesians to extract these details, but on the other side a reluctance to develop in a legendary manner any of the characters thus extracted. Such a literary dependence would also leave yet unexplained the various discrepancies that I have noted, which make sense if coming from a real-life author, but are less intelligible if deriving from a clever forger.

Paul's Last Stand

We can take up, finally, the question of the portrait of Paul sketched in these last sentences. From the standpoint of Pauline authenticity, it can readily be acknowledged that a "generational transition" is taking place—especially if it is granted that Paul saw himself as facing imminent death! But the transition is not one of adapting Pauline theology to a generation living a century after the apostle's death, since Timothy belongs to Paul's own generation! It is, rather, a matter of Paul's beloved disciple continuing in the path he had already been following during Paul's lifetime. Yes, Paul is concerned about the courage of his delegate (1:5–7). Yes, he feels abandoned and desolate as he suffers as a prisoner. So true to life is this depiction that the most plausible explanation is that, in fact, it comes from real life.

On several occasions, I have observed the striking resemblances between 2 Timothy and Philippians in setting, style, and mode of argumentation. But it is in the finely shaded nuances of mood that the comparison is most telling, for these nuances indicate a shift in perspective that is best accounted for by a change in an author's circumstances. In Philippians, Paul writes a letter of freindship to a community that he knows intimately and that is especially dear to him, not least because it has supported him in his ministry (Phil 4:10–20). In Philippians, Paul is fundamentally positive about his situation and his prospects. Although he can envisage an imminent death, he sees life as a choice available to him (1:21–24) and he sees himself as continuing in his ministry: "Convinced of this, I know that I shall remain and continue with you all, for your progress and joy in the faith" (Phil 1:25). He even views his chains as advancing the cause of the gospel, because his fellow workers have gained in confidence and are bolder in their proclamation (Phil 1:12–13). Paul is confident that he will see the Philippian community again (2:24). He has the sense—using the image of the athlete—that he has not yet reached the goal (3:12–16).

As Paul writes 2 Timothy, as I have noted, all these perceptions have dramatically shifted. His first defense was not successful (4:16). Far from emboldening his co-workers, his imprisonment now seems to make them flee and abandon him out of shame or cowardice (1:15; 4:16). Despite having some friends with him, Paul feels abandoned—it is as though Luke is the only one there with him who really counts (4:11). And instead of being worried about some fellow workers jockeying for position out of envy and rivalry (Phil 1:15; 4:1–2), in 2 Timothy Paul faces opposition from without (4:14) and from within (2:17–18; 3:6–9). Worst of all, rather than being able to express utter confidence in his delegate Timothy, as he does in Philippians (2:19–22), he is reduced in this letter to summoning Timothy's courage to continue in the ministry and even visit his teacher in prison (4:1–5, 9, 21). Paul's sense of finality and resignation is unmistakable. He does not see a return to his active work. The Lord will save him from every evil and for his kingdom (4:18), but Paul expresses no hope in a rescue from his captivity. He is sure that the word of God cannot be chained (2:9), and he continues even in his chains to proclaim the word fully so that all the Gentiles might hear it (4:17). But he no longer thinks that he will be free from chains in this life.

Are these words from the human heart, or are they the inventions of a forger's art? The reader must decide. But in 2 Timothy, the evidence supports the case for authenticity more than it does for pseudonymity. Even if the product of pious imagination, the portrait of a saint witnessing to the very end of his life and praising God even as he suffers the shame of imprisonment, rejection, and abandonment remains a powerful one, capable of stimulating both admiration and emulation.[576] But if the words we read here come from the very one who so suffered and so witnessed, then they bear even greater significance as a precious testimony to Christian readers in every age.

---

576. The reflections of H. C. G. Moule, the bishop of Durham (1841–1920) are worth reading today. If they reveal the limitations of a scholarship too little disciplined by criticism, they also show the generosity of reading available to one who embraces the text as it presents itself. See H. C. G. Moule, *Studies in II Timothy*, Kregel Popular Commentary (Reprint, Grand Rapids, Mich.: Kregel, 1977).

INDEXES

◆

Index of Scripture References

◆

INDEX OF ANCIENT SOURCES

◆

INDEX OF AUTHORS

◆